DEFINING RUSSIA MUSICALLY

Defining Russia Musically

HISTORICAL AND HERMENEUTICAL ESSAYS

Richard Taruskin

PRINCETON UNIVERSITY PRESS

PRINCETON, NEW JERSEY

Library of Congress Cataloging-in-Publication Data
Taruskin, Richard.
Defining Russia musically : historical and hermeneutical essays /
Richard Taruskin.
p.   cm.
Includes bibliographical references and index.
ISBN 0-691-01156-7 (cloth : alk. paper)
1. Music—Russia—History and criticism.   I. Title.
ML 300.T37   1997
780′.947—dc20   96-41182

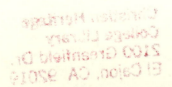

For Caryl and Karol
who have set me so many good examples

and for P. C. van den Toorn
public adversary, private pal

Music reaches its high-water mark only among men who have
not the ability or the right to argue.

—Friedrich Nietzsche, *The Wanderer and
His Shadow* (1880)

If Russia is to be saved, it will only be as a Eurasian power
and only through Eurasianism.

—Lev Gumilyov (1992)

I've no doubt that Russia has not lost the opportunity to reach
prosperity and democracy. But it can do so only under one
condition: a realization of itself as a true part of Western
civilization.

—Vassily Aksyonov (1994)

It's been very nice, the reception these stories have got,
because, broadly speaking, people have managed to respond
to them as stories rather than messages in a bottle. It's been
very nice to be a writer again. I feel like everything I say or
do is treated as an allegory of my situation. The point is that
I'm trying to not be defined explicitly by this situation.

—Salman Rushdie, on *East, West* (1994)

Russia is so Russian!

—John Updike (1966)

CONTENTS

OTHERS: A MYTHOLOGY AND A DEMURRER
(BY WAY OF PREFACE)

THE SECULAR fine art of music came late to Russia. To all intents and purposes, its history there begins in 1735, when the Empress Anne (Anna Ioan-
novna, reigned 1730–40) decided to import a resident troupe of Italian opera
singers to adorn her court with exotic and irrational entertainments. The first
such performance took place at the Winter Palace in St. Petersburg on the
empress's birthday, 29 January (Old Style) 1736. It was *La forza dell'amore e
dell'odio*, an opera seria by Francesco Araja, the leader of the troupe. That
was the beginning of secular music in Russia as a continuous, professional,
and literate artistic tradition.[1]

That tradition, although it thrived at court under a series of distinguished
maestri di cappella (Manfredini, Galuppi, Traetta, Paisiello, Sarti, Cimarosa),
was of no particular importance to Russia at large, and Russia, beyond providing a few favored foreigners with brief plum appointments, was of no
importance to it. The practice of European art music had little or no role to
play in the formation of Russian national consciousness, which did not even
begin to be a factor in Russian culture until the reign of Catherine the Great
was well under way.[2]

It was only the spread of Europeanized mores and attitudes beyond the
precincts of the court, and the increased Russian presence in Europe following
the Napoleonic Wars, that really rooted European high culture in Russian
urban centers and led beyond receptivity to actual Russian productivity in the
European arts. The institutional means for maintaining that productivity in
music were established in the 1860s, chiefly by dint of Anton Rubinstein's
heroic labors. By the last decade of the nineteenth century Russian composers
of European art music—particularly Rubinstein himself and Chaikovsky, the
outstanding early graduate of Rubinstein's conservatory—had achieved
"world" prominence and prestige. As fine a professional education in music
could be had in Russia as anywhere else on the continent, and Russia's eminence as a habitat and training ground for first-rate talent (chiefly violinistic
and pianistic talent) would actually begin to eclipse that of other nations.

[1] An earlier operatic performance on Russian soil—*Calandro*, a *commedia per musica* by
Giovanni Alberto Ristori, performed at the Kremlin palace in Moscow by a troupe of Italian
comedians from the court of Dresden on 30 November 1731—was an isolated event, not to be
duplicated in the old capital until 1742.

[2] The basic historical treatment of this watershed in Russian cultural history remains Hans
Rogger, *National Consciousness in Eighteenth-Century Russia* (Cambridge, Mass.: Harvard University Press, 1959).

And yet the profession that Rubinstein, Chaikovsky, and all those violinists and pianists followed had only just achieved legitimacy in Russia. Only since the 1860s had Russian law recognized the existence of any such animal as a "Russian composer." And only since the 1770s at the earliest had there even been such a thing as a Russian who worked professionally at music as a European fine art. If Vasiliy Pashkevich (1742–97)—Vincenzo Manfredini's apprentice, who wrote singspiels to texts by Catherine the Great's court poets and eventually by the Empress herself—turns out to have been of Russian birth rather than an immigrant Pole as his name (Paszkiewicz) suggests, then he was the oldest person to whom that description could be applied.

If not, then the distinction belongs to Maxim Sozontovich Berezovsky (1745–77), the son of a serf, who trained at court with Galuppi (first as a sopranist and then, very exceptionally, as a composer) and was sent to Bologna at the Empress Catherine's expense in 1766 to study with Padre Martini. In the event he received instruction not from Martini himself but from the latter's assistant, Stanislao Mattei; but he was awarded the diploma of the Accademia Filarmonica in 1771, one year after Mozart, and saw his journeyman opera, to Metastasio's old *Demofoonte* libretto, successfully produced in Livorno during the 1773 Carnival. (He was then summoned home to take over the Imperial Court Chapel Choir; his suicide at the age of thirty-one made him a legendary figure and, beginning in the 1840s, the subject of novels, plays, and eventually movies.) Berezovsky was thus the earliest Russian-born composer of opera; but since his opera went unheard in Russia, it cannot be said to have contributed to the development of any indigenous practice of European art music there.

The same goes for the *opere serie* of Dmitriy Bortnyansky (1751–1825), another precocious son of a serf from the same Ukrainian village as Berezovsky, who followed him to Italy and eventually succeeded him as Imperial Court Chapel choirmaster. The historical significance of both Berezovsky and Bortnyansky lay in another area; with their choral concertos they played a leading role in Westernizing the much older tradition of Russian Orthodox sacred singing (*peniye*, long distinguished in the Russian vocabulary from the secular art of *muzïka*). Yevstigney Fomin (1761–1800), who is treated at some length in the first part of this book, was a junior member of this first generation of native-born Russian practitioners of the European fine art of music, all men of low birth who pursued their careers in conditions of indentured, quasi-military service.

Accordingly, the practice, as opposed to the consumption, of art music in Russia continued to carry a social stigma well into the nineteenth century, even though Bortnyansky lived to a venerable age and acquired great fame. Rubinstein's efforts to secure an institutional base and official social recognition—the bureaucratic rank of *svobodniy khudozhnik*, "free artist," equivalent to a midlevel civil service grade—for the art he practiced were motivated in part by the self-interest of a man working under multiple social and ethnic handicaps.

Another factor that improved the social standing of art music in Russia was the rise of a generation of noble dilettante composers and performers. Among the earlier members of this cohort were the brothers Wielhorski (Viyel'gorskiy), Counts Mikhail (1788–1856) and Matvey (1794–1866), familiar to readers of Berlioz's memoirs. The elder brother composed an opera, two symphonies, and a raft of chamber music. The younger brother was a cellist of international repute. (Mendelssohn's familiar D-major sonata is dedicated to him.) He lived long enough to become Rubinstein's ally in the professional organization of St. Petersburg musical life, heading the first board of directors of Rubinstein's Russian Musical Society, which sponsored the first full-time resident orchestra in the Russian capital (from 1859), as well as the conservatory (from 1862).

A slightly younger member of this noble cohort was Alexey Fyodorovich Lvov (1798–1870), another long-serving director of the Imperial Court Chapel Choir and a cousin of the Lvov who is cast in a starring role in the first part of this book. As a composer, although he wrote operas and concertos, Alexey Lvov is remembered only for *Bozhe, tsarya khrani* (God Save the Tsar), the dynastic anthem (1833). His greater fame during his lifetime was as a violinist who appeared (gratis, of course) as soloist with orchestras throughout Europe and who played regularly in a trio with Matvey Wielhorski and Franz Liszt. (This last was a professional ensemble in that the pianist was paid—but he was paid by his noble partners, who thus qualified as patrons, not professionals; and the group appeared only at aristocratic salons.)

Later generations of the aristocratic class of Russian art-musicians included Glinka and Dargomïzhsky. The last of the line was Musorgsky, whose landowning family was impoverished by the 1861 emancipation and who therefore had to earn a living (not, it goes without saying, as a musician). Chaikovsky—native-born, conservatory-trained, full-time—was in a word Russia's first composing *professional*, and the very first native musician to achieve a position of esteem in Russian society without the advantage of blue blood or a prestigious sinecure, and without being a performing virtuoso. His professional and social status, not the spurious issue of nationalism, was what estranged him from the "kuchkists," and them from him. They all needed their day jobs and lacked his entrée to the court musical establishment.

So of course they created a mythos of authenticity that excluded him, as it excluded his ethnically suspect mentor, Rubinstein—a mystique that received massive publicity thanks to the prodigious journalistic activity of Vladimir Stasov, their promoter, and César Cui, their brother-in-arms. That myth— which authenticated "true" Russian music by a preternatural ethnic aura unrelated, indeed inimical, to the temporal institutions of the actual Russian state—reached its full formulation only in the 1880s, by which time

Chaikovsky's domination of the local musical scene was complete, when folklorism, even among the kuchkists, was actually becoming passé, and when entrepreneurial patronage was at last allowed by law to compete with the crown in the fields of theater management and music publishing.

It was just then, of course, that Russian music began making a massive bid for recognition on the world stage, and foreign champions for it began to appear. The early foreign champions—for example, Camille Bellaigue (1858–1930) in France and Rosa Newmarch (1857–1940) in England—were indoctrinated directly by Stasov and Cui; their successors—for example, Michel-Dmitri Calvocoressi (1877–1944) in France (later England) and Montagu Montagu-Nathan (1877–1958) in England—were beholden to Bellaigue and Newmarch; Gerald Abraham (1904–88) was Calvocoressi's disciple, even as many younger British champions (by now academic scholars) like Edward Garden (b. 1930) and Gerald Seaman (b. 1934) have been Abraham's. The myth lives on.

It is a myth of otherness.

Tardy growth and tardier professionalization, remote provenience, social marginalism, the means of its promotion, even the exotic language and alphabet of its practitioners have always tinged or tainted Russian art music with an air of alterity, sensed, exploited, bemoaned, asserted, abjured, exaggerated, minimized, glorified, denied, reveled in, traded on, and defended against both from within and from without. From without Russian music was (and is) often preemptively despised and condescended to (witness the vagaries of Chaikovsky's critical reception), though just as often it has been the object of intense fascination and of occasional cults and crazes (witness the same Chaikovsky's ineradicable presence in the concert hall, or the Diaghilev-ignited craze that launched Stravinsky's spectacular career).

From within the world of Russian music there has been a great tendency to celebrate or magnify "difference," in compensation for an inferiority complex that was the inevitable product of its history, but just as often in sincere certainty of Russia's cultural, even moral superiority and its salvific mission. Even Chaikovsky, approaching the height of his fame, could complain to his patroness about the "insulting tone of condescension with which they address a Russian musician" in central Europe. "You can read it in their eyes: 'You're just a Russian, *but I am so kind and indulgent that I favor you with my attention.*' The hell with them! Last year I found myself against my will at Liszt's. He was nauseatingly deferential, but a smile that never left his lips spoke the sentence I underlined above with perfect clarity. It goes without saying that by now I am less disposed than ever to go to these gentlemen on bended knee."[3]

---

[3] Letter to Nadezhda von Meck from Vienna, 27 November/9 December 1877; P. I. Chaikovsky, *Perepiska s N. F. fon-Mekk*, vol. 1 (Moscow: Academia, 1934), pp. 100–101.

Thirty years later, Rimsky-Korsakov could return from Paris crowing that "we Russian composers were veritable Mozarts compared with Richard Strauss, Debussy and Dukas," mired as the West had become by then in "decadence."[4]

Yet however alienated by temperament or by force of circumstance from the "mainstream" of fashion or success, however dependent for their promotion upon their exotic appeal, and however inferior or superior they felt in consequence, Russian musicians in the literate fine-art tradition have *always* construed their identities in a larger European context and drawn their "sentiment of being" (to cite Rousseau's definition of authenticity) from that sense of relatedness. When Miliy Balakirev, the one Russian composer who might fit anyone's narrowest definition of a "nationalist," was introduced by Vladimir Stasov to Rosa Newmarch in 1901, he sat down at the piano to play her a kind of *profession de foi* in tones: Beethoven's *Appassionata*, Chopin's B-minor sonata, and Schumann's G-minor.[5] Not a Russian note in the lot, and yet it characterizes Balakirev and his old "kuchka" far better than their usual chauvinist label. A 1909 memoir by Cui of the group's early days offers vivid confirmation:

> We formed a close-knit circle of young composers. And since there was nowhere to study (the conservatory didn't exist) our *self-education* began. It consisted of playing through everything that had been written by all the greatest composers, and all works were subjected to criticism and analysis in all their technical and creative aspects. We were young and our judgments were harsh. We were very disrespectful in our attitude toward Mozart and Mendelssohn; to the latter we opposed Schumann, who was then ignored by everyone. We were very enthusiastic about Liszt and Berlioz. We worshiped Chopin and Glinka. We carried on heated debates (in the course of which we would down as many as four or five glasses of tea with jam), we discussed musical form, program music, vocal music, and especially operatic form.[6]

—all the same issues, in other words, as were then being debated in Europe. For this was no band of mighty ostriches. What is being described here is a "Davidsbund," to use Schumann's word—a cabal of idealistic progressives opposing authority, on the one hand, and philistinism, on the other, and propagating their views through Cui's avowedly Schumannesque activity as a member of the press. Except for Glinka all the objects of their veneration were located to the west of Russia—and why not? Glinka was at this point the only Russian to venerate, precisely because he alone was on a level with the Eu-

[4] Vasiliy Vasil'yevich Yastrebtsev, *N. A. Rimskiy-Korsakov: Vospominaniya*, ed. A. V. Ossovsky, vol. 2 (Leningrad: Muzgiz, 1960), p. 423.

[5] Rosa Newmarch, *The Russian Opera* (New York: Dutton, n.d. [1914]), p. 200.

[6] "Pervïye kompozitorskiye shagi Ts. A. Kyui," in Cui, *Izbrannïye stat'i* (Leningrad: Muzgiz, 1952).

ropeans. The autochthonous music of Russia, the tonal products of the soil and its peasant denizens, were not admired and not discussed.

For wholly racialized, totalizing notions of Russian musical difference one must look to the West, to the French writers who wrote, and the English ones who alas still write, not only out of an inherited Stasovian bias but also out of internalized, unacknowledged and perhaps by now altogether unwitting colonialist prejudices. Thus in the very recent *Viking Opera Guide*, one may read of Glinka's undefined yet "totally Russian imagination" and Chaikovsky's equally undefined yet "very pronounced Russianness." And, to one's dismay, one also finds a bumblingly innocent appropriation of Balakirev's viciously anti-Semitic sally at Anton Rubinstein: "not a Russian composer, but a Russian who composes."[7]

Essential Russianness, ostensively meant (however obtusely) as a criterion of positive valuation, functions nevertheless as a fence around the "mainstream," defining, lumping, and implicitly excluding the other. One rarely finds Verdi praised for his Italianness anymore, and one *never* finds Wagner praised for his Germanness, heaven forbid, although Verdi and Wagner were as conscious of their nationality, and as affected by it creatively, as any Balakirev. In the conventional historiography of "Western music" Verdi and Wagner are heroic individuals. Russians are a group.

But of course Russia, too, was a colonialist power, and as part 2 of this book will relate, lumped and totalized its others just as resolutely, and with the same pretense of admiration. In Soviet times, too, composers from the "republics" had to wear their Russian-made native badges: witness Khachaturyan, an Armenian who never lived in Armenia but who throughout his career had to compose in Borodin's patented "Polovtsian" style. Witness, too, the manner in which national musical, and particularly operatic, traditions were bestowed upon the arbitrarily created Central Asian republics of the Stalinist imperium.

Typically, a Russian composer of the older generation, steeped in the nineteenth-century "classical" heritage, would be commissioned to "found" the operatic tradition of a Union republic, sometimes in collaboration with an indigenous composer, more often singlehandedly. Thus Sergey Nikiforovich Vasilenko (1872–1956), a Moscow composer who had studied with Taneyev, created the first Uzbek opera (*Buran*, 1939) in collaboration with his own pupil, Mukhtar Ashrafi (1912–75), a native of Bukhara. Yevgeniy Grigoryevich Brusilovsky (1905–81) was the founder of Kazakh opera, with *Kïz-Zhibek*, which inaugurated the Alma-Ata opera house in 1934. He was a pupil of Maximilian Steinberg, Rimsky-Korsakov's son-in-law. For Tajik opera Sergey Artemyevich Balasanyan (1902–82), a Kabalevsky pupil, was re-

[7] *The Viking Opera Guide*, ed. Amanda Holden, with Nicholas Kenyon and Stephen Walsh (London: Penguin Books, 1993), pp. 369, 1083, 925.

cruited; his *Shurishe Vosè* (Vosseh's Uprising) inaugurated the opera house in Stalinabad (now Dushanbe) in 1939. The founder of Kirghiz opera was Alexander Moiseyevich Veprik (1899–1958), a pupil of Myaskovsky; his opera *Toktogul* (1940) inaugurated the opera house in Frunze (now Bishkek). Finally, the opera house in Ashkabad, the capital of the Turkmen republic, opened in 1941 with the opera *Zokhre i Takhir* by Adrian Grigoryevich Shaposhnikov (1888–1967), a pupil of Glazunov.

At the very least it will be evident that ideologies of promulgation and reception affecting Russian art music have been far more explicitly formulated and acknowledged, as a rule, than those of the "universal" repertories with which the Russian product has contended; and that, often enough, such formulations have been hollow excuses, founded on garish double standards, for tendentious value judgments. "A Russian symphony? A contradiction in terms!" my most distinguished professor in graduate school could still snort not so many years ago, illustrating the point with a snatch from the beginning of Borodin's Second. "Who begins a symphony with a fermata?" he asked triumphantly. (With difficulty I resisted the impulse to come back with "da-da-da-DAA.") On the other side of an apparent ideological divide is the treatment accorded Chaikovsky's symphonies by the *New Grove Dictionary*. Except for the last of them, the only one that escapes severe censure is the Second, for the reason that it contains Chaikovsky's "most fully Russian" work.[8]

But the divide between the condemning and the excusing view is only apparent. Whether invoked in praise or in blame, the arbitrarily defined or proclaimed Russianness of Russian music is a normative criterion, and ineluctably an invidious one. If "How Russian is it?" is your critical question, then however the question is answered, and however the answer is valued, you have consigned Russian composers to a ghetto.

And so I find myself in warm sympathy with the basic complaint enunciated by Gary Tomlinson, another "historian of others," who notes, in terms borrowed from Tzvetan Todorov, a common failure to perceive difference without imputing it to inferiority, however that judgment be camouflaged by a show of indulgent approbation.[9]

---

[8] *The New Grove Dictionary of Music and Musicians*, ed. Stanley Sadie (London: Macmillan, 1980), vol. 18, p. 611. What makes the work "most fully Russian" is the fact that it incorporates quoted folk songs. That this is exclusively a Western measure of Russian authenticity is shown by Musorgsky's belittling comments about Chaikovsky's opera *The Oprichnik*, in which the conspicuous consumption of folk songs is written off as pandering—"the public demands Russian stuff from Russian artists"—by a cynic whose proclaimed worship of "pure musical beauty" masked "the aim of becoming a favorite with the public and making a name for himself" (letter to Stasov, 26 December 1872; M. P. Musorgsky, *Literaturnoye naslediye*, ed. A. A. Orlova and M. S. Pekelis, vol. 1 [Moscow: Muzïka, 1971], p. 143).

[9] See *Music in Renaissance Magic: Toward a Historiography of Others* (Chicago: University of Chicago Press, 1993), pp. 9–10, citing Tzvetan Todorov, *The Conquest of America: The*

This is already enough to adumbrate the ironic tensions that have always attended the production and consumption of Russian art music, creating a plenteous field for the historical or cultural critic to probe. There is the tension between overt agendas and covert or involuntary ones; and of course there is the old tension between "center and periphery" as one used to say, or between "the universal and the national."[10] Where academic musicology, as befit its Germanic origins, used to be tetchily (and yes, nationalistically) "center-centered," now it is much more the fashion (and much more fun) to use the discourse of "alterity" as a tool for deconstructing (particularizing and situating) the universal. All of musicology, we Rusists like to think, is getting Russian.

ANOTHER durable and fertile tension attending Russian music concerns matters of interpretation and "ownership." Owing to the historical circumstances in which Russian artists have worked, the symbology of Russian art is exceptionally rich and multivoiced. In an autocratic or oligarchical society in which political, social, or spiritual matters could not be openly aired, such matters went underground into historiography and art. The art of no other country is so heavily fraught with subtexts.

This is so obviously true in the case of Russian music as to have created, paradoxically enough, yet another obstacle to its musicological appreciation, another deterrent to its scholarly investigation. The same heavily fraught character that made Russian music so urgently communicative (and so appealing to audiences) marked it off from the academically hallowed discourse of "absolute music," greatly magnifying its aura of undesirable alterity. It was often painfully evident that techniques and approaches that were developed to serve the needs of immanent critique (style criticism, structural analysis) engaged a lot of Russian music very incompletely or trivially. Of course the music,

---

Question of the Other (New York: Harper and Row, 1984); he goes on to cite from Todorov a concomitant incapacity for acknowledging "*equality* without its compelling us to accept identity." This has an obvious analogue in the reception of Stravinsky, and the unwillingness of "mainstream" historians and theorists who have accepted Stravinsky's greatness to acknowledge his Russianness, a pattern described and illustrated more fully in the first section of chapter 13. For an extreme and very deplorable example see Claudio Spies, "Conundrums, Conjectures, Construals; or, 5 vs. 3: The Influence of Russian Composers on Stravinsky," in *Stravinsky Retrospectives*, ed. Ethan Haimo and Paul Johnson (Lincoln: University of Nebraska Press, 1987), pp. 76–140.

[10] To savor the double standards informing this noachian dualism one need only scan the table of contents in Alfred Einstein's *Music in the Romantic Era* (New York: Norton, 1947). Chapters 15 and 16, titled "Universalism within the National," treat German, Italian and French composers, plus Chopin and Liszt, evidently traveling on Nansen passports; chapter 17, titled "Nationalism," is the ghetto chapter, covering all denizens of Bohemia, Russia, Scandinavia, Holland, Belgium, Hungary, Poland, Spain and Portugal, and North America without further discrimination.

dismissed as trivial or defective, could easily take the rap for that. Or, when the music was felt to be inescapably important, the relevance of the nonimmanent could be minimized or denied.

Thus an early style-critical study of Shostakovich's late quartets, music of undoubtable weight and seriousness, begins with an explicitly antihermeneutical disclaimer, somewhat inconsistently backed up by recourse to the composer's authority: "If we can assume these works to be capable of standing on their own merits, disregarding and divorced from the composer's presumed 'intentions,' then a comparatively objective, stylistic approach, which treats each work first as an autonomous entity and only then in its relationship to other works, appears to be warranted. Indeed, the quotation with which the Introduction began [see n. 11] would seem to indicate Shostakovich's desire to let his works 'stand on their own merits' without additional help from the composer."[11]

And an important analytical study of Scriabin—thought nowadays by many theorists to be inescapably important as a way station en route to atonality—opens with a strikingly similar disclaimer, breathtakingly projected on the composer without even a pretense of the latter's assent: "Those whose attention is focused solely on the mystical aspirations of Scriabin's large works lose sight of an equally important aspect of his career: even when his harmonic practice was quite advanced and he was striving for magnificent ecstatic effects in his sonatas and orchestral works, Scriabin remained at heart a confirmed formalist. His compositions consistently reflect both his sensitivity to the finest detail and his interest in subtle, complex relationships worked out with meticulous precision."[12]

Perhaps needless to say, what is introduced merely as an "equally important aspect of Scriabin's career" is thereafter the "sole focus" of the book, completely displacing the "other" stuff. Also deserving of comment is the use of the highly (and oh, so variously) charged word "formalist" to describe the composer of works found amenable to the analyst's very formal methods. The aggressive way in which both studies, on Shostakovich and on Scriabin,

---

[11] Laurel E. Fay, "The Last Quartets of Dmitrii Shostakovich: A Stylistic Investigation" (Ph.D. dissertation, Cornell University, 1978; University Microfilms 7902266), p. 2; interpretive studies are dismissed en masse as "subjective" endeavors that "explain more about the individual author [of the interpretation] than about Shostakovich and his compositions" (p. 1). The epigraph is a comment reportedly made in conversation with the critic and musicologist Georgiy Khubov (who will be more fully introduced and discussed in the last chapter of this book) during the last year of the composer's life: "I, you understand, willingly listen to critical remarks and answer questions, but I leave the judgement of the content of my own compositions up to the musicologists." Needless to say, the author of the dissertation, who has gone on to become America's most astute commentator on Soviet music and its relationship to its multifarious contexts, has reconsidered these premises.

[12] James Baker, *The Music of Alexander Scriabin* (New Haven: Yale University Press, 1986), pp. vii–viii.

utilize the standard arsenal of contemporary "formalist" musicology—"Adlerian" style criticism, "Schenkerian" analysis, pitch-class set theory—in order to marginalize and eventually cast off the "extramusical" baggage ("politics," including the politics of the personal, in the case of Shostakovich; the "occult" or the "mystical" in the case of Scriabin) eminently validates Gary Tomlinson's call for "a brand of interpretation that does not silence, efface, or absorb the other in the act of understanding it."[13]

The name of that game is hermeneutics. It is what this book is all about.

AS CHAPTER 12 will illustrate, Scriabin attracts the silencing treatment with special rabidity. Why Scriabin?

An old joke: a black man is seen reading a Yiddish newspaper. When asked why he is reading the socialist paper rather than the communist one, he answers, "That's all I need!" To be Russian is bad enough; to be an occultist on top of that is two strikes. For many, it's been enough to declare him out: "Scriabin," scoffs Joseph Kerman, "who would have added Indian mysticism, color, and scent to the already bulging *Gesamt* of Wagnerian orthodoxy, came to nothing."[14] It is certainly arguable that an analytical method concerned only with Scriabin's "interest in subtle, complex relationships worked out with meticulous precision" also reduces him to nothing.

That is why Tomlinson, for one, ever vigilant of the rights of others, and as sensitive as any Scriabin-lover to "historians' and musicologists' hegemonic treatment of occult thought," has declared analysis, the immanent close reading of musical texts and their technical explication, to be "one of the most severe systems of discursive constraints that the modern academic disciplines have offered," an inherently "monological" practice that "can see only sameness and converse only with itself," and therefore incompatible with hermeneutics.[15]

Tomlinson wants to converse directly with others on an equal footing and so learn from them. The "paradigm" he wants to apply to musicology comes from recent highly relativistic anthropological theory, which stresses exceeding openness to difference and the cultivation of a radically nonjudgmental ("noncoercive") attitude to the knowledge gathered from informants. One can only applaud an effort to reduce the "one-sidedness" (read: closed-mindedness) of our relationship with "those we share today's world with," and to recognize the desirability of true dialogue with them.[16] It is obvious

---

[13] *Music in Renaissance Magic*, p. 9.

[14] "Wagner: Thoughts in Season," in *Write All These Down: Essays on Music* (Berkeley and Los Angeles: University of California Press, 1994), p. 264.

[15] See *Music in Renaissance Magic*, pp. 19, 230–31; for an even stronger, more general indictment of "close reading" see Tomlinson's "Musical Pasts and Postmodern Musicologies: A Response to Lawrence Kramer," *Current Musicology* 53 (1993): 18–24, esp. pp. 21–22.

[16] *Music in Renaissance Magic*, p. 13.

that such an effort has ramifications and promises potential benefits that quite transcend the bounds of mere academic practice. But Tomlinson presses his "dialogical" point further, asking "whether there can be any essential differences between historical and anthropological encounters with others."[17]

Well yes, there are. Or rather there is one big difference that simply cannot be got around. Historical others are dead. They can no longer actively construct themselves. They cannot function as "mutually" (or reciprocally) "interpreting subjects."[18] Dialogues with the dead, or with inanimate things, are metaphorical when not delusional.

Tomlinson, while making a point at the outset of disavowing personal belief in the occult practices he studies,[19] nevertheless wants dialogue with both the dead and the inanimate—or rather, he wants to converse with the dead through the inanimate medium of texts. He claims precedent for this dialogical fallacy in the hermeneutic practice of Hans-Georg Gadamer and Mikhail Bakhtin. From Gadamer he adopts the notion of the "implicit question" that arises out of the dialectical encounter between reader and text. "The voice that speaks to us from the past," Gadamer writes, "—be it text, work, trace— itself poses a question and places our meaning in openness. In order to answer this question, we, of whom the question is asked, must ourselves begin to ask questions. We must attempt to reconstruct the question to which the transmitted text is the answer."[20]

The last sentence, an acknowledged paraphrase from R. G. Collingwood, is already famous within musicology thanks to its many oft-quoted, unacknowledged paraphrases by Carl Dahlhaus.[21]

But Gadamer's "voice of the past" is a figurative voice, produced by the interpreter's imagination as he consciously attempts a speculative fusion of his own "horizon" of understanding—itself the product of interpretive tradition, among other things—with the horizon of understanding within which the text was produced. Gadamer calls the latter the "horizon of the question within which the sense of the text is determined." He explicitly cautions that it is up to the interpreter, the historian or critic, to "find the right questions to ask." These questions come not in response to an enforced mental passivity

[17] Ibid., p. 6.

[18] Ibid.

[19] *Music in Renaissance Magic*, p. 3.

[20] Hans-Georg Gadamer, *Truth and Method*, 2d ed. (1965), anonymous trans., ed. Garrett Barden and John Cumming (New York: Crossroad, 1985), p. 337; quoted in *Music in Renaissance Magic*, p. 28.

[21] Cf. Philip Gossett, "Up from Beethoven" (review of Dahlhaus, *19th-Century Music*), *New York Review of Books*, 26 October 1989, p. 21; for a general discussion of Dahlhaus's dependence on Gadamer's hermeneutical legacy, with specific reference to the idea of "reconstructing questions," see James Hepokoski, "The Dahlhaus Project and Its Extramusicological Sources," *19th-Century Music* 14 (1990–91): 221–46, esp. pp. 231–38. Gadamer acknowledges Collingwood's autobiography as the source of his "logic of the question" in *Truth and Method*, p. 333.

(as Tomlinson construes Gadamer's "opening up, and keeping open, of possibilities"), even if subjectively they appear to occur to us unbidden (whence Gadamer's temporary formulation that "questioning . . . is more a 'passion' than an action"). In fact "finding the right questions" provides the initial stimulus, in Gadamer's view, to the practice of an active, "conscious art" for which the "Socratic-Platonic dialectic" is the enduring model.

To allow oneself, as Tomlinson does, to imagine that the "questions" (in ordinary methodological language, the hypotheses) that one entertains as one reads dialectically (that is, "openly") have in fact been actively propounded by the text is to engage in precisely the pretense or delusion of omniscient objectivity that Tomlinson otherwise purports to oppose. It is, to use one of Tomlinson's favorite pejoratives, a form of solipsism in which a dialogue that has been staged and scripted entirely within the interpreter's own head is apprehended as a dialogue between two actual subjects.[22]

Tomlinson defends his construal of Gadamer with a quote: "It is more than a metaphor . . . to describe the work of hermeneutics as a conversation with the text."[23] But the phrase that Tomlinson has elided from the quote gives it a different meaning, one altogether inconsistent with Tomlinson's premises. To describe hermeneutics as conversation, the elided phrase allows, is "a memory of what originally was the case," meaning that, *in addition to being a metaphor*, this conversation is a conscious application or reconstruction of the "Socratic method," in which, one recalls, only one party actively poses questions.

From Bakhtin, the patron saint of "dialogue," Tomlinson appropriates the term *vnenakhodimost'*, "outside-locatedness" or, more simply, "outsideness" (or more esoterically, as Tomlinson prefers, "exotopy"). Tomlinson sees Bakhtin's outsideness as an insurance of intersubjectivity, the protection of the other's subjective integrity and its strangeness against the incursions of an aggrandizing "monological" interpreter who would, by the exercise of an unthinking empathy, assimilate it. And yet Bakhtin's actual usage of the term suggests that it is the preservation of the creative interpreter's integrity that is the real issue (and a risky, hence necessary, one for a Soviet writer to raise).

"There exists a very strong, but one-sided and thus untrustworthy idea," Bakhtin wrote near the end of his life,

> that in order better to understand a foreign culture, one must enter into it, forgetting one's own, and view the world through the eyes of this foreign culture. . . .
> Of course, a certain entry as a living being (*vzhivaniye*) into a foreign culture, the possibility of seeing the world through its eyes, is a necessary part of the process of understanding it; but if this were the only aspect of this understanding, it

---

[22] Quotations in this and the preceding paragraph are from *Truth and Method*, pp. 266, 301, 330, 333.

[23] Ibid., p. 331, as quoted by Tomlinson on p. 28.

would merely be duplication and would not entail anything new or enriching. *Creative understanding* does not renounce itself, its own place in time, its own culture; and it forgets nothing. In order to understand, it is immensely important for the person who understands to be *located outside* the object of his or her creative understanding—in time, in space, in culture. For one cannot even really see one's own exterior and comprehend it as a whole, and no mirrors or photographs can help; our real exterior can be seen and understood only by other people, because they are located outside us in space and because they are *others*.

In the realm of culture, outsideness (*vnenakhodimost'*) is a most powerful factor in understanding. It is only in the eyes of *another* culture that foreign culture reveals itself fully and profoundly (but not maximally fully, because there will be cultures that see and understand even more). A meaning only reveals its depths once it has encountered and come into contact with another, foreign meaning; they engage in a kind of dialogue, which surmounts the closedness and one-sidedness of these particular meanings, these cultures. We raise new questions for a foreign culture, ones that it did not raise itself; we seek answers to our own questions in it; and the foreign culture responds to us by revealing to us its new aspects and new semantic depths. Without *one's own* questions one cannot creatively understand anything other or foreign (but, of course, the questions must be serious and sincere). Such a dialogic encounter of two cultures does not result in merging or mixing. Each retains its own unity and *open* totality, but they are mutually enriched.[24]

Note again that only one party is portrayed as asking questions; that is because in the quoted passage Bakhtin, like Tomlinson, is considering diachronic encounters, but unlike Tomlinson he does not delude himself that such a dialogue can be actively intersubjective. I have quoted the passage at length because it resonates with so many other Russian formulations that will be encountered in this book, in which the self is constituted in and through the encounter with the other; and also because the difference in tone and outlook between the bold, optimistic seventy-five-year-old victim of Soviet oppression and the nervously circumspect young beneficiary of American affluence and liberalism is so pronounced.

Bakhtin does not regard his own subjective self with automatic suspicion; it is his primary tool. Indeed, one of the "principal advantages of *vnenakhodimost'*," as the coiner of the term defined it, was the insurance it provided against "loss of one's own position" in an encounter with the other.[25] Tomlinson, on the contrary, following contemporary anthropological theory (developed, of course, on the basis of synchronic study involving personal contact

[24] Mikhail Bakhtin, "Response to a Question from the *Novïy Mir* Editorial Staff" (1970), in M. M. Bakhtin, *Speech Genres and Other Late Essays*, trans. Vern W. McGee, ed. Caryl Emerson and Michael Holquist (Austin: University of Texas Press, 1986), pp. 6–7.

[25] Bakhtin, "From Notes Made in 1970–71," in ibid., p. 141.

with living informants), looks out mainly to protect the other's interests, and seeks to place his own as far as possible "in jeopardy."[26]

To be sure, Bakhtin recognizes that "one's own position" can be dogmatic and monological, or, more simply, that one's mind may be closed:

> The exclusive orientation toward recognizing, searching only for the familiar (that which has already been), does not allow the new to reveal itself (i.e., the fundamental, unrepeatable totality). Quite frequently, methods of explanation and interpretation are reduced to this kind of disclosure of the repeatable, to a recognition of the already familiar. . . . Everything that is repeatable and recognizable is fully dissolved and assimilated solely by the consciousness of the person who understands: in the other's consciousness he can see and understand only his own consciousness. He is in no way enriched. In what belongs to others he recognizes only his own.[27]

This begins to sound a great deal like Tomlinson's far from unjustified critique of ordinary music-analytical practice. Unfortunately, it also describes Tomlinson's approach to Bakhtin.

IN THE long passage cited earlier on *vnenakhodimost'*, Bakhtin raises a crucial issue for dialogical inquiry when he notes that, because of our outsideness, "we raise new questions for a foreign culture, ones that it did not raise itself." In another passage he rejects the notion that our aim should be "to understand a given text as the author himself understood it." That is good, he allows, as far as it goes, "but our understanding can and should be better."[28] It is not that we are so much smarter now, he insists, but that texts contain more than their authors can ever know.

> Powerful and profound creativity is largely unconscious and polysemic. Through understanding it is supplemented by [our present] consciousness, and the multiplicity of its meanings is revealed. Thus, understanding supplements the text: it is active and also creative by nature. Creative understanding continues creativity, and multiplies the artistic wealth of humanity. The co-creativity of those who understand.[29]

Hence Bakhtin's much quoted remark, that

> neither Shakespeare himself nor his contemporaries knew that 'great Shakespeare' whom we know now. There is no possibility of squeezing our Shakespeare into the Elizabethan epoch. . . . [Shakespeare] has grown because of that which actually has been and continues to be found in his works, but which nei-

---

[26] *Music in Renaissance Magic*, p. 6, quoting James Clifford.
[27] "From Notes Made in 1970–71," pp. 142–43.
[28] Ibid., p. 141.
[29] Ibid., pp. 141–42.

ther he himself nor his contemporaries could consciously perceive and evaluate in the context of the culture of their epoch.[30]

A creatively dialogical hermeneutics is thus not limited in its view of the other to what the other would recognize and affirm. Gadamer expresses a related thought when he says that "it is a hermeneutical necessity always to go beyond mere reconstruction," and this because "we cannot avoid thinking about that which was unquestionably accepted, and hence not thought about, by an author, and bringing it into the openness of the question."[31] Both writers broach a level of meaning that transcends the authorial subjective, and so also transcends the intersubjective.

Tomlinson broaches it too, and never sees the contradiction between it and the intersubjective model of diachronic interpretation that he is attempting to construct. In fact he broaches it in a particularly strong form derived from Michel Foucault's *Les Mots et les choses: Une Archéologie des sciences humaines*.[32] In this strong variant, which was found unconvincingly extreme when first promulgated and later modified by the author, what is called the "archeological" level of meaning, which defines the ground rules under which thought and action take place (or, as Tomlinson puts it, "the grid of meaningfulness that constrains and conditions a discourse or social practice"), is, necessarily, "largely or wholly hidden from and not articulable by the historical actors."[33] Furthermore, this level is radically distinguished from the hermeneutic level of meaning, which deals in that which was known and articulable—in other words, with what Tomlinson calls "conscious authorial [or compositional] intent."[34] Summarizing this tough dualistic view, Tomlinson asserts that "the actors themselves . . . knew what they were doing and, frequently, why they were doing it (these are the meanings interpreted by hermeneutic history); but they couldn't fully know what what they were doing did."[35]

This is rather lofty, both as regards the "actors" and as regards "hermeneutic history." It sets up, as rigid dualisms inevitably will, all kinds of invidious hierarchies of which Tomlinson, on reflection, might well disapprove (between the actors and the interlocutor, for example, or between the subjectively experienced and the objectively observed) and privileges, in its antisubjectivity, precisely that which is not available to dialogue, but only to the theorist's superior horizon. It needs to be taken down a few pegs.

---

[30] "Response to a Question from the *Novïy Mir* Editorial Staff," p. 4.

[31] *Truth and Method*, p. 337.

[32] Paris: Gallimard, 1966; trans. as *The Order of Things: An Archeology of the Human Sciences* (New York: Random House, 1970).

[33] *Music in Renaissance Magic*, pp. x, 34.

[34] Ibid. (e.g., pp. 29 ["authorial intent"], 234 ["conscious compositional intent"], etc.).

[35] Ibid., p. 34.

In the first place, as the preceding quotes from Bakhtin and Gadamer should suffice to indicate, any view of hermeneutics that reduces it to intentionalism is a willfully impoverished view. The first section ("Shostakovich and Us") of chapter 14 will be a detailed argument that intentionalism is precisely what hermeneutics is not. A properly conducted hermeneutical inquiry, it will be argued there, includes what Tomlinson calls archeology, as Bakhtin more than implies when he states that "the first task is to understand the work as the author himself understood it, without exceeding the limits of his understanding," but that the equally necessary "second task is to take advantage of one's own position of temporal and cultural outsideness" to the world of the author and the text,[36] precisely so as to determine (as Tomlinson puts it) "what what they were doing did."

In the second place, the insistence that archeological meanings are necessarily unconscious, indeed unknowable and inarticulable by historical actors and their contemporaries, is willfully exaggerated. What "goes without saying" is not for that mere reason unsayable. In his own energetic polemical activity on behalf of "postmodern" musicology, for example, Tomlinson himself has performed an effective archeology of contemporary musicological "discourse" and "social practice," attempting to get a cohort of contemporary historical actors, namely his colleagues, to see what he has already managed to unearth and articulate, namely the "grid of meaningfulness that constrains and conditions" their activity, and that he calls by the name of "modernism."[37] Those whom he has convinced have been able to see, and to name, what had been hidden without ceasing to be contemporary historical actors.

Tomlinson might be tempted to describe those who have resisted his message as preferring to remain blind, but their blindness, in any case, is not a necessary but a chosen thing, chosen precisely because confrontation with previously unchallenged and unconscious constraints can itself be quite constraining. Changes in the structure of belief and practice (or what Tomlinson, after the prodigally overquoted Thomas Kuhn, calls "paradigm shifts") come about precisely when formerly unconscious constraints become (read: are made) conscious. Although Foucault liked to imagine this process as taking place in violent, glamorous lurches, in fact it happens little by little, quite undramatically, every single day. What is truly hidden remains hidden. To

---

[36] "From Notes Made in 1970–71," p. 144. Before introducing "archeology" into the discussion, Tomlinson had offered a less restricted and more accurate if still incomplete definition of hermeneutic practice, as aiming at "the interpretation of texts so as to form hypotheses of their authors' conscious or unconscious meanings and the making of hypotheses about relationships among (and hence traditions of) texts" (*Music in Renaissance Magic*, p. x).

[37] See his "Musical Pasts and Postmodern Musicologies," cited in n. 15; also G. Tomlinson, "Cultural Dialogics and Jazz: A White Historian Signifies," in *Disciplining Music: Musicology and Its Canons*, ed. Katherine Bergeron and Philip V. Bohlman (Chicago: University of Chicago Press, 1992), pp. 64–94; and even the very text under discussion here, the introduction to *Music in Renaissance Magic*, pp. 1–43.

total darkness no one's eyes can grow accustomed. Things become visible because they are potentially so. ("Where there was id," someone once said, "let ego be.") As Foucault might have been the first to caution, metaphors like "archeology" ought not be taken too literally.

Of course it is always possible to draw the circle of hidden constraint and conditioning wider, so that, for example, it encompasses both the "modernists" and their "postmodern" critics like Tomlinson. One can even draw it wide enough to encircle Foucault himself. The purview of "archeological" meaning, in other words, can always be manipulated to fulfill its own conditions. To that extent the concept is a fiction resting on a truism. So is Tomlinson's dialogically active historical other, who is in some ways an unknowable subject, in other ways an object known all too easily and well. Their fictiveness, and their joint foregrounding of epistemological limits, are what the two concepts, otherwise so contradictory, have in common.

WE CAN all do with an occasional reminder that we can't know everything, and heuristic fictions can be useful tools indeed. The danger is that truism easily hardens into dogma, and fictions, when they are unawares believed, are easily transformed into mystique. How else explain the conclusion Tomlinson draws from his study of Renaissance magical practices invoking music, that on the other side of the insuperable barrier of alterity there is "a place where magic works." He continues, lest anyone think he is speaking in metaphors: "This I think we must accept almost as a matter of faith, faith in anthropological difference and in people's abilities to construct through language and deed their own worlds, unfettered by the world rules others have made. This is the place where Ficino's astrological songs succeeded in bringing about the effects his discussions of them described."[38]

But if that is the case, then the whole process asserted by "archeology," whereby one "episteme" (as Foucault called them), one set of unarticulated premises of knowledge, suddenly gives way to another, becomes entirely random and mysterious. Tomlinson recognizes this and takes explicit, prescriptive steps to protect the mystery:

> Our desire to ask is . . . almost irresistible: "But how, precisely, did Ficino's songs work technically? How did they change the physical relationship between him and the cosmos?" We must recognize that the voicing itself of the question is an unwarranted act of translation, a forced reshaping of Ficino's world to fit the different shape of our own. Once the question is posed we have jerked Ficino's songs into our space, into a space we control utterly. Then there is no answer but that Ficino's songs were unsuccessful in working the physical effects he envisaged for them; that they failed; that they were . . . technically unavailing if socially rewarding.

[38] *Music in Renaissance Magic*, p. 247.

So we must not ask the question that comes automatically to our lips. It is, more than most, a coercive question.[39]

Faith in difference is thus purchased at the cost of faith in scholarship. To avoid coercing the other—an aim that has arisen, to repeat, out of altogether laudable postcolonialist intentions—we must be prepared mercilessly to repress ourselves. What is so curious is Tomlinson's failure to realize how coercive are his own tactics on the others whom he addresses most directly— that is, his readers. For an appeal to faith immediately substitutes doctrinal for scholarly authority, and turns academic debate into holy war. Things take a downright Orwellian turn when Tomlinson maintains that a knowledge arising precisely out of a forcible "limiting of our investigation" in the name of faith represents "as unfettered an understanding . . . as we can attain."[40]

That is Newspeak. But it is not new. It is exactly what Blaise Pascal, in his famous high-stakes "bet," counseled rationalists to do, some three and a half centuries ago, in order to resist the devil's episteme and safeguard their soul's salvation: adopt the external forms and practices of believers, he advised, and this, eventually, *vous fera croire et vous abêtira.*[41] "It will make you believe," he promised, "and it will make you stupid." What Pascal prescribed was avowedly a dogmatic practice. With Tomlinson dogmatism has gone underground, but a suitably equipped intellectual archeologist will have little trouble in unearthing it. Our solicitude for others, in any case, can find other, less crippling, avenues of expression than the surrender of our critical faculties.

The first and most important exercise of these faculties is precisely that of deciding when others, and which others, are deserving of our solicitude. The mandatory insulation of the other's position from "coercive" scrutiny paralyzes that most essential function. We have only to substitute a name like Pol Pot for that of Ficino, or a practice like ethnic cleansing for that of astrological song, in order to see that willed abstentions from interrogation and judgment do not necessarily advance the Lord's work. Is Tomlinson's special pleading on behalf of Ficino and his divertingly exotic ways in any important sense distinguishable, say, from Henry Kissinger's notorious defense of the repression at Tienanmen Square? Do protective measures really show respect for the other? Whom shall we respect the more in the event, the Beijing students who aped the symbols of Western democracy and tried to erase difference, or those who by the exercise of force upheld the uniqueness of the Chinese political and cultural experience?

If we hold difference in reverence, will we not be led to insist upon it? Does placing a mental fence around others only protect them, or might it not con-

---

[39] Ibid., pp. 250–51.
[40] Ibid., pp. 251, 250.
[41] Blaise Pascal, "Le pari," in *Pensées et Opuscules* (Paris: Larousse, 1934), p. 62.

fine them as well? And does it protect only them, or might it not also insulate our own practices from scrutiny? How does such a romantic concern for the preservation of cultural difference differ, finally, from the concerns of a benevolent colonialist who opposes the education or the enfranchisement of native populations?

It would be well, in any event, to remember for whose sake it is that we are most commonly exhorted, in today's world, to silence "questions that come automatically to our lips" out of "faith in anthropological difference." Arguments and renunciations that at first sentimental blush can seem to safeguard the interests of the oppressed can and more often do serve the interests of their oppressors. "At the recent United Nations World Conference on Human Rights," Stephen Greenblatt has written in honorable abashment, "it was the most brutally oppressive governments that invoked 'history' and 'difference,' claiming that concepts of fairness and justice should be measured against regional particularities and various historical, cultural, and religious differences. These are the 'progressive' arguments of torturers."[42]

That is why it is so important that as scholars we treat otherness not as immutable or essential fact but as *myth*—which is not to say, in the vulgarized sense of the word, as falsehood, but as an operational fiction or assumption that unless critically examined runs a high risk of tendentious abuse. (The first section ("A Myth of the Twentieth Century") in chapter 13 is the other place in this book where an insufficiently conscious mythology will be confronted head-on.) A mythographic attitude toward otherness, and toward culture-theorizing generally, is shared especially widely among Slavists and Rusists and post-Sovietologists. We have our special reasons to condemn and to resist utopian romanticism, however novel and glamorous the packaging.[43]

THESE, then, are among the subtexts that (once you get to digging) may turn up beneath the "postmodernist" call to renounce analysis and close critical

---

[42] "Kindly Visions," *New Yorker*, 11 October 1993, p. 120.

[43] Aside from a general nausea that arises from an awareness of what happens when theoretical dogmas actually do gain control of a social practice, there is the dowdy if (for Slavists) time-honored matter of "realism" so eloquently broached by Clare Cavanagh in a shattering talk she gave at a panel devoted to "Shostakovich's Contemporaries and Their Fates in the Soviet Period" (I thank Prof. Cavanagh for allowing me to quote from the typescript): "The dead authors and books of Barthes, Foucault and Derrida can retain their purely metaphorical status only in a society that has long since lost the habit of literally destroying writers and texts for their verbal crimes against the state. If the literal meaning, in other words, of phrases like 'the death of the author' or 'of the book' is the first meaning that comes to mind, as it does for the Slavist, it undermines the very core of these theorists' arguments; it undoes our capacity to conceive of language as mere metaphoricity, or of the world as pure interpretation" ("The Death of the Book *à la russe*: Poetry under Stalin," read at the conference "Shostakovich: The Man and His Age" at the University of Michigan, 30 January 1994). It also undoes our capacity, I should say, to ignore the heartless complacency and the frivolity that informs this vein of antihumanistic theorizing.

reading in the name of fetishized difference, and the reasons why that call, seductive though it may be in the context of an overly routinized and often morally purblind professional practice, has got to be resisted and actively opposed. In the case of Gary Tomlinson himself, who has been specializing in vanished or nonliterate repertories that can offer little resistance to anyone's tactics or assertions, methodological renunciation has been minimal (though perhaps the repertorial renunciation has been exorbitant). Scholars who retain a critical interest in what I have called (after Charles Seeger) "the fine art of music"—and their readers, too, lest we forget—have more to lose.

At stake are two points of honor. One requires that we do not ask our readers to accept our findings on faith. The critical and skeptical posture we have inherited from the traditional practice of our discipline is a hard-won and precious thing, the truest trophy of positivism.[44] The other requires that we not let ourselves off easy by confusing difficult aims and tasks with impossible ones. We can admit that omniscience is impossible without giving up the project of advancing our knowledge. We can admit that our conclusions can only be held true pending falsification and still insist that falsification come by way of reasoned refutation or counterexample, not dogmatic assertion. We can admit that our individual "subject positions" are necessarily partial and limited without forgetting that those who have mounted general attacks on empiricism in the name of theoretical abstractions are subject to the same epistemological limitations as the rest of us.

In the hermeneutic essays that follow—hermeneutic in the larger, truer sense that includes archeology—I rely heavily on close textual analysis precisely because hermeneutics and musical analysis have so often and so complacently been declared, from both sides of the presumed divide, to be antagonistic. In fact, the essay that deals most obviously in archeological subtexts—the one on Stravinsky's *Svadebka*—is precisely the one that reads the text most closely. If the notes on the page cannot be an entrée to such an investigation, especially one that leads in such a hazardous direction, then I do not think we have any proper entrée at all; and as Albert Camus asked at the end of the essay that more than any other proclaimed the author's political engagement, "If we are not artists in our language first of all, what sort of artists are we?"[45]

In every essay that follows, then, I will be asking precisely the question that our new obscurantists would place off limits—"But how, precisely, did [Chaikovsky's and Scriabin's and Stravinsky's and Shostakovich's] songs

---

[44] I borrow the phrase from that excellent phrasemaker Joseph Kerman, whose insufficiently discriminating demonization of "positivism" has provided a banner under which many disciplinary faith-healers have congregated (see *Contemplating Music: Challenges to Musicology* [Cambridge, Mass.: Harvard University Press, 1985]; the quoted phrase is on p. 225).

[45] "The Artist and His Time," in Albert Camus, *The Myth of Sisyphus and Other Essays*, trans. Justin O'Brien (New York: Knopf, 1955), p. 150.

work technically?" —precisely in order to understand both the means by which the composers realized their intentions ("how [Chaikovsky's and Scriabin's and Stravinsky's and Shostakovich's] songs worked their physical effects") and also the way in which the composers were responding to issues and circumstances that, one can only presume, lay below the threshold of their conscious intending as they went about the act of composing. (For, to put it as bluntly as I have often had to do in response to bluntly reductive questioning, no, I do not imagine that Stravinsky's mind was actively fixed on Mussolini while in the very midst of scoring *Svadebka*.)

In part 1, from which the title of the book is drawn, I attempt to set questions of Russian nationality, national character, and national self-awareness (all translatable by a single capacious Russian word, *narodnost'*) in varying historical or musical contexts to discourage the usual clumsy reductive or essentialist—and ineluctably invidious—generalizations about "nationalism" (also a possible translation of *narodnost'*) without minimizing what was and is an issue of paramount mythic concern to virtually all Russians, creative artists emphatically included. Technical explication based on close observation is as indispensable to this as it is to any anti-generalizing, anti-essentializing task. The trick, as always, is to avoid reductiveness or assimilation to an arbitrary norm without losing engagement with musical particulars. The method has been as far as possible to ground analytical practice in historical information. This, too, is a reconciliation often dismissed as impossible or superfluous by those unwilling to cope with its difficulty.

THE WRITING of this book was assisted by a University of California President's Research Fellowship in the Humanities, awarded for the academic year 1993–94, my first sabbatical year since joining the Berkeley faculty. Its nucleus was a trio of lectures prepared for the Christian Gauss Seminars in Criticism at Princeton University and delivered there (together with a supplementary lecture at the music department) in November and December 1993 under the general rubric "Hermeneutics of Russian Music." The first, entitled "Chaikovsky and the Human," consisted of the closing third of chapter 11, of which the opening third had been given, under the title "Tchaikovsky: A New View," as keynote address at the International Tchaikovsky Symposium, Hofstra University, 7 October 1993. The second Princeton lecture, "Scriabin and the Superhuman," was an abridgment of chapter 12. The third, "Stravinsky and the Subhuman," corresponded to the first section of chapter 13, and the fourth, "Shostakovich and the Inhuman," corresponded to the third section of chapter 14 (originally given in October 1991 at an international conference, "Soviet Music toward the Twenty-First Century," held on the campus of the Ohio State University).

The "Notes on *Svadebka*" section of chapter 13 is built up around a harmonic analysis first constructed as part of a general study of Stravinsky's

"Russian period" (*Stravinsky and the Russian Traditions* [Berkeley and Los Angeles: University of California Press, 1996]). In its original setting, the analysis was part of a narrative tracing the development of Stravinsky's personal style and compositional technique against the background of contemporary Russian culture. The present chapter hijacks the analysis, as it were, for insertion into a much more critical context, in keeping with the way in which my thinking about the composer and his significance has evolved since 1986, when the earlier study was drafted. Some of the material indicative of that evolution was first published in a review that appeared in *The New Republic*, 5 September 1988, and in an exchange with Robert Craft in the *New York Review of Books*, 15 June 1989.

The first section of chapter 14 is based on a talk originally given as the keynote address at an international conference, "Shostakovich: The Man and His Age, 1906–1975," held at the University of Michigan in January 1994. In its present form it incorporates material first published in reviews that appeared in *Slavic Review* (vol. 52, no. 2 [Summer 1993]) and *Music Library Association Notes* (vol. 50, no. 2 [December 1993]). The middle section of chapter 14 is a much revised version of an article originally published in *The New Republic*, 20 March 1989.

The chapters in part 2, presented here under the rubric "Self and Other," are based on previously published material. Chapter 8 first appeared as an article in *19th-Century Music* (vol. 6, no. 3 [Spring 1983]), chapter 9 as an article in *Cambridge Opera Journal* (vol. 4, no. 3 [November 1992]), and chapter 10 as a chapter in volume 2 of *Storia dell'opera italiana*, ed. Lorenzo Bianconi and Giorgio Pestelli (Torino: EDT/Musica, forthcoming as of this writing); this is its first publication in the original English.

Finally, part 1 contains material first published in reviews in the *Journal of the American Musicological Society* (vol. 43, no. 1 [Spring 1990]) and the *New York Times* (12 July 1992) and in *The New Grove Dictionary of Opera*, ed. Stanley Sadie (London: Macmillan, 1992).

PART I

Defining Russia Musically
(Seven Mini-Essays)

Too many people in the past have been terrifyingly certain
about what Jewish music is or should be. . . . This
cataclysmic string of definitions warns us not to define.
—Alex Ross (1995)

CHAPTER 1

N. A. LVOV AND THE FOLK

To BEGIN WITH, Russian national consciousness was an aspect of Westernization. The same eighteenth century that witnessed the Petrine reforms and their aftermath—the construction of an Italianate "window on the West" atop the Neva marshes at the cost of untold thousands of indentured lives, the adoption of "German" technology and the quasi-militarization of civilian life in the name of the bureaucratic "service state," the importation and imitation of foreign artifacts of every description—was also the century in which the cultivated Russian elite first established a national literary language distinct from the archaic ecclesiastical idiom, first wrote up the national history, first began to look upon the livers of those indentured lives as repositories of a tradition worth knowing and preserving. At a time when the inhabitants of the Russian countryside thought of themselves simply as "Christian folk" (*krest'yanye*) or "the Orthodox" (*pravoslavnïye*) and would never have dreamed of claiming their *barin* (the owner of the land to which they were confined by law) as their countryman, the most enlightened (that is, Enlightened) and Westernized barins were already thinking of their "souls," together with themselves, as constituting the *narod*, the Russian "people." In the words of Prince Antioch Dmitriyevich Kantemir (1709–44), Russia's first belletrist in the modern Western sense and author of an influential "Letter on Nature and Humanity," noble and serf were united by "the same blood, the same bones, the same flesh."[1]

This expanded, as it were "verticalized" sense of blood kinship was a revolutionary notion in an age that had traditionally formed political solidarities entirely along class-based "horizontal" lines—lines that we would call international—of family, clienthood, and personal fealty. Nor did vertical political relations necessarily imply nationhood. When Immanuel Kant, along with the rest of the faculty of the University of Königsberg and the assembled local nobles and burghers, took a compulsory oath of allegiance to Tsar Paul I after the Russian army had annexed the city and its environs to the contiguous territory of Russia, the great philosopher had no sense that by becoming a Russian subject he had become a Russian. Nor do we. To become a subject,

[1] *Sochineniya, pis'ma i izbrannïye perevodï knyazya Antiokha Dmitriyevicha Kantemira*, ed. P. A. Yefremov, vol. 1 (St. Petersburg: Glazunov, 1867), p. 54.

an oath would do. Being a Russian, like being a noble, required the right blood.

The idea of a national identity vouchsafed by "blood, bones, and flesh"—read: common language, customs, religion, and history—was one of the many imported concepts Westernized Russia made her own in her ambitious bid for recognition on the world (well, the European) stage. Only a nation, after all, can be a nation among nations. Not for nothing, the Moldavian-born Prince Kantemir was a diplomat by profession, and spent his last dozen years—his "Letter"-writing years—abroad as the Tsarina's ambassador in England and France. And as there can hardly be any sense of the self without a sense of the other, there could be no Russian nationalism until there was Russian cosmopolitanism. "And what should they know of Russia," to paraphrase Kipling, "who only Russia know?"

It was in this urbane, aristocratic spirit that the "discovery of the folk" took place in eighteenth-century Russia, alongside similar discoveries in England (Cowper), France (Rousseau), and Germany (Herder). Among its protagonists was Nikolai Alexandrovich Lvov (1751–1803), a noble landowner and world traveler with multifarious artistic and scientific interests and the leisure to indulge them all. As a member of both the Russian Academy of Sciences and the St. Petersburg Academy of the Arts, and as the maintainer of a famous artistic salon, Lvov cultivated a wide circle of distinguished friends, among them leading poets (Gavrila Derzhavin, Vasiliy Kapnist, both his brothers-in-law), artists (Dmitriy Levitsky, Vladimir Borovikovsky), and musicians (Giuseppe Sarti, the Empress Catherine's protégé). As an architect he upheld the neoclassical conventions of his time, but in literature he was a pioneering challenger to neoclassicism in the name of "sentiment," detecting a great reservoir of spontaneous, great-hearted sincerity in the Russian peasant, whose peculiar traits defined the unique national character and whose expressive culture, of which Lvov was in his day a matchless connoisseur, could provide artists of the high culture with worthy models for emulation.

Lvov set an example for such appropriation in a verse letter to a friend and fellow littérateur, unpublished until 1933, extolling the Russian national character:

> Zaletél sokol / uzh za óblako . . .
> Chto za óblako / luchezárnoye,
> Luchezárnoye / inozémnoye,
> Lyubo tám tebe? / —v molodíkh letakh
> Na zamórskoy krai / mï v rayók glyadim,
> Bleskom ráduzhnïm / ya prel'shchálsya sam;
> No iz zá morya / vse domóy glyadel,
> Net utékh pryamïkh, / mne kazálos', tam,
> Gde nel'zyá imi / podelít'sya s kem!

Gde prolít' nel'zya / zhivotvórnïy dukh
Schast'ya rússkogo / v nedrï rússkiye.
S kem podérish' tam / bogatïrsku rech'?
S kem otvázhnuyu / gryanesh' pésenku?
Ispolínskoy dukh / nashikh ótchichets
Vo chuzhíkh zemlyakh / lyudyam kázhetsya
Sverkh"yestéstvennïm / isstupléniyem!
Da i kák yemu / ne kazát'sya tak
Vo chuzhíkh zemlyakh / vsyo po nítochke
Na bezmén slova, / na arshín shagi.
Tam sidyát sidyat, / da podúmayut,
A podúmavshi / otdokhnút' poydut,
Otdokhnúvshi uzh, / trubku vïkuryat
I zadúmavshis' / rabotát' nachnut.
Net ni pésenki, / net ni shútochki.
A u náshego / pravoslávnogo
Delo vsyákoye / mezhdu rúk gorit.
Razgovór yego / gromovóy udar,
Ot rechéy yego / iskrï sïplyutsya,
Po sledám za nim / koromïslom pïl'![2]

The hawk flew off beyond the cloud . . .
Such a radiant cloud,
Radiant, exotic,
You like it there? —When we are young
We look at land beyond the sea as if at heaven,
I myself was attracted by its rainbow gleam;
But from beyond the sea I kept looking homeward.
There are no unmixed pleasures, so it seemed to me,
Where there is no one to share them,
Where the animating spirit of Russian joy
Cannot diffuse itself in the Russian midst!
With whom there can one hold forth in speech heroic?
With whom strike up a song so bold?
The giant spirit of our forefathers
In foreign lands strikes people
As some sort of unnatural frenzy!
And how else could it appear to them?
In foreign lands all goes by design;
Words are weighed, steps are measured.
There they sit and sit, consider well,

---

[2] Z. Artamonova, "Neizdannïye stikhi N. A. L'vova," *Literaturnoye nasledstvo* 9, no. 10 (1933): 275. (The addressee is Ivan Muravyov-Apostol.)

And having considered, rest awhile,
And having rested, smoke a pipe,
And only then, so heedfully, they go to work.
They have no songs, neither do they joke.
But with our Orthodox, meanwhile,
Any undertaking blazes in his hands.
His words are thunderclaps,
From his speech sparks fly,
In his wake he leaves a cloud of dust!

The remarkable thing about this doggerel is that not only does it sing the praises of folk song, it is itself an imitation folk song, one of the very earliest representatives of what would be one of the commonest nineteenth-century poetic genres in Russia. Beyond the appropriation of folk imagery (the soaring hawk, a fixture of peasant wedding songs) and the evocation of folk antiquities (the *bogatïri*, heroic warriors celebrated in the venerable *bïlina*, Russia's then recently recovered oral epos), Lvov demonstratively cast his verse in a meter endemic to the wedding song, the type regarded by connoisseurs of his generation as the most ancient and the most indigenous of all folk poetic genres, consisting of pentasyllabic hemistichs, each with a single tonic accent on the third syllable. You could sing Lvov's poem to the tune of either of the wedding choruses in Glinka's operas (the bridesmaids' "Razgulyálasya, razliválasya" in *A Life for the Tsar*, act 3; "Lel' taínstvennïy, upoítel'nïy!" in *Ruslan and Lyudmila*, act 1) that marked a musical epoch some decades after Lvov's decease (example 1.1).

If he called it anything at all, Lvov would merely have called this meter a *pesennïy razmer* (song meter). A few decades later, when in the brief heyday of Russian romanticism folk song imitation was practiced on a grand scale, the meter would be christened the *kol'tsovskiy stikh* after Alexey Koltsov

EXAMPLE 1.1

a. *A Life for the Tsar*, act 3

[Lvov: Za - le - tel   so - kol   uzh   za   o - bla - ko...]

Raz - gu - lya - la - sya,   raz - li - va - la - sya

b. *Ruslan and Lyudmila*, act 1

[Lvov: Za - le - tel   so - kol   uzh   za   o - bla - ko...]

Lel' ta - in - stven - nïy,   u - po - i - tel' - nïy!

(1809–42), the premier lyricist of the early Russian romance.[3] Lvov's fore-shadowing of Koltsov's technique is a remarkable early testimony to the new status of the folk song (*narodnaya pesnya*) in Russian letters, and to its cultural meaning, coeval and coextensive with that of the emergent concept of *narod* itself.

Lvov's activities on behalf of folk lyric and folk epos took many forms. Macpherson-like, he confected an original *bïlina* in tonically stressed free verse about the bogatïr Dobrïnya Nikitich (although unlike Macpherson he never tried to fool anyone with it). He also collaborated with Yevstigney Ipat'yevich Fomin (1761–1800), a cannoneer's son who was far and away the ablest native-born Russian art composer of his generation, on a singspiel called *Postal Coachmen at the Relay Station* (*Yamshchiki na podstave*, 1787).[4] It opens with a pair of remarkable stylizations of the elaborately melismatic folk genre now universally known in Russia (following Lvov's coinage) as *protyazhnaya pesnya* (literally, "drawn-out song"), in authentic responsorial style replete with intoner (*zapevala*) and heterophonic chorus (*podgoloski*). The second of them, of which the first strophe is given as illustration in example 1.2, was called "The Hawk Soars Aloft" (*Vïsoko sokol letayet*).

There is nothing else like these grave, stately, intricately woven choruses in the whole literature—an embryonic literature, admittedly—of eighteenth-century Russian art music. For the most part, when proles or serfs got to do their own thing on urban stages, it was apt to be a form of cute girlish ritual (bridal shower or yuletide fortune-telling) cast in Frenchified couplets with orchestral ritournelles or, for the boys, strophic fun and games. *Yamshchiki na podstave* contains a rather celebrated example of the latter. A newlywed driver named Timofey, spared from an unjust conscription that would have separated him from his bride, Fadeyevna, whips out his balalaika and dances with her, the two of them (joined later by another dancing driver and the chorus) singing lustily the while (example 1.3).

What has attracted so much notice to this little number is the fact that the dance song the characters sing, "A Birch Tree Rustled in the Field," is familiar to concertgoers the world over thanks to Chaikovsky, who adopted it ninety years later (but not from Fomin, needless to say) for the finale of his Fourth Symphony—and also thanks (in Russia, anyway) to Balakirev, whose appropriation of it in his first Overture on Russian Themes (1858) is discussed in detail in chapter 8. Another precocious touch is the hocketing pizzicatos that

[3] See Malcolm H. Brown, "Native Song and National Consciousness," in Theofanis George Stavrou, ed., *Art and Culture in Nineteenth-Century Russia* (Bloomington: Indiana University Press, 1983), pp. 75–76.

[4] The full score is published, edited by Irina Vetlitsïna, as no. 6 in the series *Pamyatniki russkogo muzïkal'nogo iskusstva* (Monuments of Russian Art Music), Yuriy Keldïsh, general editor (Moscow: Muzïka, 1977).

EXAMPLE 1.2. Fomin, *Yamshchiki na podstave*, second chorus ("The Hawk Soars Aloft"), first verse

represent the balalaika (even though Lvov's libretto calls for a pit mandolin), anticipating by half a century the accompaniment to the oarsmen's chorus in the first act of Glinka's *A Life for the Tsar*.

Yet despite all these adumbrations of the standard Russian repertoire, there is nothing in the least "nationalistic" about Fomin's use of folklore here. His trio is an essay in "low" style as befits low-born characters. Their lowness, in fact, is given explicit emphasis by Count Lvov's libretto: they sing not in spontaneous exuberance but, at the behest of Timofey's father, to entertain and thank the noble officer who has intervened as stand-in for the Empress

EXAMPLE 1.2, *continued*

(who could not appear as a character on stage) to straighten out their predicament, and they even adapt the words, at the end of the song, to praise him, the
boys at that very moment going *v prisyadku*, into their "typically Russian"
squatting dance ("Golden days have dawned, / the fair maid and her love have
been reunited, / oh, yes indeed, reunited / by our kind commanders, / oh yes
indeed, our commanders").

EXAMPLE 1.2, *continued*

This number falls right into line, then, with contemporary European representations of the folk. Lvov and Fomin's Timofey, Fadeyevna and Yan'ka are
not so far from Simon, Jane, and Luke, the trio of rustics in Thomson and
Haydn's *The Seasons*. For that is what folklore and folklorism represented in
aristocratic eighteenth-century Europe: in a (Russian) word, *krest'yanye*, as
(yet) opposed to *narod*—rustics, as opposed to "the people," let alone "the
nation." (And to Chaikovsky, in *Eugene Onegin*, that is what they still repre-

EXAMPLE 1.3. Fomin, *Yamshchiki na podstave*, no. 8 (trio with chorus), opening ritournelle and first strophe

sented a good ninety years later: witness the serfs' choral songs and dances in scene 1, performed to entertain and thank the *barïnya*; or even more to the point, the chorus of decorative berry-picking maidens in scene 3, which frames the turning point in the drama involving the opera's "real people.")

Fomin's opening choruses are utterly different from the trio, and from any

EXAMPLE 1.3, *continued*

previous artistic representation of the Russian folk. They are in a demonstratively "high" style—the highest at which any Russian opera before Glinka ever aimed (and what truly distinguished Glinka from his predecessors, it is no longer so novel to point out, was never his sheer Russianness but the height of his style). The choruses stoutly evince the new view—a proto-Herderian view—of the folk as unself-conscious bearer of native wisdom, *lore* in its most ancient and distinguished sense. The subject matter is literally lofty; the singers do not entertain their betters but gladden or console themselves; theirs is music not for listeners but for the singers' sake—an artless art for the sake of art. And it is transcribed by the "art" composer, at his *barin*'s behest, with a reverence and an accuracy of observation that bespeaks magnanimous esteem.

It is an interesting question, though, just what it was that was being transcribed and transmitted here, as representative of the newly envisaged Russian popular spirit. One can only guess at accuracy of observation when the thing observed is no longer available for comparison, and no corroborating transcription of *Vïsoko sokol* exists. But the opening choruses in *Yamshchiki na podstave* remained for practically a century the single attempt in Russian art music to reflect in their fullness the traditions of Russian folk choral singing; and Lvov's literary description of the custom, in the unsigned preface to his folk song anthology of 1790, would remain an isolated one until the publication of polyphonic field transcriptions of *podgoloski* by Yuliy Melgunov, a Moscow pianist who in the late 1870s "discovered" the heterophonic practices Lvov had already detailed and illustrated more than eighty years before. The leading Russian experts had by then forgotten what Lvov already knew, and rejected Melgunov's transcriptions, which began appearing in 1879, as "barbarous."[5]

The choral textures in the Lvov-Fomin choruses are astonishingly faithful, for the date, to those of genuine oral heterophony. Unlike virtually any choral texture by a composer in the cultivated tradition (even those who, in the next century, purported to base their styles on native folklore), these choruses of Fomin's are genuinely heterophonic: at virtually no time can any one voice in them be unequivocally identified as the carrier of the main tune. The mode hovers between the minor (with cadences on the tonic) and the relative major (with cadences on the dominant), reproducing the salient characteristic of the so-called mutable mode (*peremennïy lad*) of genuine folklore. At the same time, aspects of the harmony show definite "Westernized" traits, such as the use of applied dominants and the harmonic minor. The easy assumption would be that, in the process of transcribing them, Fomin had corrected the *podgoloski* of his rural informants, adapting them to the habits of harmony and voice-leading he had picked up from old Padre Martini, with whom he had studied in Bologna on a government stipend in the early 1780s.

There are good reasons to distrust the easy assumption in this case. Fomin was born and died in St. Petersburg, Russia's most—indeed, only—

[5] The ill-tempered word, strange as it may seem, was Rimsky-Korsakov's, in his "Chronicle of My Musical Life" (trans. Judah A. Joffe as *My Musical Life* [London: Eulenburg Books, 1974], p. 257).

completely "European" city. Orphaned at an early age, he was admitted before his sixth birthday to the Foundling School of the Imperial Academy of Fine Arts, a charitable institution set up by Catherine II to foster a new generation of Europeanized Russian artists. His first teacher in composition there (beginning in 1777), was a German, Hermann Friedrich Raupach, who was then serving as harpsichordist and conductor in Catherine's court orchestra. On his graduation in 1782 Fomin was packed right off to Italy, where he remained until the year before his collaboration with Lvov. Where would this utterly urbane composer have heard a Russian peasant choir? What rural informants could he—or Count Lvov himself—have counted on?

The answer is suggested by Lvov's verse preface, in twenty-eight lines of flowery iambic hexameter, to the libretto, published in 1788 (without attribution) in the provincial town of Tambov. It is headed "An offering to his excellency [*yego vïsokoblagorodiyu*], S.M.M." This personage is invoked (in the familiar second person) as a muse and described as a helpmeet, most concretely in lines 10–16:

> No na golos stikhov naladit' ya ne znayu
> I dlya togo, muzh zvuchnïy, prebegayu,
> Plenyonnïy zvonkoyu ya shaikoyu tvoyey,
> Soglasnoy peniyem, a vidom na razlade,
> Yavlyayushchey organ s pokhmel'ya v maskarade,
> Veli tï golosom chudesnoy shaike sey
> Dat' silu, zhizn' i blesk komedii moyey.

> But how to set my verse to tunes I know not
> And for that, O sonorous sir, I turn to you,
> Enthralled by your clarion crew,
> Harmonious in song if motley to the eye,
> To one intoxicated a seeming organ in disguise,
> Command this splendid crew of yours with voice divine
> To lend strength, life, and sheen to this comedy of mine.[6]

The manuscript of the libretto, which established Lvov's authorship, was discovered in the archive of the neoclassical poet Derzhavin, Lvov's brother-in-law, who in 1788 was governor of Tambov;[7] and it is Derzhavin who provides the key to identifying "S.M.M." His ode-parody, "In Praise of the Mosquito" (*Pokhvala komaru*), begins with an in-joke: "Pindar sang the praises of the eagle, Mitrofanov of the hawk" (*Pindar vospevál orlá, / Mitrofánov sokolá*). The poet himself provided an explanatory note identifying

---

[6] Quoted from Yuriy Keldïsh, "K istorii operï 'Yamshchiki na postave'" (first published in *Sovetskaya muzïka*, no. 10 [1973]), in Keldïsh, *Ocherki i issledovaniya po istorii russkoy muzïki* (Moscow: Sovetskiy kompozitor, 1978), p. 133.

[7] Artamonova, "Neizdannïye stikhi," pp. 285–86.

this Mitrofanov as "the famous singer who used to sing the Russian song 'The Hawk Soared Aloft' (*Vïsoko sokol letal*)."[8]

The one corroborating document concerning this far from "famous" figure is a letter from T. P. Kiryak, the director ("inspector") of the Smolnïy Institute, St. Peterburg's most fashionable finishing school, concerning the lavish festivities organized by Potyomkin on 27 April 1791 to commemorate the Empress Catherine's recent victory over the Turks.[9] The letter refers to "a certain court counselor named Mitrofanov," who was to lead a group of "carolers" (*pesel'niki*) stationed aboard a "Chinese sloop" in a group of oarsmen's songs.[10] This Mitrofanov's midgrade civil service rank (*nadvornïy sovetnik* or "court counselor") entitled him precisely to the honorific *vïsokoblagorodiye*, as in Lvov's affably ironic dedication to "S.M.M." One may conclude from this that the two references are to the same individual.

Thus it transpires that at least one, and probably both, of the impressive choral *protyazhnïye* with which Fomin's opera begins was imparted to Lvov and his musical collaborator by a local connoisseur, S. M. Mitrofanov by name, who was Lvov's intimate acquaintance and (presumably, therefore) not too distantly his social inferior, who sang and possibly composed "Russian songs," of which "The Hawk Soars Aloft" was the best known, and who led a group of local amateurs—evidently somewhat ragtag if well liked, as both Lvov's reference (to a *shaika*, a "crew" or "gang") and Kiryak's (to *pesel'niki*, "choirfolk" or "carolers") suggest —on whose participation in performances of his singspiel (which seem never to have taken place) Lvov was counting. These were the "informants"—not rural at all, as it turns out, and not particularly lofty, one suspects—on whose renditions Fomin's high-toned transcriptions were based. It is even conceivable that Fomin worked from a score supplied by Mitrofanov, to which he may have added no more than the orchestral accompaniment.

If these surmises are correct, then Fomin probably did not adapt or adulterate his "folk" material to any great extent; in all likelihood it came to him from its urbanized source already highly adulterated. Or rather, less invidiously, its style already represented an urban redaction of a rural prototype, leading tones and all. The "enlightened" perspective from which the trained arranger approached the "natural" folk artifact predisposed him to expect, and to value,

---

[8] G. R. Derzhavin, *Sochineniya*, vol. 3 (St. Petersburg, 1886), p. 401; quoted in Keldïsh, "K istorii operï 'Yamshchiki na podstave,'" p. 134.

[9] It was for this very celebration that Osip Kozlovsky composed the choral polonaise "Thunder of Victory, Resound!" (*Grom pobedï, razdavaisya*), to panegyric verses by Derzhavin, which will figure so prominently in the discussion of Chaikovsky's neoclassicism in chapter 11.

[10] T. P. Kir'yak to I. M. Dolgorukov, first published in the almanac *Russkiy arkhiv* (1867), quoted by Keldïsh (pp. 134–35) from annotations by I. N. Rozanov to a collection of song texts (*Pesni russkiye izvestnogo okhotnika M. . .* [St. Petersburg, 1799]) thought possibly to be Mitrofanov's (I. N. Rozanov, ed., *Pesni russkikh poètov [XVIII-pervaya polovina XIX veka]* [Leningrad, 1936], p. 88).

kindred rather than alien characteristics. Sought and prized was a reinforcement of a sense of kinship ("same blood, same bones, same flesh"), not a
frisson of otherness.

The same can be said of many of the songs, and all of the arrangements, in
Lvov's "Collection of Russian Folk Songs with Their Tunes" (*Sobraniye
narodnïkh russkikh pesen s ikh golosami*) of 1790, an epoch-making compendium of one hundred Russian folk songs that was reissued in 1806 with 97 of
the original songs plus 53 new ones for a total of 150.[11] This glorious anthology, Lvov's main claim to immortality, was inspired directly by Herder's
compilations of *Volkslieder* (1778–79), from the title of which Lvov adopted
what is now the standard Russian term, *narodnaya pesnya*, for a "folk"
(= *Volk*, = *narod*) song, rather than *prostaya pesnya* ("simple song") or
sel'skaya pesnya ("rustic song").[12] In an unsigned introduction to the original
edition, Lvov called attention in self-conscious and fairly self-congratulatory
(if also self-contradictory) fashion to its unprecedented fidelity to the pecu-
liarities of the folk original, ending with a thinly veiled dig at all predecessors
and rivals:

> Anyone can easily see how hard it was to collect the tunes of these unwritten folk
> songs, dispersed over thousands of versts, and to notate them as often as not from
> the faulty singing of untrained singers. But no less difficult was the task of—
> without spoiling the folk melody—accompanying it with a correct bass, itself in
> the folk character. These tasks, however, have been accomplished with all pos-
> sible diligence, and the bass has been set almost everywhere just so; and even
> very close to what an impeccable chorus [viz., Mitrofanov's] might sing when
> performing these songs. Having thus preserved all the peculiarities of Russian
> folk singing, this collection possesses as well all the virtues of the original: its

[11] There have been six editions in all. The third (St. Petersburg: Meditsinskya tipografiya,
1815) was a reprint of the second from the same plates. The fourth edition (St. Petersburg:
Suvorin, 1896), ed. with an introduction by A. E. Pal'chikov, was the first to name Lvov,
formerly anonymous in deference to the traditions of noblesse oblige, as the collector; his identity
was attested by various letters and documents, in particular a memoir by his younger cousin
Fyodor Petrovich Lvov called *O penii v Rossii* (On Singing in Russia), published in 1834. The
fifth edition (Moscow: Muzgiz, 1955), ed. with an introduction by Victor Belyayev, is unreliable,
the texts having been purged, primarily of their religious content, for Soviet consumption. (For a
piquant example involving the famous coronation hymn from *Boris Godunov*, see R. Taruskin,
Musorgsky: Eight Essays and an Epilogue [Princeton: Princeton University Press, 1993],
pp. 300–312.) The sixth edition (Ann Arbor: UMI Research Press, 1987), ed. Malcolm H.
Brown, is a facsimile of the second edition with an invaluable apparatus (introduction and appen-
dices) by Barbara Krader and Margarita Mazo.

[12] The earliest printed collection of Russian folk songs (texts only), by Mikhail Chulkov,
issued in four volumes beginning in 1770, was called, simply, *Sobraniye raznïkh pesen* (Collection of Various Songs). The first anthology to include tunes, by Vasiliy Trutovsky (four volumes,
1776–95), was called *Sobraniye russkikh prostïkh pesen s notami* (Collection of Russian Simple
Songs with Musical Notation).

simplicity and integrity are uncompromised, whether by correcting the sometimes strange melodies or by embellishing them.[13]

These remarks had mainly to do with the contribution of Lvov's shadowy
collaborator, one "Ivan Prach" (d. ca. 1818), a Bohemian from Silesia whose
original name was either Jan Bogumir Práč or Johann Gottfried Pratsch, who
wrote the keyboard accompaniments to the tunes (as well as transcribing at
least some or, likely, most of them).[14] Pratsch settled in St. Petersburg some-
time in the 1770s and supported himself as a piano teacher to fashionable
girls, serving for many years on the faculty of the Smolnïy Institute. It has
been suggested, as a way of accounting for his involvement with the song
anthology, that Pratsch was music tutor to the Lvov family. In any event, only
Pratsch's name appeared on the title page of the collection, or in any of the
editions appearing within his lifetime, which has led to some exaggeration of
his role in selecting and organizing the contents. That job was Lvov's entirely;
the musical arranger was just a hired hand.

Pratsch's work has received harsh judgment from musicians and scholars of
a later time. His employer's generous evaluation of his "basses" will evoke a
smile from those familiar with this tradition of abuse. Yet Lvov's remarks are
amply justified by contemporaneous standards, and are even farsighted in
their attempt to relate the matter of practical harmonization to the traditions of
folk choral polyphony, even in its urbanized manifestations. Pratsch's arrangements, moreover, naive as they may seem with their right-hand doubling
of the voice and their "Alberti's" and "murky's" in the left, are much more
than mere "basses." They are convincingly artistic in a way that previous
arrangements (i.e., those in Trutovsky's collection, mentioned in n. 12,
which did assume the form of a simple melody-plus-bass on two staves)
were not.

In effect Pratsch transformed each *narodnaya pesnya* entrusted to him into
a diminutive art song with a well-wrought if conventional keyboard accompaniment prefiguring the idiom of the so-called domestic romance (*bïtovoy
romans*) of the next generation, thus actively collaborating with the "folk," in
the spirit of the Enlightenment, to produce a new genre that purposely mediated or transcended the borders between genres (read: social classes).

The stylistic traits thus arrived at manifestly reflected the tastes of the intended audience—Pratsch's pupils at the Smolnïy, for example, for whom he
elaborated several songs in variation sets, or Lvov's literary circle. For thus
catering to the haute bourgeoisie Pratsch has been roundly abused by later

---

[13] Cited from P. A. Vulfius, *Russkaya mïsl' o muzïkal'nom fol'klore: Materialï i dokumentï*
(Moscow: Muzïka, 1979), p. 78.

[14] Transliterating his name from Russian might suggest a rhyme with Bach rather than Crotch,
so the unambiguous German form will be used here from this point on; it would be a good idea to
make it standard "English" usage.

generations of scholars and musicians from standpoints by turns romantic, positivist, and Marxist-Leninist. Yet as much as folkloristically inclined musicians of the later nineteenth century, from Balakirev and Serov in the sixties to Lyadov in the nineties, may have railed against Pratsch in word or in musical deed, and however they may have striven for a more (by their lights) authentic harmonization, they all tacitly accepted his method of showcasing the native material with a decorative accompaniment for the pianoforte in the established European manner.

And that is because neither his aim nor theirs was purely (that is, merely) curatorial or documentary: the idea was to return what was the people's to the people, to make the products of oral tradition available to the literate by allowing the music of the countryside to reach the parlor piano. The dissemination of a patriotic sort of aesthetic enjoyment was the object. Romantic collector-arrangers, beginning with the so-called *pochvenniki* ("men of the soil") of the 1850s, could delude themselves that they were realizing the "inherent nature" of the folk product, or even its "soul," and could debate endlessly the proper means toward such an end.[15] But if such were truly their aim they would have kept their hands to themselves. What their quest for "the immutable primordial Russian folk song"[16] was really after, and what it never occurred to Lvov or Pratsch to crave, was exoticism—fetishized difference.

It was not until the days of institutional field collecting within an explicitly "scientific" (that is, academic and anthropological) purview—the expeditions sponsored by Tsar Alexander III's own Imperial Geographical Society in St. Petersburg (beginning in 1893), and those of the Musical Ethnographic Commission at Moscow University (around the turn of the century)—that Pratsch's presentational format, and the aesthetic it implied, would be effectively challenged. The MEC publications were "phonographic," representing the last word in hardware. They specialized in descriptive scores of what was termed *podgolosochnoye mnogogolosiye* (podgoloski polyphony). The IGS publications, in the interests of scientific chastity, eschewed accompaniments altogether, even those of peasant informants, and presented no more than a single-line melodic transcription. Ironically, of course, this was a considerable step backward from Lvov's standards of fidelity to folk performance practice. The reduction to a single definitive line reflected an unconscious utopian idealization.

---

[15] For an introduction to the debates, and the early romantic solutions, see "'Little Star': An Étude in the Folk Style," in Taruskin, *Musorgsky*, pp. 38–70; Mazo's annotations to the sixth edition of the anthology contains a sampling (on pp. 29–32) of disparaging romantic commentary on the arrangements, beginning with contemporaries who resented Pratsch's foreign birth, up to and including folklorists and historians of the early Soviet period.

[16] Boris V. Asafyev, introduction to Jacob Stählin, *Muzïka i balet v Rossii XVIII veka*, p. 8; quoted by Barbara Krader in the introduction to the sixth edition of the Lvov-Pratsch collection, p. 4.

Lvov and (following his instructions) Pratsch were not utopians or idealists. In a seemingly artless but in fact quite sophisticated fashion, they were realists whose collection "enables us," in Margarita Mazo's shrewd estimation, "to glimpse the [actual] musical milieu and to sample the [actual] musical environment which nurtured Russian composers of the eighteenth and early nineteenth centuries," without cosmetic or ideological equivocation.[17] The most immediate musical consequence of the Petrine reforms was the sudden mass transplantation of folk song, together with its singers, into Peter's newly created metropolis on the Neva. It would be naive to expect that it would escape modification in the process of transplantation; and it would be just as prejudicially invidious to regard the modified or newly minted product as inauthentic as it would be so to regard the transplanted peasant or second-generation urban dweller who sang it.

Unlike their romantic successors, Lvov and Pratsch did not entertain such prejudices. They happily included in their anthology many examples of what today's ethnographers call "literary songs," army songs, and even *rossiyskiye pesni*, "Russian (-style) songs," an early type of art song to a Russian text, dealing characteristically with "urban" sentiments like "the passion of love, previously almost ignored" (according to a contemporary witness) in song,[18] and incorporating resonances from a wide variety of surrounding musics: "arias and songs from popular European operas, French minuets, Italian sicilianas, polonaises, etc.," as Krader lists them in the introduction to the sixth edition (p. 7).

As Margarita Mazo, an exemplary postromantic ethnographer, emphasizes, these urban mongrels were not confined to the "literate" tradition. Widely disseminated in theaters, streets, and barracks, they joined the oral tradition and must necessarily have influenced genres that originated in that tradition, eventually even in villages.[19] Thus Pratsch's redactions (like Fomin's in

---

[17] Introduction to the sixth edition, p. 75.

[18] Prince Mikhail Shcherbatov, quoted in D. D. Blagoy, *Istoriya russkoy literaturï XVIII veka* (2d ed., Moscow: Prosveshcheniye, 1951), p. 59.

[19] This applies particularly to "literary songs," a genre especially despised by later collectors and discreetly soft-pedaled in the Soviet scholarly literature, which were anonymous but obviously recent orally disseminated settings of texts by contemporary authors, both known and unknown. (A choice example of an urban "literary song" is the first of the two organ-grinder tunes accompanying the episode of the street dancer in the first tableau of Stravinsky's *Petrushka*, a setting, universally known by Russians from its oral transmission, of a verse, " 'Twas on a Night in Rainy Autumn" [*Pod vecher, osen'yu nenastnoy*, 1815] by the young Pushkin.) As Mazo explains, the genre had its ironies: "Many poems by Lomonosov, Tredyakovsky, and Sumarokov [i.e., poets of the neoclassical school] earned popularity as songs, and in this form became well known to the general public of the middle and lower classes and found their way into many manuscript collections. These literary songs were as essential a part of the urban tradition then as songs written by contemporary poets are in today's [Soviet Russian] tradition. More than any other type of song, they reflected changes in public taste and musical style. Some of these songs eventually achieved a measure of popularity in Russian villages; as time went by, they became a

Yamshchiki na podstave) do not represent "simplifications . . . made to ac-
comodate the songs to European metric and harmonic practice" as much as
they "reflect urban singing traditions at the time."[20]

There is every reason to suppose, in particular, that Pratsch's notorious
leading tones, long regarded as "Western" disfigurements, were endemic to
the melodies in question at the time and in the place of their collection. If the
concepts of purity that governed the study and collection of folklore during
the romantic period were foreign to eighteenth-century (and late twentieth-
century) collectors, still less did they *ever* constrain informants. Approaching
their task without idealistic preconceptions, Lvov and Pratsch did not scruple
(the somewhat grandiose rhetoric of the preface notwithstanding) to collect
their material wherever they encountered it, chiefly in St. Petersburg and the
city's immediate vicinity—and not only from the urbanized peasants (servants and laborers) who might have been expected to retain some vestige of
rural traditions, but from their own friends and acquaintances (i.e., Lvov's
circle of artists, litterateurs, aristocratic dilettantes, not to mention "amateurs
and relatives, who were forever singing in his house"),[21] from earlier printed
and manuscript sources, and even from popular singspiels.

---

part of rural traditions and gradually absorbed some features of the local styles. The Lvov-Pratsch
collection must have played an important role in this process" (introduction to the sixth edition,
pp. 45–46).

Indeed, the ironies go even further than that. One of the "literary songs" Mazo singles out for
discussion is "How Have I Aggrieved Thee?" (*Chem tebya ya ogorchila*), classified by Lvov as a
protyazhnaya. The text had been published as early as 1781 in the collected works of Sumarokov
(who had *oskorbila* [offended] in place of *ogorchila* [aggrieved]), and, as Mazo notes, the setting
by Lvov and Pratsch is especially close to the style of an urban "romance with instrumental
accompaniment, such as became popular later in the eighteenth century." The tremendous vogue
of this particular song as household music throughout the nineteenth century is attested not only
by contemporary witnesses (Mazo cites two, one from 1809 and the other from 1912!) but also by
the number of arrangements in which it was issued, and the frequency of its adoption for variations or other sorts of reworking by composers of art music, both Russian (e.g., an early trio by
Borodin for two violins and cello [1853]) and Western (e.g., Fernando Sor, "Souvenir de Russie"
for two guitars, Op. 63 [ca. 1839]). What she does not mention is that a variant of this tune, the
very epitome of what the romantic purists of later Russian generations would have called a
poddelka (counterfeit) or a *lzhe-narodnaya pesnya* (fake song), had been adopted as the first of
the "Two Russian Themes" on which Glinka himself, to whom purists inevitably trace their line,
tried to base his unfinished symphony of 1834. For Glinka, too, then, the "literary" urban style
was quite sufficiently "*narodnïy*." (Another example of a song by Sumarokov turning up both
in the Lvov-Pratsch collection and in Trutovsky's collection of 1776–79 is discussed by
Yuriy Keldïsh in *Istoriya russkoy muzïki v desyati tomakh*, vol. 2 [Moscow: Muzïka, 1984],
pp. 167–69.)

[20] Preface to the sixth edition, p. 44; even more provocatively, Mazo suggests that such
apparent simplifications and accommodations "may be 'corrections' made not by Pra[ts]ch, but
by everyday musical practice" (p. 37).

[21] Fyodor Petrovich Lvov, *O penii v Rossii*, quoted in Yuriy Keldïsh et al., *Istoriya russkoy
muzïki v desyati tomakh*, vol. 2, p. 238. As already noted, this testimony by Nikolai Lvov's

The last point is especially significant. As many as forty songs known from seven eighteenth-century Russian operas and singspiels, by composers domestic and imported alike, appear in the collection.[22] What is important to realize is that although the assumption (even by the editors of the sixth edition) has always been that the collection was the source from which the composers of the stage works drew the tunes, most of the stage works in fact predate the first edition of the collection, and the relationship between borrower and lender is more likely the reverse.[23] The collection thus contains an untold number of what can only be described as musical "back formations" from the artistic tradition. The most obvious instance of this is Mitrofanov's celebrated song about the hawk, already encountered in its choral guise in *Yamshchiki na podstave*. It is evident that Pratsch was directed to transcribe the song directly out of the 1787 score, meanwhile adapting it for a single voice with keyboard accompaniment. Confronted with the impressive contrapuntal texture shown in example 1.2, the hapless arranger could only thread his way through it (for the most part, predictably enough, following the soprano), producing an ersatz "tune" the likes of which could never have been sung in steppe or village, or even in Peter's town (figure 1.1). It exemplifies to

---

cousin was the chief basis for ascribing the collection to Lvov, beginning with the fourth edition in 1896. It furnished the purist annotator of that edition, A. E. Pal'chikov (whose brother Nikolai was one of the first connoisseurs of *podgolosochnoye mnogogolosiye*), with one of his principal causes for complaint: Pratsch, he charged, arranged "only tunes sung to him by people invited by Lvov. This is probably why there are the inevitable major and minor in songs of an entirely different nature, and why the song harmonizations throughout are done in the manner of romances at the end of the eighteenth century" (preface to the fourth edition, p. ix, quoted in the preface to the sixth edition, p. 30). Palchikov thus backhandedly confirms Mazo's supposition concerning the actual state of the oral tradition from which the collectors drew their material.

[22] In addition to the Lvov-Fomin *Yamshchiki na podstave*, the stage pieces include the following: *Mel'nik—koldun, obmanshchik i svat* (The Miller Who Was a Wizard, a Cheat, and a Matchmaker, 1779) by Mikhail Sokolovsky; *Sankt-Peterburgskiy gostinnïy dvor* (1782), and *Fevey* (1786, vocal score arr. Pratsch) by Vasiliy Pashkevich; *Nachal'noye upravleniye Olega* (The Early Reign of Oleg, 1790) by Pashkevich, Giuseppe Sarti, and Carlo Cannobio; *Fedul s det'mi* (Fedul and His Children) by Pashkevich and Vincente Martín y Soler; and *Le astuzie femminili* (Feminine Wiles, 1794) by Domenico Cimarosa. The songs are identified, in an alphabetical list by title, in appendix C to the sixth edition (pp. 434–41) and, according to the works into which they are incorporated, in Nina Bachinskaya, *Narodnïye pesni v tvorchestve russkikh kompozitorov* (Moscow: Muzgiz, 1962).

[23] This applies as well to the many variation sets, both for keyboard (by Pratsch himself, as well as such other composers as Wilhelm Palschau and a certain Karaulov, designated "amateur" to identify him as a nobleman) and for violin (by the famous eighteenth-century virtuoso Ivan Khandoshkin), which circulated in manuscript over the decades preceding (as well as following) publication of the Lvov-Pratsch collection. Several of the keyboard sets have been published in Lev Barenboim's and Vladimir Muzalevsky's *Khrestomatiya po istorii fortep'yannoy muzïki v Rossii* (Moscow and Leningrad: Muzgiz, 1949); Khandoshkin's works are listed in Anne Mischakoff, *Khandoshkin and the Beginning of Russian String Music* (Ann Arbor: UMI Research Press, 1983).

FIGURE 1.1. Pratsch's arrangement of *Vïsoko sokol* (The Hawk Soars Aloft) (Lvov and Pratsch, *Sobraniye russkikh narodnïkh pesen*, 2d ed. [St. Petersburg, 1806], vol. 2, *protyazhnïye* no. 24)

perfection, however, what Mazo calls "the complex symbiotic relationship that existed in the late-eighteenth-century urban tradition in Russia," whereby new songs were born and style characteristics freely exchanged.[24]

Viewed in this way, from a standpoint that accepts its emphasis on currency and contemporaneity, rather than from the utopian, anachronistically cen-

[24] Introduction to the sixth edition, p. 49.

Высоко соколъ лѣтаетъ
По выше того бѣлая лебедушка
Слѣталсл соколъ съ бѣлою лебедушкой
Спрашивалъ соколъ
Спрашивалъ соколъ у бѣлой лебедушки
Гдѣ лебедь была.

FIGURE 1.1, *continued*

sorious vantage point romantic cthnographers and conventional music historians have adopted, the Lvov-Pratsch collection all at once seems to seethe
with creative life—far more so, in fact, than those later anthologies (especially the self-consciously scientific ones of the Imperial Geographical Society) that purported to embalm the artifacts of an undefiled rural tradition and
thus preserve them from the inevitable ravages of the life process.[25] Such a

[25] See Sergey Lyapunov's "Report to the Imperial Geographical Society," following the first
of its officially sponsored musical collecting expeditions in 1893 (reprinted in Vulfius, *Russkaya
mïsl' o muzïkal'nom fol'klore*, pp. 231–34.

project can only be described today as quaint, or worse. Mazo observes with engaging cheek that "modern-day ethnomusicology's notion of what is to be considered a folk song is closer to the viewpoint expressed in the LPC [Lvov-Pratsch Collection] than it is to the more exclusive views of some nineteenth-century and even twentieth-century collections."[26]

It was precisely because of that creative life, that currency and contemporaneity, that the Lvov-Pratsch collection was able, as Mazo points out, to "influence the folk tradition itself, even in the outlying regions, as a consequence of the numerous reprints of the songs taken from the LPC and published in school songbooks circulated throughout the vast reaches of Russia."[27] The collection, in other words, and uniquely, fulfilled the role its compilers (but particularly Lvov) envisioned for it, as a cultural uniter—indeed, as a creator—of the Russian nation.

This achievement gives the ultimate lie to those who, proceeding from a fastidious romantic-nationalist conception of a native spirit at once preternatural and inborn, have denied the authenticity of this greatest and most culturally significant of Russian folk song collections, owing in the first place to its urban origins and in the second to its musical arrangements having been fashioned by an ethnic alien. Any privileged conception of an "authentic Russian folk song" of course implies a similarly intransigent notion of what constitutes an "authentic Russian." Once this is grasped, Lvov's leading tones begin to look downright precious; nor will it seem impertinent to note that Balakirev, who will emerge in chapter 8 as the musician most avid to rid folk song harmonizations of their leading tones (thus as representative of his historical moment as Lvov had been two generations before), was also avid to rid Russia of her Jews. But Russia is large and contains multitudes. The work of Nikolai Lvov and his Bohemian assistant is a monument to that largeness and to those multitudes, and a memento of the Russian nation's brief flicker of Enlightenment.

[26] Introduction to the sixth edition, p. 14.
[27] Ibid., p. 76.

CHAPTER 2

M. I. GLINKA AND THE STATE

VÏSOKO SOKOL LETAYET, a serf chorus in a style a noble would recognize as lofty, was the perfect musical embodiment of the earliest, Enlightened model of Russian nationalism, purveyed by liberal aristocrats in the time of Catherine the Great. It is good to remember at the end of our bloody century that there was once such a thing as liberal nationalism even in Russia, and that it is possible for nationalism to inspire inclusive rather than exclusive sentiments. Neither nostalgic nor exotic, Fomin's chorus did not merely represent the "other," as, shorn of its leading tones and dominants, it might have done. Cast in an idiom a city-dweller or a landowner would find at once fresh and familiar, it united city and country, high and low, cosmopolitan and insular, self and other.

Such a nationalism, despite its top-down provenience, could actually work as a positive, ameliorative social force. When the peasant could symbolize not just class but nation, implying a society conceived as organically united within its national borders, he became more fully human. It became harder to justify an institution like serfdom, not only to "the West" but to oneself.

Not that one could call N. A. Lvov himself, "good" *barin* though he undoubtedly was, anything like an abolitionist yet, let alone a democrat. To confine ourselves to the evidence already before us, the very singspiel in which loving stylization of the peasant idiom as a national emblem reached its peak culminates in a celebration of the sovereign's benevolent intervention in response to supplication, reinforcing, for the benefit of all spectators, belief in the autocratic hierarchy as divinely instituted instrument of human happiness.

And yet the early Russian abolitionists such as Alexander Radishchev (1749–1802), Lvov's practically exact contemporary and social peer, came to their beliefs through the same burgeoning national consciousness, and shared Lvov's regard for peasant lore. The famous chapter ("Myodnoye Station") from Radishchev's *Journey from St. Petersburg to Moscow*, anonymously published the same year as the Lvov-Pratsch folk song anthology (also semi-anonymous, though not for the same reason), begins with a description of a village *khorovod* (to the strains of "The Birch Tree," of all national emblems!) and ends in a fit of anguish over a slave auction at which the members of a family are sold off to different buyers. Running from the scene, the author meets an American acquaintance on the stairs: "Go back," he cries. "Don't be a witness to this arrant disgrace. You once cursed the barbaric custom of selling black captives in the remote settlements of your fatherland. Go back, . . . don't be a witness to this blot of ours, and don't proclaim our shame to your fellow citizens when you speak with them about our ways!"[1]

That shame was the early fruit of *narodnost'*. National consciousness became national conscience. The history of nationalism in post-Napoleonic Russia is the story of how that liberalizing bond was undone.

THE TRICK was to associate love of country not with love of its inhabitants but with love of the dynastic state. The sundering of the one link and the forging of the other was the chief cultural and educational accomplishment of the reign of Tsar Nicholas I. The way in which, in Russia, the professional arts fell into line behind this policy is striking evidence of the oft-hushed bond between romanticism and reaction.

On the second of April, 1833, Count Sergey Semyonovich Uvarov, the Tsar's newly appointed minister of "popular enlightenment" (that is, education, as the Bolsheviks would also call it), circulated a letter to the heads of all educational districts in the Empire, stating that "our common obligation consists in this, that the education of the people be conducted, according to the Supreme intention of our August Monarch, in the joint spirit of Orthodoxy, autocracy, and nationality."[2] *Pravoslaviye, samoderzhaviye, narodnost'*: this was the troika of interdependent values to which Russians would henceforth be expected to subscribe, formulated thus, apparently, in direct rebuttal to the familiar revolutionary slogan *Liberté, Egalité, Fraternité*. In its new company, *narodnost'* would function as "a worthy tool of the government," as Uvarov put it, or, as quite accurately echoed in Soviet times, as an "ideological weapon in support of serfdom and autocracy."[3] The nation was conceived entirely in dynastic and religious terms, autocracy being related to Orthodoxy as "the ultimate link between the power of man and the power of God."[4]

This was the brand of "nationalism"—Official Nationalism (*ofitsioznaya narodnost'*) as it came to be called—that was embodied and propagated in Glinka's epochal first opera, conceived almost immediately upon promulgation of the new doctrine and as a celebration of its precepts, reaching a symbolic climax in the epilogue, a pageant of religious veneration of the nation in the person of the Tsar. It was no progressive thing.

---

[1] A. N. Radishchev, *Puteshestviye iz Peterburga v Moskvu* (Leningrad: Lenizdat, 1971), pp. 160, 163.

[2] "Tsirkulyarnoye predlozheniye G. Upravlyayushchego Ministerstvom Narodnogo Prosveshcheniya Nachalstvam Uchebnïkh Okrugov 'o vstuplenii v upravleniye Ministerstvom,'" quoted in Nicholas V. Riasanovsky, *Nicholas I and Official Nationality in Russia, 1825–1855* (Berkeley and Los Angeles: University of California Press, 1959), p. 73.

[3] Ibid., p. 74; *Entsiklopedicheskiy slovar'* (Moscow: Sovetskaya èntsiklopediya, 1964), vol. 2, p. 542.

[4] Vasiliy Zhukovsky, *Polnoye sobraniye sochineniy v odnom tome* (Moscow, 1915); quoted in Riasanovsky, *Nicholas I and Official Nationality in Russia*, p. 97.

The opera was indeed a direct response to the state ideology, mediated by one of its canonical proponents, Vasiliy Andreyevich Zhukovsky (1783–1852), author of the stout words quoted just above in defense of dynastic authority, and of the text to the epilogue of *A Life for the Tsar* as well. In addition to being Glinka's friend and mentor, he was an outstanding romantic poet, the tutor to the royal heir (the future Alexander II), and an official state censor. *A Life for the Tsar* was hatched in Zhukovsky's aristocratic literary salon, to which Glinka became attached immediately on his return to St. Petersburg from Italy in 1834. "When I declared my ambition to undertake an opera in Russian," Glinka recalled in his memoirs, "Zhukovsky sincerely approved of my intention and suggested the subject of Ivan Susanin."[5]

It was a predictable choice, even an inevitable one; for one of the cornerstones of Official Nationalism was the creation of a romantic national mythology, "a sense of the present based on a remodeled past," in the well-chosen words of a recent historian of Slavic literature. "Legend and history," he continues,

> were a pleasing combination, and one sees among some Poles and Russians of this time that odd cultural phenomenon in which a legendary past is created to antedate and form a basis for history. Not having an *Iliad* or *Aeneid*, they wrote their own mythical past from folklore. They were inspired by the poems of Ossian and by Herder's idea of creating a national consciousness out of national myths.[6]

Glinka's maiden opera, the first Russian opera that was really an opera (not a singspiel) and the earliest to achieve permanent repertory status, hence the cornerstone of the national repertory, was created out of just such a didactic mythography.

The legend of Ivan Susanin had a tenuous documentary basis: a concession conferred in 1619 by Tsar Mikhail Fyodorovich, the first Russian ruler of the house of Romanov, on one Bogdan Sobinin, a peasant from the village of Domnino in the Kostroma district, and renewed to Sobinin's heirs by every Romanov ruler all the way down to the first Nicholas, granting dispensation from certain taxes and obligations in recognition of the merits of Sobinin's father-in-law, Ivan Susanin, who, "suffering at the hands of said Polish and Lithuanian persons immeasurable torments on Our account, did not tell said Polish and Lithuanian persons where We were at the time, and said Polish and Lithuanian persons did torture him to death."[7] That is, Ivan Susanin had at

---

[5] Mikhail Ivanovich Glinka, "Zapiski" (Memoirs), in *Polnoye sobraniye sochineniy: Literaturnïye proizvedeniya i perepiska*, vol. 1 (Moscow: Muzïka, 1973), p. 266.

[6] Hubert F. Babinski, *The Mazeppa Legend in European Romanticism* (New York: Columbia University Press, 1974), p. 89.

[7] Quoted in Alexander Vyacheslavovich Ossovsky, "Dramaturgiya operï M. I. Glinki 'Ivan Susanin,'" in A. V. Ossovsky, ed., *M. I. Glinka: Issledovaniya i materialï* (Leningrad and Moscow: Muzgiz, 1950), p. 16.

the cost of his life concealed from a Polish search party the whereabouts of Mikhail Fyodorovich, the sixteen-year-old scion of an old boyar family, who had been elected Tsar by a popular assembly in February 1613, thus ending the "time of troubles" regarding the Russian succession and founding the dynasty that would rule Russia until 1917. The name of Ivan Susanin entered historical literature in 1792 and his deed was embroidered and immortalized by Sergey Glinka (the composer's cousin) in his *Russian History for Purposes of Upbringing* (*Russkaya istoriya v pol'zu vospitaniya*, 1817), since which time it went into all children's textbooks and became part of every Russian's patriotic consciousness.[8]

Parallels with Susanin's deed were suggested by the activities of peasant partisans in the Patriotic War of 1812 against Napoleon; in the aftermath of that war "Ivan Susanin" became a fixture of Russian Romantic literature (e.g., the eponymous ballad or "duma" by Kondratiy Rïleyev) and the Russian stage, including the fairly trivial musical stage of those days: e.g., Catterino Cavos's eponymous singspiel of 1815, to a libretto by Alexander Shakhovskoy, the Intendant of the Imperial Theaters, which, in accord with the conventions of its genre, allowed Susanin to be rescued by the timely arrival of Russian troops.

Glinka's opera, too, was originally to have been called *Ivan Susanin*; its eventual title was conferred upon it by Tsar Nicholas himself in return for the dedication. Before suggesting the subject to Glinka, Zhukovsky had tried to interest the historical novelist Mikhail Zagoskin (1789–1852) in contributing to the Susanin literature. This too would have been natural: with a pair of blockbuster novels that had made him a literary celebrity—*Yuriy Miloslavsky; or, The Russians in 1612* (1829) and *Roslavlev; or, The Russians in 1812* (1831)—Zagoskin had already drawn explicit parallels between two periods of civil strife, foreign occupation, and expulsion of the foe, explicitly identifying the Russian national spirit with love of the Romanov dynasty, thus prefiguring the patriotic mythography of Official Nationalism.

Except for the epilogue, which he wrote himself, and which remains one of the essential historical documents of Nikolayan state ideology, Zhukovsky farmed out the actual task of composing the text of the opera to his court colleague and protégé, Baron Yegor Fyodorovich Rozen (Georg Rosen), a Prussian from Reval (now Tallinn, Estonia) who had learned Russian in the military and who was now the secretary to Zhukovsky's pupil, the Tsarevich Alexander. Apart from augmenting the title character's household so far as necessary to obtain a standard operatic quartet, Rozen seems for the most part to have followed Rïleyev's treatment of the Susanin legend with its dramatic scene in the woods. Before Rozen's involvement in the project Count Vladimir Alexandrovich Sollogub (1813–82), the future court historiographer

---

[8] Ibid., p. 17.

then fresh from his university studies, wrote the texts for the opening choruses and for Antonida's cavatina and rondo in act 1. Another precocious protégé of Zhukovsky, Nestor Vasilyevich Kukolnik (1809–68), who had already written a five-act historical verse drama, "The Hand of the All-High Has Saved the Fatherland" (*Ruka Vsevïshnego otechestvo spasla*, 1832), on the subject of the founding of the Romanov dynasty, contributed the text for the orphan-boy Vanya's scene at the monastery gates, which was added to the opera after the première. Kukolnik would remain one of Glinka's closest friends. His name lives on today, long after his pompous nationalistic dramas have perished, because Glinka set many of his lyrics to music.

This, then, is the context into which Glinka's "patriotic heroic-tragic opera in five acts" should be placed in order to understand its "nationalism" and to avoid the misunderstandings that usually becloud discussion of it. A detailed scenario, modeled largely on the formal conventions of the contemporary Italian opera, was drawn up late in 1834 by the committee named above to guide the composer and his various librettists as they worked independently, the music frequently outrunning the text. Glinka relied as well on an unusually complete and well thought-out musical plan that reflected not only his acquaintance with French rescue operas and an aspiration to achieve "a single shapely whole"[9] but also his enthusiastic commitment to the state ideology and his determination to embody it in symbolic sounds.

As THE composer put it in an oft-quoted passage from his memoirs, his root conception of the drama underlying his first opera lay in the opposition of Russian music vs. Polish, a structural antithesis with many surface manifestations. The Poles (the "other") are at all times and places represented by stereotyped dance genres in triple meter (polonaise, mazurka) or highly syncopated duple (krakowiak); they express themselves only collectively, in impersonal choral declamation. The Russian music is at all times highly personal and lyrical. While drawing to a small extent on existing folk melodies, it is chiefly modeled on the idiom of the contemporary sentimental urban romance, in which the Russian folk melos had been put through an italianate refinery.

The chief identifying traits of this urban *style russe* are not at all far removed from those of Pratsch's folk song arrangements. They include the predominance of duple (or compound duple) time, though duple bars are often grouped very irregularly, as in the orphan Vanya's song (act 3) with its seven-bar phrases (example 2.1); cadential terminations by (sometimes heavily embellished) falling fourths or fifths (what Glinka was fond of calling "the soul of Russian music"); and a very free, seemingly unstable interplay of relative major and minor keys reflecting, again as in Pratsch's settings, what ethnomusicologists call the "mutable mode" (*peremennïy lad*) of Russian

---

[9] Glinka, "Zapiski," p. 269.

EXAMPLE 2.1

a. Vanya's song (*A Life for the Tsar*, act 3)

Allegro moderato

Kak mat' u - bi - li u ma - - la - go pten - sa,

(As they killed the birdie's mother . . .)

b. Lvov-Pratsch, *Sobraniye russkikh narodnïkh pesen, protyazhnaya* no. 21
(possible source of melody)

Akh! chto è - to za serd - tse vo mne vsyo iz - nï - lo!

(Ah, what kind of heart is mine, all despairing . . .)

c. Lvov-Pratsch, *Sobraniye russkikh narodnïkh pesen, plyasováya* (dance song) no. 25
(for alternation of three- and four-bar phrases)

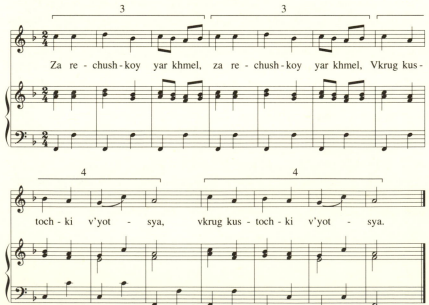

Za re - chush - koy yar khmel, za re - chush - koy yar khmel, Vkrug kus -

toch - ki v'yot - sya, vkrug kus - toch - ki v'yot - sya.

melismatic songs. The prime examples of "pure" (Italo-)Russian style in *A Life for the Tsar* are from act 1: Antonida's cavatina and the first part of the concluding trio, "Do Not Pine, Beloved" (*Ne tomi, rodimïy*) (example 2.2).

The second act is entirely given over to Polish dances. Thereafter the rhythm of the musical contrast becomes more rapid: the Poles' approach in act 3 is telegraphed by a few strategic allusions to the act 2 polonaise; their colloquies with Susanin both in that act and in act 4 are always couched (on both sides) in stereotyped generic terms. At the tensest moment in act 3, where the Poles forcibly seize Susanin and he cries out "God, save the Tsar!" Polish (triple) and Russian (duple) rhythms are briefly superimposed (example 2.3). The symbolic battle of styles is also played out in the overture, which (contrary to usual practice) was the first number from the opera to be composed.

Derivations from actual folklore in *A Life for the Tsar* are few. Susanin's first replique in act 1 is based on a coachman's song Glinka claimed to have taken down from life,[10] while a very famous song, "Downstream on the Mother Volga" (*Vniz po matushke po Volge*), reduced to a characteristic motif, accompanies the dénouement in act 4 as an ostinato. The bridesmaids' chorus in act 3 (a brilliant adaptation of an old Russian decorative stage convention to a novel dramatic purpose), while set to an original melody, is composed, as we have seen, in the pentasyllabic hemistichs of authentic Russian wedding songs, which Glinka was the first artist-composer to set in an actual quintuple meter instead of adapting it to a more conventional one. (The chorus is quoted in example 1.1, in connection with Nikolai Lvov's appropriation of the same meter for poetry.) And yet the result is still an ersatz, of course, a modified form of "Russian" compound duple, exactly as in the famous Allegro con grazia from Chaikovsky's Sixth Symphony. (As in Lvov's *pesennïy razmer* or the later *kol'tsovïy stikh* of Russian romantic poetry, Chaikovsky, like Glinka, invariably groups his fives as two-plus-three, with a strong sense of two beats to the "foot," or bar.) Wholly, if very skillfully, feigned are the choruses in act 1, to texts by Sollogub, including the one for boatmen in which an elaborate pizzicato accompaniment in imitation of balalaika strumming (anticipated by Fomin, as we have seen, in *Yamshchiki na podstave*) cunningly pits the theme of the earlier women's chorus in counterpoint against the boatmen's tune. As in *Kamarinskaya*, the orchestral fantasy that will be the subject of chapter 8, Glinka loved to work his most sophisticated technical tricks on the "naivest" material.

Far more important than the sheer amount of folk or folklike material in the score (meager, and therefore equivocal, in comparison even with the works of certain predecessors, to say nothing of later musicians in the "Glinka tradition") is the use to which such material is put. This was Glinka's great breakthrough, as another romantic literary contemporary, Prince Vladimir Fyo-

[10] Ibid., p. 271.

EXAMPLE 2.2. Glinka, *A Life for the Tsar*

a. Antonida's cavatina, act 1

Andante mosso ma ben sostenuto

(I look out over the open field, my eyes fixed on the distant river . . .)

EXAMPLE 2.2, *continued*

b. Trio (Sobinin, Antonida, Susanin) from Susanin's entrance with theme (act 1)

dorovich Odoyevsky (1804–69) was first to discern. What Glinka "proved," according to Odoyevsky, writing in the *Northern Bee* (*Severnaya pchela*, Faddey Bulgarin's newspaper, the unofficial organ of Official Nationalism), was that "Russian melody may be elevated to a tragic style." In so doing, Odoyevsky declared, Glinka had introduced "a new element in art."[11]

---

[11] "Pis'mo k lyubitelyu muzïki ob opere g. Glinki: Zhizn' za Tsarya," in V. F. Odoyevsky, *Muzïkal'no-literaturnoye naslediye*, ed. G. B. Bernandt (Moscow: Muzgiz, 1956), p. 119.

EXAMPLE 2.2, *continued*

pras - no   Do - ro - go - go dnya,

kru - shit'   se - bya

Na - re - chon - nïy   zyat'!   Mo (-yo)

(*—Do not suffer vainly, don't torment yourself, my valiant ally, my son-in-law to be!*
—How can I not suffer, not torment myself!
—Don't suffer, my darling, don't torment yourself! Don't darken this dear day in vain.)

What this meant was that Glinka had *without loss of scale* integrated the national material into the stuff of his "heroic" drama instead of relegating it, as was customary, to the decorative periphery (as did Fomin, for example, or Cavos, even at their loftiest). Of the dramatic crux, including Susanin's act 4 scena in which the national style is particularly marked, Odoyevsky wrote: "One must hear it to be convinced of the feasibility of such a union, which until now has been considered an unrealizable dream."[12] One reason why it had been so considered, of course, was that before Glinka Russian composers had never aspired to the tragic style at all. What made it feasible was that the main characters in Glinka's opera were all peasants, hence eligible, within the conventions of the day, to espouse a folkish (even an Italianized, urbanized folkish) idiom.

But that hardly made the opera socially progressive, even by the standards of a Nikolai Lvov; for the most advanced of all Glinka's musicodramatic techniques was one that enabled him to harp from beginning to end on the opera's overriding theme of zealous submission to divinely ordained dynastic authority. The epilogue, which portrays Mikhail Romanov's triumphant entrance into Moscow following the rout of the Poles, is built around a choral

[12] "Vtoroye pis'mo k lyubitelyu muzïki ob opere Glinki, Zhizn' za tsarya, ili Susanin," in Odoyevsky, *Muzïkal'no- literaturnoye naslediye*, p. 124.

EXAMPLE 2.3. Superimposed Russian and Polish rhythms (Glinka, *A Life for the Tsar*, act 3, voice parts only)

(—*I fear nothing, not even death! I will lay down my life for the Tsar, for Russia!*
—*Damned mule, shall we kill him?*
—*What good would it do?*
—*We've run others through for not knowing, so it'll serve him right*)

anthem (Glinka called it a "hymn-march") proclaimed by massed forces, including two wind bands on stage, to the following quatrain by Zhukovsky:

Slav'sya, slav'sya nash russkiy Tsar',
Gospodom dannïy nam Tsar'-gosudar'!
Da budet bessmerten tvoy tsarskiy rod!
Da im blagodenstvuyet russkiy narod!

Glory, glory to thee our Russian Caesar,
Our sovereign given us by God!
May thy royal line be immortal!
May the Russian people prosper through it!

Glinka's setting is in a recognizable "period" style—that of the seven-
teenth- and eighteenth-century *kantï*, three- or four-part polyphonic songs that
were the oldest of all "Westernized" Russian repertories (ironically, and perhaps unknown to Glinka, their ancestry was part Polish), and which in Peter
the Great's time were often used for civic panegyrics, in which form they
were known as "Vivats." The *Slav'sya* theme is motivically (that is, "organically") related to that of Susanin's retort to the Poles (example 2.3), derived
from the opening peasant chorus in act 1 (and through that relationship to the
opening phrase of the overture; see example 2.4).

But that only begins to describe its unifying role. As Alexander Serov was
the first to point out, the *Slav'sya* theme (which in Nikolayan and Alexandrine
Russia became virtually a second national anthem) is foreshadowed throughout the opera wherever the topic of dynastic legitimacy is broached (see example 2.5).[13] The approach is gradual, beginning in act 1 with a minor-mode
reference to the first two bars of the theme when Susanin (seconded by the
chorus) dreams of "A Tsar! A lawful Tsar!" In act 3, when news arrives of
Mikhail's election, paving the way to Antonida's wedding (for Susanin had
forbidden celebrating a joyous family event during the interregnum), Susanin
and his household bless their good fortune by falling to their knees in prayer:
"Lord! Love our Tsar! Make him glorious!"—and between their lines the
strings insinuate the same fragment of the *Slav'sya* theme, only this time in
the major. When later in the same act the Poles demand to be taken to the
Tsar, Susanin answers defiantly to an extended if somewhat simplified snatch
of the *Slav'sya* theme, disguised mainly in tempo:

Vïsok i svyat nash tsarskiy dom
I krepost' bozhiya krugom!
Pod neyu sila Rusi tseloy,

---

[13] See Alexander Nikolayevich Serov, "Opïtï tekhnicheskoy kritiki nad muzïkoyu M. I.
Glinki: Rol' odnogo motiva v tseloy opere 'Zhizn' za tsarya'" (1859), in A. N. Serov, *Izbrannïye
stat'i*, ed. G. N. Khubov, vol. 2 (Moscow: Muzgiz, 1957), pp. 35–43.

EXAMPLE 2.4. Glinka, *A Life for the Tsar*

a. Epilogue, "hymn-march" (no. 24), voices only

b. Act 1, opening chorus

(In blizzard, in storm)

c. Beginning of overture

A na stene v odezhde beloy
Stoyat krïlatïye vozhdi!

Our Tsar's home is a high and holy place,
Surrounded with God's staunch strength!
Beneath it is the power of all of Russia,
And on the walls, dressed all in white,
Winged angels stand guard!

Thus *A Life for the Tsar* is thematically unified in both verbal and musical dimensions by the tenets of Official Nationalism. The irony, of course, is that Glinka adapted the techniques by which he achieved this broadly developed musicodramatic plan from the rescue operas of the revolutionary period and applied them to an opera where rescue is thwarted, and in which the political sentiment was literally counterrevolutionary. No wonder, then, that the opera became the mandatory season-opener for the Russian Imperial Theaters (by law the personal property of the Tsar); and no wonder its libretto had to be superseded under Soviet power by a new one (by Sergey Gorodetsky) that replaced devotion to the Romanov dynasty with abstract commitment to national liberation (led by the popular militia of Minin and Pozharsky) and to an anachronistically secular concept of the Russian nation.[14]

And no wonder that as early as the 1860s the opera had become an embarrassment to the lately liberalized intelligentsia, and even such an ardent disciple of Glinka as Vladimir Stasov could complain that "no one has ever done a greater *dishonor* to our people than Glinka, who by means of his great music displayed as a Russian hero *for all time* that base groveler Susanin, with his canine loyalty, his henlike stupidity ["owllike" in Russian] and his readiness to sacrifice his life for a little boy whom, it seems, he has never even seen."[15]

What Glinka did was to draw upon characteristics of all the varieties of indigenous Russian music he had heard from his earliest years, not with the condescension of the sophisticate who wants to be "folksy," but with the perfectly natural ease of a musician for whom folk-song was as deeply rooted and as valid an experience as more cultivated music.[16]

[14] Here, for example, is Gorodetsky's version of the *Slav'sya* quatrain: Slav'sya, slav'sya tï, Rus' moya!/ Slav'sya tï, russkaya nasha zemlya! / Da budet vo veki vekov sil'na / Lyubimaya nasha, rodnaya strana! ("Glory, glory to thee, O Russia mine! / Glory to thee, our Russian land! / May our beloved, our native land / Be strong throughout all ages!").

[15] Letter to Mily Balakirev, 21 March 1861; M. A. Balakirev and V. V. Stasov, *Perepiska*, ed. A. S. Lyapunova, vol. 1 (Moscow: Muzïka, 1970), p. 130.

[16] David Brown, *Mikhail Glinka: A Biographical and Critical Study* (London: Oxford University Press, 1974), p. 113.

EXAMPLE 2.5. Glinka, *A Life for the Tsar*

a. Act 1, no. 4 (voices only)

b. Act 3, no. 11 (quartet)

This sentence from the first English-language biography of Glinka sums up the conventional viewpoint on *A Life for the Tsar* (as "first Russian opera"), on Glinka (as "first Russian composer"), and on Russian music as the "West's" most significant "other." The view of Russian music as "other" is obviously a Western view (albeit one that easily spreads to Westernized Russians). It is less obvious that measuring the Russianness of Russian music by its folkish quotient is also a Western, not a Russian, habit, and a patronizing

EXAMPLE 2.5, *continued*

c. Act 3, no. 12 (Susanin's arioso)

one that originates in colonialist attitudes. (Perhaps that is why it is so rife among British writers.)

Unhampered by the prejudice that Russian music must be exotic in order to qualify as authentic, it is easy to see that the difference between a *A Life for the Tsar* and earlier Russian operas, or between Glinka and earlier Russian composers, had little or nothing to do with the assimilation of folklore. It was obvious even to Glinka's contemporaries that his folkish quotient was, if anything, lower than the average mark set by his predecessors, especially the ones who churned out the trivial vaudevilles and singspiels that were the bread and butter of the Imperial Theaters.

Their most accomplished representative was Alexey Nikolayevich Verstovsky (1799–1862), whose *Askold's Grave*, an ambitious semihistorical opera in four acts (albeit with spoken dialogue), to a libretto by the patriotic historical novelist Zagoskin after his own eponymous novel, had its première a year earlier than *A Life for the Tsar* and probably deserves recognition as the most enduringly popular Russian opera of the nineteenth century. To the end of the nineteenth century there would be many who claimed that Verstovsky was the more authentically Russian composer, precisely because Verstovsky was more insularly Russian than was Glinka with his ostentatiously virtuosic "European" technique.

Among those who refused to concede Glinka's preeminence was the bitterly envious Verstovsky himself, who shortly after the 1836 première gave *A Life for the Tsar* a withering review in a letter to Prince Odoyevsky. His point was precisely that this St. Petersburger parvenu Glinka was no more (and probably a good sight less) Russian than the honest Muscovites like himself and Alexander Alyabyev (1787–1851) who had been slaving in the sweatshop of the Imperial Theaters churning out Russian operas by the bushel. "And lo! *the dawn of Russian opera has appeared* on the horizon with *A Life for the Tsar*," he snarled,

> while Alyabyev and I are sent to the garrison, for Glinka's opera marks an epoch on the Russian stage. Thus twenty years' work on the part of an individual who all that while had striven with all his might to invest the character of National Russian music in European form—all that is not worth a dime. And because of what? Because to you Lord Writers of Petersburg Moscow might as well be Podunk, and anything that might show itself there is in your opinion way beneath mediocrity. *The dawn of Russian music*, not just Russian songs—but purely national music with all the appurtenances of opera—that's long been on the horizon. The sun we haven't seen yet. And it's hardly going to appear until they all stop turning up their noses at whatever is really Russian and national. I remember Catalani's and Sontag's tears when they heard Russian melodies, but it never occurs to any of our singers to sing Grimslava's song from *Vadim* or the romance from *Tvardovsky* or the aria from *Askold's Grave* in polite society. I say

this not because they are so great but because they are truly pervaded with the characteristics of Russian music. And the melodies in them so pleased Romberg and Schwenke that one of them made a wonderful arrangement of them. I wish you'd listen again to the third act finale of *Askold's Grave*. It would shame you and convince you that the Dawn of Russian Music broke for opera in Moscow, not Petersburg. I am the first to idolize Glinka's marvelous talent, but I will not and cannot renounce my rights to primacy. True, none of my operas contain triumphal marches, polonaises, or mazurkas, but they have their inalienable virtues, achieved by dint of great experience and knowledge of the orchestra. There is nothing in them of the oratorio, nothing in them of the lyric, but these are not needed in opera; every genre has its own forms, its own limits. You don't go to the theater to pray to God. Yes, and while we're at it, a lot of it comes from not knowing how to write words. You yourself know how many (or rather, how few) writers we have who know what a musician needs. I do not see this knowledge in Rozen. The time of Italian librettos is past.[17]

And so on and on. Actually, he's quite right,[18] just as Alexander Serov, then a would-be composer also given to stewing in sour grapes, was right to contend, in his obituary for Verstovsky in 1862, that Verstovsky "strikes chords within the Russian soul that Glinka never touched."[19] It is all correct, and all beside the point.

Glinka's greatness was recognized from the beginning; and however they admired Verstovsky, their contemporaries unanimously sensed that it was Glinka who represented a "wonderful beginning" for Russian music.[20] Far from a matter of Russianness *tout court*, his greatness was seen as consisting in his unprecedented seriousness, originality, technical virtuosity, and (as a result of these) his viability on the world stage. Glinka did not invent the Russian style, but he made Russian music competitive. Through him, Russia could for the first time join the musical West on an equal footing, without excuses, as a full-fledged participant in international musical traditions, and a

---

[17] A. N. Verstovsky to B. F. Odoyevsky, December 1836; first published in *Biryuch* (Petrograd: State Theaters, 1921), quoted from Alexander Semyonovich Rabinovich, *Russkaya opera do Glinki* (Moscow: Muzgiz, 1948), pp. 170–71. Where the translation has "Podunk" Verstovsky had written Chukhloma, a town in the Kostroma guberniya, in the middle of the great Russian nowhere. Angelica Catalani (1780–1849) and Henrietta Sontag (1806–54) were among the earliest European divas to sing in Russia. *Vadim* and *Pan Tvardovsky* were earlier singspiels by Verstovsky. The cellist Bernhard Romberg (1767–1841) and the pianist Carl Schwenke (1797–1870) were a popular touring team. For the record—it will become relevant to an argument later in this book—one of the most popular numbers in *Askold's Grave*, the chorus of immured maidens in act 3, is in fact cast as a polonaise (albeit without explicit indication).

[18] Only where he says, "You don't go to the theater to pray to God" was Verstovsky dead wrong; it shows that, unlike Glinka, he did not grasp the nature of Nikolayan totalitarianism.

[19] A. N. Serov, *Izbrannïye stat'i*, vol. 2, p. 47.

[20] Nikolai Gogol, "Peterburgskiye zapiski" (1836), in *Sochineniya i pis'ma N. V. Gologya*, ed. V. V. Kallash (St. Petersburg: Prosveshcheniye, 1896), vol. 7, p. 340.

contributor to them. The old bromide that Glinka liberated Russian music by turning away from the West has it just backward. Liberation came from facing and matching, not retreating.

And yet both in Russia and in the West, then and since, it has always been important for some to represent Glinka's greatness in terms of his greater Russianness. Within Russia, this was yet a further manifestation of Official Nationalism. The extract given above from David Brown's biography was a gloss, amounting to a paraphrase, on a review of *A Life for the Tsar* by Yanuariy Mikhailovich Neverov (1810–93) that appeared in the *Moskovskiy nablyudatel'* (Moscow Observer) shortly after the première. The author of this article was then a young Moscow dilettante, a protégé of Odoyevsky, whose evaluation of *A Life for the Tsar* faithfully echoed his mentor's.[21] Neverov himself dreamed of a composing career until Otto Nicolai, to whom he applied for instruction in Vienna, discouraged his ambitions.[22] In later life he achieved some prominence as an orientalist and educational administrator, a career for which one had to be a card-carrying Official Nationalist.[23] Thus it is not surprising to find raillery, in the part of Neverov's critique that David Brown selected for glossing, against a want of true *narodnost'* in Verstovsky's works, despite an abundance of "delightful Russian tunes," owing to their "arbitrary mixture of arias, duets, and trios of all styles and all peoples in which the listener sought in vain for any unity *or dominating idea.*"[24]

It is not the mere presence of Russian melodies, however authentic, that makes for *narodnost'*, then, but the use of such melodies to evoke an all-encompassing idea of Russia: "images which are purely Russian, native," as Neverov put it, "all clear, comprehensible, familiar to us simply because they breathe a pure *narodnost'*, because we hear in them native sounds."[25] *But also* because "all these Russian images are created by the composer in such a way that *in the aggregate*, in their cohesion, they have been marshaled against the intrigues of the enemy invader, attempting to enslave the Russian land."[26] Thus Glinka, unlike Verstovsky, is truly *narodnïy* because he is ideologically, not merely decoratively, *narodnïy*. His Russians all speak in a single voice. And they speak not only for something but against something as well. Such a basis for approbation follows directly and entirely from the tenets of Official

[21] Neverov's basic judgment on the opera is straight out of Odoyevsky: "Up to now we had never heard Russian music in an elevated style; this was Mr. Glinka's creation" (Ya. M. Neverov, "O novoy opere g. Glinki 'Zhizn' za tsarya,'" in Tamara Livanova and Vladimir Protopopov, *Opernaya kritika v Rossii*, vol. 1 [Moscow: Muzïka, 1966], part 1, p. 207).

[22] Ibid., pp. 206–7.

[23] Grigoriy Bernandt and Izrail Yampolsky, *Kto pisal o muzïke*, vol. 2 (Moscow: Sovetskiy kompozitor, 1974), p. 233.

[24] Quoted from Brown, *Glinka*, pp. 112–13; italics added.

[25] Quoted from ibid., p. 113.

[26] Quoted from Livanova and Protopopov, *Opernaya kritika v Rossii*, p. 208; italics in the original.

Nationalism, and has nothing to do (as Neverov himself implies in his remarks about Verstovsky) with style per se, or with what an English writer, footlessly omniscient, will characterize as the greater rootedness or validity of the composer's own musical experiences.

Now the other historical period in which Glinka's *narodnost'* was given an ideological spin in Russia was, of course, the Stalinist period, which embodied in so many ways a resurgence of Nikolayan nationalism, especially after World War II, known in Russia, like the Napoleonic Wars that preceded the first Nikolai's reign, as the *Velikaya otechestvennaya voyna*, the "Great Patriotic War." It was during this period, the period of the early cold war, that the jingoistic critical writings of Vladimir Stasov, which strove hard to represent all Russian art as entirely autochthonous, hardened into Soviet scripture and assumed the overwhelming mandatory authority in the secondary literature against which Western writers are willy-nilly forced to react.

The Soviet literature justified investing Stasov with so much official prestige, amounting to a new Official Nationalism, by emphasizing Stasov's personal relationship with the figures he so tendentiously promoted, in music mainly Glinka and the so-called Five (whose Russian sobriquet, *moguchaya kuchka* or "mighty little heap," Stasov had actually coined).[27] A Western writer, conditioned by another sort of unconscious prejudice to value emanations from Russia in direct proportion to their perceived autochthonism will be easily taken in.

AN EXCELLENT case in point is the *Slav'sya*, the "hymn-march," in the epilogue to *A Life for the Tsar*. Its status as symbol of the Russian nation came about for political reasons unrelated to its stylistic pedigree, which, as we have observed, is of a distinctly Westernized strain.[28] Stasov may or may not have been aware of the old repertory of *kantï* on which Glinka drew for this monumental number; but he was definitely aware of, and committed to, the preposterous theory that Russian folk music preserved the modes of classical antiquity (a view that may have had its origins in the doctrine of the "third Rome" that asserted Russia's status as preserver of a Christianity unsullied by either papism or Protestantism and thus rightful heir to the spiritual leadership of the Christian world). Stasov contended that Glinka, by intuition alone, had divined the archaic system that Russian folklore preserved undefiled, and had made it the foundation of his (therefore) wholly autochthonous personal style. His music restores "none other than the system of ancient or medieval modes

---

[27] On this term and its coinage, see R. Taruskin, "What is a Kuchka?" in *Musorgsky: Eight Essays and an Epilogue* (Princeton: Princeton University Press, 1993), pp. xxxiii–xxxiv.

[28] Further on nonstylistic sources of Slavic musical nationalism, see Michael Beckerman, "In Search of Czechness in Music," *19th-Century Music* 10 (1986–87): 61–73. This important article builds in part on an unpublished 1984 paper, "Theme and Prototype in Russian Music" by Malcolm H. Brown, which I, too, gratefully acknowledge for its welcome clarification of issues usually treated in obfuscating fashion.

that Europe has long since forgotten and all other composers have forsaken," and the proof was the *Slav'sya*.

"This chorus," wrote Stasov in the year of Glinka's death,

indisputably the greatest and most perfect national anthem ever heard in Russia, has such a profound significance for the future of Russian musical art, contains the solution to so many substantial aesthetic and technical problems, that it will surely be the subject of serious specialized investigations. It affords shining proof of Glinka's genius for the way he instinctively grasped and captured the spirit and character of Russian music; instinctively, because he himself never suspected what he had wrought in this hymn. The *Slav'sya* chorus consists of several plagal cadences following one another without interruption (for which there are precedents in Chopin: e.g., the Mazurka Op. 30, no. 2, and so on); but the melody that is built on them is a stirring series of notes, moving *by step* (*mouvement par degrés* [sic] *conjoints*), so that out of thirty-four notes that make it up, there are only seven thirds, one fifth, and one sixth. Consequently, we have here a melody created purely in the style of our ancient Russian and Greek church melodies, with a harmonization consisting of medieval plagal cadences! Glinka's unconsciousness of all this is shown by the fact that in proceeding from the first cadence to the second, he made a single use of what we *now* call a minor triad (G minor) against the rules of the church modes, but the next time he omitted it and decided instead to make a direct approach from a G cadence to one on A.[29]

"Doesn't the harmony sound like a good deal of C major tonic and dominant at the beginning, with a final swing to the dominant?" asks David Brown.[30] Of course it does. That is exactly what it is. There was never a Russian harmonic tradition along the lines Stasov suggests; his analysis is pure tendentious invention. But Brown, generously or credulously as it may seem, is disposed to grant that "any Russian view must obviously be treated with respect, for Russian ears are *naturally* more sensitive to such matters than ours."[31] If Stasov analyzes the music a certain way, that means he "really heard it this way," and however impossible his assertions may be to confirm empirically, therefore, "we must take these on trust."[32] Also to be taken "on trust" is Neverov's preposterous claim (one that later Russian composers openly disputed and, in their work, refuted) that Glinka's recitatives faithfully transmit "the intonation of Russian speech."[33]

---

[29] Vladimir Vasil'yevich Stasov, "Mikhail Ivanovich Glinka" (1857), in Stasov, *Izbrannïye sochineniya v tryokh tomakh* (Moscow: Iskusstvo, 1952), vol. 1, p. 445n.; unlike the *Slav'sya*, it should be pointed out, the Chopin mazurka to which Stasov refers cadences plagally in the key designated as the tonic by the key signature. (The "plagal cadences" in the *Slav'sya* are, according to the key signature, on the dominant.)

[30] Brown, *Glinka*, p. 134.

[31] Ibid., p. 111 (italics added).

[32] Ibid., p. 134.

[33] Ibid., p. 121.

This apparent naivety has the appearance of openmindedness, but it is actually something more nearly the opposite. It is the result of a predisposition, a prejudice that has rendered the critic susceptible to a propaganda that appeals by design to prejudice. The prejudice, in Brown's case if not in Stasov's, is a special instance of perhaps the most pervasive bias in modern Western musicology, namely, the bias that sees only style and structure as "real." Thus for a modern Western writer, nationalism in music must consist in autochthonous style (and style alone); and such autochthonous style, in the case of a "national" composer, validates his music in a way that the composer personally cannot do.

Indeed, in Brown's discussion Glinka is actually granted very little in the way of personal control over his style or technique. In a remark evidently intended as benevolent, the biographer allows that "Glinka's melodic nationalism seems effortless and was, one suspects, quite artless." He goes on to admonish the reader that "it is important to emphasize this, for an examination of *A Life for the Tsar* reveals all sorts of small but very real similarities between quite separate tunes."[34]

Now a whole school of musical analysis, associated with the Austro-American scholar Rudolf Réti and a pleiad of native or naturalized British disciples including Hans Keller, Deryck Cooke, and Alan Walker, measures the greatness of a composer's achievement by the extent to which the criterion here adduced by Brown is met.[35] Réti was at pains to stress that "at least in the representative works of great musical literature," this was "essentially a *conscious* process," evidence of the composer's superior command. "The great composers," he went on, "were fully aware both of the thematic principle and of the technique through which they materialized it. As this consciousness was supported and complemented by a thorough technical training, this transforming of musical ideas into different shapes finally became the composer's customary way of expressing himself, his natural musical language."[36]

At first Brown seems to be ascribing such a shaping consciousness to the composer of *A Life for the Tsar*:

> Now, Glinka was very concerned, as he himself said and as we shall later see, to ensure that the opera made "an harmonious whole," and he set about this by creating many substantial cross-references between its component parts. Therefore might not a concern to tighten the structure have led him to fabricate these smaller thematic similarities?[37]

Yet after giving a pair of subtle examples of just the type that Réti and his disciples customarily adduce to demonstrate the conscious shaping powers of

[34] Ibid., p. 115.

[35] The foundational text for this approach to criticism is Réti's *The Thematic Process in Music* (New York: Macmillan, 1951).

[36] Ibid., pp. 233–34.

[37] Brown, *Glinka*, p. 115.

a Mozart or a Schumann, Brown decides that "what seems more plausible," after all, "is that Glinka, by focusing upon a smaller range of melodic types with certain traits in common," inherited directly and unconsciously from his folk heritage, "made the opera more of a piece than it would otherwise have been," had he relied (or been able to rely) on the promptings of a personal imagination.[38]

Consider the implications. A Russian composer in the art music tradition is assumed (or rather, doomed) to create, because he is Russian, in the manner of a peasant singer—not by effort or art but by instinct, as is only "natural for a man born and bred in different cultural surroundings, and *inheriting different racial characteristics and attitudes*."[39] While one can affect admiration, even a sort of envy, for such an artist on the romantic or neoprimitivist assumption that what is unmediated by civilization is imbued with spontaneous authenticity, such admiration is inevitably laced with condescension. Mr. Natural, with his biologically inherited attitudes, can have only a group identity. Stripped of that identity, he is stripped of all authenticity. When Glinka fails to conform to his English biographer's model of Russian group identity and group behavior, it is held very much against him, as the remarks quoted in chapter 9 about the character of Ratmir in *Ruslan and Lyudmila*, Glinka's second opera, will amply attest.

[38] Ibid., pp. 115–16.
[39] Ibid., p. 135 (italics added).

CHAPTER 3

P. I. CHAIKOVSKY AND THE GHETTO

VIEWING Glinka through the eyes of his British biographer, we begin to see why it remains the Western habit to group all Russian composers, like any others who do not hail (in a word to be much rehearsed throughout the "Notes on *Svadebka*" in chapter 13) from the "panromanogermanic" mainstream, as "nationalists" whatever their actual predilections;[1] why composers of the panromanogermanic mainstream are rarely described as nationalists whatever their actual predilections; and why, for "peripheral" composers, stylistic dependency on autochthonous folklore is taken in the West as an indispensable earnest of authenticity, a virtual requirement. It is yet another manifestation of fetishized difference. And that is why conventional musicology, perhaps alone among the humanistic disciplines, and in seeming inattention both to the most inescapable headline realities and to the most elementary moral imperatives, continues, uncritically and embarrassingly, to celebrate "nationalism."

But it is really no celebration. In conventional "canonical" historiography Russian (or Czech, or Spanish, or Norwegian) composers are in a double bind. The group identity is at once the vehicle of their international appeal (as "naifs") and the guarantee of their secondary status vis-à-vis the unmarked "universal." Without exotic native dress such composers cannot achieve even secondary canonical rank, but with it they cannot achieve more. However admiringly it is apparently done, casting a composer as a "nationalist" is pre-eminently a means of exclusion from the critical and academic canon (though not, obviously, from the performing repertoire).

---

[1] A striking example of such lumping came unexpectedly in an excellent paper, read at a recent musicological convention, introducing the theoretical thought of Sergey Ivanovich Taneyev (1856–1915). The paper emphasized Taneyev's signal contribution, one that has been tacitly appropriated by "mainstream" theorists everywhere (and will be much used in this book in the chapters on Scriabin and Stravinsky): namely, that of "introduc[ing] the use of cardinal numbers for intervals in order to effect systematic transformations of material, tonally derived formal hierarchies, and an explanation for the role of counterpoint in large forms." At the same time it was observed, irrelevantly as it might seem, that Taneyev's compositions are "without conspicuously nationalistic elements" (Gordon D. McQuere, "The Development of Music Theory in Russia: Sergei Taneev," *AMS/CMS/SEM/SMT Abstracts* [Vancouver, 1985], p. 39). When asked why this observation was called for, the speaker replied that it answered "a natural question" about a Russian composer.

The double bind operates most transparently in the case of Chaikovsky and has functioned this way since the beginning of the century now ending, when Russian music, thanks in large part to Diaghilev's promotion, began its conquest of Paris. The appealing orientalist myth of the "âme slave," the primitivistic, neo-Scythian, collective Russian consciousness played an important part in this promotion (as witness the repertoire adduced and discussed at the end of chapter 9). This mythology, and the ecstatic reaction to it on the part of the French press and public, was painstakingly nurtured and manipulated by Diaghilev once he began creating (with *The Firebird*) a "Russian" repertory earmarked expressly for a French audience. One of its unintended side effects was to aggravate the backlash against Russian composers who did not conform to the exotic stereotype purveyed by the Ballets Russes, and first among them was the composer whose Europeanized outlook and manner most nearly matched Diaghilev's own aristocratic predilections. Not until 1921 would Diaghilev dare present Chaikovsky in any but tiny doses to his audience; and when he did (with the London *Sleeping Beauty*) he nearly lost his shirt.

Even before Diaghilev, French critical antipathy to Chaikovsky ran high. Its source probably lay in César Cui's outrageously partisan survey *La Musique en Russie*, a reissue in book form of a series of articles originally published in 1878 in the *Revue et Gazette musicale*, which furnished a whole generation of French critics and writers on music with virtually their sole source of information on Russian music. Cui had dismissed Chaikovsky as "a musician of extraordinary talent, except that he abuses his technical facility," and, most unfairly, as being "far from a partisan of the New Russian school; he is more nearly its antagonist."[2]

Though this last assertion was no truer than the notion of a monolithic "New Russian school" itself, it played into the Western prejudice about exotic group identities and formed French opinion irrevocably. By 1903, the composer Alfred Bruneau—in *Musiques de Russie et Musiciens de France*, a book that slavishly recycled Cui's old "kuchkist" propaganda despite its author's having made a personal goodwill tour of Russia in 1901–2 as the quasi-official emissary of the French government—embroidered on Cui's account of Chaikovsky with astonishing animus: "Devoid of the Russian character that pleases and attracts us in the music of the New Slavic school, developed to hollow and empty excess in a bloated and faceless style, his works astonish without overly interesting us," the critic sneered.[3] Again, without an exotic group identity a Russian composer can possess no identity at all. Without a collective folkloristic or oriental mask he is "faceless."

The recent British biographers who have meant to vindicate Chaikovsky

[2] *La Musique en Russie* (Paris: Fischbacher, 1880), pp. 132, 119.

[3] Alfred Bruneau, *Musiques de Russie et musiciens de France* (Paris: Bibliothèque Charpentier, 1903), pp. 27–28.

against this sort of dismissal have not questioned the orientalist premises on which the dismissal has been based. Vindication on their terms has meant vindication as a "nationalist." That is, the critic must "succeed" where Cui and Bruneau had "failed," in uncovering Chaikovsky's all-validating group identity. So his folk song quotations are toted up and, owing to the requirements of concerto finales and operatic second acts, the stats are impressive. Passages from his correspondence evincing devotion to birch trees and mud are adduced. Benevolently, but far from benignly, Chaikovsky's Russianness, like Glinka's, is reduced to a set of "racial characteristics and attitudes" cast in rigorous opposition to those of the West.

The locus classicus for this position is the penultimate chapter ("The Russian Composer") in David Brown's four-volume biography of Chaikovsky. The author's stated aim is to "pinpoint a little of the Russianness of Tchaikovsky's music" and in so doing to provide a model that might "suggest to other present or future Tchaikovsky scholars lines of investigation they might pursue." And yet from the very beginning the focus is less on the music than on the man who made it, toward whom a typical attitude of condescension is adopted: "His was a Russian mind forced to find its expression through techniques and forms that had been evolved by generations of alien Western creators, and, this being so, it would be unreasonable to expect stylistic consistency or uniform quality."[4] The best that can be said of Chaikovsky the symphonist is that "a composer who could show so much resourcefulness in modifying sonata structure so as to make it more compatible with the type of music *nature had decreed he would write* was no helpless bungler."[5] This is what the Russians (before 1861) used to call the *krepostnoye pravo*: to the land the serf was born and on the land he shall remain.

Radical essentialism of this kind is not at all a new approach. It characterized a great deal of Victorian scholarship and has long been recognized as an aspect of romanticism that is especially liable to degenerate into racialist bombast. With no basis save bias, and in spite of all the evidence we have of Chaikovsky's social environment, his tastes, and his education, Brown insists on educing the essentials of the composer's musical style directly from "pure folksong,"[6] peasant lore, the unmediated musical mirror of "the Russian mind."[7] Chaikovsky, it is categorically asserted, was "endowed with a mind of this nature."[8] His musical style was thus innate, biologically determined,

---

[4] David Brown, *Tchaikovsky*, vol. 4: *The Final Years: 1885–1893* (New York: Norton, 1991), p. 10.

[5] Ibid., vol. 1: *The Early Years: 1840–1874* (New York: Norton, 1978), pp. 108–9; italics added.

[6] Ibid., vol. 4, p. 423.

[7] Ibid., p. 425.

[8] Ibid., p. 424

and there was simply nothing the poor man could do about it.[9] He is cast as a victim of his racial endowment, a casualty of the unbridgeable gap between "Russian instinct" and "Western method," the latter as dogmatically and reductively conceived as the former.[10]

Such a view of the Russian style and the Russian mind can only lead to an obsession with purity. When such an obsession is voiced from the Russian side, of course, we call it "nationalism." But a nationalism that insists on purity is no longer a benign or liberating nationalism. It has turned aggressive and intolerant. We will reencounter it in the old Balakirev and the young Stravinsky. When the obsession with Russian purity is voiced from the Western side, though, what shall we call it? What shall we make of the frequent chiding Chaikovsky receives from his British biographers for lapsing, for not being Russian enough?

In the finale of the Fourth Symphony, Edward Garden declares, the pure folk song (the familiar "Birch Tree") is "dragged in most inappropriately, squared off with two extra beats and ruined in the process."[11] Chaikovsky gratuitously "mars" an aria in one of his operas, Brown declares, and "turns traitor to its essential Russianness by extending it with vocal sequence and operatic cadenza."[12] There are even passages where the British biographer presumes to instruct his Russian subject in the ways of Russianness. Complaining that in one of Chaikovsky's operatic finales "loud and vapid tumult replaces genuinely inventive conflict," he notes "one precious moment of respite" where the tenor takes tender leave of the soprano:

"We will wash away our grief on mother Volga," he sings, pouring out a pure Russian cantilena supported by male chorus, as beautiful a melodic passage as any in the opera. Even here, however, Tchaikovsky cannot let slip the opportunity for harmonic "cleverness," and his sudden shift into neapolitan regions . . . compromises for a moment that Russian world so clearly conjured up in the vocal part.[13]

These are the words of a fatherly "bwana," celebrating the picturesqueness of the quaint aboriginal world he patronizes, ever watchful lest the natives,

---

[9] Hence the author's renewed insistence, having identified subtle Rétiesque thematic interconnections in Chaikovsky's symphonic output, that "to what extent Tchaikovsky was aware of creating these relationships while composing his themes is debatable" (Ibid., p. 431).

[10] Ibid., p. 436.

[11] Edward Garden, *Tchaikovsky* (London: Dent, 1973), p. 81. Brown (*Tchaikovsky*, vol. 2: *The Crisis Years: 1874–1878* [New York: Norton, 1983], p. 176) reminds us (and Chaikovsky) that Balakirev had used the tune "more correctly" in his Overture on Three Russian Themes; compare example 8.4 in chapter 8.

[12] Brown, *Tchaikovsky*, vol. 1, p. 150.

[13] Ibid., p. 147.

forsaking their essential natures, lose their exotic charm and start acting like his equals.

That is why Brown is so concerned to insist, even devoting a separately titled chapter addendum to it, upon "the Russianness of *Eugene Onegin*," the one Chaikovsky opera to have achieved supreme repertory status the world over, and a work in which the musical idiom is not stylistically marked with national character in a way that immediately advertises itself to the "Western" ear. Yet where elsewhere Brown can cite technical features in support of his diagnoses of (rustic) Russianness, here all he can do is adduce without commentary or amplification the testimony of authorities, chiefly Stravinsky and Prokofiev, to the effect that "Tchaikovsky drew *unconsciously* from the true popular sources of our race" (Stravinsky)[14] and that "*Eugene Onegin* is the most intrinsically Russian opera" in which every role "corresponded completely to the Russian character, each in its own way" (Prokofiev).[15]

Anyone who really knows Russia, or Russians, or the cultural politics of interwar Paris (where both Stravinsky and Prokofiev made their pronouncements, Stravinsky's as promotional propaganda for his boss), will know how to read these comments and deconstruct their mystique. Even old Boleslaw Przybyszewski, the hopelessly doctrinaire "vulgar-Marxist" critic whom we will encounter again in chapter 11, had it right when he spoke, albeit clumsily, of Chaikovsky as a "musical realist" who "drew his melodic style from the melodic springs of surrounding Russian reality," that is, the music of the Europeanized urban class to which the composer himself belonged.[16] With cunning insight (no "instinct" here!) Chaikovsky was able to abstract musical morphemes (what the shrewd if politically contemptible Soviet musicologist Boris Asafyev later christened "intonations")[17] from this mongrel "townsong" idiom, instantly recognizable as indigenous by Russians, but accessible to Westerners as "universal."

And it was naturally that urbanized, sophisticated, cosmopolitan Russian style that émigré modernists like Stravinsky and (at the time) Prokofiev would have sought to advance against the folkloric idiom that had become de rigueur in Red Russia, where the slogan "an art national in form and socialist in content" (in Stalin's very words) had forged a link that tainted idioms Westerners could apprehend as indicatively "Russian."[18]

---

[14] Letter to the *Times* of London on behalf of Diaghilev's *Sleeping Beauty* production; quoted in Brown, *Tchaikovsky*, vol. 2, p. 217.

[15] Giacomo Antonini, unpublished memoir quoted by Brown in ibid., p. 218.

[16] "O Chaikovskom," foreword to P. I. Chaikovsky, *Perepiska s N. F. fon-Mekk*, ed. V. A. Zhdanov and N. T. Zhegin, vol. 1 (Moscow: Academia, 1934), p. xvi.

[17] See in particular his monograph, *Yevgeniy Onegin: Liricheskiy stseni P. I. Chaikovskogo* (Moscow and Leningrad: Muzgiz, 1944).

[18] See Iosif Vissarionovich Stalin, *Voprosï Leninizma* (Moscow: Gospolitizdat, 1931), p. 137. With regard to the tainting of folklore under the Bolshevik regime, compare a widely publicized statement attributed to Shostakovich in the newspaper *Sovetskoye iskusstvo* (20 November 1938)

As IN the case of *A Life for the Tsar*, the critically relevant point about *Yevgeniy Onegin* is neither to establish nor to falsify its essential "Russian-ness," but to investigate the purposes and the results of a calculated stylistic construction. It is another matchless test case, in its way just as programmatic an effort toward defining Russia (and Russians) musically; and it has been just as comprehensively misunderstood from the outside.

In addition to the general problems Chaikovsky has had with Western connoisseurs, *Yevgeniy Onegin* has one all its own: its relationship to its literary source, one of the most revered monuments in all of Russian litera-ture. Although the snobbish solecism according to which an opera derived from preexisting literature is judged by a simple yardstick of fidelity—correspondingly exigent as the source is valued—has happily been losing ground (in the case of Russian works partly through a timely dissemination of Bakhtin's ideas),[19] in the case of Chaikovsky's masterpiece it obstinately per-sists. The opera has been the bane of Pushkin-lovers from the beginning (Tur-genev to Tolstoy: "Undeniably notable music . . . but what a libretto!").[20] By now, on the authority of the militantly tone-deaf Vladimir Nabokov, for whom "the ideal state" was one in which there was "no torture, no executions [and] no music,"[21] denigration of Chaikovsky's work has become literary dogma.

The novel's greatness is assumed to lie in its irony, vouchsafed by its glori-ously intrusive narrative voice—"a kind of spiritual air conditioner," as one commentator has colorfully put it. When that machine is turned off, as it is assumed to be in the opera, "the atmosphere becomes sticky, the underpin-nings of the wonderfully delicate, intricate, balanced structure rot, and it col-lapses. You are left with a banal, trite, and sentimental bore—which may nevertheless be a vehicle for some delightful music."[22]

This formulation shows magnificent incomprehension of what the music in an opera does—but particularly in this opera, where the music, quite simply, is the narrator. From the very first sung notes, Olga's and Tatyana's duet to the harp, the music acts as a very busy and detached mediator of situations

---

on the subject of his Sixth Symphony, then announced as the "Lenin" symphony: "I have set myself a task fraught with great responsibility, to express through the medium of sound the immortal image of Lenin as a great son of the Russian people and a great leader and teacher of the masses. I have received numerous letters from all corners of the Soviet Union with regard to my future Symphony. The most important advice contained in these letters was to make ample use of musical folklore" (quoted from Nicolas Slonimsky, "Dmitri Dmitrievitch Shostakovitch," *Musi-cal Quarterly* 28 [1942]: 431).

[19] See especially Caryl Emerson, *Boris Godunov: Transpositions of a Russian Theme* (Bloom-ington: Indiana University Press, 1986).

[20] Letter of 15/27 November 1878; quoted from Gerald Abraham, ed., *The Music of Tchaikovsky* (New York: Norton, 1974), p. 149.

[21] Vladimir Nabokov, *Strong Opinions* (New York: McGraw-Hill, 1973), p. 35.

[22] Hugh McLean, "The Tone(s) of 'Eugene Onegin,'" *California Slavic Studies* 6 (1971): 15.

and feelings. As Asafyev was the first to demonstrate in detail, Chaikovsky "sings" his opera in an idiom intensely redolent of the domestic, theatrical, and ballroom music of its time and place—its, not his—and in so doing he situates it, just as Pushkin situates the literary prototype, in the years 1819–25. And just as Pushkin's characters achieve their "reality" by virtue of a multitude of precisely manipulated codes, so Chaikovsky's express themselves through a finely calculated filter of musical genres and conventions.

To express the passions and spontaneous reactions of the characters by means of stereotyped melodic and harmonic figures, however freshly and virtuosically recombined, makes exactly the same point Pushkin makes in his novel: feelings are never spontaneous but always mediated by the conventions and constraints, as often learned from literature as from "life," to which we have adapted. Therein lie both the tragedy (the constraints) and the salvation (the adaptation) of human society.

Moreover, where the novelist must arrange things in a temporal sequence, the musician can simultaneously present and comment without recourse to digression. The best possible illustration comes at the very outset, with the eccentric "quartet" for women's voices in which that very typical period duet-romance (to an early verse by Pushkin), sung offstage by Tatyana and her sister, accompanies a speech-song conversation (unlike Glinka's speech-song, truly conversational in its contours and rhythms) between their mother, Mme Larina, and Filipp'yevna, their former wet nurse. The foreground conversation begins with an invocation to the books in Larina's life ("O Grandison! O Richardson!") and ends with a modest paean to habit ("given to us from above as substitute for happiness"; the music is quoted in chapter 10).

"It seems to me," Chaikovsky later wrote to his friend Vladimir Pogozhev, a theater official, "that I am truly gifted with the ability *truthfully, sincerely, and simply* to express the feelings, moods, and images suggested by a text. In this sense I am a *realist* and fundamentally a Russian."[23] The opening quartet in *Yevgeniy Onegin*, and the whole opera that follows, wonderfully bears out this self-characterization. The realism and the Russianness of this opera are equally profound and profoundly interrelated; and they are equally likely to be missed by those who equate realism with "formlessness" and can discern national character only in the sort of folklore that exists in *Yevgeniy Onegin* (like the "folk" itself) only as an aspect of decor.

Another example of Chaikovsky's diegetical skill—his ability at once to present and to comment—comes at the moment when the title character together with his friend, the poetaster Lensky, make their first appearance. The comically exaggerated courtly flourishes in the orchestra that accompany their

---

[23] V. N. Pogozhev, "Vospominaniya o P. I. Chaikovskom," in Igor Glebov (i.e., Boris Asafyev), ed., *P. I. Chaikovsky: Vospominaniya i pis'ma* (Leningrad: Filarmoniya, 1924), p. 77 (emphasis in the original).

bows to the Larin ladies instantly sketch their foppish histories, accomplishing much of the work of Pushkin's chapter 1, the absence of which is so often
and so severely held against the opera's libretto. In their startling anticipation
of *Pulcinella*, these "eighteenth-century" curlicues also call attention to
Chaikovsky's underappreciated mastery of the grotesque.

These points apply not only to the characters' public behavior and to the
obviously "generic" ballroom scenes but even, or especially, to their most
private and personal utterances. Tatyana's Letter Scene, the most private and
personal in the opera, is in effect a string of romances linked by recitatives:

1. "Puskai pogibnu ya" ("Even if it means I perish"): Allegro non troppo, Db
   major, 4/4, da capo form (18 bars)
2. "Ya k vam pishu" ("I'm writing to you"): Moderato assai quasi Andante, D
   minor, 4/4 strophic form (56 bars, including recits)
3. "Net, nikomu na svete ne otdala bï serdtse ya!" ("No, there is no one else on
   earth to whom I'd give my heart"): Moderato, C major, 2/4 (accompaniment
   in 6/8), da capo form (80 bars, including recits and transitions)
4. "Kto tï: moy angel-li khranitel'" ("Who art thou—my guardian angel?"):
   Andante, Db major, 2/4, da capo form (75 bars, 129 counting orchestral
   introduction and orchestral/vocal coda).

The resonances between the music of this scene and the duet-romance
within the opening quartet are many, conspicuous, and (yes, most consciously) calculated: they are the resonances between Tatyana's inner and
outer worlds. To cite the most obvious correspondence, both numbers incorporate Tatyana's leitmotif (it is the last line of each strophe in the duet, the
middle section of the last romance in the Letter Scene). But the leitmotif is
itself a bearer of the generic resonance. Beginning on the sixth degree of the
minor scale, it initiates a descent to the tonic, thus describing the interval that
more than any other defines the idiom of the *bïtovoy romans*, the Russian
domestic or household romance of the early nineteenth century. Russian
scholars have gone so far as to coin the term *sekstovïy* ("sixthy") and its derivative *sekstovost'* ("sixthiness") to denote that defining quality.[24] A pair of
melodies by Alexander Varlamov, the leading composer of romances current
at the time of *Yevgeniy Onegin*'s action, can serve as paradigm (example 3.1).
The role of Tatyana, saturated with sixths encompassing degrees $\hat{1}$–$\hat{6}$/$\hat{6}$–$\hat{1}$, or
(more characteristically) $\hat{5}$–$\hat{3}$/$\hat{3}$–$\hat{5}$, is, with that of Lensky, surely the
"sixthiest" in all of opera (example 3.2).

In the last part of example 3.2 melodic sixths are nested within a harmonic
idiom that shows a semiotically marked "sixthiness" of its own: the constant

---

[24] See Mikhail Semyonovich Druskin, *Voprosï muzïkal'noy dramaturgii operï* (Leningrad:
Muzgiz, 1952), p. 131ff.

EXAMPLE 3.1

a. Varlamov, *Krasnïy sarafan* (1832), words by Nikolai Tsïganov

Umerenno skoro (Allegro moderato)

Ne shey tï mne, ma - tush - ka, kras - nïy sa - ra - fan,

ne vkho - di, ro - di - ma - ya, po - pu - stu v iz" - yan.

b. Varlamov, *Na zare tï yeyo ne budi* (1842), words by Afanasiy Fet

Umerenno skoro (Allegro moderato)

Na za - re tï ye - yo ne bu - di,

na za - re o - na slad - ko tak spit;

EXAMPLE 3.2. "Sixthiness" in Chaikovsky's *Eugene Onegin*

a. Tatyana's leitmotif (opening of introduction)

b. Act 1, opening duet (the first sung phrase in the opera)

Tatyana

Slï - kha - lil'   vï

(Have you ever heard . . .)

c. Letter scene, beginning of first romance

Pu - skai po - gib - nu ya

(Even if it means I perish . . .)

d. Letter scene, second romance, beginning of second strophe

Za - chem, za - chem vï po - se - ti - li nas?

(Why, oh why did you visit us?)

e. Letter scene, beginning of third romance

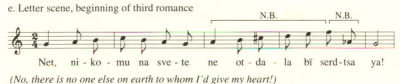

Net,   ni - ko - mu na sve - te   ne ot - da - la bï serd - tsa ya!

(No, there is no one else on earth to whom I'd give my heart!)

f. Letter scene, introduction to fourth romance

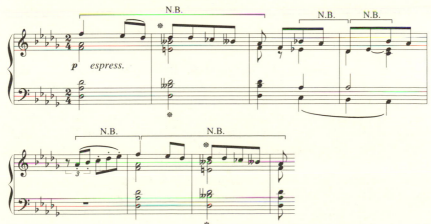

EXAMPLE 3.3. Chaikovsky, *Eugene Onegin*

a. Act 1, no. 12 (Onegin's aria)

Onegin

Mech-tam i go-dam net voz-vra - ta akh, net voz

vra - ta, ne ob-no-vlyu du-shi mo-yey!

Ya vas lyu-blyu lyu-bov'-yu bra - ta, *etc.*

(Dreams and years do not return, my soul I cannot renew! I love you like a brother . . .)

use of the minor submediant (the "flat sixth" in the major) as alternate harmonic root or tone center. This alternation can take the form of an immediate
local progression, as shown, or it can be projected in the form of a subsidiary
key governing large spans within the tonal structure. The orchestral prelude or
introduction to act 1 sets the precedent: its development section is all within
the key of the submediant, which resolves to the dominant by way of retransition. In the Letter Scene, the whole vocal coda ("Konchayu! strashno pere-
chest'," or "Finished! I dare not reread") is cast within the key of the starred
chord in example 3.2f, spelled enharmonically as A major.

The melodic-harmonic idiom is only one of many genre resonances that tie

EXAMPLE 3.3, *continued*

b. Act 3, no. 22 (finale)

(*O, take pity, take pity on me! I was so wrong! I've been so punished!*)

Tatyana's Letter Scene to the opening duet and thence to the whole world of the domestic romance. The harp-heavy orchestration of the first two sections is another. But the harp does more than evoke the sounds of domestic music-making. The inspired chords (non arpeggiato!) that punctuate the woodwind phrases in the actual letter-writing ritornello (introducing the second romance as listed above) take their place within a marvelously detailed sound-portrait of the lovesick girl, in which Chaikovsky shows himself an adept practitioner of Mozart's methods of "body portraiture," as outlined in the famous letter from Mozart to his father about *Die Entführung aus dem Serail*.[25] As in the case of Mozart's Belmonte or Osmin, we "see" and "feel" Tatyana—her movements, her breathing, her heartbeat—in her music. This iconicity shows off music's advantages especially well: what the novelist or poet must describe, the composer (unlike the dramatist, who must depend on the director and the cast) can actually present.

As to irony, did Pushkin ever make more trenchant comment than Chaikovsky, when he mocks Onegin's passionate confession to Tatyana in act

[25] 26 September 1781; *Mozart's Letters*, trans. Emily Anderson, ed. Eric Blom (Harmondsworth: Penguin Books, 1956), pp. 181–82.

EXAMPLE 3.4. Chaikovsky, *Eugene Onegin*, act 3, no. 21
(cf. example 3.2c)

U - vi̇! so - mne-n'ya net,   vlyu - blyon ya

(Alas! There is no doubt I'm in love)

3 with a fleeting reference to the music by which he had rejected her in act 1
(example 3.3)? It is not simply a matter of showing that the boot is on the
other foot: that much had already been accomplished by setting Onegin's
arioso at the end of act 3, scene 1 (example 3.4) to the melody of the first
romance in the Letter Scene (equally ironic in that Onegin, not having "heard"
that music on its earlier appearance, cannot be "quoting" it now; the reference
is entirely a narrator's aside). The allusion to the rejection music shows him
fickle and erratic; it takes the place of the lengthy passage in Pushkin's novel
in which Tatyana visits the absent Onegin's library and discovers, by peeking
at the annotations in his books, the shallowness of his soul.

The concluding confrontation between Onegin and Tatyana has been described as "a duet in the grand style,"[26] but even here the method of construction remains that of stringing romances (a technique Chaikovsky evidently
picked up from his teacher, Anton Rubinstein: compare the third act of the
latter's *Demon*). Tatyana's chief melody apes the one her husband, Prince
Gremin, had sung in the preceding scene, thus telegraphing her answer to
Onegin. Only twice, fleetingly, do the two voices mingle. It is hardly a duet at
all. Like Tatyana's total silence in response to rejection (act 1, scene 3, and,
except for her participation in ensembles, in act 2, scene 1 as well) the scene
flies in the face of operatic convention, underscoring by omission (yet another
ironic narrator's aside!) the futility of the dramatic situation. The very fact
that *Yevgeniy Onegin* contains no love duets already testifies to its singular
affinity with Pushkin's novel, air conditioner and all.

Not that there are no divergences between Chaikovsky's treatment of the
story or its characters and Pushkin's: Lensky in particular, whose sixthy act 2
aria (quoted in chapter 11) is a very serious moment, reflects a later, more
sentimental age—the age of Turgenev, so to speak, rather than Pushkin's.
But even here, the use of the modest romance form is more than just evocative; it sets distinct limits on Lensky's emotional scale. Like all the characters
in the opera, he remains a denizen of a realistic novel (one of the very earliest
to be given operatic treatment), not a historical spectacle or a well-made play.

[26] Carl Dahlhaus, *Nineteenth-Century Music*, trans. J. Bradford Robinson (Berkeley and Los
Angeles: University of California Press, 1989), p. 301.

CHAPTER 4

WHO AM I? (AND WHO ARE YOU?)

RULING OUT essentialist approaches to what defines Russia (the Russian, Russians) makes things harder, but only because it requires us to be realistic. Nothing exists in its own terms only; nothing, at least since the expulsion from Eden, is truly autochthonous. What may appear to be perceptions of essences are in reality perceptions of relationships. A biographer incautious enough to believe that he has seen Chaikovsky plain has only gazed credulously upon a construction of his own making, reflecting (like all "others") the writer's projected sense of himself.

This comes out especially clearly when David Brown identifies Chaikovsky's "natural" limitations vis-à-vis the Western "classical" symphonic tradition. The English writer's conceptualizations of that tradition are entirely idiolectal, based, one can only surmise, on the jargon of his own training. They include hollow catchphrases—"tonal dynamism," for example, or "tonal growth"—that have been coined to designate (that is, create) categories to which Chaikovsky's access is barred by "nature."[1] What the author has done, obviously, is to accept himself as a metonymy for the West, against which he has manufactured a countermetonymy named Chaikovsky.

That countermetonymy should never have been allowed to write symphonies, Brown strongly implies. But there is an early exception: the Symphony no. 2 in C minor, Op. 17 (1872), which bears the subtitle "Little Russian" because Ukrainian folk tunes are incorporated into three of its four movements. The folkloristic element is most obvious in the finale, where (in a manner paralleling that of Balakirev's overtures on Russian themes, described in chapter 8) the first "group" of a sonata design consists of variations à la *Kamarinskaya* on a dance-tune (*gopak*) called "The Crane" (*Zhuravel'*) (see example 4.1a). "Here it was that Tchaikovsky aligned himself more closely than ever before with the nationalists' ideals and practices," Brown writes.[2] The resulting success should have taught him to stay put in the ghetto, where he belonged: "It is one of the greatest causes for regret in all Tchaikovsky's work that he never again attempted something of the same sort."[3]

---

[1] "Such a command of tonal growth was utterly beyond Tchaikovsky" (Brown, *Tchaikovsky*, vol. 1: *The Early Years: 1840–1874* [New York: Norton, 1978], p. 109); "being entirely devoid of the ability to devise a planned tonal growth . . ." (ibid., p. 112).

[2] Ibid., p. 264.

[3] Ibid., p. 269.

EXAMPLE 4.1. Chaikovsky, Symphony no. 2, fourth movement

a. Beginning of variations

But there is something very peculiar about Brown's description of the piece. He gives three examples illustrating the clever changes Chaikovsky works on the tune, and another to illustrate a whole-tone progression that brought a grudging word of praise from César Cui. These are quoted as examples of Chaikovsky at his most personal, even though all of them—especially the whole-tone scale!—are patent derivations from Brown's approved models. Never quoted, but only described (and inaccurately), is the symphonic introduction to the variations set (example 4.1b).

Brown hears in this an anticipation by two years of Musorgsky's *Pictures at an Exhibition* ("Promenade" and "The Great Gate of Kiev").[4] But that must be because of the resemblance between Chaikovsky's brassy scoring and Ravel's 1923 orchestration of the Musorgsky. Once the mind is rid of prejudice—once, that is, the possibility is entertained of parallels and models

---

[4] Brown, *Tchaikovsky*, vol. 1, p. 265.

EXAMPLE 4.1, *continued*

b. Introduction

that lie outside the ghetto walls—it is hard to miss the resonance from another C-major finale to a C-minor symphony, the most famous symphony in the world (example 4.2a). And once resonances with Beethoven, the most inevitable of all symphonic models, are spotted, they proliferate. The introduction to Chaikovsky's finale simultaneously glosses or parodies the introduction to another Beethoven symphonic finale in C major, the start-again-stop-again introduction to the finale of the First Symphony, in which the constituent notes of the theme are gradually accumulated (example 4.2b).

These resonances are just as conspicuous as the ones with Glinka or Balakirev (to say nothing of actual peasant music). They would never be missed in a Schumann or a Bruckner. But in Chaikovsky they are occluded by the ethnic walls that have been erected by defenders of the "Western" mainstream, ideologically blind to the possibility of a valid or authentic relationship of receptivity between that mainstream and its Far Eastern tributary.[5]

[5] For a discussion of Chaikovsky's Second Symphony that avoids clichés about "high nationalism" and explores the work's many affinities with the international symphonic literature, one must go all the way back to Hermann Laroche's review, "Novaya russkaya simfoniya," which first appeared in the newspaper *Moskovskiye vedomosti*, 7 February 1873. There is no English translation. The most recent Russian reprint is in G. A. Larosh, *Izbrannïye stat'i*, vol. 2 (Leningrad: Muzïka, 1975), pp. 28–31. A German translation is available in Hermann Laroche, *Peter Tschaikowsky: Aufsätze und Erinnerungen* (Berlin: Verlag Ernst Kuhn, 1993), pp. 74–79.

Example 4.2

a. Beethoven, Symphony no. 5, fourth movement, beginning

b. Beethoven, Symphony no. 1, fourth movement, beginning

When such resonances are noticed by those guardians of "the West" who pose as guardians of Russia, it is usually to regret them. The *New Grove Dictionary*, for example, complains that Glinka "could not dispense with Western compositional techniques," and that therefore *A Life for the Tsar* is "basically . . . a Western opera."[6] But this is addled. All operas that are recognizably within the historical tradition of the genre are "basically Western." The "Western" techniques one employs to compose such a work are one's vehicles, not one's impediments; no composer of "art music," regardless of nationality and however nationalistic, could ever dispense with them, for they are what define his trade.

THE PROCESS of metonymy-countermetonymy also works the other way around, of course, and that is where it becomes interesting. Russian percep-

---

Most sustained is a comparison between Chaikovsky's symphony, including the finale, and Beethoven's Eighth.

[6] *The New Grove Dictionary of Music and Musicians*, ed. Stanley Sadie (London: Macmillan, 1980), vol. 7, pp. 436, 442.

tions of Russia, or Russians' perceptions of themselves as Russians, are inevitably colored by perceptions of others to the East and to the West. In the case of classical art music, of course, it can only be the West, even (as will be argued in chapter 9) when the East is the object of ostensible imitation.

But to speak here of "the West" is very much to oversimplify. The West was never perceived, except by the most incurable bigots, as a monolith but rather as an aggregate of components—some cherished, others rejected; some held to be compatible with Russian ways, others incompatible (not only with Russia but with one another). Russia was no more a monolith than was "the West"; and differences of Russian opinion often came down to differences in perceptions as to what was to be cherished and what rejected in Russia's most significant Other.

In music at least two "Wests" were always present to Russian consciousness, two "Wests" against which Russian musicians habitually defined and constructed their identities. Neverov's account of *A Life for the Tsar* is again indicative. Immediately before the preposterous assertion that Glinka's recitatives were life-drawings of native speech inflections comes a much more plausible characterization of them: "His recitatives resemble neither the German nor the Italian; they unite the expressivity and dramatic flexibility of the former with the melodiousness of the latter."[7]

This is highly resonant with a great deal of Russian thinking about Russia. The way in which Glinka's recitatives are uniquely Russian (the way, that is, in which they are unlike their Western counterparts) consists precisely in the way that they resemble their Western counterparts—or rather, the way in which they combine all that is best in them. Uniting the best of the West—or, more generally, the best of the rest—was one highly preferred way of being Russian, for it affirmed belief in the universality of Russian culture, and in its salvific mission. What Neverov modestly claimed for Glinka (and, through Glinka, for Russia) was no different from what Dostoyevsky would magniloquently declare of Russia by way of Pushkin:

Never has there been a poet with such a universal responsiveness as Pushkin. But it is a matter not only of susceptibility but also of its amazing depth—that reincarnation in his spirit of the spirit of foreign nations, an almost complete, and therefore miraculous, reincarnation. . . . This we find in Pushkin alone, and in this sense he is a unique and unheard-of phenomenon, and to my mind a prophetic one. . . . For what else is the strength of the Russian national spirit than the aspiration, in its ultimate goal, for universality and all embracing humanitarianism? . . . Not inimically (as it would seem it should have happened) but in a friendly manner, with full love, we admitted into our soul the genius of foreign nations, without any racial discrimination, instinctively managing—almost from

---

[7] Quoted from Tamara Livanova and Vladimir Protopopov, *Opernaya kritika v Rossii*, vol. 1 (Moscow: Muzïka, 1966), part 1, p. 207.

the first step—to eliminate contradictions, to excuse and reconcile differences. . . . To become a genuine and all-around Russian means, perhaps (and this you should remember), to become brother of all men, a *universal man*.[8]

For all that his conventional reputation as founder of an insular Russian school suggests otherwise, such a man was Glinka, a prodigally eclectic composer, natural heir to the full range of operatic styles and conventions practiced in his day. The elaborate first-act cavatinas in both his operas, or especially the third act of *A Life for the Tsar* with its multipartite ensembles and its monumental finale, show his mastery of what Julian Budden has called the "Code Rossini"[9]—the set of formal molds that governed the Italian opera of the *primo ottocento*—to the point where, looking back, he could poke fun at his own "creeping Italianism" (*ital'yanshchina*). At the same time, both Glinka's operas conspicuously exhibit features of the French rescue genre— the genre of Grétry, Méhul, and Cherubini, not to mention Beethoven—with its ample choruses, its reminiscence themes and its "popular" tone. As Berlioz was quick to notice, moreover, Glinka's style, especially in *Ruslan and Lyudmila*, was heavily tinged with "the influence of Germany" in the prominence accorded the orchestra, the spectacular instrumentation, and the "beauty of the harmonic fabric."[10]

That the models for his second opera included Mozart, *Die Zauberflöte* in particular, can be readily seen not only from the gaudy glockenspiel and glass-harmonica colors in the magic music but also from the act 3 finale, in which the good sorcerer Finn first intervenes like a Sarastro to break the spells woven by the evil sorceress Naína (= Queen of the Night), then stands in as a tenor to complete the vocal complement for a concluding quartet ("Teper' Lyudmila ot nas spasen'ya zhdyot," or "Now Lyudmila awaits from us salvation") that reflects something of the serene radiance of "Bald prangt, den Morgen zu verkünden." This limpidly scored, loftily diatonic ensemble, too often overlooked amid the welter of blinding exotica for which *Ruslan* is justly famed, marks Glinka as Russia's one-and-only "high classic."

What must be emphasized is that, just as Neverov's review of *A Life for the Tsar* implied, this eclecticism, far from effacing Glinka's musical Russianness, in fact *constituted* it—emphatically in the composer's own eyes, as well as in the eyes of his contemporaries. (Only his self-styled heirs disagreed; but

---

[8] F. M. Dostoyevsky, "Pushkin: A Sketch," *The Diary of a Writer*, trans. Boris Brasol (New York: Charles Scribner's Sons, 1949), pp. 978–80. A little less apocalyptically, the platform of Dostoyevsky's short-lived literary journal *Vremya* had suggested in 1861 that "the Russian idea may well be a synthesis of all the ideas that have developed in Europe" (quoted in V. V. Zenkovsky, *A History of Russian Philosophy*, trans. George L. Kline [New York: Columbia University Press, 1953], vol. 1, p. 414.

[9] *Operas of Verdi*, vol. 1 (New York: Praeger, 1973), pp. 12ff.

[10] H. Berlioz, "Michel de Glinka (*La Vie pour le czar; Russlane et Ludmila*)," *Journal des Débats*, 16 April 1845.

as we shall see in chapter 8, Balakirev's demonstrative folklorism was not without its ambiguities, being in fact the vehicle for the thoroughgoing Germanification of the "Glinka tradition.")[11] And just as Dostoyevsky implied, Glinka's programmatic eclecticism was aimed explicitly at "eliminating contradictions and reconciling differences"—specifically, the contradiction, more apparent to Russians, perhaps, than to anyone else in Europe, between the southern Catholic culture of the "Latins" and the northern Protestant culture of the "Teutons."[12]

This dichotomy was variously, but always radically and invidiously, ratified by Russian musicians and music lovers in the early nineteenth century: by the many Russian "melomanes" who enthusiastically endorsed Italy over Germany; but also by romantic idealists like Prince Odoyevsky (see chapter 10), who cast the split in lofty, somewhat puritanical terms taken over directly from German philosophers who valorized Teutonic *Geist* (*dukh* in Russian), or "spirit," over Latin *Sinnlichkeit* (in Russian, *chuvstvennost'*), or "sensuality." German music was all *dukh*, brains without beauty; Italian music was all *chuvstvennost'*, beauty without brains. Glinka resolved—yes, consciously—that his music, Russian music, would uniquely have both brains and beauty.[13]

Because he grew up in a country that lacked the institutional means for training professional composers, Glinka is habitually looked (down) upon as an autodidact and a naif. This is a serious misapprehension. Despite a late start, and despite his being, as an aristocrat, an avocational musician, Glinka had a fabulously well rounded professional education in music, but it was an education acquired the old-fashioned way, by apprenticeship and practical experience.

After childhood and adolescent music instruction in piano and violin, both on his ancestral estate and (from 1818) at the Boarding School for the Nobility

[11] This Germanification itself reflected a general cultural trend in Nikolayan and post-Nikolayan Russia; the model for Balakirev's "New Russian school" (a.k.a. the "mighty kuchka") was no native precedent but Schumann's *Davidsbund*; by the time of César Cui's critical debut, Balakirev's brother-kuchkist would define Russian music by saying that its distinctiveness came by way of German music, which it had emulated and surpassed "in depth of feeling and force of passion" (César Cui, "Opernïy sezon v Peterburge," *Sankt-Peterburgskiye vedomosti*, 3 September 1864; reprinted in Cui, *Muzikal'no-kriticheskiye stat'i*, vol. 1 [Petrograd, 1918], p. 109). By this time, the stranglehold of the court Italian Opera on St. Petersburg musical life (to be described in chapter 10) had made expedient a tactical alliance with the German school, lately given an official institutional presence in the Russian capital by Anton Rubinstein's performance and pedagogical organizations.

[12] Cf. Pyotr Yakovlevich Chaadayev's celebrated *Lettre première sur la philosophie de l'histoire* (1829), trans. Valentine Snow in Marc Raeff, ed., *Russian Intellectual History: An Anthology* (New York: Harcourt, Brace and World, 1966), pp. 160–73 (esp. pp. 164–65).

[13] The Russian predilection for brains-and-beauty eclecticism is already evident in Yevstigney Fomin's musical education: after preliminary study in St. Petersburg with the resident German, Raupach, he was packed off to Italy to finish his training with Padre Martini.

in St. Petersburg, and after teaching himself the rudiments of form and orchestration by rehearsing and conducting his uncle's serf orchestra in the classical repertory, Glinka apprenticed himself in 1828 to Leopoldo Zamboni, the principal coach for an Italian opera troupe headed by Leopoldo's father Luigi, the famous *buffo* (Rossini's original Figaro), that had come to St. Petersburg at the expense of Count Matvey Wielhorski. Zamboni schooled his local apprentice in the forms and conventions of Italian opera, as well as in elementary counterpoint ("fugues in two parts without words," as Glinka put it in his memoirs).[14] Over the next two years he also attended the rehearsals and the extremely idiomatic Zamboni-led performances of over a dozen Rossini operas.

In 1830 Glinka went abroad for an extended stay. In Milan he became personally acquainted with Bellini and Donizetti and under their supervision wrote creditable imitations of their work, publishing in addition a number of instrumental tributes to the Italian opera that included (besides several sets of piano variations) a couple of ambitious concerted compositions. Thus he acquired beauty. Then he went after brains, making straight for the Teutonic source. He spent the winter of 1833–34 in Berlin, under the tutelage of Siegfried Dehn (1799–1858), the most sought-after German pedagogue "and indisputably the first musical wizard in Europe" in his pupil's awed recollection, who through a combination of strict counterpoint and ancient lore, "not only put my knowledge in order, but also my ideas on art," as Glinka so meaningly put it in his memoirs.[15] He returned to Russia shortly before his thirtieth birthday, the possessor of a fully professional, exceptionally cosmopolitan technique. He went back to Dehn nearly a quarter of century later, at the very end of his life, for advice on how he might apply the principles of species counterpoint to Russian church chant—that is, how he might achieve a new "reconciliation of contradictions" to produce a new, distinctively Russian, style.

As the first fully equipped, native-born Russian contributor to the European fine art of music, and a nobleman with powerful court connections, Glinka worked, from every standpoint but the (in his case) irrelevant pecuniary one, under highly favorable institutional conditions, with a state-owned theater at his virtual beck and call. He could afford his accommodating, omnivorously receptive attitudes toward the musical "West."

As chapter 10 will detail, those conditions would deteriorate radically almost immediately after the première of Glinka's second opera (which goes a long way toward explaining why there was no third). Faced with unequal competition from a court-sponsored Italian opera troupe barred by explicit

---

[14] Glinka, "Zapiski" (Memoirs), in *Polnoye sobraniye sochineniy: Literaturnïye proizvedeniya i perepiska*, vol. 1 (Moscow: Muzïka, 1973), p. 235.

[15] Ibid., p. 262.

policy from performing the work of Russian composers, the generation of
Russian composers who came creatively to active life in the 1840s and 1850s
were forced into an alienated, antagonistic relationship to the very state
Glinka had happily venerated in his first opera, to its musical establishment,
and to the foreign artists it now exclusively supported.

The quintessential victim of this blatantly discriminatory phase in Russian
government arts policy was Dargomïzhsky, and it is to him that we may trace
a new phase in Russian musical self-definition vis-à-vis "the West," one of
jealous omnivorous rejection. Dargomïzhsky, some nine years Glinka's junior, also took early instruction from a member of the Zamboni troupe (Franz
Schoberlechner, a Viennese composer of Italian opera whose Russian-born
wife was a leading soprano with the company) and received from Glinka, on
the latter's return from Berlin a few years later, the notebooks in which Dehn
had set down his course of instruction in thoroughbass and counterpoint. But,
frozen out by the court-backed Italians, he recoiled from the "beauteous"
Western strain (on Donizetti's latest: "There's little to say . . . once a medal
has been stamped out and described, is there any need to describe the next
medal from the same die?"), and on encountering Wagner (through Serov,
who lent him the score of *Tannhäuser*), he recoiled from the "brainy" Western
strain as well: "unnatural . . . painful . . . *Will und kann nicht!*"[16]

What is left, after both brains and beauty have been renounced? Good character! Dargomïzhsky became a musical Diogenes, seeking "truth" in word
(the sloganeering letters for which he is so well remembered by nationalistic
historians) and in musical deed (*The Stone Guest*, after Pushkin, the very
model of "reform" opera).[17] His new, unbending stance demanding art without artifice won him a coterie of admirers in Balakirev's young circle of musical mavericks, and at least one outright imitator in Musorgsky, whose early
Marriage, after Gogol, and the first version of whose masterpiece *Boris Godunov*, were modeled on the precepts, and to some degree even on the music,
of the man Musorgsky twice called "the great teacher of musical truth."[18]

There is very little in any of these works—*The Stone Guest*, *Marriage*,
even the first *Boris* beyond its folkish or churchly set pieces—that is indicatively Russian in style; yet they, and the stylistic trend they represent, no less

[16] To his father, December 1844; to A. N. Serov, summer 1856; both in Nikolai Findeyzen,
ed., *A. S. Dargomïzhskiy (1813–1869): Avtobiografiya, pis'ma, vospominaniya sovremennikov*
(Peterburg: Gosudarstvennoye izdatel'stvo RSFSR, 1921), pp. 16, 43.

[17] For a full account see R. Taruskin, *Opera and Drama in Russia*, 2d ed. (Rochester: University of Rochester Press, 1994), chapter 5 (*"The Stone Guest* and Its Progeny").

[18] The phrase appears in the dedications to Dargomïzhsky of two of Musorgsky's naturalistic
songs of the late 1860s, when relations with Dargomïzhsky were at their closest: *Kolïbel'naya
Yeryomushki* ("Jeremy's Cradle Song," 1867) and *S nyaney* ("With Nanny," the first of the
Nursery cycle). On Musorgsky's relationship to and borrowings from Dargomïzhsky, see R.
Taruskin, *Musorgsky: Eight Essays and an Epilogue*, chapters 2 ("Handel, Shakespeare, and
Musorgsky") and 5 ("Musorgsky vs. Musorgsky: The Versions of *Boris*").

than the one (or the two) represented by Glinka, were nonetheless the product of a particular, very emphatic Russian national self-definition vis-à-vis "Europe." Thus the shared style characteristics of these odd operas amount in their way to another particular and peculiar Russian style.

How did this extremist, uniquely Russian brand of musical realism that arose out of wholesale rejection of European artifice relate to other manifestations of Russian musical nationalism? That is the crucial Musorgsky question, but it does not apply to Dargomïzhsky. *The Stone Guest*, based verbatim on Pushkin's "little tragedy" of Don Juan (1830), has a Spanish setting and a certain amount of perfunctory Spanish local color. Otherwise the music is cast, with inventiveness and expressivity of a high order, in an international lyric style that is not in itself in any way innovative. Dargomïzhsky's reform targeted institutions and genres, not style.

Musorgsky, in addition to being (after Dargomïzhsky) an institutional outsider and a rebellious rejector of European savoir-faire, was a very self-conscious stylistic innovator. His media, no less than Dargomïzhsky's or Glinka's, were those of the European tradition; and yet he was more thoroughly and profoundly obsessed than any other member of his musical generation by *narodnost'* and its full panoply of attendant historical and social issues. With him the question of the relationship between originality and tradition(s), between realism and *narodnost'*, becomes central, and it becomes complicated.

His obsessions and his historical group-identity as an insular nationalist notwithstanding, Musorgsky was far less squeamish than Dargomïzhsky about his "Western" counterparts and rivals. He studied both Wagner and Verdi with apparent fearlessness, and accepted a great deal from both of them in the process of learning the ropes of historical opera on the grand scale he favored.[19] He often twitted his kuchkist confrères on their provincial naysaying, reminding the immature Rimsky-Korsakov that Wagner, whatever his faults, aimed high and was in this, if in nothing else, worthy of emulation: "Wagner is strong, strong because he seizes art and shakes it."[20] In the thick

---

[19] See R. Taruskin, *Musorgsky: Eight Essays and an Epilogue*, pp. 267–69 (including a possible quotation from *Don Carlos* in *Boris Godunov*); Roland John Wiley, "The Tribulations of Nationalist Composers: A Speculation Concerning Borrowed Music in *Khovanshchina*," in *Musorgsky: In Memoriam (1881–1981)*, ed. Malcolm H. Brown and R. John Wiley (Ann Arbor: UMI Research Press, 1982), pp. 163–77 (on a possible quotation from *Rigoletto*); Borodin recalled that the teenaged Musorgsky could play excerpts from *Traviata* and *Trovatore* pretty much ad libitum (see Jay Leyda and Sergei Bertensson, *The Musorgsky Reader* [New York: Norton, 1947), p. 3; much later, a younger contemporary reported that Musorgsky could play through whole scenes from *Siegfried* from memory (Nikolai Kompaneysky, "K novïm beregam: M. P. Musorgskiy [1839–1881]," *Russkaya muzïkal'naya gazeta*, no. 17 [1906], col. 439; quoted in Caryl Emerson and Robert William Oldani, *Modest Musorgsky and Boris Godunov: Myths, Realities, Reconsiderations* [Cambridge: Cambridge University Press, 1994], p. 233).

[20] Fragment of a letter datable by its contents before 4 October 1867; Musorgsky, *Literaturnoye naslediye*, ed. A. A. Orlova and M. S. Pekelis, vol. 1 (Moscow: Muzïka, 1971), p. 95.

of work on *Khovanshchina*, he took time out to see the first Russian production of *Aida*. For all the practiced ironizing (especially practiced when writing to Stasov, his stern collaborator) and strained punstering, his enthusiasm at Verdi's "rough and gaudy theatricality" shows right through: "Now *maestro-senatore* Verdi on the other hand! This one does it big, he's not afraid of anything, this originator! His whole *Aida*—way to go!—it's full of everything, from everyone and even from himself. He's got *Trovatore* in there, and a little 'Mendelssohn,' and a little 'Wagner'—everything but Amerigo Vespucci."[21]

Clearly, "Europe" was something Musorgsky felt he could face up to. His self-confidence—easily (and usually) dismissed as the bluster of the callow, the ignorant, the untried—has a suprapersonal, ideological edge as well. Roll callowness, ignorance and innocence together, translate it all into Russian, and the specific nature of his Russian ideology, his national self-definition, will emerge. It is the ideology of *yurodstvo*, Holy Foolery, a state of perfect freedom from cogitation (brains) and charm (beauty), a state of perfect authenticity.

MUSORGSKY's songs of the late 1860s represent, with *Marriage*, the high-water mark of what is generally regarded as his naturalistic phase. They are a portrait gallery of life-drawn types: so, at least, the composer purported, and so they have been characterized by long-standing reputation. Among them, "Darling Savishna" (*Svetik Savishna*, 1866), one of the earliest, dedicated to brother-kuchkist Cui, is held to be especially emblematic. According to Vladimir Stasov, the composer's would-be mentor and indefatigable tribune, the song was especially truthful in that it was a virtually unmediated portrayal of an actual scene the composer had witnessed on his brother Filaret's country estate in the summer of 1865.

> Standing by the window one day he was struck by the commotion taking place before his very eyes. A hapless village idiot (*yurodivïy*) was declaring love to a young peasant girl whom he fancied, pleading with her, and abasing himself on account of his ugliness and his miserable position. He understood better than anyone else that the joys of love were not for him. Musorgsky was deeply affected. The character and the scene were strongly imprinted on his soul. Instantly there appeared to him the peculiar forms and sounds in which to embody the images that had so shaken him.[22]

A study in grotesquerie, in musical uncouthness (no brains) and calculated deformity (no beauty), the song "milked laughter" from a "tragic ferment," as

[21] Letter of 23 November 1875; Musorgsky, *Literaturnoye naslediye*, vol. 1, p. 207. The phrase translated as "way to go!"—Russian readers will smell it a mile off—is *ai-da!* On "rough and gaudy theatricality" (A. A. Gozenpud's phrase) see Taruskin, *Musorgsky: Eight Essays and an Epilogue*, p. 267.

[22] Vladimir Vasilyevich Stasov, "Modest Petrovich Musorgsky" (1881), in Stasov, *Izbrannïye sochineniya* (Moscow: Iskusstvo, 1952), vol. 2, p. 184.

the composer explained, no longer reconciling but most discomfitingly exposing contradictions, the first and foremost being that between the genteel art
song medium and the indecorous content.[23] The very complex half-comic,
half-tragic ambience that arose out of what seemed the author's unflinching
precision of observation and his refusal to intrude or comment on the scene
did strike a new note in Russian music, indeed (once it became known abroad)
in European music *tout court*. This was realism at full potency. It had the ring
and the force of truth. Alexander Serov pronounced the ultimate Russian ac-
colade: "A ghastly scene. It's Shakespeare in music."[24] In the West it would
win the composer a host of posthumous disciples, who worshiped him as a
musical god.[25]

But was he really trading in true facts? And what was the nature, or the
butt, of his harsh humor?

Consider first what came first. Like most of the texts Musorgsky set during
the period, the words of *Savishna* were of his own devising; that was part and
parcel of life-drawing as he conceived it. Set in characteristically resolute
syllabic fashion, it convinced connoisseurs (especially those familiar, from
the composer's correspondence, with his designs) that it reproduced "the in-
flexions of prose speech."[26] The use of quintuple meter, the isochronous
rhythmic beats organized by contour in inflexibly recurring measure-long
units ("modules," to use now-fashionable terminology), was also taken as
naturalism, depicting, according to the song's greatest interpreter, "the irregular walk of the limping 'innocent' [*yurodivïy*] and the hasty [i.e., breathless?]
formation of his phrases."[27] Laid out phrase by hasty phrase, the text looks
like this:

> Svetik Sávishna, / svet Ivánovna,
> Svet moy Sávishna, / sokol yásnen'kiy,
> Polyubí menya / ne razúmnova,
> Prigolúb' menya / goremíchnova!
> Oy-li, sókol moy, / sokol yásnen'kiy,
> 5 Svetik Sávishna, / svet Ivánovna,
> Ne pobrézgai tï / gol'yu góloyu,

[23] Letter to Arseniy Golenishchev-Kutuzov, 10 November 1877; M. P. Musorgsky, *Literatur-noye naslediye*, vol. 1, p. 235.

[24] Kompaneysky, "K novïm beregam," *Russkaya muzïkal'naya gazeta*, nos. 14–15 (1906), col. 365; according to Kompaneysky, who sang the song to Serov and recorded his remark, Serov immediately added, "Too bad, though, that he has such poor command of his pen."

[25] Cf. Claude Debussy, "La Musique russe et les Compositeurs français," *Excelsior*, 9 March 1911; quoted in Malcolm Brown, introduction to *Musorgsky: In Memoriam (1881–1981)*, p. 4.

[26] Gerald Abraham, "Russia," in *A History of Song*, ed. Denis Stevens (New York: Norton, 1970), p. 364.

[27] Boris Christoff, *Moussorgsky: Mélodies, Enregistrement intégral* (Paris: Pathé Marconi, 1958), commentary, p. 39.

Bestalánnoyu / moyey dóleyu!
Urodílsya vish' / na smekh lyúdyam ya,
Pro zabávu da / na potékhi im!
10　Klichut: Sávishna, / skorbnïm rázumom
Velicháyut, slïsh', / Vaney Bózhiyim,
Svetik Sávishna, / svet Ivánovna,
I dayút pin'kov / Vane Bózh'yemu,
Kormyat chéstvuyut / podzatíl'nikom.
15　A pod prázdnichek / kak razryádyatsya,
Uberútsya vish' / v lentï álïye,
Dadut khlébushka / Vane skórbnomu,
Ne zabït' chtobï / Vanyu Bozh'yego.
Svetik Sávishna, / yasnïy sokol moy,
20　Polyubí-zh menya / neprogózheva,
Prigolúb' menya / odinókova!
Kak lyublyú tebya, / mochi nét skazat',
Svetik Sávishna, / ver' mne, vér' ne ver',
Svet Ivánovna!. . .

Darling Savishna, bright falcon mine,
Love me, fool that I am,
Cosset me, miserable one that I am!
my falcon, bright falcon mine,
5　Darling Savishna, Dear Ivanovna,
Don't despise the poor, the hungry,
Misfortune is my lot!
Look how I was born to be laughed at,
To provide amusement, entertainment!
10　They shout at me, O Savishna, hear?
They cry up Johnny Fool-in-God's poor brains,
Darling Savishna, dear Ivanovna,
And they give Johnny Fool-in-God a kick,
Feed him, honor him with slaps and cuffs.
15　But on holidays when they deck themselves
With finery, you see, with ribbons red,
Then they'll give poor Johnny a crust of bread,
Not to forget old Johnny Fool-in-God.
Darling Savishna, bright falcon mine,
20　Do love me, good-for-nothing that I am,
Cosset me, lonely one that I am!
How I love thee I just can't begin to say,
Darling Savishna, believe me, or don't,
Dear Ivanovna! . . .

But this is not prose at all. Nor does it transmit any sort of spontaneous utterance. A quick glance up above, at Count Lvov's letter-in-verse in praise of Russia (quoted in chapter 1), will instantly give it away. It is an imitation folk poem in Lvov's *pesennïy razmer*, which is to say (with excruciating irony) an imitation wedding song. These ironies extend beyond the generalities of form to the specifics of wedding diction as well: *velichayut* ("cry up") in line 11 resonates with *velichal'nïye*, the mock-praises or "roasts" sung as toasts at Russian peasant wedding feasts (cf. the fourth tableau of Stravinsky's *Svadebka*); *lentï alïye* ("ribbons red") in line 16 recalls the plaiting songs sung at the bridal shower on the wedding eve (cf. the first tableau of *Svadebka*). But the irony of casting the hopeless nattering of a lovesick idiot in the strains of which he dreams, but will never hear, is only one level of the poem's resonance.

The choice of the indicatively Russian *pesennïy razmer*—or what Musorgsky, who had used it more than once before (albeit by way of ready-made *chanson russe* verses, and in musical meters that avoided quintasyllabic isochrony) would have called the *kol'tsovskiy stikh*, "Koltsovian verses"[28]— makes *Savishna*, like Lvov's letter in verse, an ironic *velichal'naya* to Russia herself. It is another instance, like Glinka's maiden chorus in the third act of *A Life for the Tsar* (the first, epochal, usage in Russian art music of literal quintuple meter to reflect the *pesennïy razmer*), of turning a decorative cliché to expressive account through irony. (Glinka's maidens arrive, right after Susanin's abduction by the Poles, to celebrate Antonida's bridal shower as in countless earlier Russian singspiels and are astonished to find her lamenting not pro forma but in earnest.)

Musorgsky hinted as much a year later when he singled out *Savishna*, among all the things he'd written, as "a rudimentally Russian production, not steeped in German profundity and routine, but poured forth on native fields and nourished on Russian bread."[29] Having written the song, Musorgsky briefly took to calling himself and even signing himself "Savishna" in his correspondence with intimates like Lyudmila Shestakova (Glinka's long-surviving sister) and Balakirev.[30] Was he identifying with the girl? Is this more evidence of complex sexuality?[31] This time the answer must be no.

---

[28] Earlier Musorgsky settings of poems cast in the *kol'tsovskiy stikh* include his very first song, "Where Art Thou, Little Star?" (*Gde tï, zvyozdochka*, 1857, rev. ca. 1863), to a text by Nikolai Grekov, and "Tell Me Why, Fair Maiden" (*Otchego skazhi, dusha devitsa*, 1858), to a text by Koltsov himself (see Taruskin, *Musorgsky: Eight Essays and an Epilogue*, pp. 56–68).

[29] To Vladimir Nikolsky, 12 July 1867; Musorgsky, *Literaturnoye naslediye*, vol. 1, p. 89.

[30] E.g., Shestakova, 5 January 1867 (*Literaturnoye naslediye*, vol. 1, p. 78). Having referred to himself throughout the letter as Savishna, Musorgsky signed it with an exaggeratedly *ur*-Slavic spelling, interpolating a superfluous "hard sign," thus: *Savish"na*, adding in a footnote, "the earthy [*pochvennaya*, better rendered as "Mother Earthly"] spelling of the name."

[31] On Musorgsky's probable homosexual orientation see Taruskin, *Musorgsky: Eight Essays and an Epilogue*, p. 30; Jane Turner, "Musorgsky," *Music Review* 47 (1986–87): 153–75.

Musorgsky identified himself not with the title character but with the song itself—or rather, with the voice within the song, the self-pitying, self-obsessed voice of the *yurodivïy*.

Yurodivïy. Holy Fool. The simpleton who speaks the truth. That was Musorgsky among composers, and that was Russia among nations. Thus *Svetik Savishna* was not just a song. It was a badge. And so, whatever its anecdotal origins and however entrenched its aesthetic reputation, it was no monument to realism. It did not fix a single, never-to-be-repeated moment in all its particularity. Rather, it created and bequeathed an archetype, one that established a creative self-image and defined a Russia.

That archetype achieved an epitomizing, immortalizing embodiment a couple of years later, in the character of the *yurodivïy*, the Holy Fool in *Boris Godunov*. Although modeled on a character in Pushkin's drama (as Pushkin's *yurodivïy* had been modeled on a story from Karamzin's history of Russia),[32] Musorgsky's *yurodivïy* is the most original conception in the opera. In the version of 1869, the *yurodivïy* appears where he had appeared in Pushkin, in the scene at the Shrine of the Blessed Basil, where with a boldness unavailable to the common folk, the Fool confronts the "Tsar-Herod" with his crime. Pushkin, for whom the Fool was just a "funny young fellow,"[33] had given him a silly little song to sing when he receives a penny in return for his prayers:

Mesyats svetit,	The moon is shining,
Kotyonok plachet,	The kitten's crying,
Yurodivïy, vstavai,	Get up, fool,
Bogu pomolisya![34]	Pray to God!

Musorgsky's Fool expands on the song somewhat (the additional words are the composer's), and, by changing over to the future tense, adds a note of unmistakable if inscrutable prophecy:

Mesyats yedet,	The moon goes its way,
kotyonok plachet,	The kitten's crying,
yurodivïy vstavai,	Get up, fool,
Bogu pomolisya,	pray to God,
Khristu poklonisya.	Bow to Christ.
Khristos, bog nash,	Christ, our God,
budet vyodro,	There will be fine weather,
budet mesyats. . .	There will be moonlight. . .

[32] For details see Taruskin, *Musorgsky: Eight Essays and an Epilogue*, p. 189.

[33] Letter to Pyotr Andreyevich Vyazemsky, 7 November 1825; J. Thomas Shaw, ed., *Letters of Alexander Pushkin* (Madison: University of Wisconsin Press, 1969), p. 261.

[34] A. S. Pushkin, *Sochineniya* (Moscow: Khudozhestvennaya literatura, 1964), vol. 2, p. 328.

Musorgsky marks the division between Pushkin's nonsense song and his own fool's prophecy with a remarkable musical change (see example 4.3a). The first quatrain is set in the three-beat meter and paired couplets of the traditional Russian dance song. Here the Fool is obviously singing—performing his song—within the action of the drama: his song is "diegetic music," as today's film critics would say, or "phenomenal music" in the apter vocabulary of Carolyn Abbate, who has so fruitfully explored the all-important operatic code of music "heard" and "unheard."[35] The Fool's song starts out as unambiguously "heard" music, and in this it resembles all the other clearly folk-marked vocal music in the first version of the opera.

When the *yurodivïy* goes over from Pushkin's original text to Musorgsky's vaticinal extension, his music undergoes a change in meter (to four-beat measures), in tonality (down a half step), in verse structure (to a disintegrating ostinato), and in cadence placement (cadential harmonies gradually losing their stable definition and flowing into an endless mudslide of chromatic side steps). The transformation describes an entropy: song collapses into speech as the Fool becomes (according to Musorgsky's direction) "distracted," or vatically entranced. At the same time, the status of the utterance becomes ambiguous: what begins as clearly "phenomenal" shades over into "noumenal music," the music of the general sonic ambience, no longer clearly "heard" by the onstage characters. The effect is to surround the words of the *yurodivïy* with a nimbus—the aura of "truth"—that disembodies them.

This remarkable musical transformation is repeated at the end of the scene, when Musorgsky's *yurodivïy* (unlike Pushkin's) reprises his song in an expanded form (example 4.3b), with new words (the composer's), in a tonic (i.e., stress-counting) folk meter that occasionally hints at the quintasyllabic *pesennïy razmer*. They are explicitly and chillingly clairvoyant with respect to the outcome of the historical drama:

> Léytes' slyózï gór'kiye,
> Plách', dushá pravoslávnaya!
> Skoro vrág pridyot / I nastánet t'ma,
> Témen' tyómnaya / neproglyádnaya.
> Gore Rusi!
> Plach', russkiy lyud,
> Golodnïy lyud! . . .

> Flow, bitter tears,
> Weep, Orthodox soul!
> Soon the enemy will come and darkness will fall,

---

[35] See Robbert van der Lek, *Diegetic Music in Opera and Film* (Amsterdam: Editions Rodopi, 1991); and Carolyn Abbate, *Unsung Voices* (Princeton: Princeton University Press, 1991), pp. 4–10.

EXAMPLE 4.3. Musorgsky, *Boris Godunov*

a. Scene at St. Basil's, first *yurodivïy* (Holy Fool) song

EXAMPLE 4.3, *continued*

me - syats . . .

b. Second (closing) *yurodivïy* song

Ley - tes' ley - tes' slyo - zï gor' - ki - ye,   plach', plach' du - sha pra - vo - slav - na - ya.   sko - ro vrag pri - dyet i na - sta - net t'ma, te - men' tyom - na - ya ne - pro - glyad - na - ya. Go - re, go - re Ru-

EXAMPLE 4.3, *continued*

si,   plach', plach' rus-skiy lyud,   go - lod - nïy   lyud!___

Darkest dark, impenetrable dark.
Woe to Russia!
Weep, Russian folk,
Hungry folk! . . .

In the second version of the opera (1872), the scene of the *yurodivïy* is plucked out of Pushkin's scene (literally ripped by Musorgsky out of his older score) and inserted into a new final scene, the one at Kromy, that has no counterpart in Pushkin. The two songs now enclose not the confrontation between idiot soothsayer and guilty ruler but the scene of popular submission to the Pretender, thus marking the hungry, frantically gullible Russian folk, not the sinful Tsar, as the tragic protagonist of the drama. The *yurodivïy*'s final disembodied prophecy now closes not a single scene but the entire opera on a note of desperate, doom-laden entropy: the disintegration of its cadential structure is now the opera's concluding harmonic gesture, casting an uncanny retrospective pall over the whole preceding action.

Whose voice is this? Who gets the last word? In Pushkin, and in Musorgsky's earlier version based directly on Pushkin, the voice of the *yurodivïy* was the voice of nemesis, invoking heavenly judgment on Boris. Placed at the end, after Boris's death and the Pretender's triumph—that is to say, after the apparent resolution of the drama—the negating entropic voice is the voice of one who knows the unhappy future, who knows that there has been no resolution of Russia's fate.

That description applies, superficially, to the *yurodivïy*, but his is not, in fact, the last "voice" that is heard. The disembodiment of his song continues after his singing stops in an orchestral postlude based on an ostinato drawn from the sighing, sixthy, semitonal "intonation" of lamentation that had accompanied the song at its beginning. The very last phrase, in the low strings, is a final, rhythmically augmented repetition of the ostinato, a double descent from the sixth to the fifth degree of the A-minor scale, that sounds after the tonic bass note has dropped out. The song, the scene, and the opera thus grind to a halt on an unaccompanied fifth degree—that is, on the dominant, the very emblem of nonresolution (example 4.4).

EXAMPLE 4.4. Musorgsky, *Boris Godunov*, orchestral postlude following second *yurodivïy* song

Whose voice is this? It is the voice of one who knows the unhappy future because for him it is the past. At one level of disembodiment beyond the visible body on the stage, it is the voice of the chronicler, the super-Pimen who has penned the opera, the composer-*yurodivïy* who sees and speaks the truth, and whose name is Musorgsky. At a further level of disembodiment it is the voice of the chronicle itself, the truth-bearing voice of history. At the ultimate level, it is the voice of Russia's self-consciousness, a voice transcending persons and people, defining the nation-*yurodivïy* whose mission it is, earned through suffering, to bear the truth to the world.

CHAPTER 5

SAFE HARBORS

ON 31 DECEMBER 1900, the last day of the nineteenth century, Nikolai Rimsky-Korsakov, Musorgsky's surviving kuchkist confrère and musical executor, universally recognized and hailed as the greatest living Russian composer, received a visit from his faithful Boswell, a banker named Vasiliy Vasilievich Yastrebtsev. Yastrebtsev asked for a fitting memento of the day, whereupon Rimsky-Korsakov wrote out the accompaniment to a passage from Spring's recitative in the prologue to his opera *The Snow Maiden* (example 5.1).

"Figure out the riddle, kind sir," he wrote as inscription, alluding to the missing words: "And it's all just light and cold brilliance, and there's no

EXAMPLE 5.1. Rimsky-Korsakov's end-of-century inscription in Yastrebtsev's album, with voice part (from *The Snow Maiden*) restored

warmth."[1] It was an apt if ruefully overstated comment on what had happened over the preceding quarter-century to his music, and to Russian music as a whole, as a result of professionalization, institutionalization, self-censorship, and what might be called the perils of safe harbor.

Rimsky-Korsakov is still identified in every history book as a member of the "Mighty Five," as they are often called in English, the maverick group of self-trained musicians who fought the good nationalist fight against German hegemony, against academic routine, and against philistine conservatism. By 1900 that group was only a memory. Its two most characteristic members, Musorgsky and Borodin, were long dead, and Rimsky-Korsakov was at the head of another school of composers altogether, one that is never mentioned in Western history texts since it does not conform to the stereotypical behavior the West expects from Russian composers.

The school Rimsky-Korsakov now headed was known as the Belyayev school, because it owed its existence to the activities and largesse of a timber merchant named Mitrofan Petrovich Belyayev, who, beginning in 1882, the year after Musorgsky's death, had endowed a magnificent publishing enterprise, two concert series, and several annual prizes for the purpose of supporting Russian art music. The patron's will made provision for the continuation of these undertakings in perpetuity: the concert series and the awards lasted until the revolution, and the publishing house, now located in Frankfurt, Germany, has lasted to this day. For composers willing and able to meet Belyayev's standards, his company offered cradle-to-grave career insurance. Anyone able to make the grade was also willing.

For all his commitment to the cause of indigenous musical culture, Belyayev's idea of musical culture was wholly formed on the Germanic academic model. An amateur violinist and violist, he was a great enthusiast of chamber music, with "absolute" symphonic works next in line, program music and concertos after that, and all vocal genres at the very bottom.[2] His notion of standards was founded on a notion of technical quality that was founded in turn on the three Rs of the musical academy—harmony, counterpoint, form. He enforced these standards through an executive committee consisting of three conservatory professors, with Rimsky-Korsakov at its head.

Rimsky-Korsakov had already been a conservatory professor for over a decade when Belyayev began his patronage activity, and by the turn of the century he was as pedantic a stickler for the academic niceties as any conservatory professor anywhere. The St. Petersburg Conservatory, which now

---

[1] V. V. Yastrebtsev, *Reminiscences of Rimsky-Korsakov*, ed. and trans. Florence Jonas (New York: Columbia University Press, 1985), pp. 275–76.

[2] Reinhold Glière, "Vstrechi s belyayevskim kruzhkom," *Sovetskaya muzïka*, no. 8 (1949): 66; for more on the Belyayev school and the "Belyayevets" mentality, see R. Taruskin, *Stravinsky and the Russian Traditions* (Berkeley and Los Angeles: University of California Press, 1996), chapter 1.

bears Rimsky-Korsakov's name, had been founded in 1862 by Anton Rubinstein over the vociferous objections of the nationalist faction. Rimsky-Korsakov had been unexpectedly named to its faculty in 1871, although, as a member in good standing of the Mighty Five, he was himself innocent of academic training. He therefore embarked on a heroic program of belated self-education that estranged him from his former circle and left him in command of a superlative academic technique he spent the rest of his life imparting to others, beginning with Alexander Glazunov and Anatoly Lyadov and ending with Igor Stravinsky. His early star pupils, Glazunov and Lyadov, both fellow professors by century's end, joined him on the Belyayev executive committee.

Thus these three composers, as pedagogues and as channelers of a fantastic Maecenas's largesse, became the all-powerful leaders of a guild, or, to use a contemporary Russian term, an *artel*, a crafts collective.[3] They brought up their pupils to exhibit their academic credentials to the point of virtuosity, and rewarded them with a place at the Belyayev feeding trough. It was as easy to deride the artel from without as it was difficult to rebel from within. Debate around it, moreover, took exactly the form debate would take about its virtual successor, the Union of Soviet Composers, with proponents emphasizing material benefits and detractors emphasizing creative freedom. Yet so powerful were the blandishments it could offer, even without any raw state power to back them up, that the Conservatory/Belyayev nexus made for an absolutely invincible establishment. The result, with the single equivocal exception of Scriabin, was the near-total absence of a Russian musical avant-garde all through the period of literary and painterly experimentation now known as the Silver Age.

There was, however, a modest sort of approved musical modernism within the establishment. Rimsky-Korsakov, who reviled Debussy and Richard Strauss, and who never tired of exhorting his pupils to avoid the sort of anarchic decadence those names represented, never gave up his sense of himself as a "progressive" musician.[4] He enjoyed experimenting with unusual harmonies—and the word "experimenting" is especially well chosen in his case, since his attitude toward musical innovation ("progress") was naively scientific in the sense that it was obsessively rigorous and fatally systematic. In the excerpt from *The Snow Maiden* given in this chapter as example 5.1, the unusual chords—not that unusual, really, just augmented triads—were deployed in a regular chromatic ascent that mirrored an equally systematic

---

[3] "Silèn" [Alfred Nurok], "Muzïkal'nïy artel'," *Mir iskusstva*, nos. 21–22 (1898): 79.

[4] For Rimsky-Korsakov on Debussy, see his diary for 1907, printed in Nikolai Rimsky-Korsakov, *Polnoye sobraniye sochineniy: Literaturnïye proizvedeniya i perepiska*, vol. 1 (Moscow: Muzgiz, 1960), p. 16; on Strauss, see the anonymous obituary memoir by a former pupil in *Russkaya muzïkal'naya gazeta* 15, nos. 32–33 (10–17 August 1908), col. 661; and on his definition of progressive (as opposed to "revolutionary"), see Rimsky-Korsakov, *My Musical Life*, trans. Judah A. Joffe (London: Eulenburg Books, 1974), pp. 285–86.

and rhythmically sequential chromatic descent in the bass, the whole accomplishing nothing but a motion from one voicing of the A-major triad to another. The progression is thus what theorists would call a "coloristic" (or "prolongational") rather than a "functional" one.

The main harmonic innovation of Rimsky-Korsakov's later years—one that he passed on directly to his pupils—was the cautious and methodical mining of the coloristic possibilities inherent in a scale of regularly alternating whole steps and half steps. In his day it was known as the "tone-semitone scale" (*gamma ton-poluton*), or "Rimsky-Korsakov scale" (*korsakovskaya gamma*); today's music theorists call it the octatonic scale because it contains eight tones to the octave.[5] It defines Russia musically at the turn of the century just as surely as "modal" folk song harmonizations had done forty years earlier.

The main reason for this preoccupation of Rimsky's was his heavy investment in fantastic and fairy-tale subject matter, for which a vocabulary of recherché yet easily apprehended harmonies and harmonic sequences was desirable (along with the sort of recondite orchestral timbres he could summon up better than any contemporary) to contrast with the diatonic and folkish idiom of the older Russian "nationalism," as a musical metaphor for the confrontation between human characters and supernatural ones, both benign and sinister. It was a tradition that went back to Glinka, but it received its strongest emphasis in Russian music during Rimsky-Korsakov's late years in reaction to conditions of Russian literary and theatrical censorship.

The composers of the Mighty Five, working at a particularly "civic" moment in Russian intellectual history that had been made possible by a relaxation of censorship under the Emancipator-Tsar Alexander II, had been drawn to themes of serious historiographical import: alongside Musorgsky's famous historical operas one could place Rimsky-Korsakov's first dramatic effort, *The Maid of Pskov* (1872), in which Ivan the Terrible not only appears and sings but is explicitly judged.[6] By contrast, in the stringent conditions that followed the liberal Tsar's assassination and that obtained throughout the reigns of Alexander III and Nikolai II, the safest course was a retreat into fantasy.[7]

Rimsky-Korsakov had made his retreat in 1900 with *The Tale of Tsar Sal-*

[5] It was christened by Arthur Berger in a seminal article, "Problems of Pitch Organization in Stravinsky" (1963), in Benjamin Boretz and Edward T. Cone, ed., *Perspectives on Schoenberg and Stravinsky* (Princeton: Princeton University Press, 1968), pp. 123–55. On its use among the Belyayevtsï see R. Taruskin, "Chernomor to Kashchei: Harmonic Sorcery; or, Stravinsky's 'Angle,'" *Journal of the American Musicological Society* 38 (1985): 72–142.

[6] See R. Taruskin, "'The Present in the Past': Russian Opera and Russian Historiography, ca. 1870," in *Russian and Soviet Music: Essays for Boris Schwarz*, ed. Malcolm H. Brown (Ann Arbor: UMI Research Press, 1984), pp. 77–146, esp. pp. 90–124.

[7] On the "retreat into fantasy" see Boris Tyuneyev, "O Cherepnine (dialog)," *Russkaya muzïkal'naya gazeta* 22, no. 15 (12 April 1915), cols. 275–76.

tan, and followed up with *Kashchey the Deathless* (1902), *The Legend of the Invisible City of Kitezh* (1904), and *The Golden Cockerel* (1907), highly colored fairy tales all. There was also a new tendency to borrow aspects of the style and form of his work, not just its subject matter, from folk models, which put Rimsky-Korsakov in touch with the movement in Russian painting today's art historians call neonationalism. To this very limited extent, then, the late Rimsky-Korsakov, and his pupils, responded to the Russian Silver Age.

To the extent that any musicians went farther in these directions during the decade that followed Rimsky-Korsakov's death in 1908, it was simply a matter of what is best called maximalism—intensifying the means employed toward accepted ends. *The Firebird*, the ballet through which Stravinsky made his early reputation, was an exact analogue to his teacher's fantastic operas, replete with a folkloric diatonic idiom representing the human characters and a coloristic chromatic one representing the supernatural. The repertory of timbres and special instrumental effects was expanded, and the arsenal of exotic harmonic *Kunststücke* grew, as the result of both a normal emulatory impulse and the special needs of Sergey Diaghilev's "export campaign," by which the Russian school had to become more demonstratively Russian than ever to satisfy the expectations of a Parisian audience, even as advanced musicians at home were waving the banner of "denationalization" as an earnest of artistic maturity.[8]

Petrushka, Stravinsky's second ballet, brought foreign-export neonationalism to its peak and made its composer's name an emblem of (Parisian) modernism. Yet even its most seemingly radical devices, like its eponymous "bitonal" chord, were direct applications of established St. Petersburg habits. (The "Petrushka chord" was a venerable guild secret that had been explicitly handed down from Rimsky-Korsakov to his pupils; Stravinsky was by no means the only one to use it).[9] *The Rite of Spring*, conspicuously more radical than its predecessors, was no less than they a maximalization of an existing practice to which it remained loyal—or rather, a synthesis of several practices: the rationalized harmonic techniques inherited from Rimsky-Korsakov, an archaistic or neoprimitivist tendency that in its maximalistic phase went by the name of Scythianism (but which is by now easy to accept as an extension of the older, tamer neonationalism), and of course the generalized Silver Age

---

[8] The term "denationalization" was made explicit in the year of *The Firebird*'s première by the critic Vyacheslav Karatïgin in (of all places) an obituary for Miliy Balakirev, the original leader of the Mighty Five, who had long outlived his relevance to the Russian musical scene. See V. Karatïgin, "Miliy Alekseyevich Balakirev 1837–1910," *Apollon*, no. 10 (September 1910): 54.

[9] See R. Taruskin, "*Chez Petrouchka*: Harmony and Tonality *chez* Stravinsky," *19th-Century Music* 10 (1986–87): 265–86, where the chord is sighted in and cited from the work of Maximilian Steinberg, who had adopted it from a late unpublished sketch by Rimsky-Korsakov himself.

rhetoric of apocalypse, of which the greatest musical exponent—and by common contemporary consent, simply the greatest exponent—was Alexander Nikolayevich Scriabin.

But even though Scriabin was a genuine theurgist, a self-appointed mediator in his art between the human and the divine, and even though, as chapter 12 will detail, he took inspiration directly from Vyacheslav Ivanov and other religious and metaphysical poets of his age, he was anything but a reckless or disheveled avant-gardist. He was the proud recipient of an elite conservatory education, spent his early years in the Belyayev incubator, and retained to the end of his career a fastidious, not to say pedantic concern for polish and finish that earned him Rimsky-Korsakov's eternal if somewhat grudging respect.[10] Not even the gawky, gangling young Prokofiev—whose early works horrified the squeamish Scriabin, and who attempted a rather callow emulation or maximalization of *The Rite of Spring* in his Scythian Suite, with its naively literalistic title—not even he could be called an avant-gardist. His loyalty, like Stravinsky's and like Scriabin's, was to the established elite culture. While he liked playing the role of an enfant terrible, he made sure that an academician could always detect his underlying allegiance to the traditional values and skills on which grades were based. This remained true throughout his life; it is utterly characteristic of Prokofiev that beneath the clangorous surface there always lay a simple harmonic design and a stereotyped formal pattern straight out of the textbook.

Thus there simply was no avant-garde in Russian music on the eve of the revolution. The most poignant example of its lack is suitably negative. When Kazimir Malevich and Alexey Kruchonïkh needed a score for their "cubofuturist" opera, *Victory over the Sun* (1913), they commissioned it from Mikhail Matyushin, a name that will not be found in any music dictionary. Why? Because Matyushin was a painter, who happened to have studied the violin at the Moscow Conservatory and played professionally for a while, and who therefore could read and write musical notation.[11] There was no professional composer in Russia who would subscribe to anything like the futurist manifesto called "A Slap in the Face of Public Taste," who would consider writing the musical equivalent of *zaúmnïy yazïk*, the "transrational language" of futurist poetry, or who would even attempt a creative career outside the established institutions of the day, unless they were new institutions that promised, like Diaghilev's Paris enterprise, to outstrip the establishment in material extravagance and social prestige.

IT WAS the Bolshevik coup that gave rise to the only musical avant-garde Russia has known in the twentieth century. To understand this fact, however,

---

[10] See, for instance, Yastrebtsev, *Moi vospominaniya o N. A. Rimskom-Korsakove*, vol. 2 (Leningrad: Muzgiz, 1960), p. 365.

[11] See *The Avant-Garde in Russia 1910–1930: New Perspectives*, ed. Stephanie Barron and Maurice Tuchman (Los Angeles: Los Angeles County Museum of Art, 1980), pp. 208–9.

one must know what an avant-garde really is. The term does not properly signify the mere possession or use of an "advanced" technique. That could be called elite modernism or modernist professionalism if a term is needed, and that term would serve to cover all the maximalistic tendencies we have been surveying. Maximalism, as we have seen, implies the extension of a tradition, which in turn implies loyalty to the tradition one is extending, even if one is extending it to the point of so-called decadence.

An avant-garde is something else. The term is military, and it implies belligerence: countercultural hostility, antagonism to existing institutions and traditions. Avant-gardes always put traditionalists on the defensive, even maximalizing or decadent traditionalists, and turn them reactionary. Compare the rhetoric deployed by our own tenured modernists (who still like to call themselves the "academic avant-garde") against the so-called Minimalists, nonaffiliated composers who represent (or who represented until their commercial co-option) a true avant-garde position in recent concert music.

To return to revolutionary Russia, it seemed at first inevitable that a workers' and peasants' government would be hostile to the art institutions of the aristocracy and the bourgeoisie, which had harbored the art of what Lenin called the "bored upper ten thousand."[12] Yet as long as an elite art was supported by its consumers, only its value was open to question, not its authenticity. Once the many are asked to support the art of the few, questions of authenticity are inevitable, along with questions of social function and social responsibility. If these questions can become so exacerbated even in relatively placid liberal democracies like ours, how much more, then, in a revolutionary socialist state? Nationalizing the theaters, the concert halls, and the conservatories was in fact one of the earliest acts of the new regime. To many elite establishmentarians, emphatically including the modernists among them, this was handwriting on the wall, and they left—the Rachmaninoffs and the Prokofievs alike.

The famous exchange between the emigrating Prokofiev and Anatoly Lunacharsky, the head of the so-called NARKOMPROS (the "People's commissariat for enlightenment"), as recorded in Prokofiev's Soviet-period memoirs, illustrates a familiar confusion. "You are revolutionaries in art," Lunacharsky is supposed to have said, "we are revolutionaries in life; we ought to work together." But Prokofiev was no revolutionary in art. Like Rachmaninoff (and like Stravinsky, who had been a voluntary expatriate since 1910), he was a traditional maximalist who saw the revolution in "life" as a threat. It was only when he became convinced that the arts policies of the Soviet state no longer posed any threat to traditional art that he decided to return.

But if Prokofiev was no revolutionary in art, neither was Lunacharsky, and neither was Lenin. They, too, were committed traditionalists in art, faithful to

---

[12] "Party Organization and Party Literature," in V. I. Lenin, *Selected Works* (New York: International Publishers, 1971), p. 151.

the petty-bourgeois tastes of the nineteenth-century intelligentsia, the social class from which they had emerged. In an oft-quoted conversation with the German Communist Klara Zetkin, Lenin had no hesitation in proclaiming himself a philistine with respect to modern art movements, and even derided the sentiment Lunacharsky is supposed to have expressed to Prokofiev. "We are good revolutionaries," he said, "but somehow we feel obliged to prove that we are on a par with 'contemporary culture.' But I have the courage to declare myself a 'barbarian.' I am unable to count the works of expressionism, futurism, cubism, and similar 'isms' among the highest manifestations of creative genius. I do not understand them. I do not derive any pleasure from them."

If Lenin had gone on to say that therefore the art of the traditional high culture was corrupt and had to be replaced with a proletarian culture, he would have qualified as an avant-gardist. But he said nothing of the kind. In fact, he said, "We must preserve the beautiful, take it as a model, use it as starting point, even if it is 'old.' Why must we turn away from the truly beautiful just because it is 'old'? Why must we bow low in front of the new, as if it were God, only because it is 'new'?"[13]

So notions of beauty did not have to change with notions of social justice. What had inspired Tsar and courtier could continue to inspirit the Soviet state. Trotsky went so far in his loyalty to Victorian aesthetics as explicitly to assert that culture was above classes—and he did so in express opposition to the notion of a specifically proletarian art.[14] The Bolsheviks were quite right to distrust modernism, of course, because modernism is often motivated by the wish to preserve exclusivity. But the premodern, the conventionally beautiful, would be retained out of affection and habit—and above all, out of national pride, which vouchsafed the especially improbable survival of the Russian classical ballet into the Soviet period: for all that it symbolized the autocracy, it was after all the world's finest.

So the Bolshevik takeover did not endanger the arts institutions of Tsarist Russia. Works overtly glorifying the Romanov dynasty, like Glinka's *A Life for the Tsar*, were of course removed from the repertory—until their librettos could be refurbished, anyway—and others were sanitized. (The peasant scene, for example, was dropped from Chaikovsky's *Eugene Onegin*, though it, too, came back under Stalin.) The difference was that the institutions of the "landlord culture" would be placed at the service of the working class.

The task was undertaken in a spirit of the frankest paternalism. The masses were to be raised to the level of the unquestioned elite culture. They were to be educated in the old bourgeois ways, right down to elementary behavior—

---

[13] Klara Zetkin, *Reminiscences of Lenin* (London: Chatto and Windus, 1929), p. 14.
[14] See Leon Trotsky, *Literature and Revolution* (New York: International Publishers, 1924), p. 14.

don't talk, don't smoke, don't crack nuts, wear a tie "so as to fit more into the atmosphere of beauty."[15] Some remarks by Lunacharsky before a performance of Glinka's *Ruslan and Lyudmila* capture the flavor: "To you, workers, will be shown one of the greatest creations, one of the most cherished diamonds in the wondrous crown of Russian art. On a valuable tray you are presented with a goblet of beautiful sparkling wine—drink and enjoy it."[16] Even chamber music, the most aristocratic music of all, was lovingly preserved and presented to the masses. New quartets sprang up, including the Lunacharsky Quartet and the Lenin Quartet. Their performing style was "externalized," as the saying then went—overdramatized, overly demonstrative, ingenuously explicit, didactic. It is the style of playing still recognizable, alas, as "Soviet."

And this raises the chief difficulty with the notion of hybridizing an avantgarde social ideology with traditional art institutions: all it produces is debased institutions. More authentic, perhaps, within the early Soviet context was another educational endeavor instigated by Lunacharsky: the so-called *Proletkult*, in which the emphasis was placed on direct musical participation —*samodeyatel'nost'*, to use the Soviet term. This type of organized local instruction had its roots in nineteenth-century "populism," the idealistic *khozhdeniye v narod*, the "going to the people" through which the educated could serve them and prepare them for responsible self-government. The many folk schools and choruses organized by the *Proletkult* were modeled on the famous St. Petersburg 'Free Music School' founded by Lomakin and Balakirev in the early 1860s. Lenin, with his suspicion of independent activity and his visceral commitment to traditional high culture, thought the movement obscurantist and threw the decisive weight of his prestige against it. It lasted only until 1923.

It was during the so-called NEP years that the genuine Soviet avant-garde emerged. During this period of economic recovery, the Party and the government declared a laissez-faire policy with respect to the arts while devoting their attention to more pressing matters of survival. A hundred flowers bloomed. As usual, one particular Venus flytrap eventually managed to gobble up the other flowers, but for a time many schools of thought did contend. In 1923 two major professional associations of musicians were organized. One, the Association of Contemporary Music (called the "ASM" after its Russian initials) comprised the traditional establishment, including the traditional maximalists. It was affiliated with the International Society of Contemporary Music and participated in the prestigious ISCM festivals. At its own

---

[15] Konstantin Stanislavsky, *My Life in Art*, trans. J. J. Robbins (New York: Meridian Books, 1956), pp. 554.

[16] *Istoriya muziki narodov SSSR*, vol. 1 (Moscow, 1966), p. 51; quoted in Boris Schwarz, *Music and Musical Life in Soviet Russia: Enlarged Edition, 1917–1981* (Bloomington: Indiana University Press, 1983), p. 15.

FIGURE 5.1. Henry Cowell, *Tiger* (1928), published in 1930 by the USSR State Music Publishing House (Muzgiz) as the second of *Dve p'yesï* (Two Pieces)

concerts the ASM featured guests like Milhaud, Hindemith, Franz Schreker, Alfredo Casella—and Henry Cowell, who published his most maximalistic piece of piano music, *The Tiger*, while touring the USSR (figure 5.1). The ASM propagandized on behalf of such major modernist events as the Leningrad production of Berg's *Wozzeck* in 1927, with the composer in attendance. (It was because he remembered this triumph of Berg's that Berg's teacher, Schoenberg, briefly considered taking refuge in the Soviet Union in the period of his persecution by the Nazis.)

The ASM's most prominent composer member was Nikolai Myaskovsky; its other main organizers were scholars and critics, including Pavel Lamm, Boris Asafyev, Victor Belyayev (unrelated to the old Maecenas), and Leonid Sabaneyev (who would soon emigrate). Its most radical representatives included Alexander Mosolóv (1900–1973), who gained a brief world notoriety for his futuristic symphonic suite *Stal'* (Steel), which included the famously cacophonous *Zavod*, known in English as "The Iron Foundry," and Georgiy Mikhailovich Rimsky-Korsakov (1901–65), the grandson of the great composer, who was an early experimenter with microtonal music. The ASM sponsored several journals and a publishing house called the Tritone, which issued Asafyev's famous futurist critique of Stravinsky.[17] The ASM was not exclusively a modernist organization, however; it represented all established traditions, not just the tradition of the new. Its membership included the latter-day "Belyayevtsï" and most conservatory professors, like Maximilian Steinberg, Rimsky-Korsakov's very conservative son-in-law, who qualified on both counts.

Now because music history in the West has traditionally been written from an elite modernist perspective, with stylistic complexity and technical innovation valued as the chief earnests of cultural authenticity, the ASM has been greatly glorified as the one bright spot in the otherwise deplorable history of Soviet music. There have been some enthusiastic Western technical studies of "Asmovsky" music, including a pioneering general survey by the German scholar Detlef Gojowy and more recent ones by Peter D. Roberts (on the piano repertoire) and Larry Sitsky.[18]

Most of the music, to judge by these surveys, is uninteresting, dividing into a sub-Scriabin wing, in which the old rhetoric of apocalypse was all too easily assimilated to a rhetoric of revolution, and a superficially antithetical futurist wing in which sub-Stravinskian, even sub-Prokofievian neoprimitivism was assimilated just as predictably to evocations of industrial or urban reality. All this music can be traced back through its models to the old Belyayev school.

There is no need for a revisionist vendetta against the ASM; despite the best efforts of its rediscoverers it is finished, forgotten and unrevivable, and many of its members suffered cruelly under Stalin.[19] But there is a need to challenge

---

[17] *Kniga o Stravinskom* (Leningrad: Triton, 1929; 2d ed., Leningrad: Muzïka, 1977), trans. Richard F. French as *A Book about Stravinsky* (Ann Arbor: UMI Research Press, 1982).

[18] Detlef Gojowy, *Neue sowjetische Musik der 20er Jahre* (Laaber: Laaber-Verlag, 1980); Peter Deane Roberts, *Modernism in Russian Piano Music*, 2 vols. (Bloomington: Indiana University Press, 1993); Larry Sitsky, *Music of the Repressed Russian Avant-Garde, 1900–1929* (Westport, Conn.: Greenwood Press, 1994).

[19] The paradigmatic case was that of Mosolov. There had always been conspicuous and disconcerting gaps in the accounts of this quintessential twenties futurist in standard reference

its status in conventional historiography as the site of a golden age or an authentic avant-garde. It was merely the phase of Soviet music that most closely conformed to the Western European modernist model, and hence most amenable to exploration and evaluation on the accepted terms of Western musicology. The ASM was *not* the Soviet avant-garde.

That distinction must be reserved for its great adversary, the Russian Association of Proletarian Musicians (called the RAPM, after its Russian initials), by now the most universally reviled faction in the history of Soviet music. Militantly countercultural, hopelessly doctrinaire, intolerant, self-righteous, the radical proletarians were the ones who wanted to throw out all sophisticated traditions and build the new Soviet music on the rubble. RAPM frightened elite modernists by portending what Maximilian Steinberg called "the annihilation of professional art and the reduction of everything to complete dilettantism."[20]

RAPM defined itself chiefly by what it opposed: it was antimodern, anti-Western, antijazz—but also antifolklore, antinationalist. The "RAPMistï" also opposed whatever was politically incorrect beyond redemption in the classical repertory both European (Wagner!) and Russian (Chaikovsky!). They stigmatized the music produced and patronized by the ASM as that of the decadent bourgeoisie, denouncing it under four general rubrics: 1) the cultivation of sensual and pathologically erotic moods; 2) mysticism (these

---

works. The article on him in the *New Grove*, for example, by the Soviet musicologist Inna Barsova, contained two statements, as follows: "Mosolov lived in Moscow until 1937," and "from 1939 to his death he lived in Moscow" (*The New Grove Dictionary of Music and Musicians*, ed. Stanley Sadie [London: Macmillan, 1980], vol. 12, p. 612). A 1989 article in *Sovetskaya muzïka*, also by Barsova, innocently titled "From the unpublished archive of A. V. Mosolov," heartbreakingly filled the gap with documents and photographs, including one of Mosolov's Gulag registration card, dated 25 August 1938, and the text of a frantic letter addressed by his former teachers, Myaskovsky and Glière, to Mikhail Kalinin, the Soviet figurehead president, in an effort—a successful effort, amazing to relate—to secure his release. (I. A. Barsova, "Iz neopublikovannogo arkhiva A. V. Mosolova," *Sovetskaya muzïka*, no. 7 [1989]: 80–92, and no. 8 [1989]: 69–75.) The unusual success of the intervention was due to the fact that Mosolov had been incarcerated not on a political charge but on a trumped-up charge of "hooliganism," brought by his enemies within the Composers' Union. Before his arrest he had, in the wake of the formal denunciation of Shostakovich, been expelled from the union (4 February 1936), an extreme measure that effectively deprived him of his livelihood, and that merited a report in the union organ. The gleefully sarcastic report is signed by the wife of Tikhon Khrennikov: Kl[ara Arnoldovna] Vaks, "Kompozitor Mosolov isklyuchen iz SSK," *Sovetskaya muzïka*, no. 3 (1936): 104. (The one prominent Soviet musician to have been "illegally repressed," as his entry in the standard Soviet music encyclopedia now reads, was the composer and theorist Nikolai Sergeyevich Zhilyayev (1891–1938), pupil of Taneyev and Ippolitov-Ivanov, close friend of Scriabin, and teacher of Khachaturyan, among many other Soviet composers. He was, unluckily, also close to Marshal Mikhail Tukhachevsky, and his downfall came in the wake of Tukhachevsky's arrest in 1937.)

[20] Quoted in Schwarz, *Music and Musical Life in Soviet Russia*, p. 102.

two corresponding to what I have called the "sub-Scriabin" mode); 3) naturalistic reproduction of the movement of the contemporary capitalist city (what is usually called futurism); and 4) cultivation of primitive, coarse subjects (these corresponding to the "sub-Stravinsky" or "sub-Prokofiev" modes).[21]

In place of all this the RAPMistï proffered revolutionary gebrauchsmusik, marchlike *massovïye pesni* ("mass songs" for group singing) set to agitational propaganda (*agitprop*) lyrics, and "operas" or "oratorios" fashioned out of medleys of such songs, often the product of collective authorship. Their names—Alexander Davidénko, Boris Shekhter, Victor Belïy—are mostly forgotten now, except when exhumed for ritual execration, but they also include Dmitriy Kabalevsky and Marian Koval, two of the great villains of Soviet music under Stalin.

Not a stellar roster, not much of a musical yield, and from 1929, when they achieved administrative power, a terrible brake on Soviet musical life. But the RAPM was nevertheless significant as the one really new tendency the Soviet state brought forth in musical art. As the Asmovsky stalwart Leonid Sabaneyev put it, however sarcastically, shortly after emigrating, "If Communist Russia has created anything original, it is the advance in the democratic direction, the appeal for 'music for all.'"[22] The avant-garde character of this seemingly reactionary appeal is important to note, because otherwise one can understand neither the style nor the sentiment that informs the music of Shostakovich, the tragic genius of Soviet music.

Shostakovich, although passively a member of the local Leningrad chapter of ASM,[23] was typical of neither organization. His music was too Asmovsky for RAPM and too Rapmovsky for ASM. On the Asmovsky side, he had an elite conservatory education and was interested in all the modernist trends of the twenties, of which many—but especially *Wozzeck* and the *Zeitoper* ("now" opera) of Křenek and Hindemith—found echo in his work. He could be a maximalist's maximalist, as in the thirteen-voice dissonant fugato from his Second Symphony. There is also a striking futurist streak in his music of the period: not just the famous factory whistle in the same symphony but also its characteristic "cinematic" montage technique, juxtaposing quickly changing "frames" in place of the linear developmental techniques one learned in school. (Not by accident, and he was not the only one, Shostakovich's first paying job as a musician was as a piano player in a silent movie theater.)

The choral finales of the Second ("October") and Third ("May Day") Sym-

[21] "Platform of the Russian Association of Proletarian Musicians" (1929), in Nicolas Slonimsky, *Music since 1900*, 4th ed. (New York: Charles Scribner's Sons, 1971), pp. 1353–57.

[22] Leonid Sabaneyeff, *Modern Russian Composers*, trans. Judah A. Joffe (New York: International Publishers, 1927; reprint, New York: Da Capo Press, 1975), p. 240.

[23] Laurel Fay, "Shostakovich, LASM and Asafiev," a paper read at the University of Michigan conference "Shostakovich: The Man and His Age," 29 January 1994.

phonies (1927, 1929) followed a RAPM stereotype, replaying the closing gestures of Beethoven's Ninth as street harangue, accompanied by a rhythm-band orchestra. At the end of the Second, the chorus begins shouting instead of singing; the passage sits ambiguously between ASM, in its maximalism, and RAPM, in its revolutionary skepticism of the symphonic tradition. The same skepticism—critiquing and undermining established genres from within—informs Shostakovich's first opera, *The Nose*, after Gogol (1928), where in place of a cavatina for the hero, Kovalyov, we hear him gargling at his sink, and where the first symphonic interlude is given over to the un-pitched percussion. One has the impression of traditions being mocked and smashed, not extended. ASM seems to have understood; Shostakovich was boycotted by its selection committee when it came to sending Soviet works abroad to ISCM festivals. (He did not need them: Bruno Walter played the First Symphony in Berlin on his own initiative, followed by Stokowski in Philadelphia; by 1928, when he was twenty-two, Shostakovich's lifelong international fame had been established.)

And yet RAPM suspected him, too, agitating against *The Nose* until its run was curtailed under their pressure in 1930. Shostakovich's genuine "prolet-kult" sympathies are evident in his loyalty all through the period of RAPM's ascendancy to the so-called TRaM theater (Theater of Working-class Youth), for which he composed a wealth of incidental music; and also in his professed hostility toward commercial "light music" (*lyogkiy zhanr*) and other opiates of the masses. Yet "lower" genres nevertheless infect a great deal of his early music, especially the First Symphony with its piano-dominated circus-galop of a scherzo. It was with Shostakovich no matter of raising the lower genre to the level of the higher. From the conservatory or Asmovsky perspective his music threatened debasement.

So it is fruitless to try to pigeonhole Shostakovich within the ready-made categories of ASM and RAPM; he was bigger than both of them. As the one major and enduring Soviet composer of the period with genuine avant-garde, not merely elite-modernist, leanings, he was unique. His is the only Soviet music of the period that seems to have a future.

And yet, as the last chapter of this book will relate in grievous detail, that future was cut short. The next phase of Soviet music, the grim one, was inaugurated by an event many unsuspecting musicians hailed with relief: the "historic April resolution" of 1932, as Shostakovich himself called it,[24] through which the Communist Party dissolved all the independent arts organizations, replacing them with the "unions" of art workers that lasted to the end of the Soviet period. Prokofiev responded to this move by accepting Soviet citizenship at last; not only for him but for every Soviet composer the unions

---

[24] S. Shostakovich, "Moyo ponimaniye 'Ledi Makbet,'" in *"Ledi Makbet Mtsenskogo uyezda," opera D. D. Shostakovicha* (Leningrad: Gosudarstvennïy Akademicheskiy Malïy Opernïy Teatr, 1934), p. 9.

seemed to offer protection and a guaranteed material security—shades of Mitrofan Belyayev! But what was at first thought to be a deliverance from the dictatorship of the meddlesome proletarianists in fact removed the last remaining obstacles to the naked exercise of totalitarian power over the arts. They were now directly subject to arbitrary Stalinist control.

Like all times of radical (in this case directed) change, this was a time of (in this case cynical) theorizing on a grand scale. The concept of socialist realism was invented (by Andrey Zhdanov) and christened (by Gorky, like Prokofiev a newly returned émigré) in connection with the implementation of the April resolution. The charter of the Union of Soviet Composers defined it as support of "the victorious progressive principles of reality, toward all things heroic, bright, and beautiful," and as struggle against "folk-negating modernistic directions that are typical of the decay of contemporary bourgeois art."[25] Thus affirmation became an enforceable requirement, along with antimodernism and—for the first time—*nationalism*, a bourgeois mystificatory concept toward which Marxian "scientific socialism," with its theory of class struggle, was hostile by virtual definition. Yet there it was, resurrected from the dustbin of history.

But then, for all its novel bureaucratic vocabulary, socialist realism really meant the institutionalization of petit-bourgeois taste at its most philistine (what Vera Dunham, in her fundamental study of Stalinist literature, identified as *meshchanstvo*, middle-class values),[26] as well as the revival of Tsarist notions of art and education in service not to class interests but to those of the state. The holy trinity of socialist-realist norms—*partiynost'* (serving the ends of the Party), *ideynost'* (high propaganda content), and *narodnost'* (nationalism)—shared the final term with the three weird sisters that a century earlier had defined the dynastic ideology of Tsarism, as formulated under Nikolai I, the most Stalinesque of all the Tsars. *Partiynost'* stood in for *samoderzhaviye* (autocracy) and *ideynost'* for *pravoslaviye* (orthodoxy). There was even a direct hint of Christian ethics à la Tolstoy in the new insistence upon universal accessibility as an earnest of authenticity.[27]

What this final requirement boiled down to in practice, however, was nothing more than the elevation of *russkaya klassika*, the standard Russian repertory of the nineteenth century—created for an imperial stage and reflecting its values, now a focus of newly reemphasized national pride, and of course greatly popular with audiences—to the status of an aesthetic and stylistic norm to which Soviet composers were expected to adhere. Chaikovsky's cen-

[25] Quoted in B. S. Shteynpress and I. M. Yampolsky, *Entsiklopedicheskiy muzïkal'nïy slovar'*, 2d ed. (Moscow: Sovetskaya entsiklopediya, 1966), p. 486.

[26] Vera Dunham, *In Stalin's Time: Middleclass Values in Soviet Fiction* (Cambridge: Cambridge University Press, 1976).

[27] For a consideration of the Tolstoyan roots of Soviet arts policy, see R. Taruskin, "Current Chronicle: Molchanov's *The Dawns Are Quiet Here*," *Musical Quarterly* 62 (1976): 105–15.

tenary in 1940 was a watershed. Alexander III's court musician was officially designated the greatest Russian composer. His work—and even his person, which took some doing—became sacrosanct. His operas were restored to their authentic form in performance, which meant ridding the Soviet stage of all manner of saving adaptations, including the famous Meyerhold "re-Pushkinization" of *The Queen of Spades*, and reinstating the servile peasant scene in *Yevgeniy Onegin* that had so offended proletarian taste.

So those who have looked (and continue to look) upon the arts policies of high Stalinism as a resurgence of RAPMism could not be more mistaken. RAPM was antimodern, all right, but it was also anticlassical. The mistake, as always, is the confusion of categories, with modernism equated with avant-garde and conservatism with reaction. Where RAPM (like Western "neo-classicism" at the opposite end of the political spectrum) was a reactionary avant-garde, the aesthetics of Stalinism exhibited the predictable conservatism of entrenched power.

One could indeed argue, against the conventional view that the abstractness of (instrumental) music exempted it from direct ideological control, that the new official philistinism affected music most directly, precisely because the paraphrasable or extractable "content" of music is usually so much less explicit than its style. Thus over the next two decades Soviet composers were subjected to an increasingly inflexible stylistic censorship, their dissonance treatment, for example, or their observance of formal conventions, being themselves regarded as potential indicators of political orthodoxy. This was truly formalism stood on its head. (What is incredible to musicians is that nonmusicians so often look upon it as benign; more than once I have been brought up short by educated people in the West, even professional intellectuals or scholars, who seem to think that censorship, anathema in other fields—theirs, for instance—is, for music, right.)

By the time of the infamous musical show-trials convened by Zhdanov in 1948, Soviet composers were exhorted simply to copy the music of Chaikovsky and the Mighty Five—which, of course, is exactly what the less imaginative members of the Belyayev school had been doing half a century before (figures 5.2a and b). We are back to our starting point, but with a difference: now it was murderous state power, not just the pecuniary blandishments of a millionaire patron, that enforced stylistic conformity. The late-Stalinist imitation of the nineteenth-century classics was skillful, literal, and unbelievable. Between 1948 and 1953, the year of Stalin's death, the style of most Soviet music became virtually indistinguishable from that of the turn-of-the-century Belyayev school, itself a sodality of epigones.

The most exemplary cases, and the most hyperbolically acclaimed, were the abject exculpatory efforts of the hobbled, terrified geriatric generation: Myaskovsky's last symphony, the Twenty-Seventh in C major, Op. 85 (1949), the recipient of a posthumous Stalin prize and for years afterward the

Грозили вы' нас перегнать,
Но вот, попробуйте... догнать!

За колесницей, слева направо:
М. В. Коваль, И. И. Дзержинский, С. С. Прокофьев,
Г. Н. Попов.

FIGURE 5.2A. "At the musical Hippodrome," a cartoon from *Sovetskaya muzika,* issue of January 1948 (actually published in February), in which the Zhdanov-convened "Conference of Soviet Musicians at the Headquarters of the Central Committee" was reported and the notorious Party Resolution on Music promulgated. In the chariot (l. to r.) are Rimsky-Korsakov, Glinka, and Chaikovsky, saying, "You threatened to surpass us, but just you try to catch up!" (*Grozili vï nas peregnat', | No vot, poprobuyte . . . dognat'!*). Trailing them on nags and hobbyhorses are (l. to r.) Marian Koval', the editor of the journal, Ivan Dzerzhinsky (composer of the hitherto highly approved "song opera" *Quiet Flows the Don*), Sergey Prokofiev, and Gavriyil Popov, a recent Stalin-Prize winner whose career was effectively smashed by the Resolution.

Загадочная картинка,
Многозначительный вид:

Глинка ли Глебова, Глебов ли Глинку.
Кто же кого здесь благодарит?

FIGURE 5.2B. Cartoon from the March issue, in which Glinka, holding the January issue behind his back, congratulates Boris Asafyev (the celebrated Soviet musicologist and member of the USSR Academy of Sciences, who wrote criticism under the pen name Igor Glebov, and who was given credit for the wording of the Resolution on Music) ostensibly for his recent (1947) Glinka biography. The caption rhyme: "An enigmatic picture, a momentous view: Glinka Glebov or Glebov Glinka, who here's thanking who?" The last line—"Kto zhe kogo zdes' blagodarit?"—plays chillingly on the proverbial rule of Cossack frontier justice (popularized by Lenin), "kto kogo"—literally, "one [does it to, gets the best of] the other," so by extension, "somebody's got to be the winner (and somebody's got to be dead)."

officially canonized model of "'correct' Soviet symphonism";[28] Prokofiev's
last symphony, the Seventh in C♯ minor, Op. 131 (1952), which also posthumously earned what by then had been renamed the Lenin Prize, but only
after a substitute "optimistic" ending had been demanded and supplied; perhaps most paradigmatically, the Concerto for French Horn and Orchestra in
B♭, Op. 91 (1950), by Reinhold Glière (1875–1956), a composer old enough
to have been an actual Belyayevets fellow traveler half a century earlier, who
had hardly modified his style since then, but who nevertheless felt the need to
make a propitiatory offering. About the Horn Concerto a contemporary critic
wrote—approvingly, it should be reemphasized—that, unlike the composer's
Cello Concerto (completed in 1946, shortly before the crackdown), "it contains practically no psychological or emotional contrasts; even, placid, and of
a cheerful character, its predominantly major tonalities, diatonic harmonies,
and bright instrumental timbres are maintained over the course of its three
movements."[29]

The work of gifted and extremely well trained composers, the music of the
post-Zhdanovite half-decade is highly palatable stuff—unless you know its
date. When you do know it, and when you know the fear and trembling that
stood behind the folksy anodynes and the smooth or stirring platitudes, it is
the most indigestible music in the world. "What were all the exulting, cheery,
dashing songs of those years all about?" wrote Daniyil Zhitomirsky, a revered
figure in Soviet musicology and a disciple of Zhilyayev, about the mass songs
of the thirties, when thousands, including his master, had perished; and, in
bitter parody of the old doctrinaire language, he asked, "What was their social
function?"[30] From the perspective of the *glasnost'* years, when Zhitomirsky
posed it, the question had an answer too obvious to bother stating. "Life is
getting better, life is getting gayer" (*zhizn' stanovitsya luchshe, veseleye*),
went the Stalinist mantra all through the years of terror. Music, too, could lie.
And if mass songs could lie in the thirties, symphonies and concertos could lie
even more impressively in the forties and fifties.

And yet they did not lie; they spoke the icy truth. In its hothouse isolation,
its servile affirmation, its cultural stagnation, and its intellectual limitation
this music faithfully mirrored the attributes of the society from which it had
been wrested. In a terrible way it, too, defined Russia.

[28] Stanley Dale Krebs, *Soviet Composers and the Development of Soviet Music* (New York:
Norton, 1970), p. 117.
[29] Marina Leonova, "Simfonicheskoye tvorchestvo Gliera," in *Reyngol'd Moritsevich Glier:
Stat'i, vospominaniya, materialï*, ed. V. M. Bogdanov-Berezovsky (Leningrad: Muzïka, 1967),
vol. 2, p. 63.
[30] Daniyil Zhitomirsky, "O proshlom bez prikras" (On the Past, Unvarnished), *Sovetskaya
muzïka*, no. 2 (1988): 103. This article was the very first response in the Soviet musical press to
Mikhail Gorbachev's fateful call for "*glasnost'*."

CHAPTER 6

AFTER EVERYTHING

THE TEEMINGLY prolific post-Soviet composer Alfred Schnittke has achieved phenomenal eminence in what may turn out to be a new world order of music. Not since Shostakovich has a composer from the Russian sphere been such a world celebrity as this son of a German-Jewish father and a Volga-German mother, whose first language was that of his parents, and who has lately made a suburb of Hamburg his home.

With such a background, Schnittke would seem to come naturally enough by his fabled eclecticism, yet the reasons for his emergence and his appeal seem nevertheless bound up with the milieu in which he was formed. Aesthetically, if not stylistically, his brand of "postmodernism" is not so far from the Soviet unmodernism of old. Ideas about art that were kept alive under Soviet power by decree, and pronounced dead by the modernist establishment in the West, have reemerged as viable now that both old regimes have collapsed.

On its surface Schnittke's music sounds anything but Soviet. He first became widely known in the West during the 1970s as a shadowy, semiunderground figure who divided his time between writing utilitarian film scores for a livelihood and unperformable masterworks "for the drawer." That romantic aura heavily influenced the early reception of his works, many of which were first performed abroad, and continues to dominate reportage about him in the wake of his voluntary exile. Echoes of the Vienna serialists, of Ligeti, of Stockhausen and Boulez abound in early scores like *Pianissimo* for orchestra, first performed at the august Donaueschingen Festival in 1969. They would have made him out a very conforming composer indeed had he been a Westerner, but coming from a Soviet composer (expected as a matter of Mayakovskian course to express public sentiments *fortissimo*) they were read as scurrilously countercultural.

The phantasmagorial, hour-long First Symphony (1972), first performed in Gorky, later the city of Andrey Sakharov's exile, was a harbinger of Schnittke's famous "polystylistic" manner, now pigeonholed (quite unnecessarily, I think) as postmodern. It is a grim riot of allusion and outright quotation, much of it self-quotation, in which Beethoven jostles Handel jostles Mahler jostles Chaikovsky jostles Johann Strauss, and thence into ragtime and rock, with parts for improvising jazz soloists. Here, too, the smashingly (and crashingly) distinctive Schnittke orchestra first announced itself, an omnivorous combine to which the harpsichord is as essential as the electric bass. All styles and genres are potentially and indiscriminately germane to this musical equivalent of a universal solvent.

Like Mahler, and of course like Ives, Schnittke envisioned the symphony as a musical universe, enfolding all that is or could be within its octopus embrace. But it is not a loving embrace. The Schnittkean Tower of Babel proclaims not universal acceptance but more nearly the opposite, an attitude of cultural alienation in which nothing can claim allegiance. Postmodernism here reduces simply to postism, after-everythingism, it's-all-overism. The symphony comes to rest on a note of desperate irony. A childishly banal violin solo, reminiscent of the crooning *yurodivïy* at the end of *Boris Godunov*, is followed by a reprise of the opening unstructured freakout, finally giving way to a sudden unison C—simplicity itself.

But a simplicity so unearned and perfunctory suggests no resolution, merely dismissal. The world of early Schnittke is Dostoyevsky's world without God, where everything is possible (and nothing matters). Within the administered world of Leninist dogma, where nothing was possible and everything mattered, this was sheer subversion.

The Concerto Grosso no. 1 (1977), the first Schnittke composition to gain a big reputation in the West, propounded things even more graphically. It deploys three distinct stylistic strata—highly disciplined and intensely fiddled neobaroque; amorphous entropic atonal; and syrupy Soviet kitsch, the last banged out on a prepared piano sounding like a cross between the Soviet radio's signature chimes and the beating of ash cans. Guess which one wins in the end. It is a chilling demonstration of "negative dialectics," resolution as degeneracy. It is also terribly funny, but who could miss the blackness of the humor? These early scores were obviously the work of a resentful, marginalized artist. To that extent, at least, they remained securely modernist in attitude.

Yet beneath the surface avant-gardism, Schnittke has at bottom always conformed, for better and for worse, to the customary outlook and manner of a Soviet composer. Since Shostakovich's death in 1975, he has increasingly cast himself—how deliberately one cannot really say—as that great figure's heir and torchbearer, and he has begun to command Shostakovich's huge and loyal following.

Like Shostakovich, Schnittke is very much the public orator. He favors genres with proven mass appeal. By now (1995) there are eight stout symphonies to his credit, and more concertos, perhaps, than any major contemporary has written. His rhetorical manner ranges from grand to grandiose. A half-hour's duration counts as short. The symphonic scores are often so bulky that they have to be printed in condensed form.

The concertos have been written almost as if in collusion with an outstanding generation of late-Soviet soloists, particularly string virtuosos—violinists Mark Lubotsky, Gidon Kremer, and the late Oleg Kagan; violist Yuriy Bashmet; cellist Natalya Gutman—who have taken them around the world. The concentration on the traditionally humanoid, voice-aping strings, so often shunned for just that reason by modernists of an earlier generation, is already a token of Schnittke's orientation. He prizes the heroic subjectivity audiences habitually identify with.

Following the pattern set by the First Concerto Grosso, Schnittkean musical arguments almost always take shape through bald, easily read contrasts. Plush romantic lyricism (at times ironic, as often ingenuous), chants and chorales and hymns (real or ersatz), actual or invented "historical" flotsam (neoclassic, neobaroque, even neomedieval), every make and model of jazz and pop—all of this and more are the ingredients. As they are stirred together, the pot frequently boils over in violent extremes of dissonance: tone clusters (a Schnittke specialty), dense polytonal counterpoint (often in the form of close canons), "verticalized" melodies whereby the notes of a tune are sounded simultaneously as a chord.

Yet however harsh or aggressive or even harrowing, the music never bewilders. Discord, heard always as the opposite or absence of concord, functions as a sign (just as it does in Shostakovich), and so do all the myriad stylistic references.

This "semiotic" or signaling aspect, a traditional characteristic of Russian music, is what makes Schnittke's music so "easily read"—or rather, so easily paraphrased on whatever terms (ethical, spiritual, autobiographical, political) the listener may prefer. Not only do Schnittke's raw materials often carry prefabricated associations, he also packs his music with symbolically recurring sonorities and leitmotifs. These include, again as in Shostakovich, the self-advertising melodic anagram of the composer's name (along with those of favored friends or soloists), as well as such hoary standbys as the B–A–C–H cipher, even (unbelievably) the Dies Irae. No other composer writing today so fearlessly recycles clichés.

The result is socialist realism minus socialism. It implies dramaturgy and aspires, beyond that, to the condition of philosophy, even oracle, meanwhile (unlike most oracles) providing built-in ponies to guarantee comprehension. The music seems ever engaged with the grandest, most urgent, most timeless—hence (potentially) most banal—questions of existence, framed the simplest way possible, as primitive oppositions (though the dialectics are no longer unremittingly negative). With a bluntness and an immodesty practically unseen since the days of Mahler, Schnittke tackles life-against-death, love-against-hate, good-against-evil, freedom-against-tyranny, and (especially in the concertos) I-against-the-world.

When the stakes are raised so high, a composer who can come up with musical matter of sufficient interest and pliancy to sustain the tension of argument over a vast Schnittkean time span can engineer a mighty catharsis indeed. And this is true however the opposing forces appear to play themselves out, whether as tragedy (the Viola Concerto, with its pathetic, brutally quashed attempts at harmonious cadence) or triumph (the Cello Concerto, with its stout hymnodic finale) or, perhaps most affectingly, at some fraught point in between (the Concerto for Piano and Strings, with its vacillating gestures toward a chorale). One who cannot come up with the right notes, of course, will produce the worst sort of bathos. That constant risk is itself riveting.

And here again Schnittke's habits bring Shostakovich's to mind. They share an ascetic predilection for (or a fatal limitation to) homely unprepossessing ideas, just this side (or even that side) of hackneyed, stretched taut (or thin). There seems to be a Tolstoyan conscience at work in their determination not to let the mere notes distract the listener from the meaning, and their unwillingness to let go of an idea until they are sure that every last listener has got the point. It certainly enhances the impression of high ethical purpose, and it also greatly increases the risk of bathos. The wonder of it all, for those receptive to the method, is how often Schnittke, like Shostakovich before him, manages to skirt the pitfall and bring off the catharsis—a catharsis a mere hairbreadth from blatancy and all the more powerful for having braved the risk.

Others will remain unmoved. Black-and-white has never been much of a moral color scheme. The music has violence galore but no sex whatever, and it is still resolutely scaled to the attention span and the reaction time of a Soviet audience. A taste for Schnittke, as for so much Russian music, requires willingness to regard music as a sweaty, warty human document; and even then, listening to one composition after another can lead to the discovery within oneself of surprising reserves of fastidiousness. Yet Schnittke's best scores, like those of Shostakovich, are reminders that the tawdry and the exalted can be near-twins at the opposite extreme from the safe and the sane.

What are the best scores? Those in which the sheer sensory experience of the medium predominates, for this immediacy is Schnittke's saving grace, the surest compensation for his crudeness, his naivety, his square rhythms and noodling ostinatos, his gooey structures. The string concertos are a natural starting point, especially as played by their intended soloists, whose visceral collective voice provided the prototype for Schnittke's musical oratory.

Two of the symphonies are engrossing. The monumental Third (1981), commissioned by the Leipzig Gewandhaus Orchestra, begins with what sounds like Wagner's *Rheingold* prelude cubed and cubed again: a musical motif derived from the natural harmonic series that ascends through a canon in which every single member of the orchestra participates individually. Out of this primal sonic soup emerges a potted history of classical music (second movement, featuring the musical ciphers of thirty-four German composers' names) that is savagely attacked by a division of anarchic rock guitars spewing feedback-distortion (third movement) and sinks back into the ooze, the canon now descending in retrograde (fourth movement). Yet there is hope:

the canon theme comes back one last time in a limpidly harmonized coda piped by an innocent solo flute.

In summary this Pandora's box parable is triteness itself, but what a texture the telling has! Among other richnesses, the Schnittke sound world is saturated with archetypal Russian tintinnabulation, produced not only by the orchestral bells and glockenspiel but by the vibraphone and even the flexatone, normally a child's toy.

And then there is the constantly strumming Schnittkean "continuo" of piano, celesta, harps, harpsichord, Hammond organ, electric guitar, electric bass, and various mallet instruments in ever-changing combos. Its descent from the Schoenberg of *Herzgewaechse* via the Boulez of *Le Marteau sans Maître* and (especially) the Stravinsky of the Requiem Canticles is clear, and very moving in its implied gesture of reconciliation; and its exaggerated presence is superbly palpable, practically tactile.

The continuo contingent comes virtuosically into its own in the Fourth Symphony (1984), actually a sinfonia concertante in the form of a colossal set of variations on three themes, ecumenically representing the Orthodox Slavonic, Roman Catholic, and Protestant liturgies respectively, with a fourth, from the synagogue, as occasional leavening. They are enunciated by a trio of keyboard protagonists (piano, harpsichord, and celesta) that play in perpetual canon at the almost-unison and the almost-octave—an invigorating counterpoint of skewed cross-relations, imaginatively educed from various medieval theories of Eastern and Western chant.

In the turbulent middle of the symphony the contrapuntal dissonances become harmonic clusters, and the writing reaches a crazed intensity that terrifies cathartically the way only rock concerts ordinarily do. In its ecumenical reach and its harsh spirituality the symphony seems a postmodern manifesto, and a masterpiece—until the sentimental letdown at the end, when all the themes are montaged in a treacly conventional choral counterpoint.

In the *glasnost'* days Schnittke was exalted in his native land by audiences hungry for formerly forbidden fruit as a religious moralist who, in the words of one critic, "pitilessly exposes the tragedy of the world in which we live and seeks salvation in God."[1] But I would prefer not to see the religious impulse as primary in his work, because more than anything else it nudges him over the edge into banality and bluster—as in the Second Symphony (1979), an unbearably maudlin six-movement meditation on the Latin Mass, inspired by a visit to the Austrian monastery of St. Florian, where Bruckner had been organist. Yet Schnittke's religious ecstasy seems to derive less from Bruckner than from Messiaen, as witness the Turangalila-like fanfares in the Gloria movement. The saccharine, contrived purity of the choral parts, confined to

---

[1] Lev Nikolayevich Raaben, *Sovetskaya muzïka 60–80 godov, v svete novogo muzïkal'nogo mïshleniya XX veka* (unpublished typescript), p. 384.

real and ersatz Gregorian melodies, descends from there into the lower celestial regions inhabited by the likes of Alan Hovhaness, especially as Schnittke shares Hovhaness's fascination with endless "oriental" melismas noodled snake-charmer fashion by oboes and their bigger brethren.

Yet even this composer's misfires are appealing in their way, because they arise out of something rare and suspect in the reticent and conflicted West, namely moral commitment. Long oppressed by an ideological dictatorship, Schnittke has survived it, and survived his nihilism. He has emerged as an upholder of what another Russian critic calls "eternal moral categories"[2]— just what progressive humanists, in countries where artists risk nothing more than public indifference or the withholding of largesse, are apt to denounce as the sheep's clothing of complacency or worse.

Such a charge will not stick to this composer. Like Shostakovich—like Solzhenitsyn, for that matter—he has earned the right to preach to us. The appeal of his music often lies less in our response to its sound patterns than in our sense of the composer's moral and political plight (and the fragility of his life, if we know about his recent strokes and heart attacks). That empathy, born of historical awareness, lends an extra concreteness, an extra force, to his musical plots and arguments—that is, to the way we construe and value his paraphrase-inviting antitheses and juxtapositions.

That is a double standard, of course, blatantly unfair to many other composers who have homely ideas and overorchestrate egregiously but are not so readily given the benefit of the doubt. But fair or no, it's human—and sanctioned by history. Even after everything, a Russian voice is still special, still privileged. Russia is still different, still other. And Russian music still has the power to define that difference.

---

[2] L. Ivanova, "Ot obryada k èposu," in *Zhanrovo-stilisticheskiye tendentsii klassicheskoy i sovremennoy muzïki* (Leningrad: LGITMiK, 1980), p. 174.

CHAPTER 7

OBJECTIVES

WHAT LINKS the very disparate chapters that follow is the constant, implicit theme that has been the explicit subject of these introductory essays: that of defining Russia musically, along with its converse, defining music Russianly.

National self-definition through music is of course right in the foreground of the trio of essays in part 2, collected under the rubric "Self and Other." I hope, however, that they will serve to complicate rather than simplify the subject or issue of Russian musical "nationalism," and that the complications will clarify. The field is rife with teasers: ironies and paradoxes that are soft-pedaled if not suppressed in conventional, reductive accounts. One of these involves the relationship between patriotism and nationalism. Sometimes, as in the case of Glinka and his first opera, described in chapter 2, the two can be coincident. At other times, as in the case of Rubinstein vs. Balakirev, described in chapter 8, they can be altogether opposed. In that chapter, moreover, a third alternative that is national without being either patriotic or nationalistic is also identified. The powerful irony explored in the chapter is the way in which the internalized other became so much more necessary a component of the actively nationalistic tendency than it had been of the merely "national."

The other in that case was Germany; the chapter shows Russia as an East turning West. The next chapter, a study of "orientalism," shows Russia as a West turning East. In both chapters there is ultimate confusion as to what is self and what is other, since Russia, poised between the unambiguously Western and the unambiguously Eastern, viewing both, and viewed by both, as other, could never locate or define its self unambiguously with respect to either.[1] Therefore, both chapters emerge as antiessentialist cautionary tales. What is "authentic" and what is "representative," in a fashion paralleling the patriotic and the nationalistic, do not necessarily converge. What is "Russian"—hence, too, what is "Western" and what is "Eastern"—can be more reliably gauged on the basis of reception than on the basis of provenance or original intent.

Chapter 10, on musical Russia vs. another "West," namely Italian opera, seems less fraught with ambiguity, at least on the surface. The other here

[1] As a recent example of this dilemma consider the coverage, by the Soviet magazine *Muzïkal'naya zhizn'*, in 1986, of the piano prodigy Yevgeniy Kissin's "Western" debut—in Tokyo.

seems a clear and present threat to self-interest, and the story seems unambiguously one of resistance rather than appropriation. But that is only if one identifies the Russian self only with Russia's musicians. From the standpoint of the Russian state, which of course defined Russian patriotism, things looked rather different, and the story is indeed (and more explicitly than ever) one of appropriation—and of the outright political exploitation of art, one of the overriding, reciprocally defining themes in the history of music as an art in Russia. And yet appropriation and exploitation are never complete; slippage and leakage of meaning—hence contests over meaning and the actual thematization of meaning—are collectively another perennial theme of that history. Russia is one country where there has never been the luxury of unmediated response. There can be no evading hermeneutics when treating art within those heavily patrolled frontiers.

After this initial trio of chapters in which nations are viewed as collective entities confronting other collectivities, the focus of the book seems to narrow, homing, in the time-honored tradition of bourgeois historiography, on individuals. In each case, however, the individual is paired with a general concept that is treated as a specifically Russian manifestation. With Chaikovsky, the "human" theme is related to the special construction the composer put upon the term in the context of Russian absolutist politics. What is often forgotten by historians of art is that by the late nineteenth century "political absolutism" and "Russia" were virtually synonymous terms. Chaikovsky's status as a sort of court musician was an integral part of his identity as (one sort of) Russian musician. The aristocratic, hence (as I maintain) basically preromantic nature of Chaikovsky's art defines that art as Russian; and that art, reciprocally, defines the society and the culture within which it was produced, and which it ardently served, as Russian.

Absolutism and autocracy are visions of an all-encompassing political hierarchy: *singleness* (or as the Russians say, *vseyedinstvo*) on the human plane. Transfer that singleness to the superhuman plane, the transcendent plane to which all that is human is other, and it assumes the aspect of the unknowable Plenitude of Gnostic philosophy, the *pleroma* Scriabin sought to disclose through an art that would by its apocalyptic revelations break the bonds of the phenomenal world and return the inner self to its native realm of light.

This urge to transcend all pluralities was a maximalization of a longstanding, highly characteristic strain of antirationalistic Russian thought going back almost a century to the Russian Schellingians, whose outstanding representative was Prince Odoyevsky—the same Odoyevsky whom we have already encountered as an enthusiastic advocate of Glinka's achievement and whom we shall encounter again as the principal "philosophical" opponent to the Italian opera. Odoyevsky's principle of *tsel'nost'* ("wholeness") lies behind the Slavophiles' *sobornost'* ("commonality" or integral union), which mutates finally into the radical *vseyedinstvo* of the Russian symbolists, many of whom (as reported in chapter 12) thought of Scriabin not only as one of their own but as the best, most potent, and most "essentially Russian" of them all.

As a radical monist Scriabin paid no attention whatever to nations or nationalism. As a theosophist, hostile to all temporal authority, he was no patriot. But only in Russia did such thinking achieve the grandiosity his work exemplifies—indeed, caps. As the culminating representative of Russian philosophical monism in its terminal occultist phase, Scriabin's art, no less than Chaikovsky's, is certifiably the product of a Russian viewpoint and a Russian moment. In its extremism, it contributed resoundingly to Russian cultural self-definition in its time.

Though rarely characterized in national terms,[2] Scriabin's achievement as described and technically explicated here is in agreement with generally accepted accounts of his intentions. Indeed, the explication aims precisely to affirm the link, often treated by analysts and critics as a source of embarrassment, between the composer's intentions and his achievement.

In the case of the young Stravinsky who was Scriabin's contemporary, the artistic product was manifestly, indeed programmatically national. A show of national character, predicated on its reception as exoticism, was the calculated basis of its international appeal. On the surface it was the old Russian ploy of parading Self as Other. (The ironic implications of this masquerade are pursued in chapter 10). And yet in this case the technical explications, particularly of *Svadebka* in the second section of chapter 13, have been aimed at problematizing the easy relationship between impulse and accomplishment that is commonly assumed. Instead of an *heureuse continuité* extending a valued past, such as Stravinsky celebrated (as "tradition") in *Poetics of music*,[3] his "Swiss period" folklorism is treated here as an unforeseen and unforeseeable response to the crisis in Russian self-definition that followed upon the postrevolutionary deracination of the upper-class intelligentsia. The continu-

---

[2] Indeed, it is still a musicographical commonplace to portray Scriabin, gratuitously, as a freak cosmopolite in the ghetto: "Curiously, [!] Skryabin was not himself nationalist in orientation" (Robert P. Morgan, *Twentieth-Century Music* [New York: Norton, 1991], p. 55); "In contrast to Stravinsky, Scriabin's musical language was not rooted in Russian national folk sources but rather in various art-music traditions" (Elliott Antokoletz, *Twentieth-Century Music* (Englewood Cliffs, N.J.: Prentice-Hall, 1991), p. 100; "Skryabin was in many ways atypical of Russian composers and he had no significant followers" (David Fanning, "Russia: East Meets West," in *Music and Society: The Late Romantic Era*, ed. Jim Samson [Englewood Cliffs, N.J.: Prentice-Hall, 1991], p. 198). To be sure, there is also the odd "vindication" restoring him to first-class ghetto status: "The opening melody of [Scriabin's] Study Op. 42 No. 2, based on the minor triad, with its limited range and *nota cambiata* approach to the 5th of the chord, is exactly in the style of a great number of Russian folk songs," etc. (Peter Deane Roberts, *Modernism in Russian Piano Music* [Bloomington: Indiana University Press, 1993], vol. 1, p. 17).

[3] Igor Stravinsky, *Poetics of Music in the Form of Six Lessons*, trans. Arthur Knodel and Ingolf Dahl (New York: Dutton, 1947), p. 74.

ity emphasized here is not that between Stravinsky's late folkloristic music and earlier Russian "nationalisms" but that between the late folkloristic music and the "neoclassical" phase that followed.

The chapters on Shostakovich deal, inescapably, with the problem of art under maladaptive totalitarian conditions. From this standpoint the treatment of Shostakovich may be viewed as complementing that of Chaikovsky, which describes a notably successful adaptation to political conditions that were arguably comparable in stringency if not as spectacularly violent in repression. In both cases it is a specifically Russian oppression that is described, and a particularly Russian response to it. For this reason, I believe that the discussion of Shostakovich offered herein may imply an answer to the tough, enduring question of why the Soviet despotism seemed to stimulate musical richness while other twentieth-century tyrannies, notably the Nazi regime, were musically barren.

It is not just that the Thousand-Year Reich lasted a mere dozen years, while the Soviet state hung on for more than seventy. (But of course there is a modicum of explanation even in that: had the Soviet state lasted only until 1929, it could have claimed no credit at all for Prokofiev; and as of that year only a single significant work by Shostakovich, his First Symphony, had been performed.) It is also that, altogether unlike the composers of Hitler's Germany, the most artistic composers of Stalin's Russia, following a calling that went back long before Stalin (one that Stalin and his cultural minions attempted, but in vain, to coopt to their exclusive purposes), actively engaged with the life around them in a way that only popular culture did by then in the democracies and dictatorships to the west.

The subject requires further research, to be sure, but it seems sufficiently evident that it was precisely the greater "autonomy" of German art—long its glory and its claim to preeminence—that rendered it sterile, merely escapist, under conditions of twentieth-century totalitarianism.[4] Under orders not to be stylistically adventurous but not required to march in step, German music marched off into oblivion. Under much more stringent orders to conform, and actively required to make civic avowals, Russian music (and that of Shostakovich above all, precisely because he was not only the most gifted but also the most bullied) acquired huge public moment and moral authority, and became the basis for a furiously contentious exegetical tradition that shows no sign of letup even after the Soviet collapse. Again, as always, the musical response to Soviet tyranny was a defining moment both for music and for Russia.

[4] See *Colloquium Klassizität, Klassizismus, Klassik in der Musik 1920–1950*, ed. Wolfgang Osthoff and Reinhard Wiesend (Tutzing: Hans Schneider Verlag, 1988); also Wolfgang Osthoff, "Symphonien beim Ende des Zweiten Weltkriegs: Strawinsky—Frommel—Schostakowitsch," *Acta Musicologica* 59 (1987): 62–104.

And again, as always, it is precisely what is special and different about the
Russian experience that makes it so instructive, so illuminating about events
and conditions elsewhere and everywhere. As the first section of chapter 14
will contend at length and attempt to illustrate, the controversies surrounding
Shostakovich's legacy are an ideal crucible for considering and working on
general problems of musical hermeneutics. No other music—none since Beethoven, anyway—so compels recognition of the essential interpretive dilemma, but also the wonderful interpretive opportunity, that musical artifacts present at their most culturally fraught: namely, in Charles Rosen's
well-found words, the dilemma "that some kind of metaphorical description is called for, and even necessary, but . . . none will be satisfactory or
definitive."[5]

The Stravinsky case is an ideal crucible for testing another sort of general
hypothesis, long associated with ethnomusicology (and, in the realm of high
culture, mainly with Theodor W. Adorno) but now widely—and, often, much
too loosely—applied to art-musical texts, namely that modes of musical organization microscopically inscribe modes of social organization. Believing as I
do, first, that this is a hypothesis, not a foundational truth to be merely asserted or assumed; second, that the burden of testing it rests with those who
see the need for it; and third, that those with the best equipment for appre-
hending the inherent logic and meaning of musical texts are apt to be least
likely to see the need for it, I have chosen for this one argument, or at any rate
for a major part of it, the medium of close musical analysis replete with
standard technical jargon. I realize that this approach may excessively try the
patience of some readers to whom the book is otherwise eagerly addressed,
and I hope that the argument is sufficiently corroborated by other, more generally accessible aspects of the discussion. Because the subject matter is tick-
lish, involving a depressingly familiar nexus of "great product and grim prejudice" (in Thomas Hodge's vivid phrase),[6] and saddling a greatly admired
figure with a burden of responsibility that is by no means universally welcomed by his devotees, I thought that I myself had better be particularly
responsible, and avoid any possible air of hit-and-run. The result is a regretta-
bly heavy chapter, perhaps, but at least I can promise that the cards are all on
the table.

The chapters on Chaikovsky and Scriabin also endeavor to reflect a Russian
light on the wider world. The redefinition of "eighteenth-century" aesthetics
so as to subsume Chaikovsky, and the concomitant rejection of the term "classical" to denote a period style or a preromantic aesthetic practice, are tested
against Mozart, partly with the help of Wye J. Allanbrook's excellent study,

---

[5] "Music à la Mode," *New York Review of Books*, 23 June 1994, pp. 59–60.
[6] "The Icon and the Hacks," *New Republic*, 8 August 1994, p. 41.

cited in chapter 11. Similarly, hypotheses about the expressive (or representational) mechanisms of Scriabin's "tonal" and "atonal" practices are tested against Wagner and Schoenberg. If the book succeeds in upholding one of its central theses, that regarding the codependence and inevitable blurring of self-definition and "other-construction," some insight into the selfhood of its "others" may hopefully emerge.

PART II

Self and Other

CHAPTER 8

HOW THE ACORN TOOK ROOT

OF ALL THE musicians of his generation, only Balakirev knew Glinka. They met around Christmas 1855, the eighteen-year-old Wunderkind from Nizhnïy Novgorod having been brought to St. Petersburg by his patron, Alexander Ulïbïshev, the famous lover of Mozart and hater of Beethoven. The boy was being presented chiefly as a piano virtuoso. As a composer he had as yet little to his credit: two unfinished chamber works, a couple of songs, the beginnings of a piano concerto. His magna opera were two pianistic vehicles: the Fantasia on Themes from *A Life for the Tsar*—mainly a transcription in the Lisztian fashion of the act 1 trio "Ne tomi, rodimïy" (Grieve not, beloved)—and the *Grande fantaisie sur airs nationales russes pour le pianoforte avec accompagnement d'orchestre composée et dédiée à son maître Monsieur Charles Eisrich par Mily Balakirev*, Op. 4.[1] These were standard popular fare of the kind that launched any virtuoso's career. It would be rash to attach any great nationalistic significance to them.[2]

And surely no such significance was attached, least of all by Glinka. His historiographical image notwithstanding, Glinka cared little for the *style russe* per se, at least at this late phase of his career (or rather, postcareer, for by 1855 he was no longer composing). Five years earlier he had written to a friend, "I have decided to shut down the Russian song factory and devote the rest of my strength and sight to more important labors."[3] But there were to be

---

[1] Eisrich was Balakirev's piano teacher in Nizhnïy Novgorod; through him the boy had made the personal acquaintance of Ulïbïshev and also his first acquaintance with Glinka's music. It was at a concert directed by Eisrich that Balakirev heard "Ne tomi, rodimïy" and was moved to make his transcription. See A. S. Lyapunova and E. E. Yazovitskaya, *Miliy Alekseyevich Balakirev: Letopis' zhizni i tvorchestva* (Leningrad: Muzïka, 1967), pp. 15–16.

[2] Compare, for example, the *Rondo brilliant* for piano and orchestra, Op. 98, by Hummel (on whose famous septet Balakirev modeled his early octet), composed for a Russian tour in 1822. Its main theme is a Russian folk song, "Zemlyanichka yagodka" (Little Raspberry), which Hummel found in the same source that had served Beethoven for his Rasumovsky quartets, the *Sobraniye narodnïkh russkikh pesen* (1790) of Lvov and Pratsch. In the course of his international career, Hummel was obliged to favor his audiences with variations and rondos on English, Scottish, German, and Dutch tunes, not to mention his Hungarian Dances, Op.23, or his German Dances with Battle Coda, Op. 25. Cf. the worklist by Joel Sachs in *The New Grove Dictionary of Music and Musicians*, ed. Stanley Sadie (London: Macmillan, 1992), vol. 8, pp. 785–88.

[3] Letter to Vasiliy Englehardt, quoted in Boris Asafyev, *Glinka* (Moscow: Muzgiz, 1947), p. 267.

no such projects. According to Vladimir Stasov's testimony, by the time Glinka met the young Balakirev he "was completely immersed in the classics—Bach, Handel, and Gluck."[4] At the beginning of 1855 he had written to the poet Nestor Kukolnik, his best friend, that "if suddenly my muse were to bestir herself, I would write something without text for orchestra; but I'm finished with Russian music, as I am with Russian winters" (like many Russian gentlemen of leisure, Glinka wintered abroad).[5] He was greatly tickled by Balakirev's Fantasia on *A Life for the Tsar* and asked to hear it whenever, in the early months of 1856, its author paid him a visit. But that, obviously, was because it flattered him.[6] There is no record of Balakirev ever having played Glinka his *Grande fantaisie* on folk themes, although he did play him the first movement of his early concerto the moment it was finished. Glinka's sister, Lyudmila Shestakova, recorded her brother's opinions of Balakirev's talent for posterity, and they are couched in terms of general and quite conventional praise—"a brilliant future," "a solid musician," and the like.[7] Twice Glinka gave Balakirev themes to set as compositional exercises, and in both cases the themes were Spanish, not Russian.[8] The young man's success with the first of these assignments occasioned Glinka's greatest encomium: he told his sister that Balakirev would make a good teacher for her daughter, since in him "I have for the first time found views that accord closely with mine in all that concerns music."[9]

Then Glinka went abroad, never to return. And the propagandists took over. In later days, when Balakirev had become an embattled symbol of Russian nationalism in music, the early contact with Glinka was played up for all it was worth. "[Glinka] received Balakirev very warmly as a composer, *especially as a composer of Russian music*," wrote Stasov in 1882; "[he] was not mistaken in seeing in this youth his heir and successor."[10] And a latter-day Balakirev disciple published Glinka's remark about his niece's musical education, with this significant (and evidently fabricated) addition: "Believe me, in

[4] Vladimir Vasilyevich Stasov, *Selected Essays on Music*, trans. Florence Jonas (New York: Praeger, 1967), p. 90.

[5] M. I. Glinka, *Pis'ma i dokumentï* (*Literaturnoye naslediye*, vol. 2) (Leningrad: Muzgiz, 1953), p. 509.

[6] "Ne tomi, rodimïy," it might well be noted, was by no means among the most obviously "national" numbers in *A Life for the Tsar*, anyway. As already observed in chapter 2, it is cast in the style of a *bïtovoy romans*, or salon romance, of a type very popular in Russia in the early nineteenth century, but of miscegenated Russo-Italian character. For more on the style of such pieces, see "'Little Star': An Étude in the Folk Style," in R. Taruskin, *Musorgsky: Eight Essays and an Epilogue* (Princeton: Princeton University Press, 1993), pp. 38–70.

[7] Lyapunova and Yazovitskaya, *Miliy Alekseyevich Balakirev*, pp. 24–25.

[8] The first was the basis for Balakirev's *Fandango-Étude* for piano, completed 14 February 1856; the second was given to Balakirev on Glinka's departure from St. Petersburg on 26 April of that year, and became the basis for the orchestral Overture on a Spanish March Theme (1857).

[9] Lyapunova and Yazovitskaya, *Miliy Alekseyevich Balakirev*, p. 30.

[10] Stasov, *Selected Essays on Music*, p. 90. Italics added.

time he will be a second Glinka."[11] These testimonials, which cast Balakirev in the role of ordained prophet of the Russian national school, reflect faithfully the turbulent milieu of Russian musical politics in the later nineteenth century, but they seriously distort the relationship between master and disciple in the light of subsequent events.

The first such event was the first major piece Balakirev composed after Glinka's death. The Overture on the Themes of Three Russian Folk Songs (usually abbreviated as the Overture on Russian Themes) was, according to the autograph of its earliest version, "begun on 19 September 1857 in St. Petersburg" and "finished in Zamanilovka at Shestakova's dacha on 26 June 1858."[12] Conceived as it were within the bosom of the Glinka circle, the overture was tribute to the memory of the great man, in the form of an equally deliberate emulation (the *mot juste* would be the Russian *ótklik*, combining response, comment, and echo) of Glinka's Fantasia for Orchestra on the Themes of a Wedding Song and a Dance Song, entitled *Kamarinskaya* (1848).

This is the work that is known to all the world as a paradigm—perhaps *the* paradigm—of burgeoning Russian nationalism in music. Chaikovsky wrote of it, in a phrase that has become a dogma, that the Russian symphonic school was "all in *Kamarinskaya*, just as the whole oak is in the acorn."[13] A Soviet musicologist has meticulously traced the genetic evolution of that oak in a volume of some five hundred pages.[14] And yet, while the historical significance of the work is every bit as great as these testimonials would indicate, Chaikovsky's simile does not seem quite right. For it suggests a spontaneous, natural germination, while the growth of the *Kamarinskaya* tradition was very much a cultivation, carefully tended and pruned in its initial stages by Balakirev, both as composer and, later, as leader of his circle. The differences between *Kamarinskaya* and the responses to it by the Balakirev school are an instructive measure of the difference between national and nationalist art.

KAMARINSKAYA was one of three *Fantaisies pittoresques* for orchestra that Glinka wrote under the spell of Berlioz and his music, whose acquaintance he had made in Paris in 1844–45. The other two—*Jota aragonesa* and *Recuerdos de Castilla*, better known as *Souvenir d'une nuit d'été à Madrid*—were, as was so typical of Glinka's predilections, of Spanish national charac-

---

[11] Grigoriy Timofeyev, "M. A. Balakirev," in *Russkaya mïsl'* (1912), quoted in Edward Garden, *Balakirev* (New York: St. Martin's Press, 1967), p. 31.

[12] E. L. Frid, "Simfonicheskoye tvorchestvo," in *Miliy Alekseyevich Balakirev: Issledovaniya i stat'i* (Leningrad: Muzgiz, 1961), p. 93.

[13] Diary entry, 27 June 1888. Quoted in David Brown, *Mikhail Glinka: A Biographical and Critical Study* (London: Oxford University Press, 1974), p. 1.

[14] Viktor Tsukkerman, *"Kamarinskaya" Glinki i yeyo traditsii v russkoy muzïke* (Moscow: Muzgiz, 1957).

ter. Clearly it was nationality, not nativism, that mattered to Glinka, as to so many artists of the early and mid-nineteenth century—including, notably, Berlioz himself, with his *Marche hongroise* and his *Carnaval romain*. Native or foreign, it was the color that mattered, not the country of origin. What was important was that themes be "characteristic," that they embody what Glinka called "positive data" (*polozhitel'nïye dannïye*),[15] and strong national coloring was a convenient way of achieving this. The situation was hardly different from what it had been in the eighteenth century or even much earlier: local color as a minor musical species providing minor musical thrills. The only thing to set the early nineteenth century apart was the greater frequency of its use, particularly in opera. But that reflected above all a change in the nature of operatic plots, settings, and characters. In instrumental contexts, national coloring was merely *pittoresque*, to use Glinka's word, an exotic element (even if native) approached simply as the source of musical enjoyment, devoid of programmatic or symbolic content. This was as true of Glinka's Russian *fantaisie* as it was of his Spanish pair. On this point he was quite explicit in his memoirs:

> At that time [i.e., while in Warsaw in 1848], I noticed quite by accident a kinship between the wedding song "From Beyond the Mountains High" [*Iz-za gor, gor vïsokikh, gor*], which I used to hear in the country, and the dance song "Kamarinskaya," which everybody knows. And all at once my imagination took fire, and . . . I wrote a piece for orchestra under the title "A Wedding Song and a Dance Song." I can assure the reader that I was guided in composing this piece solely by my innate musical feeling, thinking neither of what goes on at weddings, nor of how our orthodox populace goes about celebrating, nor of how a drunk might come home late and knock on the door so that he might be let in.[16]

The point of *Kamarinskaya*, then, was not a portrayal of Russian life or a celebration of Russian folklore but a pretext for brilliant orchestration built around a kind of abstract musical pun. Glinka did not start out by looking for some Russian themes on which to base an orchestral fantasy; they came to him unbidden—they found him, as it were. The "kinship" or hidden relationship between the two themes that prompted the composition of the work is set out in example 8.1.[17] The notes marked with asterisks in the dance song (most

---

[15] Cf. Glinka to Kukolnik, 8/18 April 1845: "In Spain I will set to work on my proposed [orchestral] *fantaisies*—the originality of the local melodies there will be of significant help to me, the more so as . . . my unbridled imagination needs a text or some positive data" (Glinka, *Pis'ma i dokumentï*, p. 276).

[16] M. I. Glinka, "Zapiski" (Memoirs), in *Polnoye sobraniye sochiveniy: Literaturnïye proizvedeniya i perepiska*, vol. 1 (Moscow: Muzïka, 1973), p. 333. The reference to the drunk alludes to the way the critic Feofil Tolstoy (Rostislav) had sought to "explain" the repeated-note brass figures at rehearsal nos. 12 and 13 to the Empress Alexandra.

[17] The source of the wedding song "Iz-za gor, gor vïsokikh" is Glinka's own notation in his memoirs. The traditional dance song "Kamarinskaya" was in widespread dissemination.

of them in strong, conspicuous rhythmic positions) correspond with the first six notes of the wedding song.

It is tempting to speculate on how this resemblance first occurred to Glinka. "Kamarinskaya" is one of a well-defined group of Russian folk *naigrïshi*, or instrumental dance tunes. These typically consist of a short (often three-measure) phrase repeated ad infinitum as the basis and framework for an open-ended series of extemporized variations, played by wedding bands, or simply by a *muzhik* on a balalaika or a concertina, to accompany a strenuous and often competitive type of male dancing (*v prisyadku*, in a squat) well known in the West as "typically Russian," thanks to its exportation by professional folk-dance ensembles (see figure 8.1).[18] The principle of ostinato, so important in Russian art music, stems from these dance-until-you-drop *naigrïshi*.[19] As we know from the recollections of his contemporaries, Glinka was fond of emulating the practices of wedding bands by improvising accompaniments to the "Kamarinskaya" tune, seated at the piano, accompanied by a partner, Chopsticks-fashion. Stasov, for one, reported that he "would keep on playing the tune for him at the top of the piano, and often asked him to repeat this or that variation (the last or next-to-last) which he had played to us. But

EXAMPLE 8.1. Folk themes in Glinka's *Kamarinskaya*

a. Wedding song

Iz - za gor, gor vï - so - kikh gor

b. Dance song, "Kamarinskaya"

ad infinitum, with perpetual variation

[18] An interesting selection of *naigrïshi* transcribed by various folklorists is given in Tsukkerman's book (see n. 14), pp. 92–111. A striking field recording of a wedding band extemporizing at full tilt on a *naigrïsh* called *Timon' ya* (a close relative of the tune Glinka used) may be heard in the set *Muzykal' nïy fol'klor narodov SSSR*, issued in conjunction with the VII International Music Congress in Moscow, 1971 (Melodiya D-030833–36).

[19] And as I have shown elsewhere, the Dance of the Earth in *The Rite of Spring* is also based on a *naigrïsh*. See my "Russian Folk Melodies in *The Rite of Spring*," *Journal of the American Musicological Society* 33 (1980), esp. pp. 533–43.

Figure 8.1. Two views of the "Kamarinskaya" dance from nineteenth-century
Russian woodcuts (*lubki*). From Tsukkerman, *"Kamarinskaya" Glinki*
(Moscow, 1957), pp. 353, 369

INTRODUCTION	WEDDING SONG	TRANSITION	DANCE SONG	WEDDING SONG *(reminiscence)*	TRANSITION	DANCE SONG *(reprise)*	CODA
Based on motive y	Four repetitions; a. all 'unisono b. melody plus accompaniment c. and d. theme in bass	Based on x as bass to y	Ostinato variations: 30 × 3 measures with retransition to wedding song	Two repetitions, plus a third, interrupted	Based on z	Ostinato variations: 12 × 3 measures + 31 × 3 measures	Fragmentation of the dance song
d $i \rightarrow VI(B\flat)$	F: begins with IV ($B\flat$)	d $iv_6 \rightarrow V$	D	F	$d \rightarrow B\flat$ (cf. introduction)	$B\flat$: $I \rightarrow vi$ (+ added sixth) D: $ii^0{}_3^4 \rightarrow V \rightarrow I$	D

DIAGRAM 8.1. Glinka, *Kamarinskaya*, form diagram

often he had already forgotten them, and instead of these, his fantasy invented still more new ones—without end."[20] Perhaps it was while thus diverting himself one day that Glinka unexpectedly found himself playing "Iz-za gor, vïsokikh gor," a tune he had long known and loved, as we know because he had previously incorporated it into his "Wedding Song" to a text by Rostopchina (1839).[21]

The way Glinka's orchestral fantasy is constructed out of the two songs is summarized in diagram 8.1. The two themes are first given in stark contrast, like a conventional introduction and allegro. But all at once, right in the middle of things, the fast theme is magically transformed into the slow one, by means of the progressive revelation of their "kinship," as demonstrated in example 8.1. It is an admirably executed maneuver, which extends over thirty-one measures, beginning at rehearsal no. 6 in the score. Its main events are summarized in example 8.2.

This feature, along with the virtuosic handling of its rather modest orchestra, has earned *Kamarinskaya* its well-deserved reputation for masterly craftsmanship. Less often noted but perhaps even more remarkable is the way Glinka derived his introductory and transitional passages from the melody of the wedding song by extracting motives from it. There are three of these, labeled *x*, *y*, and *z* in example 8.1, and each of them is exploited at some point for transitional and modulatory purposes. The opening is built entirely on a sequential treatment of *y*, which is led to a surprising conclusion on $B\flat$. This prepares, at short range, the first downbeat harmony of the wedding song (see example 8.3a). At the long range it is even more meaningful, as we shall see.

[20] Quoted in Brown, *Mikhail Glinka*, p. 273.

[21] This song is also known as "Northern Star" (*Severnaya zvezda*). The version of the folk tune in it, though in a different key, is note-for-note identical to the one in *Kamarinskaya* and was evidently the source for the latter.

EXAMPLE 8.2. Glinka, *Kamarinskaya*, transition to the wedding song after figure 6

EXAMPLE 8.3. Motivic derivations in Glinka's *Kamarinskaya*

a.

EXAMPLE 8.3, *continued*

The transition from the wedding song to the dance song is effected by a neat contrapuntal juxtaposition of motives *x* and *y* (example 8.3b). And note how the B♭ of the introduction is taken up again here by means of motive *x* and resolved to the dominant of the key of the dance song. The tonal progression is in fact a projection of the wedding song incipit. The last time *x* is sounded (in the bass), it is limited to three notes, the resolving A being withheld; twice the motive is reiterated in this guise, and then the resolution is made through an interpolated lower neighbor, G. This double-neighbor progression in the bass is then transformed chromatically to furnish the little turn figure that introduces the dance song—another instance of the tightly coordinated interplay of melodic and harmonic events.

The most significant of these events takes place in the next transitional passage—the retransition back to the dance song after the reprise of the wedding song. Here Glinka uses motive *z* to lead to an F, which is then provided with another turn figure, derived from the same motive (see example 8.3c). This identifies the F immediately as the opening note of the dance song and therefore as the fifth of the tonic scale. A modulation has thus been achieved with marvelous economy to the unexpected (but, as we have seen, hardly unprepared) key of B♭. The reprise of the dance song having been made in the twice-adumbrated key of the flat submediant, the final triumphant return to D major is effected by the same bass resolution we observed previously in example 8.3b, derived from the incipit of the wedding song, *x* (see example 8.3d).

The underlying tonal progression that lends contrast and a heightened structural unity to the dance song variations is thus shown to be structured around the opening motive of the wedding song. Here is a hidden "kinship," indeed! Such a thorough interpenetration of melodic and harmonic structures is the kind of thing one is used to finding (and therefore seeking) in Beethoven, perhaps, but hardly in the work of provincial autodidacts. The fact that the themes on which this elegant construction was based happened to be Russian folk tunes, it should be clear by now, was a secondary characteristic of the work, in terms of both its conception (as reported by Glinka in his memoirs) and its execution (as revealed in the foregoing discussion).

Yet *Kamarinskaya* was a watershed in the history of musical folklorism for all that. For it took not only the whole of its thematic material from folklore but also, to an unprecedented degree, its structural modus operandi. The three-measure *naigrïsh* motive is repeated without significant structural change some seventy-five times in the course of the two sections that are based on it. What changes is the "background," to use the term often found in the critical literature: kaleidoscopically shifting instrumental colors, harmonizations, countermelodies. *Kamarinskaya*, almost as if by accident, accomplished the feat of creating for itself a novel formal procedure both original and "organic," and one, moreover, hardly at all indebted to "German" symphonic methods. The significance of the work, which far outstripped its composer's modest intentions, lay precisely here, in its fortuitous yet symbiotic fusion of national thematic material and sui generis (or to put it as Herder might, *urwüchsige*) form. For writers like Stasov, it became the very paradigm of *svoyeobraznost'*, a Slavophile term roughly equivalent to Herder's *Urwüchsigkeit*, which became a critical watchword among champions of the Russianness of Russian music and of the Balakirev school.

But *svoyeobraznost'* has its price: it is by definition unrepeatable. It is obvious that the special features that made Glinka's fantasy a masterpiece belonged to it alone, and could not be appropriated except in a patently epigonal way. So when Balakirev came to render homage at its shrine, he wrote a piece that differed from *Kamarinskaya* as significantly as it resembled it. And the differences had largely to do with reconciling Glinka's innovatory procedures with the canons of "German symphonism."

THERE IS considerable irony in this, since what made Balakirev and his circle a truly nationalist phenomenon lay in large part in their principled opposition to musical "Germanism," as embodied chiefly in the person and activities of Anton Rubinstein and in the organizations he founded, the Russian Musical Society and the St. Petersburg Conservatory (established in 1862). Rubinstein, a virtuoso of international fame and a composer of German schooling, saw the future of Russian music in terms of professionalization under the sponsorship of the aristocracy and the stewardship of imported teachers and virtuosos. In the same year that Balakirev met Glinka, Rubinstein had published an article in the Vienna *Blätter für Theater, Musik und Kunst* called "Russian Composers," in which he first outlined this Peter the Great–like program for Russian music and first hinted at his lifelong equation of Russian musical nationalism with dilettantism, even in Glinka.[22] Although even Rubinstein's worst enemies recognized his patriotic motives,[23] and although it was also universally acknowledged that Rubinstein, both as lobbyist and as role model, was largely responsible for creating the social and institutional means through which a professional musical life might flourish in Russia, his words met with a chorus of indignation. In this chorus Russian composers insulted by his remarks, including both the aging Glinka and the youthful Balakirev, were

[22] Cf. Lev Aronovich Barenboim, *Anton Grigoryevich Rubinshteyn*, vol. 1 (Leningrad: Muzgiz, 1957), pp. 181–84. These sentiments were echoed and even intensified in Rubinstein's notorious squib "On Music in Russia," written for home consumption and published in January 1861 as propaganda for the conservatory. Cf. Barenboim, *Anton Grigoryevich Rubinshteyn*, pp. 236–39.

[23] Cf. Stasov, *Selected Essays on Music*, pp. 82–84.

joined by all manner of nationalists and Slavophiles who were particularly vocal in Russia at just this moment, thanks to the Crimean War. It may be said with some justice, therefore, that Russian musical nationalism, as a self-conscious artistic tendency, was touched off by this article by a musician for whom music was "a *German* art," and in whose opinion "a deliberately national art . . . cannot claim universal sympathy [but] awakens an ethnographical interest at best."[24]

The leaders of the anti-Rubinstein backlash were Stasov and Balakirev, the former assuming the role of public propagandist,[25] the latter that of musical functionary and educator. It was in the spirit of opposition to the German-dominated professionalization of St. Petersburg musical life, with its strong aristocratic and establishmentarian underpinning, that Balakirev gathered around him his famous "little band" of musical mavericks and autodidacts, and joined forces with Gavriyil Lomakin to organize the Free Music School as a rival and an alternative to both the Russian Musical Society and the Conservatory at once.[26] And it was no doubt partly in a spirit of rejoinder to Rubinstein's views on the inevitable immaturity and provincialism of national instrumental music that Balakirev wrote his Overture on Russian Themes of 1858 in precisely the way he did.

Unlike Glinka, Balakirev did go looking for his themes; the determination to write a symphonic work on Russian folk songs preceded the specific embodiment. The three songs he chose were all available by 1857 in published anthologies (this had not been true of the themes in *Kamarinskaya*), and this, presumably, was where Balakirev sought and found them. Example 8.4 shows the three themes as they first appear in the overture.[27] The criteria for

---

[24] Anton Rubinstein, *Muzïka i yeyo predstaviteli* (Moscow: P. Jurgenson, 1891), pp. 40, 83–84.

[25] See especially his vociferous answer to Rubinstein's "On Music in Russia," entitled "A Conservatory in Russia" (*Konservatoriya v Rossii*), which appeared in the conservative paper *Severnaya pchela* on 24 February 1861. Some extracts are given in Stasov, *Selected Essays on Music*, pp. 82–83.

[26] For details of the Rubinstein-Balakirev rivalry, see Robert C. Ridenour, *Nationalism, Modernism, and Personal Rivalry in Nineteenth-Century Russian Music* (Ann Arbor: UMI Research Press, 1981), chapter 4.

[27] Theme I, *Bïlina (Pesnya pro Dobrïnyu)*: Mikhail Stakhovich, *Sobraniye russkikh narodnïkh pesen*, vol. 3 (Moscow: M. Bernard, 1854), no. 1: "A white birch bends toward the ground, where the grass lies silky . . ." Also used by Grechaninov in the opera *Dobrïnya Nikitich*.

Theme II, *Khovorod* (ceremonial dance): Lvov and Pratsch, *Sobraniye narodnïkh russkikh pesen* (St. Petersburg: Top. Gornago uchilishcha, 1790), no. 62. "A birch tree stood in the field, all leafy it stood . . ." Also used by Fomin in *Yamshchiki na podstave*, Glinka in the Tarantella for Piano, Chaikovsky in the finale of the Symphony no. 4, and Grechaninov in the Russian Folk Dances, Op. 130.

Theme III, dance tune: Daniyil Kashin, *Russkiye narodnïye pesni*, part 3 (Moscow: Selivanovsky, 1834), no. 98. "Quite early last evening I sat down to a feast, a merry get-together . . ." Also used in the fourth tableau of *Petrushka*.

EXAMPLE 8.4. Folk songs in Balakirev's Overture on Russian Themes (1858)

their selection are obvious, if one knows *Kamarinskaya*, and show how se-
dulously Balakirev sought to model his work on Glinka's. The overture is set
in a slow-fast introduction-and-allegro scheme corresponding to that of
Glinka's "Wedding Song and Dance Song." Moreover, the pair of tunes that
together constitute the thematic material of the central allegro, though they are
finished and symmetrically structured melodies rather than *naigrïshi*, are both
built up out of three-measure rhythmic periods exactly analogous to the "Kamarinskaya" motive (these are indicated with brackets in example 8.4). This
enabled Balakirev to achieve a headlong ostinato character just as unremitting
as Glinka's—in fact more so, since there is no interrupting return to the slow
tempo; instead, the slow theme returns briefly at the end as a reprise, rounding
the composition off with a whiff of nostalgia and a suggestion of ternary form.
The body of the overture consists of a span of some 360 measures, expressed
in the form of 120 three-bar ostinato cells (mostly grouped further into six-
or twelve-bar units corresponding to the structure of the themes: cf. diagram 8.2 on page 130).

The tonal plan of the overture reflects *Kamarinskaya* as unmistakably as
does its rhythmic structure. The same tonal areas are used in the fast central
portions of both works (if we discount the return to the slow tempo in
Glinka's, which, as we have seen, has no direct counterpart in the overture):
two sharps, with a central modulatory swing to two flats. Balakirev's retransition, moreover, is based on a sequential extension of the bass $\flat\hat{6}$–$\hat{5}$ progression that had been so strikingly employed by Glinka: compare examples 8.5a
and 8.3d.

As to differences, the most obvious of them also turns out to be the crucial
one. Balakirev's piece makes use of *three* folk tunes, where Glinka had used
only two. A glance at the keys of Balakirev's allegro themes reveals the reason. In B minor and D major respectively, they are the first and second themes
of a sonata design, the very format Glinka had so resourcefully skirted in
Kamarinskaya. Just how the sonata-allegro form is overlaid to the ostinato
procedure derived from *Kamarinskaya* is shown in diagram 8.2. Key relations
are the usual ones: the second theme comes back in the tonic major in the
recapitulation, preparing the way for the reprise of the introduction; the development is the pretext for the excursion into Glinka's flat submediant.

The interesting problem was how to achieve a sense of developing form out
of a procedure as static and sectional as ostinato. So attention is particularly
drawn to the unstable sections: the bridges, transitions, and of course the
development. At least three techniques can be identified, all of them with
ample precedent in *Kamarinskaya*. One is the kind of sequential harmonic
pattern, often accompanied by syncopation that slightly blurs the three-bar
rhythmic units, already illustrated by example 8.5a. Another is the extraction
of motives from the themes. There is only one full-fledged example of this in

EXAMPLE 8.5. Motivic derivations in the Overture on Russian Themes

a.

b.

Allegro energico

EXAMPLE 8.5, *continued*

EXAMPLE 8.5, *continued*

the overture, but it is far more systematically deployed than anything in *Kamarinskaya*, in keeping with Balakirev's general expansion of form over that of his model. From the first eight notes of the allegro's first theme, Balakirev derives a motive, *x*, out of which he constructs a fanfarelike "preface" that opens the overture, preceding the introduction proper (example 8.5b). This motive and its immediate extensions provide Balakirev with very pliant material for use in the development section (the passage cited in example 8.5a is in fact derived from the extensions). In another guise, minus the repeated notes, it forms the exquisite "dissolve" by which the allegro gives way to the coda (i.e., the reprise of the slow introduction). Here, moreover, we encounter a unique motivic expansion of the third phrase of the allegro's second theme, labeled *y* in example 8.5c.

The remaining technique is that of contrapuntal juxtaposition of themes and motives. The one significant instance of this in *Kamarinskaya* has been given in example 8.3b. In Balakirev's overture there are many more, some of them quite clever. In the retransition, fragments of both allegro themes are combined over a dominant pedal (example 8.5d). And somewhat later, in the course of the recapitulation, the two halves of the first theme are telescoped (example 8.5e).

Balakirev's Overture on Russian Themes can thus be viewed as a kind of principled advance over his model both as regards sheer dimensions and as regards symphonic character and procedure. The paradoxical aspect it seems to present in its apparent rapprochement with German convention falls away if seen in the context of the historical moment. In its symphonic aspects the overture can be seen as an attempt to beat Rubinstein at his own game, or at

Allegro energico: "PREFACE" **Andante: INTRODUCTION**

Th. I: Three statements with varying harmonization

B (ends on V) B

Allegro [ostinato]: EXPOSITION

First theme	*Bridge*	*Second theme*	*Codetta*
Th. II: five repetitions	Th. II, modified	Th. III: two statements	Th. II and III juxtaposed
b	b → D b: i → vi (g) D: iv → V → iv$_4^6$	D	b/D → g

DEVELOPMENT

Reprise of "preface"	Th. II	"Preface" material (from x)	*Retransition* Contrapuntal combination of II and III
B♭*	g ⤳ D♭		Dominant pedal (F♯) †
		IV of D♭ → V C: VI♭ → V b: VI → V	

RECAPITULATION

First theme	*Second theme*	*Transition*
Th. II *ff*, then three varied repetitions	Th. III in tonic major, then relative major	Extension of III (y) over x in bass
b	B D	→ V of B

CODA: Andante

Reprise of Th. I

B

*new key signature †original key signature reinstated

DIAGRAM 8.2. Balakirev, Overture on Russian Themes (1857–58), form diagram least to demonstrate that Russian national character need imply no loss of scale or of technical sophistication—precisely what Glinka had demonstrated for opera in *A Life for the Tsar*. The work, moreover, may be seen as a conscious attempt to lay the cornerstone of a "school," something Glinka manifestly was *not* trying to do in *Kamarinskaya*. So where Glinka had aimed at nothing higher than a musical witticism, albeit the witticism of an inspired and masterly craftsman, Balakirev needed to aim at a statement of manifest "importance." And where Glinka could afford to indulge himself with a work that was sui generis in every particular, Balakirev was attempting to establish a genre, and that meant observing and handing down conventions.

But however all that may be, Balakirev's overture was still a work based on, and appealing to, "innate musical feeling," as Glinka had written of *Kamarinskaya*. There was still no hint of a program; the national character remained a purely stylistic phenomenon. As a somewhat lengthy parenthesis, more or less the same might be said of the three fairly lumpish *Fantaisies pittoresques* for orchestra that Glinka's brilliant response to Berlioz elicited as response in turn from Alexander Dargomïzhsky. All of them bear comparison to *Kamarinskaya*: they are all in introduction-and-allegro format, and they all incorporate national material, two of them native. The "jocular fantasy" (*fantaziya-shutka*) *Baba Yaga* (1862), subtitled "From the Volga to Riga," (*S Volgi nach Riga*), bears no real program, despite the titular reference to the traditional Russian witch. The idea of her flight is merely the pretext for a musical travelogue that takes us from the heart of Russia, over land and sea, to the German-speaking Baltic capital—geographical stages represented by the famous slow folk song "Vniz po matushke po Volge" (Downstream on Mother Volga), the very one Glinka had already used, far more imaginatively, to carry the dramatic turning point in *A Life for the Tsar*; by ostinato variations on a Smolensk tune, "Ukazhi mne, mati, kak belïy len slati" (Show Me, Mother Dear, How to Spread Linen), suitably provided with some weird "empirical" harmonies and strained orchestral effects to depict the Baba Yaga on her broomstick; and by the *bürgerliche Lied*, "Anna-Maria, so gehst du doch hin." Stylistic contrasts, amounting to incongruities, provide what jocularity there is to be found in this inept and disjointed piece. It was an idea Glinka had thoroughly exploited, and far more seriously, in *A Life for the Tsar*, with its Russian and Polish scenes and confrontations. Dargomïzhsky's *Kazachok* (1864), subtitled "Fantasia on the Theme of a Little-Russian Dance," is an out-and-out copy of *Kamarinskaya* of which the main section, an allegretto, is a set of ostinato variations on a Ukrainian *naigrïsh*. Like *Kamarinskaya* a "changing background" piece, it nonetheless fails to generate, much less maintain, a comparable level of musical momentum, owing largely to the fact that the *naigrïsh* on which it is based is a phrase of two-plus-two measures, lending the variations a deadly foursquareness of design from which Dargomïzhsky had not the resources of harmonic or instrumental invention to rescue it.[28] The Finnish Fantasy (*Chukhonskaya fantaziya*, 1867) was written later and is a more accomplished piece than the other two. Its thematic material, however, is non-Russian, showing Dargomïzhsky to have shared Glinka's fairly indiscriminate predilections where national character was concerned.

But none of Dargomïzhsky's overtures had anything to contribute to the growth of a nationalist school. They are essays in musical comedy and "low" style, aesthetically akin to the realistic genre romances of Dargomïzhsky's late years. From the crucial point of view of craft and professionalism they can bear comparison neither with Glinka nor with Balakirev. They are the work of an amiable "gentry" dilettante, the very epitome of what is meant by a "regional" composer, and could only add grist to Rubinstein's ideological mill. Yet however dubious their merits, Dargomïzhsky's fantasias, along with the works by Glinka and Balakirev that we have examined, constituted the whole repertoire of "Russian" orchestral music as of 1864.

IN THAT year Balakirev's second Overture on Russian Themes appeared, a work that marked as great an advance over his first in formal scope and symphonic procedure as the first had marked over *Kamarinskaya*. At the same time it exhibited a far greater determination on the composer's part to purify the national character of his style. In their symbiosis these two traits marked a new stage in the emergence of oak from acorn and led inevitably to a genuine sense of programmatic content in the music. All three elements were profoundly and complexly interrelated, and in their interrelationship added a new ideological dimension to the concept of musical nationalism—one far more deserving of the name than any previous one had been.

In the years immediately following the composition of the first overture, Balakirev had made a close study of Russian folk song with an eye toward its creative exploitation. Dissatisfied with the quality of existing published collections, and perhaps stimulated by the recent collecting and editing efforts of the so-called *pochvenniki* ("men of the soil"), Balakirev made his own collecting expedition along the Volga in the summer of 1860.[29] The songs he then collected were issued in his epoch-making volume of forty arrangements, the *Sbornik russkikh narodnïkh pesen* of 1866.

From the point of view of incipient musical nationalism the most significant aspect of the collection was the technique of harmonization Balakirev worked out. He sought and found a method that preserved, more faithfully than any previous one, two particular aspects of the folk original: the diatonic purity of

---

[28] *Kazachok* may even have taken a leaf from Balakirev's first overture; its slow introduction is preceded by a fast flourish.

[29] For a consideration of the *pochvennik* collectors and their impact on art music, see R. Taruskin, *Opera and Drama in Russia*, 2d ed. (Rochester: University of Rochester Press, 1994), chapter 4.

the minor mode—both the natural minor and what Balakirev christened the "Russian" minor, the Dorian mode as popularly conceived—and the quality of tonal "mutability" (*peremennost'*), as it is called, whereby a tune seemed to oscillate between two equally stable points of rest, as it were two "tonics." The latter often coincided with the common-practice relationship of tonic to relative minor or major (cf. the tonal relationships in the exposition of the first overture); but just as often it involved the lower neighbor to the tonic in the minor mode, what common practice defined as the flat seventh. In almost all prior collections of folk songs, and in most art music based on folk tunes, these features had been obscured by the use of the harmonic minor and of secondary dominants. Both these devices Balakirev virtually banished from his harmonizations.[30]

The first fruit of Balakirev's collecting and harmonizing activity was not the publication of 1866, however, but the second Overture on Russian Themes. Like the first overture it employed three folk songs, but this time they were all songs the composer had personally collected. Example 8.6 gives the tunes as harmonized in the 1866 anthology, along with a fourth theme used in the overture, which Balakirev had composed himself while vacationing in the Caucasus in the summer of 1863.[31]

Although—and this should be emphasized—the harmonic style of these settings was Balakirev's personal invention, it is instantly recognizable to us today as generically "Russian," thanks to its thorough assimilation into the later compositional practice not only of Balakirev himself but that of his followers Rimsky-Korsakov, Musorgsky, and Borodin, not to mention such postkuchkist epigones as Glazunov, Lyadov, and Lyapunov. The most immediately striking characteristic is the avoidance of dominant harmony—this at a time when advanced Western (read: Wagnerian) harmonic practice was based on ever more emphatic dominant prolongations. The setting of theme I (in "Russian," or Dorian minor), on which Balakirev based the slow introduction of his second overture, is particularly resolute in this regard. The low Cs of the melody are all harmonized with minor V chords, and the final cadence invokes the major IV. Also noteworthy is the articulation of the chordal

---

[30] For illustration of these points, and for further detail on Balakirev's harmonic practice after 1860, see Taruskin, "Little Star,"pp. 57–68.

[31] I (introduction): *Svadebnaya* (wedding song) from the Nizhnïy Novgorod guberniya, Knyaginsky district; *Sbornik russkikh narodnïkh pesen, sostavlennïy M. A. Balakirevïm*, no. 1. "There was no wind, then all of a sudden it blew . . ."

II (first theme): *Khorovodnaya* (round dance) from the Samara guberniya, Stavropol district; *Sbornik*, no. 2. "I'm off to Constantinople . . ."

III (second theme): *Khorovodnaya* from Pramzin in the Simbirsk guberniya; *Sbornik*, no. 22. "Merry Kate, brown-eyed Kate, dance round the room, stamp your little feet . . ."

IV (closing theme): original tune, transcribed from the score. Balakirev's authorship is attested by a presentation inscription to Stasov; see Frid, "Simfonicheskoye tvorchestvo," p. 140.

EXAMPLE 8.6. Themes from Balakirev's second Overture on Russian Themes (1863–64). Reproduced from his anthology *Sbornik russkikh narodnïkh pesen* (St. Petersburg, 1866)

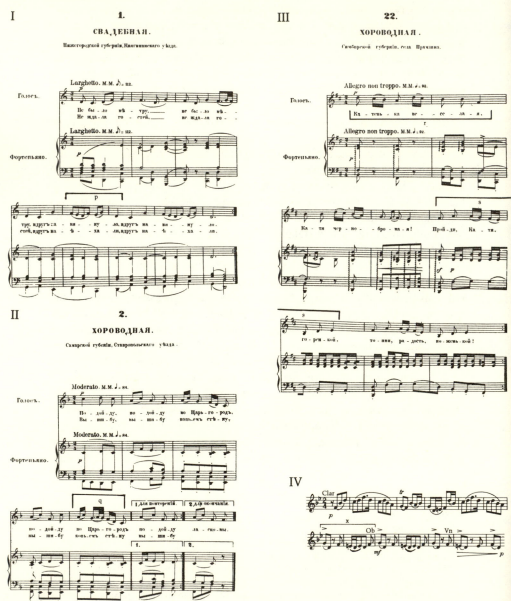

accompaniment, which emphasizes in quasi-cadential fashion every arrival at the low C, which is the *peremennost'* tone (i.e., the "alternate tonic").

It is instructive to compare this harmonization with those of the themes that had furnished the slow introduction to *Kamarinskaya* and to Balakirev's first overture, for by doing so we may observe how deliberate a cultivation this "neo-Russian" harmonic style was. In example 8.7, Glinka's wedding song is given first as he harmonized it in 1839 for his song "Northern Star," and then as it is first harmonized in *Kamarinskaya* (its first statement there being *all'unisono*). These settings derive much of their charm from the use of chromatic auxiliary tones. This harmonic feature is exploited with especial assiduity in the *Kamarinskaya* version, producing an effect in the second and third measures (the chromatic pass between A and G in both directions in the middle voice) that Gerald Abraham pinpointed over sixty years ago as one of

EXAMPLE 8.7. Glinka's harmonizations of the wedding song

"The Elements of Russian Music," at least Russian music of this particular vintage.[32] It arises not out of any response to the nature of the original melody, however, but as an outgrowth of the use of applied dominants, something Balakirev, as we have seen, tended to eschew.

The harmonization of the *bïlina* melody in the slow introduction to Balakirev's first overture is still very much within the Glinka tradition, though it gives evidence of an original and sensitive ear (and of things to come). Example 8.8 gives all three statements of the melody, at least in part, for each contributes something of harmonic interest. The melody uses six tones, equivalent to the major scale minus the seventh degree. But this is merely a structural equivalence, not a functional one, for the tune ends not on what would be the tonic of that putative major scale but rather on the lower fifth degree. Common practice dictates that this tone be treated as a dominant, and that is how Balakirev in fact harmonized the melody on its second and third appearances (examples 8.8b and c, which are immediately consecutive in the overture). In example 8.8c, he actually tacked on a cadential phrase (bracketed in the example) to steer the tune back to the proper tonic. In example 8.8b, the ending of the melody is unretouched, but the harmonization clearly identifies the concluding note as the dominant (the French sixth preparation, the cadential suspension).

The first statement (example 8.8a), however, is magical and prophetic. There are no full chords, and the two-part harmony is fraught with a delicious ambiguity. What sounds (and looks) like a sustained dominant pedal in the violins—an effect plagiarized in many later Russian pieces, perhaps most famously in Borodin's *In Central Asia* of 1880—is never resolved as such but instead is reapproached in a fashion that stabilizes it, so that one doesn't know whether to interpret the pair of chords at the end as iii–V in B major or as vi–I in a Mixolydian F♯. This ambiguous, skeletal harmony seems to be an attempt, and an inspired one, at rendering a style of folk harmony that must have been quite familiar to Balakirev from his daily aural experience in Nizhniy Novgorod (the so-called *podgoloski*, "undervoices") but that would not be reflected in the published repertoire of "scientific" folk song transcriptions until Yuliy Melgunov's first collection (1879). Also related to *podgoloski* is the way the little horn and clarinet phrases in the seventh and eighth measures foreshadow in diminution the motion of the "harmonizing" violin line, as shown by the brackets in the example. Add to that the instrumental color, which seems an imitation of such peasant wind instruments as the *rozhok* ("shepherd's horn") and the *svirel'* (panpipes), and one has a measure

[32] *Music and Letters* 9 (1928): 51–58. *Kamarinskaya* features this device very prominently indeed (see, for example, the bass between rehearsal nos. 14 and 15), and even Stravinsky makes pointed reference to such usages in the *Danse russe* from *Petrushka*—which, one should recall, is an evocation of St. Petersburg in the 1830s (see the passage seven measures before no. 43). But cf. the "orientalist" usage discussed in the next chapter.

EXAMPLE 8.8. Balakirev's harmonizations of the *bïlina* theme

of Balakirev's unprecedentedly open-eared approach to the tonality and the sonority of Russian folk song.

What was a unique and exceptional passing phenomenon in the first overture became the rule in the second, and even began to govern long-range tonal organization. Like the wedding song in *Kamarinskaya*, the slow theme of the introduction in the second overture begins with an *all'unisono* statement, but the final pair of measures is fully harmonized. The whole gesture is then immediately repeated, forming parallel periods (example 8.9). The cadence of the first period is harmonized very much like the setting in the folk song anthology of 1866 (cf. example 8.6): a plagal cadence through a major IV,

EXAMPLE 8.9. Balakirev, second Overture on Russian Themes, mm. 5–25

evoking the "Russian minor." The second period has a different termination, however. The pair of horns picks up the A♭ (the lower neighbor, or *peremennost'* tone) on its first appearance, and the continuation is transposed down a step so that the A♭ is tonicized at the end, again through a plagal—that is, dominantless—cadence. Thus the tonal "mutability" of the original melody is reinforced through a tonal progression in the overture. To a degree unprecedented in music Russian or otherwise, tonal properties of folk music have been allowed to govern those of art music.

In keeping with his general avoidance of dominant harmony in the minor mode, Balakirev does not employ a single authentic cadence over the course of the introduction, only plagal ones. And these are often deployed in chains suggesting the use of a term like "applied subdominant," as at the very end of the introduction, in which a progression along the "circle of fourths" leads back from the *peremennost'* tone (A♭) to the tonic for the final cadence: A♭– E♭–B♭.

Like the first overture, the second is cast in the form of a sonata-allegro embedded within a larger ABA form, effected by a concluding reprise of the introduction as coda (see diagram 8.3). And here, too, the principle of *peremennost'* affects the tonal plan. Whereas in the first overture Balakirev's formal procedure had created no tonal ambiguity, because the key of the introduction and that of the "first theme" had been parallel tonics (B major/minor), he now invoked a "Lisztian" third relation between the B♭ minor of the introduction and the D major of the first theme. Thus a sonata form in D is ambiguously embedded within an ABA structure in B♭. These are—not at all by accident, of course—the very keys on which the famous modulation in *Kamarinskaya* had turned, and as a matter of fact the transition from the end of the introduction to the beginning of the sonata-allegro is patently modeled on that modulation, with the highly characteristic difference that Balakirev goes directly from ii$_3^4$ to I, eliding out the dominant harmony and (by touching G in the bass) turning the progression in effect into a plagal cadence. Compare example 8.10 with example 8.3d.

The *peremennost'*-like "stalemate" effect between the regions of B♭ and D is enhanced by using B♭ minor as the key of the second theme (theme III) and its parallel major as the key of the closing theme (theme IV). Balakirev symmetrically completes the key scheme, moreover, by starting the development section in F♯ major: a full rotation of major thirds is thus achieved.[33] Structurally important dominant relations occur only twice: in the preparation of the second theme in the exposition, and in the retransition to the recapitulation. Yet even in those places *peremennost'* relations play a part, for in both cases the dominant pedal is approached by the use of theme I, harmonized as in its second appearance in the introduction, with tonic progressing to lower neighbor, which then functions as dominant.

But alongside this "declassicalization" of key relations—something that was going on in the West as well, along different lines—there is a remarkable growth in symphonic style, measured (as the nineteenth century measured it) in terms of motivic development and "thematic dramaturgy." As example 8.6 shows, from each of his themes Balakirev quite systematically extracted at least one motivic cell to furnish material for transitions and development (they are labeled *p*, *q*, *r*, and *s*). Thanks to the greatly increased reliance on this technique, the second overture contains a far greater amount of tonally unstable, dynamic writing than the first, full of excellently sustained tonal tensions and free at last from the stranglehold of ostinato phrasing, which had been practically the sole means of propulsion in the first overture (as it had also been, of course, in *Kamarinskaya*). The phrase structure of the second overture is newly pliant and unpredictable. All themes are presented Beethoven fashion, with momentary departures leading back to climactic statements.

---

[33] Something similar had occurred in the development section of the first overture, which was based on symmetrical minor-third relations: B♭, G minor, and D♭. Cf. diagram 2.

Larghetto, 3/4: INTRODUCTION

Th. I	I	p: sequential repetitions over pedal	I(climactic)	p	I(cf. beginning of development)	codetta: expansion of plagal cadence over harp arpeggios
bb	*perememmost'* modulation to Ab, through plagal cadence		bb		bb (over Gb pedal)	Ab → eb → bb

Allegro moderato, 4/4: EXPOSITION   3/4: L'istesso tempo   2/4

Transition	*First theme*	*Bridge*		*Second theme group*	*Codetta*
q	Th. II q II q II q *ff*	Th. I p I,	I, † sequentially developed	Th. III q r s III r *ff*	Th. IV
D:ii$^{\varnothing\,4}_{\;\;3}$	D G g D	d g→F pedal	bb	Ab bb Bb bb	Bb

DEVELOPMENT   *Retransition*

Th. II q II q	I+q, III+I s q
F# b~~~C#(Db)	b~~~† ~~~ A pedal

RECAPITULATION

First theme	*Second theme*	*Codetta*
Th. II q	Th. III (climactic)	Th. IV ("x" in timpani)
	"Q"	*
B+y	r q s in various combinations	g(over Bb pedal) ~~~ ~~~ ~~~ D → Db ~~~ (over A pedal)
D G major/minor (over D pedal)	bb, g d	D

CODA: Tempo I°

Th. I, p. plagal cadences over fragments of II, III and q

bb

*cf. *Kamarinskaya*, final modulation   †*Peremennost'* relationship

DIAGRAM 8.3. Balakirev, second Overture on Russian Themes (1863–64), form diagram

EXAMPLE 8.10. Balakirev, second Overture on Russian Themes, transition to the Allegro

And as has often been observed in the literature, Balakirev's motivic work is exceedingly resourceful and sophisticated, especially as regards contrapuntal juxtapositions. These often involve combinations of one or another of the extracted motives with theme I, which functions throughout the overture as a kind of motto, somewhat on the order of the wedding song in *Kamarinskaya*.[34] An example from the development section shows two linked instances of the procedure. The first of them maps a collage of motivic fragments onto a "Dorian" plagal progression of the type established in the introduction; the second is for its time (and place) a remarkably linear bit of writing (example 8.11a).

The very end of the overture is another memorable collage: an extension of theme II leads to a final poignant recollection of motive *q* (and even the final pizzicatos are thematic: cf. m. 4 of theme II), the whole attended by recollections of theme IV in the form of the harp accompaniment and the use of Lydian E♮s. If these collages seem merely "decorative," compare example 8.11b, showing the modulatory bridge from the first theme to the second in the recapitulation. This is a "functional" passage if ever there was one, serving admirably the symphonic requirement of linkage.

In his second Overture on Russian Themes Balakirev did what many then (and even now) considered the impossible: he constructed an extended, sustained piece of symphonic music wholly out of folkloric material. Unlike *Kamarinskaya* or the first overture, the piece is ample, even imposing in its dimensions and its complexity of design. No longer is there any trace of

[34] The most palpable borrowing of this kind from *Kamarinskaya* is the unexpected return of theme I as bridge to the second theme in the exposition.

EXAMPLE 8.11. Balakirev, second Overture on Russian Themes, from the development section

EXAMPLE 8.11, *continued*

ostinato variation in its structural scheme, though its line of descent from *Kamarinskaya* could not be more direct, and though there remain countless details of scoring, harmony, and general facture betraying its indebtedness to Glinka's example.[35] But Glinka's whimsicality has been replaced by an urgent earnestness of purpose. And where the older composer had sought to entertain, his disciple now seeks to impress with his powers of construction and to exalt with his sense of climax and peroration. *Kamarinskaya* and the first overture had remained close in concept to their sources: their impulse and "content," quite simply, had been song and dance. The second overture marked such an advance in the symphonic dimension and variety of pacing, such a radical reweighting of structural priorities in favor of transition and development, departure and arrival, as to amount to a difference not merely in degree of technical mastery (for Glinka's could hardly be excelled) but in actual kind.

Indeed, the second overture's dominant impression is that of narrative, or what Balakirev later termed "instrumental drama"—the first such piece to have been completed by any Russian save the Germanophile Rubinstein. And when such a composition is based upon "characteristic" material of any kind, the question immediately raised is not "What is it?" but "What's it about?" Or, to make this rather loose thought somewhat more rigorous, in terms of Meyer's well-known formulation: the "kinetic-syntactic" processes of Balakirev's second overture are so highly developed as inevitably to lend a "connotative" dimension to the national material.[36] The piece seems no longer to be a *Fantaisie pittoresque* guided solely by "innate musical feeling." It *means* something; it is in some sense—but what sense?—a statement about Russia.

This impression, already strongly conveyed by the qualities of the second overture's structure and style, is amply confirmed by the work's compositional and publication history. Yet even here we shall confront some paradoxes—paradoxes that suggest that the programmatic quality is in fact an absolute, with an a priori existence independent of the specific programmatic content. This programmatic element—brought about by the conjunction of a highly elaborated and kinetic structure with a highly characteristic thematic content—was, moreover, an essential contributing factor to Balakirev's authentic nationalism.

---

[35] To cite one last example of this indebtedness: Balakirev makes his transition from the sonata-allegro to the coda (reprise of the introduction) by invoking Glinka's dropping semitone progression (cf. example 8.3d), approaching B♭ minor from D major (in $^6_4$ position) through its relative D♭.

[36] Cf., inter alia, Leonard B. Meyer, "Universalism and Relativism in the Study of Ethnic Music," *Ethnomusicology* 4, no. 2 (1960): 49–54.

THE PERIOD of exacerbated musical politics immediately preceding the founding of Rubinstein's Conservatory in 1862 coincided with what was generally a turbulent moment in Russian political and social life—the aftermath of the Crimean War and the multiple far-reaching reforms of the early reign of Alexander II. A typical incident of those years was a series of student demonstrations at the beginning of the 1861–62 academic year that led to a great number of arrests and the temporary closing of the three leading Russian universities, those at St. Petersburg, Moscow, and Kazan (where Balakirev had briefly studied). From his London exile the "radical democrat" Alexander Herzen greeted this outbreak of political activism among the youth of Russia with an enthusiastic editorial in his émigré journal *The Bell* (*Kolokol*), entitled "The Giant Wakes!" The article ended with an impassioned call to the students at the shut-down institutions:

> In Russia the universities are closed, in Poland even the churches have been shut down, defiled by the police. There is neither light of reason nor light of religion! Where would they thus lead us in the dark? . . . So, where will you turn, brave youths, you who have been shut out from your studies? Where, indeed?
>
> Listen closely, since darkness does not prevent hearing: from all sides of our enormous fatherland, from the Don and from the Urals, from the Volga and the Dnepr a moan is growing, a rumble is rising—it is the beginning of a tidal wave which is boiling up, attended by storms, after a horribly fatiguing calm. *To the people! With the people!*—That's where you belong.[37]

Stasov, who as an official of the St. Petersburg Imperial Public Library had privileged access to censored literature, was a regular reader of Herzen's *Kolokol*, and its active tribune among his circle of intimates. In the early sixties, he bombarded the young Balakirev with radical reading matter, and for a time the latter was so receptive to it as to have actually contemplated an opera on a subject drawn from Chernïshevsky's "nihilistic" novel *What Is to Be Done?*[38] According to a letter often quoted by Soviet historians, Stasov associated the conception of Balakirev's second overture with their reading "The Giant Wakes!" together, and in particular with Herzen's image of the rising tidal wave.[39] Nor is there any reason to doubt that this was the case; the reference occurs in a private communication in the form of an allusion to a mutually remembered event. And Balakirev had himself gone "to the people" the year before and "listened closely" to their folk-musical utterances. To associate musical populism with political liberalism had natural attractions for a young

---

[37] "Ispolin prosïpayetsya," *Kolokol*, no. 110 (1 November 1861), reprinted in Alexander Herzen, *Sochineniya*, vol. 7 (Moscow: Izdatel'stvo Akademii nauk SSSR, 1958), p. 392.

[38] Cf. letter of Balakirev to Stasov of 27 April 1863 (Lyapunova and Yazovitskaya, *Miliy Alekseyevich Balakirev*, p. 90).

[39] Letter of 11 October 1869. A. S. Lyapunova, ed., *M. A. Balakirev i V. V. Stasov: Perepiska*, vol. 1 (Moscow: Muzïka, 1970), p. 270.

maverick musician who was engaged in battle with a musical establishment dominated by the aristocracy and staffed chiefly by Germans. The image of the rising wave may well have played a part in predisposing Balakirev's musical imagination toward the dramatic and dynamic character by which his second overture so conspicuously differed from his first.

Indeed, and perhaps ironically, it was the thought of Herzen's wave of popular unrest that first aroused Balakirev's interest in Beethoven—the fount and origin of "German symphonism"—as a model. Soon after reading "The Giant Wakes!" Balakirev wrote to Stasov of his discovery, at a soirée at Cui's, of Beethoven's *Consecration of the House* Overture. "I'll tell you its program," Balakirev promised, rather enigmatically. "*Very interesting!* There is even a boiling tidal wave attended by storms.[40] Despite this evident enthusiasm, Balakirev seems to have done nothing further about the project of setting Herzen's wave to music for a year and a half after writing this letter.[41] When the overture was first performed, moreover, neither Alexander Serov's witheringly unfavorable review nor Cui's predictably enthusiastic one made any reference to programmatic content, aquatic or otherwise.[42]

But when in 1869 Balakirev finally published the work, five years after that first performance, he called it a "musical picture" and gave it the patently programmatic title *1000 Years*. This alluded to the recently celebrated millennium of the quasi-legendary founding of the Russian state at Novgorod by the Varangian Prince Rurik in A.D. 862. No evidence survives to suggest that either Balakirev or Stasov had any such idea in 1862, nor did Balakirev provide any clue in letter or preface to the specific relationship between title and music in 1869. But some indication of what he (or Stasov) may have had in mind can be found in a letter in which Stasov described to Balakirev a proposed design for the title page of the published score:

> On the left there will be a drawing of "primeval Russia"—Moscow, or perhaps one of the autonomous princely cities; and finally, as if disappearing in the distance, "modern times"—some city, a rushing locomotive, telegraphs, some new buildings (only, it goes without saying, not the Senate and not the Admiralty).[43]

This is pretty far from a rising wave of popular discontent. In fact it rather flies in the face of the previous conception, putting meliorism in place of social criticism. Nor is there anything in the score to connect with such a program,

[40] 4 January 1862 (ibid., p. 181). According to the editorial notes to the correspondence, Stasov red-penciled at this point in the margin, "Beethoven was a prophet!" (ibid., p. 408).

[41] The first extant sketches for the overture were jotted down in July 1863. Cf. Lyapunova, *Balakirev i Stasov: Perepiska*, p. 420.

[42] For Serov's review see A. N. Serov, *Kriticheskiye stat'i*, vol. 4 (St. Petersburg: Tip. Departamenta udelov, 1894), p. 2020. Cui's is in César Cui, *Izbrannïye stat'i* (Leningrad: Muzgiz, 1952), pp. 18–19.

[43] 17 December 1868 (Lyapunova, *Balakirev i Stasov: Perepiska*, p. 262). In the end this design was rejected in favor of a more conventional Russian landscape.

since none of the themes is any more archaic or modern than any of the others. Stasov, it is true, made a rather blatantly ex post facto attempt in an article of 1882 to justify the program of *1000 Years* by fixing upon what we have called theme IV, the one composed by Balakirev himself ("the emerging new life is expressed in an enchanting, truly inspired melody of wondrous beauty").[44] But the dodge is transparent, and one can readily agree with one Soviet writer, who finds in the second overture "neither drama nor history; it is merely a picture, a picture of Russia as seen through the eyes of a 'man of the sixties' [i.e., a progressive thinker], one who has felt the powerful strength, the spiritual beauty and the poetic gift of the 'awakening' populace"[45]—an interpretation that takes the putative inspiration via Herzen quite nicely into account without pressing too insistently for specific programmatic content.

So why the change of title? Conceivably it was requested by the publisher, but it more likely reflected a change of heart. The nervous breakdown that interrupted Balakirev's career took place right around this time, and was coupled with his well-known spiritual crisis and the attendant shift in his political sympathies. In fact, the vicissitudes of the second overture's program were only beginning. Upon his return to musical life in the 1880s, Balakirev reissued a number of early works in revised editions. *1000 Years* was one of these. It was retouched (rather inconsequentially) in 1884 and brought out by Bessel in 1890 with a new designation—"symphonic poem," a new title—the old Slavonic *"Rus' "*[46] and a new and detailed program, quite explicitly (if mendaciously) set out in a preface (signed and dated 14 February 1886), as follows:

> The unveiling in 1862 in Novgorod of a monument to the Russian millennium was the occasion for the composition of the symphonic poem *Rus'*, which was originally published by the local music dealer A. Johansen under the title *1000 Years: A Musical Picture*. As the basis of the composition I selected the themes of three folk songs from my own anthology, by which I wished to characterize three elements in our history: the pagan period, the Muscovite order, and the autonomous republican [*udel'no-vechevoy*] system, reborn among the Cossacks. Strife among these elements, expressed in the symphonic development of these themes, has furnished the content of the instrumental drama, to which the present

[44] Stasov, *Selected Essays on Music*, p. 95.

[45] Frid, "Simfonicheskoye tvorchestvo," p. 136.

[46] Not *Russia*, as it is usually rendered in English. Balakirev was quite explicit on this point in a letter to Stasov of 8 February 1886, in which the proper wording of the French titular material was discussed. "Shouldn't the Slavonic *Rus'* be translated into the Latin *Russia* (on the order of Liszt's *Hungaria*)? Otherwise, if we translate it as *Russie*, it will mean 'Rossiya' [i.e., the modern name for the country], which I do not want" (A. S. Lyapunova, ed., *M. A. Balakirev i V. V. Stasov: Perepiska*, vol. 2 [Moscow: Muzïka, 1971], p. 82). In English, of course, "Russia" should be avoided for the same reason that "Russie" is to be avoided in French. Best leave the title untranslated.

title is far better suited than the previous one, since the author had no intention of drawing a picture of our thousand-year history but only a wish to characterize some of its constituent elements. In republishing this work with the firm of Bessel and Co., I have reorchestrated it and significantly amended it.[47]

But all that was really amended was the program; the music was hardly touched. And the amendment amounted this time to a volte-face. Far from either a social protest or a melioristic panorama, we are now faced with a Slavophile glorification of Russian antiquity, particularly of those quasi-communal forms of social organization that were maintained avatarlike by the Cossacks, for which they were admired by pan-Slavists and reactionaries, and for which they were reviled by every progressive or liberal element. And Balakirev went even further. In the last edition of the score to come out within his lifetime (Zimmerman, 1907), he amended the sentence beginning "Strife among these elements . . ." to read: "Their strife, culminating in the fatal blow dealt all Russian religious and national aspirations by the reforms of Peter I, has furnished the content of the instrumental drama."[48]

What an anomaly this is: from its putative beginnings in Herzen, the ideological content of Balakirev's overture (or picture, or symphonic poem) has swung 180 degrees to the right. For so had his outlook: from a "man of the sixties" the composer had become a xenophobic reactionary of the Nikolai II era. He even went so far as to claim, in a letter to a Czech Slavophile acquaintance, that his intention in composing *Rus'* had been "to depict how Peter the Great killed our native Russian life."[49]

Now there is if anything even less in the actual thematic content of the second overture to support the specific program of *Rus'* than there is to support that of *1000 Years*. Both programs were concocted ex post facto. But while they cannot be reconciled ideologically either with each other or with the original stimulus in Herzen, all three contents have in common a principled commitment to native, not merely national, character as a source of artistic inspiration, and beyond that, to the use of such material as a kind of civic deed. And all three ideological contents require for their musical support the highly kinetic symphonic form Balakirev called "instrumental drama." All three interpretations of the music of the second overture might seem equally plausible, without considering the history of the piece. But applied to the first overture, which lacks what I have called the programmatic quality, all would appear equally absurd. So the radical expansion of form Balakirev achieved in his second overture can be seen now as an effort to accommodate an ideological, not merely evocative, content. And this effort was demanded by a commitment to artistic nationalism that the aristocratic composer of *Kama-*

[47] Quoted from Lyapunova, ed., *Balakirev i Stasov: Perepiska*, vol. 2, p. 279.
[48] Quoted from Frid, "Simfonicheskoye tvorchestvo," p. 132.
[49] To. I. Kolař (1907). Ibid.

rinskaya not only lacked but despised, and one, moreover, that anticipated—and how ironically, given Balakirev's eventual politics!—the arts policies of the Soviet state. Nor is this the first time the antecedents of Soviet aesthetics have been located in surprisingly un-Marxian terrain.[50] Glinka's acorn has yielded some strange and bitter fruit.

BUT ALL that is quite another story. Balakirev's Russian overtures, particularly the second, were hardly devoid of more immediate issue. The two members of his circle who shared his gift for instrumental composition took them repeatedly as a model. Closest of all was the Overture on Russian Themes, Op. 28 (1866), by the twenty-two-year-old Rimsky-Korsakov. It is practically a plagiarism: scored for almost precisely the same orchestra as the second overture, it is cast in precisely the same form, sonata-allegro on two themes framed by a slow introduction and postlude on a third. It relies in its development section on the same contrapuntal-collage techniques, and is even based on a third-relation as tonal axis (except that it goes in the opposite direction: D–F♯ instead of D–B♭). Even in so mature a composition as the "Russian Easter" Overture (*Svetlïy prazdnik*, 1888), Rimsky followed the Balakirev model with scarcely a departure. One might also mention the first movement of his Symphony no. 1 (1862), in which the tune "Down by Mother Volga" is given a very kinetic treatment, or even the first movement of his Symphony no. 3 in C (1873), in which Rimsky used a symmetrically third-related key scheme adapted from Balakirev's second overture: in the exposition the second theme comes in E major, and it is recapitulated in A♭.

We have already noted the similarity between the beginning of Borodin's *In Central Asia* and the introduction to Balakirev's first overture. The sustained dominant pedal in the high violins persists (with one brief departure) for some ninety measures, finally giving way to a texture of sustained winds over rapid pizzicato strings. This latter instrumental idea was employed by Balakirev in both his overtures: in the first at rehearsal no. 4, in the second at two measures after no. 1. It was so widely copied thereafter as to become a veritable *style russe* cliché. The culmination of Borodin's "musical picture" (for that is what he called it, after *1000 Years*) is a contrapuntal combination of the two main themes, the first of which, moreover, is always presented in key rotations by thirds.

In a famous letter to the singer Lyubov Karmalina, Borodin averred that among the members of the quondam Balakirev circle "individuality is beginning to gain the upper hand over school."[51] In spite of this, his *Central Asia*,

---

[50] For a consideration of the Tolstoyan background of much Soviet aesthetics, see my review of Molchanov's *The Dawns Are Quiet Here* in *Musical Quarterly* 62 (1976): 105–15.

[51] 1 June 1876. S. A. Dianin, ed., *Pis'ma A. P. Borodina*, vol. 2 (Moscow: Muzgiz, 1936), p. 107.

written several years after the letter, shows the extent to which Balakirev had in fact succeeded in establishing a school with his Russian overtures. And for all Balakirev's xenophobic rejection of the West, the soil he tended would have remained barren without the fairly liberal application of German fertilizer. The impulse to write an imposing symphonic work based on Russian folk songs is at least as much a Westernizing impulse as a nationalistic one, else why not leave the folk songs to the folk? In a sense it was the very opposite of what Herzen had called for. Balakirev had not gone "to the people." He had brought the people into the high culture, embodying their musical artifacts in works meant not for them but for an educated urban elite, whose criteria of musical value and importance (like Balakirev's own) were irrevocably formed on the instrumental music of the German classics and of such moderns as Schumann and Liszt. Their methods and techniques of formal construction and thematic-motivic elaboration were what gave Balakirev the equipment he needed to turn Glinka's sprouting acorn into a rooted tree.

The final irony is the rapidity with which the oak became petrified. As early as the 1890s followers of Balakirev's methods had turned his style into a rigidly formulaic, superprofessionalized canon, fostered by the conservatory under Rimsky-Korsakov and Glazunov, and by the lavishly endowed publishing house, concert series, and annual prize competitions underwritten by Mitrofan Belyayev. Balakirev himself, owing to the interruption in his career and his subsequent commitment to musical as well as political reaction, became his own chief epigone.

In the 1860s and 1870s, however, the ambivalence of Balakirev's position was for the most part lost on his fellow kuchkists, especially the remaining pair, Cui and Musorgsky, who were vocal composers at heart. They saw only the battle against the short-range enemies, "rootless cosmopolitans" and colonizers like Rubinstein and Serov. There is a rather puzzling, if seldom noticed, reference to Balakirev's second overture near the end of a very long letter that Musorgsky wrote to him about Serov's *Judith*. The letter is dated 10 June 1863, about a month before Balakirev began concentrated work on the piece. The part that is relevant to our present concern runs as follows: "Will you finish your Russian overture by winter? I would like very much to hear it. I feel that I will love it above all your other works; judging by what I already know of it, it will be very much to my taste, and besides it is the first thing of yours untainted by Germany."[52] But what could he have known of the work? Clearly, nothing more than the themes (and only the ones collected along the Volga at that; the original theme IV had not yet been invented), and perhaps something of the style of their harmonization. This much, certainly, *was* anti-German—and was in fact pronounced *ganz falsch* by a German professor in Prague.[53]

[52] M. P. Musorgsky, *Literaturnoye naslediye*, vol. 1 (Moscow: Muzïka, 1971), p. 70.
[53] Cf. the letter from Balakirev to Musorgsky 11/23 January 1867, quoted in Garden, *Balakirev*, p. 57.

But in the light of the finished product, especially when compared to *Kamarinskaya*, Musorgsky's pronouncement is fairly risible. And when Cui asserts, in his review of the second overture's first performance, that it was "completely novel in form,"[54] one feels one is confronting "kuchkism" in the quick: the critic's attention, like Musorgsky's, is entirely on the piquant details, not on the underlying structure. (One could say as much about the composer of *William Ratcliff*.) For form was the one area in which Balakirev was far from an innovator. He was a consolidator, a synthesizer who at last managed to reconcile Russian themes with what Musorgsky derisively called "German transitions."[55] By these efforts and by the example of his overtures he made the soil of Russian instrumental music fertile. Without him the acorn might have remained an acorn.

[54] *Izbrannïye stat'i*, p. 18.

[55] Cf. his letter to Rimsky-Korsakov of 5 July 1867, in which he described his *St. John's Eve on Bald Mountain*: "The general character of the thing is heated, there are no longueurs, transitions are compact, without German preparations, which lightens things considerably" (*Literaturnoye naslediye*, vol. 1, 87).

CHAPTER 9

"ENTOILING THE FALCONET"

THIS CHAPTER originated as a contribution to a symposium organized by the Dallas Opera and Southern Methodist University around the Opera's production of Borodin's *Prince Igor* in November 1990. Because many Soviet guests had been invited, the poster and program book were printed in English and Russian side by side. I found that the word "orientalism" in my title had become *tema vostoka*—"the Eastern theme"—in translation, even though *orientalizm*, or more commonly, *orientalistika*, are perfectly good Russian words (well, Russian words, anyway). It was a sensible precaution. "The Eastern theme" is neutral: from a paper with that phrase in the title one expects inventories, taxonomies, identification of sources, stylistic analysis. "Orientalism" is charged. From a paper with that word in the title one expects semiotics, ideological critique, polemic, perhaps indictment. The translator was quite right to err on the side of innocuousness, rather than saddle me with a viewpoint I might not wish or manage to live up to.

Yet orientalism in Russian art music, and especially in opera, is the topic this chapter addresses, not "the Eastern theme." One could not possibly do the latter justice in anything less than a book, what with the hundreds of Russian operas, ballets, tone poems, instrumental pieces, and songs with oriental subject matter that appeared over a rough century between Catterino Cavos's *Firebird* and Stravinsky's.[1] Any adequate taxonomy of this richly variegated material would first have to separate it into what we might call intra-imperial and extra-imperial categories (which already raises the specter of orientalism), dividing the intra-imperial, following the movements of the Russian army, into Siberian, Caucasian, and Central Asian phases, cutting the extra-imperial first into vastly unequal Near and Far Eastern shares, and then apportioning the Near Eastern into Arabian, Persian, Turkish, and Levantine strains. So prevalent for a while was the "Eastern theme" that when Vladimir Stasov, the great mythologizer of Russian music, looked back in 1882 at "Twenty-Five Years of Russian Art" (the title of one of his most famous essays), he could name "the oriental element" as one of the four distinguishing—and, of course, progressive—features of what he called the

---

[1] The genre had a quaint eighteenth-century forerunner in *Fevey* (1786), a singspiel by Vasiliy Pashkevich to a libretto by Catherine the Great, which sports a chorus of "Kalmyk" (Mongolian) kumiss-drinkers.

"New Russian school," the others being skepticism of European tradition, "striving for national character," and "extreme inclination toward 'program music.'"[2]

Leaving taxonomy for another day, then, we are left with orientalism: the East as a sign or metaphor, as imaginary geography, as historical fiction, as the reduced and totalized other against which we construct our (no less reduced and totalized) sense of ourselves. As Stasov implied, as we knew to begin with, and as we have been forcibly reminded of late, it is not possible to separate this constructed East from "the real one." The East is the East only to the West: the very act of naming it is already constitutive and heavily invested, consciously or not, with theory. The history of "the Eastern theme" is thus willy-nilly a facet of the history of ideas, and there can be no investigation of it that is not both itself an ideological critique and subject to ideological critique in its turn.

The only question is how overt shall we make our critique, and how bluntly accusatory. If I had wanted to put my enlightened scholarly and human perspective on display by attacking the subject of the Dallas symposium it would have been all too easy. I could have pointed out that throughout *Prince Igor*'s notorious eighteen-year gestation (1869–87) its plot was being uncannily reenacted in real life: Russia was just then competing avidly with Britain in what Kipling (and others) called the Great Game, a protracted imperialist war in Central Asia against a Muslim Holy League led by the Khan of Bokhara. I could have shown that, along with most of educated Russia, Borodin and Stasov enthusiastically endorsed this war, which came to an end only with the Soviet debacle in Afghanistan. As evidence I could have cited virtually all the differences between the libretto—or, better yet, Stasov's original scenario—and its literary source, the twelfth-century epic known as "The Lay of Igor's Campaign" (*Slovo o polku Igoreve*).

As regards the relations between the Russians and their antagonists, the Polovtsï, there were two main inventions: on the one hand there was the egregious Ovlur—an unidentified name in the *Lay* but in the opera a turncoat "good Indian" straight out of Fenimore Cooper—who arranges Igor's escape; on the other, there was the interpolated love intrigue between Igor's son Vladimir, who does exist in the *Lay of Igor's Campaign*, and Khan Konchak's daughter, "Konchakovna," who does not. Later, it will be evident that Konchakovna was an absolutely essential character for the sake of her music. The pretext for her invention, however, was very slim: just a few lines in the

---

[2] "Dvadtsat' pyat' let russkogo iskusstvo: Nasha muzïka," *Vestnik Yevropï* (six installments, 1882–83), reprinted in V. V. Stasov, *Izbrannïye sochineniya v tryokh tomakh* (Moscow: Iskusstvo, 1952), vol. 2, pp. 522–68; the discussion of the four points is on pp. 525–29. For a translation, see Piero Weiss and Richard Taruskin, *Music in the Western World: A History in Documents* (New York: Schirmer Books, 1984), pp. 390–94.

Lay between Khans Gzak and Konchak in which they briefly consider "entoiling the falconet by means of a fair maiden" as Nabokov translated it.[3]

Stasov's scenario ended with an epilogue Borodin never composed, in which the wedding of Vladimir and Konchakovna was celebrated after a second, successful campaign. It was a transparent derivation from the last scene of Glinka's *Ruslan and Lyudmila*, the opera on which *Prince Igor* was modeled in countless ways great and small. Except for the final chorus, which would have incorporated the last few lines of the *Lay* (including the famous concluding Amen), the epilogue had no precedent in Russian literature or history, yet it epitomized the scenario's ideology: while in captivity Igor would not assent to a marriage that would make his son a Polovtsian, even postponing his escape to prevent it; and yet he rejoices at home in the same marriage when it "annexes" the Khan's daughter as a Russian and a Christian.

Thus *Prince Igor*, which chiefly differs from the more innocently "magical" *Ruslan* precisely by virtue of its aggressive nationalism, finally made overt the pervasive subtext to nineteenth-century Russian essays in orientalism: the racially justified endorsement of Russia's militaristic expansion to the east. "We go with trust in God for our faith, our Russia, our people," the operatic Igor anachronistically proclaims, very much in the spirit of Tsar Alexander II. As a matter of fact, Borodin's exquisite "musical picture," *V Sredney Azii* ("In the Steppes of Central Asia"), was explicitly composed—along with Musorgsky's orchestral march "The Taking of Kars" and Chaikovsky's lost "The Montenegrins Receiving the News of Russia's Declaration of War on Turkey"—to glorify Alexander's expansionist policy. It was intended as an accompaniment to one of a series of *tableaux vivants* planned in celebration of the Tsar's silver jubilee in 1880.

These, then, are some of the points I might adduce were I interested in "unmasking" *Prince Igor* or in making Stasov and Borodin out as a pair of feckless "orientalists." But that would be a bore, and so I will not mention them. Yet (to drop the Ciceronian mask and don another) just as the prosecutor knows that the jury cannot really disregard the inadmissible evidence just because the judge has so instructed them, I do intend these "unmentioned" points to equip us with a context, and a subtext. If one is going to talk about oriental style as a sign, one must specify its referents.

Foundation thus laid, I shall try from here on to let the music speak for itself by way of examples chosen and arranged so as to let a certain semiotic point emerge. Again, I have scamped the inventory and the taxonomy. Some kinds of musical orientalism passed the Russians by. There is no Russian equivalent to Félicien David's symphonic ode *Le Désert*, famed for its transcription of the muezzin's call to prayer; Islam as such seems to have left the Russians cold. There are many kinds of specifically Russian musical oriental-

---

[3] *The Song of Igor's Campaign*, trans. Vladimir Nabokov (New York: Vintage, 1960), p. 70.

ism that I will not mention either. Some, like biblical orientalism, while very prominent and telling, are not particularly relevant to *Prince Igor*. Others, like the representation of oriental military hordes, or of barbarian magnanimity, are very pertinent indeed. But instead of covering the whole field with a thin film, I prefer to concentrate on one aspect and get somewhat beneath the surface.

As ALREADY suggested, Russian orientalism can be divided into periods roughly corresponding to the phases of Russian imperial expansion. The heyday of Russian romanticism, as every lover of Pushkin and Lermontov knows, coincided with the Caucasian campaigns. One of the best-loved souvenirs of that period (best loved by musicians, anyway), was an untitled lyric by Pushkin dating from 1828:

> Ne poy, krasavitsa, pri mne
> Tï pesen Gruzii pechal'noy:
> Napominayut mne onye
> Druguyu zhizn' i bereg dal'nïy.
>
> Uvï! napominayut mne
> Tvoyi zhestokiye napevï
> I step', i noch'—i pri lunye
> Chertï dalyokoy, bednoy devï.
>
> Ya prizrak milïy, rokovoy,
> Tebya uvidev, zabïvayu;
> No tï poyosh'—i predo mnoy
> Yevo ya vnov' voobrazhayu.
>
> Ne poy, krasavitsa, pri mne
> Tï pesen Gruzii pechal'noy:
> Napominayut mne onye
> Druguyu zhizn' i bereg dal'nïy.
>
> Sing not in my presence, O beauty,
> Thy songs of sad Georgia;
> They remind me
> Of another life, a distant shore.
>
> Alas! they remind me,
> Thy cruel melodies,
> Of steppes, of night—and 'neath the moon
> The features of a poor far-off maid.
>
> This lovely, fateful vision
> I can forget on seeing thee;

But you sing—and before me
I envision it anew.

Sing not in my presence, O beauty,
Thy songs of sad Georgia;
They remind me
Of another life, a distant shore.

Between 1829 (the year of the poem's publication) and 1909 at least twenty-six settings of it were published by Russian composers (and a couple of non-Russians, too, such as Pauline Viardot, who set it as a concert vehicle for her Russian tours).[4] We shall consider three, beginning with the one by Glinka, the patriarch himself, which he published in 1831 at the age of twenty-seven, five years before his first opera, *A Life for the Tsar*, was performed and he became a "nationalist." Subtitled "Georgian Song," it incorporates the first two stanzas of the poem (See example 9.1).

According to the composer's memoirs, the melody of this song, which he learned from the poet and playwright Alexander Griboyedov, was an authentic Georgian tune, the very one to which Pushkin reputedly composed the poem.[5] From the music alone there is no way of guessing that. Nothing about the song sounds the least bit exotic. The diatonic melody seems perfectly ordinary to Western ears, Glinka's harmonization humdrum, the prosody straightforward. Already we have a warning that musical orientalism is a matter not of authenticity but of conventions—conventions that had not yet been established by 1831.

Now compare Balakirev's setting, published under the actual title "Georgian Song" a generation later in 1865 (see example 9.2). It has Eastern export written all over it. The melody is full of close little ornaments and melismas with telltale augmented seconds (even though the singer—that is, the speaker of the lines—is not supposed to be an oriental), and the beautiful woman has evidently brought her band with her. It is easy to find authentic recorded prototypes for this setting, much as we can imagine Balakirev, who spent a good deal of time in the Caucasus, encountering them in situ. Folkways FE 4535 ("Folk Music of the USSR," compiled by Henry Cowell) has two conveniently consecutive cuts, the first of which exemplifies the melodic style, the second the oriental orchestra with its characteristic drum pattern.[6]

The interesting thing is that these "prototypes" are Armenian, with strong Turkish and Persian influences, not Georgian. Georgian folk music does not sound anything like them, or like Balakirev's "Georgian Song," and obvi-

---

[4] For the complete list see Georgiy Ivanov, *Russkaya poèziya v otechestvennoy muzïke*, vol. 1 (Moscow: Muzïka, 1966), p. 288.

[5] Mikhail Ivanovich Glinka, *Memoirs*, trans. Richard B. Mudge (Norman: University of Oklahoma Press, 1963), p. 47.

[6] Side 3, bands 5 ("Machkal," duduks instrumental) and 6 (Shirak Folk Dance with Tara).

EXAMPLE 9.1. Glinka, *Ne poy, krasavitsa* (1831)

EXAMPLE 9.1, *continued*

ne   cher-tï da - lyo - koy, mi - loy de -vï,   mi - loy de   vï.

ously Balakirev knew that perfectly well. But he wanted us to get the point, and that meant sacrificing real verisimilitude—pardon the pleonasm—to something higher, or at least more legible—what Russians call *khudozhest-vennaya pravda*, "artistic truth." The critic Hermann Laroche, pondering the matter of what I have called biblical orientalism, put it this way: "In what does [Alexander] Serov's masterly characterization of the extinct Assyrians [in his opera *Judith*] consist, or [Anton] Rubinstein's of the ancient Semites [in his "sacred opera," *The Tower of Babel*]? Obviously in one thing only: the composers have successfully reproduced *our* subjective idea of the Assyrians and the Semites"—as Balakirev reproduced his contemporaries' idea of the contemporary orient, indeed as romantic composers, increasingly a rare breed in Russia, usually did.[7]

So far we have had an example that was authentic but not exotic, and one that was exotic but not authentic. It is the latter that we take for verisimilar, hence "truly" oriental. But Balakirev's setting has little going for it except its seeming verisimilitude, an infusion of stereotyped local color that connotes little and does nothing to redeem what might seem a negligent reading of the poem.[8] If that seems an injustice, compare a third setting of Pushkin's poem, the most famous one, written by Rachmaninoff another generation later in 1892 (the same year as the Prelude in C♯ minor), when the composer, a prodigy of nineteen, had just been hatched from the Moscow Conservatory (see example 9.3).

---

[7] Hermann Laroche (German Larosh), "'Der Thurm zu Babel' Rubinshteyna," in Larosh, *Muzïkal'no-kriticheskiye stat'i* (St. Petersburg: Bessel, 1894), p. 117.

[8] "Might seem," since on deeper reflection it might also seem a manifestation of a characteristic ambivalence that Russian composers (unlike French or German one) felt toward "the Eastern theme." Russia was a contiguous empire in which Europeans, living side by side with "orientals," identified (and intermarried) with them far more than in the case of the other colonial powers; and, as we have already learned from Stasov, oriental coloration was one of the ways by which the composers of the "New Russian school" strove to distinguish themselves from those of Western Europe. It was simultaneously and ambiguously a self-constructing and an other-constructing trait. This irony will find echo at the end of the chapter.

EXAMPLE 9.2. Balakirev, *Ne poy, krasavitsa* (1865)

Rachmaninoff's setting is far less verisimilar than Balakirev's and makes no pretense at authenticity. Yet with hardly an augmented second it speaks the sign language of Russian orientalism in a highly developed form, adding a great deal to our experience of the poem. We can trace that language back to Glinka (though not to his "Georgian Song"), passing optionally through Balakirev but necessarily through Borodin and *Prince Igor*, which was first per-

EXAMPLE 9.2, *continued*

pe - sen Gru - zi - i pe - chal' - noy:

Na - po - mi - na - yut mne o - ne   Dru - gu - yu

zhizn'   i   be - reg dal' - (nïy)

formed only two years before Rachmaninoff composed his song. The young
composer was evidently emulating the opera, although the opera was not the
source of the tradition in which he was participating. Rachmaninoff was also
probably responding to Balakirev's setting, to judge from the way the voice,
on its first entrance, dramatically interrupts the melody with a recitative, interpreting the first line of the poem, with its request not to sing, as an actual
command to leave off singing.

His setting also has conspicuous melismas: not little decorative authentic-
sounding ones like Balakirev's, which sound strange in the mouth of the poet-

EXAMPLE 9.3. Rachmaninoff, *Ne poy, krasavitsa*, Op. 4, no. 4 (1892)

EXAMPLE 9.3, *continued*

Example 9.3, *continued*

EXAMPLE 9.3, *continued*

Ne poy kra-sa-vi-tsa pri mne tï pe-sen

Gru-zi-ï pe-chal'-noy: na-po-mi-na-yut mne o-

ne _____ dru-gu-yu zhizn'; i be-reg dal'-noy.

EXAMPLE 9.3, *continued*

speaker, but great sweeping ones that have a motivic consistency deriving
from the opening neighbor-note. The neighbor-note motif is usually sounded
in pairs or in threes, with ties that connect resolution tones to the next preparation tone. The result is a syncopated undulation that is sounded in conjunction
with two other distinctive musical gestures to complete a characteristic semiotic cluster: a drone (or drum) bass such as even Glinka had suggested, and—
most important of all—a chromatic accompanying line that in this case steadily descends along with the sequences of undulating melismas.

To anyone privy to the tradition on which it depends, the song's opening
ritornello quite specifically conjures up the beautiful oriental maiden the song
is about—not the one singing, but the one remembered. And the ritornello
also tells us that she was the poet-singer's erotic partner; for the cluster of
signs (undulating melisma, chromatic accompanying line, drone) evokes not
just the East, but the seductive East that emasculates, enslaves, renders passive. In a word, it signifies the promise of the experience of *nega*, a prime
attribute of the orient as imagined by Russians. The word, originally spelled
with a "yat" (a vowel confiscated by the Bolsheviks after the revolution) and
drawled voluptuously by those who know that fact, is usually translated as
"sweet bliss," but it really connotes gratified desire, a tender lassitude (or
"mollitude," to rely once more on Nabokov's vocabulary).[9] In opera and
song, *nega* often simply denotes s–e–x *à la russe*, desired or achieved.

The syncopated undulation itself is iconically erotic, evoking languid
limbs, writhing torsos, arching necks. The drum bass and the melismas are an
echo of the stereotyped musical idiom Balakirev had primitively evoked,
nega's necessary ticket of admission (for Russian necks do not arch and
writhe). It is the descending chromatic line—neither iconically nor stylistically verisimilar, but a badge worn by exotic sexpots all over Europe (only
connect with a certain Habañera)—that completes the picture of the seductive East. The climax of the song—undeniably a climax despite the soft

[9] See *Eugene Onegin: A Novel in Verse by Aleksandr Pushkin*, trans. from the Russian, with a
commentary, by Vladimir Nabokov (New York: Pantheon, 1964), vol. 2, p. 186, where Nabokov
speaks of the word's "emphasis on otiose euphoria and associations with softness, luxuriousness
[and] tenderness." As an alternative he proposes "dulcitude."

dynamic—occurs at the setting of the last two lines, when the chromatic line is suddenly transferred from the middle of the texture to the voice part, at the top. It is by no means a unique or original touch; in fact it is rather typical. Indeed, everything about Rachmaninoff's setting is both typical and extreme. No masterpiece of the genre, it lays the *nega* on with a trowel, what with the threefold sequential repetition of the undulating melisma, and particularly with a chromatic line that descends through almost an entire chromatic scale. When it comes to suggesting *nega*, less can definitely be more.

HAVING ARRIVED at Rachmaninoff's locus classicus by way of antecedent settings of Pushkin's "Georgian Song," let us turn around and press back again in time, to discover the origins of the particular orientalist trope it embodies. Borodin has been already named as immediate precursor. Before getting to *Prince Igor* it will be useful to have a look at a little-known spinoff from the opera, a posthumously published song entitled "Arabian Melody" (*Arabskaya melodiya*), composed in 1881 at the request of the contralto Darya Leonova. It is a harmonization of a "khasid" (*qasida*), a North African improvisatory vocal solo to the text of a classical Arabic poem, which the composer found in a book his librarian friend Stasov procured for him, Alexandre Christianowitsch's *Esquisse historique de la musique arabe aux temps anciens* (Cologne, 1863). In the source the melody is labeled "Insiraf Ghrib," meaning a fast section from a *qasida* performed in the evening. Notwithstanding, Borodin's setting is a slow one, marked *Andante amoroso* (alternating, it is true, with piano ritornelli marked *Allegro passionato*). The text, about the lover's sweet death in love, is Borodin's paraphrase of Christianowitsch's French translation of the Arabic original. Translated into suitably archaic Italian, it could pass for a madrigal text. The melody is another oriental tune, like that of Glinka's "Georgian Song," that happens to coincide with a normal Western diatonic mode and so does not immediately give away its origin to the Western ear. What marks Borodin's song as "oriental" is the snaking chromatic accompanying line, so obviously related to the one in Rachmaninoff's "Georgian Song." While the song is often performed by male singers (notably Boris Christoff in a well-known recording), it is important to keep in mind that it was written for a contralto; the voice range, too, was a marker, as we shall see. Borodin would never have composed such a song for a bass (see example 9.4).

Where Rachmaninoff's chromatic line made a straightforward descent, Borodin's is serpentine, adding a new dimension of erotic undulation. The point at which the change of direction takes place is very significant. The line descends to the fifth degree, then passes chromatically up to the sixth, then down again through the same interpolated half step, joined now by a middle voice that proceeds to repeat the same double pass twice, not counting a couple of extra undulations between the fifth degree and its chromatic upper

EXAMPLE 9.4. Borodin, "Arabskaya melodiya," second strophe

EXAMPLE 9.4, *continued*

smert' slad - ka   mne, smert' ot   stra - sti k te - be.

neighbor. When the climax is reached ("But even death is sweet to me, the death born of passion for thee"), the rhythm of the undulation is excited into diminution and begins to spread out to neighboring scale degrees, ontogeny thus foreshadowing phylogeny, as we know from Rachmaninoff.

The reversible chromatic pass between the fifth and sixth degrees is in fact the essential *nega* undulation, as a little snatch from the Chorus of Polovtsian Maidens at the beginning of *Prince Igor*'s second act will prove (see example 9.5). Brief as it is, this little passage summarizes with great economy everything we have learned thus far: the text is about creature comfort and gratified desire (in this case the image of nocturnal dew following a sultry day is acting as *nega*-surrogate); the sopranos contribute the melodic undulation, here a sort of pedal; the altos contribute the harmonic undulation, from the fifth degree to the sixth and back through a chromatic passing tone each way; and the orchestral bass instruments supply the drum/drone. Even the ritornello at the end is a marker, for it is played on the English horn. We will encounter that timbre again.

Now we are equipped to get the full message from the most famous music in all of *Prince Igor* (see example 9.6). The famous "Polovetsian Dance" displays the whole cluster—melodic undulations tied over the beat, a chromatic pass between degrees 6 and 5, pedal drum/drone, English horn timbre—just as they are displayed in the "oriental" theme that confronts a Russian one directly in the "musical picture" *In Central Asia*. The theme makes its first appearance, predictably enough, as a long English horn solo. Illustrated here is the final statement, in which the chromatic inner voice grows to encompass a whole scale, as in Rachmaninoff's modeling of it, and is climactically repeated in an outer voice, in this case the bass (see example 9.7). It was a telling touch—and again, a typical one—to extend the length of each phrase to five bars through one extra languorous undulation ("please, just once more . . ."). What it tells us is why those hedonistic Central Asians were simply no match for the purposefully advancing Russians.

EXAMPLE 9.5. Borodin, *Prince Igor*, no. 7 (ten bars before figure 2)

EXAMPLE 9.6. Borodin, *Prince Igor*, no. 17 (four bars after figure 2, orchestra only)

EXAMPLE 9.7. Borodin, *In Central Asia*, mm. 175–92

What I have been calling the "markers" have long been recognized as essential features of Borodin's personal style (compare Ravel's *A la manière de Borodine* for piano [1913], where they all pass in review). They did achieve what we might call maximum strength in Borodin—who, by the way, though the illegitimate son of a Georgian nobleman, was born in St. Petersburg and never visited the orient—but they were none of them his invention. Compare the beginning of the Maidens' Dance from act 2 of Anton Rubinstein's *The Demon*, composed in 1871 after Lermontov's famous romantic poem set in Georgia (see example 9.8). It, too, could be titled "A la manière de Borodine." Or, conversely, Ravel's piano piece could have been entitled "A la manière de Rubinstein."

But both would have been misnomers; the origin of the style, as of so much in Russian music, lay in Glinka—in particular in the third act of *Ruslan and Lyudmila*, the opera Glinka based on the mock epic Pushkin had written between 1817 and 1820 during the first flush of Russian orientalism. The setting of Glinka's third act is the magical garden of the sorceress Naína, who keeps a chorus of sirens handy to enchant errant heroes. It goes without saying that these seductresses sing oriental tunes of promiscuous origin. Their first is called the Persian chorus, and it set the tone for all the exercises in *nega*-evocation that we have been examining (see example 9.9). Here is the fount

EXAMPLE 9.8. Rubinstein, *Demon*, act 2, Maidens' Dance

EXAMPLE 9.9. Glinka, *Ruslan and Lyudmila*, no. 12, mm. 93–112
(Naína's part omitted)

and origin, the passage that established the voluptuous undulation and the chromatic pass as emblems to be displayed by oriental singing or dancing girls in future operas and songs. Glinka claimed the melody was truly a Persian one that he heard sung by a Persian-born secretary in the St. Petersburg Ministry of Foreign Affairs. The claim must be true, because Glinka was not the only one who used the tune; it also figures in the middle section of Johann Strauss's *Persischer Marsch*, first played in Vienna's Volksgarten in December 1864 to welcome the visiting Shah. To compare Strauss's boisterous march with Glinka's dreamy chorus is revealing: what made the chorus a marker of *nega* and a model for generations to come were the elements Glinka brought to it, not any "oriental" essence. As a recent impassioned authority has observed, "Orientalism overrode the Orient."[10]

NOWHERE is this dictum better corroborated than in the archetypal embodiment of oriental luxuriance in Russian opera: Ratmir, the first of Naína's victims in the magic garden. He is an easy mark. One of three suitors in quest of the abducted Lyudmila, Ratmir is a young Khan of the Khazars, a nomadic Turkic tribe, famous for its eighth-century conversion to Judaism, and indigenous to areas lately acquired as of 1817 by the Russian empire. Pushkin introduces him as being "full of passionate daydreams," and that is why he fails in his quest: he simply cannot keep his mind on it. The fact that he is cast as a trouser role for a contralto has been ascribed to the composer's insistence on writing a major part for Anna Vorob'yova, the singer who made a sensation in the trouser role of Vanya the orphan boy in Glinka's first opera, *A Life for the Tsar*. But the contralto timbre also symbolized the torpid and feminized East.

Ratmir's big aria in act 3 of *Ruslan* shows him literally torpid, wandering into Naína's garden in a state of exhaustion, complaining that "sultry heat has replaced the shade of night," and longing for the sweet bliss of sleep. At this point he is musically characterized by a pedal bass, by the melismas he sings, and by an ornate English horn obbligato—in other words, by the trappings of local color. The melody is supposedly a Tatar (i.e., Mongol) tune Glinka had learned from the great seascape painter Ivan Aivazovsky; a near relative of it figures in David's *Le Désert* (see example 9.10).

This is obviously no characterization of a hero. It is the portrait of a loser, and so will the same set of markers characterize the ill-fated Georgian Prince Sinodal thirty years later in Rubinstein's *Demon*. Though a traditional tenor, Sinodal becomes an honorary contralto, emasculated by his Ratmirish melismas and the pedal bass. Note, too, the extraordinary economy of the English horn obbligato, which dooms the singer as lover even before he opens his mouth (see example 9.11). When the bass moves it does so in order to reestablish the tonic through the chromatic pass we have learned by now to

[10] Edward W. Said, *Orientalism* (New York: Pantheon, 1978), p. 196.

EXAMPLE 9.10. Glinka, *Ruslan and Lyudmila*, no. 14 (Ratmir's cavatina)

associate with *nega*. This, too, is something Sinodal shares with Ratmir—though not in the example we have so far examined.

For all his impotence Ratmir is a noble character, and to Glinka that meant Ratmir's big musical number had to get the full cantabile-cabaletta treatment. We have seen the opening cantabile. Now for the cabaletta, in which Ratmir has one of those "passionate daydreams" of his, mopishly recalling his harem. It has raised many eyebrows, this cabaletta, for it is cast as no oriental dance but in what Glinka frankly marks "Tempo di valse." Glinka's most recent biographer wrings his hands over the "stylistic non-sequitur" here, by which "the languishing oriental, approaching the height of passion, is converted into a waltzing Westerner." "Glinka," he concludes, "betrayed Ratmir badly in *Ruslan and Lyudmila*," and this proves that he was "simply unable to express real physical passion in music."[11]

Is "real physical passion" what Ratmir is all about? Of course not. Ratmir is an avatar of *nega*, the passive, feminine embodiment or enjoyment of "molles délices," as Nabokov has it.[12] Let us recall what constitutes *nega* in music at a minimum: tied or syncopated melodic undulations, and the reversible chro-

[11] David Brown, *Mikhail Glinka: A Biographical and Critical Study* (London: Oxford University Press, 1974), p. 223.

[12] *Eugene Onegin*, vol. 2, p. 186.

EXAMPLE 9.11. Rubinstein, *Demon*, act 1, scene 3 (Sinodal's arioso)

EXAMPLE 9.12. Glinka, *Ruslan and Lyudmila*, no. 14 (cabaletta)

matic pass between the fifth and sixth degrees of the scale. And now look at
the offending waltz—in which the text, not by Pushkin but by a poetaster
named Valerian Shirkov, makes a rare, explicit reference to *nega*. Leaving
that term untranslated so that it may incorporate all its associations, the words
are these: "A wondrous dream of quickening love rouses the fire in my blood;
tears scald my eyes, my lips burn with *nega*." Susan McClary might wish me
to say something at this point about autoeroticism,[13] but I will be true to my
promise and let the music do the speaking (see example 9.12).

The voice part is nothing but syncopated neighbors and appoggiaturas that
could easily be extended into Rachmaninoff's quintessential oriental
melisma, and the English horn does nothing but signal the chromatic pass,
immediately reversed in the bass so that it becomes a harmonic undulation—a
veritable mug. Far from playing the character false, the waltz is another locus
classicus of oriental languor seen through European—well, Eurasian—eyes.
Again, orientalism overrides the orient. Putting the two halves of Ratmir's
aria together we have a complete catalog of the devices that would be mined

[13] Compare her remarks on Don José's "Flower Song" from *Carmen*, in *Feminine Endings:
Music, Gender, and Sexuality* (Minneapolis: University of Minnesota Press, 1991), pp. 59ff.

by Russian composers bent on depicting that languor all the way to Rachmaninoff and beyond.

And now for the climax. Ratmir never achieves it; it had to wait until *Prince Igor*, in which the ultimate Ratmir surrogate finally made his/her appearance. Konchakovna is unique in the annals of opera: an ingénue role played by the throatiest contralto imaginable. Ratmir's voice range, as we see, has by now become an indispensable signifier. In the act 2 love duet with Vladimir, Igor's son (the ostensible heroic tenor), her voice coils all around and beneath his to startling effect. The falconet is indeed "entoiled by means of a fair maiden"—and emasculated. Nor had there ever been such an emphasis on raised fifths, flattened sixths, and chromatic passes in general. Rather than compile a tedious list, let us just note a few salient points.

At the very beginning of the excerpt (see example 9.13), which is cast over the harmony of the dominant ninth, Konchakovna's part obsessively applies the flattened sixth to the fifth while Vladimir, having gone through a variety of other passes, finally adopts hers at the fermata; she then turns around and makes another pass at him, from raised fifth to sixth, while he yelps in response, his répliques narrowed down to the sign of chromatic passing in its minimal, most concentrated form—what we might call the very morpheme of *nega*. The orchestral bass meanwhile gives out one of those complete chromatic descents that signal *nega* at full sensual strength. Again, she entoils him and he replicates her pass; they reach their first climax on a question ("Will you/I soon call me/you your/my wife?"), supported in the orchestra by a prolonged harmony rooted on the flat sixth, which finally makes affirmative— indeed climactic—progress through the dominant to the tonic. The change from question to affirmative reply itself takes the form, for Vladimir, of a chromatic inflection (the earlier sustained high A♭ now trumped by sustained high A♮). And while they hold their final notes the orchestra harps repeatedly on the hypnotic undulation of fifth degree and flattened sixth. Vladimir is now thoroughly lost: Ratmirized, his manhood *nega*ted, rendered impotent with respect to his (and his father's) mission, he must be left behind. No less than Ratmir, he has been the victim of a sinister oriental charm.

AND NOW, a few parting ironies. While something that could certainly be indulged for its own sake as soft porn, the orientalist trope associated with *nega*—a flexible amalgam of ethnic verisimilitude, sensual iconicity, characteristic vocal or instrumental timbres and Glinka-esque harmony—nevertheless functioned within the Victorian conventions of its time. In most of the examples discussed (and in any number of others) *nega*, associated with the orient, is held up as a degenerate counterpart to more manly virtues associated with Russians. It marked the other—marked it, in fact, for justified conquest.

With this in mind, a list of the Russian compositions through which Sergey

EXAMPLE 9.13. Borodin, *Prince Igor*, no. 12 (duet), eighteen bars after figure 3 to the end

EXAMPLE 9.13, *continued*

EXAMPLE 9.13, *continued*

Example 9.13, *continued*

EXAMPLE 9.13, *continued*

Diaghilev and his ballet company conquered Paris in their first two *saisons russes* (1909–10) makes droll reading. Besides the Polovetsian Act from *Prince Igor*, they include the "Apparition of Cleopatra" from Rimsky-Korsakov's opera-ballet *Mlada*; the Dances of the Persian Slave Girls from Musorgsky's opera *Khovanshchina* (presented, like the *Mlada* music, in an omnium gatherum choreographed by Mikhail Fokine under the title "Cléopâtre"); the Arabian Dance from *Ruslan and Lyudmila*, presented as part of another Fokine *salade russe* entitled "Le Festin"; Rimsky-Korsakov's *Sheherazade*, choreographed by Fokine to a murder-in-the-harem scenario by Alexander Benois; and Stravinsky's *Firebird*, the first original ballet Diaghilev ever commissioned. Clearly, *nega* was having a field day in Paris, and Stravinsky's first ballet was created in part to supply a new infusion of semi-Asiatic exotica-cum-erotica, the sex lure that underpinned Diaghilev's incredible success.

Of course, *nega* had a meaning for the French vastly different from what it meant to the Russians. For the French it meant Russia, for to them Russia was East and Other. The heavy emphasis on oriental *luxus* in his early repertory was something Diaghilev had calculated coldly, one could even say cynically. It accounts for the disproportionate popularity of Russian musical orientalia in the West to this day, and for the notion (abetted, of course, by Stasov's influential propaganda) that it was one of the main modes of Russian musical expression, if not (next to folklore-quoting) the dominant one. The ploy eventually held Diaghilev captive, preventing him from presenting to the West the musical artifacts of Europeanized Russia, beginning with Chaikovsky's operas and ballets, with which he personally identified. *That* Russia has always been despised in the West as inauthentic. It is one more reason why Chaikovsky, who outside of one little dance in *The Nutcracker* and one little aria in his opera *Iolanta* never mined the orientalist vein (and who alone among the major Russians has therefore gone practically unmentioned in this chapter), is still considered somehow less Russian—ergo, less valuable—than Musorgsky or Rimsky-Korsakov or Glinka.

And yet, as we have had ample opportunity to observe, the orientalist trope comprises far more than ethnic verisimilitude, and Chaikovsky, once this is realized, turns out to have been by no means immune to its lure. He made telling and (by now, to us) obvious recourse to it, quite early in his career, in the love themes from *Romeo and Juliet* (1869; revised, 1870, 1880), written just as the composer was getting over his infatuation with the soprano Desirée Artôt, the one woman known to have aroused his sexual interest, who had disappointed him by marrying the Spanish baritone Mariano Padilla y Ramos.

The frank sensual iconicity of this music is often remarked. Usually it is the throbbing, panting horn counterpoint that is so recognized; but the themes evoke *nega* just as surely by means of the strongly marked chromatic pass between the fifth and sixth degrees, and the first love theme (the one generally

associated with Romeo) features, on its first appearance, the equally marked
English horn timbre (example 9.14a). Juliet responds to Romeo's advance by
mirroring his descending chromatic pass with an ascending one that is then
maintained as an oscillation (or better, perhaps, an osculation), while Romeo's ecstatic reentry is prepared by reversing the pass and linking up with
the striking augmented-sixth progression that had launched Chaikovsky's
"balcony scene" to begin with (example 9.14b). At the climax, delayed until
the recapitulation, Chaikovsky enhances carnality by adding one more chromatic pass at the very zenith of intensity to introduce the last full statement
from which the love music will then gradually subside (example 9.14c).
Steamier than this Russian music would not get until Scriabin discovered
Tristan, a good three decades later.

As to the source of the steam, we have corroboration from the best of
witnesses. In a marvelously cruel letter to Chaikovsky (1/13 December
1869), Balakirev, the inspirer and the dedicatee of Chaikovsky's "Overture-
fantasia" and of course a connoisseur nonpareil of musical orientalism, reacted to the four main themes of the work, which Chaikovsky had sent him for
inspection while composition was still in progress. Here is what he had to say
about the big love theme:

EXAMPLE 9.14. Chaikovsky, *Romeo and Juliet* (1869 version)

EXAMPLE 9.14, *continued*

. . . simply enchanting. I often play it and have a great wish to kiss you for it. It has everything: *nega*, and love's sweetness, and all the rest. . . . It appears to me that you are lying all naked in the bath and that Artôt-Padilla herself is rubbing your tummy with hot scented suds. I have just one thing to say against this theme: there is little in it of inner spiritual love, only the physical, passionate torment (colored just a wee bit Italian). Really now, Romeo and Juliet are not Persian lovers, but European. . . . I'll try to clarify this by example. I'll cite the first theme that comes to mind in which, in my opinion, love is expressed more inwardly: the second, A♭-major, theme in Schumann's overture *The Bride of Messina*.[14]

Indeed, Schumann's long wet noodle of a love theme, which reaches no climax, does seem as if by design to moderate the orientalism of Chaikovsky's, diluting the chromatic passes and replacing the lascivious English horn with a chaste clarinet.

Balakirev's letter confirms the surmise that Chaikovsky used the orientalist trope metonymically, to conjure up not the East as such but rather its exotic sex appeal. The little tease about Artôt is provocative indeed, precisely because it is so plausible. If, as Balakirev seems to suggest, Chaikovsky had cast himself as Romeo to Artôt's Juliet, then the theme becomes a self-portrait. And if so, then it is another instance where, in a manner oddly peculiar to the Russian orientalist strain (and one that, unhappily, can give encouragement to essentialist assumptions), the eastward gaze is simultaneously a look in the mirror.

[14] Sergey Lyapunov, ed., *Perepiska M. A. Balakireva s P. I. Chaikovskim* (St. Petersburg: Zimmerman, 1912), pp. 49–50.

CHAPTER 10

ITAL'YANSHCHINA

EARLY EXPOSURE

During the night of 11/12 March 1801 (Old Style), Tsar Paul I of Russia was strangled in his bed by members of his retinue, acting either under orders or with the consent of the heir apparent, who would reign gloriously for a quarter century as Alexander I. Shortly thereafter, Paul's protégé, Giuseppe Sarti, the last in the brilliant line of Italians who served as musical directors to the imperial court and chapel in the eighteenth century, left Russia and was not replaced. At the beginning of the nineteenth century, Russia was all at once without a court Italian opera theater. It would take almost half a century before Italian opera would regain its mandate.

Early in Alexander's reign, in 1803, the public theaters of Russia were reorganized under a crown monopoly that lasted until 1882. Theatrical enterprises could no longer be undertaken as private speculations. All theaters became the property of the crown and were directly administered by the government. In St. Petersburg the official chain of command went from the autocrat through the governor-general of the city to a steering committee that oversaw the daily operation of the theaters and decided matters of repertory and personnel. As part of this reorganization, four public theaters were established in St. Petersburg. Tsar Alexander had already concluded a contract with Antonio Casassi, a dancer who had been working in Russia since 1780 and who had since 1792 been custodian of the Imperial Theaters under Catherine the Great, to form an Italian opera troupe for the capital, for which a new house—the *Noviy maliy teatr* (New Little Theater)—was constructed on the Nevsky Prospect. In 1803 the building was purchased by the government, and Casassi's troupe nationalized as one of the four theaters created under the new plan. The three other theaters—Russian, French, and German—presented spoken plays as well as musical ones; the Italian theater alone was to be reserved for operas. Named as its musical director was the Venetian Catterino Cavos (1776–1840), who had been on the staff of the Imperial Theaters since 1798, and who was also put in charge of opera and ballet spectacles at the *Bolshoy kamenniy teatr* (Great Stone Theater), the Russian-language house. The *Noviy maliy* repertoire consisted exclusively of opera buffa, mostly revivals from the court theater of Catherine the Great, and by "her" composers (Paisiello, Martín y Soler, Cimarosa; works of Salieri and Portogallo were also performed.)[1]

Casassi's superannuated enterprise lasted only until 1807; of all types of spectacle, Italian opera at this, one of its historic low points, had the least to offer the newly emergent Russian urban paying public. All the other theaters, by contrast, were flourishing, and musical plays were in every case the main attraction. Most fashionable by far was the French company, which performed for the public at the *Bolshoy kamennïy*, and for the court at the Hermitage and at Peterhof, the Tsar's retreat. Their repertoire—*opéras comiques*, rescue operas, vaudevilles by Dalayrac, Grétry, Isouard, Méhul, Catel, and Cherubini (and one Russian, Alexey Nikolayevich Titov)—was fresh and exciting, and there were two stars at the helm: François-Adrien Boieldieu, who in seven years as musical director (1804–11) presented the Russian public with some dozen premières of his own; and Charles Louis Didelot, who choreographed the ballets, for which a veritable craze developed. (Daniel Steibelt was also associated with the French opera from 1808, and stayed on in St. Petersburg until his death fifteen years later.) There was also a popular French theater in Moscow, as every reader of *War and Peace* will recall. And the same reader will not need to be reminded that French opera in Russia came to a sudden halt with the Patriotic War of 1812, and was never revived. (The last production in St. Petersburg had been Spontini's *La Vestale*, which opened on 13 January 1811, just three years after its Paris première.)

Between 1812 and 1829 operas were given in St. Petersburg only in Russian and German. This did not mean that the French and Italian repertories were altogether neglected. It was the German company, for example, that first introduced Russian audiences to Rossini (*Tancredi*, 1817). The Russian opera also presented Rossini in translation, along with works by Paer and Fioravanti. The Russian-language production of *Don Giovanni* in 1828 (with the title role transposed for the tenor Vasiliy Samoylov) was a direct stimulus on Pushkin's "little tragedy," *The Stone Guest* (1830), later set to music by Dargomïzhsky.

A word about Cavos: from the time of his appointment as music director at the *Bolshoy kamennïy* he cast his lot totally with the Russian opera so far as composition was concerned, and wrote all his mature operas to Russian librettos, many by Prince Alexander Shakhovskoy, a popular playwright of the time, who was also the *éminence grise* on the Imperial Theaters Committee. (Cavos also collaborated with Didelot on a number of French-style ballets

---

[1] Information in these paragraphs from Robert-Aloys Mooser, *Annales de la Musique et des Musiciens en Russie au XVIIIme Siècle*, vol. 3 (Geneva: Editions du Mont-Blanc, 1951); and Yuriy Keldïsh, "Opernïy teatr," in Yury Vsevolodovich Keldïsh, Olga Yevgeniyevna Levashova, and Aleksey Ivanovich Kandinsky, eds., *Istoriya russkoy muzïki*, vol. 4 (Moscow: Muzïka, 1986), pp. 25–61 (also "Khronologicheskaya tablitsa," pp. 354–406).

after the latter's return to Russia in 1816.) Thus despite his nationality Cavos does not properly figure in the history of Italian opera at all, even in Russia.

THE EARLIEST more or less continuous Italian opera enterprise in nineteenth-century Russia was based in neither capital but in the Black Sea port city of Odessa, where a state theater for opera and ballet was opened in 1809. In that year a small troupe of Italian singers and dancers led by an impresario named Montavani, featuring the celebrated *buffo cantante* Luigi Zamboni (1767–1837, the very one who would later create Rossini's Figaro) and his daughter Gustavina as prima donna, appeared in the city and began giving performances of opera buffa. They were officially engaged for the new theater beginning the next season, and returned regularly (except for the plague year 1812–13) until 1820, when they were lured to Moscow.[2] From 1821, Italian opera in Odessa was managed by Luigi Buonavoglia, whose chief claim to fame was having written the libretto for Paer's *Agnese di Fitz-Henry* (1809), one of the most popular operas of the period. It naturally figured in his first Odessa season (the next year it would be performed in the capital in Russian translation). Among the artists in Buonavoglia's roster was Adelina Catalani, sister-in-law of the world-renowned Angelica.[3] During his year of exile in Odessa (1823–24) Pushkin was an enthusiastic fan of Buonavoglia's company ("In the evenings I don't go anywhere except to the theater," he wrote a friend),[4] and recalled what he encountered there for the first time in a supplement ("Fragments of 'Onegin's Journey'") that did not make it into the definitive text of *Eugene Onegin*:

> No uzh temneyet vecher siniy,
> Pora nam v Operu skorey:
> Tam upoítel'nïy Rossini,
> Yevropï baloven—Orfey.
> Ne vnemlya kritike surovoy,
> On vechno tot zhe, vechno novoy,
> On zvuki l'yot—oni kipyat,
> Oni tekut, oni goryat,
> Kak potselui molodïye,
> Vsyo v nege, v plameni lyubvi,
> Kak zashipevshego Ai
> Struya i brïzgi zolotïye . . .

---

[2] Yakov S. Katsanov, "Iz istorii muzïkal'noy kul'turï Odessï (1794–1855)," in Boris Solomonovich Shteinpress, ed., *Iz Muzïkal'nogo proshlogo: Sbornik ocherkov* (Moscow: Muzgiz, 1960), pp. 393–459, esp. p. 407.

[3] Ibid., p. 408.

[4] J. Thomas Shaw, trans. and ed., *The Letters of Alexander Pushkin* (Madison: University of Wisconsin Press, 1967), p. 136.

No, gospoda, pozvoleno l'
S vinom ravnyat' *do–re–mi–sol*?

But the blue evening grows already darker.
Time to the opera we sped:
There, 'tis the ravishing Rossini,
Darling of Europe, Orpheus.
To severe criticism not harking, he
Is ever selfsame, ever new;
He pours out melodies, they effervesce,
They flow, they burn
Like youthful kisses, all
In mollitude, in flames of love,
Like the stream and the golden spurtles of Ay
Starting to fizz; but, gentlemen,
Is it permitted to compare
Do–re–mi–sol to wine?[5]

By the end of Pushkin's stay, at least eight Rossini operas had been performed in Odessa—and pretty skimpily, the great poet's enthusiasm notwithstanding. In 1820, the roster of the theater orchestra had been raised (!) to
sixteen. Only at the end of Pushkin's season did Buonavoglia manage to increase it again, to twenty-four.[6] As for the singing, one disgruntled melomane
compared the troupe to "a nomadic tribe who, having been around to all the
provincial stages [of Italy], to Bologna, Siena, Ferrara and elsewhere, is finally bringing its worn-out talents our way."[7] Perhaps the nadir was reached
in December 1827, with *Don Giovanni*, a disastrous one-night stand.[8] By
1830, despite a number of bankruptcies and a whole series of new managers,[9]
standards would be much improved (to judge by the same witness). The number of Rossini operas in active repertory would reach thirteen. New productions of Rossini would continue over the next decade, although from 1830
first Donizetti and then Bellini would come to dominate the repertoire.

The Odessa Italian opera reached its peak in the season 1844–45, when
Luigi Ricci took over the theater, introducing the works of Verdi (beginning
with *I Lombardi*), and bringing with him some first-class singing talent,
though as usual with provincial houses, it was talent either past its prime—for
example, Giuseppina Ronzi de Begnis—or before it. Into the latter category

---

[5] Aleksandr Pushkin, *Eugene Onegin*, trans. Vladimir Nabokov (New York: Pantheon, 1964),
vol. 1, p. 343.

[6] Katsanov, "Iz istorii muzïkal'noy kul'turï Odessï (1794–1855)," p. 412.

[7] Ibid., p. 411.

[8] See Tamara Nikolayevna Livanova and Vladimir Vasilyevich Protopopov, *Opernaya kritika
v Rossii*, vol. 1, part 1 (Moscow: Muzïka, 1966), p. 101.

[9] See Katsanov, "Iz istorii muzïkal'noy kul'turï Odessï (1794–1855)," p. 410.

fell the twins Franziska (Fanny) and Ludmilla (Lidia) Stolz, the elder sisters of the great Verdian soprano Teresa Stolz, with whom Ricci shared a notorious *ménage à trois* that led to his dismissal. (His operas, however, stayed in the repertory.) Another high point came in May 1851 with the appearance (as Norma) of Teresa Brambilla, two months after she had created the role of Gilda in *Rigoletto*. By this time there were thirty-five musicians in the pit.[10] The solo flautist was Antonio Sacchetti, whose son Liberio (1852–1916) would occupy the chair in music history and aesthetics at the St. Petersburg Conservatory for many years.

The Italian opera at Odessa, the longest-lasting if least remembered public enterprise of its kind in Russia, was a casualty of the Crimean War. It closed its doors for the last time in 1855.

"AND IS IT TRUE," wrote Pushkin from Odessa to his friend and fellow poet Anton Delvig in St. Petersburg, "that Rossini and Italian opera are coming where you are? My God! They are the representatives of heavenly paradise. I'll die of longing and envy."[11]

No, they were not coming just yet. Before taking on the capital, Zamboni and Co. (in reconstituted and much improved vocal shape) stopped off in Moscow, under the auspices of the old capital's loftily aristocratic Society of Music Lovers (*Obshchestvo liubiteley muzïki*; its directors included the Princes Yusupov, Dolgorukiy, and Golitsïn), which subsidized their appearances with a public stock issue. (What made it legal was the Tsar's own participation; Alexander bought ten shares and threw in an additional subsidy of 30,000 rubles per annum.)[12] They opened at Apraksin's Theater the evening of 12 November 1821 with *Il Turco in Italia*, the first Rossini ever to reach Muscovite ears. Though it developed a cult following among the fashionable, the Italian theater in Moscow never managed to turn a profit. It held on for only six seasons, until May 1827.

Our principal witness to the impression it made is Prince Vladimir Odoyevsky (1804–69), then at the very beginning of a distinguished literary career. (Like the poet and playwright Griboyedov, his contemporary, Odoyevsky was a dilettante composer as well.) His was the minority viewpoint—that of the Hoffmannesque or "Mozartean" opposition to the "Rossinists." Summing up the Italians' third Moscow season (1823–24), Odoyevsky listed their pros and cons from the frankly idealistic, Germanophile vantage point that was typical of literary Russians of the period (Pushkin, the greatest of literary Russians, was here as ever atypical):

---

[10] Ibid., p. 420.

[11] *Letters of Pushkin*, p. 143.

[12] Abram Akimovich Gozenpud, *Russkiy opernïy teatr XIX veka (1836–1856)* (Leningrad: Muzïka, 1969), p. 660; Vladimir Fyodorovich Odoyevsky, *Muzïkal'no- Literaturnoye naslediye* (Moscow: Muzgiz, 1956), p. 535.

One has to admire the Italian singers' artistry, their enviable flexibility of voice, likewise the all-around presentableness of the Italian enterprise, which affords the Muscovite educated class one of its favorite pleasures. For the sake of all this it might be possible to forgive the theater's excessive attachment to Rossini. But will our descendents (for whom alone we labor, as has been said) believe us when we say that in all the four years of the troupe's presence in our midst not a single Mozart opera has been given at the Italian theater![13]

As if to mollify their critics, Zamboni and Co. did put on *Don Giovanni* the very next year (31 January 1825) as a bénéfice for their prima donna, Luigia Anti (1800–1837). The production had its drawbacks; the title role was sung (as was then usual) by a tenor, with consequent damage to ensembles. But the veteran director's Leporello filled Odoyevsky with delight, allowing him the hope that "in our great city *Don Giovanni* were the turning point in that disease known as Rossinism."[14]

The disease having died out in Moscow of its own accord, the Italians continued northward to the imperial city, whither they were summoned by Count Matvey Wielhorski, St. Petersburg's leading musical patron. They opened with Rossini (*Il barbiere* and *Cenerentola*) at the *Bolshoy kamenniy* during the winter of 1828; their first full season in the capital would commence on 17 January of the next year. The troupe continued to feature their director, Zamboni, now aged sixty-one but still "the best of all his kind" in the words of Alexander Ivanovich Vol'f, the great chronicler of the St. Petersburg stage, "thanks to whom Rossini's comic operas pleased the melomanes even more than the rest" of the repertoire.[15] Another veteran of the Moscow campaign was the bass Domenico Tosi (d. 1848), who would spend the rest of his life in St. Petersburg, eventually joining the Russian opera troupe and (with legendary ineptitude) creating the role of Farlaf in Glinka's *Ruslan and Lyudmila*. Glinka himself, then in his twenties, was very friendly with the Italian artists during their St. Petersburg engagement, and in 1828 apprenticed himself for a while to Leopoldo Zamboni, the director's son, who was acting as the group's principal coach.[16] Among the newly engaged singers was the dramatic soprano Sophie Schoberlechner (1807–64), Russian-born daughter of Filippo Dall'Occa, a Bolognese musician (pianist and cellist) and voice teacher long resident in St. Petersburg. Her husband, the Austrian composer Franz Schoberlechner, composed a vehicle for her appearances in the Russian capital (*Il Disertore per l'Amore*), which was duly performed during the troupe's second St. Petersburg season.

---

[13] Odoyevsky, *Muzïkal'no-Literaturnoye naslediye*, p. 87.

[14] Ibid., p. 95.

[15] Alexander Ivanovich Vol'f, *Khronika peterburgskikh teatrov s kontsa 1826 do nachala 1855 goda*, part 1 (St. Petersburg: tip. R. Golike, 1877), p. 20.

[16] Mikhaíl Ivanovich Glinka, *Literaturnïye proizvedeniya i perepiska*, vol. 1 (Moscow: Muzïka, 1973), p. 235.

There would be only three such seasons. Despite a massive dose of contagion (eighteen different Rossini operas; eleven in 1829 alone) and despite year-round exposure (with summer seasons at the resort of Kamennïy Ostrov), the disease Odoyevsky sought to cure with Mozart never infected St. Petersburg at all. The Italian opera "failed to attract a large public or arouse the slightest enthusiasm," in the measured words of Vol'f, who placed the blame squarely on the performers. "Italian opera cannot withstand mediocrity; experience has proved this."[17] During the season 1830–31, Vol'f recorded, "the deficit mounted and mounted, until maintaining the costly troupe became impossible."[18] For the next dozen years neither Russian capital would hear any opera in Italian.

Even in translation, Italian opera fared poorly. A few rustic and sentimental perennials held the boards—notably Fioravanti's *Le Cantatrici villane* (*Derevenskiye pevitsï* in Russian) and Paer's *Agnese* (*Otets i doch'*, after its subtitle, "Il Padre e la Figlia"), without both of which, it seemed, no St. Petersburg season was complete—but novelties tended, as before, to be French. The Rossini repertoire reverted to those few standards that had been introduced in Russian before the Italian visit. Vol'f echoed in retrospect the *Schadenfreude* many were feeling at the time: "Our singers, ready for anything, set pluckily to making up their fioriuras under Cavos's guidance, nor did they fall on their faces; Rossini's *Cenerentola* and *Derevenskiye pevitsï* were heard with great pleasure, and nobody missed the far more artful renditions of the Italians."[19] Osip Petrov, the great Russian bass, then at the beginning of his career, was found a worthy, even a surpassing replacement for Zamboni in the basso-buffo roles.

ONSET

Another reorganization of the Imperial Theaters took place in 1829, reflecting the character of Tsar Nikolai I (reigned 1825–55), Alexander's younger brother, who, in the words of a prominent historian, "often bypassed regular channels, and . . . generally resented formal deliberation, consultation, or other procedural delay."[20] According to an ukase issued on 29 April, the cumbersome Imperial Theaters Committee was abolished. Its duties and powers were now concentrated in the office of a single Intendant of the Imperial Theaters, who reported directly to the Minister of the Imperial Household.[21] In effect, this placed the Imperial Theaters under the direct personal

---

[17] Vol'f, *Khronika peterburgskikh teatrov s kontsa 1826 do nachala 1855 goda*, part 1, p. 23.
[18] Ibid., p. 26.
[19] Ibid., p. 29.
[20] Nicholas Riasanovsky, *A History of Russia* (London: Oxford University Press, 1963), p. 360.
[21] Vol'f, *Khronika peterburgskikh teatrov s kontsa 1826 do nachala 1855 goda*, part 1, p. 23.

control of the Tsar, and under the financial control of the autocrat's personal exchequer. Questions of budget, repertoire, and personnel were subject to the Tsar's personal review; it was a prerogative Nikolai and his successors took seriously and exercised energetically. All questions of ordinary censorship aside, no theatrical work could see production without the Tsar's personal approval and implicit (often active) cooperation. It was something no critic could afford to forget. Nor could composers: Alexander Dargomïzhsky chose the subject of his first opera (*Esmeralda*, after Hugo) only after being persuaded by his friend Vasiliy Zhukovsky (not only a great poet but also a government censor) that his first choice, *Lucrezia Borgia*, could never be produced in Russia.[22]

Nikolai's ordinary censorship, meanwhile, was of a spectacular strictness. His accession having been opposed by an attempted palace coup in favor of his brother Konstantin (the so-called Decembrist revolt), Nikolai lost no time in instituting controls that almost rivaled the insanely repressive policies of his father, Paul. Among them was an immediate edict (promulgated 14 December 1825) that banned all "rescue operas" of the kind popularized in revolutionary France, and all operas with overtly antityrannical plots. Even *La Clemenza di Tito*, proposed for production in 1826 (possibly as a veiled hint to Nikolai to deal leniently with the Decembrists), was banned.[23] In addition, all operas with biblical plots were prohibited in keeping with the Orthodox Church's strictures against the secular depiction of religious themes, a ban that extended even to the inclusion of ecclesiastics (of any denomination) among the cast of characters. Thus Rossini's *Mosè in Egitto*, first performed in Russia in 1829, had to be disguised as *Pietro l'Eremita*, as it had been some years before in London. (When the expanded French version, sung in Italian, reached the Russian capital in 1853, it was in the guise of *Zorà*, again following London.) After 1848 restrictions became tighter yet: even when sung by Russian singers (i.e., in individual scenes or arias at benefit performances), some operas (*Lombardi*, *Ernani*) could be performed only in the original language[24]—a restriction reminiscent of that which until recently controlled the concert performance of sacred music in the USSR. The Nikolayan censorship outlasted Nikolai. *Les Vêpres Siciliennes*, as in Italy, was given in Russia (from 1857) as *Giovanna de Guzman*. (An incidental mark of the favored treatment accorded *La Forza del destino* on its world première in St. Petersburg in 1862 would be the fact that, by special—and precedent-setting— dispensation, its Franciscans, Padre Guardiano and Fra Melitone, would be undisguised.)

[22] Nikolai Findeyzen, ed., *A. S. Dargomïzhskiy (1813–1869): Avtobiografiya-Pis'ma-Vospominaniya sovremennikov* (Peterburg: Gosudarstvennoye izdatel'stvo, 1921), p. 5.

[23] Gozenpud, *Russkiy opernïy teatr XIX veka (1836–1856)*, p. 712.

[24] Gozenpud, *Russkiy opernïy teatr XIX veka (1857–1872)* (Leningrad: Muzïka, 1971), p. 180.

Few of the alterations mentioned thus far were uniquely imposed in Russia; censorship was a fact of theatrical life throughout Europe. That Nikolai's censorship was still and all the strictest may be seen in the case of *Guillaume Tell*—a touchy subject everywhere but France, but nowhere as touchy as in St. Petersburg. An alternative libretto, by J. R. Planché, had been prepared for London and afterward also used in Berlin and elsewhere. It was called *Andreas Hofer*, after the leader of the Tyrolean resistance to Napoleon. Yet even Hofer, despite his devotion to the Austrian Emperor, struck Nikolai as a dangerous example (and the events depicted too recent). A new libretto, set in the distant and innocuous fifteenth century, had to be concocted just for Russia by Rafaíl Mikhailovich Zotov, the head of repertory for the Imperial Theaters: drawing on Walter Scott's then-recent *Anne of Geierstein*, Zotov came up with *Karl Smelïy* ("Charles the Bold"), under which title the opera was given its St. Petersburg première in 1836.[25] Later, when the opera would be performed in Italian, Zotov's translated libretto (*Carlo il Temerario*) remained *de rigueur*. Thus such notorious Soviet adaptations as that by which Nikolai's favorite Russian Opera, *A Life for the Tsar*, was cleansed of its Tsarism had ample Tsarist, indeed Nikolayan, precedent.

Another Nikolaian ukase, issued two years earlier, had established a schedule of payments for theatrical authors and artists. Works were divided for purposes of emolument into five categories, as follows:

1. original tragedies and comedies in verse in five or four acts, or the music of "large operas" (4,000 rubles or 1/10 of receipts, whichever was greater)
2. original tragedies and comedies in verse in three acts, or prose plays in three or four acts, translations of tragedies and comedies in verse in five or four acts, or the music of "medium-sized operas" (2,500 rubles or 1/15 of receipts)
3. original comedies, tragedies, and dramas in verse in two acts or one, or in prose in three acts, translations of tragedies and comedies in verse in three acts, original vaudevilles in three acts, or the music of "small operas" (2,000 rubles or 1/20 of receipts)
4. original dramas or comedies in prose in two acts, translated dramas or comedies in verse in two acts or one, translations of excellent dramas in three or two acts, original vaudevilles in two acts or one (1,000 rubles or 1/30 of receipts)
5. translated vaudevilles and brief prose plays (by arrangement, not to exceed 500 rubles).[26]

These terms are of significance in the present context chiefly because they did *not* apply to foreign authors, nor were visiting artists' fees subject to the ordinary pay scale of the Imperial Theaters.

[25] Ibid., p. 78.
[26] Vol'f, *Khronika peterburgskikh teatrov s kontsa 1826 do nachala 1855 goda*, part 1, p. 17.

HISTORIANS of the Russian operatic stage now agree that the turning point for Italian opera in Russia came in January 1836—ironically enough, the same year (though not the same "season") as the première (in November) of Glinka's *A Life for the Tsar*, which laid the cornerstone for the development of a Russian national operatic school. Between that cornerstone and that development there would be a long wait; by contrast, the repercussions of the banner year for Italian opera were immediate. It was *Semiramide*, Rossini's last Italian opera and his most heroic, chosen by Cavos for his own bénéfice against the wishes of the Imperial Theaters Directorate,[27] and with his protégée Anna Vorob'yova (1816–1901) in the trousers role of Arsace, that tipped the scales for Italy. Vorob'yova had a fantastic personal success, the production turned an unheard-of profit, and it finally aroused a loyal following for Italian opera on the part of a public that had spurned the same repertoire in native renditions only a few years before. Nikolai Gogol, who happened to spend the year in the capital and wrote a theatrical diary, was among those amazed: "*Semiramide*, to which the public has been indifferent for the past five years [i.e., since Zamboni's troupe had last presented it], all at once enraptures the same public now that Rossini's music has become virtually an anachronism."[28]

In the wake of this epochal production, the tide began to turn at last away from the French repertoire and toward the Italian when it came to selecting novelties for the Russian opera (and for its surviving rival, the German) to produce. In 1836–37, besides *A Life for the Tsar* there were five new productions in the two houses combined. Of these, four were Italian. In 1838–39 it was four out of six; in 1839–40, five out of eight; 1840–41 (Russian figures only), three out of four. Beginning the next season, the Donizetti craze belatedly hit the Russian capital, and new productions would be for a while either by local composers or by the one Italian.

Perhaps even more significant, the proportion of operatic performances in St. Petersburg to straight dramatic ones—a proportion that had plummeted after the Italians had quit St. Petersburg in the early thirties—now began to rise, and by the early forties actually overtook the spoken drama.[29] Soviet historians have speculated that this sudden dominance of Italian opera was due to its greater political safety, given the strictures of the Nikolaian censorship, whether compared with its French counterpart or with the straight dramatic theater.[30] But though this may have had something to do with the number of productions and performances, it cannot account for the full houses and

[27] Anna Vorob'yova memoirs, quoted in Gozenpud, *Russkiy opernïy teatr XIX veka (1836–1856)*, pp. 751–52.

[28] Nikolai Vasilyevich Gogol, *Sochineniya i pis'ma* (St. Petersburg: tip. Prosveshcheniye, 1896), vol. 7, p. 338.

[29] Gozenpud, *Russkiy opernïy teatr XIX veka (1836–1856)*, pp. 719–20.

[30] Gozenpud, *Russkiy opernïy teatr XIX veka (1857–1872)*, p. 101.

the enthusiasm Gogol, among many others, wonderingly described. Over a single decade the Russian capital had turned from a town inexplicably unsusceptible to Italian music into one unexpectedly insatiable for it—and it had all been due to domestic, not imported, productions.

BUT NOW the Italians struck again, and decisively, for they had an invincible ally. In 1843, Giovanni Battista Rubini, the greatest tenor of the age but now getting past his prime, made a joint tour of Germany and the Netherlands with Liszt. Liszt, who had had a triumph in St. Petersburg the year before, now suggested (how cynically one cannot tell) that it was time for the forty-nine-year-old singer to conquer the cultural hinterland to the north and east. The ground had been broken for him at the beginning of the 1841–42 season, when the forty-four-year-old Giuditta Pasta had appeared with the Russian Opera in the title role of *Norma*, which she had created a decade earlier. In her honor, the other singers, all regular members of the Russian and German opera troupes, learned their roles in Italian, as they did for *Semiramide, Tancredi*, and *Anna Bolena*, the other operas in which Pasta appeared. In Vol'f's recollection: "She astounded everyone with her style, but her singing turned out to be highly unsatisfactory. The greatly renowned prima donna's voice was already jolly well shot."[31]

If the aging Pasta had had a fiasco, the occasion of her appearance was nonetheless an event, and the aging Rubini was eagerly welcomed in her train. Arriving in St. Petersburg during Lent, he began with concert appearances. On the reopening of the theaters, he took the title role in the Russian Opera's production of Rossini's *Otello*. Connoisseurs of Italian singing, who knew enough to regard the roulades and trills, the frequent resort to head voice, the *messa di voce*, the *portamento*, and the rest of Rubini's affectations as being as endemic to "the style and character of Italian music as the ogives are endemic to Gothic architecture,"[32] greeted Rubini with enthusiasm. To most of the audience, however, Rubini's "way of singing predominantly in falsetto . . . seemed at first a bit strange."[33] But when the great tenor appeared in Bellini (*Pirata, Puritani, Sonnambula*), and especially as Edgar in *Lucia*, a role in which his performance was already a legend, and one that exploited his mannerisms as if by design, resistance evaporated: "Not only our melomanes but the whole uninitiated crowd went into an indescribable ecstasy. . . . St. Petersburg had never heard anything like it, and it dawned on everyone how such singing, so full of passion and feeling, was supposed to affect one. It would be no exaggeration to say that the whole house wept."[34]

---

[31] Vol'f, *Khronika peterburgskikh teatrov s kontsa 1826 do nachala 1855 goda*, part 1, p. 98.

[32] Unsigned review in *Panteon*, quoted in Gozenpud, *Russkiy operniy teatr XIX veka (1857–1872)*, vol. 2, p. 190.

[33] Vol'f, *Khronika peterburgskikh teatrov s kontsa 1826 do nachala 1855 goda*, part 1, p. 106.

[34] Ibid.

Tsar Nikolai was waiting for this. He immediately appointed Rubini "director of singing" to the crown and, through his Intendant, Prince Pyotr Vol-
konsky, bade the Italian return in the fall of 1843 with a troupe, on terms no
artist could refuse: a personal fee of 80,000 rubles for a season to last from
October to February (= ca. 2,000 per performance; by contrast, Osip Petrov,
the highest-paid singer in the Russian troupe, still received the scale decreed
for Russian artists in 1827: 4,000 rubles—or, as paid in the 1840s in terms of
a reformed currency, precisely 1,142 silver rubles—per annum).

At a stroke, Nikolai had made his capital one of the operatic centers of
Europe, on a par with Paris, Vienna, and London; and he had identified himself in the eyes of world as an enlightened despot. These must be understood
as his objectives. Much has been made, especially by Soviet historians, of the
tyrant's scorn for all things Russian; and it is true that among the "enlightened" aristocracy of the period (and of course not only in Russia), a "national"
style could only mean an uncultivated or a rustic style. This may explain why
no one expected much from the Russian Opera; from the aristocratic point of
view it was a contradiction in terms. (And hence those comments overheard at
the première of *A Life for the Tsar* and widely reported thereafter: "C'est de la
musique des cochers"; "C'est mauvais; on entend cela dans tous les cabarets";
and so on.)[35]

Yet snobbery cannot alone explain the hugely expensive enterprise Nikolai
now undertook. It was first and foremost a diplomatic move. And, in a way
that can only look perverse if approached (as it usually is) from anachronistic
vantage points, it was a patriotic venture as well. To understand it as such we
may look to one of the Tsar's chief spokesmen, a journalist, censor, and
police informer named Faddey Bulgarin (1789–1859). Writing in his own
reactionary newspaper, *The Northern Bee* (*Severnaya pchela*), Bulgarin justified the enterprise in terms that must have reflected Nikolai's own thinking:

> Let's admit it: without an Italian opera troupe it would always seem as if some-
> thing were missing in the capital of the foremost empire in the world! There
> would seem to be no focal point for opulence, splendor, and cultivated diversion.
> In all the capitals of Europe the richest accoutrements, the highest tone, all the
> refinements of society may be found concentrated at the Italian Opera. This can-
> not be changed, nor should it be. The more noble delights, the greater the
> good. . . . Consequently, [the Italian Opera] not only satisfies our musical crav-
> ings but nourishes our *national pride*.[36]

And so it came about that St. Petersburg became the home of two opera
theaters (three for a season, but the Germans were soon squeezed out) with
two repertories, two languages, and two audiences. As the novelist Pyotr

---

[35] Cf. ibid., p. 56.

[36] *Severnaya pchela*, 1843, no. 220; 1844, no. 249 (both quoted in Gozenpud, *Russkiy
opernïy teatr XIX veka (1857–1872)*, vol. 2, p. 184).

Boborïkin put it in his memoirs, "At the Russian Opera you would find visitors from the provinces, bureaucrats (especially from the Office of Provisions next door), officers, and kids from school," while in the Italian Opera you would find "all of court-attached, diplomatic, military, and titled St. Petersburg."[37]

Though a little overdrawn, the essential accuracy of this observation is attested by César Cui. As a student he used to buy standing room for the Italian Opera (at twenty-five kopecks), in the "amphitheater" behind the balcony ("where there was a splendid view of the Bolshoy Theater's chandelier, and also of the performers' feet whenever they approached the footlights"). Upon receiving his officer's commission, he found it "unseemly" to be seen with the students in the amphitheater, yet "seats in the Bolshoy were beyond my pocket." The solution was to attend the Russian theater, the Mariyinsky, where prices were lower, "so I migrated thither, all the more so since I had just met M. A. Balakirev and learned from him of the existence of Russian composers."[38]

Meanwhile, just how unfashionable the Russian Opera became in the heyday of the Italian can be learned from an irritated memoir by Dargomïzhsky, who overheard a Count Bludov remark to a Princess Manvelova: "Ne chantez vous pas quelque chose de la Roussalka, *on dit* que c'est charmant." Added Cui, who printed the memoir and italicized the "on dit": "*Rusalka* had by then been given fifteen times or so, but he had never thought to buck the fashion and set foot in the Russian opera house."[39]

FRENZY

When Rubini reappeared in October, he had a hand-picked cast in tow headed by Giuseppe Tamburini (who also received 80,000 rubles) and the young Pauline Viardot (65,000 rubles). It was widely rumored that of the remaining artists at least one—Assandri, a prima donna "whose singing was as ugly as her appearance was beautiful," according to the memoirs of one of Nikolai's confidants[40]—had been hand-picked not by Rubini but by the Tsar, who had seen her in Warsaw. The Italian singers completely monopolized the winter season of the "Russian Opera"; only two Russians—Osip Petrov and the Ukrainian-born baritone Semyon Gulak-Artemovsky (later the composer of some locally popular singspiels)—were allowed to share the boards with

---

[37] *Za polveka*, quoted in Tamara Livanova, *Opernaya kritika v Rossii*, vol. 2, part 3 (Moscow: Muzïka, 1969), p. 153.

[38] "Iz moikh opernïkh vospominaniy," in César Cui, *Izbrannïye stat'i* (Leningrad: Muzgiz, 1952), pp. 510–25, esp. pp. 512, 517.

[39] Ibid., p. 404.

[40] Alexander Nikitenko, quoted in Gozenpud, *Russkiy opernïy teatr XIX veka (1857–1872)*, p. 185.

them. All the bénéfices went to the Italian stars. Viardot and Tamburini made sensations. The former, in a stroke of public-relations genius, interpolated Alyabyev's popular romance "The Nightingale" (*Solovey*) into the lesson scene in *Barbiere*. St. Petersburg went mad:

> Two subscriptions—one for thirty performances on Mondays and Fridays, the other for fifteen on Wednesdays—were sold out in an instant. At performances in which Viardot and Rubini took part, people who had never in their lives been higher up than the *bel étage* now congregated in the balconies and the gallery. In the lobbies all one heard was talk of "The Nightingale," and how Viardot had sung it with the purest Russian accent, or of *Sonnambula*, in which she vied with Rubini and moved everyone to tears in the awakening scene. In all this there was not the slightest affectation; serious people, connoisseurs of music (not even excluding Glinka himself) were no less carried away than the high-society dilettantes.[41]

Considering the malicious irony with which Glinka described the Imperial Italian Opera in his memoirs, this testimony is valuable. The reasons for Glinka's later disaffection, and the even more extreme disaffection of succeeding generations of Russian musicians, had only partly to do with musical (or dramatic) values.

The next season more world-class artists joined the roster: Marietta Alboni, Jeanne Castellan, Agostino Rovere. Subscriptions were increased to forty and twenty performances; with bénéfices, the season total came to seventy-six. The rage for Italian opera had become a mania, and the behavior of the Russian audience had achieved parity with that of audiences to the west. Vol'f describes flying wreaths and bouquets ("Until then St. Petersburg had not known the floral frenzy [*tsvetobesiye*]," he comments); loges turned into political and diplomatic meeting places (one was dubbed "la fosse aux lions"); other loges providing competing showcases for society belles.[42] The public divided into warring factions over the prime donne. Viardists and Castellanists interfered with performances, exchanged blows. Satirists had a field day—though they had to be careful to aim their darts at melomanes from the ranks of the merchant class or the civil service, not the nobility. One such was the young Nikolai Nekrasov, who wrote a long essay in the *Literaturnaya gazeta* on the way the rage for Italian operas was transforming life in the Russian capital:

> Everybody has begun to sing!
>
> You have a notion to take a stroll on the Nevsky—"Uu-na for-ti-ma [*sic*] lag-rima, uuu-na . . ." booms out behind you; you look into a coffee shop—

[41] Vol'f, *Khronika peterburgskikh teatrov s kontsa 1826 do nachala 1855 goda*, part 1, p. 107.
[42] Ibid., p. 112.

roulades à la Tamburini meet you even on the stairs. You drop in on a family of
your acquaintance, even one that lives all the way out on the Vïborg side of town,
and they'll immediately sit their daughter at the piano and force her to squeal her
way through an aria from *Norma* or some other opera. You turn into the remotest
little alleyway you can find, and you won't go ten steps before you meet up with
an organ grinder, who, seeing you from afar, has lost no time in starting up the
finale to *Pirata* in full expectation of a munificent reward.[43]

Highly placed Russian dilettantes began offering operas to the Italian
troupe. Alexey Fyodorovich L'vov (1798–1870), the personal adjutant to the
Tsar and the director of the Imperial Court Chapel Choir, whose chief claim to
fame was having composed the Tsarist national anthem (*Bozhe, tsarya
khrani*) some years earlier, was one of these. He had the libretto of his opera
Bianca und Gualtiero translated from German into Italian expressly for the
purpose of having it performed in the Russian capital. "Despite the participation of Viardot, Rubini, and Tamburini," Vol'f notes, "this score attained
what is called a *succès d'estime*."[44] (Audiences, in fact, railed at having domestic imitations diluting their subscriptions, and the Tsar obligingly forbade
further performances of operas by Russian composers at the Italian opera after
the season of 1848–49.)[45] Otherwise the repertory for 1844–45 (Rubini's last
season) consisted entirely of Rossini (four operas), Bellini (four), and Donizetti (seven). The Russian Opera, in a state of near-total neglect, had a repertory of only seven works in all (by Glinka, Verstovsky, Weber, Meyerbeer,
Hérold, Auber), and a season of only thirty performances, on Sundays only.

After one more season of attempting to compete (or rather, coexist) with
the Italians, the Russian Opera was finally "banished" to Moscow (autumn
1846), leaving the St. Petersburg operatic stage entirely in the hands of the
foreign troupe. Until 1850 the Russian troupe would appear in the Russian
capital only for short guest seasons in the spring, after the Italians had gone
home. It was an arrangement that has lived ever since in various sorts of
infamy in the historiography of Russian music, both in the late nineteenth-
century "nationalist" telling and in the more recent Soviet one. From 1850 the
Russian capital again supported the two troupes full-time, though hardly on an
equal basis.

Never again, for one thing, would the Russian opera sing at the *Bolshoy
kamennïy*. Its rather skimpy schedule of performances was worked into the
time available between dramatic spectacles at the so-called Alexandrinsky
Theater, the chief house for Russian drama, and between the clowns and the

---

[43] Quoted in Tamara Livanova, *Opernaya kritika v Rossii*, vol. 1, part 2 (Moscow: Muzïka,
1967), p. 66.

[44] Vol'f, *Khronika peterburgskikh teatrov s kontsa 1826 do nachala 1855 goda*, part 1,
p. 112.

[45] Gozenpud, *Russkiy opernïy teatr XIX veka (1857–1872)*, p. 208n.

bareback riders at the Circus Theater (*Teatr-tsirk*), which latter eventually became their home. The troupe was miserably equipped, miserably paid, thoroughly demoralized. *A Life for the Tsar*, the showpiece of the Russian repertoire, was done so poorly during this worst of all periods that the composer himself, as his sister has related, could not bear to sit through it.[46] Glinka, much embittered in his late years by artistic conditions in Russia, and creatively paralyzed by frustration, would not live to see a change.

Meanwhile, the subsidized Italian troupe was reorganized both as to personnel and as to repertoire. Rubini had retired, and Viardot, having been seized with whooping cough toward the end of the 1845–46 season, would not return to Russia until 1852. Of the original stars only Tamburini remained. The St. Petersburg prime donne in the late forties were Teresa de Giuli-Borsi and Erminia Frezzolini (the latter greeted on her debut by a delirious press reception, to which Vladimir Stasov, later such a shrill opponent of the Italian opera, made a rapturous contribution);[47] the primi tenori Carlo Guasco and Lorenzo Salvi; both Filippo Colini and Filippo Coletti sang baritone roles. (By this time the stars were receiving 100,000 rubles per annum apiece, a sum that, equaling 55,000 gold francs, made St. Petersburg the most lucrative operatic venue in Europe.) As these names already suggest, the main repertory innovation was the advent of Verdi, beginning with *I Lombardi* in the fall of 1845 ("O mia letizia," sung by Salvi, scored an instant hit).[48] The immediate post-Viardot seasons brought *Ernani* and *I due Foscari* (1846–47), and *Giovanna d'Arco* (1849–50). Verdi productions in the fifties would include *Nabucco* (1851, as *Nino*), *Rigoletto* (1853), *Macbeth* (1854, as *Sivardo il Sassone*), *Il Trovatore* (1855), *La Traviata* (1856), *Luisa Miller* and *Les Vêpres siciliennes* (both 1857, the latter as *Giovanna di Guzman*).

The repertory expanded in a different direction during the 1849–50 season when the troupe presented *Les Huguenots*, sung in Italian to a disguised libretto under the title *I Guelfi e i Ghibellini* (four years later *Le Prophète* would arrive, disguised as *L'Assedio di Ghent*). *Les Huguenots* was chiefly a vehicle for the St. Petersburg debuts of Mario and Grisi, who created sensations in this and other operas (including *Don Giovanni*) of a kind that Vol'f, looking back in 1877, insisted had never been equaled since.[49] Mario (himself of noble birth) became the personal protégé of the Tsar.

An indication of how a privileged theatrical enterprise could flourish under Russian conditions (viz., an autocracy that owned all theaters directly, subsidized them from the Tsar's private purse, and administered them through the

---

[46] Lyudmila Shestakova, "Posledniye godï zhizni i konchina Mikhaíla Ivanovicha Glinki," quoted in Livanova, *Opernaya kritika v Rossii*, vol. 2, part 3, p. 12.

[47] Gozenpud, *Russkiy opernïy teatr XIX veka (1857–1872)*, p. 178.

[48] Vol'f, *Khronika peterburgskikh teatrov s kontsa 1826 do nachala 1855 goda*, part 1, p. 116.

[49] Ibid., p. 141.

civil service) was given the next season, when the critic Bertold Damcke, having dared find deficiencies in Mario's performances, found himself deprived of his forum (the French-language *Journal de S-t Pétersbourg*) at the instigation of Alexander Gedeonov, the Intendant of the Imperial Theaters, who had secured the assistance of the Ministry of Foreign Affairs (i.e., the censorship) to protect the huge financial investment the state treasury had made in the singer. In a similar case, a threatened hissing party was dissuaded by a counterthreat of police action.[50]

The Tsar was known to meddle personally in matters artistic, if in his considered opinion they seemed to warrant political control (and in Russia—then as later—the line between the artistic and the political domains was blurrier than anywhere else). A case in point, related by Anton Rubinstein, who witnessed it, sheds some light as well on the blurry relations between matters of church and matters of state in Nikolai's Russia. The Tsar was attending the première of *Le Prophète*:

> In the intermission following the coronation scene, [His Majesty] Nikolai Pavlovich came onto the stage, approached Mario, conversed with him, made some flattering remarks about his performance and then asked him to remove his crown. Nikolai Pavlovich broke the cross off the crown and gave it back to the dumbfounded singer.[51]

In Russia, where orthodoxy and autocracy went hand in hand, it was unacceptable that the leader of an insurrection be shown sporting a cross.

New artists of the fifties, the great decade of the Imperial Italian Opera, included the then as yet unknown Enrico Tamberlik (who at his benefit in December 1850 "acquainted us with the C♯ [in *Otello*] that would later gain him a European reputation"),[52] Giorgio Ronconi, Luigi Lablache (then at the dusk of his career and mainly confined to buffo roles), Tacchinardi-Persiani (also noticeably in decline), Achille de Bassini, Medori, Pozzolini, Nantier-Didier, Lagrua, Brambilla—to list only those discussed individually in Budden's *The Operas of Verdi*. Two not named there but who must be mentioned here were Enrico Calzolari (1823–88) and Angiolina Bosio (1830–59), who made their mature careers (if Bosio can be said to have had a mature career) almost entirely in Russia. Calzolari, a *tenor di grazia* who appeared in no fewer than fifty-four operas on the St. Petersburg stage between 1853 and 1871,[53] carried an official title as "First Singer of Their Imperial Majesties."

[50] Ibid., p. 148.

[51] Anton Rubinstein, "Avtobiograficheskiye rasskazï, 1829–1867," in Lev Aronovich Barenboym, *Anton Grigor'yevich Rubinshteyn: Zhizn', artisticheskiy put', tvorchestvo, muzïkal'no-obshchestvennaya deyatel'nost*, vol. 1 (Leningrad: Muzgiz, 1957), pp. 397–421, esp. p. 412.

[52] Vol'f, *Khronika peterburgskikh teatrov s kontsa 1826 do nachala 1855 goda*, part 1, p. 155.

[53] See the list in Viktor Adolfovich Bernatsky, "Iz zolotogo veka ital'yanskoy operï v Peterburge," *Russkaya starina* 168 (1916): 17–24, 276–83, 434–56, esp. pp. 279–80.

As for Bosio, it was she who replaced Viardot as St. Petersburg's special darling. She never sang in Italy past the age of eighteen, but had made her prior reputation in Paris and London, as well as America. Engaged for the 1855–56 season on terms only St. Petersburg could afford, she made her debut there as Gilda, a role she had created for Covent Garden. An overnight sensation, she reigned for four years as the great Russian Verdi heroine. Vol'f's 1884 recollection of Bosio as Violetta is full of loyal nostalgia: "Since Bosio no one has sung the role here to such perfection, not excepting Patti."[54] Serov, an avowed opponent of the Italian Opera, went further, attributing whatever success *La Traviata* had achieved in Russia to Bosio alone: "Right now," he wrote in 1856, "this opera is attracting and will continue to attract a crowd, because Mme Bosio as Violetta sings marvelously, working wonders with this music. Given such a bewitching performance one will sometimes give the composer credit for subtlety and tenderness in the dramatic characterization, as well as beautiful ideas. Yet without Mme Bosio you wouldn't find such qualities in this score with a microscope."[55]

The idealized affection in which Bosio continued to live in Russian memory had to do with the romantic circumstances of her sudden illness and Violetta-like death in St. Petersburg, caused by pneumonia at the end of the season of 1858–59. She was twenty-eight. Some idea of the devotion she inspired may be gained from an unlikely source, the memoirs of an impressionable youth of the period, Prince Pyotr Kropotkin. The famous anarchist recalled:

> When the prima donna Bosio fell ill, thousands of people, chiefly of the youth, stood till late at night at the door of her hotel to get news of her. She was not beautiful, but seemed so much so when she sang that young men madly in love with her could be counted by the hundred; and when she died, she had a burial such as no one had ever had at St. Petersburg before.[56]

Other decidedly nonfrivolous types who worshiped Bosio included the poet Nikolai Nekrasov, once so condescending toward the Italian opera, who memorialized his heroine in sentimental verse ("Daughter of Italy! With Russian frost / How hard to harmonize the noonday rose"); and—most surprising of all—the radical writer Nikolai Chernïshevsky, whose somewhat paradoxical relationship to the Italian Opera will be a matter to examine more closely further on. Yet despite such deviant modes of reception, the Italian Opera never ceased to be Russia's "official" opera, the artistic emblem of the Russian court and aristocracy.

---

[54] Vol'f, *Khronika peterburgskikh teatrov s kontsa 1826 do nachala 1855 goda*, part 2 (St. Petersburg: tip. R. Golike, 1877), p. 110.

[55] Alexander Serov, *Izbrannïye stat'i*, vol. 2 (Leningrad: Muzgiz, 1957), p. 414.

[56] Peter Kropotkin, *Memoirs of a Revolutionist* (Boston: Houghton, Mifflin, 1899), p. 119.

AN OUTSTANDING illustration of its status was the way it came to Moscow. After the Zamboni troupe's failed attempt to establish itself in the second city, there had been no Italian opera to speak of there until 1844, when the Moscow Intendant of the Imperial Theaters (Alexey Verstovsky, himself a distinguished composer of Russian operas) had invited the Odessa troupe up for a guest tour featuring Lorenzo Salvi, who had not yet sung in St. Petersburg, as star performer. A subscription was gotten up to establish a regular troupe the next year on the coattails of the brilliant first season at St. Petersburg, but it had to be discontinued after a single season. From 1845, Moscow had relied for its Italian opera on the occasional touring provincial company, even as the star-studded Imperial troupe was hitting its stride in St. Petersburg.[57]

But in the late summer of 1856, there was an occasion—a doubly official one—for which Italian opera on a grand scale was deemed indispensable: the opening of the newly restored Moscow Bolshoy Theater, celebrated amid the festivities attending the coronation of Alexander II. The whole Italian troupe, headed by Calzolari, Lablache, De Bassini, and of course Bosio, was sent down from St. Petersburg to inaugurate the theater. Between 20 August and 27 September they gave more than twenty performances of eight operas by Bellini, Donizetti, and Verdi.[58] Thus did the Russian Empire celebrate its great occasions of state.

Thereafter, for the duration of Alexander II's reign, the Moscow Italian Opera (a branch office of the St. Petersburg company) would inhabit the second city's Bolshoy Theater. For a time, as in St. Petersburg, it would totally eclipse the Russian. Regular subscription seasons began in 1861, at the initiative of Leonid Fyodorovich Lvov, Verstovsky's successor as Intendant of the Moscow Imperial Theaters, whose brother had composed that old ersatz *Bianca e Gualtiero*. The early seasons, on a lowish budget, were for the most part starless. The level of performance was consequently no match for St. Petersburg, but it was apparently good enough for Lev Tolstoy, who attended the Moscow Italian opera regularly in his younger, not yet art-hating days. His diaries record a few laconic reactions, mostly favorable: "Even the music was very pleasant" (on Rossini's *Mosè*); "I was up to understanding and enjoying the first two acts but then I got tired" (on *Guillaume Tell*). *Faust*, on the other hand, was "stupid."[59]

From 1868 the Moscow seasons, indeed the Bolshoy Theater itself, became the bailiwick of the impresario Eugenio Merelli, son of Bartolomeo Merelli, the old dictator of La Scala and Donizetti's old librettist. It was Merelli who succeeded in engaging Desirée Artôt, who enlivened the Moscow scene and captured the heart of that unlikeliest of suitors, Chaikovsky (hired to write

[57] Information in this paragraph from Gozenpud, *Russkiy opernïy teatr XIX veka (1857–1872)*, vol. 2, pp. 239–41.

[58] Livanova, *Opernaya kritika v Rossii*, vol. 2, part 3, p. 44.

[59] Ibid., p. 192.

recitatives for Auber's *Fra Diavolo*, performed, in Italian, as Artôt's bénéfice in January 1870). A single appearance of Tamberlik (as Manrico) in October 1870 and the guest tours of Adelina Patti beginning the next season were the artistic high points of the official Italian Opera's Moscow branch.

SUBSIDENCE

So it has been two decades now (or nearly) that the Russian Opera has suffered extraordinarily from the prevalence among the public of a taste for a foreign opera, an Italian one. There are an abundance of people in St. Petersburg who, having held loges by subscription at the Italian Opera for fifteen years running, have hardly even heard of the existence among us of a Russian opera theater, have no idea that there is such a thing as *Ruslan and Lyudmila*, or Dargo-mïzhsky's *Rusalka*, and only just heard *A Life for the Tsar* by chance because they wanted to see the inside of the new Mariyinsky Theater. There can be no denying that *Italian* opera, excellently performed by wonderful *Italian* singers, is a fine thing, even an aesthetic one; it can give much enjoyment to the most enlightened taste. Rubini, Lablache, Tamburini, Malibran in the epoch of their greatest brilliance managed to turn even Goethe's head, as is plain from his letters to his wife. There can be no denying that such a dainty dish . . . ought to be part of the luxurious life of all the great world capitals. Neither Paris nor London could do without its Italian opera; in Vienna, too, and in Berlin the Italian opera appears frequently. But what a difference compared with us! Berlin, Vienna, Paris all put *their own* opera first.[60]

So would St. Petersburg, ere long. In 1859 a seeming disaster befell the Russian opera troupe. The Circus Theater, their home since their return from Muscovite exile, burned down. Yet it was a blessing in disguise, for it enabled the dawn of a new era. Arts policies under Alexander II were more favorably disposed to the national company. Active patriotic propaganda in the wake of the Emancipation and, especially, the Polish uprising of the early sixties (not to mention the many plots and attempts on the life of the Tsar) led to the cultivation of native Russian art as an instrument of state ideology. The period around 1860 was also a time of intensive professionalization in all phases of Russian musical life, led by the indefatigable Anton Rubinstein. Accordingly, a new and very well appointed theater was built on the old Circus site expressly for the Russian opera and ballet troupes: the legendary Mariyinsky (in Soviet times the Kirov), which opened its doors in 1860.

Still, the first two seasons of the new decade were dominated by Verdi's presence in the Russian capital. On the surface this brought new luster and legitimacy to the city as a center for Italian opera; at the same time, though, it

---

[60] "Opernïy repertuar v S.-Peterburge," *Iskusstva*, no. 2 (1860); quoted in ibid., part 4 (Moscow: Muzïka, 1973), p. 273.

brought certain festering matters to a head. Both Verdi's trips were connected with the staging of the opera that the new Intendant of the Imperial Theaters, Andrey Ivanovich Saburov, had commissioned from him. Had it not been for Emma Lagrua's illness and subsequent loss of her voice, *La Forza del Destino* would have had its première in the early months of 1862. As it was, it had to wait until October (November, New Style), when Leonora was sung by Caroline Barbot, a singer new to St. Petersburg whom Verdi himself had recommended for the part. Nevertheless, there was a major Verdi première during the earlier season: *Un Ballo in Maschera*, in a strong performance by many of the same singers who would eventually do *Forza*—Tamberlik, Graziani, Nantier-Didier. Verdi's well-publicized presence in the city added a special naive excitement to the performances of all his works; here the Russian capital showed itself still, *au fond*, a gawky provincial town:

> From 24 November—that is, from the day of Verdi's arrival in St. Petersburg— each performance of his operas *Traviata* (4 December [1861]), *Trovatore* (6 December), *Un Ballo* (9 December) invariably finished with long, loud, abundant yet futile calls for the composer. Blessed with a congenial personality, *un uomo aggradevole sociale*, as his Italian chums would have it, a merry companion in the circle of his friends but at all times modest, Verdi avoids official manifestations of approval, he recoils from ovations. It might easily have been true that on the evenings in question the maestro was not even in the theater, for, as is well known, he prefers to listen to the works of others. We wish to say only that not one of these calls for him went by without some comical misadventure or, in one case, a strange (to put it tactfully) outcome. On Wednesday, 6 December, the calls for Verdi were especially insistent. The voice of Tamberlik, who tried to announce that the maestro was not present in the theater, was completely drowned out by the redoubled demands for his appearance. In order to put a stop to all the vain shouting, it was necessary to send out the esteemed prompter of our Italian opera troupe, Sgr. Garignani, with the same news. As soon as the multitude of Verdians caught sight of a man on stage in an ordinary suit instead of a costume, all thunder rained down upon him: "Bravo Verdi! Evviva il maestro! Bravissimo!" No matter how hard Sgr. Garignani tried to convey, by word or gesture, that he was not Verdi, it was all in vain. Triumphant applause accompanied him into the wings.[61]

Yet this delirium did not repeat itself the next November: *Forza* did not take hold. Pyotr Sokalsky, a Ukrainian composer who was then reporting on St. Petersburg musical life as correspondent for a Moscow newspaper, wrote of "satisfaction in the parterre and the loges, dissatisfaction in the foyer and

---

[61] Matvey Stepanovich Lalayev, "Ital'yanskaya opera v Peterburge," *Sovremennik* 91 (January 1862), quoted in Livanova, *Opernaya kritika v Rossii*, vol. 2, part 3, pp. 298–99.

the gallery."[62] By 1881 *Forza* would have only nineteen performances in the city of its première, while *Ballo* would amass ninety-two.

Indeed, that gala première turned in the end into a rather equivocal and ill-presaging event, owing chiefly to resentments over finances and payments—not only the actual expenses, but the invidious double scale that consigned Russian performers and composers to an essentially unsupported existence on the fringes of their own country's artistic life. It was a situation comparable to that which obtained in America in the first half of this century and bred the same hostilities. Verdi had been paid 60,000 francs (= 33,000 rubles) at a time when the statutory limit for compensation to a Russian artist for a single performance (even if that meant composing the score) remained fixed just where it had been set at the beginning of Nikolai's reign some three and a half decades before. In addition Verdi was granted an expense account of 5,000 rubles and a per-performance honorarium of 806 rubles 45 kopeks.[63] As a result, most Russian musicians had their knives out, and just about everyone's perception of the opera's quality was measured against, and colored by, their perception of the wastefulness of the enterprise. Thus Vol'f, normally a dispassionate chronicler:

> Saburov had made a show of generosity at the expense of the state exchequer and paid Verdi 60,000 gold francs plus traveling expenses. Everyone was expecting miracles for such money, and meanwhile the opera turned out to be the famous composer's weakest work. At the first performance Verdi was much applauded and called for, of course, out of courtesy, but subsequently there was hissing to be heard and poor receipts. As a result the sixty thousand turned out to have been thrown out the window for the sake of Saburov's desire to gain fame in Europe as an enlightened patron of the arts.[64]

Alexander Serov, never dispassionate, was even blunter:

> Maestro Verdi was mistaken in his opinion of the northern barbarians. The "Scythians" have judged his new opera, against all expectation, at its true worth. It was not hissed throughout out of sheer courtesy, out of hospitality. You can't very well abuse someone you yourself have invited. But woe betide any Russian composer who may appear before the St. Petersburg public with such an opera. He won't get a production like the one Verdi was given, not even in his dreams! His score will appear before the court in all its poverty. People are always a hundred times stricter with one of their own, who comes without benefit of fash-

---

[62] *Moskovskiye vedomosti*, no. 245 (9 November 1862); quoted in ibid., part 4, p. 305.

[63] A. Dmitriyeva, "Peterburgskaya opera Verdi," *Muzïkal'naya zhizn'*, no. 8 (1988): 19–21, esp. p. 19.

[64] Vol'f, *Khronika peterburgskikh teatrov s kontsa 1855 do nachala 1881 goda* (St. Petersburg: tip. R. Golike, 1884), p. 118.

ion or fame. What would follow such a fiasco would be nothing short of scandal. . . . And rightly so![65]

This was a turning point. The later sixties were a period of marked decline for the St. Petersburg Italian opera. The repertoire was ossifying, growing stale. There were no composers on the Italian horizon to compare with Verdi or his predecessors. The novelties in the seasons between *Forza* and the next Verdi première (*Don Carlo* in 1869, another fiasco that according to César Cui demonstrated "the total collapse of the Italian school and the facelessness of its great maestro")[66] were either ephemerae by Bottesini (*Chatterton*), Pedrotti (*Fiorina*), Ricci (*Rolla, Crispino e la comàre*), or Cagnoni (*Don Bucefalo*, which proved, again according to Cui, that "even the Italians despise their music and caricature it"); or they were the work of non-Italians (Gounod, Boieldieu, David, Meyerbeer). Interest in Wagner, meanwhile, was given a great boost by his personal appearances in St. Petersburg and Moscow in 1863, much trumpeted by Serov, if not the greatest surely the most prolific music critic Russia (if not the world) had ever seen. St. Petersburg would not see a Wagner opera on stage, however, for another half decade.

Italian performing talent seemed, at least from the vantage point of Russia, to be declining along with composition. In his account of the 1864–65 season, Vol'f notes that "there has been a general cooling toward the Italian opera, probably on account of the shortage of stars of the first magnitude in the female roster."[67] A couple of seasons later the situation had grown worse: "There has been no change in personnel, and all the same operas were performed. Everyone complained about the monotony of the repertoire and began to talk as if the very costly Italian opera were altogether superfluous."[68] By the middle of the 1866–67 season, rumors were rife that it would be the last. César Cui reacted with predictable self-congratulation: "What is most pleasing in this is the fact that the Italian Opera died a natural death, not a violent one. . . . Thus St. Petersburg turns out to be the first capital that will do without Italian opera. The foreign press is applauding us. One newspaper has even invoked that well-known verse of Voltaire's, 'C'est du Nord, à present que nous vient la lumière.' "[69]

Though reports of its demise were on this occasion premature, the fortunes of the Italian troupe continued to decline. In an article summing up the 1868–69 season, Cui could crow that whereas the Italian opera had ended the season

[65] Serov, *Izbrannïye stat'i*, vol. 2, p. 515.
[66] Cui, *Izbrannïye stat'i*, p. 148.
[67] Vol'f, *Khronika peterburgskikh teatrov s kontsa 1855 do nachala 1881 goda*, p. 121.
[68] Ibid., p. 123.
[69] Cui, *Izbrannïye stat'i*, p. 87.

with a deficit of 200,000 rubles, the far less expensive Russian opera, riding the crest of a new-won popularity, had shown a profit of 60,000.[70] Yet it was not the Russian Opera that was giving the Italian its stiffest competition but the French theater, enjoying a new burst of popularity thanks to what a horrified Kropotkin called "the putrid Offenbachian current" that "infected all Europe":

> Both [the Italian Opera and the Russian] were now found "tedious" and the cream of St. Petersburg society crowded to a vulgar theater where the second-rate stars of the Paris small theaters won easy laurels from their Horse Guard admirers, or went to see *La Belle Hélène*, which was played on the Russian stage, while our great dramatists were forgotten.[71]

What staved off the inevitable for a while was the arrival out of the blue of the young Adelina Patti, she of the "marvelous metallic voice and mechanical, supernatural perfection of coloratura technique,"[72] at the tail end of the otherwise disastrous season just described. The phenomenal general intoxication she produced has been immortalized by ridicule in Musorgsky's hilarious *Peepshow* (*Rayok*), composed the next year. There, it is Feofil Tolstoy (1810–81)—a dilettante composer of markedly Italianate leanings (his *Il birichino di Parigi*, mounted by the Italian Opera in 1849, had provoked Nikolai's ban on native products) but better remembered for the music criticism he wrote under the pseudonym Rostislav—who is shown in the throes of Pattimania. She had her detractors (Cui: "The first time I heard her I was bowled over by her vocal prestidigitation; the second time I listened with indifference to her familiar tricks; thereafter I slept").[73] But the rabidity she inspired was unprecedented, infecting even some of the Italian Opera's most outspoken foes. The most stiff-necked of all, Alexander Serov, actually composed for Patti an *Ave Maria d'una penitente* (figure 10.1, overleaf), which the diva sang in his memory following his sudden death in 1871.

As long as Patti was there to sing it, there would remain an avid audience in the Russian capital for the Italian Opera's traditional repertoire. Rossini, Donizetti, Bellini, all bloomed anew. When she sang Zerlina, even *Don Giovanni* was a popular opera. All at once the Italian opera was again the hottest ticket in St. Petersburg. The troupe's finances were shipshape, prospects ever bright. The old ironizing commenced once more; thus Chaikovsky: "Is it not flattering to our national pride, when all is said and done, that at a time when so many capitals, directing their envious glance at the northern barbarians, are forced to content themselves with their homegrown (albeit excellent) opera,

[70] Ibid., p. 149.
[71] *Memoirs of a Revolutionist*, pp. 119–20, 252.
[72] Cui, *Izbranniye stat'i*, p. 514.
[73] Ibid.

FIGURE 10.1. Alexander Serov's tribute to Adelina Patti, composed in 1869, published (by "B. [recte V.] Bessel, Sᵗ Pietroburgo") in 1870, and sung in the composer's memory by the dedicatee in 1971 (Asafyev collection, Russian National Library, Moscow)

Figure 10.1, *continued*

we possess Italians with Patti at their head?"[74] But then came the evening of 1 February 1877, Patti's bénéfice in the role of Gilda:

> The beneficiary was greeted with the customary triumph and showered with flowers. The opera went better than ever; everyone noticed that the beneficiary was singing and acting with an ardor that was not only unusual, but uncharacteristic of her, especially her scenes and duets with [the primo tenore, Ernest] Nicolini. Among those who noticed was the prima donna's husband, the Marquis de Caux, who was sitting as always in the first row in on the right aisle. As soon as the second act was over he ran straightaway into the wings and fell upon Patti with reproaches for her brazen public coquetry. The stormiest scene imaginable ensued; the enraged diva hurled her jewels in her husband's face and threw him out of her dressing room, declaring she would no longer live with him. The intermission, meanwhile, had gone on at unheard of length. Baron [Karl] Kister [1821–93; Intendant of the Imperial Theaters, 1875–81] succeeded with effort in getting the evening's beneficiary to calm down and finish the opera. As a result of the scandal there was a trial *en séparation de corps et de biens*; the Marquis purchased his freedom by agreeing to pay his rapacious wife a million and a half francs. After this neither Patti nor Nicolini ever returned to St. Petersburg.[75]

Which doomed the Italian Opera there. It hobbled along for a few more seasons on second-rate singers and third-rate repertoire (Marchetti, Gammieri). In 1879 the company "made a concession to the Zeitgeist," as Vol'f put it,[76] and essayed *Tannhäuser* with Emma Albani as Elsa and Antonio Cotogni as Wolfram. The next year *Lohengrin* followed, without an international star save Cotogni. But here the Italian Opera was following the Russian, which had produced both Wagner operas years before and (particularly in the choral and orchestral departments) performed them better. Vocally, the Russian troupe had improved to the point where the two companies were close to meeting in the middle. As a matter of fact, the Russian Opera was by then competing with the Italian on the latter's home ground. It maintained three Verdi operas in repertory (the three one would expect: *Rigoletto, Traviata,* and *Trovatore*) and had the temerity to add *Aida* to its roster only one season later than the Italian troupe (1876–77). Verdi's opera "was received just as well in the Mariyinsky Theater as in the Bolshoy."[77] The ultimate turnabout came in 1880, when by special dispensation the Italian Opera marked the twenty-fifth anniversary of the reign of Alexander II with a performance of the specially translated "*La vita per lo Tzar.*" A bass from the Russian opera (Vladimir Vasilyev, known as "Vasilyev I") was lent for the occasion to render the role of Susanin. Another Russian opera presented in the eighties by the

[74] P. I. Chaikovsky, *Muzïkal'no-kriticheskiye stat'i* (Leningrad: Muzïka, 1986), p. 33.
[75] Vol'f, *Khronika peterburgskikh teatrov s kontsa 1855 do nachala 1881 goda*, p. 137.
[76] Ibid., p. 139.
[77] Ibid., p. 136.

Italian troupe in St. Petersburg (and only by it) was Anton Rubinstein's *Nerone*, which had been written to Jules Barbier's libretto for the Paris Opéra.

The death knell was sounded by the accession of Alexander III, the "Bourgeois Tsar," whose jingoistic arts policies precisely reversed the double standard his grandfather Nikolai had imposed forty years before, and who in 1882 decided to abrogate the crown monopoly on theaters, leading to a great proliferation of private theatrical enterprises (professional and amateur), quite a few operatic ones among them. (Those of Sergey Ivanovich Zimin and the railroad tycoon Savva Ivanovich Mamontov achieved particular eminence; it was Mamontov who gave Chaliapin his start.) Without the support of the crown and the high aristocracy, an imported Italian opera was untenable. As Ivan Vsevolozhsky, the new Intendant, put it at a meeting with the artists of the Mariyinsky Theater in September 1881, it was now the policy of the Imperial Theaters that "Russian opera . . . occupy within Russia the same place as is accorded national operas in the West."[78] Accordingly, the permanent Italian opera troupes in both Russian capitals were disbanded—first in Moscow (1882), and then in St. Petersburg (1885). The *Bolshoy kamennïy* theater was razed and rebuilt as the St. Petersburg Conservatory, whose opera workshop now occupies the space in which the première of *Forza* took place. From Alexander's reign up to the present day, pride of place in the Russian operatic repertory has gone to the native product—by the 1880s a national school of world caliber, whose chefs d'oeuvre had already begun to be exported—and all opera of whatever provenance has been sung in Russian.

IMAGE

I am willing to admit that no *self-respecting* capital can do without an Italian opera. But as a Russian musician can I, listening to Mme Patti's trills, forget for even one moment the humiliation our native art suffers in Moscow, where it can find neither space nor time for its support? Can I forget the pitiful way in which our Russian opera has been forced to vegetate, when we have in our repertory several operas of such quality that any other *self-respecting* capital would show them off as priceless treasures? They'll tell me by way of answer that when there is a Patti to be had in Moscow, it's ridiculous even to think about Russian opera. But to refute such an objection I need only point to Vienna, Berlin, Paris, Brussels, Munich, Dresden, and Prague. As far as Mme Patti herself is concerned, I am not in the least astonished at the ecstasies she calls forth, and I laugh at the purists who speak of her with feigned indifference only because the pleasure of hearing her costs so much. Mme Patti is a ravishing phenomenon; phenomenons are expensive and for the simplest of reasons—they are rare. No one who heard

---

[78] Gozenpud, *Russkiy operniy teatr XIX veka (1873–1889)* (Leningrad: Muzïka, 1973), p. 222.

Mme Patti, as I did, on Saturday last, 6 November, in *Il Barbiere di Siviglia*, will complain at what he had to shell out in order to obtain such enjoyment. Her singing in this opera boggled my mind. In the enchanting beauty of her voice, the nightingale purity of her trills, the fabulous lightness of her coloratura there is something superhuman. Yes, exactly: superhuman.[79]

So wrote the moderate and evenhanded Chaikovsky in 1871, at the beginning of his short career as a newspaper reviewer, summing up the Russian response to Italian opera as well as any single commentary might do. In his effort to see both sides he touches upon practically every theme: the social status of the genre, the specific pleasures (in the Russian way of seeing things, nonmusical pleasures) to be gained from it, the importance of star performers to its success. But above all, he emphasizes the harm its presence was doing, given the specific political and economic conditions in which art was supported and purveyed under the Russian autocracy.

The uniformity, as well as the extremity, of the resistance to Italian opera on the part of Russian musicians—and particularly the ones who matter to us now—is surely the uniquely significant part of the story of Italian opera's reception in the Empire. It was no mere concomitant to "nationalism," that ever-ready ersatz category by means of which facile historiography continues to marginalize all European artistic activity east of the Danube. It went far deeper than that into matters of heart and belly that always precede matters of mind and taste. Quite simply, practitioners of the very new (and, until the 1860s, socially unrecognized) profession of "composer" in Russia could ill afford to see merit in that which posed a grave and present threat to their existence. Were there no state-supported Italian opera to contend with, torturing them at once with professional frustration and creative isolation, it is unlikely, moreover, that composers of Russian opera would have proven so prone to assume those radically pure aesthetic and stylistic stances for which they live in history, if not on stage. The opposition in Russia seems at times a caricatural one between "opera without music" and "opera without singing."

There has, in any case, always been a special Russian high-mindedness about the arts, and never more than in the nineteenth century. Partly it was the result of the early popularity in Russia of German idealistic philosophy. Partly it was a response to the pressure of a despotic censorship: at a time when open political, social, or economic debate was impossible, serious discussion of public policy had to go on in the guise of literary and artistic criticism—and creation. Nowhere else did artists feel such an uncoerced pressure to be citizens. (Coercion came later.)

We shall see that many members of the so-called intelligentsia were at their least intelligent when the subject was music. But music had its own intelligentsia, every bit as idealistic and puritanical within its own domain as their

---

[79] Chaikovsky, *Muzïkal'no-kriticheskiye stat'i*, pp. 32–33.

more overtly politicizing counterparts. And that is how one must understand the young Chaikovsky—thought by many in the West to be a "Westernizer," and no one's idea of a "Wagnerian"—when he writes:

> I consider the Italian opera with all its attributes to be a matter that has nothing to do with the higher purposes of art, a matter in the highest degree antimusical. In the Italian opera it is not the singers who exist to perform musical works of art, but rather the music that discharges a purely official duty in furnishing something for this or that artist to sing. In the face of such a reversal of means and ends can one make any serious critical evaluation of repertory?[80]

Indeed, the important critics—Serov, Cui, Laroche, Stasov—did not waste many words on the Italian opera. They treated it as something beneath their notice, except when it came to making invidious comparisons. Considering the popularity of what they were ignoring, it was a notably quixotic position they were affecting, with predictable consequences so far as their influence was concerned. Thus we have a situation in which the public and the idealistic musical intelligentsia stood resolutely back to back—a quintessentially "romantic" situation.

Since romanticism is neither a trait nor a movement prominently associated with Russia, some background may be desirable. Prince Odoyevsky, the Moscow littérateur, can be our focal point. On the basis of his collection of stories entitled *Russian Nights* (1844) he is often called the Russian E.T.A. Hoffmann; and indeed, Odoyevsky's whole outlook is Hoffmannesque in its extreme commitment to an antirationalist, anti-utilitarian idealism derived, like Hoffmann's, from Swedenborg and Schelling. It was the old story of *Geist* (in Russian, *dukh*) vs. *Sinnlichkeit* (in Russian, *chuvstvennost'*), entailing a commitment to German instrumental music as the highest and most philosophical of all the arts.

Among the stories in *Russian Nights* are two musical tales, one entitled "The Last Quartet of Beethoven," the other "Sebastian Bach." The only Italian operas Odoyevsky recognized were those written by the German-speaking Mozart; and among these *Don Giovanni*—minus the final sextet, of course—was singled out by the Russian Hoffmann (exactly as it had been by the German one) for its exemplary romanticism. Odoyevsky propagated his musical views prolifically: his collected writings on music fill a volume of some seven hundred pages, and he was active also as a musical antiquarian. His education, his philosophical commitments, his early adherence to "absolute music," and—not least—his social eminence, all made Odoyevsky a natural leader of the opposition to Italian opera. No one played a greater role than he in shaping nineteenth-century "intelligent" taste.

Odoyevsky's first onslaught against the Italian taste took the form of a

---

[80] Ibid., p. 35.

scene in a satirical novella entitled "Vexing Days" (*Dni dosad*), which he
published in 1823, aged nineteen, in the *European Courier* (*Vestnik Yevropï*),
one of the major intellectual journals of the time. The story's central episode
depicts Moscow's brief dalliance with Italian opera as brought to the city by
the Zamboni troupe, emissary of spiritual emptiness. A Count Gluposilin
("Strength-and-Stupidity") is holding forth to young Arist, the author's surrogate, on the merits of Rossini during a performance of *Tancredi*. (They listen
to the arias, converse during the recitatives.) "Di tanti palpiti," the moment
everyone has been waiting for, proves too much for Arist:

> —"What!" I shouted, "Tancredi is singing an ecossaise, and a pretty poor one at
> that! And everyone is delighted with it??"
> —"Calm down," Gluposilin remonstrated, on the verge of anger, "you want to
> quarrel with the whole world. Don't you know, kind sir, this aria is so good
> that every gondolier in Italy is singing it!"
> —"I quite agree," I answered him coolly. "This is a fine aria for a gondolier; but
> for Tancredi it won't do at all. Do Mozart and Méhul write their operas like
> that? With what simplicity and strength they depict the slightest tinge of char-
> acter! You won't find Tancredi expressing his joys and sorrows like any old
> gondolier with them!"
> —"Enough already! Forgive me," Gluposilin insisted, "but this aria is first-rate!
> It's beyond argument, beyond argument!" . . . I had my revenge on Glu-
> posilin. . . . For the whole duration of the performance I tormented him with
> my doubts. When, for example, he went into ecstasies at roulades and trills, I
> stopped him cold with the remark that they were being done to the words *Io
> tremo, i miei tormenti, il mio dolente cor*. Another time I pointed out to him
> that Argirio really shouldn't be using a dance tune to tell Amenaide *Non ti son
> più genitor*; and so on. . . . I spent the evening angry at myself for under-
> standing Italian, angry at the singers for their distinct enunciation; it took away
> half my pleasure.[81]

Four and a half decades later Odoyevsky was still at it. His rage at the
destructive popularity of Italian music—fed, to be sure, by culture snobbery
and religious bigotry, but also by outrage at the lack of outlet for the work of
Russian composers—reached its peak in 1867 with a blistering tirade against
the installation of Merelli's permanent troupe in the Bolshoy Theater. *Can
Italian opera further our artistic education by so much as a hair?* he asked
rhetorically (using his own italics), and thundered in response:

> But the ignorance of the majority of the Italian singers who come here passes
> all belief. Not only do they not understand, they do not even know about any-
> thing else in the musical world outside their own so-called music, which is to say
> an effeminate, sickly, constantly lying sort of music that depends on vocal acro-

---

[81] Cited from Livanova and Protopopov, *Opernaya kritika v Rossii*, vol. 1, pp. 312–13.

batics and banal effects; or else it is based, as in the Papal Choir, on the shameful mutilation of men—the pitiful result of that leaden yoke that has always weighed upon poor Italy. It is the song of slaves, forced through their tears to entertain a company of Metternichs or else King Bomba.

What have these wanton moans to do with our healthy, virginal, scrupulous musical environment? In all likelihood tawdry, empty Italianate sonorities would knock all sense out of our national feelings, they would teach us to listen with a straight face and without disgust to the various rattling noises that issue forth from dolls; these dolls dance with their voices on a tightrope (a fairly difficult operation, but so much the worse), and meanwhile one doll passes itself off as Norma, another as Semiramide, a third as Francis I, and all of a sudden (or so I hear) as Don Carlos, too.[82]

Odoyevsky ended his screed with a plea: "Man cannot live on 'verdyatina' alone." The epithet, formed by adding to Verdi's name a suffix denoting some sort of edible animal flesh (as in *telyatina*, "veal", from *telyonok*, "calf"), permanently enriched the Russian lexicon of musical invective. The connotation is of something tasty but cheap. (A memoir by an old Mariyinsky Theater hand recorded a comment by the eighteen-year-old son of the leading basso of the Russian Opera Company on scanning the repertory for the season 1900–1901: "Again this verdyatina!" sniffed Igor Stravinsky.)[83] It was Odoyevsky (though many claimed credit) who called *La Forza del Destino* a "polka in four acts."[84] Another typical Odoyevsky coinage was *vzbellinit'sya*, which plays on the verb *vzbelenit'sya*, meaning "to become enraged after ingesting henbane (*belena*)." Just so were Bellini's corybantic followers driven mad.[85] Odoyevsky's many sallies at the expense of the Italian opera—its composers, its singers, above all its audience—set the tone for decades of high-minded Russian raillery.

Glinka, Odoyevsky's exact contemporary, was by contrast a true connoisseur of Italian vocal music and singing, and a serious student of it. After his early, desultory lessons with the younger Zamboni, Glinka went in pilgrimage to Milan in the early 1830s to continue his studies. There he became acquainted with Bellini and Donizetti and wrote some very creditable imitations of their work. His earliest publications, issued during his Milanese period, comprised a number of instrumental tributes to the Italian opera. In addition to several sets of piano variations they included a couple of ambitious concerted compositions: a "Divertimento brillante" for six instruments on themes from *La Sonnambula*, and a "Serenata" for seven on themes from *Anna Bolena*.

[82] "Russkaya ili ital'yanskaya opera," in Odoyevsky, *Muzïkal'no-Literaturnoye naslediye*, p. 314.

[83] Eduard Stark, *Peterburgskaya opera i yeyo mastera* (Leningrad: Muzgiz, 1940), p. 15.

[84] Odoyevsky, *Muzïkal'no-Literaturnoye naslediye*, p. 289.

[85] David Lowe, "Vladimir Odoevskii as Opera Critic," *Slavic Review* 41, no. 2 (Summer 1982): 306–15, esp. p. 310.

Italianate style would be for Glinka a permanent acquisition and a principal resource.

Yet by the time he established his reputation as an opera composer, and especially by the time it came to write his memoirs, Glinka had come to regard, or at least to advertise, his Italian apprenticeship as something long outgrown, and expressed himself on the subject of Italian music and singing with an irony that amounted, at times, to bitterness. At the first rehearsal of *A Life for the Tsar*, Vorob'yova recalled, the composer made a point of asserting his hostility to all Italian music, gratuitously informing the cast that he had never once attended the opera in St. Petersburg, "even though I know that you recently put on *Semiramide* very successfully."[86] In the memoirs, he let no opportunity go by to remind the reader of his mature indifference to "virtuosité," even when recalling the gala première of *Anna Bolena*, which he had been privileged to attend at La Scala.[87] About Rubini's fateful St. Petersburg debut in 1843, he waxed derisive: the tenor was "*not* Jupiter [as Count Wielhorski, among others, had called him] but a ruin. . . . He sang either with much too much strength or else you could hardly hear him; you might say he just opened his mouth while the audience sang his pianissimo for him, which made them feel great, of course, so they applauded with fervor."[88]

In the memoirs, Glinka ascribed his aversion to "Italian 'songbirds' and fashionable Italian music" to the miscarriage *Don Giovanni* had suffered at the hands of Rubini and company, during the first St. Petersburg Italian season.[89] But frustrations and discouragements of a more personal kind also contributed to his changed attitude. Glinka was the first Russian composer to experience directly the unfortunate effects of Tsar Nikolai's arts policies. In 1849, Frezzolini had wished to sing Antonida in *A Life for the Tsar* at her bénéfice but was prevented from doing so by the edict that had just come down banning performances of Russian works by the Italian troupe ("Gloire à M. Tolstoi!" poor Glinka muttered in his memoirs,[90] referring to the composer of the work whose fiasco precipitated the decree). This meant that Russia's premier composer was deprived by Nikolai's frankly discriminatory policies of the kind of lavish production and first-class vocal talent that only the Italian Opera could then provide. Being treated like a second-class musical citizen in his own country deeply wounded him, contributed to the creative block that plagued him in his last decade, and caused him forever to associate the Italian Opera with what he saw as his own failed career. According to his

[86] Quoted in David Brown, *Glinka* (London: Oxford University Press, 1974), p. 80.

[87] Glinka, *Memoirs*, trans. Richard B. Mudge (Norman: University of Oklahoma Press, 1963), p. 61.

[88] Ibid., pp. 176–77.

[89] Ibid., p. 180.

[90] Ibid., p. 217.

sister, Glinka left Russia for the last time in 1856 spitting on the ground and hoping "never to see this vile country again."[91]

Dargomïzhsky, Glinka's younger contemporary, had even better reason to feel this way. His career was dogged from the outset by the favoritism shown the Italian Opera in Russia. Having completed his first opera, *Esmeralda*, in 1839 (to the libretto Victor Hugo had prepared from *Notre-Dame de Paris* around 1831 for Louise Bertin), he waited eight full years for its production by the Imperial Theaters. By the time the bureaucratic (i.e., censorship) formalities had been cleared, the Italians had come to town, and, as we learn from an agonized letter from Serov to Stasov (14 September 1844), "until the craze for the Italians is past, [Intendant Alexander] Gedeonov will not accept any opera from anyone for anything on any terms, on account of which Dargomïzhsky has received a point-blank refusal."[92]

The reason for Serov's agony was the refusal, by Vladimir Zotov, the son of the director of repertoire under Gedeonov and a successful playwright, even to consider collaborating with Serov on an operatic project in view of the production embargo. As for *Esmeralda*, it finally saw the light of day in 1847—but only in Moscow, during the Russian Opera's "exile." Dargomïzhsky's opera had its St. Petersburg première in 1851, twelve years after its submission. As the composer relates in an autobiographical sketch, Tamburini tried to secure it for his bénéfice at the Bolshoy; but as in the case of Frezzolini and *A Life for the Tsar*, he was refused on account of the 1849 ban.[93]

As Dargomïzhsky's late, notoriously slogan-filled letters attest, his attraction to the extreme notions of musical realism for which he is best remembered today was in large measure a ferment of sour grapes. In any case, his recorded opinions of Italian music are even more condescending than the norm. In an 1844 letter to his father from Paris, after a number of detailed descriptions of French operas he had chanced to see, there is this addendum: "At the Théâtre des Italiens I also heard *Linda di Chamounix* by Donizetti. About this there is nothing much to say. First of all, you'll hear it in St. Petersburg; but second, once a medal or a coin has been stamped out and described, is there any need to describe the next medal or coin that issues from the same die and the same machine?"[94]

Alexander Serov, for his part, maintained an unswerving, quite unapologe-

---

[91] L. I. Shestakova, "Posledniye godï zhizhni i konchina Mikhaíla Ivanovicha Glinki," in A. Orlova, ed., *Glinka v vospominaniyakh sovremennikov* (Moscow: Muzgiz, 1955), p. 309.

[92] "A. N. Serov, Pis'ma k V. V. i D. V. Stasovïm," ed. Abram Akimovich Gozenpud and Vera Alekseyevna Obram, in *Muzïkal'noe nasledstvo*, vol. 1 (Moscow: Muzgiz, 1962), pp. 65–312, 129.

[93] Findeyzen, *A. S. Dargomïzhskiy (1813–1869)*, p. 6.

[94] Ibid., p. 16.

tic loyalty to Rossini throughout his career as critic, even if he did feel the need indirectly to admit its irrationality. He closed a warm obituary tribute to the Swan of Pesaro by invoking Montaigne: "There you have my opinion; I do not offer it as good, all I can say is that it is mine." To which he added, with telltale defiance, "If I may be permitted on this occasion to alter Montaigne's words a bit, I would say: "There you have my opinion of Rossini. I find that it is *correct* and doubt whether anyone can prove to me that it is not."[95]

To proclaim an admiration for Rossini—by way of exception—was a common tactic among Russian critics of Italian opera in the latter nineteenth century. (Not that such an admission was necessarily insincere: Vladimir Stasov, the flagrantly partisan tribune of Glinka and the Five, was incautious enough to have asserted in an early article, written in the throes of infatuation with Frezzolini and published—five years after *Ruslan and Lyudmila!*—in 1847, that "Il Barbiere di Siviglia [was] the best opera of the first half of the nineteenth century." Luckily for his later reputation, the article was unsigned.)[96] Admitting to a love of Rossini lent credence to one's dismissal of his successors, particularly the Italian standard-bearer of the 1850s, whom Serov was pleased to greet as follows:

> In the case of Verdi's operas it seems to us that their posters are never printed as they should be. Whether in *Ernani* or in *I Lombardi* the leading character is not the one listed on the poster. The leading character is the *big bass drum* and its allies, the copper cymbals, followed by the *chorus* (unison) and only then Charles V, Ernani, or whoever, in the order listed.[97]

The sole merit Serov was willing to grant the Italian Opera was its role in the development of musical taste, that is, of lay connoisseurship.[98] (Similarly, Mily Balakirev—admittedly not a composer of opera and so not in direct competition with the Italians—allowed that the Italian Opera was "the best school for Russian singers.")[99] Other critics, even those known for their conservatism, disputed this. Herman Laroche (1845–1904), a critic of the next generation famous for his hostility to the modern music of his day, saw the Italian Opera nevertheless as a brake, a closer of the public ear. Even in a period of decline, he wrote in 1874, Italian opera continued to hold the masses in thrall with an obsolescent repertoire, crudely sung. Unlike most critics, Laroche gave the credit for this accomplishment not to the star singers but to the composers who established the genre's hegemony in the 1840s, whose expert yet cynical creative methods he compared with those of the French

---

[95] Serov, *Izbrannïye stat'i*, vol. 2, p. 468.

[96] Stasov's authorship was established on the basis of his correspondence with Serov: see Gozenpud, *Russkiy opernïy teatr XIX veka (1857–1872)*, pp. 178–79.

[97] A. N. Serov, *Stat'i o muzïke*, vol. 1 (Moscow: Muzïka, 1984), p. 85.

[98] Ibid., p. 82.

[99] Quoted in Bernatsky, "Iz zolotogo veka ital'yanskoy operï v Peterburge," p. 17.

"roman-industrie" as exemplified by such perennially popular authors as Dumas père or Eugène Sue: "The reason [for its success] lies in the music itself, in the powerful talent of its composers, but above all in their smartly calculated, adroitly implemented, purely practical methods, in their thorough knowledge of the listener in all his weaknesses and cravings."[100]

Particular interest attaches to the way in which César Cui—in an ambitious general survey of contemporary operatic schools dating from 1864, the year of his critical debut—attempted quasi-technically to analyze for his readers the ways and means of Italian opera, and justify his contempt for it. At the time of writing, Cui was still very close to Balakirev and the other members of the original Five, and his early critical pieces reflected the discussions that animated the meetings of the circle that would eventually produce *Boris Godunov*, *Prince Igor*, and *Snegurochka*. The strong idealist bent already encountered in the writings of Odoyevsky, with its rigid opposition of spirit and sensuality, may still be observed in Cui; but now it is cast in terms of a musical dichotomy, that between harmony (German) and melody (Italian). While a somewhat hackneyed distinction, what makes it noteworthy is the extreme confidence with which Cui constructs an idiosyncratic hierarchy of musical elements in accordance with an unstated—and unmusical—agenda:

> A musical idea consists of melody, harmony, and rhythm. Of these three elements the most important is harmony (i.e., the combination of several tones with one another) because of its rich variety and the profound impression it makes on the listener. In melody (the succession of tones one after another) there can be no great variety. They all consist of the same twelve tones; all possible sequences of these tones have long since been exhausted. A great multitude of melodies have been written; it would be impossible to create a new one. Salvation must be sought in harmony and in working-out, i.e., *the gradual development of musical ideas*. It is precisely these last-named elements that the Italians have failed to cultivate *at all*. Their harmony hardly goes beyond those chords that any amateur might pick out at the piano or on the guitar.
>
> There is even less development of musical ideas among the Italians than there is beauty of harmony. They have *not the slightest idea* of working-out. Italian music has barricaded itself behind some kind of Chinese wall. It neither knows nor wants to know what is going on on the outside. It is entirely satisfied with self-congratulation. The present trend in German music is entirely alien and unknown to it. Development of musical ideas it calls "erudition" and in its helplessness to aspire to it scorns it and brands it dry. That is why Italian operas, consisting entirely of melodies and devoid of harmonic interest or any development at all, are so extremely boring and monotonous. Once you know two, you know them all.

[100] Herman Laroche, *Izbrannïye stat'i*, vol. 3 (Leningrad: Muzïka, 1976), p. 128.

Quod erat demonstrandum! The upshot of this description (which goes on to charge Italian opera with stereotyped forms, disregard for the meaning of the text, hackneyed and noisy orchestration, and, above all, neglect of recitative, the chief bee in Cui's bonnet) is that "for a *cultivated musician* Italian opera hardly exists." The main focus of attack now shifts to the audience and its darlings. Here Cui's arguments are less original, but he does make an accurate prediction:

> The audience for Italian opera consists not of music lovers but of lovers of singing who all unawares confuse the two. I'll go further yet: most of these gentlemen don't even care about singing. They'd rather just hear beautiful vocal sounds, perfectly executed roulades. A single high note seized by Tamberlik, a scale sung by Fioretti transports them into the same ecstasy as any aria, with this difference only, that in the aria there are more scales and high notes. Maintaining the Italian opera costs the Imperial Theaters enormous sums. Doing away with the Italian opera would be beneficial to the development of the public taste, for Italian music is a form of stagnation. . . . But in spite of everything, doing away with the Italian opera will be *impossible* until we have our own *singers of equal quality*. It is hard to demand of a dilettante that he forgo the charms of good performance or persuade him that the beauties of a really worthy work of art can survive a bad one. We do not consider the lovers of Italian music to be incapable of enjoying a less superficial kind of music, so long as it may be heard in a good performance. Then they will see that melody and passion are not the sole property of the Italians, that in other schools they also exist and are even more expressive and profound.[101]

Having indicted Italian music as stagnant, and having therefore specifically denied Verdi any essential novelty vis-à-vis his more decorous predecessors, Cui wonders what kind of a future such an art (and such an artist) might possibly have. Twenty-five years later he had an answer: "*Don Carlos, Aida, Otello* represent the progressive collapse of Verdi's creative powers even as they testify to a progressive turn in the direction of new forms, founded upon criteria of dramatic truth" such as enlightened anti-Italianate critics like Cui had been demanding all along.[102] Italian opera, in short, could improve only at the cost of its own destruction as a distinctive genre.

The other members of the Five had little to add to this analysis. As long as the Italian Opera troupe enjoyed its official support, their public face was, and could only be, one of implacable idealistic opposition. Their private predilections could be less predictable. Borodin's memoir of his first glimpse of the young (indeed, teenaged) Musorgsky showed him "extraordinarily polite and well-bred. The ladies were making a fuss over him. He sat at the piano and,

---

[101] Cui, *Izbrannïye stat'i*, pp. 32–34; emphases original.
[102] Ibid., p. 415.

coquettishly throwing up his hands, played excerpts from *Trovatore*, *Traviata*, etc. very sweetly while the circle around him buzzed in chorus: 'charmant, délicieux!' and so on."[103] (Borodin himself, it seems, knew *Il Barbiere di Siviglia* by heart and could regale companions with it at the piano to their hearts' content.)[104] Stravinsky, whose father often shared the concert platform with Musorgsky, recalled being told by his parents that the composer of *Boris Godunov* "was a connoisseur of Italian operatic music and that he accompanied concert singers in it extremely well."[105]

After 1885, when Italian opera had ceased to be an aggravated political issue in Russia, one could afford to relax a bit. Thus Vasiliy Yastrebtsev, Rimsky-Korsakov's Boswell, recorded an evening's conversation in 1893 in which "Rimsky-Korsakov, Lyadov, Glazunov and [the music publisher] Belyayev had talked about the Italian composers. How surprised (perhaps even indignant!) the followers of the New Russian school would have been to hear their idols unanimously extol Verdi and Rimsky-Korsakov praise Donizetti, particularly *Lucia*! In the view of Nikolai Andreyevich, Donizetti was not only extremely gifted; his style of composing had a special elegance which set him apart from the others."[106] By then St. Petersburg had heard the work of Ponchielli (*La Gioconda* and *I Lituani* had figured in the last seasons of the Italian Opera, and *Gioconda* had been part of the Maryinsky repertoire since 1888), as well as the *veristi* (*Manon Lescaut* and *Cav-&-Pag* had their premières in 1893), and the conversation Yastrebtsev recorded doubtless expressed a measure of unexpected nostalgia.

THE RECEPTION of Italian opera among the literary and the politically active intelligentsia was quite another story. We have already noted Pushkin's purely epicurean delight in Rossini, and there were many like him. Vissarion Belinsky (1811–48), one of the founders of Russian utilitarian aesthetics and hence the opposite of an epicurean, was carried away in spite of himself by Rubini. During the latter's spring tour in 1843, Belinsky went to every performance of *Lucia*, and wrote to Vasily Botkin, his intellectual confidante, that Rubini was

> a terrifying artist. In the third act I wept such tears as I had not wept in many a year. I'm going again to hear it today. The scene where he tears the ring away

[103] Sergei Aleksandrovich Dianin, ed., *Pis'ma A. P. Borodina*, vol. 4 (Moscow and Leningrad: Muzgiz, 1950), p. 297.

[104] Serge Dianin, *Borodin* (London: Oxford University Press, 1963), p. 25.

[105] Igor Stravinsky and Robert Craft, *Conversations with Igor Stravinsky* (Garden City, N.Y.: Doubleday, 1959), p. 45.

[106] Vasiliy Vasilyevich Yastrebtsev, *Reminiscences of Rimsky-Korsakov*, ed. and trans. Florence Jonas (New York: Columbia University Press, 1985), p. 47. *Lucia*, we learn from Rimsky-Korsakov's posthumously published autobiography, had been a childhood favorite (*My Musical Life*, trans. Judah A. Joffe [London: Eulenberg, 1974], p. 12).

from Lucia and calls upon heaven to witness her perfidy is fearful, horrible. . . .
I realized that all the arts have the same laws. Heavens, what a sobbing voice—
so much feeling, such a flaming lava of feeling erupts from him, it is enough to
drive you mad.[107]

For some it was a guilty pleasure. The poet and critic Apollon Grigoryev
(1822–64) proclaimed at length his inability to understand his own preference
for *Lucia* over *Ruslan*.[108] But there was another dimension to the Italian opera's popularity with the "thinking" public. In order to understand it we must
take into account a curious and seldom-reported fact, stated most succinctly
by Prince Kropotkin. Writing of his school years in the 1850s, which happened to coincide with the heyday of the Italian Opera as a Russian institution, he recalled that it was

> in some strange way intimately connected with the radical movement, and the
> revolutionary recitatives in *Guillaume Tell* and *I Puritani* were always met with
> stormy applause and vociferations which went straight to the heart of Alexander
> II; while in the sixth-story galleries, and in the smoking room of the opera, and at
> the stage door the best part of the St. Petersburg youth came together in a com-
> mon idealist worship of a noble art. All this may seem childish; but many higher
> ideas and pure inspirations were kindled by this worship of our favorite artists.[109]

No other theater could offer such an outlet for forbidden sentiment, least of
all the Russian opera as it was then; for the Russian opera, despite the view
propagated by the historiography of a later time, was a politically ultraconservative institution. *A Life for the Tsar*, its linchpin, was the very epitome of the
Nikolaian doctrine of "Official Nationality," as we have seen, celebrating the
blimpish trinity of Orthodoxy, Autocracy, and Patriotism. (Just compare that
with *Liberté, Égalité, Fraternité*!) The later national school, as exemplified
by Serov, Balakirev, Chaikovsky, Cui, and (increasingly) Musorgsky, was
equally wedded to reactionary political ideals. Of all the famous Russian composers, only Rimsky-Korsakov could be fairly called a "liberal," and even he
did not show his colors until 1905. Meanwhile, at the Italian Opera, to quote
the memoirs of another old enthusiast:

> Ovations were especially strong when they gave some slight pretext for hints of
> what then passed for a liberal drift. Tamberlik would be forced to repeat the
> phrase "Cercar la libertà!" in *Guillaume Tell* three and even five times. Later on
> Graziani and Angiolini would have a similar success with the duet in *Puritani*
> that ends with the words "Gridando libertà!"[110]

---

[107] Quoted in Livanova, *Opernaya kritika v Rossii*, vol. 1, part 2, p. 35. Turgenev commented
that Belinsky's infatuation with Rubini's singing was born not of any musical appreciation but
only in response to the tenor's pathetic and dramatic qualities.

[108] See his article "Russkiy teatr" in Dostoyevsky's journal *Epokha* (5 March 1864).

[109] *Memoirs of a Revolutionist*, p. 120.

[110] Konstantin Skalkovsky, *Vospominaniya molodosti* (St. Petersburg, 1906), p. 113.

Even Cui, staunch military man that he was, looked back indulgently on these demonstrations, calling them "an innocent manifestation of sixties liberalism."[111] But they were more than that. As long as the radical students of the 1850s and 1860s could congregate in the passages and the uppermost gallery of the Bolshoy Theater and, standing in what Kropotkin called "a Turkish bath atmosphere," shout their approval of Tamberlik or Angiolini, they could enjoy a sense of solidarity that was barred to them in any other sphere of Russian public life. Nowhere but at the Tsar's own Italian Opera, in other words, did Russian radicals have the right of assembly.

Just as important, the Italian opera was the one form of theater in which everyone, from titled nobleman to anarchist, could find something on which to fasten with enthusiasm. Vol'f, looking back on this time from the politically turbulent 1870s, wrote with quaint nostalgia of the palmy days of the early Italian seasons, when everyone took pleasure in the opera side by side, albeit each in his own way. "In our time such a universal enthusiasm would be unthinkable," he sighed. "One must take into account that in those days there were no social factions [!], and thus the intellectual elite lived through literature and the arts alone."[112] Though the case as he makes it is far overstated, Vol'f was correct to point out that the Italian Opera was a potent unifier of the social fabric in midcentury Russia. This was at once something useful to those concerned with maintaining the social status quo, and something precious if illusory to those concerned with overthrowing it. Hence the intense nostalgia for the Italian Opera in its golden age that informs so many memoirs of Grand Duke and anarchist alike, and hence the myriad evocations of those magic evenings that inform so many passages in the works of Russian authors, be they reactionary or radical.

A case in point as concerns the radical faction is Nikolai Chernïshevsky, often taken for the prototype of the "nihilist" Bazarov in *Fathers and Children*, Turgenev's famous novel of "social factions." Chernïshevsky's discussion of music in his early utilitarian-realist tract *The Aesthetic Relation of Art to Reality* is revealing. Even as he condemns "artificial singing" (his term for art music) by comparison to the "natural singing" of folk music, it is clear that all his notions of the former are based on Italian opera, the only kind of art music with which he was familiar, and which thus became for him the paradigm of musical artistry ("deliberate, calculated, embellished with everything with which human genius can embellish it"). Chernïshevsky has no conception whatever of instrumental music (for idealists, the higher kind). His "proof" of the superiority of vocal music was worthy of the Bolshoy parterre: "as soon as the singing starts, we cease to pay attention to the orchestra."[113]

[111] Cui, *Izbrannïye stat'i*, p. 515.

[112] Vol'f, *Khronika peterburgskikh teatrov s kontsa 1826 do nachala 1855 goda*, part 1, p. 107.

[113] N. G. Chernïshevsky, *Selected Philosophical Essays* (Moscow: Foreign Languages Publishing House, 1953), pp. 347, 348.

In *What Is to Be Done?*—his notorious novel of 1863 advocating free love—Chernïshevsky has his heroine, Vera Pavlovna, fall asleep musing angrily at having missed *La Traviata* owing to her lover's negligence: ". . . as if he didn't know that when Bosio is singing you can't get two-ruble tickets at eleven o'clock! . . . I'd go to the opera every night, even to something bad, as long as Bosio were singing." On falling asleep she dreams of meeting Bosio (strangely mixed at first with the contralto De Meric, who often sang Maddalena to Bosio's Gilda in *Rigoletto*). The singer performs a romance to words by Pushkin ("But where did Bosio find the time to learn Russian?"), urging Vera Pavlovna on to the enjoyment of love. For Chernïshevsky, then, it was Bosio who, bringing Violetta to life with her art, symbolized the licentious sentiments to which Verdi's heroine gives voice in the first act, sentiments from which the Russian radical sought to purge all moral stigma. Bosio, who like Viardot enhanced her popularity by giving free concerts for students,[114] did her unwitting bit to encourage radical interpretations like this, as Viardot had done before her.

Yet there were limits. Viardot's success with the students had been her undoing in Russia. Her biographer leaves it an unexplained mystery why the great singer did not return to St. Petersburg for the season 1853–54 (or any time thereafter), despite having announced plans to do so.[115] Vol'f reveals that she had in fact been banned for having "excessively electrified the youth."[116] And that is why the hopelessly smitten Ivan Turgenev had to pursue her through the length and breadth of Europe. Turgenev, though his involvement with the Italian Opera thus had a special personal intensity, can stand here for that class of Russian littérateurs on the right who admired it as a representative of high aristocratic and "universal" (read: cosmopolitan) culture that put the pretensions of all merely local composers everlastingly to shame. Unremittingly hostile to the Russian national school, Turgenev satirized it in a number of his novels (*On the Eve*, *Smoke*) and allowed himself to become embroiled in endless controversy with Stasov, its great tribune, on account of his unregenerate opinions, particularly as regarded Dargomïzhsky's last opera, *The Stone Guest* (after Pushkin).

This was an opera written programmatically and polemically against every Italianate tradition and for that reason the great hobbyhorse of the "New Russian school." Defending himself against Stasov's insinuation that he remained faithful to outmoded forms of art merely out of submission to authority, Turgenev affirmed delight in the old "recitatives and arias not because authorities praise them but because at the first sound of them my tears begin to flow. And

114 Gozenpud, *Russkiy opernïy teatr XIX veka (1873–1889)*, pp. 158–59; see also Cui, *Izbrannïye stat'i*, p. 514.

115 April FitzLyon, *The Price of Genius* (London: John Calder, 1964), pp. 299, 300.

116 Vol'f, *Khronika peterburgskikh teatrov s kontsa 1826 do nachala 1855 goda*, part 1, p. 164. He also notes that Mario, a notorious philanderer, had been banned at the same time as a threat to public morals.

it is not authorities that compel my contempt for your *Stone Guest*, which I had the patience to sit through not once but twice, and in no 'doubtful' rendition but in a masterly traversal of the vocal score. . . . It will ever remain one of the great mysteries of my life how intelligent people like you and Cui . . . can find in these pitiful peeps and chirps—what? not just music, but a work of genius that will usher in 'a new era of music'!!?!! Really now, is this not just unconscious chauvinism?"[117]

Another Russian writer who strongly favored Italian opera was the famous playwright Alexander Ostrovsky; his often stormy relations with the many Russian composers who were attracted by his work could be (in fact, have been) the subject of an interesting book.[118] What made relations stormy was the frequent divergence of viewpoint between the librettist, who despite his reputation as a "progressive" writer and a connoisseur of folklore was eager to transform his plays into vehicles for Italianate vocalism, and the composers with whom he worked, who were of course mostly hostile to any such idea. For this reason Ostrovsky's collaborations with Chaikovsky and Serov were notable fiascos; the composer with whom he got on best was Vladimir Kashperov (1826–94), the outstanding (and practically the only) Russian emulator of the Italian school in the latter nineteenth century, and Ostrovsky made something of a laughingstock of himself for pushing Kashperov's work so strenuously with unsympathetic Russian conductors.[119]

ECHOES

Before *A Life for the Tsar* there were no true Russian operas. Russians like Berezovsky and Bortnyansky had composed Italian operas in the eighteenth century, but these were composed on Italian soil and performed only in Italy. Opera performed in Russia to Russian texts (even if composed by Cavos) meant only singspiels or *comédies mêlées d'ariettes*.[120] Echoes of Italian opera entered Russian music at first through song. It was the work of the "three Alexanders"—romance composers Alyabyev (1787–1851), Varlamov (1801–48) and Gurilyov (1803–58)—who truly "mingled the Russian *mélos* and the reigning Italianism with the most carefree and charming ease," as Stravinsky put it of a later composer,[121] and in so doing laid the stylistic

---

[117] Letters of 15/27 March and 14/26 May 1872, printed in Stasov, "Dvadtsat' pisem Turgeneva i moyo znakomstvo s nim," *Severnïy vestnik*, no. 10 (1888): 145–67, esp. pp. 166–67.

[118] E. M. Kolosova and Vladimir Filippov, *A. N. Ostrovskiy i russkiye kompozitorï* (Moscow and Leningrad: Iskusstvo, 1937).

[119] Memoir by Mikhail Ippolitov-Ivanov in *Ostrovskiy i russkiye kompozitorï*, p. 79.

[120] The best discussion of these musical plays may be found in Simon Karlinsky, *Russian Drama from Its Beginnings to the Age of Pushkin* (Berkeley and Los Angeles: University of California Press, 1985), chapter 5 ("The Age of Catherine: Comic Opera and Verse Comedy").

[121] Igor Stravinsky, *Poetics of Music in the Form of Six Lessons*, bilingual ed. (Cambridge, Mass.: Harvard University Press, 1970), p. 122. Stravinsky was speaking of Dargomïzhsky's *Rusalka*.

foundations on which the operas of Glinka would be erected. Curious reminiscences of Italian opera can also be found in some of the early printed collections of Russian folk songs with accompaniments—for example, those of Daniyil Kashin (1833) and Ivan Rupin (1831, published under the name "Rupini")—where the melismata of the so-called "drawn-out song" (*protyazhnaya pesnya*) are rendered in a fashion distinctly redolent of Italianate fioritura. This hybridized style persisted in Russian romances throughout the century, and produced a real masterpiece in Chaikovsky's "Was I Not a Blade of Grass?" (*Ya li v polye da ne travushka bïla?*), Op. 47, no. 7.

The style of the Italianized *protyazhnaya* underlies the roles of both of Glinka's operatic heroines—Antonida and Lyudmila—and may be savored at its height of expressivity in the trio *Ne tomi, rodimïy* ("Do Not Grieve, Beloved") in the first act of *A Life for the Tsar*, the number Balakirev so successfully arranged for piano. In *Ruslan and Lyudmila*, Italian styles are used as elements of characterization. The noble title pair have extended solo numbers (Lyudmila's act 1 cavatina, Ruslan's act 2 aria) that go through Italianate progressions of tempos and in Lyudmila's case entail a high level of virtuosity. (Viardot smuggled Lyudmila's cavatina into the *Bolshoy kamennïy* theater by interpolating it into the *Barbiere* lesson scene in 1852.) Farlaf, Ruslan's ridiculous rival, has a rondo (act 2) in purest buffo style, created for Tosi. Buffo patter-singing—in Russian, *skorogovorka*—modeled on Farlaf would remain a stock item for basses in Russian comic operas like Rimsky-Korsakov's *May Night* or Chaikovsky's *Vakula the Smith*, both after Gogol; it was thus indirectly the Italian opera's most enduring legacy for Russia. A resonance of a more specific kind occurs in the first act of *Ruslan*: a quartet in canonic style (*Kakoye chudnoye mgnoven'ye*, "What Uncanny Flash?") following upon Lyudmila's abduction, modeled directly on "Fredda ed immobile," from *Il Barbiere*. In turn it provided the model for a similarly motivated ensemble in the third-act finale from Chaikovsky's *The Oprichnik* (1873).

Except for out-and-out imitators like Aleksey Lvov, F. Tolstoy, and Kashperov, there is no later Russian composer of opera whose Italianate borrowings are as plain as Glinka's. The Francophile Dargomïzhsky was as indifferent to Rossini and Co. as he would later be to Wagner. It is an oft-noted paradox that Alexander Serov began writing his first completed opera, *Judith*, to an Italian text prepared at his request by one Ivan Antonovich Giustiniani, an *improvisatore* resident in St. Petersburg. But that is to be explained as a matter of ambition rather than stylistic or aesthetic affinity. Serov wanted his opera to be performed by the stellar international cast of the St. Petersburg Italian Opera, and thence to be exported to western Europe. Dissuaded at first by the refusal of Emma Lagrua to sing the title role, and finally by the inflexible ban on performances of native works by the Italian troupe, he reworked the opera to a Russian text. Only two spots in the finished opera give any evidence of Italianism. One is the final hymn of praise (act 5), where the triumphant heroine rejoices in virtuosic roulades. The other is ironic: Judith makes her seductive and insincere appeal to Holofernes in act 3 by means of a sly parody of Bellinian melody.

Serov's next opera, *Rogneda*, contained a sugary part (Ruald) written for Fyodor Nikolsky (1828–98), a Milan-trained tenor whose extraordinary vocal powers did much in the 1860s to enhance public esteem for the Russian opera. Nikolsky was widely compared with Tamberlik, and for exploiting the singer's prowess Serov found himself accused of hypocrisy and (what was worse) banality. Thus Cui:

> To each his own: our public loves Italian melodies. Fine. There's no blaming Mr. Serov for writing them. But what is altogether no good is the routine Italian construction of his melodies. . . . And after the end of the duet, *piano*, we get a final B♭—the crudest trick in the book for getting the audience to applaud. Mr. Serov himself affects to despise C♯s. But the whole difference is only that Sgr. Tamberlik *has* a C♯, and all Mr. Nikolsky has is a B♭.[122]

Elsewhere Cui commented on the general tendency of Serov's development by sneering, "After *Judith* Mr. Serov wrote *Rogneda*—good. But when after *Rogneda* he finally writes *La Traviata*, only then will his genius achieve its full wingspread."[123] "Italianism," for the likes of Cui, had become merely a generalized term or mode of abuse.

And it was misplaced. The intense cultivation of historical drama by playwrights and composers alike in the 1870s ensured that the prime Western model for Russian opera would be French. Serov thought of himself as a Wagnerian, but no one can fail to see that his model of (perhaps unconscious) choice was Meyerbeer. Chaikovsky's operatic output is specifically Gallic at all levels of style and tone, from the grand Scribian extravaganza (*The Oprichnik*, *The Maid of Orleans*) to the more modest scale endemic to the Théâtre Lyrique (*Eugene Onegin*, *Iolanta*). For him the Italian opera was decidedly passé as a source of style or a model of procedure (as it remained for Rimsky-Korsakov, who only really hit his stride as a composer of operas in the 1890s).

There is, however, one fascinating Italianate resonance in Chaikovsky— fascinating for its indirectness. Along with the rest of musical St. Petersburg, Chaikovsky, then an impressionable conservatory pupil, attended the glamorous première production of *La Forza del Destino*, and it is not surprising to find an echo of Verdi's overture, with its sledgehammer symbolism, in Chaikovsky's earliest symphonic poem, *Fatum*, the very title of which resonates with the title of the famous opera. Verdi's muttering flat-sixth reminiscence motif punctuates Chaikovsky's lyrical theme to the same semantic

---

[122] César Cui, *Muzïkal'no-kriticheskiye stat'i*, vol. 1 (Petrograd, 1918), p. 55.

[123] "Zhurnal'nïye tolki o 'Rognede' g. Serova," *Sankt-peterburgskiye vedomosti* (1866), no. 14.

effect, albeit not as a within-the-work ("introversive") reminiscence but as an "intertextual" one (examples 10.1a–b). After Chaikovsky destroyed this youthful effort (posthumously reconstructed from parts and published in 1896), he cannibalized the lyric theme in the climactic duet for the star-crossed lovers in *The Oprichnik*, an opera very much concerned with the force of destiny (example 10.1c). Thus Verdi's opera continued to reverberate in Chaikovsky's, but only through a symphonic intermediary, and "semantically" rather than stylistically.

It has been claimed that Musorgsky's *Boris Godunov* owes a specific debt to *La Forza del Destino* for character models: Varlaam/Melitone, Idiot/Trabuco.[124] Yet the characters in question were both present in the Pushkin play from which Musorgsky's libretto closely derived. On the other hand, the opening of the Scene at the Fountain (act 3, scene 1) in the second version of Musorgsky's opera, where the False Dmitri unaccountably sings Pushkin's stage directions ("Midnight . . . in the garden . . . by the fountain") in a fashion much ridiculed by littérateurs at the time, may well be an unconscious echo of the opening of the third act of *Don Carlos* ("A mezza notte, ai giardin della Regina, sotto gli allor della fonte vicina"), which had had its St. Petersburg première precisely when Musorgsky was beginning work on *Boris*. Even here, though, the resonance is textual, not musical. Yet it is not inconceivable that Verdi's example helped wean Musorgsky from the extremist-realist incubator in which his talent had, in somewhat one-sided fashion, been nurtured. Though a good "kuchkist" would have been loath to admit it, Verdi may thus have played a significant part in leading Musorgsky to the "rough and gaudy theatricality"[125] that has ensured his opera's survival as a world classic when so much of the Russian radical purism that provided its immediate environment has passed into history.

At the other extreme, the self-declared Russian Italianists have also been forgotten. The only one worth recalling here is Kashperov, Ostrovsky's favorite. A protégé of Glinka's, Kashperov studied with his mentor's mentor, Siegfried Dehn, in Berlin but gravitated afterward to Italy, where he lived for eight years (1857 to 1865) and had three operas produced: *Maria Tudor*, on a text by Ghislanzoni (Milan, 1859); *Rienzi*, to his own translation of Wagner's libretto (Florence, 1863); *Consuelo*, after George Sand (Venice, 1865). These

---

[124] Julian Budden, *The Operas of Verdi*, vol. 2 (New York: Oxford University Press, 1979), p. 520. The most sustained attempt to establish a Verdian presence in Musorgsky is Robert W. Oldani's in Caryl Emerson and Robert William Oldani, *Modest Musorgsky and Boris Godunov: Myths, Realities, Reconsiderations* (Cambridge: Cambridge University Press, 1994), pp. 235–39. See also R. John Wiley, "The Tribulations of Nationalist Composers: A Speculation Concerning Borrowed Music in *Khovanshchina*," in Malcolm H. Brown, ed., *Musorgsky: In Memoriam, 1881–1981* (Ann Arbor: UMI Research Press, 1982), pp. 163–77, where Marfa's répliques in the "love requiem" in the fifth act of *Khovanshchina* are traced to Gilda's "Lassù in cielo" from *Rigoletto*, act 3.

[125] Gozenpud, *Russkiy opernïy teatr XIX veka (1873–1889)*, vol. 3, p. 74.

EXAMPLE 10.1

a. Verdi, Overture to *La Forza del Destino*, figure C

b. Chaikovsky, *Fatum*, eight bars after figure 3

EXAMPLE 10.1, *continued*

c. Chaikovsky, *The Oprichnik,* act 4, Duet, nineteen bars after figure 70

were the first operas by a Russian produced in Italy since the eighteenth century. Kashperov returned to Russia at Nikolai Rubinstein's invitation, to join
the faculty of the newly formed Moscow Conservatory, where he was professor of singing from 1866 to 1872. It was in Moscow that he joined forces
with Ostrovsky, whom he had met several years before in Italy. The playwright eagerly arranged his own most famous and most "typically Russian"
work, *The Storm (Groza)*, as a numbers libretto for Kashperov to set in his
wonted Italian (pre-Verdian) manner. The opera was produced at the Mariyinsky in 1867. Serov, who was about to embark on a collaboration of his own
with Ostrovsky that would result, after many vicissitudes, in his third opera,
The Power of the Fiend (Vrazhya sila), reviewed *The Storm* with what must
seem unbelievable tactlessness to anyone unfamiliar with the general tenor of
nineteenth-century Russian journalism:

> Whether it was the result of the hoary prejudice that an operatic canvas must
> remain *far removed* from dramaturgical criteria and automatically debase any
> subject it touches, or whether it was the desire to match the text to the capabilities
> of the composer, or yet whether it was because of his own Italianate predilections
> and inspiration, the fact remains that A. N. Ostrovsky has weakened his play

enormously in adapting his text for the opera, and has hardly helped the cause of *serious* operatic standards in so doing.[126]

The standards Serov had in mind, it goes without saying, were those of realism as then understood in Russia, and which may be boiled down to a Chernïshevskian aphorism: "Emotion and form are opposites."[127] Instead of "form," great specificity of time and (national) location were prized and striven for. Ostrovsky's goals were different; he had in fact skillfully adapted his dramatic structure to the demands of Italian operatic form, confident that the musical scale thus achieved would heighten emotional intensity sufficiently to compensate for the attendant loss in dramatic motivation and subtlety. The story was stripped down to the love intrigue, which, denuded of its social and cultural milieu (which today will inevitably strike the reader as the play's most essential component), is reduced to a typical (that is, "universal") triangle of fickle woman, spineless paramour, and ridiculous cuckold. Several roles—including Kabanova, the heroine's mother-in-law, often viewed by literary critics as the play's central character—are virtually eliminated. (Kuligin, the "conscience" of the play, is replaced by the chorus.)

In fashioning the libretto, Ostrovsky sought to gather into big arias the individual, scattered speeches and admissions of the lovers Boris and Katerina. Thus the opera begins right off (except for a conventional genre chorus) with an aria by Boris in which he sets forth at length his hopeless love for Katerina, which in the play is revealed gradually in dialogues and soliloquies spread over two acts. Katerina's two scenes with her friend Varvara, one before and one after her husband's departure in the play, are combined in the opera into one enormous *scena* that begins the second act (thus balancing Boris's aria in the first). These numbers are broadly set, Italian-style, in a sequence of increasingly rapid tempos.

The other main ploy in constructing the libretto was to end each of the four acts with an ensemble finale. The first act of the play, which offered no such possibility, was pretty much cut. The first act of the opera ends with the departure of Tikhon, Katerina's husband (act 2 in the play). Ostrovsky constructed a long farewell scene centering around Tikhon's parting words to each of five characters in turn: a series of little linked duets that in Kashperov's setting conform to what Glinka had once sarcastically described as "typical Italian" behavior: "Instead of A, then B, then A plus B, one character sings A, the other also A, and then together the same A in thirds and sixths."[128]

---

[126] Serov, *Izbrannïye stat'i*, vol. 2, p. 73.

[127] *Selected Philosophical Essays*, p. 346.

[128] Reported by Serov in a letter to Stasov, 14 February 1843; *Muzïkal'noe nasledstvo*, vol. 1, p. 204. Observations on the Kashperov-Ostrovsky *Groza* are based on the separately published libretto (Moscow, 1867) and the piano score of Kashperov's music (without voice), arr. Alexander Dubuque (Moscow: P. Jurgenson, n.d.).

César Cui did his best, as critic, to write off the work of "Il signor maestro Kasperoff" as a joke.[129] Serov, in greater detail, and with characteristic humorlessness, made a similar point. Kashperov, in his description, "belongs to the category of 'naïve' composers: for him an opera is a collection of *vocal pieces and ditties à la Donizetti et Pacini*, accompanied by an orchestra à la Donizetti et Pacini; and the libretto exists for the purpose of somehow motivating the arias, duets, and so on for the prima donna, the contralto, the tenor, and the baritone." Such music and such a dramaturgy, he went on, "is just as appropriate as the song of the Volga boatmen would be in *Lucrezia Borgia*." As for the playwright/librettist's own participation in the venture, "If A. N. Ostrovsky has given up one of his best creations to serve *such* an enterprise, that is his own affair. That from an opera written with such ideals nothing could come but a profanation of his play, is once again as clear as day."[130] One could scarcely hope to find a better or more typical delineation of "literary" vs. "musical" thinking on the subject of opera in nineteenth-century Russia. Audiences by 1867 seemed to be tending toward Serov's line; Kashperov's opera did not enter the Mariyinsky repertory.

As a postscript we may cite what appears to be the very last instance of a Russian composer of any stature adopting an Italian model for opera: Sergei Rachmaninoff's *Aleko* (1892), written as a graduation exercise from Moscow Conservatory to an assigned text by Vladimir Nemirovich-Danchenko, based on Pushkin's long narrative poem "The Gypsies" (*Tsïganï*). It so happens that Kashperov had also written his first, heavily Italianate, opera on the same romantic subject some forty years earlier (the libretto was by the revolutionary writer Nikolai Ogaryov—further testimony to the strange predilection Russian radical thinkers had for Italian or Italianate opera). That opera had never been staged, and there was no chance Rachmaninoff could have known it. But everybody in Moscow knew and was talking about *Cavalleria rusticana*, which had its first performances there in 1891 and was revived just as Rachmaninoff set to work on *Aleko*. Geoffrey Norris has pointed up the extensive parallels between the two operas' librettos.[131] Rachmaninoff even inserted an orchestral intermezzo to accompany the breaking of the dawn, corresponding exactly (and gratuitously) with Mascagni's famous "Intermezzo sinfonico."

By and large, it is clear that Russian composers practiced what they preached where Italian opera was concerned. An account of the echoes of German or (especially) French opera in the work of Russian composers would

---

[129] "Muzïkal'nïye zametki," *Sankt-peterburgskiye vedomosti*, no. 304 (1867).

[130] Serov, *Izbrannïye stat'i*, vol. 2, pp. 76–77.

[131] "Rakhmaninov's Student Opera," *Musical Quarterly* 59, no. 3 (July 1973): 441–48, esp. pp. 447–48.

be many times the length of this one. The reason was as much a matter of timing as one of aesthetics. The rise of the Russian opera had coincided with the decline of the Italian. And yet its very absence testifies to the importance of the Italian opera in defining, and constructing, the Russians' musical *samopoznaniye*, their sense of an art-musical self.

PART III

Hermeneutics of Russian Music:
Four Cruxes

CHAPTER 11

CHAIKOVSKY AND THE HUMAN

A CENTENNIAL ESSAY

CONSERVATIVE AND CONVENTIONAL

An Italian orphan girl is brought up as the ward of an English baronet on his country estate. Another ward of the manor, a young man training for the ministry, loves her. She toys somewhat cruelly with him but loves her guardian's nephew, a careless young officer who toys with her in turn, and who at his uncle's instance is courting a haughty beauty far above the orphan girl's station. The well-born couple's engagement is announced, and the orphan girl is devastated. The officer, perceiving that his fiancée is annoyed by the orphan girl's attentions to him, callously suggests that his uncle marry her off to the young preacher. The preacher, knowing how this plan will upset his beloved, sends her a desperate disclaimer that only mystifies and alarms her. The baronet, oblivious of her feelings, broaches the idea of a double wedding, expecting her to be delighted. Instead, of course, she is crushed. The officer, having mollified his bride and secured her agreement, asks the orphan girl to meet him alone, intending to explain the situation. The bride teases her viciously about her unrequited love, driving her into a jealous frenzy. On her way to her appointment with the officer she goes to a certain cabinet and draws out a dagger, intending to kill him. When she arrives at the appointed place, however, she finds him lying dead, the victim of a sudden seizure. She hurries back to the manor, informs everyone of what she has found, and faints away. The preacher picks her up to revive her, finds the unused dagger in her pocket, and quietly replaces it. The orphan girl runs off and hides herself on a neighboring farm, where the preacher eventually finds her. He tells her that he alone knows her secret, that she could never have gone through with the murder, that she is innocent and safe. In gratitude, she marries the man who loves her, who, having at last acceded to a vicarage, has now gained all his heart's desires. But she soon expires in childbirth. As the author of the tale puts it, "the delicate plant had been too deeply bruised, and in the struggle to put forth a blossom it died."

The author is George Eliot. The tale is "Mr Gilfil's Love-Story," the second of the three novellas in Eliot's first book, *Scenes of Clerical Life* (1858). But for a fatal glass of water, or a dose of mysterious cholera-simulating poison, or something, the story would very likely have been turned into an opera by Pyotr Ilyich Chaikovsky in collaboration with his brother Modest. To his friend Hermann Laroche, Chaikovsky pronounced Eliot's tale "perfect for opera"[1] and even, shortly before his death, sketched a fragmentary scenario, which survives in his archive.[2] On the way to Mr Gilfil the composer rejected two proffered librettos from Modest, both adapted from translations by the romantic poet Vasiliy Zhukovsky. *Nal and Damayanti*, after the Hindu *Mahabharata*, went on from Chaikovsky to Arensky. *Undina*, after La Motte Fouqué's water nymph tale, on which subject Chaikovsky had already written and burned an opera, went on to Rachmaninoff, who sent it back to Modest, where it stayed. Both times the composing Chaikovsky complained to the literary Chaikovsky that the subject was "too far from life" and that he wanted something more like *Cavalleria rusticana*.[3]

Is "Mr Gilfil's Love-Story" like *Cavalleria rusticana*? That depends on how you look at it. It is not nearly as much like Mascagni's opera as Pushkin's poem "The Gypsies," the basis of Rachmaninoff's maiden opera, briefly discussed in the previous chapter, which deliberately played up the resemblance to what was then the hottest new operatic property.[4] In Eliot's story the jealous murder is only a fleeting wish, not a deed. On the other hand, Eliot's tale, like the play by Giovanni Verga on which Mascagni drew, has a resolutely, indeed emphatically prosaic setting, not a romantic gypsy locale like Pushkin's. Yet Pushkin hovers in the background to Chaikovsky's choice nevertheless. Far more conspicuous than any affinity for *Cavalleria rusticana* are the correspondences in "Mr Gilfil's Love-Story" to Pushkin's novel *Eugene Onegin* and his novella *The Queen of Spades*—and, even more specifically, to Chaikovsky's operatic treatments of them.

Several plot similarities surely caught Chaikovsky's eye. The relationship between the officer and the orphan girl closely parallels that between Onegin and Tatyana in Pushkin's novel. The officer is characterized as an Oneginish rake: "To find oneself adored by a little, graceful, dark-eyed, sweet-singing woman, whom no one need despise, is an agreeable sensation, comparable to smoking the finest Latakia."[5] There are even a couple of passages in which

[1] "Otlichno mozhno bïlo bï napisat' operu"; see G. A. Larosh, "Na pamyat' o P. I. Chaikovskom," in E. Bortnikova et al., ed., *Vospominaniya o P. I. Chaikovskom*, 4th ed. (Leningrad: Muzïka, 1980), p. 352.

[2] Covering the second and third acts only, it is printed in *Muzïkal'noye naslediye Chaikovskogo* (Moscow: Izdatel'stvo akademii nauk SSSR, 1958), p. 153.

[3] See his letters to Vladimir Davïdov (11 April 1893) and to Modest (17 April 1893), in P. Chaikovsky, *Polnoye sobraniye sochineniy; Literaturnïye proizvedeniya i perepiska*, vol. 17 (Moscow: Muzïka, 1981), pp. 79, 85.

[4] See Geoffrey Norris, "Rakhmaninov's Student Opera," *Musical Quarterly* 59 (1973): 441–48.

[5] George Eliot, *Scenes of Clerical Life*, ed. Thomas A. Noble (Oxford: Clarendon Press, 1985), p. 114. Further page references to this source will be made in the text.

the rake tries to console the smitten girl with the offhand promise of a brother's love, as in Onegin's answer to Tatyana's letter, the central set piece of scene 3 in Chaikovsky's opera (or, as in Chaikovsky's answer to Antonina Milyukova's letter, the central set piece in the drama of his life).[6] More striking yet is the fairly lengthy scene in which the distraught orphan girl is put to bed by the kind but uncomprehending housekeeper, as Tatyana is put to bed by Fillipyevna, her old nanny; and then both girls, unable to sleep, get out of bed and spend the night at the window (though Eliot's heroine, unlike Pushkin's, feels no hope and writes no letter). These surface resemblances, though they may have arrested the composer's attention, are minor. The major correspondences are two: one structural, the other attitudinal.

Caterina Sarti (known familiarly as Tina), Eliot's orphan girl, is Italian; and, being Italian, she sings. Eliot's story has a pervasive soundtrack of vocal music. It is more than a decorative fixture, also more than a fixer of local or period color. It defines social relations. In a kind of *Upstairs, Downstairs* routine, we first hear Tina, seated at the harpsichord at the behest of her guardian, Sir Christopher Cheverel, regaling a party—the very party at which the officer is being seen off in pursuit of his bride—with

> Sir Christopher's favourite airs by Gluck and Paesiello [*sic*], whose operas, for the happiness of that generation, were then to be heard on the London stage. It happened this evening that the sentiment of these airs, "*Che farò senza Eurydice?*" and "*Ho perduto il bel sembiante*" [from Paisiello's *Amor vendicato* (1786)] in both of which the singer pours out his yearning after his lost love, came very close to Caterina's own feeling. But her emotion, instead of being a hindrance to her singing, gave her additional power. (P. 96)

A couple of chapters later, we hear Sir Christopher's housekeeper ask his gardener, as they sit with the other servants before the fire, to regale them with what the author describes as "a remarkably *staccato* rendering of 'Roy's Wife of Aldivalloch,'" a Scottish song by Neil Gow, the great fiddler, urging him on with the remark that "I'd rather hear a good old sung like that, nor all the fine 'talian toodlin'" (pp. 107–8). Already we must suspect that these two, and the other servants, will show Tina a greater sympathy and understanding than those ostensibly closer to her.

At the other end of the tale music serves again as emotional outlet, when, to pass "the long feverish moments before twelve o'clock," when she is to meet with Captain Wybrow, the officer, Tina rushes to the harpsichord: "Handel's

---

[6] "If you will be satisfied with a quiet, calm love, rather the love of a brother, then I make you my proposal," as his widow recalled his words. See Antonina Chaikovskaya, "Vospominaniya vdovï P. I. Chaikovskogo," *Russkaya muzïkal'naya gazeta* 42 (1913): 918; quoted in Alexander Poznansky, *Tchaikovsky: The Quest for the Inner Man* (New York: Schirmer Books, 1991), p. 212. More than likely the composer was deliberately paraphrasing his character's words (unless his widow was doing the paraphrasing in retrospect).

'Messiah' stood open on the desk, at the chorus 'All we like sheep,' and Caterina threw herself at once into the impetuous intricacies of that magnificent fugue. In her happiest moments she could never have played it so well; for now all the passion that made her misery was hurled by a convulsive effort into her music" (p. 154).

And finally, music is the healing force that revives Tina's wounded spirit sufficiently, if not to save her, then at least to enable her to recognize and respond to the preacher's—that is, Maynard Gilfil's—claim on her heart. A minor character named Ozzy, Gilfil's nephew, carelessly strikes a note on the harpsichord with his riding whip about a week after the catastrophe. It is the first musical tone Tina has heard since the fateful day.

> The vibration rushed through Caterina like an electric shock: it seemed as if at that instant a new soul were entering into her, and filling her with a deeper, more significant life. She looked round, rose from the sofa, and walked to the harpsichord. In a moment her fingers were wandering with their old sweet method among the keys, and her soul was floating in its true familiar element of delicious sound. . . . Presently there were low liquid notes blending themselves with the harder tones of the instrument, and gradually the pure voice swelled into predominance. . . . Caterina was singing the very air from the *Orfeo* which we heard her singing so many months ago at the beginning of her sorrows. It was *Che farò*, Sir Christopher's favourite, and its notes seemed to carry on their wings all the tenderest memories of her life, when Cheverel Manor was still an untroubled home. The long happy days of childhood and girlhood recovered all their rightful predominance over the short interval of sin and sorrow.
>
> She paused, and burst into tears—the first tears she had shed since she had been at [Gilfil's sister's home]. Maynard could not help hurrying towards her, putting his arm round her, and leaning down to kiss her hair. She nestled to him, and put up her little mouth to be kissed.
>
> The delicate-tendrilled plant must have something to cling to. The soul that was born anew to music was born anew to love. (P. 183)

These are very Chaikovskian situations and effects. Both *Eugene Onegin* and *The Queen of Spades* have scenes of girlish singing that, while seeming at first no more than decorative, acquire crucial musical and dramatic significance later on. In *Eugene Onegin* it is the duet for Tatyana and her sister Olga (to the words of an early verse of Pushkin's), at the opera's very outset, which contains Tatyana's leitmotif (already featured in the orchestral prelude) and which establishes the "realistic" period idiom—the idiom of the domestic romance (*bïtovoy romans*)—that will define the opera's setting and also resonate in the music of all the principals through its characteristic contour (or morpheme, corresponding to what Boris Asafyev would later call *intonatsiya*) outlining the interval of a minor sixth. That interval is now known in Russia as the "Lensky sixth," after that character's famous act 2 aria, "Kuda, kuda vï

EXAMPLE 11.1. Lensky's aria (Chaikovsky, *Eugene Onegin*, act 2, scene 2)

(What has the breaking day in store for me?)

udalilis'" ("Whither, ah whither are ye fled"; see example 11.1), but it also permeates Tatyana's part (her letter scene in particular), the reminiscences of genre music linking her most private and "spontaneous" emotions at once touchingly and ironically to the conventions of thought and behavior that govern them.[7] And Chaikovsky gives us his version of Eliot's *Upstairs, Downstairs* routine when he follows the opening domestic romance with the two folk songs sung by serfs—one "drawn out" (*protyazhnaya*), the other a dance (*plyasováya*) that inspires Olga to emulate the peasants' unaffected spirit and despise a bit her overly reflective sister.

In *The Queen of Spades*, which the Chaikovsky brothers deliberately set back in time from the early nineteenth century of *Eugene Onegin* to the late eighteenth of "Mr Gilfil's Love-Story," a genre duet in period style (on verses by Zhukovsky) opens the second act, sung by the female protagonist, Lisa, and her confidante, Pauline. Pauline, asked to sing again, complies with an unaccountably gruesome song (on verses by Konstantin Batyushkov) about a doomed maiden. That song then takes its place in the network of sinister doubles that stalk this most haunted of all operas when Gherman, the obsessed young officer, surprises Lisa later in the scene, his entreaties to her uncannily replaying the "intonations" of Pauline's song, thus forecasting Lisa's doom (example 11.2).

Predictably, then, Chaikovsky's scenario incorporated or adapted most of the musical moments in "Mr Gilfil's Love-Story." In fact, having somewhat schematically enhanced their symmetry, he structured the whole scenario around them. Act 1 was to contain the two arias, newly composed by Chaikovsky, presumably in an adapted period style such as he had employed

---

[7] See R. Taruskin, "Yevgeny Onegin," in *The New Grove Dictionary of Opera*, vol. 4, ed. Stanley Sadie (London: Macmillan, 1992), pp. 1193–94.

EXAMPLE 11.2. Chaikovsky, *The Queen of Spades*

a. Pauline's romance (act 1, scene 2)

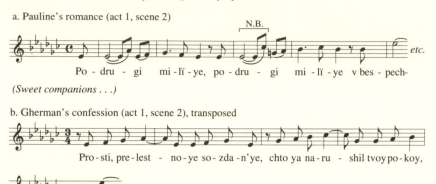

(Sweet companions . . .)

b. Gherman's confession (act 1, scene 2), transposed

(Forgive me, adorable creature, for disturbing your peace)

in his Pushkin operas. The climax of act 2 was to be the highly compressed and intensified scene of attempted murder, which in Chaikovsky's version takes place in the presence of the entire household and is organized around a reprise of the second aria from act 1, during which Tina "gets so carried away, that to everyone's astonishment (somewhat as in [Scribe's and Legouvé's] *Adrienne Lecouvreur*) she really attacks the Captain, unexpectedly seizing a dagger and hurling herself at him, but just as she comes running the Captain emits a shriek and dies."[8] Act 3 is organized around a reprise of the first aria, initiated by Gilfil in an effort to bring Tina around. "She listens attentively, begins singing, then weeps, regains her composure, and all ends auspiciously though with a tinge of melancholy. She does not become Gilfil's bride but does give him reason to hope she might yet come to love him."[9]

Thus the next opera Chaikovsky might have written, had he lived, would have maintained and possibly intensified his familiar reliance, as much a structural as a dramaturgical reliance, on genre set pieces and their reprises. Like so much else about Chaikovsky's style and modus operandi, these devices are often looked upon as naive or hackneyed. Indeed they are conservative and conventional. Everything about Chaikovsky, from his political views to his social deportment and attitudes to his musical tastes, was conservative and conventional, which is one of the many reasons why of all the great composers of the nineteenth century Chaikovsky has always been the easiest one for twentieth-century people to condescend to—in a conventional sort of way.

[8] *Muzïkal'noye naslediye Chaikovskogo*, pp. 153–54.

[9] Ibid., p. 154. It is not quite clear whether this was in fact to be the end of the opera.

A similar attitudinal conservatism and conventionality informs a great deal of Victorian literature, which of course is why it appealed so strongly to Chaikovsky. The narrative strategy in "Mr Gilfil's Love-Story" actually thematizes the celebration of convention and its uses, reminding one of similar thematizations in Chaikovsky. The dramatic events recounted earlier in straightforward chronological order are actually nested in the story within a very complex series of flashbacks, so that the reader's attitudes toward the plot are never naive but are constantly subjected to manipulation by the author. The novella's first sentence begins, "When old Mr Gilfil died, thirty years ago, there was general sorrow in Shepperton." Gradually, at first through a collage of picturesque anecdotes and dialect sound bites, we learn of his long, quiet, solitary career as a country pastor, of his quaint, somewhat absent ways, of his routined and repetitious modus vivendi, his "caustic tongue, and bucolic tastes, and sparing habits." But also we learn of his calm satisfactions—dog, hearth, pipe, gin—and of the undemonstrative kindness and the unshowing probity that made his parishioners hold him in respect and even in affection, though they seldom thought of the old bachelor, especially in his last reclusive years.

Only then do we learn, at first by following his housekeeper into a locked room in Mr Gilfil's house, that he had not always been a bachelor and that there was a corresponding "secret chamber in his heart, where he had long turned the key on early hopes and early sorrows, shutting up for ever all the passion and the poetry of his life" (p. 84). The story we know at last commences, but it too is narrated with many flashbacks and detours, and an epilogue returns us to Mr Gilfil's old age, giving us one last look at "the dear old Vicar," who, "though he had something of the knotted whimsical character of the poor lopped oak, had yet been sketched out by nature as a noble tree" (p. 186).

What do we think of, if we are thinking Chaikovsky? We think of Mme Larina and her wistful al fresco ruminations at the very beginning of the operatic *Eugene Onegin*, set as a recitative conversation with Fillipyevna in counterpoint against the opera's first set piece, the idiom-defining domestic romance sung by her daughters within the house, offstage. It is a commentary on the old romance itself, turning this quite unprecedented quartet or double duet for women's voices (a tour de force, incidentally, of art-concealing contrapuntal artistry) into a simultaneous text and gloss—an explicit meditation on one of the novel's paramount themes, the relationship between life and literature, between spontaneous feeling and mediating convention, between— if a bit of once-modish language may be excused—signifiers and signifieds. These are just the aspects of Pushkin that literary people fancy inaccessible to music, or at least to Chaikovsky; but that is another mark of the condescension we so easily feel toward this astonishing genius—a condescension that will richly repay examination for what it can tell us about ourselves.

The Larina/Fillipyevna side of the opening quartet culminates in a maxim Pushkin had adapted from his contemporary Chateaubriand: *Privïchka svïsshe nam dana, zamena schastiyu ona* ("Habit is given to us from above as substitute for happiness"). It could serve equally well as a motto for *Eugene Onegin* or for "Mr Gilfil's Love-Story." Its importance to Chaikovsky can be gauged from the prominence and the placement he gave it. And as long as we are so used to reading Chaikovsky's compositional choices autobiographically, we cannot pass over the proximity of *Eugene Onegin* to the central tragedy of the composer's life, his bootless marriage, and the way "Mr Gilfil's Love-Story," too, concerns one central dramatic event that irrevocably marks and distorts a life, turning a noble tree into a poor lopped oak. Chaikovsky did tend in certain self-pitying moments to look back on his life that way, or so certain oft-quoted letters would seem to indicate, and one could certainly make the familiar claim that he was drawn to Eliot's tale out of a sense of emotional kinship—or "identification," to use the standard terminology of hack criticism—with the title character.

QU'EST-CE QUE LE CLASSICISME?

The question remains, and will always remain, how critically *significant* such an observation is. It is of course a familiar question, one of the cursed questions of modern criticism, associated most conspicuously with another Eliot, the one with initials for a nom de plume, who was always after us to ignore "the man who suffers" in our pursuit and veneration of "the mind which creates."[10] But how could such a behest be heeded in the case of the composer of a *Symphonie pathétique*, an explicitly designated "symphony of suffering," who wrote in a famous letter elicited by his patron that his composing was "a musical cleansing of the soul, which boils over with an accumulation that naturally seeks its outlet in tones, just as a lyric poet will express himself in verse"?[11] If Eliot proclaimed that "it is not in his personal emotions, the emotions provoked by particular events in his life, that the poet is in any way remarkable or interesting,"[12] and if Chaikovsky proclaimed that his personal emotions were in fact the sole subject of his work, then the only conclusion available to critics obedient to Eliot's authority—and for a long time that

---

[10] See T. S. Eliot, "Tradition and the Individual Talent (1919), in *Selected Prose of T. S. Eliot*, ed. Frank Kermode (New York: Harcourt Brace Jovanovich/Farrar, Straus and Giroux, 1975), p. 41. The word *significant* is italicized above in homage to Eliot's insistent habit in that essay.

[11] To Nadezhda Filaretovna von Meck, 1 March/17 February 1878; Chaikovsky, *Polnoye sobraniye sochineniy; Literaturnïye proizvedeniya i perepiska*, vol. 7 (Moscow: Muzgiz, 1962), p. 124.

[12] "Tradition and the Individual Talent," p. 43.

meant virtually everybody—was that Chaikovsky's work was in no way remarkable or interesting.

That is why many of us would like to see a bit of immanent criticism applied at long last to Chaikovsky, however passé such a practice may otherwise be deemed in today's critical climate. I have been surreptitiously doing just that in my comments about genres and conventions—codes tacitly, which is to say impersonally, agreed to in advance by the producers and the receivers of a work of art. It holds for the setting in *Eugene Onegin* of Chateaubriand's maxim about the virtues of habit, which is to say salubriously conventional behavior. Chaikovsky set it off as a sudden little canon, a genre set piece in miniature (example 11.3). Here the simple contrapuntal form represents its meaning—that is, becomes *significant*—according to a time-honored code: "Es ist der alte Bund," as Bach had put it, fugally, many years before. It is the old constraint: if feeling is to be significantly expressed, it must be mediated through significant forms—that is, forms that function as conventional signifying codes. And that presupposes their intelligibility, which of course implies predefinition. If, as has been claimed, and as I agree, Chaikovsky is the great "poet of everyday life," and a "genius of emotion," it is because he knew how to channel life and emotion with great power and precision through coded forms.

Chaikovsky's reliance on conventions and established genres implied a certain attitude toward his audience, one that he never hesitated to make explicit. Let us return for a moment to *Cavalleria rusticana*, the opera he held up as a model to his brother against the fantasy or mystical subjects Modest kept pressing on him. His caution that an opera subject not stray too "far from life" is often interpreted as evidence of the composer's need, a need often presented as infantile, to "identify" personally with his subjects. But compare his characterization, given in an interview with a St. Petersburg reporter in November 1892, of Mascagni, and the secret of the Italian newcomer's success:

> People are wrong to think that this young man's colossal, fabulous success is the result of clever publicity. No matter how much you publicize the work of a nonexistent or ephemeral talent, you'll accomplish nothing. There is just no way of forcing the whole European public to simply croak in fanatical delight. Mascagni, it's clear, is not only very gifted but also very smart. He realizes that nowadays the spirit of realism, the harmonization of art and the true-to-life, is everywhere in the air, that Wotans, Brünnhildes, and Fafners do not in fact excite any real sympathy on the part of the listener, that human beings with their passions and woes are more intelligible and tangible to us than the gods and demigods of Valhalla. Judging by his choice of subject, Mascagni operates *not by force of instinct* but *by force of an astute perception of the needs of the contemporary listener*. Accordingly, he does not behave like some Italian composers who

EXAMPLE 11.3. Larina and Filippyevna, duettino (Chaikovsky, *Eugene Onegin*, act 1, scene 1)

try to look as much as possible like Germans and who seem ashamed of being the children of their fatherland. Instead, he illustrates his chosen life dramas with true Italian suppleness and charm, and the result is a work of near-irresistible fascination and appeal for the public.[13]

How very bourgeois, we are apt to think; or, if we are true Slavists, how very Alexander III! To the avowed conventionality we have already noted, Chaikovsky now adds a calculated bid for audience appeal of a kind that we have long been taught to despise as pandering. This, too, is echoed in the "Gilfil" scenario, when Chaikovsky pointedly invokes *Adrienne Lecouvreur*, a proven crowd-pleaser, as object of deliberate emulation. In the St. Petersburg interview, Chaikovsky lists his personal pantheon of contemporary composers—one that so jars with our inherited notions of canon as to make Chaikovsky's notoriously equivocal canonical status seem only inevitable and fair. He writes Brahms off altogether, along with Goldmark, Bruckner, the young Richard Strauss, and Moritz Moszkowski ("who works, despite his Slavic name, in Germany"), and unreservedly praises Saint-Saëns, Delibes, Massenet, Grieg, Svendsen, Dvořák, and in the latter's train Zdeněk Fibich, Karel Bendl, Karel Kovařovic, and Josef Bohuslav Foerster. Who are these people? With a couple of exceptions this seems a roll call of third-raters. Chaikovsky seems to be asking to be included in their number, and we have by and large been ready, nay eager, to oblige. Within his own—Russian—artistic milieu, Chaikovsky seems by his own confession the very personification of what historians of Russia like to call the Era of Small Deeds.

Of course the chief god in the Chaikovskian canon is a composer of undisputed canonicity, indeed the very touchstone of musical greatness. But Chaikovsky's worshipful attitude toward Mozart is usually dismissed as a sentimental mistake, based on what is presumed to have been a superficial acquaintance,[14] on a par with his nostalgic and disreputable pastiche evocations of that nineteenth-century fairyland known as "the eighteenth century." The *New Grove Dictionary* pronounces Chaikovsky's Mozartianas, and his "neoclassical" tendency generally, to be inauthentic, even "inglorious," and compares it invidiously with the neoclassicism of Stravinsky: "For whereas the latter, in his neo-classical works, subjected styles from the past to his Russian flair for creative caricature as a means of further self-discovery, Tchaikovsky turned to the 18th century as a means of escape from himself."[15]

---

[13] G[rigoriy Anatol'yevich] B[lokh], "Beseda c Chaikovskim," *Peterburgskaya zhizn'*, no. 2 (1892); in P. I. Chaikovsky, *Muzïkal'no-kriticheskiye stat'i*, 4th ed. (Leningrad: Muzïka, 1986), p. 319. Italics added.

[14] "Čajkovskij affirme avoir adoré ce dernier [Mozart] toute sa vie, mais, le *Don Juan* excepté, il ne le connaît alors que superficiellement" (Vladimir Fédorov, "Čajkovskij, Musicien Type du XIXᵉ siècle?" *Acta Musicologica* 42 [1970]: 63).

[15] *The New Grove Dictionary of Music and Musicians*, ed. Stanley Sadie (London: Macmillan, 1980), vol. 18, pp. 619, 615.

And yet, if we open the same *New Grove Dictionary* to Daniel Heartz's very sophisticated article entitled "Classical," we do not find the usual bromides about autonomy or equilibrium or purity or sobriety. Instead we find a historically grounded emphasis on high technical skill and on universality of appeal, the latter construed in terms of cosmopolitanism, in terms of mastery of all genres, and, most significantly, in terms of a pair of attitudes educed from the influential writings of the French critic Henri Peyre. The first is "happiness in remaining within certain conventions or at least not straying too far from them—conventions that were bound to please and aid the public"; and the other, closely related, defines "the 'classical' artist, regardless of the field or period," as one who "worked in complicity with his public, attempting to fulfil its expectations, and was not afraid to be pleasing or to submit to society's conditions."[16]

These are precisely the attitudes we have noted in Chaikovsky—the very attitudes, ironically enough, that have, along with so much else, led to his misprizing. How is it that "classical" attitudes, attitudes describing what is by definition a standard of excellence, should have become tinged with opprobrium? More particularly, am I proposing that we regard Chaikovsky as a "classical" artist?

I am not. The term "classical," in all its music-historical and music-critical usages, has long been a prime candidate or target for deconstruction, if not for destruction outright; and I aim to contribute herewith, to the best of my ability, to that long overdue project. I hasten to point out, though, that the attributes Peyre and Heartz cite as "classical" are indeed attributes Chaikovsky shared with Mozart and with Mozart's contemporaries, and, more generally, with the aristocratic musical culture of the eighteenth century; and that, consequently, Chaikovsky's kinship with the Viennese master runs deeper than mere pious veneration or stylistic parody. And I would also contend that the line from Mozart to Chaikovsky is, both for reasons implicit in the Heartz/Peyre formulations and for reasons having to do more generally with politics and history, a more direct line than the one that connects Mozart and his contemporaries with the composers more commonly perceived, within the purview of conventional music history, as their successors. In fundamental ways that go far beyond matters of "style" or "form," and that amount to the very opposite of "escape from himself," Chaikovsky was very much a Mozartean composer.

But hardly a "classical" one; for neither was Mozart. The term is an anachronism. It was born for music in the nineteenth century in the heat of aesthetic battle, and it only cooled into the familiar, purportedly neutral style-critical category in our own century. The qualities that Henri Peyre calls "classical"

---

[16] Ibid., vol. 4, p. 450; the source of Peyre's formulations is his book *Qu'est-ce que le Classicisme?* (Paris, 1935).

are that only in contrast to the so-called "romantic." Both terms, but particularly the "classical," which was not used in the period of its current application, are intelligible today only in their artificially constructed binary relationship. But the qualities Chaikovsky shared with Mozart can be constructed in other dialectical contexts as well.

Historically the most applicable or appropriate opposition is that between *Zivilisation* and *Kultur*, the binarism that midwifed the birth both of romanticism and, in the early nineteenth century, of German artistic self-consciousness as well. In this pair the former term, "Zivilisation," stood for the culture of the prerevolutionary European aristocracy and the values of the Enlightenment. It necessarily implied what Daniel Heartz calls the artist's "easy relationship with the expectations of the consumer."[17] *Kultur* was the specifically romantic and specifically Germanic discourse of *Innigkeit*, the discourse of "self-discovery," to put it in New Agey, *New Grove*ian terms. It celebrated the idiosyncratically personal and the artist's unique subjectivity, presupposing a producer-oriented musical ecosystem that quickly coalesced into a cult around the heroic personality of Beethoven the great symphonist. The discourse of *Kultur* radically dichotomized the qualities of *Geist* and *Sinnlichkeit*, spirituality and sensuality, the former being associated with pure, disinterested artistry and the genres of "absolute" and "universal" instrumental music in which the Germans claimed supremacy; whereas the latter was associated with "civilized"—that is, French—manners and with music that served the base ambitions of performers and the frivolous appetites of spectators, the epitomizing genre for Russians, as we have seen, being the Italian opera.[18]

All at once the public was the enemy. The worst thing an artist could now do, under the dispensation of *Kultur*, was the very thing Haydn and Mozart most wanted to do and were so successful at doing: namely, "to please." Schumann, the exemplary *Kultur* critic, wrote darkly of "the poisoned flowers"—which we might translate suitably as "les fleurs du mal"—that tempted and threatened artists: "the applause of the vulgar crowd and the fixed gaze of sentimental women."[19]

The vulgar, the sentimental, and the feminine—put them all together and they spell Chaikovsky, as viewed through a Teutonizing, which is to say, a "universalizing," lens. For it has certainly been the triumph of the Germanic outlook that, propagated at first through the proliferation of Germanic conservatories throughout Europe and America, and then through the establishment

---

[17] *The New Grove Dictionary of Music and Musicians*, vol. 4, p. 450.

[18] See the discussion of Vladimir Odoyevsky's opera criticism in the previous chapter, pp. 215–17.

[19] Review of trios by Alexander Fesca, in R. Schumann, *Gesammelte Schriften*, ed. Heinrich Simon, vol. 3 (Leipzig, n.d.), p. 115; quoted in Sanna Pederson, "On the Task of the Music Historian: The Myth of the Symphony after Beethoven," *Repercussions* 2, no. 2 (Fall 1993): 20.

of the academic discipline of musicology on the German university model, what had been constructed at first as a national code of values has indeed been universalized in the discourse of what we call "classical" music.

And that is precisely why the word "classical" is so ambiguous, so disingenuous, and so useless for music history. Like "romantic," it is code for a set of values; but unlike "romantic" (and like, say, "authentic"), it is loaded with a contemporary freight of connotation that is wholly unrelated, even opposed, to historical reality. Heartz, among many others by now, has noted that the composers we now call "classical" were in fact described as "romantic" by their younger literary contemporaries such as E.T.A. Hoffmann. "But this means little," writes Heartz, "because anything they perceived as imaginative, deeply moving, and colourful, including the music of Haydn and Mozart, automatically became 'romantic.'"[20]

On the contrary, I would say it means a great deal, because it gives us a model by which we can understand the later assimilation of Haydn, and especially Mozart, to the anachronistic paradigm of "classicism."

What Hoffmann and his contemporaries actually accomplished was the assimilation of Mozart and Haydn to the mythology (or the "invented tradition," as the phrase lately goes among culture historians)[21] associated with the Beethoven cult. In one of its aspects the meaning of that tradition or asserted mainstream remained constant, while in another it underwent a radical change. The constant factor was its specific identification with Germany, vouchsafing the musical supremacy of the *Kulturnation*. The radical change, which actually resulted in a split within the German national culture, was the shift from regarding the Viennese trinity of Haydn, Mozart, and Beethoven as the beginning of an artistic tendency that continued into the present—that being the position that originated with Hoffmann and reached its peak with Wagner and the "New German school"—and the view that cast the Viennese trinity as the protagonists of a Golden Age—of purity, of autonomy, of "absoluteness"—from which German music had subsequently declined, that being the position associated with Brahms and Hanslick, thence with most conventional academic historiography.[22] That is the discourse on which our notion of "the classical period," and of the Haydn-Mozart idiom as "the classical style," depends.

Chaikovsky obviously has no part of that. As long as we apply the word

[20] *The New Grove Dictionary of Music and Musicians*, vol. 4, p. 451. See also, inter alia, Leo Treitler, "Mozart and the Idea of Absolute Music," in *Music and the Historical Imagination* (Cambridge, Mass.: Harvard University Press, 1989), pp. 176–214.

[21] See Eric Hobsbawm and Terence Ranger, eds., *The Invention of Tradition* (Cambridge: Cambridge University Press, 1983).

[22] For extensive substantiation of the influence of this mythology on historical writing into our own day, see the quotations from Lang, Einstein, Arnold Whittall, and Nicholas Temperley in Pederson, "On the Task of the Music Historian," pp. 6–9.

"classical" to the composer with whom he preeminently identified (an application, be it said, that considerably distorts Mozart by exaggerating the importance of his late symphonies), Chaikovsky's claim of kinship with Mozart will remain suspect and inadmissible. To redefine the word "classical," following Peyre and Heartz, to denote the congeries of aesthetic and social attitudes to which the discourse of romanticism was a reaction, is merely polemical; and it has the undesirable side effect of obscuring the survival of those attitudes into the nineteenth century and beyond. Better to scuttle the loaded modifier and concentrate on the attitudes themselves.

"Give Us Beauty, Only Beauty!"

When this is done, the congruence of Chaikovsky's aesthetic with the discourse identified by Heartz and Peyre is virtually self-evident, and largely explains what seem not only his own quirky personal predilections, but those of many other Russians. Like most other Russians, Chaikovsky felt a powerful aversion to Wagner, while never denying Wagner's greatness (a concession, as we shall see, that cost him little). Despite his aversion, he attended the première Bayreuth *Ring* in 1876 and actually covered it in a series of quite respectful articles for the Moscow newspaper *Russkiye vedomosti*. To his brother Modest, however, he wrote later in exasperation that "the conglomeration of the most complex and recherché harmonies, the colorlessness of everything being sung onstage, the interminable dialogues, the pitch-darkness in the theater, the lack of any interest in the poetry or the story—all this simply exhausts the nerves." Music had no business doing that, he insisted. "Before," he wrote, Mozart no doubt foremost in his mind, "music strove to delight people—now they are tormented and exhausted." This remark has been interpreted to characterize Chaikovsky's romanticism vis-à-vis Wagner's incipient modernism.[23] Wagner's, however, was the romantic attitude, educed directly out of the Beethoven cult. (Compare the weeping Berlioz's retort, in the old story, to the neighbor at the Beethoven concert who inquired why he did not leave: "Madame, do you think I am here to enjoy myself?") Chaikovsky was true to the aesthetics of the Enlightenment, or to what he took to be the Franco-Italian aesthetic of enjoyment. In either case, it was a preromantic discourse to which he steadfastly adhered.

And that is why he couldn't stand Wagner's supposed antipode, either. Toward the music of Brahms, despite some outwardly cordial social encounters with its author late in life, Chaikovsky never made the slightest pretense of respect. Alongside many generalized manifestations of annoyance and boredom, he left a couple of pricelessly revealing observations about Brahms,

---

[23] See Poznansky, *Tchaikovsky*, p. 181, from which the translation of Chaikovsky's letter has been adapted.

one technical, the other aesthetic. The technical remark, made in private correspondence with his patron, was prompted by Brahms's Violin Concerto,
which Mme von Meck, who also hated it, had sent him to inspect. According
to Chaikovsky, Brahms "never expresses anything, or if he does, he fails to
do it fully [*nikogda nichego ne vïskazïvayet, a yesli vïskazïvayet, to ne
doskazïvayet*]. His music is made up of little fragments of something or
other, artfully glued together."[24] The aesthetic pronouncement may be pieced
together from a pair of letters to that very important friend of Chaikovsky's
later years, the Grand Duke Konstantin Konstantinovich.

> Isn't Brahms, in essence, just a caricature of Beethoven? Aren't his pretensions
> to profundity, strength, and power detestable, when the content he pours into
> those Beethovenian forms is so pitiful and insignificant?[25] [But no,] one cannot
> call Brahms's music weak and insignificant. His style is always lofty; he never
> chases after external effect, nor is he ever banal. He is all seriousness and no-
> bility of purpose, but the chief thing—*beauty*—is missing."[26]

These are extraordinarily telling statements. The first of them turns on its
head, as if recasting from the opposite perspective, the most commonly regis-
tered objection to Chaikovsky's own symphonic style. And more than that, it
homes in unerringly on what recent "objective" historiography has pinpointed
as the essential crux of nineteenth-century compositional practice.

As Carl Dahlhaus so influentially defined it, that problem was "the relationship between monumentality and sophisticated thematic manipulation," or,
more specifically, the "principle of evolving a monumental and 'teleological'
form from an inconspicuous motive, which does not even appear as a theme at
first, but only attains the function of a theme gradually and unexpectedly by
virtue of the consequences drawn from it."[27] Dahlhaus is describing the process of "artfully gluing together little fragments of something or other" so as
to achieve an impression of "profundity, strength, and power"—a method of
which Chaikovsky, while never granting its premises or its desirability, immediately recognized in Brahms the supreme master.

In the traditional mythology of the symphony, the Beethovenian ideal became a problem for "romantic" composers because of their uncontrollable
lyric impulse, an impulse that seduced them away from the serious spiritual
tasks set by their predecessor, toward the decorative and the sensual—in a
single word, the feminine. Chaikovsky, of course, has always been a major

[24] Letter dated Rome, 18 February/1 March 1880; Chaikovsky, *Polnoye sobraniye
sochineniy; Literaturnïye proizvedeniya i perepiska*, vol. 9 (Moscow: Muzgiz, 1962), p. 56.

[25] 21 September 1888; ibid., vol. 14 (Moscow: Muzïka, 1974), p. 542.

[26] 2 October 1888; A. A. Orlova, comp. and ed., *P. I. Chaikovskiy o muzïke, o zhizni, o sebe*
(Leningrad: Muzïka, 1976), p. 218.

[27] Carl Dahlhaus, *Nineteenth-Century Music*, trans. J. Bradford Robinson (Berkeley and Los
Angeles: University of California Press, 1989), pp. 156, 154.

offender. After reproducing the familiar program of the Fourth Symphony (a program Chaikovsky never published but educed out of Beethoven's Fifth and the *Symphonie fantastique* for the solitary benefit of the woman who paid his bills), Alfred Einstein offered these reprimands: "As Tchaikovsky let himself be led in his creative work by melodramatic and sentimental programs such as this, he seldom succeeded in a complete mastery of form. And as he was a neurotic, yielding unreservedly to his lyric, melancholy, and emotional ebullitions, he marked most distinctly a last phase of Romanticism—exhibitionism of feeling."[28]

Dahlhaus, though he characteristically confined himself to what he thought of as technical matters, was hardly less severe about the same symphony's "stylistic pretensions." About the main theme of the first movement, he noted that it

> is hardly suitable, at least by Beethovenian standards, for establishing a symphonic movement spanning hundreds of measures. The fact that this theme reaches an ecstatic *fortissimo* in a development section emerging directly from the exposition has little or no bearing on its weaknesses as the mainspring of a symphonic movement [i.e., Chaikovsky's mere success, like the bumblebee's at flying, does not override the theoretical inevitability of his failure]. . . . According to the rule established by Beethoven, the principal theme of a symphonic movement had a dual function: when broken down into particles, it served as material for the development section; when reconstituted, it served as the development's triumphant goal and destination. Tchaikovsky has spread this dual function over two different themes: an *andante* motive, which, though capable of serving as the climax of a development section, is not itself amenable to development, and a *moderato* motive, which can be drawn into a thematic process but is incapable of appearing as the main theme except at exposed locations protected by the *andante* motive. To put it bluntly, the grand style fundamental to the genre has been split into a monumentality that remains a decorative façade unsupported by the internal form of the movement, and an internal form that is lyrical in character and can be dramatized only by applying a thick layer of pathos.[29]

Is this the same Dahlhaus, one has to wonder, who in another context protested that "no-one had a burden to bear because Beethoven wielded authority in music"?[30]

Two points demand immediate elaboration. The first is that Chaikovsky, egregiously though his music may have failed to match the asserted Beethovenian standard, is not alone in this or even unusual. The whole history of the nineteenth-century symphony is traditionally narrated, even within the Ger-

---

[28] *Music in the Romantic Era* (New York: Norton, 1947), p. 316.

[29] *Nineteenth-Century Music*, p. 266.

[30] Carl Dahlhaus, *Foundations of Music History*, trans. J. B. Robinson (Cambridge: Cambridge University Press, 1983), p. 9.

man jurisdiction, and not only by Dahlhaus, as a devolution, with Brahms the miraculous, saving exception. The *New Grove* entry on the nineteenth-century symphony, by Nicholas Temperley, laments Schubert's "ill-concealed preference for melody" and holds "the chief source of weakness in the symphonies of Mendelssohn, Schumann and Tchaikovsky" to be the difficulty they all encountered in trying "to discipline the lyrical urge," with the result that in the period from Beethoven to Brahms "even the most skilful technician was hard put to it to conceal his lack of genuine interest in the 'symphonic' aspect of his work."[31]

The other point, of course, is that the traditional narrative of the nineteenth-century symphony takes one contemporary viewpoint and represents it as a universal ideal. That there were other contemporary viewpoints, perhaps representing other traditions and ideals, is evident from the disparaging passages already cited from Chaikovsky's letters on Brahms, whose shortcomings and whose reputation, it is only sporting to point out for the sake of symmetry, represented in Chaikovsky's view the decline of German musical culture.[32] These passages suggest that Chaikovsky's deviations from the Beethovenian, or at least the Dahlhausian, straight-and-narrow were perhaps conditioned less by a lack of symphonic aptitude or interest than by the wish to "express something fully."

A hint as to the source of Chaikovsky's views, and the tradition in which he might more profitably be placed, comes, most unexpectedly, in the same *New Grove* article by Temperley, even as it continues its lament:

> Mozart, in his E-flat and G minor symphonies, nos. 39 and 40, had left examples which, however tightly constructed, still made their chief effect by an almost continuous outpouring of spontaneous melody, enriched by inventive touches of harmony and orchestration. As the public accustomed itself to the complexities of Mozart's idiom, its rich lyricism, rather than its architectural strength, appealed most strongly to a Romantic generation; and it was this that was imitated and extended, sometimes to the detriment of structural factors.[33]

Leaving aside the fruitless task of deciding what was advance and what decline, let us welcome the suggestion, resonant as it is with many of our previous observations, that in the history of the symphony, too, there may have been a Mozartean tradition that bypassed the Beethovenian on its way into the nineteenth century, and that Chaikovsky may have been one of its legitimate heirs.

The other main idea that emerges from Chaikovsky's remarks on Brahms, what I have called the aesthetic point, is even more pregnant. It consists in the

---

[31] *The New Grove Dictionary of Music and Musicians*, vol. 18, p. 456.

[32] See, inter alia, his letter to von Meck from Vienna, 26 November/8 December 1877; P. I. Chaikovsky, *Perepiska s N. F. fon-Mekk*, vol. 1 (Moscow: Academia, 1934), p. 99.

[33] *The New Grove Dictionary of Music and Musicians*, vol. 18, p. 455.

radical dichotomization of *beauty*, on the one hand, and a whole discourse of profundity/strength/loftiness/seriousness/power—in a word, of *greatness*—on the other. As before, the distinction was perceived at the time in national terms, and so we had best translate our operative term into German: *das Erhabene*. In *The Birth of Tragedy*, Nietzsche, newly aflame with Wagner-mania, reserved his greatest scorn for those who evaluate music "according to the category of beauty," for that was a standard proper not to an art of sounds in motion (or anything else in motion) but only to the static visual arts. Named and derided in this connection was Otto Jahn, whose biography of Mozart was a bible to Chaikovsky; conspicuously unnamed, of course, was the arch-recusant Hanslick, who had had the effrontery, as late as 1854, to author an entire tract "On Musical Beauty" (*Vom Musikalisch-Schönen*), still notorious for its transgressions against the nineteenth-century grain.[34]

These transgressions arose out of a stubborn adherence—from the German national perspective an outmoded and treasonable adherence—to the ideology of the Enlightenment, which is to say the ideology of *Zivilisation*, which is *really* to say the ideology of the hated French. The result, Nietzsche asserted, in a phrase that has acquired a chilling resonance, was an *entartete Kunst*, a "degenerate art." "Let us but observe these patrons of music at close range, as they really are, indefatigably crying: 'Beauty! beauty!'" the philosopher taunts. "Do they really bear the stamp of nature's darling children who are fostered and nourished at the breast of the beautiful, or are they not rather seeking a mendacious cloak for their own coarseness, an aesthetical pretext for their own insensitive sobriety?"[35]

Once again we are dealing with a discourse—the discourse of "great music"—that began as a particular (and an extreme) national and philosophical outlook, but that has been so triumphant in music history and criticism (thence disseminated through "music appreciation"), becoming in the process of its triumph so thoroughly decontextualized and universalized, that it has tended to become invisible *qua* discourse. It reached an epitome of sorts in a longish testamentary book by Alfred Einstein, one of the founding fathers of American academic musicology, who was also for many years a practicing newspaper critic in Germany. We already know something of his opinion of Chaikovsky. This book, a veritable primer of pop romanticism, is called *Greatness in Music*, and Chaikovsky is subjected in it to the usual pro forma abuse, passim. The word "beauty" appears in this book only once, and when it does, it is held at arm's length in scare-quotes, the literary equivalent of tweezers. This single mention is found in the penultimate paragraph of Einstein's three-hundred-page treatise, in which the author purported to enunciate at last "the solution to our problem," that is, the problem of defining great-

---

[34] Friedrich Nietzsche, *The Birth of Tragedy out of the Spirit of Music* (1868), trans. Walter Kaufmann (New York: Vintage, 1967), p. 100.

[35] Ibid., p. 120.

ness. "The most impressive building in New York," Einstein wrote, "is Radio City. Is it 'beautiful'? Certainly not in a traditional sense, because it does not trouble itself about tradition and 'beauty.' It has the power and the security of a natural object."[36]

That power and security is indeed the condition to which the "serious" German music of the nineteenth century aspired. It all went back to the eighteenth-century revival of the ancient discourse of the Sublime (one way of translating *das Erhabene*), which was defined in explicit opposition to the more recent and familiar concept of the Beautiful. For Edmund Burke they presented "a remarkable contrast." What is beautiful is "comparatively small," as well as smooth, polished, light, and delicate. The sublime is, well, *great*. And what is to be perceived as great must be not only big but rugged, negligent, dark, gloomy, solid, massive. "They are indeed ideas of a very different nature, one being founded on pain, the other on pleasure," Burke concluded.[37] "Before, music strove to delight people—now they are tormented and exhausted," Chaikovsky complained.

The history of music in the nineteenth century—especially the Dahlhausian nineteenth century, which lasted until the First World War—could be written in terms of this contrast: in terms, that is, of the encroachment of the sublime upon the traditional domain of the beautiful, of the "great" upon the pleasant. In such a history Wagner would assume the familiar role of Hegelian protagonist; but Chaikovsky's role would be much enlarged over conventional historiographical accounts, for he would now be cast as the Great Recusant, the chief resister, forever faithful to the Mozartean premise that "music, even in the most terrible situations, must never offend the ear, but must please the hearer, or in other words must never cease to be music."[38] By contrast, the natural objects to which Alfred Einstein still made latter-day obeisance—and preeminently the mountains with which romantic artists and poets and philosophers were perennially obsessed—achieve their security, and are able to wield their uncanny power over our imaginations, precisely because they are unconcerned to please us. For this reason, Beethoven, whose Ninth Symphony was the first of the musical mountains, was reproached by his younger contemporary Louis Spohr, exactly as Chaikovsky reproached his older contemporary Brahms, for lacking a sense of beauty.[39]

Chaikovsky's own commitment to beauty—even to the mere *joli*—and all

---

[36] Alfred Einstein, *Greatness in Music*, trans. César Searchinger (New York: Oxford University Press, 1941; reprint, New York: Da Capo Press, 1976), p. 287.

[37] Edmund Burke, *A Philosophical Enquiry into the Origin of our Ideas of the Sublime and the Beautiful*, in Peter le Huray and James Day, *Music and Aesthetics in the Eighteenth and Early Nineteenth Centuries* (Cambridge: Cambridge University Press, 1981), pp. 70–71.

[38] Letter to his father, 26 September 1781; *Mozart's Letters*, trans. Emily Anderson, ed. Eric Blom (Harmondsworth: Penguin Books, 1961), p. 182.

[39] See *Louis Spohr's Autobiography, translated from the German* (London: Longman, Green, Longman, Roberts, and Green, 1865), vol. 1, 189.

that the word implied could be as militant as anyone's rejection.[40] We have evidence of that commitment both from the outside and from the inside. From without, there is the outraged Musorgsky's report to Vladimir Stasov, the correspondent most dependable to share his outrage, on meeting his mincing Moscow counterpart, who presumed to preach to him what he, Musorgsky, regarded as the hypocritical "religion of absolute beauty," a religion that, Musorgsky presumed, only masked an altogether worldly "aim of winning a name and some public acclaim." "Give us musical beauty—only musical beauty!" (*Podaite muzïkal'nuyu krasotu—odnu muzïkal'nuyu krasotu!*) Musorgsky has his Chaikovsky ranting, paraphrasing Nietzsche's derision of Jahn and Hanslick almost word for word[41]—and this in the very next letter after the one in which he had made (also to Stasov, of course) his most militant profession of "realist" faith: "the artistic representation only of beauty" (*khudozhestvennoye izobrazheniye odnoy krasoti*), he had written, "is churlish childishness—art in its infancy."[42]

From within, there is Chaikovsky's no less militant profession to *his* most dependable confidant. "What a joy it is to be an artist!" he wrote to Mme von Meck. "In this sorry age we are living through, art and art alone can distract us from hard reality. Sitting at the piano in my cottage [at Kamenka, his sister's Ukrainian estate], I am totally isolated from all the tormenting questions that weigh upon us all. Perhaps this is selfish of me, but each serves the common good in his own way and art, in my opinion, is a human necessity. Outside of my own musical sphere I am in any case incapable of being of service to my fellow man."[43]

And hence his craving, so suspect in Musorgskian eyes, to meet his fellow man's expectations. Of a work in progress he wrote to his brother that, although it was going slowly and painfully, "it seems likely to be successful. I am almost certain that [it] will please."[44] He knew no other measure of fulfill-

[40] On the importance of *le joli* (as well as on "the tasty" [*vkusnoye*]) see Chaikovsky's 1880 letter to Mme von Meck about *Carmen* in Orlova, *P. I. Chaikovskiy o muzïke, o zhizni, o sebe,* pp. 125–26.

[41] Letter of 26 December 1872; M. P. Musorgsky, *Literaturnoye naslediye,* ed. A. A. Orlova and M. S. Pekelis, vol. 1 (Moscow: Muzïka, 1971), pp. 142–43. This is the letter in which Musorgsky showed his contempt for Chaikovsky by referring to him as "Sadïk-Pasha," the pseudonym of the Polish writer and adventurer Michal Czajkowski (1804–86), much reviled in Russia as a Crimean War turncoat—i.e., a bad Russian.

[42] Letter of 18 October 1872; ibid., p. 141.

[43] 30 April 1878; *Perepiska s N. F. fon-Mekk,* vol. 1, p. 315. The allusions "this sorry age" and "hard reality" are oblique references to the trial of the revolutionary Vera Zasulich, who had made an attempt on the life of Fyodor Trepov, the governor of the St. Petersburg district, and to its outcome (that is, her acquittal), which to Chaikovsky signaled the breakdown of public morality in the name of futile liberalism. "What a pity for our poor, kind sovereign," he had written on 13 April, "who so sincerely desires what is good and who meets with such killing disappointments and setbacks" (ibid., 299).

[44] To Modest Chaikovsky, 26 September 1883; Chaikovsky, *Polnoye sobraniye sochineniy; Literaturnïye proizvedeniya i perepiska,* vol. 12 (Moscow: Muzïka, 1970), pp. 243–44.

ment as a composer than that: "Something told me," he wrote after a particularly successful première, that his work "was going to please the audience, even touch it to the quick. I was both overjoyed and afraid. But what happened exceeded my expectations by far. Such a triumph I had never experienced; I saw that the audience was aroused en masse and beholden to me. These moments are the best adornments of an artist's life. For their sake, living and toiling are worth the while."[45]

Later in the same letter Chaikovsky expresses a familiar ambivalence: "I wanted to go away and hide somewhere; a longing for freedom, quiet, solitude gained the upper hand over the satisfaction of my artistic self-esteem." It was his wonted "misanthropy," as he loved to call it, his need to withdraw. But whatever the causes of these alienated feelings, and whatever their strength, as an artist Chaikovsky was a thoroughly social being. His idea of art was based on service—a sense of social connectedness and obligation (not unmixed, naturally, with dreams of social conquest) to which, insofar as he was conscious of having one, he willingly subordinated his purely artistic conscience. Thus while, as the product of a conservatory education, he inevitably shared the prejudice, imparted to him by his revered and forceful teacher, Rubinstein, that "the symphonic and chamber varieties of music stand much higher than the operatic,"[46] he nevertheless persisted as an operatic composer and ultimately came to identify himself primarily as such. For, as he put it to his patron (in a passage that, as one can imagine, was well publicized in the Soviet literature), "opera and only opera brings you close to people, allies you with a real public, makes you the property not merely of separate little circles but—with luck—of the whole nation."[47]

Again, of course, there was ambivalence; only two weeks later Chaikovsky was contrasting himself with a familiar negative counterpart, and again one may observe a fascinating amalgam of irony and self-irony: "To restrain oneself from writing operas is heroism of a sort, and in our time there is such a hero: Brahms. . . . Brahms is worthy of respect and admiration. Unfortunately, his creative gift is meager and does not measure up to the scope of his aspirations. Nevertheless, he is a hero. I lack that heroism, and the stage, with all its tawdriness, attracts me withal."[48]

EXEMPLARY—BUT OF WHAT?

Brahms's "heroism," it is all too easy to note, was a heroism to which few aspired before the nineteenth century, and Mozart least of all. If Beethoven

---

[45] To Mme von Meck, 18 January 1885; ibid., vol. 13 (Moscow: Muzïka, 1971), p. 25.

[46] To Mme von Meck, 1879; *P. I. Chaikovskiy o muzïke, o zhizni, o sebe*, p. 117.

[47] To Mme von Meck, 27 September 1885; Chaikovsky, *Polnoye sobraniye sochineniy; Literaturnïye proizvedeniya i perepiska*, vol. 13, p. 159.

[48] To Mme von Meck, 11 October 1885; ibid., p. 171.

achieved it in greater measure, it was not so much that he aspired to such a thing but that, as *Fidelio* taught him, his talent suffered a limitation.

Yet once again Chaikovsky had put a prophetic finger on the very nub of the problem—our problem with him, and his with us. For no composer ever conformed less to, or more staunchly resisted, the myth of the artist hero—the surrogate or advance guard for the myth of the heroic German nation—that steadily gained in momentum and in prestige as the nineteenth century wore on, and which reached its dubious triumph in the artistically maladapted twentieth century. As the discourse of romanticism achieved its maximalized expression in what we now look back on as the modernist period, the dichotomies we have so far encountered, all of them variations on the same theme, took on an even more radical aspect. What had formerly been expressible as a cleavage between national schools, or between the cultivation of the beautiful and the cultivation of the sublime, or between the aesthetic of enjoyment and that of contemplation, or between the aesthetic of pleasure and that of disinterestedness, or between the discourse of enlightenment and that of transcendence, or of utility vs. autonomy, or of convention vs. originality, social accommodation vs. social alienation, opera vs. symphony, motley vs. wholeness, melody vs. motive—all this eventually came down to a gross discrimination between the serious and the popular, or even more grossly and peremptorily, into that between art and entertainment.

Chaikovsky, needless to say, comes down in every case on the wrong side of this ideological divide, which is at bottom one between an idea of art oriented toward its audience, hence centered on social reception, public meaning, and human intercourse, and an idea of art oriented at once toward its makers— hence centered on private, hidden, or ineffable meanings—and, finally, toward their product, hence centered on idealized or "absolute" notions of ontology and structure. These last were crystallized in a fictive concept of classicism to which, in a final if paradoxical move, the vastly heterogeneous art of the nineteenth century was cast in retrospect as a fictive conceptual antithesis.

Hence the image of "Čajkovskij, Musicien Type du XIXᵉ siècle"— Chaikovsky, the exemplary nineteenth-century musician—which I cite in French after Vladimir Fédorov, the Russian-born, Paris-based *doyen* of music librarians, who submitted a paper with that title for publication in *Acta Musicologica*, the organ of the International Musicological Society, to serve as the basis for a session of the society's Colloquium on Nineteenth-Century Music, held at the French town of Saint-Germain-en-Laye, near Versailles, in September 1970, of which a transcript was later published in the same journal.[49] This conference, which in Fédorov's own rather disgusted words "went hay-

---

[49] Fédorov, "Čajkovskij, Musicien Type du XIXᵉ siècle?" pp. 59–70; and Georg Knepler (chair) et al., "Čajkovskij, Musicien Type du XIXᵉ siècle?" in "Actes du Colloque de Saint-Germain-en-Laye: Études sur la Musique du XIXᵉ siècle," *Acta Musicologica* 43 (1971): 205–35.

wire" (*ist schief gegangen*),[50] was revealing indeed—not for its insights on Chaikovsky, about whom nothing much of relevance was said, but for the light it shed on the musical and musicological mentality of its own time, and on Chaikovsky's status as cultural touchstone.

Even Fédorov's original paper, though it displayed a certain bravado in bringing Chaikovsky up for musicological discussion, approached him with palpable squeamishness. It was clear that to discuss Chaikovsky as an emblematic nineteenth-century figure was to put the nineteenth century on trial.[51] An enormous emphasis was placed on the "hysteria" and psychopathology of man and times alike. The composer was portrayed as not just musically sensitive, but as "maladivement sensible à la musique"; he had "un sensibilité musicale presque morbide"; he submitted to music and to musical influences "avec peu de discernement."[52] He was a credible candidate for "exemplary" composer thanks chiefly to the catholicity of his range. Because he had tried his hand at virtually every contemporary genre, every genre could be sampled through him in a representative nineteenth-century guise. And yet the quality of that representation was explicitly, fastidiously, even histrionically placed beyond the bounds of discussion.[53]

The essence of Fédorov's argument for treating Chaikovsky as a synecdoche for the music of his century was that his "language" and his "idea of music" were "purely post-Beethovenian," a notion that depended heavily on the mythology of classicism. "Would it not be perfectly ridiculous," Fédorov suggested, "to try and say what he had to say with the balance and the sobriety of classical form?" For Chaikovsky, Fédorov maintained, music "is in no wise a pure music that plays with sounds, themes, structures." Rather,

> it serves above all to transmit, and to transmit as directly and clearly as possible, *his* state of mind, *his* emotions, *his* psychology, *his* thoughts, *his* philosophy. Man—Chaikovsky himself or any one of his fellows, it matters not—is his central musical preoccupation. This man is locked in perpetual combat with an implacable "fatum" that prevents him from achieving full self-realization, from being happy, from loving freely, from communing with his fellow creatures, from rejoicing in things as they are, from taking easy pleasure in the beauty of this world.[54]

It follows, then, that his music, and especially his symphonic music, "is biographical, psychological, programmatic above all."[55]

[50] Knepler et al., "Čajkovskij, Musicien Type du XIXe siècle?" p. 235.

[51] Fédorov, "Čajkovskij, Musicien Type du XIXe siècle?" p. 60.

[52] Ibid., pp. 60, 62, 62n.

[53] Ibid., p. 64.

[54] Ibid., pp. 66, 64–65; italics added in translation.

[55] "Sa musique symphonique est avant tout biographique, psychologique, à programme" (ibid., p. 65).

What we are dealing with, in short, is what the French call *un bête d'aveu,* "a confessing animal," and I am surprised that M. Fédorov did not summon the term himself to describe the man whom elsewhere he will describe as "the most lachrymose composer of his century."[56] Yet here one notes a familiar paradox. If Chaikovsky was indeed the most lachrymose composer of his century—or the most confessional, or the most (or indeed the least) anything—then he is no longer representative of it, hence not exemplary after all, unless one is looking not for the typical but for the stereotypical.

Which of course turned out to be the case. Having first accepted, or constructed, a stereotype of the nineteenth-century artist, formed evidently in the image of quasi-confessional and faux-confessional writers like Alfred de Musset (whose *Confession d'un Enfant du Siècle* of 1836 is probably more often cited as the "exemplary" romantic artwork than any other), Fédorov assimilated Chaikovsky to the prefabricated image, thus establishing him by fiat as an artist whose only subject was himself.[57]

In order to turn him into a synecdoche, however, Chaikovsky himself had to be synecdochically rendered: reduced to his last three symphonies; or actually to only two of the three; or rather, as we have seen, to the subtitle of one and a letter about the other, the most famous letter he ever wrote.[58] For the sake of conformity to the prefabricated image the greater part of Chaikovsky's output had to be ignored, and the whole of his correspondence had to be read in light of the one favored text. In fine, in order for Chaikovsky to become the exemplary nineteenth-century composer it was first necessary for him to disappear, leaving a tabula rasa on which each participant in the ensuing symposium could inscribe whatever fantasies and prejudices he pleased about the nineteenth century, and about Russia.

Thus what mainly distinguished that event was the ease with which the symposiasts found it possible to ignore everything Fédorov had said. Boris Yarustovsky, representing Soviet opinion, insisted that Chaikovsky was a good Russian and a progressive ("for a genius, one way or another, always serves the future").[59] An American musicologist wanted to transfer the "ex-

[56] Ibid., p. 69.

[57] For an explicit statement to this effect, see Fédorov's introductory remarks in Knepler et al., "Čajkovskij, Musicien Type du XIXᵉ siècle?" p. 206; and yet at the same time, in the spirit of the "objective" musicology of that period, Fédorov insisted that "Chaikovsky's personality be deliberately left as far as possible in the shade."

[58] See n. 11. For the most recent complete translation of the letter see *"To My Best Friend": Correspondence between Tchaikovsky and Nadezhda von Meck 1876–1878,* trans. Galina von Meck, ed. Edward Garden and Nigel Gotteri (Oxford: Clarendon Press, 1993), pp. 183–88.

[59] Knepler et al., "Čajkovskij, Musicien Type du XIXᵉ siècle?" pp. 212–13. For a different sort—an earlier and purer sort—of Soviet Chaikovsky criticism, see Boleslav Pshibïshevsky (Przybyszewski), "O Chaikovskom: Kompozitor i èpokha," *Sovetskoye iskusstvo,* no. 42 (1933); reprinted as the introduction to the first volume of the Chaikovsky–von Meck correspondence (P. I. Chaikovsky, *Perepiska s N. F. fon-Mekk,* vol. 1 [Moscow and Leningrad: Academia,

emplary" title to Dvořák, as the representative of a "more varied and universal" (because slightly more westerly or Germanic?) musical language.[60] An Italian participant wanted to view Chaikovsky as an anticipation of the *fin de siècle*, decidedly an end precisely because (*pace* the Russians) his music betrays no presentiment of crisis.

And inevitably, as the most comprehensive crux of aesthetic prejudices about the nineteenth century, the "problem" of kitsch was raised aggressively, and refused to go away. Without actually naming Chaikovsky as a kitsch composer, the Belgian "music sociologist" Robert Wangermée held him responsible for the proliferation of musical kitsch in the twentieth century (even as his importance was otherwise characteristically denigrated for having "exerted practically no influence on the composers of the twentieth century—at least on those who are mentioned in the history books"). Precisely for this reason, Wangermée suggested, "it might indeed be useful to say that Chaikovsky is the exemplary musician of the nineteenth century."[61]

In so arguing, however, Chaikovsky's most sneering accuser displayed the fatal lack of historical perspective that is so typical of Whiggish historiography. He failed to consider the history of his own position.[62]

1934], pp. vii–xviii). The essential vulgar-Marxist move is the transformation of Chaikovsky's obsession with fate, still regarded as his central theme, into a class obsession: "Of patrician origin and education, . . . he is distinctly aware of the doom that awaits his estate, the inevitable destruction of his class, and experiences it as implacable fate. . . . 'Fatum,' the pessimistic consciousness of doom, is the leitmotif of all his best works" (pp. ix–x). Of course the last three symphonies remain the prime exhibits (p. xiii: "He had the courage to look historical truth in the eye and sing himself and his class a formidable requiem: the 'Pathetic' Symphony"). Chaikovsky is linked with Tolstoy as genius tragedian of a doomed social class. It was a form of rehabilitation—or, rather, a concession to both artists' invincible popularity. Unlike the weaker members of his class, the rationalization went, who tried to save themselves with a cheap seigneurial show of liberalism (*deshoven'kim barskim liberal'nichaniyem*), Chaikovsky faced up to his class fate with courage; his work possesses the "life-affirmation" required by socialist realism and can inspire rather than mortify the Soviet audience: "For the new class draws from the tragedy of the departed not despondency but new strength towards its own self-fulfillment" (p. xvii).

[60] Knepler et al., "Čajkovskij, Musicien Type du XIXe siècle?" p. 215.

[61] Ibid., pp. 222, 224.

[62] Prefiguring Dahlhaus's better-known attempt, Wangermée tried, in keeping with his "sociological" approach, to assimilate Fédorov's catchphrase, "musicien type," to a famous heuristic model of Max Weber's: the *Idealtypus*, or "ideal type." But where Dahlhaus correctly understood the notion as a complex or a cluster of characteristics (comparable to the Wittgenstein model of "family resemblance," first posited with reference to the notional class of games) that shows up in actual cases only in part, but which may be used as a reference category to demonstrate the relatedness of phenomena that may not actually have any elements in common, Wangermée used the term as a mere synonym for "prototype" or "stereotype." Not surprisingly, therefore, he dismissed it as "peu operante . . . pour expliquer une réalité artistique dans toute sa complexité" (Knepler et al., "Čajkovskij, Musicien Type du XIXe siècle?" p. 224). For Dahlhaus's most explicit formulation of the concept see his *Realism in Nineteenth-Century Music*, trans. Mary Whittall (Cambridge: Cambridge University Press, 1985), especially the conclusion (pp. 120–

Kitsch, in Wangermée's formulation, denotes a type of music that mimics high art while remaining in actuality a form of applied or functional art. The operative category, then, is function or its absence, and so the distinction between art and kitsch depends in turn on the Kantian definition of the aesthetic as that which lacks function but has purpose.[63]

Wangermée cast the ancient split as one between *la musique de création* and *la musique de consommation*: creators' music vs. consumers' music. The former is self-referential, disinterested, and autonomous. Its loyalty is to the perpetual development of its own resources, a heroic task that requires the sacrifice of public appeal.[64] The latter courts public and material success, requiring the sacrifice of musical "evolution" or progress.[65] "The evolutionary level of the language that kitsch most willingly utilizes is that of Chaikovsky," Wangermée asserted, and that is why "it is no exaggeration to say that Chaikovsky is the spiritual father of that form of musical kitsch most peculiar to the twentieth century." But Chaikovsky, he then added, exchanging the Darwinist posture for a more frankly political one, "was himself not very audacious by century's end."

Such a composer, finally, cannot be called a creator, for he produces only *musique de consommation*. Such music, Wangermée declared in an especially dated passage (and one that came with particularly bad grace from a "sociologist"), "does not interest musicologists at all: it's just a music that constantly repeats itself, but which is not destined to last; it is created for the present, not for the future."[66] It could only have been because his music so patently defied this prediction of ephemerality that Chaikovsky, as a nineteenth-century composer, had to be exempted from the twentieth-century category for which Wangermée held him responsible.

And yet it is obvious that Wangermée's "twentieth-century" critique is founded wholly on nineteenth-century premises. His jeremiad is an only slightly updated replay of Nietzsche's old attack on beauty, the updating consisting chiefly in the fashionable Darwinist-cum-positivist insistence on the need for the language of music to evolve in perpetuity, whatever the cost to the consumer—an emphasis particularly fashionable in the period that was coming to an end around 1970, the era of Darmstadt and the so-called negative dialectic. But Darwin and Auguste Comte, the sources of M. Wan-

---

23); for a critique see Philip Gossett, "Carl Dahlhaus and the 'Ideal Type,'" *19th-Century Music* 13 (1989–90): 49–56.

[63] Or, in Kant's original wording, that which lacks an external end (*Zweck*) but has "purposiveness" (*Zweckmässigkeit*). See the *Critique of Judgement*, trans. J. H. Bernard (New York: Hafner Press, 1951), p. 73.

[64] Knepler et al., "Čajkovskij, Musicien Type du XIXe siècle?" p. 223.

[65] Ibid.

[66] Ibid., p. 223.

germée's philosophy, were as nineteenth-century thinkers every bit as "exemplary" as Wagner and Nietzsche.

The fundamental error, then, shared equally by Fédorov, Wangermée, and virtually every participant in the ill-fated conference, was to mistake their nineteenth-century critique of an eighteenth-century aesthetic for a twentieth-century critique of a nineteenth-century aesthetic. That misapprehension, coupled with a tendentious sampling of his output, is what made Chaikovsky for them, as for most of us, an "exemplary" nineteenth-century artist, when all the while he was in effect the last of the great eighteenth-century composers.

IN THE MARGINS

Vladimir Fédorov seemed to sense that this was the case, but managed (literally) to marginalize the unwelcome thought. After describing Chaikovsky's symphonic output, with its "exemplary" lyricalizing, dramatizing, and subjectivizing of an exemplary "classical" genre, he let drop a curious aside: "There remain, in the margins, his suites, the *Capriccio [italien]*, the *Serenade* [for strings] and so on; plus a few pastiches. Chaikovsky gives the impression here of all at once remembering that there are other kinds of music besides his, and in certain cases, other kinds than those of his century."[67]

But why in the margins? Simply because they do not match the stereotype? And what can it mean to say that a sizable group of compositions by Chaikovsky represents a kind of music other than "his"? There is, on the contrary, good reason to regard these works—all of them written, as it happens, in a midcareer clump between 1878 and 1884—as a watershed in his creative development and, concomitantly, as indications of personal and artistic maturation. Indeed, if we decide, experimentally, so to regard them—to make the suites, say, rather than the symphonies, our lens through which to view the composer—we shall see another pattern emerge, another model, another sort of *musicien type*.

If we accord central importance to the suites, moreover, we shall be acting in accordance with the composer's own strongly held views. For all their insignificance in the eyes of today's commentators, Chaikovsky held these works to be among his most essential and characteristic achievements. The three quotations cited earlier as evidence of the central Chaikovskian aesthetic—the untimely aesthetic of the beautiful and the pleasing—were strategically selected to support this claim. They refer, respectively, to each of the three orchestral suites in turn.[68]

---

[67] Fédorov, "Čajkovskij, Musicien Type du XIXe siècle?" p. 68.

[68] That is, Opp. 43 (1878–79), 53 (1883), and 55 (1884). *Mozartiana*, Op. 61 (1887), though now commonly designated Suite no. 4, was not so designated by the composer; indeed, during his

Except as a string of extracts from a stage work, the orchestral suite is not often considered to be a proper nineteenth-century genre. As a form "in the margins," as Fédorov says, it is often associated with marginal composers; or rather, it often serves historians as a means of marginalizing them. Thus, the *New Grove Dictionary* all too typically notes that "during the last decades of the century, composers of peripheral countries (especially northern ones) found the suite a congenial form for music of an exotic or nationalistic flavour."[69] Chaikovsky's name, it need hardly be added, is prominent in the list that follows.

Yet, so far from the "peripheries," the nineteenth-century orchestral suite originated in Germany, evidently in the wake of the Bach-Gesellschaft edition.[70] Two specialists quickly emerged: Franz Lachner (1803–90), who wrote seven orchestral suites between 1861 and 1881, and Joachim Raff (1822–82), who wrote four between 1863 and 1877. The other main pre-Chaikovskian practitioner was Massenet, one of Chaikovsky's favorites, who beginning in 1865 had written five suites of characteristic pieces for orchestra before Chaikovsky wrote his first, and who composed two more, in 1879 and 1881.

The first wave of suite writing, in the 1850s, had concentrated on the keyboard, and mainly consisted of outright imitations of the Bachian dance forms. One of the earliest such works was by Chaikovsky's teacher, Anton Rubinstein.[71] Yet even at the outset, "imitation" was not quite the right word: the cultivation of the "olden style" prompted a great deal of pseudo-modal harmonic piquanterie that could scarcely have been less plainly anachronistic to its practitioners than it is to us now, just as the "folk" style of the period was a knowing, sophisticated invention whose bona fides did not at all depend

---

lifetime the very absence of a Suite no. 4 from his catalog furnished the pretext for the punning sobriquet "Fourth Suite" (*chetvyortaya syuita*), coined by his brother Modest, and later on every St. Petersburg gossip's lips. It referred to the retinue (*svita*) of young male relations and friends— "Modest's gang," as Nina Berberova put it—with whom Chaikovsky spent his time on his late visits to St. Petersburg, and who "all more or less lived off him." See Chaikovsky's letter to Vladimir Naprávník from Paris, 15/3 June 1893, Chaikovsky, *Polnoye sobraniye sochineniy; Literaturnïye proizvedeniya i perepiska*, vol. 17, p. 109; also Nina Berberova, "Looking Back at Tchaikovsky," *Yale Review* 80, no. 3 (July 1992): 70; and cf. Poznansky, *Tchaikovsky*, chap. 27 ("The 'Fourth Suite'").

[69] *The New Grove Dictionary of Music and Musicians*, vol. 18, p. 349.

[70] See the discussion, by Robert Pascall, in *The New Oxford History of Music*, vol. 9, ed. Gerald Abraham (Oxford: Oxford University Press, 1990), pp. 560–72, esp. pp. 562–64. This is the only even moderately extended discussion of the nineteenth-century suite in the standard literature; the word "suite" is absent even from the index in such other period surveys as Dahlhaus, *Nineteenth-Century Music*, and Leon Plantinga, *Romantic Music* (New York: Norton, 1984).

[71] Op. 38 (1855): Prelude, Minuet, Gigue, Sarabande, Gavotte, Passacaille, Allemande, Courante, Passepied, Bourrée.

upon actual resemblance to the putative model.[72] It was the pretext it offered for sophisticated harmonic and (in the case of orchestral pieces) timbral invention that justified the "suite caracteristique" and ensured its popularity. It was above all an epicurean genre.

In this lay the essential difference between the late nineteenth-century orchestral suite and the contemporary symphony, which it often closely resembled both in the number of its movements and in their sequence. By the time Chaikovsky began composing orchestral suites, the retrospective was only one in a range of typical or potential components, along with national song and dance, character pieces, marches, and, especially, what might be termed "scherzoids", items of calculated grotesquery. Not even "sonata forms" were excluded, although they were not predictably placed in the initial position.

What was predictable was fancy harmony, bedight, highly textured orchestration, antic rhythm, and formal idiosyncrasy. Creating unusual hybrids and variations on the basic types was one of the pleasures of the genre for composers, and Chaikovsky (like Fabergé, the imperial jeweler) particularly excelled at creating irresistibly useless "objets de fantaisie." Indeed, he wrote to Mme von Meck that the main attraction of the suite for him as a genre was "the freedom it offers the author not to be bound by any traditions, conventional techniques, or established rules."[73] It was, or could be, imaginative play of a kind not explicitly celebrated since the end of the eighteenth century, when the notion of music as affording "a simple original pleasure" like "the smell of a rose, or the flavor of a pineapple" was one of the means by which the ancient doctrine of art as imitation of nature was dethroned.[74] That aesthetic, as far in its sensualism from the romantic concept of "absolute music" as it was in its autonomism from the old imitation theory, lived on *sub rosa* through the whole romantic century, and Chaikovsky's suites show him, despite his present reputation as a confessionalist, to have been one of its most avid cultivators.

Chaikovsky's first contribution to this epicurean and, it could seem, frivolous genre was the very next major composition he embarked upon after confiding to Mme von Meck his very striking thoughts, already cited, about the best way he as an artist could serve his fellow creatures.[75] What might

[72] See "'Little Star': An Étude in the Folk Style," in R. Taruskin, *Musorgsky: Eight Essays and an Epilogue* (Princeton: Princeton University Press, 1993), pp. 38–70.

[73] 16 April 1884; Chaikovsky, *Polnoye sobraniye sochineniy; Literaturnïye proizvedeniya i perepiska*, vol. 12, p. 352. He went on, "It's only a pity that there is no Russian word that could replace the word *syuita*, which sounds terrible in Russian. I have thought a great deal about this and cannot come up with anything."

[74] The quoted phrases come from Thomas Twining, *Aristotle's Treatise on Poetry, Translated, with Notes on the Translation, and on the Original; and Two Dissertations, on Poetical, and Musical, Imitation*, 2d ed. (London, 1812), p. 66.

[75] See n. 43. The only items Chaikovsky composed wholly during the four months that intervened between the letter of 30 April 1878 and the composition of the First Suite, begun on 15/27

look trivial from one ideological perspective—from that committed to the sublime—appeared nothing short of restorative from another. The consoling distraction the composer experienced in the act of creation could be passed along directly to the consumer. Once again the composer identified with his social peers and their human interests rather than flaunting his own disinterested (*zwecklos*) or alienated circumstances.

The decision to put together a suite "in Lachner's manner" actually followed the composition of the Scherzo, which eventually became the fifth of its six movements, and which the composer at first must have envisioned as the kernel of a new symphony.[76] What prompted the switch to a suite may well have been the character of the music that emerged, full of special orchestral effects, string-wind hockets, rhythmic contrasts and superimpositions (hemiolas, "three-over-twos"), sequences of accented chromatic auxiliaries over pedals, and other conspicuous patterning devices. But Chaikovsky's scherzos had been conforming to that mold for some time. The one in the Third Symphony (1875) is just as much a *pièce caracteristique*—a hocketing moto perpetuo requiring a virtuosic execution and full of harmonic spice, including several complete descending whole-tone scales à la Glinka (that is, à la *Ruslan*) in the bass. (The second movement of the five-movement symphony, a parody Ländler marked "alla tedesca," which Chaikovsky regarded as a second scherzo, corresponds to another characteristic suite-movement type.) And the scherzo in the Fourth Symphony is of course Chaikovsky's most famous (and determined) orchestral tour de force. The way he shoehorned a description of it into the symphony's "confessional" program, as outlined for Mme von Meck at her request, is telling:

> The third movement does not express definite feelings. These are, rather, capricious arabesques, fugitive images that pass through one's mind when one has had a little wine to drink and is feeling the first effects of intoxication. At heart one is neither merry nor sad. One's mind is a blank: the imagination has free rein, and it has come up with these strange and inexplicable designs. . . . Among them all at once you recognize a tipsy peasant and a street song . . . then somewhere in the distance a military parade goes by. These are the completely unrelated images that pass through one's head as one is about to fall asleep. They have nothing in common with reality; they are strange, wild, and incoherent.[77]

The program, in short, is the absence of a program, that is to say of paraphrasable content, in favor of "pure imaginative play" or capricious imagery

---

August, were the Album for Children (24 Easy Pieces for Piano, Op. 39) and the functional Liturgy of St. John Chrysostom, Op. 41. The Piano Sonata in G, Op. 37, in progress at the time of the letter, was completed on 26 July/7 August.

[76] See his letter to von Meck, 25 August 1878; *Perepiska s N. F. fon-Mekk*, vol. 1, p. 421.

[77] Letter from Florence, 17 February/1 March 1878; Chaikovsky, *Polnoye sobraniye sochineniy; Literaturnïye proizvedeniya i perepiska*, vol. 7 (Moscow: Muzgiz, 1962), p. 126.

or even sheer sensory *frisson*. (And note that the imagery is presented as metonymic: a strain of folkish melody conjures up a peasant; a bit of brass music conjures up soldiers.) But what is presented as the exceptional movement—the consoling distraction, perhaps—in the symphony would constitute the rule in the suite, and therein lies the generic difference.

The opening movement of the First Suite, the first item conceived specifically as part of a suite, did indeed follow the Lachnerian neobaroque model: it is a prelude (or, as Chaikovsky actually put it, an *Introduzione*) and fugue in D minor.[78] The prelude opens with what sounds in fact like the beginning of a fugue: an unaccompanied line for the bassoons in a snaking chromatic manner that evokes the Bachian pathos style (typified by the all-chromatic B-minor fugue subject from the first volume of the *Well-Tempered Clavier*, Chaikovsky's probable model). It will indeed eventually be developed in a fugato, but first it is juxtaposed with a striking contrast of imagery: a fluttering accompaniment figure in muted strings that unmistakably evokes the image of a *pirouette* or an *entrechat*, hence, metonymically, a ballerina (example 11.4). The counterpoint of the archaic and the balletic is suggestive indeed. We will come back to it.

Neobaroque stylization returns in the last movement, a gavotte, which, like many of its nineteenth-century fellows, has four beats to the bar and lacks the two-quarter pickup that was its chief eighteenth-century identifying mark. The fugue subject is reprised at the end (brilliantly, in D major) to package the whole confection in a single box. Otherwise the contents of the box are characteristically variegated yet elegantly balanced: besides the scherzo there is an intermezzo (*andantino semplice*) to supply an internal point of rest; a *marche miniature* for the treble instruments alone (the lowest note being the A below middle C), punctuated by high-pitched percussion (triangle, glockenspiel);[79] and, in second place, a movement entitled *divertimento* that is actually a waltz, added as an afterthought when Chaikovsky realized, upon sending the suite off to the publisher, that all its movements were in duple meter.[80] From then on, waltz movements would be de rigueur (but then they were hardly less so in Chaikovsky's symphonies).

Although an addendum, the divertimento in Chaikovsky's first orchestral suite is in a way its most typical movement. By the time he wrote it the composer had a fully clarified idea of what suite-composition meant to him. It

---

[78] Five of Lachner's seven orchestral suites have fugues as either first movement (nos. 2 and 6) or finale (nos. 1, 4, and 7).

[79] The original plan was to call this movement the "March of the Lilliputians" and the gavotte the "Dance of the Giants." See the composer's letter to his brother Modest, 13 November 1878, quoted in Modeste Tchaikovsky, *The Life and Letters of Tchaikovsky*, ed. Rosa Newmarch (New York: Vienna House, 1973), p. 324.

[80] See his letter to Pyotr Ivanovich Jurgenson, 9 August 1879; P. I. Chaikovsky, *Perepiska s P. I. Yurgensonom*, vol. 1 (Moscow and Leningrad: Muzgiz, 1938), p. 109.

EXAMPLE 11.4. Chaikovsky, Suite no. 1, beginning of Introduzione (solo bassoon and strings *con sordini*)

meant the cultivation of the rare, the refined, and the exquisite. From this point of view the quintessential moment in the first suite is the "variation"— the word should retain its balletic connotation as well as its classicizing one— for a trio of flutes in triplets against a pair of bassoons in duplets that so strikingly anticipates the "Danse des mirlitons" Chaikovsky would later write for the actual ballet stage. Taken as a whole, the first suite set the pattern that would apply to them all: an interpenetrating mélange of neobaroque stylization, contemporary dance music, *pièces caracteristiques*, and scherzoids. It was tacitly dedicated to Mme von Meck, whose tastes, the composer wrote, the suite was calculated to gratify.

The high point of genre interpenetration and imaginative disport came in the Second Suite, Op. 53, originally subtitled "Suite caracteristique." A major work by any standard of measurement (forty minutes' running time, an augmented orchestra), it was the main creative product of the year 1883, and the composition to which Chaikovsky referred in the letter expressing to Modest his confident expectation of "pleasing." It is in its way one of Chaikovsky's emblematic works, not least because of its fascinating first movement, of which the title must not be divulged until Vladimir Fédorov's essay has been quoted one last time. Characterizing his "Musicien Type du XIXe siècle," Fédorov asserted that music, for a such a self-absorbed and self-exhibiting artist, could "in no wise" be "a pure music that plays with sounds, themes, structures." In the original French, he said, "en aucune façon elle n'est pour lui une musique pure qui joue avec les sons, les thèmes, les structures."[81]

The long first movement of Chaikovsky's second orchestral suite is entitled "Jeu de sons." (Is there any comparable work from the period that so thematizes its emancipation from expressive content?) In fact, the piece is an ironic, even satirical, play of structures. An introduction and allegro, it is the one movement from the Chaikovsky suites that makes obvious sonata-form gestures, but it continually mocks its own formal proclivities even as it revels in composerly virtuosity. The development section is an elaborate fugue on the first theme from the exposition. The recapitulation is achieved by, as it were, doubling the fugue, introducing the second theme in counterpoint with the first.

That second theme, incidentally, is of a pronounced folklike character. It fits right into its original formal slot, since folklike lyrical "subsidiary" themes were by the 1880s a symphonic cliché. But it is grotesquely out of place on its academically contrapuntal reappearance, the more so for being scored with deliberate ungainliness for the bass instruments. Another burlesque touch is the detaching of the codas, to exposition and recapitulation alike, by means of abrupt percussion wallops, stunned pauses, and resumption at a new tempo. At the very end the tender lullaby music of the introduction unexpectedly resurfaces, casting the whole piece retroactively into an absurdly disproportionate ternary form—or is it Chaikovsky's version of a French overture?

These juxtapositions of incompatible formal and expressive gestures are the very substance of the music. When Shostakovich does something of the sort, we call the result "Gogolian." The term fits Chaikovsky's second suite at least as well. And yet the disjunctions do not in any way impel or suggest a fabular paraphrase.[82] They are juxtapositions of qualities—of flavors, one might say—rather than of actions or events. In the second movement, the obligatory waltz (here an evanescent orchestral fantasy of the *valse oubliée* type), a structural transition is accomplished, uniquely, through a "play of timbres" alone. To describe the music as deviant or un-Chaikovskian for that reason is

---

[81] Fédorov, "Čajkovskij, Musicien Type du XIXe siècle?" p. 65.

[82] If this observation is accepted as correct, Chaikovsky's "scherzoids" and suite-grotesques would seem to offer a counterexample to the familiar claim made by musical narratologists (Carolyn Abbate, for example, or Anthony Newcomb) that "we, as listeners, create patterns of events in time that will make sense of musical discontinuities; any tear in the musical fabric creates a space into which the constructed story must rush, heading off the vertigo of threatened meaninglessness" (Andrew Dell'Antonio, Richard Hill, and Mitchell Morris, "Classic and Romantic Instrumental Music and Narrative" [report of a colloquium held at Stanford University and the University of California at Berkeley, 27–28 May 1988], *Current Musicology* 48 [1991]: 44).

no more justified than it would be so to describe the equally singular Pathetic Symphony.

The slow fourth movement, "Rêves d'enfant," is the suite's center of gravity. It presents the contrast of wakeful consciousness and dream through a contrast of A-minor lullaby and fantastical pointillism in the magical key of the tritone antipode, E♭ minor, colored by fleeting hints of what nowadays we sometimes call "tonal octatonicism" (the embellishment of a diminished-seventh chord with passing tones to produce a scale of alternating tones and semitones). This exquisitely realized composition is one of Chaikovsky's palpable masterpieces—if, that is, the idea may be entertained of a masterpiece of instrumental color, orchestral texture, and harmonic contrivance. Such an idea was certainly thinkable one hundred years ago, when Alexandre Benois founded the whole *Mir iskusstva* ("World of Art") aesthetic on perceptions he gratefully apprehended as coming to him from Chaikovsky, in whose music—not just the ballets and operas, but in "whatever Chaikovsky I heard, wherever I could, at concerts and at home performances"—he discovered not only that aristocratic retrospectivism (he called it "passé-ism") that could, he thought, lead Russian art out of its cul-de-sac of bourgeois utilitarianism, but also "that mixture of strange actuality and compelling invention," that "world of captivating nightmares that exists behind our backs and remains forever inaccessible," that "genuine Hofmannesquerie" (*podlinnaya gofmanov-shchina*) that informs Chaikovsky's suites to an extent perhaps unequaled in the whole realm of instrumental music, and that is epitomized above all, perhaps in "Rêves d'enfant."[83]

Today such values are far less likely to receive endorsement. For Chaikovsky's most recent British biographer the suites, which cannot be easily read as confessional (a mode Benois would in any case have dismissed as utilitarian), are for that reason "among the most explicit reflections" of a "creative trough" brought on by the stresses of homosexual guilt and the disastrous attempt to deal with it through marriage, which had left Chaikovsky "emotionally withdrawn, even impaired," facing "a barrier between him and his own music." Although a certain originality is granted to a few movements, including "Rêves d'enfant" (which receives a modicum of praise for anticipating the style of Benjamin Britten), the general verdict is tautological: because the suites deviate from type (that is, from the habits of the "Musicien Type"), "the result is always second-rate Tchaikovsky."[84]

---

[83] A. N. Benua, *Moí vospominaniya* (Moscow: Nauka, 1980), vol. 1, p. 654.

[84] David Brown, "Tchaikovsky," *The New Grove Dictionary of Music and Musicians*, vol. 18, p. 619, and *Tchaikovsky: The Years of Wandering 1878–1885* (New York: Norton, 1986), pp. 12, 230. Although, as noted, the suites are not easily read as confessional, Brown nevertheless manages in the later publication so to read them, or at least to hint at the existence in the suites of the sort of "private, hidden, or ineffable meanings" that entitle them to consideration as

Yet color, texture, and contrivance were for Chaikovsky first-rate values. Indeed, "colorlessness" was the evil that he feared most in egalitarian philosophies such as "nihilism" or, what he took to be its synonym, "communism."[85] It is only when the store Chaikovsky set by color is appreciated that his brand of "nationalism" becomes comprehensible. Again, the second orchestral suite furnishes indispensable instruction.

Russian folk character, in two fastidiously differentiated manifestations, informs the "Scherzo burlesque," the third movement of the suite. Again it is a matter of "strange, wild, and incoherent" juxtapositions that in their avoidance of linearity—of "German transitions"—manage to evade the tendency of "kinetic-syntactic" structures (like that of Balakirev's Second Overture on Russian Themes, discussed in chapter 8) to "connote" à program or a story. Urban street music, in the guise of an accordion quartet witlessly working their tonic and dominant buttons, is countered in the de facto "trio" by the most meticulous and true-to-life facsimile Chaikovsky ever fashioned of rural peasant singing, one that extended, in the manner of what was then the avant-garde fringe of musical ethnography, to the reproduction not only of a melody but of its heterophonic performance practice, or what was then known as "folk harmonization" (example 11.5). Whether directly or through the work of these new ethnographers,[86] Chaikovsky was aware of the practice. In a letter written a few months before beginning work on the suite, he informed his publisher that "peasants never sing a song (except for the intoning phrase [*zapev*]) in real unison, but always with subordinate voices that form simple chord combinations."[87]

---

musique de création—which must be why the suites fare a bit better in the biography than they do in the *New Grove* article. (In both the First Suite and the Second, Brown suggests that the thematic content embodies abstruse references in cipher to names and places of concurrent biographical significance: see *Tchaikovsky: The Years of Wandering*, pp. 62–63, 241–42.)

[85] See his letter to Mme von Meck of 16 April 1883: "What you say about communism is absolutely true. A more senseless utopia, anything more contrary to human nature, is inconceivable. And how dull and unbearably colorless life would surely be were this material equality ever to gain ascendency" (Chaikovsky, *Polnoye sobraniye sochineniy; Literaturnïye proizvedeniya i perepiska*, vol. 12, pp. 123–24). The Soviet editors note, out of concern for their readers, that "Chaikovsky was not sufficiently discerning in political or social matters," but the bromide that artists are by nature "unpolitical" or politically "naive" is not confined to the Soviet Union; cf. Fédorov: "Je doute fort d'autre part que C. ait été réellement sensible aux événements politiques et sociaux russes de son temps ou que ces événements aient eu un influence directe sur son oeuvre" (Knepler et al., "Čajkovskij, Musicien Type du XIXᵉ siècle?" p. 213). *Directe* is the necessary precaution or amulet that turns falsifiable assertion into impregnable truism.

[86] E.g., Yuliy Melgunov's collection, entitled *Russkiye pesni, neposredstvenno s golosov naroda* ("Russian Songs Direct from the Voices of the People"), of which the first volume had appeared in 1879 (Moscow: Lissner and Roman), just in time for a couple of its items to be incorporated into Musorgsky's *Khovanshchina*.

[87] To P. I. Jurgenson, 2 February 1883; Chaikovsky, *Polnoye sobraniye sochineniy; Literaturnïye proizvedeniya i perepiska*, vol. 12, p. 47.

EXAMPLE 11.5. Chaikovsky, Suite no. 2, Scherzo burlesque, m. 206

A notation survives among the sketches for the suite, dated 3 July 1883, containing two songs Chaikovsky took down from the duet-singing of his servant Alyosha Sofronov and a laundry woman who was working that day in his house. From this evidence it has been plausibly supposed that Chaikovsky took down the scherzo melody, harmonization and all, from something he chanced to overhear.[88] It is a found object. And it is altogether appropriate that such a rough-hewn artifact should have gone into the suite, where it provided another eccentric color or flavor to set beside the accordions. Within Chaikovsky's stylistic range, only that genre was hospitable to the "false" unisons and cadential occurses that the composer displays here with such relish, and which, though he quoted more Russian folk melodies than any compatriot save Rimsky-Korsakov, are not to be found in any of his other works. In seeming paradox, and with unerring taste, the canny composer saw how appositely the unrefined peasant style could harmonize, as a condiment, with the rare, the recherché, and the epicurean.

Flavor, relish, condiment, taste . . . were one looking for the perfect put-down, one could sum it all up in Brecht's trusty pejorative, *culinary*.[89] With it, Brecht meant to reduce all art that was disengaged from social activism to the level of complacent, socially regressive, voluptuary aestheticism. But this was just another surfacing, and a particularly hawkish one, of the old heroic discourse of transcendence. Brecht stands here in the old Teutonic line, with Beethoven, Nietzsche, Wagner, and all those other audience-tormentors who saw art as an agency of world transformation.

Chaikovsky stood proudly in the other line, the line that sees art as an agency of world enhancement. He explicitly celebrated the "culinary," or, as he put it, the "tasty" (*vkusnoye*) in art. Here, too, he could claim Mozart—his Mozart—as a forebear. The set of arrangements for orchestra called *Mozartiana*, Op. 61 (1887), unofficially but not inappropriately known as his "Suite

---

[88] Boleslav Isaakovich Rabinovich, *P. I. Chaikovskiy i narodnaya pesnya* (Moscow: Muzgiz, 1963), p. 16; the notations (the second polyphonic) are reproduced on p. 139.

[89] See Bertolt Brecht, "Uber die Verwendung von Musik für ein episches Theater," trans. (as "On the Use of Music in an Epic Theatre") in John Willett, ed., *Brecht on Theater* (New York: Hill and Wang, 1964), pp. 84–90; the passage about "culinary" music is on p. 89.

no. 4," commemorates a Mozart who shared Chaikovsky's taste for delectable, often retrospective parody. Apart from the sentimental "Preghiera" (third movement), based on Liszt's 1862 piano transcription ("A la Chapelle Sixtine") of *Ave verum corpus*, K. 618, Chaikovsky's selection emphasized Mozart the keyboard confectioner. The mock-fugal Gigue (K. 574), and the purplish Minuet (K. 576b), finely (over)spiced and (over)laden caricatures of obsolete genres, serve as the opening pair of movements, while the finale is one of Mozart's jokiest pieces, the Variations K. 455 on "Unser dummer Pöbel meint" (or "Les hommes pieusement") from Gluck's *Die Pilger von Mekka* (or *La rencontre imprévue*), bumpkinry of the urbanest sort. A series of inspired "wrong" chords in the fourth variation (the first harmonized bass note perpetually reidentified—now as root, now as fifth, now as third—and inflected, finally missed) show Mozart deploying matchless wit and craft for no other purpose than *pour amuser*, flattering the taste and discernment (yes, the breeding) of his hearers, as a host might flatter a guest with a choice wine (example 11.6). That, for Chaikovsky, was precisely the point and the "lesson" of this music, as he testified both in word (an author's note calling the connoisseur's attention to Mozart's brilliant detail work) and, by adding his own piquant details of orchestral color to Mozart's, in compositional deed.

Was such an art disengaged? Complacent? Was its practitioner "apolitical" (as well as asexual)?[90] He was neither, of course; but his politics was a politics of affirmation rather than the kind of politics we have been conditioned by the artistic discourse of late, late romanticism to regard as politics, namely the politics of alienation, contention, and resistance. The politics of aristocracy is as much a politics as any other, and Chaikovsky—the maturest Chaikovsky, at any rate—was the preeminent aristocratic musician of the nineteenth century. He was the last of the court composers, and his work was the very last great musical flowering of European court art—all of which is only to restate more straightforwardly the characterization ("in effect the last great eighteenth-century composer") with which the present discussion of the orchestral suites was somewhat coyly broached.

THE IMPERIAL STYLE

He was all this because he lived in the one surviving absolutist state in Europe—in effect, the last great eighteenth-century state—and worked, like hardly another composer of his time, under virtually eighteenth-century conditions. He was the beneficiary of patronage beginning in 1876 and spent the

---

[90] Treatment of Chaikovsky as asexual (a defense against horror of his sexual deviance, as the "apolitical" assumption is a defense against horror of his—or Stravinsky's; see chapter 13—unpalatable political loyalties) is particularly rife among his British biographers, beginning with Edward Garden, who informs his readers that, as a homosexual, Chaikovsky was "unable to feel sexually aroused" (*Tchaikovsky* [London: Dent, 1973], p. 17).

EXAMPLE 11.6. Mozart, Variations K. 455, fourth variation

last five years of his life, from 1888, as Russia's uncrowned composer laure-
ate, receiving a crown stipend and enjoying the freedom of the Tsarist musical
establishment in a fashion that put him altogether beyond rivalry. This meant
particularly that he became a virtual composer-in-residence at the Russian
Imperial Theaters, forging in direct collaboration with the Mariyinsky conductor Eduard Nápravník, with the ballet master Marius Petipa, with the Intendant Ivan Alexandrovich Vsevolozhsky, and in indirect collaboration with

Tsar Alexander III himself, a personal friend, what George Balanchine has aptly christened the Russian Imperial style[91]—a style that had an enormous impact, it should be emphasized again, on the artists, poets, and musicians of the so-called Silver Age, a time that witnessed a massive recrudescence of aristocratic taste. Had Chaikovsky lived a normal span of years, which would have taken his lifetime virtually up to the revolution (and let us not forget that his elder brother Ippolit managed to outlive Lenin), he would surely have been one of that brilliant period's guiding geniuses—as in a way, through his acknowledged influence on Benois, he already indirectly was.

The beginnings of the imperial style, and its first culmination, can be located precisely in the orchestral suites. The letter (quoted earlier) in which an ecstatic Chaikovsky described to Mme von Meck his greatest public triumph, concerned the première of the Third Suite, Op. 55, which took place under the most prestigious circumstances imaginable: a subscription concert of the court-sponsored Imperial Russian Musical Society, guest conducted by Hans von Bülow. This suite was in a strangely direct way bound up with Chaikovsky's feelings about his country, about the Russian autocracy, and about the person of the sovereign—feelings that were intense, reciprocated, and symbiotic.

Chaikovsky had many friends and acquaintances within the Tsar's close circle, had executed his first commission on Alexander's behalf long before the beginning of his reign (with his early Festival Overture on the Danish national anthem, Op. 15, composed in 1866 on the occasion of the crown prince's wedding to the daughter of King Christian IX of Denmark), and furnished both the official march and the official cantata for his coronation in 1883.[92] He met the Tsar face to face when summoned to the royal residence at Gatchina in March 1884 to receive the Vladimir Cross, a high civil honor. The immediate occasion was the double première of the patriotic opera *Mazepa*, over which the St. Petersburg Mariyinsky and the Moscow Bolshoy had fought, and which had had simultaneous productions at both main state houses, introduced three days apart. The Tsar personally ordered from Nápravník, the Mariyinsky conductor, a new production of *Eugene Onegin*, to be mounted not at the Mariyinsky but at the Bolshoy Kamennïy Teatr, the "Great Stone Theater" where since the 1840s the Imperial Italian Opera, the very nerve center of Russian aristocratic arts patronage, had enjoyed an absolute hegemony. Alexander wanted to demonstrate his commitment to nurturing native talent, and Chaikovsky's was the native talent to be nurtured before all others.

[91] See Solomon Volkov, *Balanchine's Tchaikovsky: Interviews with George Balanchine* (New York: Simon and Schuster, 1985), p. 127.

[92] Chaikovsky also made a special arrangement of the final "Glory" (*Slav'sya*) chorus from Glinka's *A Life for the Tsar*, with a segue into Lvov's official Tsarist hymn (*Bozhe, tsarya khrani!*) for a total of three coronation commissions.

Dazzled by the sovereign's attention, Chaikovsky wrote to Mme von Meck that he left Gatchina feeling "a great rush of energy, burning with impatience to undertake some great new task."[93] He began working on the third orchestral suite in April. Although the suite is made up of familiar ingredients—waltz, scherzo, character pieces—their ordering is somewhat unusual. The first movement is an Elégie; the ensuing waltz is a "Valse mélancolique." The scherzo that follows is mainly quiet, ghostly, a little macabre, with a virtually pointillistic trio highlighting what sounds like a distant drum and bugle corps. Except for the scherzo's final chord, a calculated shock, the first three movements all end in whispers.

And all three are counterbalanced, indeed overrun, by the fourth movement, an enormous set of symphonic variations that Chaikovsky, during his brief and belated career as celebrity conductor, frequently performed as an independent concert piece. It begins with the customary retrospective nod. The theme is square-cut, ternary, "classical." The first few variations are full of allusions, beginning with an appropriation of Haydn's filigree technique, as in the "Surprise" Symphony or (more to the point) the "Emperor" Quartet. The third variation, for flutes, clarinets, and bassoons, is an homage to Mozart's serenades. The fourth is a jocular Dies Irae, by then (ten years after his friend Saint-Saëns's *Danse macabre*) a standard *objet de fantaisie*. Next comes the fugue without which a suite is not a suite, followed by a gigue.

Beginning with the seventh, the variations are of the "character" type, and for a while the movement is a veritable culinary extravaganza *à la russe*: peasant song, church chant, competitive dance. But then Leopold Auer steps figuratively into the pit for the obligatory violin cadenza, and the music begins to converge on imagery not merely of "Russia" but specifically of the Russian imperial court. The genial Variation 10, a 3/8 waltz for the violin soloist marked "un poco rubato," is a play on the various meanings of "variation." Here it is a ballerina's solo turn that is evoked, culminating in a series of *jetés* straight out of the second act of *Swan Lake* (example 11.7). The *danseur noble* then enters to partner the ballerina for the impassioned Variation 11, their *pas de deux*, its harmonies given extra poignancy by being played entirely over a tonic pedal that, at the very end, is nudged down through the flat submediant, the quintessential Chaikovskian passion-flower, to the dominant.

And just as the variations movement counterbalances its three predecessors in the suite, so the final variation, a "great rush of energy" in three-quarter time marked *moderato maestoso e brillante*, counterbalances and overruns the eleven that have preceded it in the set. Ending with five blazing pages marked *sempre fortissimo*, it is the music that, as the composer had foretold (or as "something" had foretold to him), lifted its first audience—an audience repre-

---

[93] Letter of 13 March 1884; Chaikovsky, *Polnoye sobraniye sochineniy; Literaturnïye proizvedeniya i perepiska*, vol. 12, p. 336.

EXAMPLE 11.7. Chaikovsky, Suite no. 3, fourth movement (Tema con variazioni), no. 10, m. 23

senting the cream of St. Petersburg society—to its feet. It could not fail, for it is a magnificent polonaise.

Four days after the première, Chaikovsky was asked to attend the Tsar's command production of *Onegin* on its fifteenth showing, at which time he once again received the sovereign's personal compliments. These honors brought forth in the favored artist a veritable ecstasy of dynastic patriotism, something that has little to do with nationalism as we currently understand the term, although it did find outlet, both verbally and artistically, in ardent manifestations of love for the fatherland and its institutions.

An especially strong verbal manifestation came in a gently reproving letter to Mme von Meck, written a few weeks after the events just recounted. What begins as an innocent paean to the "incomparable" Russian winter landscape, offered in response to his patron's equally innocent complaint about Russian mud, quickly modulates—through a transitional paragraph that begins, "it seems to me, my dear, that in general you look too sullenly and despairingly upon Russia"—into a startling explosion of political bile, in which Chaikovsky heaps scorn on institutions of representative government, on legal principle, on any limitations upon autocratic rule. "In any event" he concludes,

> I am convinced that the well-being of large political entities depends not on *principles* and *theories* but on the chance accession of individuals, whether by birth or by other causes, to the head of government. In a word, only *a human being* can serve *humanity*, not whatever principle he may embody. The question now is whether we have such a human being, on whom we may rest our hopes. My answer is: yes, and that human being is our *sovereign*.[94]

[94] 5 March 1885; ibid., vol. 13, pp. 44–45.

"It's not that I have gone over to the ultraconservative camp," Chaikovsky hastened to assure his conventionally liberal-minded correspondent, but in fact his bilious little tract could just as well have been authored (indeed, probably *was* largely authored, if indirectly) by his old jurisprudence schoolmate Prince Vladimir Meshchersky, the editor of the reactionary newspaper *Grazhdanin* (The Citizen), which, like Chaikovsky, received subsidies from the Tsar. One of the most valuable achievements of Alexander Poznansky's recent biography of Chaikovsky has been its much fuller illumination of the composer's relationship with this particular friend (known to all biographers for his role in helping the composer through the dreadful aftermath of his wedding).[95] As a personality as well as a public figure, Meshchersky is greatly pertinent to the evaluation of the composer's career with regard to various noteworthy issues, including that of homosexuality and its social consequences. An openly practicing homosexual to an extent that Chaikovsky never contemplated becoming, Meshchersky was actively protected by the Tsar from persecution, and relied on that protection. (The significance of this parallel for evaluating the persistent allegation that Chaikovsky, discovered in a pederastic liaison, was forced to commit suicide at the behest of the Tsar, working through an honor court of jurisprudence-school alumni, will be obvious.)[96] Clearly, the Tsar's patronage was especially important to those of his protégés whose private lives might otherwise inspire odium or make them vulnerable to personal threat, and bound such protégés all the more ardently to their sovereign and all that he stood for.[97]

An equally strong manifestation of Chaikovsky's dynastic patriotism, and a far more eloquent one, was the third orchestral suite. To understand how this was so, it is necessary to know something about the very special history of the polonaise in Russia.

Throughout its history the polonaise was preemininently a courtly phenomenon, perhaps the most elevated of all court ballroom genres for the way it straddled the line between dance and processional. Its three spacious, strutting beats were characteristically subdivided by two and four, the resulting pat-

---

[95] See Poznansky, *Tchaikovsky*, esp. pp. 365–67, 481–83.

[96] For a summary of the debate surrounding the circumstances of Chaikovsky's death, and a consideration of its cultural significance, see R. Taruskin, "Pathetic Symphonist: Chaikovsky, Russia, Sexuality and the Study of Music," *New Republic* 212, no. 6 (6 February 1995): 26–40.

[97] Indeed, it was precisely the relative tolerance for homosexuality, among other forms of *libertinage*, in aristocratic circles that accounts for the intense identification with the patrician class and the reactionary politics that is so noticeable among known nineteenth-century Russian homosexual men; see Simon Karlinsky, *The Sexual Labyrinth of Nikolai Gogol* (Cambridge, Mass.: Harvard University Press, 1976; reprint, Chicago: University of Chicago Press, 1992), pp. 56–57, for a discussion and a list that includes Chaikovsky's own one-time lover, the poet Alexey Apukhtin. The related aristocratic, or once-aristocratic, preference for decorative and sensual art, which looms so large in the present characterization of Chaikovsky, is another trait often associated with a gay sensibility.

EXAMPLE 11.8. Chopin, Polonaise Op. 40, no. 1 (1838)

terns of eighths and sixteenths often being organized in quasi-military tattoo or fanfare figures (example 11.8). Military, or ceremonial, or just plain noble associations were as strong or stronger than the genre's national origin in establishing its signification for art music, especially in Russia with its exceptionally strong and durable court traditions. Thus by the time the polonaise was used by Glinka, at the beginning of the second act in his opera *A Life for the Tsar* (1836; example 11.9a), to characterize the Poles (or rather, the Polish nobility) in opposition to the Russians (or rather, the Russian peasantry), it had already served Glinka's older contemporary Alexey Verstovsky, in the entr'acte to act 3 of his opera *Askold's Grave* (1835; example 11.9b), to set the scene at the palace of the Kievan (that is, Russian) Prince Vïshata.

The polonaise was established as a type—that is, a *topos*—in Russian art music by Osip (Iosif) Antonovich Kozlovsky (1757–1831), a Polish nobleman who served as an officer in the Russian army and who, following the Russo-Turkish wars, came to St. Petersburg in the entourage of Prince Grigoriy Alexandrovich Potyomkin, the chief minister to the Empress Catherine the Great. Kozlovsky's great specialty was polonaise writing; indeed, he seemed to be able to turn anything he touched into polonaises, including themes from popular quintets by Pleyel, even Mozart arias.[98] His signal contribution to the history of Russian music was the triumphal polonaise, a cantatalike choral panegyric in which he collaborated with the leading court poets of the day, especially Gavrila Romanovich Derzhavin, who authored the text for the most famous of these works, entitled "Thunder of Victory, Resound!" (*Grom pobedï, razdavaisya!*), first performed at a fête given by Prince Pot-

---

[98] An orchestral polonaise by Kozlovsky after Mozart's terzetto "Mandina amabile" (K. 480) is recorded on Melodiya Stereo 33 C 10-12743-4 (1981).

EXAMPLE 11.9

a. Glinka, *A Life for the Tsar,* act 2, no. 5: Pol'skiy (Polonaise)

b. Verstovsky, *Askold's Grave,* act 3: Entr'acte and Maidens' Chorus (no. 10)

yomkin on 28 April 1791 to celebrate the conclusion of the war (example 11.10a).[99]

This item achieved tremendous popularity, especially after the partitions of 1793 and 1795, when Russia joined Prussia and Austria in swallowing up the land of the polonaise. The victory that thundered through Kozlowski's martial strains now included victory over Poland, and the old Polish aristocratic dance now symbolized Russia's ascendancy. This "occidentalist" irony helped spawn a host of imitations that made Kozlowski's polonaise the prototype of an indigenous Russian genre, and tied the parade-ceremonial polonaise "irrevocably to the theme of [Russian] patriotism."[100] Between 1791 and 1833— the date of *Bozhe, tsarya khrani!*—Kozlovsky's polonaise served as the Russian state's quasi-official anthem for ceremonial occasions.

The culminating choral refrain, "Slav'sya sim, Yekaterina!" (Be glorified by this, O Catherine), is known to all Russian operagoers, because Chaikovsky appropriated it (to a corrupted version of the music that he evidently drew from oral tradition) at the climax of act 2 in *The Queen of Spades*, to accompany Catherine's near-appearance (example 11.10b).[101]

This striking specific allusion—one of many in *The Queen of Spades*, that masterpiece of surrealism—should not, however, be allowed to occlude the generic resonance that polonaises had not only in the work of Chaikovsky but, partly through him, in the work of other Russian composers as well. It often replaced the march where a specific overtone of official pomp was wanted. Thus the familiar "Procession of the Nobles" (*Shestviye knyazey*) in Rimsky-Korsakov's opera-ballet *Mlada* is cast as a polonaise, minimally disguised by pseudo-archaic *ur*-Slav "modality" (example 11.11a), just as the opening choral pageant in the introduction to Borodin's *Prince Igor*, though it ostensibly portrays a twelfth-century ceremony, is also tacitly (and inevitably) a polonaise (example 11.11b). Freestanding orchestral polonaises were frequently the response to official commemorative commissions, for instance Lyadov's pair of polonaises, in memory of Pushkin (C major, Op. 49, 1899) and Anton Rubinstein (D major, Op. 55, 1902), both composed to accompany the unveiling of monuments.

---

[99] The piece is headed "Polonaise quadriglia et choeur," the quadrilles being instrumental interpolations between reprises of the polonaise, illustrating sounds of battle, the Turks, and the liberated territories (a "Moldavienne"). See "Recueil d'airs choisis, Français, Russes, Italiens, et Polonaises avec Choeurs et sans Choeurs, composés par Joseph Koslovský Amateur, a St. Petersbourg" (MS without siglum in the library of the University of California at Berkeley), part 4 (Polonaises), no. 1. "Grom pobedï, razdavaisya" minus the interpolated quadrilles (and 3/8 "allemandes" or *deutsche Tänze*, precursors of the waltz), is included in Semyon Lvovich Ginzburg, ed., *Istoriya russkoy muzïki v notnïkh obraztsakh*, vol. 1 (Moscow: Muzïka, 1968), pp. 428–33.

[100] A. M. Sokolova, "O. A. Kozlovskiy," *Istoriya russkoy muzïki v desyati tomakh*, vol. 4 (Moscow: Muzïka, 1986), p. 98.

[101] She is greeted by those onstage, but could not actually appear to the audience, owing to a regulation forbidding the appearance of members of the Romanov dynasty as theatrical characters; since the Revolution a well-bedizened extra usually makes an entrance as the curtain falls.

EXAMPLE 11.10

a. Kozłowski, *Grom pobedï, razdavaisya!* (Polonaise-quadriglia), refrain

(*Be glorified by this, O Catherine, be glorified, thou tender mother of ours!*)

EXAMPLE 11.10, *continued*

b. Chaikovsky, *The Queen of Spades,* act 2, no. 15, culminating chorus

Chaikovsky's "imperial" style was virtually defined by the polonaise. Perhaps, in light of the chorus in *The Queen of Spades*, it could go without saying that Chaikovsky's earlier portrayal of Catherine the Great's court in his opera *Vakula the Smith* after Gogol (1874; revised as *Cherevichki* in 1885) was effected by means of a choral polonaise: it was virtually an automatic association, mandated on this occasion by Yakov Polonsky's libretto, which had been commissioned by the Russian court itself, and which Chaikovsky set as one of the entrants in a prize contest.[102] (It is definitely worth mentioning,

---

[102] For a consideration of that libretto and its political significance, see R. Taruskin, *Musorgsky: Eight Essays and an Epilogue*, pp. 342–47.

EXAMPLE 11.10, *continued*

though, that Rimsky-Korsakov's opera, *Christmas Eve*, on the same Gogol story, loudly though it advertised its divergence from Chaikovsky's treatment in favor of the literary original, nevertheless followed Chaikovsky in this ineluctable convention although Gogol had not called for it.) Even *Eugene Onegin*, that most intimate of operas, has its one moment of pomp, and that moment (the beginning of act 3) is a polonaise (example 11.12).

That brilliant polonaise, of course, is paired conceptually with another dance in *Eugene Onegin*, the modest waltz that introduces act 2 (example 11.13). The pairing underscores the social trajectory of the drama, from the milieu of the dowdy rural landowners personified by Mme Larina (Tatyana's mother), to whom Onegin feels superior, to that of the high urban aristocracy,

EXAMPLE 11.11

a. Rimsky-Korsakov, *Mlada* (1892), act 2, scene 3, *Shestviye knyazey*
("Procession of the Nobles")

Allegro moderato e maestoso

Example 11.11, *continued*

b. Borodin, *Prince Igor*, introduction, figure 10

(Brothers, let us sit upon our swift steed and behold the blue sea!)

EXAMPLE 11.12. Chaikovsky, *Eugene Onegin*, act 3, scene 1 (no. 19)

personified by Prince Gremin (her husband), by whom he is outclassed. In a more abstracted way, the same trajectory is described by the Third Suite, in which the "Valse mélancholique," with its tinge of subjective malaise, is relieved by the synergetic festivity of the final polonaise, a festivity no longer disturbed, as the festive finale of the Fourth Symphony is disturbed, by Byronic ruminations. The figurative court pageantry in the suite provides the consolation that the peasant holiday had failed to deliver in the symphony, because it was the dynastic state, as embodied in the bravura polonaise, rather than mere ethnicity, as embodied in the symphony's folk dance variations, that represented an authentic Russian *sobornost'*, a truly sustaining human collectivity.[103]

[103] A similar progression, from modest waltz to resplendent polonaise, can be read in the Third Symphony (1875), the work that gives perhaps the earliest intimation of Chaikovsky's imperial style. It can be read most easily in Balanchine's inspired decapitated version, which—as

EXAMPLE 11.13. Chaikovsky, *Eugene Onegin*, act 2, scene 1 (no. 13b)

MOZART REDUX

So Chaikovsky believed. Or so he fervently wished to believe, and fashioned his imperial style to bolster his faith, expressing it in a manner that once again

---

"Diamonds," the final act of the triptych *Jewels* (1967)—has become better known within the world of ballet than the score alone has ever been to concert audiences. Without the weighty, motivically intricate first movement, the remaining four stand revealed as Chaikovsky's true first suite (or "Suite no. 0," perhaps, à la Bruckner), and its waltz-polonaise dialectic would become a Chaikovskian paradigm.

allied him with his adored Mozart—allied him more closely, more significantly, and more artfully, I would contend, than any contemporary could claim.

Surely the most illuminating recent study of Mozart is Wye Jamison Allanbrook's. In *Rhythmic Gesture in Mozart*, a study of *Le Nozze di Figaro* and *Don Giovanni*, she has decisively laid to rest the myth of classicism to which Mozart had been assimilated in the nineteenth century. She accomplished this feat by showing that Mozart's music—far from an embodiment of idealized contentless form, an autonomous structure from which (according to one influential definition) "is excluded every sort of music that undertakes to lead the listener's feeling in too definite, too individual a manner"[104]—actually guides the listener's associations at every point through a series of well-defined, socially established semiotic conventions, of which the chief ingredient is the dance. She gives more than enough examples, moreover, to substantiate the claim that these codes governed not only the composition and reception of opera, where there is always a component that may, if desired, be classified (and marginalized) as "extramusical," but the composition and reception of "abstract" instrumental music as well, proving in fine that there is nothing abstract about it. The impulse to abstraction or "absolutism," she contends and proves, was something that came into music as a by-product of romanticism, with its impulse toward transcendence, and was read back on the music of the so-called classical period in the process of its canonization — which is to say (in stronger terms than Allanbrook might approve) its hijacking in support of the Germanic myth of the hero-composer.[105] That was a myth Mozart never had to reject, for he never knew it. Chaikovsky knew it and rejected it.

Why dance? Because the purpose of music for Mozart, as for Chaikovsky, was, in Allanbrook's words, "to move an audience through representations of its own humanity."[106] The metaphorical (or, more properly, metonymical) use of rhythmic gesture derived from the ritualized movement of social dance represented human behavior at its most expressive and fully realized, and did it in the most direct and corporeal way possible. "In the dancer," as Allanbrook writes, "movement and affect become one."[107] The assumption underlying this premise, of course, is that humans are at their most human not *au naturel*, and not as individuals, but as members of groups—all right, *classes*—whose feelings and actions are mediated through social convention.

---

[104] Friedrich Blume, *Classic and Romantic Music*, trans. M. D. Herter Norton (New York: Norton, 1970), p. 10; quoted in Wye Jamison Allanbrook, *Rhythmic Gesture in Mozart* (Chicago: University of Chicago Press, 1983), p. 381.

[105] See Allanbrook, *Rhythmic Gesture in Mozart*, most explicitly in the introduction and the afterword (pp. 1–9, 326–28, and the notes on pp. 329–31 and 380–81).

[106] Ibid., p. 16.

[107] Ibid.

It is an aristocratic assumption, to which, as we have had ample opportunity to observe, Chaikovsky, a privileged member of perhaps the most hierarchical society that existed in late nineteenth-century Europe, assented in
every conceivable way. As he put it to Mme von Meck, not only classes but
class warfare was the natural and necessary scheme of things: "All of life,
after all, is a struggle for existence, and if we allow that this struggle may
cease to be,—then life, too, will cease to be, leaving only meaningless proliferation."[108] And, as we have seen, he valued in the Russian autocracy a society that was organically human from the top all the way down, rather than one
organized according to some abstract political principle.

We have already had a number of indications that Chaikovsky sought in his
music to represent the dance of life. In this he knew, or rather felt, that he was
Mozart's follower. Thanks to Allanbrook's brilliant exposition, we may extend and corroborate the insight in very particular ways. Drawing on many
historical witnesses, Allanbrook was able to work out a scheme correlating
the social dances of the eighteenth century according to a social scale, roughly
classified as high, low, and "of medium character." The highest was the
courtly minuet, the lowest was the rustic contredanse. At the beginning of the
eighteenth century, these two dances inhabited wholly different social realms,
and their social connotations were well enough remembered in Mozart's day
so that his Don Giovanni (the title character, that is, in what was not by
coincidence Chaikovsky's favorite opera) could engineer a sort of social anarchy by ordering that the two be played simultaneously—together with a
"Teitsch," a speedier, hence even more loutish variety of contredanse—in the
famous mélange of three orchestras in the act 1 finale of the opera named
for him.

By century's end, enough social mixture had taken place so that the minuet
and the contredanse were commonly danced on the same social occasions.
They were, in fact, the vastly preponderant genres of social dance by
Mozart's time. Not at all coincidentally, they were the two dances that survived, frequently as a pair, in the so-called classical symphony—the minuet,
as everybody knows, slotted in by name, the contredanse often informing the
rondo (or *Kehraus*) finale. In Allanbrook's work they become a useful antithesis for analyzing the social and expressive dialectic of the Mozartean style.

A similar pair, as we have seen, governs the Chaikovskian dialectic. What
is not so obvious is its specific relationship to the Mozartean. The evolution of
the contredanse, through the *Deutsche Tanz* or Teitsch, into the waltz is traced
by Allanbrook, who notes how in the second movement of Mozart's C-major
Quintet, K. 515, "the waltz's exuberance serves as a foil for the serpentine

[108] 16 April 1883; Chaikovsky, *Polnoye sobraniye sochineniy; Literaturnïye proizvedeniya i
perepiska*, vol. 12, p. 124.

minuet."[109] The waltz is the "lower" member of Chaikovsky's pair, too; and its "higher" counterpart, the polonaise, has some striking affinities with its courtly predecessor—that is, with the statelier varieties of the minuet, exemplified in the *Don Giovanni* montage—as regards metrical structure, affect, and social meaning. Both are broadly beaten dances in triple time, the breadth of the beat reflecting exaltation in both the affective and social domains. The minuet, no less than the polonaise, easily accommodated the military *topos*.[110] The tempo relation between the Chaikovskian waltz and the Chaikovskian polonaise is roughly that between the Mozartean contredanse or Teitsch and the courtly Mozartean minuet. Indeed, so close are the two stately dances in rhythmic character that whenever, in the course of one of his Catherine-the-Great divertissements, Chaikovsky meant to write a minuet (e.g., Zlatogor's "Kak tï mila, prekrasna!" [no. 14d] in the second act of *The Queen of Spades*, or "His Highness's" [*Svetleyshiy's*] "Blagopoluchno li vï sovershili put'?" [no. 21] in the second act of *Cherevichki*) he instinctively gave it a polonaiselike stamp that could only have strengthened its social and affective import in his hearers' ears (example 11.14).

But of course the whole point of Allanbrook's study, and the emerging point of this one, is that social dances do not merely portray themselves in art-music contexts but provide a vocabulary of topoi that can signify in a more generalized or figurative way. Nor is the purpose of the dance-derived *topoi*, or of the rhythmic gestures associated with them, confined to mere celebration of the social order, however important such a purpose may have eventually become to Chaikovsky, if not to Mozart.[111] When dance functions as social indicator, as it does so emphatically in *Eugene Onegin*, it is not merely denotative but also connotative, symbolizing not only social milieus but also mores and their attendant constraints. The act 3 polonaise metonymically represents the *noblesse* that will oblige Tatyana to refuse the entreaties of the man she loves, the same man who had disdained her in her waltzing days. It telegraphs the end of the story—an end that leaves no one, except possibly old Prince Gremin, happy.

So the waltz/polonaise antithesis in *Eugene Onegin* embodies moral conflict, and represents it to the audience, through the trope of metonymy, in terms of a social environment in which the audience and the composer are co-participants. It is an attempt, as Allanbrook put it of the Mozartean method, "to move an audience through representations of its own humanity." In

---

[109] *Rhythmic Gesture in Mozart*, pp. 63–66; the quoted phrase is on p. 66, describing an example given on pp. 36–37.

[110] Ibid., pp. 35–36.

[111] Yet as Allanbrook wisely insists, Mozart's acceptance of, and reliance on, received conventions do ultimately disclose a conservative social attitude. *Figaro*, she writes (p. 194), "filled with joy and wit, and yet a certain resignation, is not a revolutionary's manual, nor a facile witness to an aphorism about true friendship knowing no bounds. Mozart had no desire to obliterate class distinctions, because for him the way to the most important truths lay through the surface of things as they are."

EXAMPLE 11.14

a. Chaikovsky, *The Queen of Spades,* act 2, no. 14d

b. Chaikovsky, *Cherevichki,* act 2, no. 21

Chaikovsky's time such a method was known as realism. "It seems to me," Chaikovsky wrote in 1891 to an official of the Imperial Theaters, "that I am truly gifted with the ability *truthfully, sincerely, and simply* to express the feelings, moods, and images suggested by a text. In this sense I am a *realist* and fundamentally a Russian."[112] Now we know how the trick was done, and from whom (not a Russian) Chaikovsky had learned it.

[112] To Vladimir Petrovich Pogozhov, 6 January 1891; Chaikovsky, *Polnoye sobraniye sochineniy; Literaturnïye proizvedeniya i perepiska*, vol. 16a (Moscow: Muzïka, 1978), p. 17. Italics original.

EXAMPLE 11.15. Chaikovsky, Suite no. 3, fourth movement (Tema con variazioni), no. 12: Finale. Polacca

Nor was a text a necessity for Chaikovsky's metonymical realism to work its effects, any more than it was for Mozart's. The supreme embodiment of the waltz/polonaise antithesis in Chaikovsky, and the most generalized and figurative, occurs in a work we have as yet considered only through the distorting lens of Germanocentric criticism. In order fully to appreciate its semiotic properties, it would be well to place it in conjunction with a work already described. Example 11.15 reproduces the characteristic fanfares that signal

EXAMPLE 11.15, *continued*

the arrival of the culminating polonaise in the third orchestral suite; and example 11.16 will remind the reader of the most famous fanfare Chaikovsky ever wrote.

Fatum! The dread motto theme from the Fourth Symphony, composed concurrently with *Eugene Onegin* in 1877–78, turns out to be yet another unadvertised polonaise. It is easy enough to see how the attributes of the genre

EXAMPLE 11.16. Chaikovsky, Symphony no. 4, first movement, beginning

might be appropriated for such a purpose: first of all the military *topos*, connoting bellicosity, hostility, implacability; then, too, the idea of grandiosity and invincible power, derived from political awe; and finally, perhaps, the idea of impersonality, dwarfing individual concerns, as the collectivity of the dominion dwarfs the individual subject.

That subject, of course, is represented by the first theme (example 11.17), explicitly designated as being *in movimento di valse* but notated in compound meter (9/8) so that three waltz measures are in effect coordinated with one measure of the polonaise just as three measures of Teitsch are coordinated with the Don Giovanni minuet. This rhythmic relationship is essential to the dramaturgy of the symphony's first movement, which is expressed in terms of the rhythm, so to speak, of the genre opposition. What is first expressed as a radical contrast becomes a superimposition during the development section, with its three terrifying collisions of subject theme and Fatum theme (mm. 253, 263, 278; example 11.18). The submission of waltz to polonaise—of subject to fate—is palpably denoted in the coda, when the waltz is reprised for the last time in a triple augmentation—that is, at the speed of the polonaise, one measure of the former now corresponding exactly to one measure of the latter, and therefore no longer a waltz at all (example 11.19).

The fate theme, then, inspires, or expresses, a sublime terror; but unlike the romantic sublime, which depends on a perception of uncanniness, of removal from ordinary human experience, the Chaikovskian sublime depends, as always, on concrete imagery explicitly derived from shared human experience.

But of course there is a major difference between the polonaise in the Fourth Symphony and the other Chaikovskian polonaises that we have sampled. The difference, quite simply and obviously, is one of affect. Where the usual polonaise affect is triumphant and celebratory, this one is alarming. It expresses not joyous community but fearful alienation. And if the polonaise in the Third Suite is read as affirming the composer's allegiance to the Tsarist state, which the polonaise is said to represent, what are we to make of the apparent political contradiction here?

But there is a contradiction only if we imagine the composer as being,

EXAMPLE 11.17. Chaikovsky, Symphony no. 4, first movement, Moderato con anima (♩. = in movimento di valse)

unlike the rest of us, a wholly changeless entity (and only if we imagine musical signification as a wholly fixed and static, quasi-lexical convention). If we regard the polonaise in the Fourth Symphony as being, like the polonaise in *Eugene Onegin*, an emblem of social mores and the constraints they impose, then the traditional biographical reading of the movement receives newly concrete support; for Chaikovsky had, in marrying, bowed to social constraints—that is, to internalized social pressures—with disastrous results. He had good reason to feel temporarily alienated from society, and good reason to embody such feelings artistically in a threatening polonaise, even as he could later celebrate his happy *rétour à la vie*, under the aegis of his benevolent sovereign, with a triumphant re-embracing of the same *topos*. The use of the imperial—or imperious—dance genre makes both the menace and the triumph legible, and that remains the point.

If Chaikovsky described the symphony theme as representing not the destructive pressure of social norms but simply blind, indifferent Fate, he was not only following an established musical convention (for who could hear a unison fanfare at the beginning of a symphony and not think of Beethoven's Fifth?) but also being true in all likelihood to his subjective perception of what threatened him, regarding Fate, as Freud famously put it, "as a substitute for the parental agency," that is, for what, casually following Freud, we all now call the superego, the locus of what we may anyhow, without fear of anachronism, call internalized social pressure.[113]

It's something we all carry around with us, at least if we are a part of Chaikovsky's potential audience. And so the "biographical" reading of the symphony, as Chaikovsky surely intended, is in fact collectively autobiographical. It creates community, if only a community of anxiety. So that must be why stern Tolstoy so valued Chaikovsky as an artist, even if there was "something not quite clear about him" as a man.[114] And that is why this symphony and this composer, though we may read at length about their faults

---

[113] *Civilization and Its Discontents*, trans. James Strachey (New York: Norton, 1961), p. 73.
[114] Tolstoy to his wife, 26 or 27 October 1893; quoted in Poznansky, *Tchaikovsky*, p. 605.

EXAMPLE 11.18. Chaikovsky, Symphony no. 4, first movement, the three collisions

EXAMPLE 11.18, *continued*

EXAMPLE 11.19. Chaikovsky, Symphony no. 4, first movement, m. 404

EXAMPLE 11.20. Chaikovsky, *The Queen of Spades*

a. Act 1, no. 3

(At last God has sent us a lovely sunny day!)

in any textbook but a Russian one, have never left the repertory and continue to annoy the conscience of those who guard the canon.

By the time we reach Chaikovsky's brief last period, the one ushered in by *The Queen of Spades*, the deployment of rhythmic gesture has become so virtuosic that it can encompass irony, and through irony, terror. The same polonaise rhythms that celebrate the crown in the opera's second act make many unadvertised appearances in the elaborate network of foils and doubles that stalk Gherman, the maniacal protagonist, and turn the opera into an early landmark of Russian symbolism. The whole central action of the first scene—beginning with the chorus of promenaders admiring the brilliant weather (another polonaise metonymy; example 11.20a) but continuing through the fatal encounter of Gherman, Lisa, and the Countess—is played against a steady throb of polonaise pulsations. So is the unbearably suspenseful scene in the

EXAMPLE 11.20, *continued*

b. Act 2, no. 16, m. 247 ("The Countess falls asleep")

(Slavsya sim Yekate . . .)

c. Act 3, no. 24, m. 24

(*Tomsky [to Prince Yeletsky]: Rely on me!*
Chorus: Ah! Hermann! Why so late, pal? Where've you come from?)

Countess's boudoir, directly before her lethal confrontation with Gherman, in which the ticking time-bomb of an ostinato (example 11.20b) is derived directly from the climactic Kozlovsky quotation ("Be glorified, O Catherine!") in the ballroom scene, as the countess, falling asleep, makes invidious comparison of balls recent and long past. The last unadvertised polonaise is the one that informs the game room chorus at the beginning of the last scene (example 11.20c), in which a final reprise of the Countess's reprise of the Kozlovsky motif heralds Gherman's entrance for what will be his own lethal encounter with Fatum.

The hallucinatory atmosphere of *The Queen of Spades* invades the Pathetic Symphony at several strategic points, of which one again evokes the rhythmic gesture of the polonaise. The middle section of that uncanny *lyrisches Intermezzo* that forms the second theme group in the first movement is accompanied by unmistakable polonaise figures—unmistakable even with four beats to the bar (example 11.21a). Prokofiev did not mistake them, and recalled them in the explicitly labeled common-time polonaise he composed for the Andrey-meets-Natasha ballroom scene in *War and Peace* (example 11.21b). In both cases the distorted yet familiar rhythmic gesture enables the audience to experience along with the characters—the lovers in *War and Peace*, the subject-persona in the Pathetic Symphony—a calculated atmosphere of unreality, which is to say of a reality made strange by powerful emotion.

IF THE culminating argument in this chapter, which relies so enthusiastically on Allanbrook's study of Mozart, seems to cast Chaikovsky in a special receptive relationship to the Viennese master he worshiped, it has been a purposeful hyperbole. It would be fairer, perhaps, to say that Chaikovsky was the eager recipient of, and participant in, a tradition that goes back to or passes through Mozart in a way that the Germanic tradition, reverently though its claim of descent from the "classical masters" has been ratified in conventional historiography, does not. It is the Franco-Italianate line that included Rossini, Bizet, Auber, Adam, and Chaikovsky, with Verdi, was its preeminent late nineteenth-century representative.[115] It is the line of which the prime theater of operation remained literally the theater, and which drew its musical imagery not from visions of transcendence but from the stock of daily life. It made a virtue of eclecticism, was therefore acutely conscious of style and tone as semiosis, but remained nonchalantly transparent to models and sources and

[115] To assess Chaikovsky's relationship to Verdi in a way that is especially relevant to the present discussion, compare his early symphonic poem *Fatum*, and its cannibalization in the last act of his opera *The Oprichnik*, with the overture to *La Forza del destino*, of which Chaikovsky, as a twenty-two-year-old conservatory pupil, attended the première production along with the rest of artistic and polite St. Petersburg (see example 10.1 in chapter 10).

EXAMPLE 11.21

a. Chaikovsky, Symphony no. 6, first movement, m. 101

(Cf. examples 11.8 and 11.10b:

b. Prokofiev, *War and Peace,* act 1, scene 2, figure 51

EXAMPLE 11.21, *continued*

attached relatively little importance to the fashioning of a personal style. (We have seen this in Chaikovsky's willing—and openly avowed—emulation even of so relatively undistinguished a contemporary as Lachner.) It remained loyal to the idea of the beautiful as the pleasing, including the sensuously pleasing. It sought community with its audience, and respected its audience's humanity.

In this company Chaikovsky was the foremost symphonist, but his view of the symphony, like Mozart's, remained true to the theater—though just how true we will probably continue to underestimate until Chaikovsky meets his Allanbrook. And he passed the view along to Mahler, who enthusiastically conducted *Eugene Onegin*, and whose idea of the symphony as *Welttheater* owed a crucial debt to Chaikovsky, for which reason Mahler, too, long paid a critical price for his unabashed eclecticism and for his alleged "mannerisms" and vulgarity.[116]

Owing to the ideological dichotomies of the nineteenth century and their largely unconscious internalization in twentieth-century criticism and historiography, Chaikovsky's Mozartean inheritance, like some kind of fallen aristocratic pedigree, is now looked upon askance as "popular" or, worse, "commercial."[117] There is truth in that judgment: the aesthetics and the practices of

[116] The Chaikovskian stylistic resonances in Mahler's First Symphony are all that are usually recognized by critics and historians today, and they are noted, with eyes averted, as something to be excused in a young composer. But the dramatic—or dramatized—structure of Mahler's Second Symphony (especially of the opening *Totenfeier*), which would henceforth define the Mahlerian, is hardly thinkable without the precedent of Chaikovsky's Fourth and Sixth Symphonies.

[117] More sophisticated or self-conscious historians, like Dahlhaus or his ideological mentor, August Halm, have deliberately revived the dichotomies. See August Halm, *Von zwei Kulturen der Musik* (Munich: Georg Müller Verlag, 1913; 3d ed., Stuttgart: Klett, 1947); Carl Dahlhaus,

Mozart's day were in some conspicuous and important ways closer to those of our contemporary pop culture than to those of what we now call "classical music."[118] But as consciousness of that kinship has been repressed, so recognition of its survivals has been stigmatized. To the extent that Chaikovsky is viewed as an heir to the legitimate "classical" (which is to say, the invented preromantic) tradition, he can be viewed only as its debaser, easily marginalized on the basis of nationality or sexuality (and recent research has exposed the links between the two marginalizing strategems).[119]

Sergey Diaghilev, for whom Chaikovsky was a great composer but an unexportable commodity, spoke with feeling on one occasion about the decline of the Russian aristocracy. "The end of a way of life is at hand. Isolated, boarded-up estates, palaces horrible in their dying magnificence, strangely inhabited by today's pleasant, average folk who could never bear the burden of yesterday's splendors."[120] That is how one tends, in benevolent moods, to look down upon Chaikovsky even now: as a pleasant, average sort trying impertinently to do a hero's work. Why do we condescend to him? Because like Mozart he would not condescend to us.

Nineteenth-Century Music, chapters 1 and 2; the best critique remains Pederson's "On the Task of the Music Historian: The Myth of the Symphony after Beethoven," but also see Stephen Blum, "In Defense of Close Reading and Close Listening," *Current Musicology* 53 (1993): 41–54.

[118] See R. Taruskin, "A Mozart Wholly Ours," *Musical America* 110, no. 3 (May 1990): 32–41; reprinted with an update in R. Taruskin, *Text and Act: Essays on Music and Performance* (New York: Oxford University Press, 1995), pp. 273–91.

[119] Taruskin, "Pathetic Symphonist," contains a summary.

[120] "V chas itogov," *Vesï* 2, no. 4 (April 1905): 45–46.

CHAPTER 12

SCRIABIN AND THE SUPERHUMAN

A MILLENNIAL ESSAY

PUTTING SCRIABIN TOGETHER

Ostanovís', prokhózhiy! V sikh stenákh
Zhil Skryábin i pochíl. Vsyo kámen' strógiy
Tebé skazál v nemnógikh pis'menákh.
Poséyan sev. V rodímïkh glubinákh
Zvezdá zazhglás'. Idí zh svoyéy dorógoy.[1]

Stop, passerby! Within these walls
Scriabin lived and found his resting place.
Stern stone in letters few has told you all.
The seed is sown. In our primeval depths
A star is lit. Now go your way.

The poet Vyacheslav Ivanov (1866–1949), one of Alexander Scriabin's closest late associates and the man who may have understood him best of all his contemporaries, wrote these lines a year after the composer's untimely and bathetic death in 1915. In letters very few indeed they tell us all. For Ivanov and the other poets and thinkers of the Russian avant garde (if not for Russia's musicians, who had no avant garde), this musician had been a prophet, his art a revelation. More than a prophet even, he had been for them a demiurge, a virtual divinity, cast after death by Ivanov, his chief mythologizer, as a light to illuminate our interior firmament as the lyre of slain Orpheus shines in the sky above us, placed there in mythic times by the god Apollo. It was an inevitable outcome. Scriabin was the sole musician of his time and place to cast himself in the Orphic image, to invest his art with the attributes of ecstatic and redemptive religion, and to channel through it intimations not merely of phenomenal appearance but of ultimate noumenal truth. His art, more explic-

---

[1] Vyacheslav Ivanovich Ivanov, "Ko dnyu otkrïtiya pamyatnoy doski na dome Skryabina" (Lines written to commemorate the unveiling of a memorial plaque on Scriabin's former domicile), *Muzïka*, no. 254 (11 March 1916).

itly than that of any other composer, was (or became) a gnosis, a way of attaining and imparting occult knowledge.

His brother-in-(common)law and close confidant, the émigré musical philosopher Boris de Schloezer (1881–1967), characterized Scriabin's uniqueness in terms that, though paradoxical from the standpoint of conventional aesthetics, will resonate powerfully—and corroborate, as it were, from the other side—the terms employed in characterizing Chaikovsky in the preceding chapter. For Schloezer, Scriabin was the only truly *romantic* musician Russia ever produced, precisely because his artistic vision was, in "classical" terms, art-transcending, hence inartistic. "An artist of genius," he wrote, Scriabin nevertheless was determined

> to cease to be an artist, to become a prophet, a votary, a predicant. Yet such appellations would have been unacceptable to Scriabin, for he refused to admit that his design reached beyond art, that he violated the frontiers of art and thus ceased to be an artist. On the contrary, he argued that the commonly accepted view of art was too narrow, its true meaning lost, and its significance obscured. It was his destiny to restore art to its original role; consequently he was much more an artist than any other, because to him art was the religion of which he was the sacristan.[2]

As in our discussion of Chaikovsky, Schloezer explicitly casts the difference between the "classic" and "romantic" temperaments as the difference between the impulse of world enhancement and that of world transformation. Although he develops the distinction from the standpoint of a partisan, which is to say invidiously, it is enormously productive. Subtract the animus and it is incandescent:

> Generally speaking, for a classicist, art is only an interlude, a celebration of some sort; it interrupts the course of time and serves as a break in the routine of life. It is an intermission, after which life resumes its course and returns to "serious business" as if nothing had changed. The goal of a romantic, on the other hand, is to erase such a distinction. A romantic definitely desires that everything be changed, with art not merely an entr'acte but a celebration that goes on, that overflows into everyday existence and integrates with it in order to illuminate and, in effect, transform it. For a romantic, the main purpose is to convert a work of art into a means of action, not only on the aesthetic plane but also on the plane of reality. The two worlds coalesce in this conception; the intention is to impart to artificial products of the creative imagination the status of real events (or likewise, to impart to real events the status of the imaginary). This is the clue to the importance of *Parsifal*. (Pp. 311–12)

[2] Boris de Schloezer, *Scriabin: Artist and Mystic*, trans. Nicolas Slonimsky (Berkeley and Los Angeles: University of California Press, 1987), p. 234. (Originally published as *Skryabin: Lichnost', Misteriya* [Berlin: Grani, 1922]). Further page references will be given in the text.

Even Chaikovsky, or especially Chaikovsky, precisely because his name had become synonymous with the self-absorbed and self-exhibiting confessional mode associated in the popular imagination with romantic artists, was for Schloezer a prototypical classic—that is, a composer in the Italianate mold who saw his art above all as decorative (and who, of course, detested *Parsifal*). His expressive side, from the truly romantic (religious and philosophical) perspective, was little more than a manifestation of what is condemned by our contemporary religious romantics as "secular humanism," the blasphemous installation of humanity, and its celebration, in place of the divine. Schloezer is contemptuous: "The sentimentality, the pathos that permeate [Chaikovsky's] music are but the excesses of his Italianism. He abandons himself all too willingly to his emotions, and he is complacent in his emotional flights" (p. 313).

As for the remaining composers of nineteenth-century Russia, they were, many of them, committed to a positivistic nationalism (Balakirev), or an equally positivistic realism (Dargomïzhsky, Musorgsky), that was just as barren from Schloezer's (and, we may assume, Scriabin's) perspective as Chaikovsky's decorative emotionalism. By century's end, Russian music was largely committed to a quite hidebound and more obviously "classical" academicism (Rimsky-Korsakov, Glazunov, Taneyev). Above all, every Russian composer except Scriabin explicitly rejected Wagner as an artistic role model, while Scriabin not only embraced him but attempted to surpass him.

The culture of romanticism, then—the culture of which Scriabin was the prophet, the votary, and the predicant—was a "dynamic and revolutionary" culture that proceeded "from culture to life" in the sense that it was endowed with "fluidity, mutability, and mobility," and its mission was to change the world (p. 280). The culture of "classicism," its dialectical antipode, was thus for Schloezer neither the culture of Greece and Rome nor that of the eighteenth century, but the cultural attitudes of the world around him, which is still to say, the world around us. Its course is "from life to culture." Schloezer's description is terrifying:

> Classical culture is fundamentally materialistic and static; herein lies the ever-present danger of its degeneration into fetishism and formalism. . . . For the classical mind the world of culture, though manufactured by man, possesses an objective reality equivalent to the world of nature's. . . . Its system of values comprises a conglomeration of manufactured objects that tend to assume an autonomous existence, forming a rigid world often hostile to man's emotional life. Products of man's creative labor are separated from their makers and embark on an independent development outside the sphere of human action. . . . In classical cultures, in which workers and masters labor together, the future is conceived as an accumulation of cultural values, a development and reinforcement of the

system whose ultimate aim is perfection in isolation. But such an absolute ideal is manifestly unattainable, for the road leading to it must be infinite. This notion is the crux of the idea of infinite progress. (Pp. 280, 284, 287)

This is a devastatingly accurate portrait of what is still a major strain in contemporary high culture, the culture of modernism. The best proof of its accuracy is the reception Scriabin's music has met with since Vyacheslav Ivanov made his roseate prediction in verse. Alas, the seed did not take root. The light went out. We no longer know this man. Only fifteen years after Ivanov penned his stanza, the young white hope of a new Russia's music told a foreign correspondent that "we regard Scriabine as our bitterest musical enemy, . . . because Scriabine's music tends to an unhealthy eroticism. Also to mysticism and passivity and escape from the realities of life."[3] The great ban on all artistic pathos and pretense that came in reaction to the cataclysmic events Scriabin (and a host of other artistic maximalists) could with hindsight be said to have foretold killed interest in him except on the part of a few fossilized votaries and predicants, cranks and dilettantes.[4] He became just another screwball "decadent" for whose gangrenous grandiosity an antidote could be found in *die neue Sachlichkeit*; or else a charlatan, perpetrating musical hypnosis, as Boris Asafyev put it in his *Book about Stravinsky*, which celebrated the figure regarded by the 1920s as Scriabin's great musical antipode, whose music possessed a "sharpness and iron discipline" that promoted "robust social health."[5] Stravinsky himself, though in his early period a somewhat abashed admirer of Scriabin, later declared the older composer to be

[3] Rose Lee, "Dmitri Szostakovitch: Young Russian Composer Tells of Linking Politics With Creative Work," *New York Times*, 20 December 1931; reproduced in facsimile in Eric Roseberry, *Shostakovich: His Life and Times* (New York: Hippocrene Books, 1982), p. 79; reprinted in David Ewen, ed., *The Book of Modern Composers*, 2d ed. (New York: Knopf, 1956), p. 380.

[4] The main keeper of the flame in Russia was the composer's son-in-law, the pianist Vladimir Sofronitsky (1902–63); and yet the spiritual aspects of the music, even in Sofronitsky's vivid performances, were written off in the Soviet milieu as the products of material hallucinogens. In a memoir by the Soviet émigré pianist Mark Zeltser, Sofronitsky "would walk to the piano with a slow, distracted gait, then, before playing, apply a black handkerchief to his nose. In musical circles, there were rumors about what was on Sofronitsky's handkerchiefs, or in them." (Quoted by Joseph Horowitz, "Disks: 26 Scriabin Pieces," *New York Times*, 11 November 1986.) Faubion Bowers, aide-de-camp to General Douglas Macarthur during the occupation of Japan and later a prolific arts journalist, was for a long time a devoted proponent of the composer, with two major publications to his credit: *Scriabin* (2 vols.; Tokyo and Palo Alto: Kodansha International, 1969); and *The New Scriabin: Enigma and Answers* (New York: St. Martins Press, 1973). His work, too, while that of an enthusiast, has tended to (as Schloezer would say) "fetishize" the sounds of the music ("the music itself," as we are now inclined to say) while relegating the occult aspect of Scriabin's creativity to the status of pathology or, in any case, something "extramusical."

[5] *A Book About Stravinsky*, trans. Richard F. French (Ann Arbor: UMI Research Press, 1982), pp. 158, 22.

"without a passport," adding rootless cosmopolitanism to the list of Scriabin's sins.[6]

Since his centennial in 1972—quite grandly observed in the USSR, where Scriabin the visionary tone poet was eventually rehabilitated, along with many other turn-of-the-century artists of an apocalyptical bent, as an incognizant harbinger of the revolution, but elsewhere hardly at all—scholarly interest in Scriabin has somewhat unexpectedly begun to revive, albeit on a new and somewhat contradictory footing. A few German and Anglophone music theorists and composers, with one significant Soviet forerunner, have been conducting serious and systematic investigations into Scriabin's evolving musical style and techniques, demonstrating not only its "iron discipline" but its surprisingly rationalistic—or, at least, easily rationalized—theoretical basis.[7] Another scholarly cohort, including historical musicologists, art historians, and literary critics, has endeavored to insert Scriabin into his cultural surroundings, seeking parallels that might explain his idiosyncrasies even as they aid comprehension of the so-called Russian Silver Age, of which Scriabin now appears to be a particularly concentrated representative.[8]

[6] The remark, made in an interview with Scriabin's former amanuensis, Leonid Sabaneyeff, was reported by Boris de Schloezer in his *Igor Stravinsky* (Paris, 1929), of which an abridged translation by Ezra Pound first appeared in *The Dial* 85, no. 6 (1929), and then in Edwin Corle, ed., *Igor Stravinsky* (New York: Duell, Sloan and Pearce, 1949), pp. 33–91. The quoted remark is at the very beginning, "whereupon," as S. A. Evreinow, an old Scriabin hand, drolly observed, Schloezer "started a discussion about the sources of Stravinsky's musical inspiration"; see the notes to "A Collection of Compositions for the Piano by Alexander Scriabin" (Paraclete Music Disc no. 101 [East Haven, Conn., 1958]).

[7] This new analytical literature begins with Varvara Dernova, *Garmoniya Skryabina* (Leningrad: Muzïka, 1968), a revision of the author's 1948 thesis, of which a translation has been published by Roy J. Guenther as "Varvara Dernova's *Garmoniia Skriabina*: A Translation and Critical Commentary" (Ph.D. dissertation, Catholic University of America, 1979). (Dernova published a preliminary report of her findings as "Nekotorïye zakonomernosti garmonii Skryabina," in Yu. Tyulin, ed., *Teoreticheskiye problemï muzïki XX veka*, vol.1 [Moscow: Sovetskiy kompozitor, 1967], and a summary of them as "Garmoniya Skryabina," in S. Pavchinsky and V. Tsukkerman, ed., *A. N. Skryabin: Sbornik statei* [Moscow: Sovetskiy kompozitor, 1973], pp. 344–83; for an English summary see Roy J. Guenther, "Varvara Dernova's System of Analysis of the Music of Skryabin," in Gordon D. McQuere, ed., *Russian Theoretical Thought in Music* [Ann Arbor: UMI Research Press, 1983], pp. 165–216.) Highlights post-Dernova include Gottfried Eberle, *Zwischen Tonalität und Atonalität: Studien zur Harmonik Alexander Skrjabins* (Munich: Katzbichler, 1978); Hanns Steger, *Der Weg der Klaviersonate bei Alexander Skrjabin* (Munich: Wollenweber, 1979); Jay Reise, "Late Skriabin: Some Principles behind the Style," *19th-Century Music* 6 (1982–83): 220–31; George Perle, "Scriabin's Self-Analyses," *Music Analysis* 3 (1984): 101–24; and James M. Baker, *The Music of Alexander Scriabin* (New Haven and London: Yale University Press, 1986).

[8] This literature includes Martin Cooper, "Aleksandr Skryabin and the Russian Renaissance," *Studi musicali* 1 (1972), condensed in M. H. Brown and R. J. Wiley, ed., *Slavonic and Romantic Music: Essays for Gerald Abraham* (Ann Arbor: UMI Research Press, 1985), pp. 219–40; Ralph Matlaw, "Scriabin and Russian Symbolism," *Comparative Literature* 31 (1979): 1–23; Malcolm H. Brown, "Skriabin and Russian 'Mystic' Symbolism," *19th-Century Music* 3 (1979–80): 42–

While the insularly musical project and the broadly cultural one have each made considerable headway, the two camps have yet to recognize a common cause, let alone find a suitably interdisciplinary method for approaching one of the most "interdisciplinary" composers who ever lived. Indeed, in keeping with the "classical" assumptions long regnant in the academy, the two projects have been operating in deliberate isolation and mutual suspicion, and this has inevitably hampered them both.

The musicians, heir to deeply entrenched traditions of positivistic style criticism and aesthetic formalism such as Schloezer presciently described, have insisted on viewing Scriabin "in an atmosphere free of the incense that clouded the minds of his earliest admirers," as one representative writer puts it, remarking further that "it would be a pity if appreciation of the music required us to follow Scriabin into this world of cosmic 'hocus-pocus.'"[9] So hostile have musicologists become to the cultural environment in which Scriabin's music arose, and to the purposes it originally addressed, and so ready have they become to diagnose such purposes as symptoms (at best) of "mild megalomania," that one highly visible review of Schloezer's study in Slonimsky's translation amounted to little more than a howl of protest at its very appearance, beginning with the remark that "the publication of this book now . . . is as silly as the book itself, and no more comprehensible," and granting only that "as a historical document, Schloezer's work has a certain deplorable importance." The sole question the book managed to provoke in the reviewer's supremely closed mind was, "What can have possessed the Oxford University Press?"[10]

But this question prompts another: in the face of such a rejection of its cultural meaning, reflecting (again, as Schloezer predicted) a general narrowing of purview that excludes hermeneutic inquiry in the name of a debased "classical" notion of "absolute music" that disgusted and enraged its com-

---

51; and I. L. Vanechkina and B. M. Galeyev, *Poèma ognya: Kontseptsiya svetomuzïkal'nogo sinteza A. N. Skryabina* (Kazan: Izdatel'stvo Kazanskogo Universiteta, 1981). There have also been some important Soviet documentary publications, including a large book of letters (A. N. Scriabin, *Pis'ma*, ed. A. V. Kashperov [Moscow: Muzïka, 1965]); and a documentary chronicle: M. P. Pryashnikova and O. M. Tompakova, *Letopis' zhizni i tvorchestva A. N. Skryabina* (Moscow: Sovetskiy kompozitor, 1985).

[9] Hugh Macdonald, *Skryabin* (London: Oxford University Press, 1978), pp. 14, 10. In a centennial "tribute" to the composer, Macdonald took off from the following premise: "Nothing is easier than to pour ridicule upon Skryabin's gradual and finally total self-delusion. Ever since the bubble of his persona was so rudely pricked in the 1920s . . . his quasi-religious convictions have been under relentless fire from the few critics who have paid him any attention at all, and must be eliminated from any possibility of serious consideration, now or even in the future." ("'Words and Music by A. Skryabin,'" *Musical Times* 113 [1972]: 22.)

[10] David Murray, "Distorted Vision," *Musical Times* 128 (1987). The diagnosis of "mild megalomania" also comes from this article. (Schloezer's book appeared in England under the Oxford University Press imprint, by arrangement with California.)

poser,[11] what has attracted so much scholarly attention to this music? James M. Baker has given an answer that may be taken, within the domain of academic music theory, as authoritative. Having launched his sustained, indeed relentless technical inquiry into what academic analysts call the "structure" of the music by observing that "Alexander Scriabin would have resented being remembered merely as a composer," Baker concludes what must thus be counted a three hundred–page insult to Scriabin's self-image by salting the wound: "Although his visions were the primary motivation for his experimentation and innovation, what remains today is his music. Scriabin's art survives because he was a master of the craft of musical composition. Much as he might have been disappointed, it is through the study of his musical structures that *we can best know him* today."[12]

Yet this answer has to be regarded, finally, as an evasion, since the phrase I have put in italics obviously ought to read "we wish to know him." It is Baker who has decided that Scriabin can and ought to be assimilated to "classical" culture, with its attendant formalism and its fetishizing of material sound objects. It is Baker who has decided that autonomous existence may be ascribed to these products of the composer's creative labor. What is the purpose of the assimilation? Is it merely an epicurean proposition? Is its goal the enjoyment of a sensuously alluring artifact without any cultural strings attached? Is it the rationalization of a solipsistic bond (a bond perceived as "intersubjective") with a somewhat disreputable object to which one has nevertheless grown emotionally attached?

These would indeed be good "classical" objectives, but there is something else, something more compelling—and something that was also clairvoyantly foreseen by Schloezer. The subtitle to Baker's doctoral dissertation (Yale University, 1977), on which his book is based, accurately reflecting both the eventual book's narrative strategy and its thesis, reads, "The Transition from Tonality to Atonality." This phrase neatly summarizes the significance Scriabin's music has assumed for contemporary music theorists, who see its progressive and remarkably trackable stylistic evolution as embodying in microcosm the essential musical progress myth of the twentieth century. Scriabin's musical legacy seems a providential validation of that fashionable teleology, embodying Schloezer's "classical" values of "infinite progress" and autonomous "perfection in isolation."

Baker's "techno-essentialist" survey is the most comprehensive analytical treatment Scriabin's music has yet received. His book is a mine of informa-

---

[11] "I cannot understand how to write *just* music now," Scriabin exclaimed to Sabaneyeff. "How boring! . . . People who *just* write music are like performers who *just* play an instrument. They become valuable only when they connect with a general idea. The purpose of music is revelation. What a powerful way of knowing it is!" (quoted in Bowers, *The New Scriabin*, p. 108).

[12] *The Music of Alexander Scriabin*, pp. vii, 270.

tion. Yet by confining its purview to the "accrual of technical innovations along a smooth, linear course," such an account of the music must leave out what is most interesting and (I would argue) most significant about it.[13] The case of Manfred Kelkel is also symptomatic. While researching *his* doctoral dissertation (for the advent of techno-essentialist historiography has made Scriabin a capital dissertation composer), Kelkel was the first to study in analytical detail the numerous sketches Scriabin made in the last two years of his life for the *Predvaritel'noye deystviye*, the "Preparatory Act" to the great *Misteriya* that was to have brought not only Scriabin's creative career but the history of the world to a cataclysmic close.[14] Having made a preliminary survey of the sketches, Kelkel rushed into print to announce that it was Scriabin, not Alfredo Casella and not Alban Berg, who had been the first to write "aggregate simultaneities," that is, chords containing all twelve notes of the chromatic scale.[15]

This race-to-the-patent-office mentality is characteristic of techno-essentialist historiography and its values.[16] All conventional music history, whatever the period, is now written in this way; that is precisely what makes it conventional. And in the wake of what is often termed the second wave of modernism—the scientistic one that took shape during the cold war, and in response to it—techno-essentialist values have been a guiding stimulus on musical composition as well.

But as scholars and composers alike have grown increasingly aware, it can be a trivializing standard of value, and it has certainly trivialized Scriabin even as it has rescued his academic prestige and promoted investigation of his technical routines. Most of the recent work on him has concentrated on the highly patterned sound surface (even where the authors have professed to be describing or explicating "structure"), with the result that we are more inclined than ever to regard an ornately crafted Scriabin composition as "some imperial Fabergé jewel," in the words of Robert Craft, fixated as we now are on the level of "the flammiferous ornaments, the trills, tremolos, arpeggios,

---

[13] I borrow the term "techno-essentialist," as well as its capsule definition, from Christopher Williams, who coined it in a penetrating review-essay, "Of Canons and Context: Toward a Historiography of Twentieth-Century Music," *Repercussions* 2, no. 1 (Spring 1993): 31–74 (the full definition is on p. 42).

[14] The dissertation was published as *Alexandre Scriabine: sa vie, l'esoterisme et le langage musical dans son oeuvre* (Paris: Champion, 1978).

[15] Manfred Kelkel, "Les esquisses musicales de l'*Acte préalable* de Scriabine," *Revue de Musicologie* 17 (1971): 40–48.

[16] Compare the conclusion of Macdonald's article on Scriabin in *The New Grove Dictionary of Music and Musicians*, where the composer is praised for having "initiated a new musical language, as Schoenberg and Debussy were doing at much the same time, no less radical and advanced than theirs, and like them breaking decisively with tonality. His sketches for the *Acte préalable* (1914–15) reveal him experimenting with 12-note chords, which is just one reason for supposing that, but for his early death, his standing as a major figure in 20th-century music would be all the more conspicuous" (vol. 17, p. 373).

glissandos, appoggiaturas and other musical sequins."[17] It is Scriabin, in other words, who now reaps the "culinary" laurels to which Chaikovsky, despised as a confessionalist but in fact a closet "classic," actually aspired.

———

GIVEN THAT the meaning of music remains one of the cursed questions of aesthetics, it is not surprising that empirical musical studies have retreated from it, even when a music so formidably coded and laden as Scriabin's has been the object in view, instead focusing doggedly on descriptive categories ("structure" and "style"), and insisting that any other dimension (but particularly every interpretive dimension) is "subjective" or "extramusical," and therefore beneath professional notice.[18] Nor is it hard to understand why studies concerned with cultural backgrounds so often fail to do justice to musical particulars. Professional discourse on music having become so forbiddingly technocratic, it is no wonder that cultural historians, and even music historians, have steered clear of the analytical literature on Scriabin. As a result, their studies have been biographical in the main, rarely venturing any critical comment on the work beyond occasional, nervously dismissive obiter dicta to the effect (to quote the author of one such study) that "it is hardly likely that [Scriabin's] grandiose vision could be communicated musically."[19]

The only cultural study of Scriabin to attempt any interpretation of the work in light of the uncovered background is that of Martin Cooper, who, ignorant of the analytical literature, had to content himself with gestural parallels, such as Scriabin's frequent use of motifs that could be compared with quasi-shamanistic *zovï* (summons) and *prigovorï* (spells) such as one finds in much Russian poetry of the period, especially Balmont's. But Scriabin was not the only composer at the time to write fanfares. Many, even Baker, have noted Scriabin's sonic analogies to various qualities of light (not to mention his

[17] Craft, "Scriabin Centenary," in *Prejudices in Disguise* (New York: Knopf, 1974), p. 187.

[18] Once again Macdonald is at the phobic extreme. His remarks on the *Poème de l'extase* are typical: "The task of elucidating the metaphysical significance of poem and music (if any) I gladly leave to others. The poem leaves a taste of wordy mystical nonsense that can hardly enhance the value of the two compositions. The only common notions which can be traced with any clarity are those basic emotive and pictorial states on which all programme music has thrived: melancholy, joy, struggle, longing, and so on, leaving Skryabin's more personal ideas of creativity and mystical divination to the *merely subjective* interpretation of both composer and listener." And, "The *Poem of Ecstasy* is a masterly work because Skryabin was still governed by the surviving rigours of symphonic structure; if it had been composed a year or two later, it would have been a less concise and less compelling reflection of that far from masterly poem, or even—and this is the more forbidding thought when we recall the weakness of the First Symphony's finale—a setting of it. As if he was somehow conscious of his commitment to instrumental music, words were left out of his scheme of things. When he tried to impose them on his music the results were *inescapably subjective*" ("'Words and Music by A. Skryabin,'" p. 25, italics added).

[19] Matlaw, "Scriabin and Russian Symbolism," p. 22.

notoriously rigorous but apparently nontransmissible pitch-color synesthesia), and nocturnal hallucinations, as if only Scriabin used trills and tremolos.

Most cultural interpreters of Scriabin's work have not ventured even this far. They have mainly confined themselves to the amassing of quotations testifying to a general kinship of ideals between the composer and some of the poets and thinkers who were his contemporaries. This can be valuable only as the prelude to a musical discussion that so far has not been forthcoming. To allege that ideals professed in common are in some sense latent in the art-works regardless of medium is merely to propound a truism.

Worse, those who have explored Scriabin's relationship to theosophy or to theurgic symbolism have tended to assimilate the composer to the poets. This has actually meant at times examining or analyzing Scriabin's amateurish poems in preference to his music. Since as a poet Scriabin produced mainly cheap imitations of his friends Balmont, Baltrushaitis, and Ivanov, it is not difficult to construct tautological correspondences connecting their work (and Bryusov's) with Scriabin's. In an age when "Gesamtkunstwerk" remained a rallying cry in Russia as nowhere else, when poets such as Balmont pro-claimed themselves makers of "inner music," and when composers like Scriabin tried their hand at poetry, one can all too easily assume that Russia's radical poets, artists, and composers traveled one path, arms happily linked, all fully conscious of one another's activity and joyously abetting it—and that discussion of one medium (invariably the literary) can subrogate them all. The music, inevitably, gets lost in the tautology.

Nor does the surmise stand up to any empirical or documentary test. Con-sider Andrey Belïy, who alone among the theurgic symbolists possessed some technical knowledge of music, and who was the one most inclined self-consciously to preach (and even, as in his verbal "Symphonies," to practice) formal correspondences between poetry and the art of tones. Belïy, it turns out, had no interest at all in the poet-musician whom Vyacheslav Ivanov called "the ultimate artistic genius of our time." Indeed, he despised Scriabin, whom he met only once, at the home of Margarita Morozova, Scriabin's patron. In a funny memoir of the occasion, after mocking Scriabin's over-fastidious appearance and deportment, Belïy described his conversation: "All the while the little white fingers of his pale little hand kept jabbing out chords of some kind in the air: his pinkies took the 'Kant' note, his middle finger would trace the 'Culture' theme, and all at once—whoops!—a leap of the index finger over a whole row of keys to the one marked 'Blavatsky.'"[20] So much for the notion that Zeitgeist automatically crosscuts media, or that kin-dred theurgic spirits inevitably recognize one another.

And yet when Belïy wrote his programmatic essay 'On Theurgy,' pub-

---

[20] Andrey Belïy, *Mezhdu dvukh revolyutsii* (Leningrad, 1934), pp. 348–49. When it came to Scriabin's piano playing, Belïy professed to find it "more light than profound."

lished in 1903 in Filosofov's and Merezhkovsky's religious-philosophical journal *Novïy put'*, he inevitably focused the discussion on music.[21] If it astonishes us that he chose as paradigm an innocent, early, and innocuous set of character pieces (*Stimmungsbilder*, Op. 1) by Nikolai Medtner, the poor man's Rachmaninoff, that only goes to show that for a theurgic symbolist even a tepid piece of music was warmer than a hot poem. Tendentiously (and perhaps unconsciously) echoing a famous remark of Felix Mendelssohn, Vyacheslav Ivanov summed up the potent advantage of music over poetry, and the futility of attempting to paraphrase it: "Where we monotonously blab the meager word 'sadness' (*pechal'*), music overflows with thousands of particular shades of sadness, each so ineffably novel that no two of them can be called the same feeling." Music, "the unmediated pilot of our spiritual depths," is thus at once the most sensitive of the arts and the most inherently prophetic, "the womb in which the Spirit of the Age is incubated."[22]

But of course this encomium is as applicable to Medtner's music as it is to Scriabin's, as it would be to any music that aspires in romantic fashion to ineffability (that is, to the "condition of music"). Belïy's choice of Medtner as exemplar was dictated by their close personal friendship, which also explains why the only piece of music ever published in a symbolist journal was again a work of Medtner's: a setting of a Belïy poem (*Epitafïya*, Op. 13, no. 2) that appeared in Nikolai Ryabushinsky's *Zolotoye runo* (The Golden Fleece) in 1908.

Scriabin also saw music as superseding poetry, his own as much as anyone's. Once he had composed the music for it, he suppressed his verbal "Poèma ekstaza," never allowing it to appear in concert programs.[23] (Of course it does regularly so appear nowadays, and is much analyzed in the "cultural" literature about the composer.[24]) If there is to be assimilation, then maybe it should be poetry that is assimilated to music. Nobody has yet figured out a way of doing this.[25]

[21] Belïy, "O teurgii," *Novïy put'* 1 (1903): 100–123.

[22] Ivanov, "Skryabin," in *Pamyatniki kul'turï: Novïye otkrïtiya* (Yearbook of the Scientific Council of the History of World Culture, Academy of Sciences of the USSR), 1983 (Leningrad: Nauka, 1985), p. 114; and Ivanov, "Vzglyad Skryabina na iskusstvo," ibid., p. 103. The passage about "sadness" is clearly disingenuous; Ivanov knew as well as the next poet that poetry obtains its "thousands of particular shades" by means of imagery, not by mere vocabulary.

[23] Let this be the answer to the odious comments quoted in n. 18.

[24] Along with the rest of Scriabin's creative writings, it is published in Mikhail Gershenzon, ed., "Zapisi A. N. Skryabina" (with a foreword by Schloezer), *Russkiye propileyi*, vol. 6 (Moscow: Sabashnikov, 1919), pp. 97–247 (the *Poèma èkstaza* is on pp. 176–91). An English translation appears in Bowers, *Scriabin*, pp. 131–35.

[25] The best try so far has been Lawrence Kramer's in *Music and Poetry: The Nineteenth Century and After* (Berkeley and Los Angeles: University of California Press, 1984), the first and concluding chapters of which outline a theory of what Kramer calls "structural rhythm," by which he identifies temporal unfolding as the essential shared property "through which we constitute the expressive process that our concrete reading or listening experience acts out," and, therefore, as

And yet perhaps the relationship between music and poetry is not quite the issue. Perhaps that intractable, distracting question may be finessed, and a more direct path sought to an integrated perspective on Scriabin, one that will at last put together the fragmentary insights that the musical analysts and the cultural historians have severally vouchsafed. Schloezer's writings on the composer, and, even more, a trio of incandescent essays by Vyacheslav Ivanov that have only just come belatedly to light, offer the best clues to how such an integration might be accomplished.[26]

What they suggest, in necessary conjunction with the musical-technical observations that Dernova, Kelkel, Reise, and Baker have more recently contributed, are answers to such basic questions as what motivated Scriabin's stylistic development and guided it along the specific path it took; what meanings Scriabin's compositions embody (and how, specifically, they are embodied); and why it is important, after all, that Scriabin was a Russian composer.

The rest of this chapter is a first attempt, an *Acte préalable*, toward constructing that integrated perspective. Proceeding from a striking formulation by Ivanov—whom I have come to trust as an interpreter of Scriabin (if not, as once assumed, an "influence" on him)—and relying in part on some of the recent analytical disclosures, the argument will pursue the ramifications of Ivanov's rather abstract conceptual thought into the world of concrete musical particulars where Scriabin lived his creative life, but where Ivanov never trod. So as to maintain an interdisciplinary reach, limits will be set on the use of technical language; but so as not to sacrifice the desired specificity of musical reference, discussion will have to begin at a very basic level.[27]

---

the "level . . . that under certain conditions can form the basis for the tandem interpretation of a poem and a composition" (p. 9). Kramer's musical and poetic interpretations, however, strike me as being not so much tandem as parallel. They do not really rely upon or complete one another; at best they are demonstrations, by no means unprecedented, of how poets and composers can obtain comparable effects. I also wish Kramer had not given in to old-fashioned new-critical squeamishness about representation, retreating from that academically disreputable ("merely subjective") and suspiciously "surface" terrain into the more hidden, "deeper," professionally sanctified, putatively objective and verifiable (but, I persist in thinking, metaphorical and self-constituting) domain of "structure." My discussion will focus unabashed (except to the extent that this footnote evinces abashment) on simpler dimensions of meaning that academic critics have tended to snub.

[26] They are: "Natsional'noye i vselenskoye v tvorchestve Skryabina" (The National and the Universal in Scriabin, 1916), "Vzglyad Skryabina na iskusstvo" (Scriabin's View of Art, 1915), and "Skryabin" (1919), all published with an introduction and commentary by I. A. Mïl'nikova in *Pamyatniki kul'turï: Novïye otkrïtiya* (Yearbook of the Scientific Council of the History of World Culture, Academy of Sciences of the USSR), 1983 (Leningrad: Nauka, 1985), pp. 88–119.

[27] For a fuller technical discussion of the analytical issues, and a preliminary outline of the new perspective (made without benefit of Ivanov), see my review of the books by Baker and Schloezer to which reference has been made in preceding footnotes, in *Music Theory Spectrum* 10 (1988): 143–69.

CONSTRUCTING THE DESIRING SUBJECT

On 25 February 1919, Vyacheslav Ivanov made a short speech to introduce a Scriabin recital by the great pianist and teacher Alexander Goldenveyzer (1875–1961). Taking as his point of departure the dicta, redolent of the religious philosopher Vladimir Solovyov's precepts, that "communality [*sobornost'*] must be realized in art, and the artwork must become a life experience [*sobïtiye zhizni*; cf. the German *Erlebnis*]," and correlating them implicitly with the recent political revolution, he proclaimed that "Scriabin has expressed in music the most profound idea of the present day," which he then promised to define. Practically the whole speech thereafter is devoted to a divagation of a familiar kind on the virtual impossibility of putting a musical message into words; but, just as one is about to give up hope, Ivanov suddenly squeezes the promised definition out in blindingly succinct form. Here it is:

> The content of Scriabin's work may be defined, it seems to me, as a threefold idea, a threefold emotion, a threefold vision:
> 1) The vision of surmounting the boundaries of the personal, individual, petty "I"—a musical transcendentalism.
> 2) The vision of universal, communal mingling of all humanity in a single "I"—or the macrocosmic universalism of musical consciousness.
> 3) The vision of a violent breakthrough into the expanse of a free new plane of being—universal transformation.[28]

The first of these propositions is the one that is probably most difficult to conceive on the simple gestural level, but it is also the one for which we have the firmest corroboration from the composer, who once remarked to his disciple Sabaneyeff that in his late sonatas he had at last managed to transcend the realm of human emotion.[29] It is on the transcendence of the petty "I" (the *malïy 'ya'*) that most of the musical observations that follow will be predicated, rather than on notions of macrocosmic commingling (easily understood, at least preliminarily, in terms of the wordless chorus in *Prometheus* or the plan for the *Misteriya*, in which there were to be no spectators, only participants), or transformatory breakthroughs (for a preliminary idea of that, just listen to the end of *Poème de l'extase* or, a bit less straightforwardly, that of *Prometheus*). Examples will be drawn mainly from Scriabin's symphonies, presumably his best-known works, and the sketches for the *Acte préalable*.

For a fully adequate demonstration, a line of critical investigation such as I wish to initiate with the present discussion would have to begin with the exposition of the most elementary musical and aesthetic premises. To save a bit of time, let us begin instead with Wagner. It was their common response to Wagner, together with Schopenhauer and Nietzsche (usually supplemented if

---

[28] *Pamyatniki kul'turï* 1983, p. 115.
[29] Quoted in Bowers, *Scriabin*, vol. 2, p. 231.

not replaced altogether by trots and by oral dissemination),[30] that underlay the spiritual and aesthetic kinship between Scriabin and the theurgic symbolists. But what was a common, eventually commonplace response among Russian thinkers and poets was a very rare response among Russian musicians, and this is what so distinguished Scriabin as a composer. What distinguished him as a Russian Wagnerian, of course, was that he could inherit from Wagner not only a philosophical attitude but also a musical technique. And, finally, what distinguished Scriabin from Wagner himself was his instrumental orientation, stemming from his activity as a piano virtuoso.

Yet he did not write conventional program music; possibly excepting the Third Symphony, known as the "Divine Poem," his music rarely embodied a parallel verbal scenario or a paraphrasable narrative content. As time went on he increasingly shunned such adulteration, eventually protecting his art from debasing paraphrase, as we have seen, by actively suppressing the verbal analogue to his own "Poem of Ecstasy." In this he remained true to the older, original concept of "absolute music," which, far from implying formalism, envisioned an instrumental music capable of directly incorporating and transmitting all the ineffable—which is to say, nonparaphrasable—expressive and metaphysical content at which the nature-imitating arts could only hint.

This immanent, inchoate expressivity was multifariously embodied and transmitted, and, it goes without saying, an expressive critique of music must be correspondingly multivalent. But we shall focus this discussion on what most nineteenth-century artists considered the chief means of its realization: harmony, or, more precisely, fluctuations in harmonic tension. Tension, to define it tautologically, is that which demands resolution. There are two main criteria by which tension achieves resolution in the musical tradition Scriabin inherited. One, which we may call the contrapuntal criterion, and which has a thousand-year history in Western musical practice, involves the resolution of dissonance into consonance (example 12.1).

The other, which we may call the functional criterion, and which has a

EXAMPLE 12.1. The contrapuntal criterion

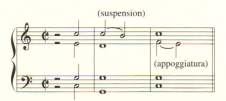

(suspension)

(appoggiatura)

[30] In the case of Wagner the chief trots were Edouard Schuré, *Le Drame musicale* (Paris, 1876; reprinted in 1886), and Henri Lichtenberger, *Richard Wagner: Poète et penseur* (Paris, 1898), which was partially serialized (as "Vzglyadï Vagnera na iskusstvo") in Diaghilev's magazine *Mir iskusstvo* in 1899.

much shorter history (becoming fully elaborated only in the seventeenth or eighteenth century, depending on one's criterion of fullness), involves syntactical relationships among the degrees of (what we call) the diatonic scale. To account for these relationships theoretically is a complicated task, though any explanation of functional differentiation would have to emphasize the fact that the diatonic scale is structurally asymmetrical. To illustrate the criterion, however, is simple, for to the extent that we have learned by exposure to identify scale degrees (even if we have not been taught to name them), we all respond to music in accordance with the functional criterion. The two criteria, contrapuntal and functional, though synergistic and almost never unmixed in practice, are nonetheless conceptually independent, as one may illustrate by demonstrating the functional criterion without using any dissonances (example 12.2).

Another name for the functional criterion is "tonality." Music is tonal if we are able to identify the notes we hear as degrees, and if the degrees are syntactically related according to certain model progressions. The two most important syntactical relations are those involving scalar half steps, known as leading tones, and those involving the basses of close-spaced chords, known as roots. We expect the half steps to sound as direct successions, and we expect the chord roots to follow in a sequence known as the circle of fifths. (Both criteria were met in example 12.2, which is why the final resolution was so ineluctably anticipated.) Any deviation from this model is interpreted as a deviation from a norm, which creates tension. And tension, to repeat, demands eventual resolution.

By the nineteenth century, composers knew and frequently employed elaborate strategies for delaying resolution and, concomitantly, increasing tension. That is one of the things that makes music sound "expressive." These strategies often involved the inflection, rather than the direct progression, of scale degrees. This technique is called "chromaticism," from the Greek for color, which suggests analogy between a spectrum of minutely altered harmonies and the spectrum of visible shades. There is also the transformation of degrees, which implies a change in the background scale according to which

EXAMPLE 12.2. The functional criterion

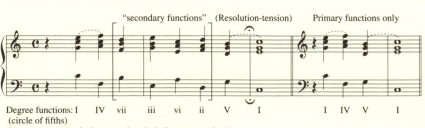

Degree functions: I   IV   vii   iii   vi   ii   V   I   I   IV   V   I
(circle of fifths)
[uppercase numerals denote major triads, lowercase minor]

they are identified. This technique is called "modulation" and produces a widened range of navigational possibilities among chords and functions. (The "navigation" metaphor is prompted by Wagner, who likened his range of potential functional relationships to a "sea of harmony.")

When dissonance is added to harmony, it enhances the tendency toward resolution, illustrating the synergy between the contrapuntal and functional criteria of harmonic tension. A chord like the one shown in example 12.3, which implies—and thus demands—a specific resolution to a preenvisioned point of repose, exemplifies what is known as the dominant function. At a minimum, it consists of three tones: a root, which must eventually progress along the circle of fifths to what is called the tonic; a leading tone, which must progress through a half step to the same tonic; and a tone that is dissonant both with respect to the root (from which it lies seven scale-steps apart) and with respect to the leading tone (from which it differs by the interval known as the tritone), which produces the tension in need of immediate resolution. (An additional tone may be added to "complete" the so-called dominant seventh chord without altering its quality either as to dissonance or as to function (example 12.4). The contrapuntal criterion creates the need to resolve; the functional criterion specifies the resolution that will satisfy the need.

We have gone back to basics after all, but only to the extent needed in order to understand Wagnerian and Scriabinesque harmony as expressive media. Such harmony arises in, embellishes, and prolongs the tense dominant function. Both Wagner's harmonic innovations and Scriabin's were specifically geared toward producing more elaborate embellishments and more extensive prolongations of that function (or, to put it another way, more elaborate and extended ways of delaying resolution), relying on the learned behavior of listeners to identify with the harmonic tension thus increased and thus to expe-

EXAMPLE 12.3. Minimal dominant seventh

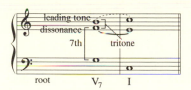

EXAMPLE 12.4. "Complete" dominant seventh

rience it as intensified affect, or emotion. As there are any number of ways in which a resourceful composer can embellish and prolong harmonic functions, so there is an endless range of potential emotional interpretations of these devices, all falling under the general rubric of tension and resolution. The greater the accrued tension, the greater the emotional release or payoff on resolution.

The locus classicus, of course, is the prelude to *Tristan und Isolde*—the prelude, not the opera, for as an instrumental piece the prelude qualifies as absolute music, in which the expressive and metaphysical content is immanent, not applied. Of course the title prejudices our reception, and I doubt whether there are many guinea pigs available, among those following this discussion, who have never heard the opera. But I believe it may be shown nevertheless that (given the conventions of composing and listening on which both the composer and his intended audience relied, and on which we rely to this day for interpreting tonal music) the expressive content is indeed immanent, not applied.

The opening of the prelude will also illustrate two points of great importance for understanding Scriabin's creative evolution. The first is that individual chords increasingly came to be regarded in nineteenth-century harmonic practice as objects, compositional premises in their own right; and second, that this became possible because, owing to the vastly enhanced range of chromatic inflection and tonal modulation that Wagnerian practice admitted, the functional interpretation of harmony became increasingly contextual—or, in other words, that harmonic tensions became subject to an increasingly wide range of potential resolutions.

The tendency of chords to become objectified entities is best illustrated by the propensity of individual chords, in the late nineteenth and early twentieth centuries, to acquire nicknames by which musicians, and not only musicians, informally refer to them. And the first such chord, as everybody knows, was the one given in example 12.5, from the second measure of the prelude to *Tristan and Isolde*. It has become something of a sport among musicologists to sight the "Tristan chord" in music by earlier composers, all the way back, if I am not forgetting anybody earlier, to the German opera composer Reinhard Keiser, an older contemporary of Handel. It is a mug's game, because the chord, while dissonant, has a place in perfectly ordinary diatonic usage (example 12.6).

EXAMPLE 12.5. Tristan chord

EXAMPLE 12.6. Diatonic occurrence of its enharmonic equivalent

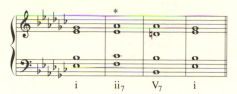

$$i \qquad ii_7 \qquad V_7 \qquad i$$

In this progression the Tristan chord deserves no special nickname—in fact it is not even the Tristan chord. Its context, and especially the nature of its resolution, are what create its special quality (example 12.7). What makes the chord startling (and name-worthy) in Wagner's usage is the fact that its constituent pitches cannot all be referred to the scale implied by its three-note introduction: in other words, some degree has been inflected (making the chord "chromatic"); or in still other words, not all the notes in the chord can be identified as degrees, which makes the chord tonally ambiguous. Vast rivers of ink have been spilled in debating its tonal status. The most economical explanation is one that identifies its "alto" pitch as inflected; when that pitch is "corrected" to a diatonic degree, the chord becomes a so-called diminished seventh on the leading tone of the background scale invoked at the outset—a chord that, by dint of an ordinary diatonic progression, may be further "corrected" to an ordinary dominant seventh (example 12.8).[31]

EXAMPLE 12.7. Prelude to *Tristan und Isolde*

Langsam und schmachtend (slow and languid)

EXAMPLE 12.8. "Normalization" of the Tristan chord

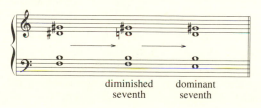

diminished   dominant
seventh   seventh

[31] The locus classicus for this economical functional interpretation of the Tristan chord is William J. Mitchell, "The Tristan Prelude: Techniques and Structure," *Music Forum* 1 (1967): 162–203.

EXAMPLE 12.9. First resolution of
the Tristan chord (cf. example 12.7,
end of m. 2)

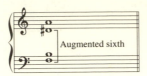

That explanation has become popular, but in my opinion it is inadequate. It is not (or not just) that the interpretation is too "normalizing," but that by identifying the chord with the harmony to which in context it appears to resolve, it denies the listener's perceptual experience (an experience on which, as I am arguing, the music's celebrated conceptual significance depends). Better take things, at first, as they are presented. The first note to move away from the enigmatic harmony is the top note, the behavior of which mimics that of the unaccompanied note on the downbeat of the previous measure, which moves by half step from a less stable putative degree (the sixth) to a more stable one (the fifth). If the soprano motion away from the Tristan chord is interpreted as a leading tone resolution, then we are left with a chord that is still dissonant but unambiguously functional.

The remaining dissonance is called an augmented sixth (example 12.9). (Chords containing augmented sixths for some forgotten historical reason sport pseudonational denominations in conventional theory parlance. The one created by the first resolution of the Tristan chord happens to be called the French sixth.) Being the product of a resolution, it is palpably less tense than the Tristan chord itself, though it is still a long way from repose. But to say that it is unambiguously functional is to say—recalling the definition of the functional criterion—that its regular resolution is foreseen. That resolution is to the dominant function—still one step from repose (example 12.10). And the way Wagner actually directs that resolution confirms our analysis of the first resolution, for it proceeds through a chromatically inflected dissonant note on the downbeat that resolves, like the one creating the French sixth, only after the rest of the chord is struck (example 12.11).

The beauty of harmonic functions is that, with training, we can learn precisely to measure the distance of functional chords from the tonic; and even without training, we may perceive and respond to that changing distance in vaguer relative terms—which is precisely what is meant by attending to the myriad fluctuations in harmonic tension that enable music to evoke for us the "thousands of particular shades" of emotion to which Vyacheslav Ivanov referred, our response to them being the mechanism through which the music becomes the "pilot of our spiritual depths." We may roughly discriminate four

EXAMPLE 12.10. Conventional
resolution of the French sixth

→ V

EXAMPLE 12.11. Parallelism
in "Tristan" progression

→ V₇

levels of tension in the opening phrase of the prelude to *Tristan und Isolde*: the
dissonant, chromatic, functionally ambiguous Tristan chord, impinging in
startling fashion on its preparation, represents the maximum; its first resolution, to a French sixth, produces a chord that is still chromatic, still dissonant,
but no longer functionally ambiguous—and therefore one degree less tense,
as we may put it for the sake of argument; the next resolution produces a
"complete" dominant seventh chord—still dissonant but neither chromatic
nor ambiguous, hence less tense by another noticeable degree; the implied
resolution of that chord will produce ultimate repose. And since we know
what it will be (we all hear it in our mind's ear, but it is given anyhow in
example 12.12), Wagner in fact leaves it for our inner ear to supply, so that
the actual sounding music retains a restless harmonic tension at all times,
virtually until the end of the opera, when all the accumulated pressure is at last
discharged in Isolde's cataclysmic *Verklärung* ("Transfiguration"), popularly
known as the *Liebestod*, the death-by-love or, in plainer language, the
orgasm.[32]

[32] The reading presented here of the Tristan chord as an embellished augmented sixth harmony
moving through a "Phrygian progression" to the dominant is roughly congruent with that proposed by Donald Francis Tovey in the eleventh edition of the Encyclopaedia Britannica (1911)
and adopted subsequently by many other analysts in the Anglo-American tradition (see, inter alia,
Walter Piston, *Harmony* [New York: Norton, 1941], p. 279). For an absorbing survey of analyses
of the opening of the Tristan prelude (including several nonfunctional or "post-tonal" views, and
even some that try to accommodate the passage to the key of E♭ minor, where, as shown in
example 12.6, the "Tristan chord" has a diatonic function) see Jean-Jacques Nattiez, *Music and
Discourse: Toward a Semiology of Music*, trans. Carolyn Abbate (Princeton: Princeton University Press, 1990), pp. 222–33. A less formal comparison of viewpoints can be found in Milton
Babbitt, *Words about Music* (Madison: University of Wisconsin Press, 1987), pp. 146–58. The

EXAMPLE 12.12. Implied resolution of "Tristan" progression

French sixth   V   [I]

In this way Wagner was able to transmit through the sound of the music the underlying idea that motivated the action of the opera. As he put it himself in a famous program note, it is this: "yearning, yearning, unquenchable, ever-regenerated longing—languishing, thirsting; the only redemption—death, extinction, eternal sleep!"[33] Notice how Wagner's redundant use of synonyms aspires to the effects of his musical nuances; but whereas we cannot measure and therefore cannot experience the exact difference between yearning and longing, we can measure and experience the difference between a Tristan chord and a French sixth, and between a French sixth and a diminished or a dominant seventh. That is the advantage in precision that Ivanov sensed in music, and envied.

As a child of my time, I have proposed a behavioral model for the workings of musical expression; as a child of his, Wagner believed with Schopenhauer that the palpable and measurable nuances of music were the ultimate, autochthonous reality of feeling, realer than the world of appearances. We may now be inclined to view musical events as metaphors for emotional ones, but for Wagner it was just the opposite: not only the action of his operas but the emotions portrayed or conveyed therein were the metaphors in his view, the music the palpable reality. Tristan's desire for Isolde and hers for him symbolized and gave a phenomenal context for the desire of the dominant for the tonic, not the other way around. (Hence from now on, in keeping with this extreme musical idealism, I shall describe musical phenomena not in terms of the listener's reaction to them but in terms of the tendencies and propensities—i.e., the "wishes" or the "will"—of the tones themselves.) Wagner's own definition of his music dramas was "deeds of music which have been made visible." To penetrate, as we have attempted here, from the visible dramatic surface to a contemplation of the hidden musical depths was literally—shifting now into Vyacheslav Ivanov's terms—to proceed *a real-*

---

objective in both these discussions is meta-analytic: they aim not to adjudicate the analytical questions at issue but to explore (and in the case of Nattiez to assess as musical representations) a wide range of analytical discourse.

[33] Richard Wagner, *Nachgelassene Schriften und Dichtungen* (Leipzig, 1885), trans. Piero Weiss, in Piero Weiss and Richard Taruskin, *Music in the Western World: A History in Documents* (New York: Schirmer Books, 1984), p. 377.

ibus ad realiora, "from the real to the more real."[34] It was left to Scriabin to strip away the vestiges of *realia*—and also to strip away the egoistic tyranny of desire, what Ivanov called the extinguishing of the *malïy 'ya,'* the "little 'I.'"

EXTINGUISHING THE DESIRING SUBJECT

We have made a closer examination of the Tristan prelude than we shall have the time to make of any one Scriabin composition. But now we have a model— Scriabin's own model—by which to measure his achievement, and a vocabulary with which to describe it. From his practice we may discern his concept of what it was that made the Wagnerian harmonic mechanism tick, and how it could be adapted to serve changing expressive or representational purposes.

From the beginning there were differences as well as affinities. What is a true but not necessarily a pertinent observation about the Tristan progression from the Wagnerian standpoint becomes absolutely essential from Scriabin's: all the chords that have figured in our discussion of it—the Tristan chord itself, the dominant seventh, the diminished seventh, and the French sixth— contain at least one tritone. That interval, which eventually became the prime or even sole active ingredient in Scriabinesque harmony, fascinated Scriabin by virtue of its functional ambiguity. In common practice the tritone is considered dissonant, but unlike the other dissonances it has not a single common-practice resolution but a dual one: its two tones resolve like leading tones in contrary motion, either by moving inward to a major third or outward to a minor sixth (example 12.13). This ambivalence arises from the fact that the tritone exactly bisects the octave and consequently shares two properties with the octave itself. First, it is inherently symmetrical, which means it cannot be "inverted"; when mirrored (i.e., turned upside-down) it simply replicates itself. And second, when transposed by its own intervallic distance it again replicates itself (example 12.14). These two properties, which in the case of the tritone or octave are really two ways of describing the same phenomenon, are now often called inversional and transpositional *invariance*, and harmonic invariance is the key to Scriabin's special musical universe.

Its inversional and transpositional invariance is what makes the tritone such a curiously passive interval. The way in which it will seek its resolution depends on external stimuli—that is, the notes that accompany it. We have already seen that it is a part of the minimally expressed dominant function: a defining root, and a tritone consisting of the leading tone and a tone creating a dissonant seventh against the root. The leading tone will seek its resolution by ascent, the seventh by descent. Yet because of the tritone's symmetrical properties, by changing the defining root we can cause an exchange of the two

[34] For glosses on Ivanov's term see B. G. Rosenthal, "The Transmutation of the Symbolist Ethos: Mystical Anarchism and the Revolution of 1905," *Slavic Review* 36 (1977): 616; also Andrey Belïy, "Realiora," *Vesï* 5, no. 5 (May 1908): 59–62.

EXAMPLE 12.13. Resolutions of tritone/diminished fifth

EXAMPLE 12.14. Inversional and transpositional invariance of tritone

functions; what had been the leading tone tending upward will become the seventh tending downward, and vice versa (example 12.15).

It will take no more than a moment's thought to realize that the two roots that accomplish this transformation must themselves lie a tritone apart. The direct progression formed by these two chords—chords sharing a tritone in common, their roots lying a tritone apart—has been recognized, beginning with the Soviet theorist Varvara Dernova, who christened it the tritone link (*tritonovoye zveno*), as the essential Scriabin progression (example 12.16). Notice that the resolution tendencies in the harmonic tritone are continually contradicted and recontradicted by the bass progression. This easy reciprocity of function attenuates the harmony's "functionality," turning it qualitatively from an active tendency into a latent or passive one. Although there is continual root activity, there is no functional progression.

We seem to examine or experience a single "floating" harmony (as Schoenberg might have said) from a dual perspective, something the Russian theorist Boleslav Yavorsky analogized to moving from two-dimensional to three-dimensional musical space—which in turn is something Scriabin himself adumbrated in a remark reported to Dernova by the composer Georgiy Mikhailovich Rimsky-Korsakov (grandson of the famous composer): "You have to be able to walk around a chord" (*nado, chtobï akkord mozhno bïlo oboyti krugom*).[35]

Until one of the root notes leaves the tritone treadmill and proceeds along the circle of fifths (or, in a pinch, by a semitone), the eventual destination of the tritone is in doubt, and one can even forget that the tritone *has* a destination. A quality of hovering, of time-forgetful stasis, altered consciousness, or

---

[35] Dernova, "Garmoniya Skryabina," p. 352.

EXAMPLE 12.15. Alternative cadential harmonizations of tritone

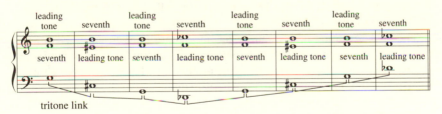

trance, can be induced. At a minimum, suspended harmonic animation of this kind is one extremely potent means of prolonging and embellishing the dominant function. It is a more radical means than Wagner ever resorted to, or needed—and a more subversive one, for it contains the seeds of the eventual neutralization of that function, indeed of "function" itself, and its veritable extinguishing.

To illustrate all these points, we may examine the motto beginning of Scriabin's Symphony no. 3, the "Divine Poem" (example 12.17). It seems to have gone unremarked until now that, despite the vastly differing affect, this passage seems to have been modeled quite directly on the opening of the *Tristan* prelude. In both cases an unaccompanied preparatory melody lasting one measure leads into a startlingly dissonant chromatic chord containing a tritone, urgently demanding an unspecified resolution. Scriabin's chord is the more radical of the two, since it is an ad hoc harmonic structure with no common-practice standing at all. Where Wagner's chord could be described

EXAMPLE 12.16. Scriabin's "tritone link"

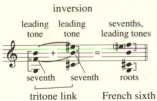

EXAMPLE 12.17. Scriabin, *Divine Poem*, first movement, mm. 1–4 (figuration and arpeggiation omitted in mm. 3–4)

taxonomically as a half-diminished seventh chord, or functionally as a "French" augmented sixth with one of its intervals unconventionally altered by contraction, adding to its dissonance and intensifying the affect of egoistic desire, Scriabin's chord may be viewed as a "German" augmented sixth (homologous to the dominant seventh) with one of its intervals unconventionally altered by expansion, adding to its dissonance and intensifying the affect of egoistic self-assertion (example 12.18).

The most striking parallel between the two openings is the specific way in which the first chord is prepared. Wagner leaps up from the tonic note to the sixth degree, which in the minor mode is a half step above the fifth, passes through the fifth to a complementary half step below—that is, to the chromatically inflected fourth degree, the "altered" note that gives the Tristan chord its name-worthy color. Scriabin's opening exactly inverts Wagner's procedure, in a fashion (one can't help speculating) prompted by the magniloquent exordium to Chopin's B♭-minor sonata (example 12.19). The melody leaps down to the chromatically inflected fourth degree, proceeds through the fifth to a complementary half step above—that is, to the sixth degree, which, the mode being major, must also be chromatically inflected to preserve the half-step relationship.

The first resolution of Scriabin's "ad hoc" chord is to an unsullied consonant triad (the trumpet, meanwhile, performing a characteristic Scriabinesque *zov* or "summons" motif), enhancing the promise of what the symphony's program note calls "joyous and intoxicated affirmation," to be wholly attained only

EXAMPLE 12.18. The "Scriabin sixth" and its common-practice source

EXAMPLE 12.19. Chopin, Sonata Op. 35, opening

in the last movement, when the Nietzschean hero—the trumpet—at last comes fully into his, or its, own. Before citing the music, I quote once more from the program, which though actually penned by Boris de Schloezer's sister, Tatyana, Scriabin's mistress (much as Liszt's writings, including programs, were often the work of Liszt's mistress, the Princess Sayn-Wittgenstein), transmits the composer's intentions well enough to have had his endorsement: "The free, powerful man-god," the program relates, "appears to triumph; but it is only the intellect which affirms the divine Ego, while the individual will, still too weak, is tempted to sink into Pantheism."

And now the music. Just as in the Tristan prelude, the first phrase is seconded by a sequential repetition. But unlike the second phrase of the Tristan prelude, the repetition is no mere intensifying iteration. It terminates not in another affirmative cadence, as it might well have done, but dissolves in a tritone link that palpably weakens its thrust (example 12.20). It is followed, in all-too-craftsmanly a fashion, by a second tritone link calculated to prepare the main key of the first movement, thus to launch a conventional sonata form that is interrupted, in a manner reminiscent of Franck's Symphony in D minor, by periodic recollections of the opening motto. These reminiscences must surely have been written, or at least improvised, before the actual opening passage, for they demonstrate the genesis of the ad hoc chord—a chord that the composer continued to exploit to the point of mannerism, and that has earned the sobriquet "Scriabin sixth."[36]

The first reminiscence takes place in E♭ major, the classically mandated key of the second theme in a C-minor sonata movement. The local tonic is held out in the treble instruments while the bass instruments proclaim the motto in the new key. At the moment when the theme reaches the fifth note, the inflected lower neighbor tone or appoggiatura to the fifth degree, the trumpet-hero joins in to sound the complementary inflection above. The two voices, trumpet and bass, proceed in contrary motion through the fifth and on to the opposite or reciprocal inflection, thus producing the "Scriabin sixth" (example 12.21). It is a symmetrical, simultaneous exchange of functions

---

[36] Macdonald, *Skryabin*, p. 37.

EXAMPLE 12.20. Scriabin, *Divine Poem*, first movement, from m. 5 (figuration and arpeggiation omitted as in example 12.17)

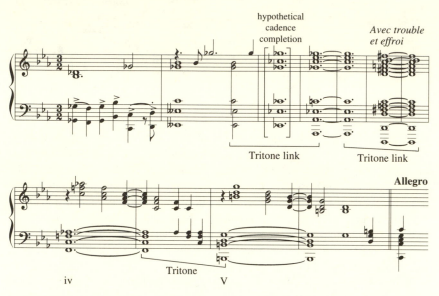

(known technically as a *chiasmus*, from the Greek for cross), comparable to that involving the two tendency tones over the tritone link. It gave Scriabin a big idea, for in the music following the "Divine Poem," simultaneously sounding (rather than successive or progressive) symmetrical relations become the primary means for embellishing or prolonging the dominant function.

The obvious next step was simply to combine the two members of the tritone link into an aggregate, producing nothing else but a French sixth, one of only two chords in common practice (the other being the diminished-seventh chord) to contain two tritones, the one corresponding to the sustained tendency tones in the tritone link, the other to the complementary roots.

EXAMPLE 12.21. Scriabin, *Divine Poem*, first movement, figure 11

Chords consisting of two tritones have exactly the same invariance properties as a single tritone, but twice as many of them (that is, they are inversionally invariant on two axes and transpositionally invariant at two intervals), and hence could further enhance Scriabin's developing methods of dominant embellishment and prolongation. Of the two possible chords, only the French sixth suited his present purpose, not only because of its Wagnerian associations but because it was generically related to the "Scriabin sixth," and could even be combined with it. The two chords had three tones out of four in common. Put together, their total of five tones would immediately have suggested to Scriabin, heir to a special Russian tradition of "fantastic" harmony, that with the addition of a single remaining tone he would have a chord that expressed the dominant function by encompassing all the members of what was known in Russia (where it had a history extending all the way back to Glinka) as the "scale by whole tones" (*gamma tselïmi tonami*) (example 12.22).

This was a momentous discovery. The whole-tone aggregate contained three tritones, thus absolutely maximizing the potential for harmonic (that is, inversional and transpositional) invariance. Simply put, every possible position of the chord was intervallically, hence functionally, identical to every other one. No matter which of its members was in the bass, no matter by which of its constituent intervals it was transposed, the pitch and interval content of the chord never varied. It was a chord, in other words, that could be endlessly "walked around," that could be mined for a great variety of symmetrical constituents (the tritone itself, the augmented triad, the French sixth, the "incomplete" dominant ninth, plus a number of ad hoc unclassified combinations), that offered a veritable infinity of possibilities for motion without functional harmonic progression or resolution, but that could be resolved at will to a functional tonic merely by allowing any of its constituent tones to proceed by half step (i.e., as a leading tone) or by fifth (i.e., as a root). And all these

EXAMPLE 12.22. Accumulation of whole-tone scale with dominant function

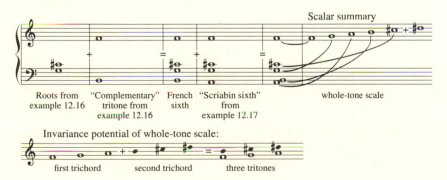

possibilities are in effect doubled by the fact that there are two whole-tone scales—that is, two complementary samplings of the twelve pitches of the chromatic scale, one corresponding to the even-numbered tones counted from any given starting point ("zero pitch"), the other to the odd—between which progressions could freely take place without resolving tension.

In giving this description of the potential behavior of the six-tone extended dominant chord—that is, its invariance and resolution properties—I have in fact given a description of the actual behavior of the *Poème de l'extase* (Symphony no. 4), Op. 54, Scriabin's most famous composition. It is very much a sequel to the "Divine Poem," again casting the solo trumpet as Nietzschean protagonist to the point where symphony becomes a virtual concerto, requiring a credit to the performer. Its Tristanesque affinities are too conspicuous to be missed. There are, to be sure, a few actual quotations from the prelude to Wagner's opera of a kind that surfaced like a reflex in the output of many composers of mystical-erotic bent (cf. just about any work by César Franck). But the main affinity is all-encompassing: like Wagner's opera, Scriabin's symphony consists in most general terms of a single fundamental gesture, an agonizingly prolonged structural anacrusis that at the very last moment achieves cataclysmic resolution/consummation. That consummatory gesture is the ultimate reality, the noumenon, for which sexual union, the creative act, the birth of the world—that is to say, the imagery of Scriabin's superseded verbal composition of the same name—had been the conceptual or phenomenal metaphors.

The music is thus laden with a profusion of apparently contradictory meanings (triumph and annihilation; procreation and cosmic parthenogenesis; birth and death), meanings that can be best clarified from the perspective of Ivanov's "threefold vision," which encompasses both the transcendence of the individual person and the breakthrough to a new plane of being. The extinction or dissolution of the individual ego—the *malïy "ya"*—is ideally adumbrated in the six-tone dominant chord, for its component tones actually constitute a symmetrical scale whose intervals are all equal and whose degrees, therefore, are all equidistant, structurally undifferentiated, and hence not subject to functional classification. As we have seen, it is on the possibility of scale-degree identification that fully conscious identification of the ego with harmonic fluctuations, and their translation into emotional response, depends.

The functional relationships in the *Poème de l'extase* are thus reduced to a single essential dualism: an almost infinitely extended, graded, and variegated dominant that in its ceaseless flux and nuance is almost palpably sensuous, and a crushingly asserted tonic, tantalizingly glimpsed and tasted in advance, but for the most part withheld. Indeed the dualism is more than just a harmonic functional relationship; it is the interaction between two planes of consciousness. The one, represented by the whole-tone scale, begins inchoate, undifferentiated, selfless, but—as the trumpet's increasing prominence and the ever longer and more insistent dominant pedals announce—coalesces and concentrates itself into an overwhelming manifestation of desire; the other, represented by the diatonic scale, suggests Ivanov's breakthrough to universal consciousness. Since we are constantly reminded that the whole-tone, functionally undifferentiated harmonies are in fact elaborations and prolongations of a single primal function—the dominant function, the most directed harmonic tension of all—the reconstitution of the ego at the same time presages the transcendence of desire. The triumphant—even triumphalist—climax at the end of the symphony is in fact the dawn of satiety and quiescence, as Scriabin's later compositions will disclose.

But in this case a musical illustration will be worth at least ten thousand words. The opening of the *Poème de l'extase* (example 12.23) recapitulates some of the cadential gestures encountered at the beginning of the "Divine Poem." A series of unusual chromatic chords, each a subset of a whole-tone scale, are quietly resolved by semitone to the C-major triad, thus establishing C major as tonic, thereby foreshadowing and planting expectation of the ultimate breakthrough. Actually, only the first chord is unproblematically

EXAMPLE 12.23. Scriabin, *Poème de l'Extase*, Op. 54, abstract of beginning

resolved (mm. 1–6). Its four tones (five, counting the central pitch of the melodic motive, which comes from the same whole-tone collection) all move by contrary motion "inward," resolving by half step (i.e., as leading tones) to tones of the C-major chord, except for the note G, which is common to both chords and remains stationary. The whole gesture, exactly as in the "Divine Poem," is then repeated at the transposition of a perfect fourth higher, reinforcing the impression of resolution of dominant to tonic.

The whole-tone chord thus arrived at is drawn from the complementary whole-tone collection, but it is resolved to the same C-major harmony as before by a complementary "outward" contrary motion (with C now the stationary common tone), thus as it were announcing the functional equivalence of the two whole-tone collections (mm. 7–10). The C-major harmony now contains a dissonant seventh, however; tension is not fully discharged, and it will continue to accumulate until the final shattering gesture.

A third cadential approach now supervenes, its tension augmented by the full simultaneous presentation of the whole-tone collection in m. 12, to which notes from the complementary collection are then added, creating a real sense of clash. The first of these clashing tones is A (in the flute), immediately taken up by the trumpet, making its bow as protagonist. It is sustained through a crescendo, which is another way of reinforcing tension, while the bass instruments force the issue by sounding G, the traditional dominant of C major. Under this pressure, the notes of the one whole-tone scale give way to the other in a fashion that approximates a traditional dominant preparation (musicians will call it a II–V progression). At the height of the crescendo, the trumpet, after a pair of attention-grabbing leaps that amount to a *zov*, makes the final approach to the dominant, dramatically resolving E to D♯, which functions in context as the augmented fifth of a dominant ninth chord on G, another chord that consists of five of the six notes of a whole-tone scale. The pressure toward resolution has by now grown intolerable.

It is relieved, however, in only one voice, albeit the most important one. The bass resolves dominant (G) to tonic (C) along the circle of fifths, but the tones of the augmented dominant ninth (including G, which is picked up by the violas) remain suspended over the tonic. The trumpet's D♯, it is true, is silenced for a while but returns in the cellos at the downbeat of m. 22, having been introduced by a full whole-tone scale, sounded by the harp, glissando. The clarinet, at the same time, makes a dramatic leap to a high *A*, the ninth of the ninth chord. So we have, in effect, a mixed color—augmented dominant ninth over tonic pedal—arising out of a mixed function, one of those ineffably graded sensuous nuances for which the *Poème de l'extase* is so famous. The mixture produces a sense of disorientation in the listener, and will be exploited for that purpose throughout the composition, becoming one of its most characteristic harmonies. It could even be called the "*Extase* chord," as indeed Scriabin seems to have recognized when he used it, a short time later, to end a piano piece called "Désir" (Op. 57, no. 1) (example 12.24).

EXAMPLE 12.24. Scriabin, "Désir,"
Op. 57, no. 1, final chord

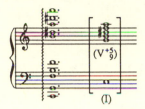

Let us take a walk around this chord. Like so many Scriabin harmonies, it contains a French sixth (the top four notes if the dominant ninth component of the chord is laid out in close spacing), which, as we know, is distinguished for its properties of invariance when inverted or transposed. Let us, then, invert the chord and transpose its members. The obvious axis for such an inversion is the top note, A, the note strategically spotlit by the clarinet leap. This is what happens when we perform the operation:

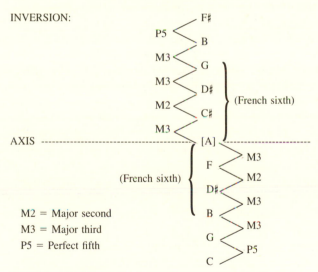

INVERSION:

M2 = Major second
M3 = Major third
P5 = Perfect fifth

TRANSPOSITION (bracketed notes transposed an octave):

		[B]	
F♯	=	F♯	
		[C♯]	
[B]			
G	=	G	
D♯	=	D♯	
[C♯]			
A	=	A	

EXAMPLE 12.25. Manipulations of *Extase* chord

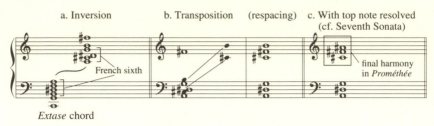

Scriabin never used the chord thus arrived at in the *Poème de l'extase*, but he must have performed the operations shown here at some point, for the chord formed by inverting the "*Extase* chord" is the most famous Scriabin chord of all, the one christened the "Chord of Prometheus" by Sabaneyeff in a famous article published in 1912 in Wassily Kandinsky's almanac *Der blaue Reiter* and known in the English-speaking world since at least 1916 as the "mystic chord."[37] The chord is traditionally represented in the Scriabin literature with C as its bass note, but the pitch level derived above is in fact the one with which *Prométhée* begins and on which it dwells for the whole of its thematic exposition (example 12.26). This coincidence enhances the likelihood that Scriabin derived the chord experimentally, as we have done, by taking a walk around the characteristic *extase* harmony. His surviving sketches—particularly those for the *Acte préalable*—do give concrete evidence of such procedures.

But while he must have found its color as strikingly evocative as we do, and therefore filed it away for future use, there could be no question of incorporating the new harmony into the *Poème de l'extase*, because it cannot interact structurally with diatonic tonality—even as a "mixed function"—and hence had nothing to contribute to that work's poetic design. It implies no resolution; it generates no harmonic tension. It can be endlessly walked around, but it implies no forward motion, creates no desire. Though mildly dissonant, it is wholly static and quiescent, and there can be no ego identification with it.

And precisely this is implied by the name Scriabin himself gave this most quintessentially Scriabinesque of harmonies. At an early rehearsal of *Prométhée*, Rachmaninoff, stunned at the sound of it, asked Scriabin, "What are

---

[37] Cf. L. Sabanejew, "'Prometheus' von Skrjabin," *Almanach der blaue Reiter*, ed. W. Kandinsky and F. Marc (Munich: Piper Verlag, 1912), which is a translation by Kandinsky (corrected at Kandinsky's request by Schoenberg) of Leonid Sabaneyev, "Prometey," *Muzïka*, no. 1 (Moscow, 1910); for the probable origin of the English byname see Arthur Eaglefield Hull, *Scriabin: A Great Russian Tone-Poet* (London: Kegan Paul, 1916; 2d ed., 1927), chapter 9, "The Mystic Chord," in which the name is attributed to "the composer's disciples," probably meaning Sabaneyev (2d ed., p. 106).

EXAMPLE 12.26. Scriabin, *Prométhée*, abstract of beginning (note transpositions by minor thirds [t3] and multiples)

you using here?" Scriabin answered, "The chord of the pleroma."[38] The pleroma, a Christian Gnostic term derived from the Greek for "plenitude," was the all-encompassing hierarchy of the divine realm, located entirely outside the physical universe, at immeasurable distance from man's terrestrial abode, totally alien and essentially "other" to the phenomenal world and whatever belongs to it.[39] What we know as the mystic chord, then, was de-

---

[38] This anecdote is related by Igor Boelza in "Filosofskiye istoki obraznogo stroya 'Prometeya,'" in *Razlichnïye aspektï tvorchestva A. N. Skryabina*, abstracts of papers read at a conference organized at the Scriabin museum, Moscow, 6–7 January 1992 (pp. 18–19). My thanks to John Bell Young for providing a copy.

[39] Scriabin would have encountered the term in Blavatsky's *Secret Doctrine*, where it is variously associated with such Promethean concepts as "Spiritual Fire" and "Astral Light," and with

signed to afford instant apprehension of—that is, to *reveal*—what was in essence beyond the mind of man to conceptualize. Its preternatural stillness was a gnostic intimation of a hidden otherness, a world and its fullness wholly above and beyond rational or emotional cognition.

But what produced this uncanny stasis? Though not so named by Scriabin, his "chord of the pleroma" was indeed a mystic chord; as to structure and expression alike it has long remained an enigma. Many ad hoc theoretical explanations of its structure have been proposed. Its note spelling (also, as here, very likely the fortuitous product of the walk-around) has given rise to the persistent notion that it is a construction of fourths, such as Schoenberg was experimenting with (and describing in his *Harmonielehre*) around the same time that Scriabin was at work on *Promethée*. But that is chimerical: two of the "fourths" in the Prometheus chord are augmented (i.e., tritones), another is diminished (hence, in the absence of functional degree identification, ineluctably a third in perceptual terms), and the chord's harmonic basis is clearly the French sixth formed by its four lowest members, the most basic Scriabin harmony of all. It has also been described (again by Sabaneyeff in the *Blaue Reiter* article) as originating in the higher partials of the harmonic series; but that curiously persistent notion merely begs the question, as any complex or dissonant harmony could be so described.

Adequate explanation of the chord's esoteric structure had to await the detection and theoretical investigation of the so-called octatonic scale, now recognized as a prime structural resource in late nineteenth- and early twentieth-century Russian music, first extensively employed by Rimsky-Korsakov and thereafter by his pupils, conspicuously including Stravinsky (example 12.27). It consists of alternating half steps and whole steps, for a total of eight tones to the octave, hence its English name;[40] in Russia it was known as the *gamma ton-poluton*, the "tone-semitone scale."[41] Scriabin almost certainly discovered it upon returning to Russia—and particularly to St. Petersburg, where the "Rimsky-Korsakov school" was flourishing—for the première of the *Poème de l'extase* in 1909, ending a long sojourn abroad, during which time he was quite out of touch with musical developments in his homeland. Upon discovering the scale—informally known as the "Rimsky-Korsakov scale" (*korsakovskaya gamma*) in St. Petersburg—Scriabin quickly realized its ideal suitability to his own poetic needs.

---

angelic androgyny. (See Helene Blavatsky, *The Secret Doctrine* [London: Theosophical Publishing Company, 1888], pp. 79, 196.) My thanks to Mitchell Morris for the references.

[40] It was christened by Arthur Berger in what has proved a seminal article, "Problems of Pitch Organization in Stravinsky," *Perspectives of New Music* 2, no. 1 (1963): 11–42; reprinted in B. Boretz and E. T. Cone, ed., *Perspectives on Schoenberg and Stravinsky* (Princeton: Princeton University Press, 1968), pp. 123–55.

[41] For the historical background see R. Taruskin, "Chernomor to Kashchei: Harmonic Sorcery; or, Stravinsky's 'Angle,'" *Journal of the American Musicological Society* 38 (1985): 72–142.

EXAMPLE 12.27. The three octatonic collections, represented as scales derived from intercalated minor-third cycles (diminished seventh chords), following Scriabin's favored orthography

What made it so was its tremendous invariance potential—a potential pretty much unplumbed by its earliest explorers, beginning with Liszt, but one that greatly enriched Scriabin's musical and poetic resources, making his art even more "suprapersonal and superreal"[42] than ever. Where the asymmetrical diatonic scale has one and the symmetrical whole-tone scale has three, the octatonic scale has four self-reversible tritones. The scale is not symmetrical but periodic; that is, it reproduces itself at every second degree. Like the whole-tone scale, the octatonic scale harbors two French sixths; and they do not overlap in pitch content, which means that the octatonic scale can afford an even greater sense of nonprogressive, "hovering" harmonic movement—movement-within-stasis—than the whole-tone. That special symmetrical harmony known as the French sixth, consisting in essence of a double tritone, continues as before to be Scriabin's prime avenue of commerce between scales. But now, in *Promethée*, commerce is between two static, nonprogressive pitch collections—the symmetrical whole-tone and the periodic octatonic. The diatonic scale, with its functionally differentiated degrees and its strong drive to resolution, has by now been virtually eliminated from the mix. It remains present at times behind the scenes, as it were, directing some vestigial local harmonic progressions along the old circle of fifths. But for the most part we are entirely in the world of *realiora*, represented by a unique musical idiom in which there is a strong sense of harmonic fluctuation and root movement—walking, indeed darting, around and between chords and scales—but in which any sense of harmonic direction and potential closure has been weakened to the point of virtual extinction. The chief harmonic sonority remains recognizably a modified dominant chord in intervallic structure, but there is virtually no dominant function to perform. Where there is no

[42] Cf. Igor Stravinsky and Robert Craft, *Expositions and Developments* (Garden City, N.Y.: Doubleday, 1962), p. 114.

dominant function, of course, there can be no complementary tonic function either. Hence the widespread notion that Scriabin's visionary late music is "atonal."

Yet Scriabin's actual practice explicitly contradicts such a notion. Our final technical observations will attempt to resolve the seeming paradox.

The "chord of the pleroma" contains six tones, of which four, as we know, form a modified dominant (French sixth) chord. Of the two remaining tones, one is referable along with the French sixth to the whole-tone scale, while the other may be referred, together with the same French sixth, to the octatonic scale. Hence the uncanny stasis of the chord, balanced as it is on a sort of cusp between two nonfunctional pitch collections. Because ego identification with musical process conventionally depends on functionally directed harmony, we are on the verge of not merely the intimation, or the representation, but the actual experience of ego transcendence. We are on the threshold of the sublime: a mode of feeling that can be said to have begun in music with the opening of Beethoven's Ninth Symphony, which famously caused Nietzsche to imagine himself "floating above the earth in an astral dome, with the dream of immortality in his heart."[43]

What holds us back is Scriabin himself, and what is holding Scriabin back is an evident lingering need to impose a sense of dynamic unfolding, of teleological form on the composition—perhaps, too, a wish to repeat the grandiose success of the *Poème de l'extase*, even though his evolving musical means and aesthetic aims had rendered such a rhetoric of hyperbole superfluous. The built-in dynamic of functional tonality having been transcended, harmonic tension can only be generated factitiously, contextually. In order, therefore, to give *Promethée* a shape comparable to that of the *Poème de l'extase*, the composer devises countless means both great and small to establish a sense of conflict between the whole-tone and tone-semitone scales, to situate the former as auxiliary to the latter, so to prepare and finally consummate a factitious resolution of the pleroma chord.

At the highest, most "structural" level, Scriabin fashions his modulatory scheme (more simply, his scheme of transpositions) in conformity with the invariance properties of the octatonic rather than the whole-tone scale. The first "moving" harmonization of the opening *zov* motif, with the chord roots transposed along a circle of minor thirds (= tone + semitone), is a case in point (example 12.28). (This is the transposition under which the octatonic scale, but not the whole-tone scale, is invariant.) Certain seemingly local devices, however, turn out to be far more telling on the long-range structure of the composition, for they show how the seemingly contradictory end of the piece is in fact implicit in the beginning.

---

[43] Friedrich Nietzsche, *Menschliches Allzumenschliche* (1878), quoted in Leo Treitler, "'To Worship That Celestial Sound,'" *Journal of Musicology* 1 (1982): 166.

EXAMPLE 12.28. Scriabin, *Prométhée*, m. 131 (arpeggiated figures reduced to block harmony)

There is no a priori reason to regard either of the non–French sixth tones of the pleroma chord—either the one exclusively referable to the whole-tone scale or the one exclusively referable to the octatonic scale—as less stable than the other. Neither, in this context, demands or presages any particular functional resolution. Yet either might be factitiously resolved by half step (i.e., leading tone) to achieve a chord wholly referable to the one scale or the other. If the F♯ were so resolved, either up to G or down to F, the chord would be an unalloyed whole-tone chord. The downward resolution would be presumably the resolution of choice, for it would lead to a full representation of the whole-tone scale; but the matter is moot, because no such resolution is ever made. Similarly, the B (top note as initially voiced) might be resolved either up to C or down to B♭/A♯ so as to achieve a fully (though not exhaustively) octatonic harmony. Again the downward resolution seems the preferable one, since the chord so achieved would be one that has an independent distinction in Scriabin's late work. It is the chord that furnishes much of the harmonic substance of the Seventh Sonata, one of Scriabin's most pervasively octatonic compositions. But the Seventh Sonata is a later composition than *Prométhée*, and so the observation might seem anachronistic.

Yet the Seventh Sonata harmony originated somewhere, after all; and if we look back at the *zov* motif in example 12.26, we can witness its birth. Played against the pleroma chord, the *zov* already suggests the priority of the octatonic scale over the whole-tone, because it starts on the F♯, the one non–whole-tone component of the chord, and returns to it through a quasi-cadential descending half step from G. There is no question, then, that the F♯ is being treated, and can only be interpreted, as a harmonically stable tone. The *zov* reaches its apogee on the note B, the non-octatonic note. And behold: the B is resolved by the same cadential descending half step to B♭ before proceeding down to G. Because the B♭ is the only note in the *zov* motif that is not a constituent of the pleroma chord itself, we have strong evidence, it seems, that Scriabin regarded and therefore treated the melodic B as harmonically unstable. The pleroma chord, we are thus led to assume, is an octatonic harmony with an appoggiatura. Let us note further that when the appoggiatura is resolved, the top three notes of the resulting chord now comprehend an ordinary major triad rooted on F♯, the specifically non–whole-tone member of the original pleroma chord.

Now as anyone who knows *Promethée* will have just recalled, that triad is the harmony to which the last, exhaustively walked-around pleroma chord gives way at the blazing if disconcertingly arbitrary conclusion of the piece. It is arbitrary because there is not enough of traditional harmonic function left in the *Promethée* idiom to give it a necessity at all comparable with its cataclysmic prototype in the *Poème de l'extase*. It is not a functional cadence at all. And yet, as we now see, it is by no means unprepared; it is "planted" at the very outset, in fact, exactly the way the concluding C-major harmony had been planted in the opening cadential gesture of the earlier composition.

So what is its status if it is not a cadence? Minus the sense of resolution, of tension relieved, we are left with a sense of sudden elevation—or, in the language of the Russian theurgic symbolists, of a *poryv*, a transporting burst. That is something of which Scriabin's music was always full. Rapid ascents and a predilection for high registers are conspicuous in his music from the moment he became interested in explicitly sublime moods and occult revelation. They assumed the role of ersatz cadential function from the moment Scriabin dispensed with conventional tonal resolutions. This happened for the first time in the Fifth Sonata, the companion piece to the *Poème de l'extase* (example 12.29); almost the identical gesture is repeated at the piano soloist's first entrance in *Promethée* (example 12.30), thus forging a link between Scriabin's first piece to cast off conventional trappings of tonal closure and his last piece to retain them. It is a gesture to which Ivanov makes explicit reference, relating it on the one hand to the *Sursum corda*, the heart-lift at the Elevation (Anaphora) of the Latin Mass,[44] and on the other to Scriabin's constant striving to transcend the human.[45]

The result of the final breakthrough to the *realiora*—at any rate the last one Scriabin lived to accomplish—may be glimpsed in the sketches for the *Acte préalable*, and in particular in the twelve-tone chords Kelkel was the first to discover and report. Kelkel reported them as a technical breakthrough. We can see them now as a spiritual breakthrough as well. A twelve-tone chord is literally *vselenskoye*, universal, and in its literal plenitude, exhausting the pitch-class vocabulary of the tempered tuning system, it is, more literally than the so-called mystic chord could ever be, a representation of the pleroma.

---

[44] "Natsional'noye i vselenskoye v tvorchestve Skryabina," *Pamyatniki kul'turï* (1983): 98. It seems altogether likely, in this connection, that Ivanov (and surely Scriabin) recalled Liszt's "Sursum corda," the last piece in the collection *Années de Pélerinage*, which contains one of Liszt's most radical harmonic effects (and one quite prophetic of Scriabin): a French sixth chord suddenly "composed out" at the climax into a blazing passage of whole-tone scales.

[45] "Vzglyad Skryabina na iskusstvo," *Pamyatniki kul'turï* (1983): 104.

Example 12.29. Scriabin, Sonata no. 5, Op. 53 (1907), beginning

There can be no question of progression; the universe has nowhere else to go. A twelve-note harmony is the ultimate invariant harmony. It can be neither transposed nor inverted. It is everywhere, and everything, at once.

Thus it is significant that Scriabin came to his twelve-note chords by extending the harmonic explorations we have already traced. The eight distinct twelve-note chords tabulated by Kelkel are not undifferentiated clusters of semitones but are laid out registrally in ways that emphasize and combine older invariant structures. One, for example, in a sketch dated 29 December 1914, places two French sixth chords, equivalent to the content of an octatonic scale, in distinct registers that would no doubt have been further distin-

EXAMPLE 12.30. Scriabin, *Prométhée*, m. 31, piano part only

guished in timbre when orchestrated. The four remaining tones of the chromatic scale, equivalent to a diminished seventh chord, are placed atop the French sixths, in a third contrasting register (example 12.31). The twelve notes have been in effect partitioned into three separate inversionally and transpositionally invariant harmonies, each containing two inversionally and transpositionally invariant tritones for a "universal," all-encompassing total of six.

Since it is harmonic progression that had always articulated the structural rhythm of music, which is to say its sense of directed unfolding in time, a music based on universal invariant harmonies becomes quite literally timeless, as well as emotionally quiescent. The two qualities, invariance and timelessness, insofar as we are equipped to interpret musical messages, are in fact aspects of a single quality of quiescence, expressed respectively in two

EXAMPLE 12.31. Universal chord from Scriabin's *Acte préalable*

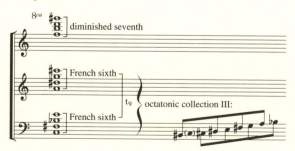

musical dimensions, the "vertical" and the "horizontal." We seem to experience an eschatological revelation, a gnosis that only music may impart: the full collapse of time and space and the dissolution of the ego. It was a dissolution at which the composer deliberately aimed, as we learn from Schloezer. Far from the solipsist of the *Poème de l'extase*, the author of the *Mysterium* "no longer dwelt on his own role; what was uniquely important to him was the act itself, and he was willing to be dissolved in it" (p. 269). This transcendence of the human, as authors from Swedenborg to Balzac to Blavatsky had foretold, amounted to the final transcendence of the world.

Eschatological Torsos

After such an experience of world transcendence there is not much that one can do for an encore. Beyond "universal" chromaticism musical maximalism could hardly proceed, and it is small wonder that modernism's next step forward should have been a (classicizing) retreat. Yet it is worth noting that the other great "transition to atonality," the one made around the same time as Scriabin's by the Viennese, was not just a parallel musical exploration but had a parallel spiritual dimension as well. Schoenberg also felt himself to be Wagner's Orphic heir. He even had a tenuous connection with Russian symbolism (and, more tenuously yet, with Scriabin) through his friend Kandinsky. And he too, at the outset at least, felt the breakthrough to atonality as a transcendence of the human plane, a direct experience of the sublime. With Schoenberg, too, there was a literary parallel intimating the essence and the purpose of his music, though it was only music (in its "absoluteness") that was capable of fully realizing the expression.

To Schoenberg the vision came from Emmanuel Swedenborg via Balzac's philosophical novel *Séraphîta* (1835), "perhaps the most glorious work in existence," as the composer put it to Kandinsky.[46] The long central chapter of this book is given over to a purported exposition of Swedenborg's life and teachings, as related to Wilfrid, a man of thirty, and Minna, a girl of seventeen, by an androgynous ethereal being with whom both are in love and who in the last chapter ascends to an angelic estate. The two lovers, who are left to share the love they bore for the angel, are privileged to witness the assumption and are vouchsafed a vision of heaven:

> Wilfrid and Minna now understood some of the mysterious words of the being who on earth had appeared to them under the form which was intelligible to each—Séraphîtus to one, Séraphîta to the other—seeing that here all was homogeneous. Light gave birth to melody, and melody to light; colors were both light

[46] Letter of 19 August 1912; Arnold Schoenberg and Wassily Kandinsky, *Letters, Pictures and Documents*, ed. Jelena Hahl-Koch, trans. John C. Crawford (London: Faber and Faber, 1984), p. 54.

and melody; motion was number endowed by the Word; in short, everything was at once sonorous, diaphanous, and mobile; so that, everything existing in everything else, extension knew no limits, and the angels could traverse it everywhere to the utmost depths of the infinite.[47]

This is the vision that inspired Schoenberg, the experience that he tried to capture with his radical new style. Partly it is a familiar matter of synesthesia and fusion of media, such as Schoenberg attempted to realize with his famous "tone-color melodies" and with the coordination of lighting and music in his tiny expressionist opera *Die glückliche Hand* (1913), the composition most directly stimulated by his friendship with Kandinsky. But in one composition, begun slightly later, Schoenberg tried to find an explicit musical analogue to the everything-in-everything, directionless, limitlessly traversable heavenly space so provocatively described by Balzac. His ideal, set forth in italics, was a *unity of musical space [that] demands an absolute and unitary perception.* In elaborating this vision, he referred directly to the source of his inspiration, comparing the "musical space" he envisioned, and that he sought through atonality to realize, with "Swedenborg's heaven (described in Balzac's *Séraphîta*)," where "there is no absolute down, no right or left, forward or backward." In such a musical space, Schoenberg went on,

> Every musical configuration, every movement of tones has to be comprehended primarily as a mutual relation of sounds, of oscillatory vibrations, appearing at different places and times. To the imaginative and creative faculty, relations in the material sphere are as independent from directions or planes as material objects are, in their sphere, to our perceptive faculties. Just as our mind always recognizes, for instance, a knife, a bottle, or a watch, regardless of its position, and can reproduce it in the imagination in every possible position, even so a musical creator's mind can operate subconsciously with a row of tones, regardless of their direction, regardless of the way in which a mirror might show the mutual relations, which remain a given quality.[48]

What was sought, then, was an infinitely collapsible, unitary, or (as we might say now) invariant space corresponding in its way to Scriabin's collapsed and suspended time. Schoenberg was at pains to note that this unity of musical space was something that the composer of genius achieves without conscious effort (as a "gift from the Supreme Commander"), pointing to an arcane structural relationship—by inversion, significantly enough, "the way in which a mirror might show" it—between the main themes of his own early Chamber Symphony, Op. 9 (1906), which only presented itself to his conscious understanding "about twenty years later."[49] In one work, however,

---

[47] Honoré de Balzac, *Séraphîta* (Blauvelt, N.Y.: Freedeeds Library, 1986), p. 173.

[48] "Composition with Twelve Tones (1)" (1941), in Arnold Schoenberg, *Style and Idea*, ed. Leonard Stein (Berkeley and Los Angeles: University of California Press, 1975), p. 223.

[49] Ibid., pp. 222–23.

Schoenberg strove consciously to effect an actual occult disclosure through the consummate unification of musical space, and this was the work (or so Schoenberg recollected it) that midwifed if not the birth then at least the conception of the twelve-tone technique.

According to a letter he sent Alexander von Zemlinsky late in 1913, Schoenberg intended for a while to follow up *Die glückliche Hand* with a grandiose operatic trilogy on the subject of *Séraphîta*, for which Marie Pappenheim, the librettist of *Erwartung*, had agreed to prepare a libretto.[50] Alternatively and concurrently, he planned a vast choral symphony, emulative of Mahler's "Symphony of a Thousand," for which the earliest surviving sketch, dated 27 December 1912, is a recitative labeled "Seraphita."[51] The culminating movement, for which the text was finished in January 1915, was a counterpart to the mystical final chapters ("Le Chemin pour aller au ciel" and "L'Assomption") in *Séraphîta*, and (as Webern, to whom Schoenberg may have disclosed his plan, was quick to discern) it contained several plain or covert textual references to Balzac's novel, of which one—the Archangel Gabriel's opening speech, "Whether right, left, forward or backwards, up or down— one has to go on without asking what lies before or behind one"—resonates as well with Schoenberg's later description of his Balzac-inspired "absolute and unitary" musical space.[52]

We know these words as the opening lines of the text of the oratorio *Die Jakobsleiter*, with *Moses und Aron* one of the great Schoenbergian torsos. Long before its first fragmentary performance (Vienna, 16 June 1961) or publication (Los Angeles: Belmont Music Publishers, 1974), as reconstructed from Schoenberg's sketches by his pupil Winfried Zillig, the work had achieved a legendary status not (to put it as Schoenberg might have done) so much for "what it was" as for "how it was made."[53] In a letter to Nicolas Slonimsky (3 June 1937), which Slonimsky published that very year in the first edition of his compendium *Music since 1900* (New York: Charles Scribner's Sons), having called special attention to it in the preface, Schoenberg wrote that the first of many *Vorversuche*, or preliminary gropings, toward his "method of composing with twelve tones happened about December 1914 or at the beginning of 1915 when I sketched a symphony, the last part of

---

[50] Letter of 21 November 1913, quoted in Alan Philip Lessem, *Music and Text in the Works of Arnold Schoenberg* (Ann Arbor: UMI Research Press, 1979), pp. 178, 229n.40, by courtesy of O. W. Neighbour, the owner of the document. According to Neighbour's article on Schoenberg in *The New Grove Dictionary of Opera* (London: Macmillan, 1992), vol. 4, p. 237, Schoenberg first entertained the idea of a *Séraphîta* opera in 1912, which would place it even closer to the period of his closest involvement with Kandinsky and the *Blaue Reiter*.

[51] Lessem, *Music and Text in the Works of Arnold Schoenberg*.

[52] See H. H. Stuckenschmidt, *Arnold Schoenberg: His Life, World and Work*, trans. Humphrey Searle (New York: Schirmer Books, 1978), p. 243.

[53] See his oft-cited letter of 27 July 1932 to Rudolf Kolisch, in Arnold Schoenberg, *Letters*, ed. Erwin Stein, trans. Eithne Wilkins and Ernst Kaiser (Berkeley and Los Angeles: University of California Press, 1987), p. 164.

which became later the 'Jakobsleiter,' but which never has been continued. The Scherzo of this symphony was based on a theme consisting of the twelve tones. But this was only one of the themes."[54]

In a sketch for an essay that was set down around 1948 and published two years later, Schoenberg gave some more details, and showed how the twelve-tone theme actually survived into the oratorio, which he began to compose in its final if unfinished form in 1917:

> I had contrived the plan to provide for unity—which was always my main motive: to build all the main themes of the whole oratorio from a row of six tones— C♯, D, E, F, G, A♭. These were probably [?] the six notes with which the composition began, in the following order: C♯, D, F, E, A♭, G. When after my retirement from the University of California I wanted to finish *Die Jakobsleiter*, I discovered to my greatest pleasure that this beginning was a real twelve-tone composition. To an ostinato (which I changed a little) the remaining six tones entered gradually, one in every measure. When I built the main themes from these six tones I did not bind myself to the order of their first appearance. I was still at this time far away from the methodical application of a set. Still I believe that also this idea offered the promise of unity to a certain degree.[55]

Was it merely a coincidence that the fateful hexachord, or six-tone row ("C♯, D, E, F, G, A♭") on which the beginning of *Die Jakobsleiter* was built (example 12.32) should have been an octatonic scale segment? Yes and no. It is unlikely that Schoenberg had the specific awareness of the octatonic scale as a compositional resource that the Russian composers of Scriabin's and Stravinsky's generations possessed—but it is not out of the question, for many of Schoenberg's writings, beginning with the *Harmonielehre* of 1911, show a detailed technical acquaintance with the works of Liszt, and it is altogether possible that Schoenberg had deduced the nature and the properties of the scale from Liszt's usages the way Rimsky-Korsakov had previously deduced them.[56] What is certain is that, given the goal of a unified musical space, Schoenberg actively sought a group of tones with an intervallic structure that would be invariant under inversion, and that criterion is satisfied by the six-tone octatonic segment.

The crucial move that made the opening of *Die Jakobsleiter* a *Vorversuch* for the twelve-tone technique was the immediate combination of the ostinato drawn from the octatonic fragment with the complementary hexachord (F♯, A, B♭, B, C, E♭)—that is, the remaining six tones necessary to complete the

---

[54] "Letter from Arnold Schoenberg on the Origin of the Twelve-Tone Method of Composition," in Nicolas Slonimsky, ed., *Music since 1900*, 4th ed. (New York: Charles Scribner's Sons, 1971), p. 1315.

[55] "Composition with Twelve Tones (2)," *Style and Idea*, pp. 247–48.

[56] The process of Rimsky-Korsakov's deduction is traced in Taruskin, "Chernomor to Kashchei."

EXAMPLE 12.32. Schoenberg, *Die Jakobsleiter*, opening ostinato

full chromatic gamut. This hexachord, too, is (inevitably) inversionally symmetrical—which is to say that its intervallic structure, being (unavoidably) identical to that of its counterpart, is also invariant when inverted. And Schoenberg actually demonstrated this property, by displaying the second hexachord as a pair of three-note chords, the one quite conspicuously the inversion of the other, that are sounded piecemeal but then sustained in the winds while the strings continue to sound the first hexachord as an ostinato running beneath (example 12.33).

This situation—the partitioning of the complete chromatic aggregate into mutually exclusive, harmonically symmetrical (or inversionally invariant) registral segments, one of them octatonic—is already highly reminiscent of the twelve-note constructions in the almost contemporaneous sketches for Scriabin's *Acte préalable*, which—one hastens to point out—not only could Schoenberg not have known at the time, but he could never have learned about during his lifetime.[57] But the resemblance is striking, and Schoenberg's next move made it closer yet.

EXAMPLE 12.33. Schoenberg, *Die Jakobsleiter*, complementary hexachord and derivative harmonies

[57] Much later, in 1922, while engaged in polemic with Josef Matthias Hauer over the question of priority in the "discovery" of the twelve-tone technique, Schoenberg claimed to have been "inspired by Scriabin's procedure as described in *Der blaue Reiter*" when he expressed the aggregate harmony in the form of two complementary hexachords in *Die Jakobsleiter*. But if he had indeed been prompted in this way by Scriabin's example, it was a striking instance of creative misreading, because Sabaneyev's article (see n. 37), although it does present the mystic chord in

As soon as the two wind chords have been completed in the higher register, and are being sustained there, the string ostinato running beneath accelerates into a rhythmic diminution, which is then treated as a stretto. That is, different instruments enter in counterpoint with different orderings of the six tones of the hexachord that are so calculated that after six such entries all six constituent tones are continuously present in the texture (example 12.34). Chalk up another aggregate simultaneity, another musically represented pleroma! Just as in the *Acte préalable*, we now have a completely saturated and completely symmetrical—which is to say a completely unitary, completely invariant and functionally quiescent—musical space. And just as in the *Acte préalable*, this construction exists and was motivated not simply as a technical feat—though that is how it has been touted in most conventional historiographical and analytical accounts[58]—but as a metaphor for a spiritual condition, or (to put it more bravely, and more truly in terms of its conception) as a medium for occult revelation. It is a foretaste of Swedenborgian heaven.[59]

That heaven is reapproached in the wordless interlude preceding the second part of *Die Jakobsleiter*, the part that Schoenberg never wrote. As with Scriabin, the ultimate revelation was never accomplished. But the interlude begins (mm. 563f.) with a return of the opening hexachord, now laid out as an actual octatonic scalar segment introducing the vocalise of the liberated soul, which begins with a fresh permutation of the same hexachord and extends it into the full chromatic ether. The principle on which the dodecaphonic principle chiefly depended, that of perpetual chromatic circulation equally encompassing the horizontal (melodic) and the vertical (harmonic) dimensions (so that there is "no absolute down, no right or left, forward or backward") was born.

---

the guise of a six-note scale segment or hexachord, describes no technique of complementation or aggregate formation. See Schoenberg's marginal annotations to Hauer's article "Sphärenmusik," transcribed in Bryan R. Simms, "Who First Composed Twelve-Tone Music, Schoenberg or Hauer?" *Journal of the Arnold Schoenberg Institute* 10 (1987): 124 (English), and 132, n. 15 (German). My thanks to Gregory Dubinsky for this reference.

[58] E.g., by Babbitt in *Words about Music*, pp. 10–16, 57–58.

[59] Another who arrived independently around the same time at aggregate harmonies (or "total harmonies," as he called them) as a means of representing or inducing transcendent experience was the Russian composer Nikolai Obukhov (1892–1954), often thought of as a Scriabinist, but one who did not know Scriabin personally and could not have known the *Acte préalable* sketches. See, for example, his song *Kolïbel'naya* (1918; published as *Berceuse d'un bienheureux* by Rouarte Lerolle, Paris, in 1921), of which excerpts are reprinted in Peter Deane Roberts, *Modernism in Russian Piano Music* (Bloomington: Indiana University Press, 1993), vol. 2, pp. 150–51. The piece begins with three different widely spaced aggregates, partitioned like Scriabin's into polychordal layers. Finally, compare Charles Ives's contemporaneous pleromic torso, the "Universe" Symphony, mainly sketched between 1911 and 1915. A page of sketches, reproduced on p. 295 of Stuart Feder's "psychoanalytic biography," *Charles Ives: "My Father's Song"* (New Haven: Yale University Press, 1992), shows the building up of a sustained aggregate sonority by means of a quintessentially (if unwittingly) Schoenbergian progression of tritones and perfect fourths (example 12.35).

EXAMPLE 12.34. Schoenberg, *Die Jakobsleiter* mm. 1–8

↑ Aggregate harmony from this point

EXAMPLE 12.35. Ives, "Universe" Symphony, harmonic sketch (see n. 59)

So it is not enough, never enough, to attribute early twentieth-century maximalism—of which the grandiose unfinished, and perhaps unfinishable, eschatological torsos of Schoenberg, Scriabin, and Ives stand as preeminent musical mementos—simply or solely to a "pressure within the art."[60] The arts are not detached from the rest of existence or experience; they receive and react to pressures from many sources. Not only their contents, but also their forms and procedures—including the procedure of detaching them from the worldly—arise in response to worldly pressures. "What form will religious sentiment assume? What will be its new expression?" asked Balzac in the preface to *Le Livre Mystique*, of which *Séraphîta* was a part. "The answer is a secret of the future."[61] That future is now past to us, and the religious sentiment has again become a secret. But it is as a vision of human perfectibility, at the very least, a vision of "ascent to a higher and better order,"[62] that we may look upon, and take inspiration from, the early atonal vision.

The quoted phrase formed the conclusion of Schoenberg's letter to Slonimsky, describing what Schoenberg saw as the victory of the twelve-tone technique. It could just as well have been a citation from *Séraphîta*. As Webern revealed, Schoenberg justified his explorations on a specifically Balzacian, occult basis. The surmounting of the major-minor dichotomy was for Schoenberg no mere technical breakthrough but a spiritual ascent—a *poriïv*—to a superhuman condition: "Double gender," he proclaimed, "has given rise to a

[60] Igor Stravinsky, in Igor Stravinsky and Robert Craft, *Conversations with Igor Stravinsky* (1959; reprint, Berkeley and Los Angeles, 1980), p. 113. See the next chapter for a gloss.

[61] Balzac, *Séraphîta*, p. vii.

[62] Slonimsky, *Music since 1900*, p. 1316.

FIGURE 12.1. Jean Delville's title page for Scriabin's *Prométhée*
(1912): "The fire that blazed in his eyes rivaled the rays of the sun"
(Balzac, *Séraphîta*)

higher race!"[63] No less than Scriabin, then, Schoenberg spoke in the voice of
the vatic androgyne, as the text of *Die Jakobsleiter* and the mesmerizing title
page of *Prométhée* (by the Belgian theosophical artist Jean Delville) jointly
declare (figure 12.1). ("The fire that blazed in his eyes," wrote Balzac of his
angelic messenger, "rivalled the rays of the sun; he seemed not to receive but
to give out light.")[64]

[63] Anton Webern (quoting Schoenberg), *The Path to the New Music*, ed. Willi Reich, trans.
Leo Black (Bryn Mawr, Pa.: Theodore Presser, 1963), p. 37.
[64] Balzac, *Séraphîta*, p. 24.

The cold war rationalization and academization of dodecaphony caused that voice to grow cold and that face to grow dim. "As you read," said one of Balzac's characters of Swedenborg, "you must either lose your wits or become a seer."[65] By now we have long since consigned Scriabin to the former estate, that of lost wits, but we have been unwilling to consign Schoenberg to either category. Instead he sulks in positivistic limbo, his methods venerated but his deeds ignored. But it is precisely the academic despiritualization of dodecaphony—more broadly, of atonality—that has led to its widespread, and justified, rejection.

Indeed, it is precisely the rationalization and refinement of dodecaphonic technique to the point where it has become a kind of abstract numerical logic that has brought attack from those who question the cognitive relevance of its logical concepts. Twelve-tone music has come to seem a conceptual game to which listeners can never gain perceptual access. Those who attempt to finesse the problem by placing the blame on the inexperience of listeners (their "incompetence," to speak cognitively), invariably come across as special pleaders.[66]

It is only when the original conception of atonality as a transrational, uncanny discourse is recognized, and its nature as a medium of revealed—which is to say undemonstrable—truth is grasped, that aesthetic apprehension can begin. It bears the aura of the sublime (Séraphîta: "Why, if you believe in number, should you deny God?"),[67] and the sublime purges and terrifies. It is important, therefore, to refresh our memory of atonality's motivating liminal impulses. Renewed contact with the early atonalists, with Scriabin, and with the sources of their inspiration, can help restore perspective, but only if they

---

[65] *Séraphîta*, p. 67. Anent Scriabin, one may rely on Wilfrid's defense of Séraphîta (p. 102): "I will not dispute her madness, so long as you do not dispute her superiority."

[66] Andrew Mead, for example, argues that in order to listen meaningfully to twelve-tone music "we must be able in some sensible way to perceive aggregates," that is, to parse and segment individual statements of the full chromatic gamut. "While I shall not deal with that issue here," he continues, "I think it reasonable to assume that we do so by hearing their boundaries, as signalled by the recurrence of pitch-classes," and claims that this entails nothing more than "simply . . . to reinterpret the significance of certain simple perceptual acts" ("Twelve-Tone Organizational Strategies: An Analytical Sampler," *Intégral* 2 [1991]: 93–168, esp. pp. 96–97). Mead ignores the sizable literature of that burgeoning branch of cognitive psychology known as music perception, in which reported experimental results have repeatedly disconfirmed the reasonableness of his working assumption. On the cognitive opacity of serial music see Fred Lerdahl and Ray Jackendoff, *A Generative Theory of Tonal Music* (Cambridge, Mass.: MIT Press, 1983), pp. 296–301; also Fred Lerdahl, "Cognitive Constraints on Compositional Systems," in John A. Sloboda, ed., *Generative Processes in Music* (Oxford: Clarendon Press, 1988), pp. 231–59.

[67] Balzac, *Séraphîta*, p. 126. One writer who recognizes the sublime, noncognizable nature of atonal music, but who nevertheless attempts a desperate reconciliation with academically more respectable viewpoints ("classical" ones, in Schloezer's terms) is Michael Hicks, in "Serialism and Comprehensibility: A Guide for the Teacher," *Journal of Aesthetic Appreciation* 25, no. 4 (Winter 1991): 77–85.

are "put together again." At the very least it should be apparent that musicians who dismiss Scriabin's spiritual vision as "cosmic hocus-pocus," and literary investigators who assume it impossible that a spiritual vision could be "communicated musically," are cut off equally from the vision and from the music. It is only the music that can communicate the vision, but only if we have vision enough to receive the communication.

CHAPTER 13

STRAVINSKY AND THE SUBHUMAN

A MYTH OF THE TWENTIETH CENTURY:
THE RITE OF SPRING, THE TRADITION OF THE NEW, AND "THE MUSIC ITSELF"

I

"IN THE ARTS an appetite for a new look is now a professional requirement, as in Russia to be accredited as a revolutionist is to qualify for privileges," wrote Harold Rosenberg, the champion of action painting, in 1960. Densely packed with ironies intended and unintended, Rosenberg's marvelous sentence encapsulates the atmosphere in which many members of the generation now reaching seniority in the arts and the academy were educated. Indeed, it is tempting now to look back on that period as if on some kind of Brezhnevite stagnation, in which yesterday's antitraditionalist sloganeering was appropriated to defend today's reactionary traditionalism, and in which loyalty to the new was professed in order to resist change. The attempt to marry the Permanent Revolution to the Great Tradition led to a vast proliferation of newspeak and doublethink, for as Rosenberg went on to observe, "the new cannot become a tradition without giving rise to unique contradictions, myths, absurdities."[1]

We are still living with them. The historiography of art—and particularly, it seems, of music—remains the most stubbornly Whiggish of all historiographies, despite long-standing maverick opposition.[2] That historiography is still a Tradition-of-the-New narrative that celebrates technical innovation, viewed as progress within a narrowly circumscribed aesthetic domain. The hermetic

---

[1] Harold Rosenberg, *The Tradition of the New* (Chicago: University of Chicago Press, 1982), p. 9. Although I begin with an appreciative nod toward Rosenberg, who coined my titular phrase and whose writing I admire, I am well aware that he would not wish me for an ally. The questions I will be asking would immediately mark me in his eyes for a "kitsch critic" (or worse, a "community critic"), because they refuse his principal tenet that "the gesture on the canvas was a gesture of liberation, from Value—political, esthetic, moral" (p. 30).

[2] The most conspicuous early voice was Leo Treitler's; see his "On Historical Criticism" (1967) and "The Present as History" (1969), both reprinted in *Music and the Historical Imagination* (Cambridge, Mass.: Harvard University Press, 1989).

and formalist side of this paradigm and the heroically individualistic, asocial side of it remain sources of dissatisfaction to those of us who believe that this manner of accounting for the production and the value of artworks has had a deleterious influence on that very production and that very value.

Awareness has been growing that the two sides of the enduring paradigm are codependent, that in both aspects the resulting narratives have been tendentiously exclusionary, and that the ideology of the cold war, which sanctioned the association of logical positivism with democracy and of formalism with the defense of political freedom, has been to a long-unrecognized extent its artificial life-support system.

The influence of the cold war on modernist attitudes in Rosenberg's field has been energetically documented of late, sometimes with a tinge of conspiracy theorizing.[3] The single noteworthy attempt of this kind so far in the field of music so far has been Martin Brody's "'Music for the Masses': Milton Babbitt's Cold War Music Theory," in which Babbitt's scientism is somewhat benignly explained as a defense, on the part of a thinker formed (and scarred) by the "dangerously irrational" ideological battles of the 1930s, against a priori (which is to say political) constraints on conceptualizing "the nature and limits of music" and against the political exploitability of any "looser," less intransigently rationalistic discourse.[4]

Will the end of the cold war bring an end to all these redemptive mythologies and exclusionary strategies? Will we finally get beyond the poietic fallacy that focuses all attention on the making of the artwork, hence on the person (and the putative freedoms) of the maker? Will we see that artists' shoptalk is not invariably the best model or medium for criticism? Will we allow that the context of technical innovation in the arts need not be confined to the history of art? Will we accept that what an artist will experience as "an irresistible pull within the art"[5] may have sources in the wider world, including some of which the artist may not be wholly aware, and that it is the historian's or the critic's job to describe them, however fallibly?

---

[3] See, for example, Serge Guilbaut, *How New York Stole the Idea of Modern Art*, trans. Arthur Goldhammer (Chicago: University of Chicago Press, 1983); or (with special reference to the CIA-funded Committee for Cultural Freedom) Peter Coleman, *The Liberal Conspiracy* (New York: Free Press, 1989).

[4] *Musical Quarterly* 77 (1993): 161–92. Brody captures well the central, characteristic paradox: the actual assertion of privilege and orthodoxy through an apparent argument for pluralism (or "cultural freedom"). His argument might have been strengthened by a more critical examination of Babbitt's claim that his premises are "value-neutral" (see p. 165), and a more explicit recognition that where Babbitt speaks of "music" (as having a "nature" and "limits," as being "autonomous," as having "individuation") he usually means "musicians," or, more simply, "Babbitt."

[5] Igor Stravinsky, in Igor Stravinsky and Robert Craft, *Conversations with Igor Stravinsky* (Garden City, N.Y.: Doubleday, 1959), p. 127. He was speaking of the "hiatus" created by "'atonality,'" which "Marxists," as he imagined them, ascribed to "social pressures."

A major deterrent to enlarging the purview of art history and criticism along these lines is the unwholesomeness of what might be discovered, and the intolerable implications such discovery may be seen to harbor. Formalism is seen as a bulwark against such a threat. Its defenders have tended to impugn the motives of skeptics, who are suspected of genius-envy and, more sweepingly, of hostility to the integrity of the individual. As one who has investigated, and who has felt it important to investigate, Stravinsky's alarming political affinities, and drawn fire in consequence, I can well appreciate the qualms expressed by the author of a recent inquiry into the occultist well-springs of modernist poetry. "This study is not a postmodern critique of modernism," he felt it necessary to declare. "It is not my intention to unveil the errors, self-deceptions, and vices of those geniuses whose impossibly great achievements oppress us all."[6]

He knows that he is in for censure from a "scholarly community [that] considers it poor form to dwell upon such an aberration" as occultism, and the history of Scriabin research, sketched briefly in the preceding chapter, shows that the musicological community has been similarly disposed. "Yeats's occultism," he continues, "has been a subject not to be raised in polite company. To do so could only serve to discredit an accredited genius of the modern age and give aid and comfort to the enemies of the modernist enlightenment."[7] Again, Scriabin scholarship bears this observation out. Those who wish to see Scriabin promoted from accredited crank to accredited genius are precisely the ones least able to cope with what, in this case, were the composer's acknowledged allegiances and his professed purposes. These have been stigmatized and marginalized, as we saw in the previous chapter, precisely in the name of enlightenment.[8]

Anxious resistance to contextualizing Scriabin seems understandable enough. His inseparability from fin de siècle occultism has made his canonical status in the West incurably insecure. And yet when it comes to a central, uncontested and incontestable genius of modern music like Stravinsky, resistance is only magnified, especially when that looming cultural context involves more than what can be dismissed as private folly but links up with great public evils, like fascism and anti-Semitism, that have had gruesome public consequences.

Unlike Scriabin's occultism (or Schoenberg's, for that matter), Stravinsky's fascism and his anti-Semitism were not, as a rule, matters the composer saw fit explicitly to thematize in his work. Although he did choose to set a couple of anti-Semitic texts in his American years, the texts do not seem to have been

---

[6] Leon Surette, *The Birth of Modernism: Ezra Pound, T. S. Eliot, W. B. Yeats and the Occult* (Montreal and Kingston: McGill-Queen's University Press, 1993), p. 4.

[7] Surette, *The Birth of Modernism*, p. 9.

[8] See James M. Baker, *The Music of Alexander Scriabin* (New Haven: Yale University Press, 1986), and R. Taruskin, review of same, *Music Theory Spectrum* 10 (1988): 143–69.

selected for the sake of their anti-Semitism.[9] Stravinsky never made a setting of the *Giovinezza* or the *Horst Wessel Lied* (but he did set *The Volga Boatmen's Song* on commission from the liberal post-Tsarist pre-Bolshevik provisional government of Russia in 1917, and he set *The Star-Spangled Banner* on his own initiative in 1941).

In the absence of any explicit indication from the composer, it cannot suffice merely to assert that his social circumstances and political attitudes ineluctably shaped his musical output. That amounts to no more than a truism, impervious to falsification and therefore empty of information. As in the case of sexuality—say, Chaikovsky's or Schubert's (to cite issues of lively currency)[10]—the burden of proof must rest with those who assert the critical relevance of the connection, and such relevance can only be usefully substantiated in specific terms: what circumstances? what attitudes? how have they shaped which works?

To the extent that the argument is advanced in terms of generalities (on the level, that is, of "theory"), adherents of the formalist or autonomist position will always be able to maintain, on the basis of its specificity, the superiority of context-free "essential" knowledge;[11] nor will they be in any way shaken in their belief that such knowledge, being purely "aesthetic," engages the artwork without mediation and, hence, obviates any need for interpretation.[12]

[9] These texts are found in the *Cantata* (1952) and *A Sermon, A Narrative and a Prayer* (1961); see R. Taruskin and Robert Craft, "Jews and Geniuses: An Exchange," *New York Review of Books*, 15 June 1989, pp. 57–58.

[10] The most informative account of Chaikovsky's sexuality can be found in Alexander Poznansky, *Tchaikovsky: The Quest for the Inner Man* (New York: Schirmer Books, 1991); for the backlash see Paul Griffiths, "The Outing of Peter Ilyich," *New York Times Book Review*, 5 January 1992, p. 24; on the treatment of the theme by the composer's biographers, see R. Taruskin, "Pathetic Symphonist," *New Republic*, 6 February 1995, pp. 26–40; on its potential critical application see Henry Zajaczkowski, "Tchaikovsky: The Missing Piece of the Jigsaw Puzzle," *Musical Times* 131 (1990): 239–42, and "On Čajkovskij's Psychopathology and Its Relationship with His Creativity," in *Čajkovskij-Studien*, vol. 1, ed. Thomas Kohlhase (proceedings of the Internationales Čajkovskij-Symposium, Tübingen, 23–28 October 1993) (Mainz: Schott, 1995); also R. Taruskin, "Tchaikovsky, P. I.," *The New Grove Dictionary of Opera* (London: Macmillan, 1992), vol. 4, p. 667. On Schubert, see Maynard Solomon, "Franz Schubert and the Peacocks of Benvenuto Cellini," *19th-Century Music* 12 (1988–89): 193–206; Susan McClary, "Constructions of Subjectivity in Schubert's Music," in Philip Brett, Elizabeth Wood, and Gary Thomas, eds., *Queering the Pitch: The New Gay and Lesbian Musicology* (New York: Routledge, 1994), pp. 205–34, and *19th-Century Music* 17, no. 1 (Summer 1993), a special issue ("Schubert: Music, Sexuality, Culture") with contributions by Rita Steblin, Maynard Solomon, Kristina Muxfeldt, David Gramit, V. Kofi Agawu, Susan McClary, James Webster, and Robert Winter.

[11] Compare a typical dictum of Carl Dahlhaus: "If one Bach fugue is a tonal reflection of the principle of manufacture, then so is another. The individuality of the entities, which constitutes their very essence, is not within the reach of social decoding, at least at present" ("The Musical Work of Art as a Subject of Sociology," in *Schoenberg and the New Music*, trans. Derrick Puffett and Alfred Clayton [Cambridge: Cambridge University Press, 1987], p. 236).

[12] Compare Pieter van den Toorn: "The question of an engaging context is an aesthetic as well as an historical and analytic-theoretical one. And once individual works begin to prevail for what

Yet even when successfully demonstrated, the connection between music and its historical situation or between music and the wider world of ideas is not self-evidently enhancing or illuminating. Pursued one-sidedly, it can amount to a debased form of the intentional fallacy—debased in the sense that it is not even the composer but a mere surrogate, the researcher, who now claims the privileged authority of the creator. Just as undesirably, it can reduce works to the status of exemplification. Works can and certainly do survive their immediate contexts, and it is the hermeneutic position itself that would uphold their right to change (that is, to be reconstituted) accordingly. Again, cases must be judged on their merits, with due reckoning of gains and losses.

It is when works "survive" into the twilight zone of decontextualization—or recontextualization within the formalist canon—that losses can seem most decisively to outweigh gains. Often, and paradoxically, it is the very radicalism of modernist art that is supposed to vouchsafe its transcendence of historical contingency. Reacting to my own historical investigations concerning Stravinsky's patrimony and stylistic evolution (and, as often happens, attributing to me stronger claims than I would care to make), Pieter van den Toorn has declared himself to be "not all that certain that this early Russian heritage is invariably the most useful context within which to position the terms of Stravinsky's musical particularity," because "what may astonish most about this music is not the ties that bind it to its immediate past but the distance that separates it from that past."[13] Certainly; and yet neither the ties that bind nor the distance that separates can be realistically gauged without specific knowledge of what van den Toorn and many others would evidently prefer to ignore.

Among those who have most loudly chanted the praises of amnesia was Stravinsky, whose squeamishness about his past, and whose rewritings of it, have become legend.[14] By the latest (cold war) phase of his career, the amnesia, formerly applied selectively and opportunistically, had become a generalized defense against all "extramusical" association. The following exchange from the first book of "Conversations" with Robert Craft is indicative:

---

they are in and of themselves and not for what they represent, then context itself, as a reflection of this transcendence, becomes less dependent on matters of historical placement. A great variety of contexts can suggest themselves as attention is focused on the works, on the nature of both their immediacy and the relationship that is struck with the contemporary listener" ("Context and Analytical Method in Stravinsky," in *Music, Politics, and the Academy* [Berkeley and Los Angeles: University of California Press, 1995]), p. 196. The impersonal constructions attributing agency to inanimate objects and notions (contexts suggesting themselves, individual works taking hold and prevailing, etc.) are characteristic of this line of thinking, even indispensable to it.

[13] Ibid., pp. 195–96.

[14] See R. Taruskin, "Stravinsky and the Traditions: Why the Memory Hole?" *Opus* 3, no. 4 (June 1987): 10–17.

R.C. Have you ever thought that music is, as Auden says, "a virtual image of our experience of living as temporal, with its double aspect of recurrence and becoming?"

I.S. If music is to me an "image of our experience of living as temporal" (and however unverifiable, I suppose it is), my saying so is the result of a reflection and as such is independent of music itself. But this kind of thinking about music is a different vocation altogether for me: I cannot *do* anything with it as a truth, and my mind is a *doing* one. . . . Auden's "image of our experience of living as temporal" (which is also an image) is above music, perhaps, but it does not obstruct or contradict the purely musical experience. What shocks me however, is the discovery that many people think below music. Music is merely something that reminds them of something else—of landscapes, for example; my *Apollo* is always reminding someone of Greece. But in even the most specific attempts at evocation, what is meant by being "like" and what are "correspondences?" Who, listening to Liszt's precise and perfect little *Nuages gris*, could pretend that "gray clouds" are a musical cause and effect?[15]

The first thing to note, in attempting to unpack this remarkable little document, is that the phrase of Auden's from which the composer is at such pains to distance himself is in fact a paraphrase—a knowing paraphrase, one has to think—of some famous pronouncements by Stravinsky himself. In his Parisian autobiography of 1936, *Chroniques de ma Vie*, Stravinsky followed his famous fighting words about music's powerlessness "to *express* anything at all" with an honorable attempt to define not only what music was not, but also what it is. "Music," he then wrote (or had his ghostwriter write),

is the sole domain in which man realizes the present. By the imperfection of his nature, man is doomed to submit to the passage of time—to its categories of past and future—without ever being able to give substance, and therefore stability, to the category of the present. The phenomenon of music is given to us with the sole purpose of establishing an order in things, including, and particularly, the coordination between *man* and *time*.[16]

A dozen years later, at lunch at the Raleigh Hotel in Washington, D.C., on 31 March 1948, Stravinsky surprised Robert Craft, whom he had just met and who recorded it in his diary, with the "marvelous remark" that "music is the best means we have of digesting time." The Stravinskys' other luncheon guest that day was W. H. Auden.[17]

For the interwar and the postwar Stravinskys, then—the Stravinskys whose

---

[15] Stravinsky and Craft, *Conversations with Igor Stravinsky*, p. 15.

[16] Igor Stravinsky, *An Autobiography* (New York: Norton, 1962), p. 54. The ghostwriter of this book was Walter Nouvel, an old Ballets Russes hand.

[17] Robert Craft, *Stravinsky: Chronicle of a Friendship* (New York: Knopf, 1972), p. 6.

thirdhand Bergsonian remarks Auden admired and improved upon—music, even if it did not "express," nevertheless signified, and what it signified was of the most primal human significance.[18] The cold-war Stravinsky was more exigent; he insisted not on music as metaphor but on "music itself."

That is a very strange notion indeed, "music itself." Its history has yet to be written, but it does not seem to be a very long one. In the sense in which the cold-war Stravinsky used the term, it does not seem to extend back more than a decade or two before Stravinsky used it. The term has nothing to do with the nineteenth century's "absolute music," with which it is now often mistakenly interchanged; for the absoluteness of absolute music, as Wagner (yes, Wagner) first envisioned it, was an absolute expressivity, not an absolute freedom from expression.[19] Stravinsky's first approximation to the term came in a little talk he took around beginning in 1935 to introduce the concerts at which he and his son Sviatoslav (Soulima) gave the initial performances of the *Concerto per due pianoforti soli*. "There are different ways of loving and appreciating music," he would say:

> There is, for instance, the way that I would call self-interested love, wherein one demands from music emotions of a general sort—joy, sorrow, sadness, a subject for dreaming on, forgetfulness of ordinary existence. But that devalues music by assigning it a utilitarian end. Why not love it for its own sake? Why not love it as one loves a picture, for the sake of the beautiful painting, the beautiful design, the beautiful composition? Why not admit that music has an intrinsic value, independent of the sentiments or images that it may evoke by analogy, and that can only corrupt the hearer's judgment? Music needs no help. It is sufficient unto itself. Don't look for anything else in it beyond what it already contains.[20]

These are clearly related concepts. Yet to speak of "aimer la musique pour elle-même," or to say that "elle suffit à elle-même," is not at all the same as speaking of "la musique elle-même," something of which Stravinsky does not

---

[18] For the discussion on which the two quoted remarks depend, see Pierre Souvtchinsky, "La notion du temps et la musique," in the special Stravinsky number of *La Revue Musicale*, no. 191 (May–June 1939): 70–81; Stravinsky paraphrased it (with due attribution) in his Harvard lectures later that year: see Igor Stravinsky, *Poetics of Music in the Form of Six Lessons*, trans. Arthur Knodel and Ingolf Dahl (Cambridge, Mass.: Harvard University Press, 1970), pp. 38–43.

[19] Wagner coined the term in an 1846 commentary to Beethoven's Ninth Symphony, where he wrote that the instrumental recitative in the fourth movement, "already almost breaking the bounds of absolute music, . . . stems the tumult of the other instruments with its virile eloquence." The absoluteness of absolute music (or, as Dahlhaus paraphrases it, "objectless instrumental music") lies in its "endless and imprecise expressiveness," an idea Wagner locates in Ludwig Tieck's description of symphonic music: "insatiate desire forever hieing forth and turning back into itself." See Carl Dahlhaus, *The Idea of Absolute Music*, trans. Roger Lustig (Chicago: University of Chicago Press, 1989), p. 18.

[20] "Quelques Confidences sur la Musique" (1935), reprinted in Eric Walter White, *Stravinsky: The Composer and His Works* (Berkeley and Los Angeles: University of California Press, 1966), p. 539.

yet seem to have the notion. He is still speaking (Kantianly, one might almost say) of pure motives and pure attitudes—of "aestheticism," if you like—but not, as yet, of pure essences. (He could hardly have been doing that before concerts in which his Three Tableaux from *Petrushka*, played by Soulima, shared the program with the new concerto.)

The special congeries of notions expressed by tautological terms like "music itself," "the music itself," "music as music," and so on, came later, at least to Stravinsky. And they came to him in America. They coincide with his serial period. (Indeed, he made a point, in a passage elided from the Auden discussion quoted earlier, of exempting the sort of music he was then composing from Auden's metaphors, even insofar as he accepted them: "If I understand 'recurrence' and 'becoming,'" he now stipulated, "their aspect is greatly diminished in serial music.")

So what was this new notion of "music itself," of which the music of the cold-war period was the best and purest exemplar? Commonplace though the phrase has become in everyday parlance, intuitively though we may feel we understand it, its definition is intractably elusive—or perhaps it would be more accurate to say protean; for it is never defined except by its context, and its context is invariably one of negation. In Stravinsky's response to Craft, "music itself" is defined as being *not* "the result of a reflection;" it is *not* evocative; it is *not* a correspondence; it is "below" the terms of Auden's generalization (so it's not that), and "above" such particular things as landscapes and clouds (so it's none of those, either). But what is it?

Impossible to say—which is precisely why the term has become indispensable in certain kinds of metamusical discourse. It is the great instrument of rejection. In Joseph Kerman's *Contemplating Music*, for example, a book that had as its objective precisely the redefinition of musicology's domain and its methodology so as to put it in closer touch with "the music itself," the concept is wielded like a bazooka. "Music itself," or "music as music," or, less often, "music in its own terms," we learn, does not consist in facts about music; or in autonomous systems or structure; or in historical generalizations; or in texts ("the bare score"); or in "moments in a hypothesized evolutionary process," or in "art 'objects' susceptible to objective manipulation," or in bibliographical minutiae, or in analytical minutiae, or in music-in-culture or music-in-society, or indeed in any exclusive context.[21]

What's left? Kerman has excluded the general and the particular, the autonomous and the contextual, the whole and the part. And still, his negatives do not equal Stravinsky's negatives, nor do they suggest similar positive intuitions, except insofar as both writers seem to eliminate the reflective and associate "music" (Kerman tacitly, Stravinsky openly) with some kind of primary,

[21] See Joseph Kerman, *Contemplating Music* (Cambridge, Mass.: Harvard University Press, 1985), pp. 55, 73, 115, 119, 139, 145, 163, 164, 171, 180, 190.

inarticulate, implicitly incommunicable activity. In Kerman's case the residuum is performing and listening; these are the activities to which his envisaged musicology (or "criticism") is accessory. In Stravinsky's case the privileged activity, naturally enough, is composing (for him, plain *doing*). For both of them, ultimately, "music itself" is a chimera, for it is half of a binarism—one hand clapping—of which the other half is the "extramusical." As in any binarism, neither term can mean anything in the absence of the other. Each, therefore, is fashioned out of its relationship to the other. (The music itself is that which is not extramusical; the extramusical is that which is not the music itself.) And as always, the need for such constructions lies in the actions—and the exclusions—that they enable.

So maybe it were better to say that rather than being merely chimerical, the indefinable but indispensable notion of "music itself" acts as a *cordon sanitaire*, a quarantine staking out a decontaminated space within which music can be composed, performed, and listened to in a cultural and historical vacuum, that is, in perfect sterility.

II

The question remains as to why the quarantine is deemed necessary. Rather than go on theorizing about it, let us observe it in action. Stravinsky's early masterpiece *The Rite of Spring* is the perfect test case: because its reputation has achieved genuinely mythic proportions; because the mythology of *The Rite* has generated a huge and many-sided literature; and because so much of that literature is so easily and instructively falsified.

The myth is an eclectic compound of at times contradictory elements. There was the work's sensationally nasty Paris première. ("The real thing—a big 'Paris' scandal!" critics marveled or scoffed. "Things got as far as fighting," the composer laconically reported in a letter home.)[22] There were the many cheap imitations it inspired. (Robert Craft called *The Rite* "the prize bull that inseminated the whole modern movement.")[23] There was the durable enigma of its technical premises, inspiring a clamor of irreconcilable analytical hypotheses. The myth of *The Rite* is at once a myth of iconoclasm and a myth of virgin birth; a myth of disruption and a myth of advancement; a myth of artistic synergy and a myth of musical autonomy. Several books have been devoted to the work by now;[24] but to appreciate the myth as such it would be

[22] Leonid Sabaneyev, "Vesna svyashchennaya," *Golos Moskvï*, 8 June 1913; Stravinsky to Maximilian Steinberg, 20 June/3 July 1913, in L. Dyachkova, ed., *I. F. Stravinskiy: Stat'i i materialï* (Moscow: Sovetskiy kompozitor, 1973), p. 474.

[23] Robert Craft, "'The Rite of Spring': Genesis of a Masterpiece," in Igor Stravinsky, *The Rite of Spring: Sketches 1911–1913* (London: Boosey and Hawkes, 1969), p. xv.

[24] Allen Forte, *The Harmonic Organization of "The Rite of Spring"* (New Haven: Yale University Press, 1978); François Lesure, comp. and ed., *Le Sacre du Printemps: Dossier de Presse*

better to look, at the outset, not at the specialized literature or the cutting edge of research but at the textbooks that transmit and cement the conventional wisdom about *The Rite* and about modernist music in general.

Stravinsky's score is always a prime exhibit, and usually *the* prime exhibit, in the early chapters of textbooks on twentieth-century music. Two such textbooks, both straightforwardly entitled *Twentieth-Century Music*, have been published in the last few years, and can be fairly said to represent the current academic-critical consensus. The one by Elliott Antokoletz opens with a boldly formulated assertion of long-established facts:

> An unprecedented departure from established musical traditions characterizes much of the music composed during the first decade of the twentieth century. . . . No changes of musical style or technique have ever produced such a sense of historical discontinuity as those that gave rise to our own era. This condition may be traced directly to the radical change in the basic premises of the musical language itself, a revolutionary transformation stemming most prominently from the works of Ives, Scriabin, Debussy, Bartók, Stravinsky, and members of the Vienna Schoenberg circle.[25]

This is a venerable saga. It has been handed down from bard to bard over many a year, but by now we all know it isn't true. The music of the first decades of the present century, encompassing the outputs of all the figures named in the concluding honor roll, is far more appropriately viewed as a maximalizing phase within the traditions established over the course of the preceding century than as a departure from them. (To add to the topsy-turviness of the standard account, when the real breaks came, in the 1920s, it was necessary to disguise them, then and since, as a recovery of historical continuity.)[26] Thanks to the recent work of many scholars, in what amounts to a burgeoning historiographical and analytical revolution, this is now very easy to see.[27] It takes far more intellectual effort, in fact, to go on maintaining the

---

(Geneva: Minkoff, 1980); Pieter C. van den Toorn, *Stravinsky and "The Rite of Spring": The Beginnings of a Musical Language* (Berkeley and Los Angeles: University of California Press, 1987); Shelley C. Berg, *Le Sacre du printemps: Seven Productions from Nijinsky to Martha Graham* (Ann Arbor: UMI Research Press, 1988).

[25] Elliott Antokoletz, *Twentieth-Century Music* (Englewood Cliffs, N.J.: Prentice-Hall, 1992), p. viii.

[26] See R. Taruskin, "Revising Revision," *Journal of the American Musicological Society* 46 (1993): 114–38, and "Back to Whom? Neoclassicism as Ideology," *19th-Century Music* 16 (1992–93): 286–302.

[27] Antokoletz himself, in his specialized work, has made a fundamental contribution toward revealing the stylistic continuity between early twentieth-century "new music" and what came before. See his *The Music of Béla Bartók: A Study of Tonality and Progression in Twentieth-Century Music* (Berkeley and Los Angeles: University of California Press, 1984), especially the introductory and concluding chapters (pp. 1–25, 312–28). In this work he has followed on that of George Perle: see, inter alia, the latter's article "Berg's Master Array of the Interval Cycles,"

existence of (or perhaps more to the point, simply to go on maintaining) the wall between the modernist Mighty Handful and their antecedents. Yet as contemporary scholarly performance still attests, many think the effort worthwhile. Partly, no doubt, it is to keep up the status of the modernist giants as giants. Praising famous men—or rather, praising self-made men—will remain on the agenda until those perpetually rising middle classes quit rising. It won't be anytime soon (and I've done my share and can't promise I'll stop).

But there is something else at work here, too. The myth of the revolutionary transformation acts as another sort of *cordon sanitaire* around the thing transformed—that is, as Antokoletz so resonantly puts it, "*the music*al language *itself*." If rupture with the historical past is accepted as a given—if, for example (as van den Toorn insists in his subtitle), *The Rite of Spring* is assumed to represent "the *beginning* of a musical language" rather than an extension or a maximalization or a culmination—then study of "the basic premises" of modern music can proceed on an entirely inferential basis, and an entirely sequestered one. The "autonomy" of the analytical act is protected. The advantage of such an approach—the gain, as it were—consists precisely in what is lost from it.

Stravinsky knew this first and best. As early as the 1920s (the time, as I say, of the real "breaks"), Stravinsky was busily revising the history of *The Rite* and erasing its past. It was in 1920 that he first told an interviewer that the first inspiration for the ballet had been not a vision of its final dance (as he had previously stated) but a musical theme, and that consequently he had written "un oeuvre architectonique et non anecdotique."[28] Over the next fifty years he continually reinforced the notion that *The Rite of Spring*, of all things, was a "purely musical" work. Perhaps influenced to some degree by the triumph he experienced in 1914 ("such as *composers* rarely enjoy," he recalled in old age), when Pierre Monteux conducted the score in the Salle Pleyel to a reception as tumultuous as the first had been, but enthusiastically positive, he averred categorically that "I prefer *Le Sacre* as a concert piece."[29]

Many have followed him in this preference. And even if matters of preference are laid aside, it is undeniable that, as van den Toorn points out at the very beginning of his study of the ballet, "for the greater part of this century our knowledge and appreciation of *The Rite of Spring* have come from the concert hall and from recordings."[30] For many if not most spectators, visual

---

Musical Quarterly 63 (1977): 1–30. With particular reference to Stravinsky, see R. Taruskin, "Chernomor to Kashchei: Harmonic Sorcery; or, Stravinsky's 'Angle,'" *Journal of the American Musicological Society* 38 (1985): 72–142.

[28] Michel Georges-Michel, "Les deux Sacres du printemps," *Comoedia* (11 December 1920), quoted from Truman C. Bullard, "The First Performance of Igor Stravinsky's *Sacre du Printemps*" (Ph.D. dissertation, University of Rochester, 1971), vol. 1, p. 3.

[29] Igor Stravinsky and Robert Craft, *Expositions and Developments* (Garden City, N.Y.: Doubleday, 1962), pp. 164, 165.

[30] Van den Toorn, *Stravinsky and "The Rite of Spring,"* p. 1.

exposure to the work comes after years of tremendous stagings before the mind's eye under the stimulus of the powerful music, and is often disappointing. Van den Toorn goes on to aver, with Stravinsky, that these facts of life and history justify the relegation of all impedimenta—"the scenario itself, the choreography, and, above all, the close 'interdisciplinary' conditions of coordination under which the music is now known to have been composed"—to the limbic category of "the 'extra-musical.'" "Like pieces of a scaffolding," he ingeniously observes, "they were abandoned in favor of the edifice itself."[31]

And yet we note a familiar diction, betokening a familiar discourse, in the elemental opposition of the "extramusical" scaffold to "the edifice *itself*," and wonder how access to the latter is to be gained. The answer, it turns out, is no surprise. We reach the edifice itself by rigorously excluding all that does not conduce directly to "pure musical delight."[32] And what is that? Van den Toorn quotes the cold-war Stravinsky: "The composer works through a perceptual, not a conceptual process. He perceives, he selects, he combines, and is not in the least aware at what point meanings of a different sort and significance grow into his works. All he knows or cares about is the apprehension of the contours of form, for form is everything."[33]

Form is everything. That seems about as definitive and as extreme a declaration of formalist principles as could be desired. And yet van den Toorn actually manages to exceed the latter-day Stravinsky's formalism in two distinct ways. The first is by explicitly identifying the listener's viewpoint and role with those attributed by Stravinsky to the composer, something Stravinsky never thought to do. "One need merely substitute listener for composer in the above quotations," van den Toorn observes, "and the reasoning becomes impregnable."[34] It is not reasoning that is impregnable here, however, but a tautology. The second strategy, inadvertent though it may have been, was misquotation. The last sentence in the extract, as published by Craft and Stravinsky, reads as follows: "All he knows or cares about his apprehension of the contour of *the* form, for *the* form is everything."[35] As a Russian speaker, to be sure, Stravinsky must have dropped his definite articles in English every day. But what a difference they make to the sense here! What Stravinsky evidently intended as a description of a particular act (composing) is transformed by van den Toorn into a universal aesthetic stance.

It transpires, then, that van den Toorn's hypothetical listener is not really identified with this particular (or any particular) composer. He inhabits a hermetically sealed world of his own making, and he would like to rest there undisturbed for the sake of the pleasure to be derived by bonding, as it were

[31] Ibid., p. 2.

[32] Ibid., p. 7.

[33] As quoted by van den Toorn on p. 18.

[34] Ibid., p. 19.

[35] Stravinsky and Craft, *Expositions and Developments*, p. 116 (italics added).

intersubjectively, with the music he hears. In a later article van den Toorn makes this point yet more explicit:

> The source of the attraction, the source of our conscious intellectual concerns, is the passionate nature of the relationship that is struck. But this relationship is given immediately in experience and is not open to the inquiry that it inspires. Moments of aesthetic rapport, of self-forgetting at-oneness with music, are immediate. The mind, losing itself in contemplation, becomes immersed in the musical object, becomes one with that object.[36]

The music itself, then, is really *the music myself*. "Leave me alone with me," is van den Toorn's ultimate plea to historians and students of culture, and he speaks for a broad cohort. It is a perfectly reasonable request, coming from a listener. Is it reasonable when it comes from a scholar? Or do scholars have other responsibilities, public ones?

The formalist strategy just examined—that of authorizing the preoccupation with "music itself" by identifying the listener's concerns with those of the composer—lies behind the analytical commonplace that to understand (or, more precisely, to comprehend) something is to give an account of its making. A prominent music analyst was recently provoked by a hostile reviewer into formulating this perception as a maxim (albeit in the form of a question): "How can anyone know *what* something is—i.e., be in a position to make aesthetic judgments about it—without knowing *how* it is made?"[37] To say this, of course, is to contradict a fundamental precept of Arnold Schoenberg, one of the founders, as a theorist, of the modern practice of musical analysis, and one of the primary objects, as a composer, of the analytical practices here upheld. In a letter to his brother-in-law, the violinist Rudolf Kolisch, who had worked out an exemplary formalistic analysis of Schoenberg's Third Quartet, the composer wrote, "I can't utter too many warnings against overrating these analyses, since after all they only lead to what I have always been dead set against: seeing how it is *done*; whereas I have always helped people to see: what it *is!*" And he admonished Kolisch in particular that an accounting of the manufacture of music "is not where the aesthetic qualities reveal themselves."[38]

But then, Schoenberg did not at the time possess the notion of "the music itself," and, unlike Stravinsky, he did not live long enough to pick it up. Returning to a recent writer like Antokoletz and his discussion of *The Rite of Spring*, we will not be surprised to find its purview, like van den Toorn's,

---

[36] "Politics, Feminism, and Music Theory," *Journal of Musicology* 9 (1991): 276.

[37] Derrick Puffett, letter to the editor, *Times Literary Supplement*, 20–26 July 1990, p. 775. The provocateur's response: "I take it that [Puffett] knows the recipes of all the meals he enjoys" (Michael Tanner, letter to the editor, ibid., 27 July–2 August 1990).

[38] Letter of 27 July 1932; Arnold Schoenberg, *Letters*, trans. Eithne Wilkins and Ernst Kaiser, ed. Erwin Stein (Berkeley and Los Angeles: University of California Press, 1987), p. 164.

resolutely purged of the "extramusical." The subject and scenario have been boiled down to the single remark that the ballet is "highly ritualistic"; but even that little trace is immediately turned into a characterization of "the music itself": "In this highly ritualistic ballet, we find the most thorough-going use of narrow-range melodics, based on nonfunctional diatonic modality, and constant repetition of short rhythmic motives or phrases in the typically irregular meters of Russian folk music."[39] For the rest, the description of *The Rite* is a description of its manufacture, covering the "generation" not only of the individual work but also of the way in which "Stravinsky transforms and expands the Russian folk-music properties into an abstract set of pitch relations to form his own personal contemporary musical language."[40] Both curious and typical is the identification of Stravinsky's putative practical methods of construction with theoretical generalizations made many years after the fact by George Perle ("interval cycles") and Pieter van den Toorn ("octatonicism"). Method is inferred from "structure" and then attributed to the composer, whose work is thus rationalized and rendered abstract.

And harmless. What is chiefly objectionable about such analysis is not its anachronism or its purloining of the composer's authority. What is chiefly objectionable is its propensity to normalize and, in yet another way, sanitize. To perceive regularities and familiar patterns beneath a complicated or unusual surface (for all that it contradicts the myth of disruption) is evidence of analytical acumen; and so regularity of pattern is prized and sought, and inevitably found. Consider Antokoletz's parsing of the opening bassoon solo in *The Rite* in such a way as to demonstrate its "structural balance" and its character as a "closed off" formal scheme (figure 13.1).[41]

Stravinsky's adaptation of a Lithuanian folk melody is cut up into four segments, of which the first and last are held to be a rhythmic palindrome $(1 + 4 : 5 + 1)$, and the middle pair are held to be a hemiola $(2 \times 3 : 3 \times 2)$. By separating the sixth note (A with fermata) from the sixteenth-note group, Antokoletz's segmentation contradicts Stravinsky's phrasing, ignores the obvious melodic parallelism, and occludes the very cadential structure the segmentation is supposed to be revealing. As to the middle pair, hemiolas are only hemiolas when they take up the same amount of (notated) time. And besides, the separation of the two segments is entirely an artifact of the bar

[39] Antokoletz, *Twentieth-Century Music*, p. 94.

[40] Ibid., p. 96.

[41] Ibid., pp. 95–96. Antokoletz purports here to develop ideas proposed by Pierre Boulez in his article "Stravinsky demeure" (1951), first published in *Musique russe*, ed. Pierre Souvtchinsky, vol. 1 (Paris: Presses Universitaires de France, 1953), pp. 151–224, later collected and published in Pierre Boulez, *Notes of an Apprenticeship*, trans. Herbert Weinstock (New York: Knopf, 1968), pp. 72–145 (in a section entitled, revealingly enough, "Toward a Technology"). Boulez's parsing, however, is not the same as Antokoletz's, and is not necessarily subject to the strictures entered herein (see "Stravinsky demeure," p. 158; *Notes of an Apprenticeship*, p. 79).

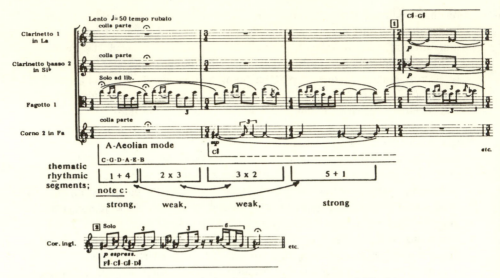

FIGURE 13.1. Elliott Antokoletz's analysis of the opening measures of *The Rite of Spring* (*Twentieth-Century Music* [Englewood Cliffs, N.J.: Prentice-Hall, 1992], p. 95)

placement, a notational convenience that both the phrasing and the explicitly demanded "tempo rubato" conceal from the ear. The whole analysis is a fiction designed to produce a specious, sanitary ("classical"?) regularity. I would call it a white lie.

Tendentious segmentation is in fact a standard feature of analysis that purports to reveal "the music itself."[42] What is revealed instead is a germ-free vivarium, entirely "closed off," as Antokoletz says, from the world in which the music was composed and in which it is experienced. This utopian harmony seems maladapted, to say the least, to Antokoletz's general view of twentieth-century music as a "revolutionary transformation," an "unprecedented departure," and a product of "historical discontinuity," all of which, at first blush, connote violence. But on reflection it is all the more apparent that a reading of twentieth-century music as "closed off" from the past is precisely what is necessary to clear space for such utopian visions of rational order as modern analysts propose. Reading such analyses with even minimal historical awareness is discomfiting. One can only wonder why such well-behaved music should have evoked protests at its first performance.

[42] This ground has been thoroughly gone over with reference to pitch-class set analysis of *The Rite*. See R. Taruskin, review of Forte, *The Harmonic Organization of "The Rite of Spring,"* in *Current Musicology*, no. 28 (1979): 114–29, esp. pp. 121–26; Forte, "Pitch-Class Set Analysis Today," *Music Analysis* 4 (1985): 29–58, esp. pp. 36–37; and the exchange of letters to the editor in *Music Analysis* 5 (1986): 313–37.

Robert Morgan's analysis of *The Rite*, in his similarly titled textbook, is similarly normalizing and sanitizing. He describes the famous ostinato chord from the "Augurs of Spring" as being only superficially what it appears to be, namely, "a combination of two triadic structures, a dominant seventh chord built on E-flat and a major triad on F-flat." Such a description (which Stravinsky, it should be noted, never outgrew) attempts an accommodation with the perceptual, if not the conceptual, norms of an earlier practice, and therefore violates a cardinal precept of the modernist myth. Rather, Morgan says, the chord is "an integrated sonority with octatonic qualities" because it is "largely, though not exclusively, drawn from the scale Eb–E–F♯–G–A–Bb–C–Db–Eb ."[43]

Morgan's two descriptive comments are in contradiction: one posits integration, the other ("largely, though not exclusively, drawn . . .") posits eclecticism, but an eclecticism that is never acknowledged or accounted for, because Morgan never says where the part of the chord comes from that is not drawn from the octatonic scale he adduces. The discrepancy between the object and its description is swept under the rug.[44] The function of the "Augurs" chord, as Morgan describes it, is likewise normative and reassuring: "the chord provides a basic pitch reference, or tonal focus, for the entire section: twice interrupted by contrasting segments, it returns in unaltered form," while "even the interruptions reveal the influence of this chord."[45] So again one wants to ask, Why the great Paris scandal? Why did things get as far as fighting?

Morgan does try to account for the initial reaction by admitting "the harshness of *The Rite*," owing to its "high level of dissonance and chromaticism."[46] He may have been responding to Arnold Whittall's very salutary reminder, in an article entitled "Music Analysis as Human Science?" that, whatever the analytical premises from which it is approached, "what is most significant" in *The Rite* "is the existence and dominance of discords."[47] This does need saying nowadays, and it does evoke the early reception of the work: after the first

[43] Robert Morgan, *Twentieth-Century Music* (New York: Norton, 1991), p. 97.

[44] Similarly, in the seminal article in which the octatonic scale was christened, Arthur Berger infers from a passage in *Svadbeka* (*Les Noces*) the as yet unnamed "referential collection of eight pitch classes" that "accounts for it all—with a few exceptions so marginal as scarcely to require mention (some dozen tones, mainly ornamental)" ("Problems of Pitch Organization in Stravinsky" [1963], in *Perspectives on Schoenberg and Stravinsky*, ed. Benjamin Boretz and Edward T. Cone [Princeton: Princeton University Press, 1968], p. 132). Since nowhere are criteria stated by which the structural and the ornamental are distinguished, one must conclude that referability to the referential collection is the tacit criterion, one that bends the argument, characteristically, into a circle. The "ornamental" pitches, of course, have since proved "structural" by reference to another analytical template (see the next section of this chapter).

[45] Morgan, *Twentieth-Century Music*, p. 97.

[46] Ibid.

[47] Arnold Whittall, "Music Analysis as Human Science? *Le Sacre du Printemps* in Theory and Practice," *Music Analysis* 1 (1982): 50.

Russian performance (under Koussevitzky in Moscow in February 1914), the critic Vyacheslav Karatïgin wrote in amazement (and only slightly hyperbolically) that "from beginning to end there is not a single pure triad."[48] Whittall goes on to propose that "as a portrait of human savagery, the tragic power of *Le Sacre* may depend precisely on the freedom for conflict to be expressed by the most immediate and effective means." This sounds like a plea to restore the "extra-musical" dimension that van den Toorn and the others so zealously exclude. And yet even Whittall cannot envision an analytical practice that goes beyond "the music itself." It's the nature of the beast to exclude the world, he finally agrees, in what seems to me a very pessimistic conclusion. "It may indeed be the case," he concedes, "that the 'rules' of the game can only be discovered if the discords are 'translated' into some other medium, in which they can be examined without the psychological burden of their true character and quality. For *Le Sacre* remains an explosive work, and analysis may be impossible unless the score is first defused."[49]

Yet the myth of *The Rite* demands reinstatement of its explosiveness, and analysts are thus in a quandary. One way out is to imagine *The Rite* in a dual aspect: as being one thing historically, quite another thing "essentially." Those committed to maintaining the high disciplinary walls that now separate "musicology" from "music theory" seem to have no trouble with such a divided consciousness. The division, furthering methodological purity, is seen as a necessary ablution, a cleansing-of-the-hands that must precede the delicate operation by which "the music itself" is isolated and dissected. The sterility of the theoretical discipline is itself seen as evidence of its superior condition. Thus, asks V. Kofi Agawu, summarizing the case for institutional isolation,

> Has not *the most influential* historical work always needed theory, whereas the best theoretical work rarely depended on the insights of *conventional* history? On present showing, we might say that theory is theory and history is history, and that although they may meet or clash sometimes, they remain separate disciplines. To this writer at least, that ain't such a bad thing.[50]

I have no problem with Agawu's notion of a music history in need of theory. One cannot visit the bathroom without theory. In my own scholarly work, for all that I am classified, at least by Agawu, as a "historian," I certainly have had need of theory, have freely helped myself to it, and even contributed to it. As for theory in no need of history—well, that's his problem. But the divided consciousness Agawu asserts as healthy is what provides

---

[48] "Sed'moy kontsert Kussevitskogo," *Rech'*, 14 February 1914.

[49] Whittall, "Music Analysis as Human Science?", p. 50.

[50] V. Kofi Agawu, "Does Music Theory Need Musicology?" *Current Musicology* 53 (1993): 98. The italics in the first sentence are added. Reread the sentence without the italicized words to appreciate the author's sophistry to the full.

writers like Morgan with a way out of the quandary to which I have referred. Morgan prefaces his normalizing, sanitizing account of *The Rite* as a score with a paragraph devoted to *The Rite* as an event, in which a familiar fable is related:

> If the Paris productions of *The Firebird* and *Petrushka* established Stravinsky as a major composer of international reputation, the score for his third Diaghilev ballet, *The Rite of Spring*, made him the most widely recognized composer of his age. The premiere of *The Rite* in Paris on May 29, 1913, is probably the most famous (or notorious) premiere in the history of music. The ballet's scenic evocation of pagan Russian rituals elicited from Stravinsky a score of unprecedented primitive force, in which music seemed to be distilled to its rhythmic essence, hammered out by the orchestra with unrestrained percussive intensity. Shaken by the radical nature of both score and ballet, the opening-night audience was in an uproar from the beginning, with those both for and against shouting at one another in heated debate. The noise level was so high that most of the music remained inaudible; yet if nothing else, the sensational aspect of the event placed Stravinsky at the forefront of the musical revolutions of the time. For contemporary listeners of *The Rite*, as for those of the first atonal works of Schoenberg, music could never be the same again.[51]

III

Not a bad achievement for inaudible music. But again, as always, the myth accommodates contradictions. That is what myths are for. The reality was different. As the ballet historians Joan Acocella, Lynn Garafola, and Jonnie Greene have put it, "The original *Rite of Spring* was no sooner made than it was laid aside." With a sophistication that knows no peer in the musical literature on the work, they go on to observe that "therefore while in the historical record we call it a ballet, the way we actually know it is as a collection of ideas: ideas leading up to its creation, together with ideas leading away from the circumstances of its production."[52] These remarks come at the outset of a remarkable essay entitled "*The Rite of Spring* Considered as a Nineteenth-Century Ballet," in which the authors do what in the musicological literature seems to be unthinkable: they insert the work into a context defined by the past, not the future. They perceive no break with tradition, but manifold extensions of it. They go so far, in fact, as to interpret the reception history of *The Rite* as "a history of the twentieth century's coping with its inheritance from the nineteenth" (p. 71). This is fabulously succinct and discerning, and

---

[51] Morgan, *Twentieth-Century Music*, pp. 95–96.

[52] Joan Acocella, Lynn Garafola, and Jonnie Greene, "*The Rite of Spring* Considered as a Nineteenth-Century Ballet," *Ballet Review* 20, no. 2 (Summer 1992): 68. Further page references to this source will be made in the text.

provides the best possible context for considering the sanitizing efforts I have been describing.

What did that nineteenth-century legacy consist of? First of all, of course, it comprised primitivism, the belief that the qualities of primitive or chronologically early cultures are superior to those of contemporary civilization, or as the ballet historians put it, that "it is those things that are least socialized, least civilized—children, peasants, 'savages,' raw emotion, plain speech—that are closest to truth" (p. 68). Primitivism is often touted, especially in discussions of *The Rite of Spring*, as one of those twentieth-century revolutions that cut our age off from the past, but it has a very long history indeed. (As the ballet historians shrewdly note, "it is one of the chief teachings of the New Testament.") It was a core constituent of romanticism, against which the modern (and again, especially *The Rite*) is so often and so wrongly construed as a break. The idea of primitive immediacy of consciousness, of at-oneness with the world, was at the very heart of the German romantic concept of culture—*Kultur*—as opposed to the false *Zivilisation* of the Enlightenment (that is, of France), and became the most basic component of the Germans' construction of their national identity.[53] At the other end of the nineteenth century, the end that provided *The Rite* with its immediate background, the idea surfaced with particular force in Russia, where in a curious semantic switch, the cognate word, *kul'tura*, was associated with Enlightenment, and a good *ur*-Slavic antonym, *stikhiya*, was pressed into service in the name of primitive romantic immediacy.[54] All this was brought to a head by the same sense of impending catastrophe that seized political and social thinkers in the aftermath of the Emancipation with its great uprooting of the peasantry, and horror at "the mockery that urban poverty made of the promises of the Industrial Revolution" (p. 68). "In our hearts," wrote the poet Alexander Blok in 1908, "the needle of a seismograph has twitched."[55] It was in the name of a maximalized primitivism that nineteenth-century romanticism gave way to twentieth-century revolutionary politics.

Maximalized and desentimentalized primitivism leads to that bleak vision known as biologism, "the belief that life is fundamentally its physical facts:

---

[53] For a stimulating discussion of this dichotomy (in the light of its formulation by the German sociologist Norbert Elias) and its implications for the historiography of music, see Sanna Pederson, "On the Task of the Music Historian: The Myth of the Symphony after Beethoven," *repercussions* 2, no. 2 (Fall 1993): 5–30. See also Celia Applegate, "What Is German Music? Reflections on the Role of Art in the Creation of a Nation," *German Studies Review* (Winter 1992), special issue ("German Identity"), pp. 21–32.

[54] For an especially pertinent discussion see Vyacheslav Ivanov (representing *kul'tura*) and Mikhail Gershenzon (representing *stikhiya*), "A Corner-to-Corner Correspondence" (1920), trans. Gertrude Vakar, in Marc Raeff, ed., *Russian Intellectual History: An Anthology* (New York: Harcourt, Brace and World, 1966), esp. pp. 374–75, 398.

[55] "Stikhiya i kul'tura," in A. Blok, *Sobraniye sochineniy v shesti tomakh* (Moscow: Izdatel'stvo "Pravda," 1971), vol. 5, p. 283.

birth, death, survival" (p. 68) and that anything else is mere ornament and palliative, a lie. Many were those who immediately saw this in *The Rite* and were afraid. Jacques Rivière, the editor of the *Nouvelle revue française*, who wrote the most prescient of all reviews of the ballet, concluded the review with the flat statement that beneath its "sociological" exterior "there is something even more momentous, there is a second meaning, more secret, more frightful: *ce ballet est un ballet biologique*." And, he continued,

> it is not just the dance of the most primitive man, it is also the dance before there was man. . . . There is something profoundly blind in this dance. There is an enormous question being carried about by all these creatures moving before our eyes. It is in no way distinct from themselves. They carry it about with them without understanding it, like an animal that turns in its cage and never tires of butting its forehead against the bars. They have no other organ than their whole organism, and it is with that that they carry on their search. They go hither and thither and stop; they throw themselves forward like a load, and wait. . . . Nothing precedes them; there is nothing to rejoin. No ideal to regain. . . . Just as the blood within them, without any reason save its pumping, knocks against the walls of their skulls, so they ask for issue and succession. And little by little, by dint of their patience and persistence, a sort of answer comes, that is also nothing other than themselves, which also meshes with their physical being, and which is life.[56]

It was the great thrust of the nineteenth-century science of anthropology to demystify mythology, to demote myths from the status to which occultists, like the post-Wagnerians and the symbolists (and, of course, Scriabin), wished to reelevate them—the belief that myths represented "a record of contact between mortals and the *au delà*"[57]—to that of metaphor for grim biological realities. It was the project of Sir James Frazer, for example, in his *Golden Bough*, to strip away the anecdotal content of myths and the metaphorical content of rituals, and reveal the ruthless rites of propitiation that lie behind them—the very thing that *The Rite of Spring* exposed. So where Scriabin's occultism sought to elevate human consciousness above the human plane, the "second sense" of *The Rite of Spring* plunged it down beneath, suggesting the prehuman or subhuman reality that civilized consciousness cloaks but does not replace.

It was a threat not only to poetic mythologism but to the sanctity of revealed religion as well. As Leon Surette observes,

---

[56] Jacques Rivière, "Le sacre du printemps," *La Nouvelle revue française*, November 1913; quoted from Bullard, "The First Performance of Igor Stravinsky's *Sacre du Printemps*," vol. 3, pp. 271–74.

[57] Surette, *The Birth of Modernism*, p. ix.

Frazer's findings reduced the putatively unique event of Christ's passion, death, and resurrection to just one of hundreds, perhaps thousands, of such deaths and resurrections that have been enacted around the world from the earliest times. Frazer's revelation that the solemn Christian mass is a survival of bloody ritual murder and ritual cannibalism—even though he was careful to avoid explicitly drawing this obvious conclusion—can clearly count as the revelation of a secret history.[58]

And there it was, no longer secret, on the stage of the Théâtre des Champs-Elysées. As Acocella, Garafola, and Greene observe about the Chosen Maiden, "Had the community simply sat down and eaten her, this would have made a difference of tone but, arguably, not of meaning" (p. 68). In that case they would have been celebrating the Eucharist.

Now before proceeding any further, the obvious objection must be addressed, that everything that the trio of ballet historians and I have been discussing belongs to the "extramusical" layer of *The Rite*, the "scaffolding," as Pieter van den Toorn says, that has been rightly discarded over time in favor of the music, "the edifice itself." But Stravinsky's contribution is not so easily separable from the rest. And the metaphor of the edifice is all wrong because it suggests permanence, whereas Stravinsky's music has undergone change— the first and most decisive change being precisely its detachment from its original context.

When Acocella, Garafola, and Greene say that the "original" *Rite* was "laid aside," we can assume that they mean Nijinsky's *Rite*, not Stravinsky's. The original choreography was not only laid aside but forgotten. Deliberately suppressed by Diaghilev following Nijinsky's departure from his company, and replaced in 1920 by Massine's, it was only painstakingly and (necessarily) fairly speculatively reconstructed by Millicent Hodson in the 1980s for performances beginning in 1987 by the Joffrey Ballet.[59] After a hiatus of three-quarters of a century, the Nijinsky choreography possessed little more than an archeological or (early modernist) period interest for most observers, and was found inadequate by many dance critics.[60] Nijinsky's contribution, it is clear, has played a negligible role in the ballet's history.

---

[58] Ibid., p. 57.

[59] On this reconstruction and its sources see Millicent Hodson, "The Fascination Continues: Searching for Nijinsky's *Sacre*," *Dance Magazine* 54, no. 6 (June 1980): 64–66, 71–75, and "Nijinsky's New Dance: Rediscovery of Ritual Design in 'Le Sacre du Printemps'" (Ph.D. dissertation, University of California at Berkeley, 1985), "Nijinsky's Choreographic Method: Visual Sources from Roerich for *Le Sacre du printemps*," *Dance Research Journal* 18, no. 2 (Winter 1986–87): 7–15, and "*Sacre*: Searching for Nijinsky's Chosen One," *Ballet Review* 15, no. 3 (Fall 1987): 53–66; Arlene Croce, "Footnotes in the Sands of Time," *New Yorker*, 23 November 1987, pp. 140–48; Robert Craft, "The Rite: Counterpoint and Choreography," *Musical Times* 129, no. 1742 (April 1988): 171–76 (but also R. Taruskin, letter to the editor, *Musical Times* 129, no. 1746 [August 1988]: 385).

[60] And in particular, by Joan Acocella: "Who can say whether 'Le Sacre du Printemps' was in fact the great modernist masterpiece that it is now claimed to be? Perhaps it was something more

What binds all productions together, of course, is the uniform presence of the score, which thus seems all the more compellingly to assume the standing of essential "edifice," to which everything else, including the transitory plastic and visual embodiments, remains parasitic and, ultimately, excrescent (the "scaffolding").

And yet that score, too, was at first "laid aside." The handful of performances it received in May and June of 1913 by the Ballets Russes in Paris and London was followed by the two Russian concert premières (Moscow and St. Petersburg) under Koussevitzky the next February, and, finally, Monteux's triumphant performance at the Salle Pleyel in the spring.

And that, for a long time, was it. It took a long while for the score to achieve the awesome reputation we now assume it possessed from the beginning. In 1913 it was not the primary object of attention. The most cursory perusal of the Paris reviews of the original production, conveniently collected in Truman C. Bullard's dissertation, reveals that it was the now-forgotten Nijinsky choreography, far more than Stravinsky's music, that fomented the famous "riot" at the première. Many if not most reviews fail to deal with Stravinsky's contribution at all beyond naming him as composer. And, as most memoirs of the première (and even Morgan's account of it) agree, a lot of the music went unheard, which did not dissuade the protesters in the least. In the words of one reviewer, "at the end of the Prelude the crowd simply stopped listening to the music so that they might better amuse themselves with the choreography."[61] And the crowd managed to turn Stravinsky against Nijinsky, giving him his first reason for wanting to cleanse his score of "extra-musical" taint.

The score was not published until 1921—that is, not until Nijinsky's contribution had been scratched and Stravinsky had begun, in tendentious interviews, the process of purifying the music. Only then did the score's victorious career begin in any real sense. The composer's squeamishness was conditioned in part, no doubt, by the initial "failure" of the work as a ballet, a failure the composer felt alongside the choreographer all through the war years, his so-called Swiss period. Throughout that time, for all that it was instantly his most notorious work, thoughts of *The Rite* were tinged for Stravinsky with thoughts of defeat. Briefly despondent in the fall of 1913, he unburdened himself in a remarkably—indeed, practically uniquely—self-revealing letter to Alexandre Benois, a letter that betrays not only the extent of

---

like the shaggy, dull, pseudo-folkloric thing that we saw in the Joffrey Ballet 'reconstruction.' Many of those who were disappointed by the Joffrey version simply concluded that its flatness was due to its having been put together from such scrappy evidence—in other words, that it wasn't really Nijinsky. But who knows?" ("After the Ball Was Over," *New Yorker*, 18 May 1992, p. 98).

[61] Louis Vuillemin, "Le Sacre du Printemps," *Comoedia* 7, no. 2068 (31 May 1913); quoted from Bullard, "The First Performance of Igor Stravinsky's *Sacre du Printemps*," vol. 1, p. 144.

Stravinsky's emotional dependence on Diaghilev but also the extent of his fear about his own creative future in the wake of the *Rite* fiasco:

> Ah, my dear, this last offspring of mine even now gives me not a moment's peace. What an incredible storm of teeth-gnashing rages about it! Seryozha [Diaghilev] gives me horrible news about how people who were full of enthusiasm or unwavering sympathy for my earlier works have turned against this one. So what, say I, or rather, think I—that's how it ought to be. But what has made Seryozha himself seem to waver about *Le Sacre*? —a work he never listened to at rehearsals without exclaiming, "Divine!" . . . To tell the truth, reviewing my impressions of his attitude toward *Le Sacre*, I am coming to the conclusion that he will not encourage me in this direction. This means I am deprived of my single and truest support in the matter of propagandizing my artistic ideas. You will agree that this completely knocks me off my feet, for I cannot, you understand, I simply *can not* write what they want from me—that is, repeat myself—repeat anyone else you like, only not yourself!—for that is how people write themselves out. But enough about *Le Sacre*. It makes me miserable.[62]

Here we get an inkling of what it was that caused Stravinsky to take refuge from the "extramusical" in "the music itself"—a creative swerve that colored all the rest of his career. His reasons need not be our reasons. And yet we seem to have our own reasons for laying the "original" *Rite* aside and purging its music. We want to forget the ways in which Stravinsky's music participated in the great stripdown from *kul'tura* to *stikhiya*, from humanism to biologism—ways that have always been salient and that used to be acknowledged, but that the music-analytical enterprise has striven hard to hush up. In the absence of a perceived threat, denial would have been superfluous.

As observed in the preceding chapter with respect to Scriabin's late music, the attenuation of functional harmonic relationships entailed a knowing loss in the power of music to represent desire, hence subjectivity. Both Scriabin and Stravinsky were happy to give up what the symbolist poet Vyacheslav Ivanov called the *malïy 'ya,'* the "petty 'I,'" in the interests of, in the one case, the transcendent dissolution of the ego and, in the other, the absorption of the individual consciousness in the collective. As Rivière noted with his customary percipience, the nonprogressive harmony and the relentless foregrounding of the *corps de ballet* went together in the representation of "l'homme au temps où il n'existait pas encore comme individu," mankind without individuals: "The beings [on stage] are still attached; they move in groups, in colonies, in flanks; they are in the grip of a frighteningly indifferent society; they are devoted to a god that they collectively comprise and from which they do not yet know how to distinguish themselves."[63]

[62] Letter of 20 September/3 October 1913; Dyachkova, ed., *I. F. Stravinskiy: Stat'i i materialï*, pp. 477–78.

[63] Cited from Bullard, "The First Performance of Igor Stravinsky's *Sacre du Printemps*," vol. 3, p. 271.

Where Scriabin represented the eschatological collapse of time and space in a music that was highly mobile in its darting root movements within an inversionally and transpositionally invariant harmonic matrix, Stravinsky's music in *The Rite* was of a kind that prompted critic after critic in Russia to resort to the word *nepodvizhnost'*—immobility—to describe its character and affect. The long stretches of arrested root motion and pulsing rhythm that analysts of "the music itself" now prefer to rationalize as structurally unifying—that is, reassuringly fulfilling a traditional formal mandate—was originally heard (and is still easily heard) as the annihilation of the subject and the denial of psychology.

Along with this immobility went a calculated formal disunity and disjunction—*drobnost'* in Russian, meaning the quality of being a sum-of-parts. Study of Stravinsky's sketchbook shows just how deliberate this calculation was. Motivic or even full-blown thematic relations that were salient in early sketches were ruthlessly attenuated as the music was "refined."[64] The "art of transition" between sections is famously eschewed in favor of abrupt, lurching shifts, often coming, as Elliott Carter once observed, "at a point where the statement of an idea is incomplete," or even of a section.[65] The very ending of the first tableau is similarly unprepared, coming as a shocking halt rather than a conclusion. There is little recall of the past in this music, and little forecasting of the future; in any case, there is far less than is customary in concert music, which is the category, in the opinion of Stravinsky and the analysts, to which we are now supposed to assign *The Rite*.

The absence of recall and forecast is an absence of memory—precisely what Rivière described in characterizing the subhuman corps (and what Nietzsche, in a famous essay, defined as the crucial lack—or freedom—that sets the animal kingdom apart from mankind).[66] Carter sensed this characteristic

[64] This observation applies in particular to the "Games" in the first tableau, the "Game of Abduction" (*Igra umïkaniya*, called the "Jeu du rapt" in the published score) and the "Game of Cities" (*Igra dvukh gorodov*, or "Jeu des citées rivales"). They were included in the scenario in response to a single passage in the Kievan Primary Chronicle—see R. Taruskin, "*The Rite* Revisited: The Idea and the Sources of Its Scenario," in *Music and Civilization: Essays in Honor of Paul Henry Lang*, ed. Edmond Strainchamps and Maria Rika Maniates (New York: Norton, 1984), pp. 183–202—and were originally sketched as a unit, with many thematic ideas in common. Later Stravinsky had no hesitation in detaching the "Game of Abduction" from its companion and inserting it in a much earlier position in the score. Not only are the earlier thematic associations obscured but the new placement also disrupts the thematic links that had unified the pair of dances ("Les Augures printaniers" and "Rondes printanières") between which the "Game of Abduction" now intrudes. Full details in R. Taruskin, *Stravinsky and the Russian Traditions* (Berkeley and Los Angeles: University of California Press, 1996), pp. 951–53.

[65] Untitled memoir in "Stravinsky: A Composers' Memorial," *Perspectives of New Music* 9, no. 2–10, no. 1 (1971): 3.

[66] See Friedrich Nietzsche, *Vom Nutzen und Nachteil der Historie für das Leben* ("On the Use and Misuse of History for Life"), in the second volume of *Thoughts out of Season* (*Unzeitgemässe Betrachtungen*): "Man says 'I remember,' and envies the animal that forgets at once, and watches each moment die, disappear in night and mist, and disappear forever. Thus the animal lives

in Stravinsky's music, too. It was a perception that began with the repetitive folk-tale plots of *Renard* and *Histoire du soldat*, both adapted from the collection of the nineteenth-century ethnographer Alexander Afanasyev.

> In these two stories, the characters on stage and the audience are dealt with as if they had no memory, as if living always in the present and not learning from previous events—a dramatic situation that suggests the puppet world, like that of Punch and Judy, as the authors certainly intended, and also in a larger sense inescapable fate and universality of action such as that in the Everyman plays or that of the shades in the Hades of Gide's libretto for *Perséphone* who ceaselessly repeat the gesture of living.
>
> Whatever the intention, this kind of almost disjointed repetition immeasurably increases the pathos of both works. In fact, I came to believe, as I studied the soldier's part [for a performance under Lukas Foss], that it was just because of this curious plot repetition, especially as it is coupled with music, that, although almost continually different in tiny details, is always drawing attention to its repetitive form.[67]

In *The Rite*, unlike *Histoire du soldat* with its very reflective title character, the elimination of memory does not increase the sense of pathos. Rather, it makes pathos impossible. And that may be why even Carter resisted the *drobnost'* of *The Rite*, preferring to view its harmonic ostinatos as "structures" that "characterize and unify each dance," and even speculating, as he suggested to Stravinsky (who declined to respond), that "all the chords in the *Sacre* were related to one source chord," which he thought he had discovered in the Introduction (where such a thing belonged).[68]

Indeed, the global unifier in *The Rite* has been an analytical unicorn or philosophers' stone, avidly hunted, found, asserted. Always, it turns out, some transient recurrent feature has been seized upon and exaggerated to the status of "universality," as when Robert Moevs asserted that the whole ballet is in the key of D minor,[69] or when Messiaen and (following him) Boulez reduced it all to a rhythmic "cell."[70] I, too, have been susceptible to this need,[71] and, I'm sure, one of the reasons why Allen Forte chose *The Rite* for

---

unhistorically: it hides nothing and coincides at all moments exactly with that which it is; it is bound to be truthful at all times, unable to be anything else" (*Werke*, ed. Karl Schlechta, vol. 1 [Munich: Carl Hanser Verlag, 1954], p. 211).

[67] Carter, untitled memoir, pp. 3–4.

[68] Ibid., pp. 4–5.

[69] Robert Moevs, review of *The Harmonic Organization of "The Rite of Spring"* by Allen Forte, *Journal of Music Theory* 24 (1980): 103.

[70] In Boulez, "Stravinsky demeure."

[71] Cf. the discussion of the three-note "*Rite* chord," in Taruskin, *Stravinsky and the Russian Traditions*, pp. 939–48.

his first full-dress demonstration of his highly abstract "set-theoretic" technique of harmonic analysis is because through its use he was able to propose solutions to the famous enigma. The search for the global unifier, I am convinced, is not motivated only by analytical preconceptions or by the wish to give *The Rite* the academic respectability that is obviously its due. Nor is it only or mainly the prestige that comes to any successful solver of standing problems that motivates the constant search. It is a case of resistance to a threat that goes far beyond the disciplinary limits of musicology.

That threat is hinted at in a third Russian word that was often applied to *The Rite* when it was new: *uproshcheniye*, simplification. *The Rite*, for all its novelty and its inscrutability and the dazzling virtuosity of its orchestral presentation, is not a complex score. Elaborate analytical procedures can make it look far more complicated than it is, even if that complexity is introduced only in order to be whittled down in turn to an orderly structural scheme.[72] Why is this felt to be desirable? Because a rational complexity is far less disquieting than a mystifying simplicity. Stravinsky's radical simplification of texture, his static, vamping harmonies, and his repetitive, ostinato-driven forms were the perfect musical approach to the primitivist ideal—the resolute shedding of conventional complexities of linear thought and their replacement by long spans of unchanging content, accessible to instant, as it were gnostic, apprehension and eliciting a primitive, kinesthetic response.

Was this stripdown truly an *uproshcheniye*, a "second" simplicity, a synthesis vouchsafing a higher integration of thought and feeling? Or was it merely what the Russians call an *oproshcheniye*, a dehumanizing retreat from intellectual engagement and an impoverishment of culture? That is a question that has never really gone away. It gave rise to a controversy that continued to swirl about Stravinsky almost to the end of his career, until preoccupation with "the music itself" and with the technology of its production, a preoccupation Stravinsky did everything in his power to abet, managed to marginalize it at last.

The view of Stravinsky as an apostle of *oproshcheniye*, of course, is the view associated with Adorno, for whom Stravinsky's simplified forms and ego-annihilating ostinatos spelled "permanent regression." Adorno, unfairly as it may seem, seized upon an early Berlin review of *Renard* that interpreted Stravinsky's primitivism (or "infantilism," as he preferred to call it) as "an affirmative ideology," and noted that such an interpretation "later appeared in Germany in a sinister context."[73] Yet how unfair is it, really, inasmuch as we know now, far better than Adorno could have known it, that when that sinister

---

[72] For a lunatic-fringe example of this tendency, see Roman Vlad, "Reihenstrukturen im *Sacre du Printemps*," *Musik-Konzepte* 34–35 (1984): 4–64.

[73] See Theodor Weisengrund-Adorno, *Philosophy of Modern Music*, trans. A. G. Mitchell and W. V. Blomster (New York: Seabury Press, 1973), pp. 165–67.

affirmative surfaced in Germany, Stravinsky was highly susceptible to its allure?[74]

Ultimately we have to ask what kind of a drama *The Rite* embodies—that is, to what category shall it be assigned? We have seen that Arnold Whittall associated its shocking musical qualities with "tragic power" and the expression of "conflict." But is that not a sentimental reading, one that identifies with the Chosen One in a manner supported neither by the scenario nor by the score? Was not the dance critic Andrey Levinson closer to the mark when he called *The Rite* "an icy comedy of primeval hysteria"?[75] And was not Jacques Rivière correct when he called special attention to the absence of conflict, even at the dénouement? The Chosen One, he exclaimed, betrays no "personal terror" at all, even though we developed humans in our humanism cannot help assuming that such terror "must fill her soul." On the contrary,

> She carries out a rite; she is absorbed into a social role, and without giving any indication of comprehension or interpretation, she acts according to the will and under the impact of a being more vast than she, of a monster full of ignorance and appetite, of cruelty and darkness. . . . Mankind is dominated by something more inert than itself, more opaque, more constraining—namely, society with its fellows.[76]

It is with that opaque, constraining force that Stravinsky's crashing orchestra, in the "Danse sacrale," is clearly identified, and in its terrible dynamism it persuades us—nay, coerces us—to share its point of view. Rarely has an antihumanist message been so irresistibly communicated.

Even the ballet historians seem to offer a sentimental reading of *The Rite* when they write that "the girl is forthrightly sent to her death in order to benefit the community" and add that "the situation could hardly be more horrible" (p. 69). On the contrary, the sacrificial dance is presented as anything but horrible—and that's what's horrible. The ballet presents and even celebrates an absolute absence of compassion as the necessary correlate of the absence of "psychology," of human subjectivity. The Chosen One, after all, is one of those beings initially presented in the first tableau as an *Adolescente*, described by the composer (in a text he repeatedly attempted to disavow in his

---

[74] The primary published document here is Stravinsky's correspondence with B. Schotts Söhne, his German publisher, in I. Stravinsky, *Selected Correspondence*, ed. Robert Craft, vol. 3 (New York: Knopf, 1985), pp. 217–72. See also my editorially titled article "The Dark Side of Modern Music," *New Republic*, 5 September 1988, pp. 28–34, and "Back to Whom?" (cited in n. 26).

[75] Andrey Levinson, "Russkiy balet v Parizhe," *Rech'*, 3 June 1913.

[76] Quoted from Bullard, "The First Performance of Igor Stravinsky's *Sacre du Printemps*," vol. 3, pp. 271–72. This passage is of course ironically reminiscent of Stravinsky's later strictures on musical performance (especially on "execution" as opposed to "interpretation"). See the sixth chapter of Stravinsky, *Poetics of Music in the Form of Six Lessons*.

interwar and cold-war phases) as being "not fully formed: their sex is unique and double, like that of a tree."[77] This hermaphroditism is at the opposite evolutionary extreme from the androgyne, the perfected being toward which the art of Scriabin (and the early Schoenberg) aspired. It is the mark of an unformed, insensate, and expendable creature, and the ballet's music, no less than its "extramusical" components, mark her for pitiless forfeiture.

Now these are among the troubling aspects of *The Rite* that the discourse of "the music itself" evades. That discourse is by no means confined to academic analysis. It dominates public criticism of classical music as well, and the evasion, when challenged, can turn quite explicit, as when Samuel Lipman of the *New Criterion*, responding to *New York Times* pieces about Prokofiev and Tchaikovsky, denounces my "attempt to write about music by writing about something else very much not music."[78] One senses the same sort of evasion in recent performances of the *The Rite*—one might even say, in its contemporary performance practice—where emphasis is placed on fleet precision and on an athletic virtuosity that defies or ignores the crushing strain the music was meant to evoke, and that it achieved far more dependably when it actually strained the capabilities of its performers.[79]

The work becomes all the more troubling when one reflects, as Adorno did, on other manifestations of that special congeries of ideas that *The Rite* embodies. The discussion by Acocella, Garafola, and Greene, following that of Rivière, emphasized the darker aspects of primitivism—biologism, sacrifice of the individual to the community, absence of compassion, submission to compulsion, all within a context defined by Slavic or Russian national folklore. Now here is a list drawn up by a prominent contemporary social philosopher in an attempt to detail the "coherent cluster of values and ideas" that, he maintains, governed the policies of the Nazi regime: "nationalism, biologism, communalism, hierarchy, corporatism, acceptance of authority, territoriality, aggression, rejection of compassion." I hope it is evident that these hair-raising correspondences are not adduced in order to establish guilt by association. As Professor Gellner put it of his list, "This cluster did not simply spring out of the head of Hitler [or, I'll add, out of Stravinsky's]; it has its roots in European history and ideas, and deserves investigation."[80] That is precisely what I would like to maintain about *The Rite of Spring*.

Rigorous musical analysis of a professional caliber must have a place of honor in any such investigation, for the music plays the primary role in carry-

[77] Igor Strawinsky, "Ce que j'ai voulu exprimer dans Le Sacre du Printemps," *Montjoie!* 29 May 1913, p. 1; reprinted in Lesure, ed., *Le Sacre du Printemps: Dossier de Presse*, p. 14.

[78] Samuel Lipman, *Music and More: Essays, 1975–1991* (Evanston, Ill.: Northwestern University Press, 1992), p. 14.

[79] See R. Taruskin, "Stravinsky Lite, Even *The Rite*," *New York Times*, Arts and Leisure section, 22 December 1991, pp. 29, 36

[80] Ernest Gellner, "Mind Games," *New Republic*, 22 November 1993, p. 38.

ing whatever cluster of values and ideas *The Rite* or any other Stravinsky composition may embody to our minds and hearts. Can such an analysis be accomplished without "defusing" the work, as Arnold Whittall suggests it must? I hope that as the boundaries between "history" and "theory," between historiography and criticism, and between "the extramusical" and "the music itself" continue to soften, and eventually dissolve, we will find it less difficult to believe that it can.

NOTES ON *SVADEBKA*

Every form of art has its starting point in reality and its finishing point in music.

> —Andrey Belïy, *Symbolism* (1910)

. . . For two weeks or so
a woman matchmaker kept visiting
my kinsfolk, and at last
my father blessed me. Bitterly
I cried for fear; and, lamenting, they unbraided
my tress and, chanting, they led me to the church.
And so I entered a strange family.

> —Alexander Pushkin, *Eugene Onegin* (1833)

Two rivers have flowed together,
Two matchmakers have come together,
They thought a thought about a blonde tress:
"How shall we divide the braid in two?"

> —*Songs Collected by P. V. Kireyevsky*, no. 999

Fair maids, cooking whizzes, pot smashers, proud matrons, thin old grannies, puny brats, zany rogues, and piddling scoundrels: SING YOUR SONGS!

> —*Songs Collected by P. V. Kireyevsky*, no. 806

On the fate of Russia now depend not only the fate of the newly self-conscious cultures of Asia but also European culture's way out of its current crisis of individualism—its way out or *death*.

> —Lev Platonovich Karsavin, "Fundamentals
> of Politics" (1927)

THIS portion of chapter 13 is specially dedicated to the memory of Dmitry Pokrovsky, to whose performances of *Svadebka* tribute is paid within, who died unexpectedly in Moscow on 29 June 1996. Our friendly disagreements about Stravinsky's relationship to Russian folklore led to many stimulating exchanges, both private and public, from which I profited greatly.

The Problem

THE FIRST thought of a scenic representation of the *svadebnïy obryad*, the elaborate Russian peasant wedding ritual, came to Igor Stravinsky in 1912, while he was composing the second tableau of *The Rite of Spring*. The first performance of *Svadebka*, subtitled "Russian choreographic scenes with singing and [instrumental] music," took place in Paris (under the title *Les Noces villageoises*) more than a decade later, on 13 June 1923. No other work would ever occupy Stravinsky even half as long. No other work would ever be as important to him. In *Svadebka* Stravinsky reinvented in his imagination the Russia that had, over the course of the ballet's gestation, been lost to him in life.

It was another "icy comedy"—an elegantly detached, non-narrative collage presentation of a ritual action that ends, like its predecessor, in a scene of virgin sacrifice. The difference was that it was drawn from an exceedingly well documented living tradition, or at the very least from customs that survived in living memory, rather than from a quasi-mythical archaic lore. It sought validation in ethnological fact (Belïy's "starting point in reality"), but, like *The Rite*, it refused to be bound by any limits such validation might imply. Its reality, like that of *The Rite*, was ultimately one created, not received. But it was a *Rite* in black and white—the literal black and white of four keyboards, plus percussion.

Finding this scoring was what took Stravinsky all that time. It superseded many preliminary versions that had tried in one way or another to reproduce the actual sounds of Russian folk instruments—one of them combined a pianola, a harmonium, and two Hungarian cimbaloms—and gave the composer what he called the "perfectly homogeneous, perfectly impersonal, and perfectly mechanical" medium by which he could do justice to the depiction of a sacrament enacted with the "profound gravity and cool inevitable intention" that, in the words of a contemporary folklorist, befit any artifact of "remorseless, inelastic tradition."[1] Despite its considerable clangor, not to mention the rowdy doings in its fourth tableau, *Svadebka* makes an impression quite unlike the terrifying *Rite*. Whereas the earlier "pagan" ballet was orgiastic and biological, *Svadebka* is a work of dignity and reserve, finally of religious exaltation (specifically Orthodox, Stravinsky insisted).[2] At a time of upheaval and ruin it offered a restorative view of the only eternity humans can know—

[1] Igor Stravinsky and Robert Craft, *Expositions and Developments* (Berkeley and Los Angeles: University of California Press, 1981), p. 118; Jeffrey Mark, "The Fundamental Qualities of Folk Music," *Music and Letters* 10 (1929): 287–88.

[2] See his cranky remarks in the margins of Asafyev's discussion of *Svadebka* (as "the embodiment of the ancient cult of fertility and reproduction") in *Kniga o Stravinskom* (Leningrad: Triton, 1929), described in Robert Craft's foreword to the English translation: Boris Asaf'yev, *A Book about Stravinsky*, trans. Richard F. French (Ann Arbor: UMI Research Press, 1982), pp. xiii–xv.

the eternity of customs. At a time of existential trauma it offered the solacing prospect of life as liturgy.

What *The Rite* and *Svadebka* have fundamentally in common is Stravinsky's lifelong antihumanism—his rejection of all "psychology." The sacrificial virgin in *The Rite* does her fatal dance with animal fearlessness, and the community accepts her ceremonial murder without remorse. In *Svadebka*, the bride laments at the outset and the groom leers in conclusion (to a variant of the same melody) not because spontaneous feeling so prompts them, but because the immemorial script so decrees.

There was of course a dark side to this celebration of the unquestioned subjection of human personality to an implacably demanding—and, by Enlightened standards, an unjust—social order; and in the awful decades of economic disaster and nationalistic totalitarianism that followed the First World War, the dark side came out into the open (as it seems to be doing again, in the wake of the cold war). Whether it irrevocably taints Stravinsky and his work, as T. W. Adorno insisted, is something we have to decide in keeping with our own liberal traditions. The tension between nostalgia for the security of community and the obligations of enlightened individualism lives not only in *Svadebka* but in ourselves as, contemplating it, we are emotionally swayed by its potent advocacy of what may appear on rational reflection to be a parlous message. The anxious thrill of moral risk that attends the experience of *Svadebka* is one of the things that has kept it alive, and one of the marks of its creator's fearful potency.

That potency arises out of a miraculously successful transcendence of the particular. The musical and textual content of *Svadebka* underwent a process of streamlining and abstraction as stringent as that to which the scoring was subjected. Originally the composer planned a detailed narrative scenario in three acts, constructed out of the work of the romantic-nationalist "Slavophile" ethnographers of Pushkin's time—Ivan Sakharov, A. V. Tereshchenko, Pyotr Kireyevsky. Act 1 was to have depicted the *Smotreniye*, the Bride Show, at which the groom's matchmaker inspects the prospective bride and strikes a bargain by a literal striking of hands (*rukobit'ye*) with the bride's father. The second act was to have had three scenes. The first, in two parts, would have depicted the bride's lament and the groom's ritual of exorcism; the second, also in two parts, would have shown the hair-plaiting ceremony at the bridal shower (*devichnik*) and the preparations for the ritual bath of purification; the third would have taken place at the bride's house right before the departure for church. Act 3 was to show the wedding feast itself.

In the end, seizing on Kireyevsky's song no. 999 (one of the epigraphs given at the head of this section), which he adopted for a while as an actual epigraph to head his score, Stravinsky rejected narrative in favor of what the formalist anthropologists of his day called a "morphological" (and what we today, following a related antihumanistic discourse, would call a "structural-ist") reading of the Russian folk tradition. Elements from the peasant rite were freely extracted and juxtaposed to create a vivid artistic shape in two great metaphorical waves. Tableaux 1 and 2, centering metonymically on the bride's and groom's coiffures, depict the "rivers"; tableau 3 (the old act 2, scene 3) shows their confluence: that is the first wave. Tableau 4 (the old act 3), as long as all the rest combined, depicts the wedding feast (*krasnïy stol*, literally "the bonny table") and aims with mounting excitement at the procreative consummation, for the sake of which the rite exists. The progressive insinuation of the opening melody from the first tableau into the concluding pages of the fourth adds a new metaphorical level, and the imitation of bells proclaiming eternity to the same strains at the very end caps the point.

Stravinsky's music abstracts three styles of peasant singing. Lament (*plach*) and chant (*peniye*), as contrasted by Pushkin in the passage from *Eugene Onegin* quoted above as an epigraph, provide the material for the first wave. (Stravinsky copied exactly the description of the Russian lamenting style—a three-note formula, sung with wailing timbre and vocalized breathing, and decorated with yodels—that he found in Vladimir Dahl's dictionary of the "living Great-Russian language," one of the great monuments of romantic-nationalistic scholarship.)[3] Songs (*pesni*), as in the wedding jester's exhortation in the penultimate epigraph above, form the substance of the second wave. The unportrayed church ceremony forms the watershed that divides the waves; a suggestion of its music, the product of another tradition entirely, comes in the middle of the second tableau, with a duet for two basses accompanied by the female chorus that is modeled on an authentic church chant, and that was first sketched in 1915 for a projected ballet called *Liturgiya*.

Otherwise, except for the melody that brings the fourth tableau to its culmination, a lyrical folk song that Stravinsky laboriously took down from the singing of his friend Stepan Mitusov, the tunes in *Svadebka*, however ethnographically authentic they may sound, are of Stravinsky's own invention. By the time he wrote *Svadebka* the composer, it seemed, could more easily make up a genuine Russian folk tune than look one up.

And there is the paradox of *Svadebka*. On the surface it seems to represent a pinnacle of Russian nationalism in music, thus confirming and conforming to a familiar prejudice (more a Western prejudice than a Russian one!) as to what Russian music ought to be. On investigation, it turns out that while the texts Stravinsky set were scrupulously drawn from ethnographic sources, the scenario and the music belong to no actual folk tradition but to an imaginary one.

---

[3] Dahl's description: "The bride does not sing, but wails [*ne poyot, a plachot*], lamenting her maiden beauty, her raven tresses, her freedom, pleading for her mother's intercession, and so on. . . . Practically throughout Russia there is a single monotonous motive [*napev*], the repetition of three tones, the last being stretched out." Vladimir Dahl, *Tolkovïy slovar' zhivogo velikorusskogo yazïka* (St. Petersburg, 1863–66), s.v. "plakat'" (to cry).

They are not Russian in any literal sense but are so intensely imagined that, in their concentration, they emerge as more Russian than the real thing. They fulfill the requirements not of ethnography but of mythography. Beginning with the real, they proceed to something realer than the real, reproducing the trajectory (*a realibus ad realiora*) to which Vyacheslav Ivanov summoned all the artists of Russia in the turbulent time of aesthetic, political, and (he hoped) spiritual transformation through which they were living.[4] As we know, Ivanov saw the epitome of this trajectory in Scriabin. *Svadebka* is unquestionably another epitome of the same transcendent maximalism. But how did Stravinsky, who had remained aloof from avant-garde literary circles in Russia, arrive at it? How did Stravinsky's transcendent vision, which retained a much more palpable connection with its "starting point in reality," compare with Scriabin's? What were its sources, what were its means of realization, and what were its implications—for him, for his contemporaries, and for us?

EURASIA

Over the long years of *Svadebka*'s gestation, the whole idea of Russian nationalism, indeed the very notion of the Russian nation, had undergone a profound crisis as the result of the revolution that cut the nation loose from the political autocracy and religious orthodoxy that had formerly defined it, and the postrevolutionary emigration that had cut vast portions of educated Russian society adrift from the land itself. Where the briefly empowered liberals, and then the Bolsheviks, promulgated wholly secularized states on models developed in the enlightened and humanist West, the Bolshevik victory and the consequent uprooting of the intellectual class produced a reactionary ferment that reached its spectacular if politically ineffectual crest not in Russia itself but in the exile communities that careened westward through Sofia, Belgrade, Prague, Berlin, and finally Paris. Though the migration perforce was centrifugally westward, the cultural reaction to the revolution produced the most resolutely, indeed savagely anti-Western moment in all of Russian intellectual history. *Svadebka* may profitably be viewed as the very crest of that wave.

As the Bolshevik victory represented the ultimate triumph of the progressive, materialist, secularizing, and Westernizing strain in nineteenth-century Russian politics, so the émigré reaction maximalized the romantic-nationalist, antiliberal, theocratic, and autochthonist strain, as transmitted from Gogol (not the story-telling genius of *Dead Souls* or *The Overcoat* but the religious reactionary who authored *Selected Passages from Correspondence with*

---

[4] See Bernice Glatzer Rosenthal, "The Transmutation of the Symbolist Ethos: Mystical Anarchism and the Revolution of 1905," *Slavic Review* 36 (1977): 610–26; an exhaustive gloss on Ivanov's phrase is given by Andrey Belïy in "Realiora" ("Na perevale, XII," *Vesï* 5, no. 5 [May 1908]: 59–62).

Friends) to the Slavophiles of the 1840s and 1850s (on whom Stravinsky relied for his folk-poetic texts) to Dostoyevsky (of the *Writer's Diary* and the "Dream of the Grand Inquisitor") to the bizarrely neoprimitive Christian writer Konstantin Leont'yev (who wanted to see Russia "frozen" out of time so as to evade the decay that historical evolution inevitably guaranteed). The maximalist phase arrived with the short-lived movement known as Eurasianism (*Yevraziystvo*) that thrived proudly as a widely noticed faction among the intellectual émigrés of the twenties before declining in the thirties into apocalyptic neo-Bolshevist and neofascist splinters. It is with the Eurasianists, many of whom were among his closest friends and associates, that it will be profitable to associate the Stravinsky of the decade, and the self-enclosed ("Swiss") creative period, that followed *The Rite of Spring*.

The intellectual genealogy just outlined is the one that the Eurasianist movement explicitly and enthusiastically claimed for itself. "For us Eurasianists," read the unsigned leader in the first volume of their philosophical organ, the *Eurasian Record*, "it would be gratifying in the highest degree to regard ourselves as located in the same Orthodox and Russian spiritual succession that included the Slavophiles, and Gogol, and Dostoyevsky, and Leont'yev." Yet "at the very moment when it became time to put our thoughts and words on paper," the essay continued, "our consciousness was so affected by an immediate sense of ongoing catastrophe that all exoteric spiritual influences were dulled, and our consciousness was remade by our personal experience of what had happened."[5] This was in its way a perfect representation of maximalism, conscious at once of a formative heritage and of a transformative burst or rush—what a Scriabinist would call a *porïv*. It produced in Eurasianism the most radically reactionary "ideocracy" (as they called it) in the history of Russian ideas.

This was no "white émigré" philosophy. It preferred almost anything to a Romanov restoration. The Russian monarchy, diluted and compromised by liberal admixtures of constitutionalism, had fallen away, thought the Eurasianists, from its Orthodox mission. It had become Europeanized, infected with what one of the founders of Eurasianism called "Romano-Germanic" legalism in place of the primitively organic forms of social organization that sustained the prefeudal, nomadic Slavic tribes, and that still survived among the non-Russian peoples inhabiting the half-European, half-Asian landmass united by the Russian empire. This landmass was *Yevraziya*, "Eurasia," and Russia could renew its spirit only by turning away from Romano-Germanic Europe and facing inward, acknowledging the kinship of all the peoples that occupied

---

[5] *Yevraziyskiy vremennik*, vol. 3 (Berlin: Yevraziyskoye knigoizdatel'stvo, 1923), p. 5. The volume is designated "third" because it followed two other collections of Eurasianist writings—*Iskhod k vostoku: Utverzhdeniya yevraziytsev* (Sofia: Rossiysko-bolgarskoye knigoizdatel'stvo, 1921) and *Na putyakh* (Berlin: Helicon, 1922)—but it was the first to be issued under the name (*Eurasian Record*) by which it would be known as a periodical journal until the end of the decade.

"Turan," the great steppe that extended from the Carpathians to the Pacific. Russia was Slavic in language only. Its religion was that of the Byzantine empire, of which it was the only independent Christian survivor, and its cultural heritage (reflected in its customs and, particularly, its music) was therefore "Turanian," or, in more up-to-date linguists' terms, Ural-Altaic.[6]

These theories were the brainchildren of Prince Nikolai Sergeyevich Trubetskoy (1890–1938), a precociously influential and original linguist specializing in phonology (and, possibly not by coincidence, the scion of an ancient boyar clan long distinguished in scholarship), whose ideas about Russian culture, partly inherited from his philosopher father and fully promulgated, in collaboration with the geographer Pyotr Savitsky, by the time he reached his thirtieth year, begat not only the Eurasianist movement but also, through Trubetskoy's disciple Roman Jakobson, the whole field of structural linguistics. The first specifically Eurasianist publication was a pamphlet by Trubetskoy called "Europe and Humanity" (*Yevropa i chelovechestvo*), published in Sofia, Bulgaria, the first Russian émigré population center to the west of the motherland, in 1920.

It was in this tract that Trubetskoy radically challenged the claim of enlightened European culture to humanist universality, relativizing it as merely one form of chauvinism ("panromanogermanic") among others, and issued a call to Russians that they rally, in opposition to the imported liberal culture that had brought disaster to their state, around a new, more authentic and salvific *samopoznaniye*—that is, a more accurate and authentic self-realization based on their non-European heritage.

The key to the essential Russian character, for Trubetskoy, lay in Russian ethnicity, and the key to Russian ethnicity lay in pre-Slavic prehistory, best reflected in the world of the present by the structure and (Trubetskoy's specialty) the phonology of the Turkic languages of Central Asia. The manner in which Trubetskoy managed to educe a theory of essential national psychology out of phonological data is breathtakingly virtuosic—or, at any rate, virtuosically tendentious, reminiscent of the "philological mysticism" that marked a great deal of maximalized nationalist thinking in postwar Europe (particularly Nazism "in its early 'runic' stage").[7]

"The Turkic languages are very closely related," the author begins,

---

[6] Ironically enough, the old name of the Turan steppe has been revived by the post-Soviet republic of Kazakhstan, precisely so as to distance itself from the Russian-dominated Soviet Union. See, for example, "Turanbank: Integrating into the World's Banking Community," an advertisement in the *New York Times*, 2 May 1994, p. A7. ("The historic name, Turan," it is there revealed, "is the name of the lands stretching from the Black Sea to the Altai Mountains," which limits the term's application to present-day Kazakh territory. "It is also the name of one of the oldest civilizations in the region.")

[7] Further on this comparison see James Billington, *The Icon and the Axe: An Interpretive History of Russian Culture* (New York: Vintage, 1970), p. 760.

especially if one ignores the foreign words (Persian and Arabic) that have pene-
trated the languages of the Muslim Turks in huge numbers. In comparing the
individual Turkic languages to one another, one easily discerns one general linguistic type, which emerges most vividly among the Altais. This type is characterized by an extraordinary harmoniousness [*stroynost'*]. The phonological content of the words is regulated by a series of laws, which in purely Turkic,
nonborrowed words admit of no exceptions. Thus the vowels in every word are
subject to laws of "vowel harmony": if the first syllable of the word contains one
of the "back" vowels (*a, o, ï, u*), then all the other syllables of that word, however many there may be, must contain one of these back vowels; if the first
syllable contains one of the "front" vowels (*ä, ö, i, ü*), then all the other syllables
must necessarily contain one of these front vowels. The mixture of back and front
vowels among the syllables of a single word is not admitted; each word is either
completely "back-voweled" or completely "front-voweled." Analogous laws regulate the use of "dark" vowels (that is, those formed by bringing the lips forward:
o, u, ö, ü) and bright (that is, those not formed by bringing the lips forward: *a, ï,
ä, i*). In the most typical Turkic languages equally strict and inflexible rules also
regulate the use of consonants in a word: some consonants (e.g., *k, g, l*) are
allowed only in "back-voweled" words, while their palatalized counterparts are
allowed only in "front-voweled" words; some (e.g., *d, b, g, j, z, zh*) are allowed
only between vowels (or between *r, l, m*, and *n* and a vowel), while others (e.g.,
t, p, k, ch, s, sh) are not allowed in precisely these positions and so on.

Thus despite its comparatively rich total inventory of sounds, the language
appears to be phonetically monotonous. Owing to the strict subjection of the
whole phonological system to the laws outlined above, the number of possible
phonological combinations is limited, and in connected speech the same phonological combinations are constantly repeated. Speech acquires a distinctive phonological unity, creating a certain acoustical inertia (something like tonal inertia
in a musical composition). The same harmoniousness and pedantic observance of
uniform laws is noticeable in the grammar of Turkic languages as well. This
grammar, strictly speaking, knows no "exceptions." All nouns are declined in a
single manner: variations come about only according to the laws of phonological
harmony already described. All verbs are conjugated similarly. The sober economy of this grammatical inventory is striking; there is no grammatical category
without logical or material justification, nor is there any arbitrary division by
gender.[8]

Trubetskoy goes on to describe similar constraints on Turkic syntax, ver-
sification, and literary forms, and from these linguistic observations—all con-

---

[8] Prince N. S. Trubetskoy, "O turanskom elemente v russkoy kul'ture," *Yevraziyskiy vremennik* 4 (1925): 354–55; reprinted in N. S. Trubetskoy, *K probleme russkogo samopoznaniya:
Sbornik statei* (Paris: Yevraziyskoye knigoizdatel'stvo, 1927), pp. 36–37. Henceforth citations to
both editions will be made in the text, with dual page references.

verging on an impression of "comparative poverty and rudimentariness in the basic speech material on the one hand, and the subordination of all speech to schematic regularites both in its phonology and its formal aspects," amounting to "a remarkable consistency and clarity of construction"—he arrives at a description of what he calls the Turkic "psychic profile" (p. 357/38).

> We will not be mistaken if we say that all Turkic intellectual activity is ruled by a single basic psychological factor: clear schematization of comparatively restricted and rudimentary material. From this it is admissible to draw conclusions about Turkic psychology itself. The typical Turk does not like to become enmeshed in subtleties or intricate details. He prefers to operate with basic, clearly perceptible forms, and to group these forms in clear and simple patterns. . . . It would be a mistake, however, to think the Turkic mind particularly inclined toward schematic abstraction. . . . The patterns on which, as we have seen, Turkic intellectual activity is formed are in no way the product of philosophical abstraction, nor do they even bear any trace of purposeful reflection. On the contrary, they are subconscious and exist in the mind as the unapprehended rationale for that psychic inertia, according to which all the elements that make up the psyche arrange themselves in this, as opposed to that, manner. This is possible thanks to the singular elementalness and simplicity of these patterns. . . .
>
> The psychology, described here, of the typical Turk also defines the lifestyle [*zhiznenniy uklad*] and worldview of its carriers. The Turk loves symmetry, clarity, and stable equilibrium. But he loves it as a given, not as a requirement. . . . Once having come to believe in a certain worldview, having turned it into a subconscious law defining his behavior, or into a universal system, and having achieved in this way a condition of stable equilibrium on a clear foundation, the Turk rests content and holds fast to his beliefs. Looking upon a worldview precisely as the firm basis of spiritual and moral equilibrium, the Turk in that very worldview manifests lethargy and stubborn conservatism. (Pp. 362–63/41–43)

And now the sleight of hand. "The psychological profile of the Turkic tribes that we have sketched above," the author assures the reader, "may be regarded in its general features as a profile of all 'Turanians'" (pp. 364/43)— including, of course, the Eurasian-Russians, even if they do not share with their fellow "Turanians" the linguistic base on which Trubetskoy's whole psychological edifice had been erected. Trubetskoy relies on analogy to cloak a subtle shift of gears from psychological description to social prescription.

> As regards the social and cultural values of people belonging to the Turanian psychological type, one can only rate them positively. The Turanian psyche imparts cultural stability and strength to the nation, affirms cultural and historical continuity, and creates conditions that favor the constructive husbanding of the nation's might. (P. 370/47)

All that is best and most positive in Russian history can be accounted for according to this romanticized psychological model; all that is worst is the fault of Peter the Great, whose attempt to modernize the country through the importation of Western technology brought instead the disastrous infusion of Romano-Germanic toxins. Again there is sleight of hand in Trubetskoy's linkage of "Turanian" sensibility with Orthodox faith.

One cannot fail to note manifestations of normative Turanian psychology in pre-Petrine Muscovite Russia. The whole way of life in which religion and daily life were one—in which state ideology, material culture, art, and religion were indivisible parts of a single system that was neither expressed theoretically nor formulated consciously, but that nevertheless inhabited everyone's subconsciousness and defined both the sentient life of each and the transcendent being of the nation as a whole—all this carries the unmistakable impress of the Turanian psychological type. Precisely this it was that held old Rus' together and gave it stability and strength. . . . Unquestioning submission is the foundation of Turanian statehood, it is consistent, and extends in concept even to the highest ruler, who automatically thinks in terms of unquestioning submission to whatever higher principles may reign in the life of each subject. In ancient Rus' such a regulating principle was the Orthodox faith, understood as an organic coupling of religious dogma and rites with the particular orthodox culture, the specific manifestation of which is the political system with its hierarchical social structure. And precisely this higher principle, the same for every subject as for the tsar himself, rather than any principle of abject slavery, knit Rus' into one indivisible and regulated whole. Orthodox faith in the old-Russian understanding of the term was precisely the framework of consciousness that enclosed everything—private life, political system, and universal being. And insofar as that framework of consciousness was not the object of conscious theoretical thought, but the subconscious basis for all spiritual life, it is impossible to ignore the obvious parallel with what was said above about normative Turanian psychology. So what if Russia received Orthodoxy not from Turanians but from Byzantium? So what if Orthodoxy actually countered "Tatarism" in Russian national consciousness? All the same, the relationship of the Russian individual to Orthodox faith, and the actual role that that faith played in his life, were both distinctly founded on Turanian psychology. Precisely by dint of the Turanian makeup of his psyche the ancient Russian was unable to separate his faith from his daily life, or consciously distinguish nonessential elements from religious manifestations, and precisely for this reason he seemed such a weak theologian when he came in contact with the Greeks. That psychological contrast between Russians and Greeks in their approach to faith and ritual arose precisely out of the circumstance that the ancient Russian national character harbored deep-seated Turanian ethnic and psychological elements that were altogether alien to Byzantium. (Pp. 370–72/48–49)

The affirmative value here attached to unthinking submission, and the suggestion that national salvation awaited the revival of the nonreflective, "organic" wholeness of Turanian psychology, or antipsychology, could scarcely resonate more self-evidently with the old *kul'tura/stikhiya* debates, or with the sacrificial ethos of *The Rite of Spring*. Trubetskoy's special contribution was to give old-fashioned neoprimitivist thinking the appearance of grounding in modern empirical science (here, linguistics). That scientific veneer lent a new luster to the old messianic call: "Consciousness of belonging not only to the Aryan, but to the Turanian psychological type is indispensable for every Russian who aspires to personal and national self-realization" (pp. 375/51).

The kinship between Trubetskoy's conclusions and the spiritual premises of Stravinsky's 1913 ballet (composed before there was such a thing as the Eurasianist movement so called) illustrates a striking parallel but does not in itself provide evidence of a direct link. There is more evidence that Eurasians drew inspiration from Stravinsky than vice versa. By the mid-1920s, Stravinsky was a god in their pantheon. The last, and in some ways the most distinguished of the major Eurasianist journals was *Vyorstï* (Milestones), published in Paris from 1926 to 1928 under the editorship of a millionaire heir to a sugar fortune named Pyotr Petrovich Suvchinsky, known (as "Pierre Souvtchinsky") to all Stravinskians as one of the composer's lifelong intimates.[9] Suvchinsky had been (with Savitsky and Trubetskoy) one of the co-editors of the *Eurasian Record*, as well as the journal's publisher (and, indeed, the bankroller of the entire Eurasianist movement). He and Stravinsky met in Berlin in the fall of 1922, shortly before the *Eurasian Record* was launched and shortly before *Svadebka* at last achieved performance. (Stravinsky was stranded for a few weeks in the German capital while awaiting the much-postponed arrival of the Soviet steamer that was carrying his mother out of Petrograd into permanent emigration.) The Eurasianist maecenas sent the composer a note following this first meeting: "The knowledge that you live on this earth helps me to go on."[10]

Eurasianist fealty to Stravinsky was confirmed in the very first issue of *Vyorstï*, which contained a lengthy article, "The Music of Igor Stravinsky," by the newly emigrated Arthur Lourié (Lur'ye), who would play a role in Stravinsky's life over the next decade comparable to that played in the 1950s and 1960s by Robert Craft. Lourié's *Vyorstï* piece, and a later one more narrowly focused on *Mavra* and *Oedipus Rex*, were the only major essays ever

---

[9] The co-editors of *Vyorstï* were Prince Dmitriy Svyatopolk-Mirsky (who as "D. S. Mirsky" wrote the standard English-language history of Russian literature) and Sergey Efron (an unusual Eurasianist sympathizer because he was a Jew). The masthead proclaimed "the close collaboration" of such prominent émigré littérateurs as Alexey Remizov, Marina Tsvetayeva (then Efron's wife), and the existentialist philosopher Lev Shestov.

[10] Suvchinsky to Stravinsky, 21 November 1922; Vera Stravinsky and Robert Craft, eds., *Stravinsky in Pictures and Documents* (New York: Simon and Schuster, 1978), p. 658.

published by the Eurasianists on music or a musician. His portrayal of Stravinsky and his cultural significance emphasizes the familiar Eurasianist theme of Russian messianism. According to Lourié, Stravinsky had transformed himself from a "Russian" composer into a "universal" one precisely by virtue of having successfully rid himself of what was covertly European in his ostensibly nationalist style. "In Russia *The Nightingale* already evoked a howl of despair," Lourié maintained, "so completely did it withdraw from the Korsakovian pseudonational opera that had risen from a German yeast." The composers of the mighty kuchka had "poured Russian wine into German bottles," which made them mere purveyors of exotica. It had remained for Stravinsky to "break the ties that connected Russia with Western Europe," as a result of which "for the first time Russian music lost its 'provincial,' 'exotic' quality and . . . has become a thing of capital significance, at the very helm of world music."[11]

Lourié's rapturous description of *Svadebka* as a work that "restores a lost equilibrium" strikingly recalls Trubetskoy's nostalgic exegesis of the Turanian "spiritual and moral worldview." Stravinsky's choral ballet, wrote Lourié, "is a mysterium of Orthodox daily life" (cf. Trubetskoy, "the ancient Russian was unable to separate his faith from his daily life"). It is "dynamic in musical terms, but in the emotional level it is saturated with the tranquility and quietude of an icon" (cf. Trubetskoy's advocacy of Turanian mental "lethargy"). Was this anything more than enthusiastic appropriation ex post facto? Or was there a deeper link between Stravinsky's spiritual and moral worldview and that of his new admirers?

SIMFONIYA

Not only did such a link exist, but exploring it will guide us willy-nilly far beyond spiritual and moral parallels, right into the technical heart of Stravinsky's masterpiece. *Svadebka*, it may indeed be shown, was a deliberately crafted representation in unmediated musical terms of the Turanian worldview described by Trubetskoy in the more indirect medium of words, embodying the "symmetry, clarity, and stable equilibrium" of "the Turanian psychological [or rather, antipsychological] type" and depicting the "organic coupling of religious dogma and rites with daily life, the specific outcome of which is the [Russian-Eurasian] political system with its hierarchical social structure." *Svadebka* is the one musical composition that may be placed alongside the works of Gogol, Dostoyevsky, Leont'yev, and the Eurasianists themselves in the annals of Russian "ideocratic" thought.

The missing link was Lev Platonovich Karsavin (1882–1952), a man Stravinsky knew very well in Russia, who in emigration became an elder

---

[11] "Muzïka Stravinskogo," *Vyorstï*, no. 1 (1926): 124, 126, 134.

statesman of the Eurasianist movement and its "principal religious thinker."[12] A historian of religious philosophy by training, Karsavin was a precociously eminent professor at the University of St. Petersburg, appointed to chairs in religion and philosophy before he had reached the age of thirty. As the brother of Tamara Karsavina, Diaghilev's first prima ballerina, he was acquainted with the whole circle of participants in the great impresario's theatrical enterprises. Not only that, the Karsavins lived in the apartment directly above that of the Stravinsky family, in an elegant building reserved for artists of the Imperial Theaters, all during the years of the composer's first (local) fame. In emigration, Karsavin established a family connection with Suvchinsky, who married the philosopher's middle daughter, Marianna. In the 1930s he was appointed by the neofascist Smetona government of Lithuania to a professorship at the University of Kaunas. He was arrested after the Soviet postwar reannexation of Lithuania and died of tuberculosis in a Stalinist labor camp.

Karsavin's closest association with Stravinsky came in the spring of 1911, during the merry days immediately preceding the Rome premiere of *Petrushka*, in which Tamara Karsavina created the role of the Ballerina. The two Karsavins were part of a group that included, besides Stravinsky, the painters Alexander Benois and Valentin Serov, all of whom "lived in the same hotel and almost never parted."[13] Every party to this idyllic interlude left tender memoirs of it, even the normally crusty Stravinsky.[14] By 1911, Karsavin's adaptation of Slavophilistic historical and religious thinking was already reaching its maximalist phase, as was Trubetskoy's.[15] Not only these biographical circumstances but also many detailed and idiosyncratic ideological affinities identify Lev Karsavin as a thinker whose proto-Eurasianist, "ideocratic" impact on Stravinsky came early enough to have affected both the conception and the realization of *Svadebka*.

In his radical monism, Karsavin was as frankly mystical a thinker as Scriabin. "Amid the multiplicity of things," as Masaryk put it long ago in *The Spirit of Russia*, "the mystic endeavors to grasp unity, and more directly, to grasp *the one*."[16] Karsavin indeed saw this endeavor as a manifestation of "the

[12] Nicholas Riasanovsky, "The Emergence of Eurasianism," *California Slavic Studies* 4 (1967): 47.

[13] Benois to Ilya Zilbershteyn, 9 March 1959; in I. Zilbershteyn and G. Samkov, *Valentin Serov v vospominaniyakh, dnevnikakh i perepiske sovremennikov*, vol. 1 (Leningrad: Khudozhnik RSFSR, 1960), p. 431.

[14] There are in fact two such memoirs by him: Stravinsky, *An Autobiography* (New York: Simon and Schuster, 1936), pp. 51–52; and Igor Stravinsky and Robert Craft, *Expositions and Developments* (Garden City, N.Y.: Doubleday, 1962), p. 27.

[15] See the introduction to *Yevropa i chelovechestvo*, where this foundational Eurasianist text, published in 1920, is characterized by the author as containing thoughts "that had taken shape in my consciousness ten years ago" (p. iii).

[16] Thomas Garrigue Masaryk, *The Spirit of Russia: Studies in History, Literature and Philosophy*, trans. E. and C. Paul (London: George Allen and Unwin, 1919), vol. 2, p. 259. Masaryk

spirit of Russia," and one of the cardinal differences between the Russian temper and the individualistic, legalistic "Romano-Germanic" spirit of Europe, which, whether in its empirical guise or its rationalistic one, was ever given to making distinctions. In his foundational tract "The East, the West, and the Russian Idea," written in direct response to the revolutionary events of 1917–18, Karsavin sought to establish "the ideal of all-in-one [*vseyedinstvo*]" as the essential differentiater of East and West, not only defining Russia as against Europe, but also Orthodoxy as against Catholicism—to say nothing of Protestantism, the rise of which split Western Christendom literally into a dualism. The Catholic Church, Karsavin argued, was a kind of state, replete with a quasi-monarchial social hierarchy and even a territory, set up in opposition, or as a counterpart, to secular authority. But such an antithesis, like every antithesis, is blasphemous:

> One cannot acknowledge the categorical supremacy or primacy of the ecclesiastical hierarchy, because the secular is also from God. . . . But neither can one limit the sphere of action of each power or regard them as complementary, for these spheres by the very nature of the church are indivisible, or (which is the same thing) divisible only abstractly, rationalistically. Therefore, . . . Orthodoxy can only aspire to an ideal condition, insisting on the proximity of all its empirical realizations. The ideal consists in the mutual penetration of church and state, their mutual dissolution, as it were, in the true body of Christ, something never achieved as yet on earth.[17]

Hence the uniquely Byzantine-Russian dogma that church, state, and nation are one—or rather, that state and nation are mystically subsumed and united by church. (Compare Trubetskoy on the principle of submission, and on the Orthodox faith as "the framework of consciousness that enclosed everything—private life, political system and universal being.")[18] Man cannot create unity merely by suppressing diversity. "To achieve the unity of mankind, so that mankind might be like the church, what is necessary is the unbroken interaction of all persons, based on simultaneous self-affirmation and self-surrender," Karsavin declared, and elaborated as follows on this seemingly paradoxical vision of social utopia *à la russe*:

---

continues, in an explicitly gnostic (and Scriabinesque) formulation: "Even the dualism of the ego and the non-ego is to be transcended."

[17] L. P. Karsavin, *Vostok, zapad i russkaya ideya* (Petrograd: Academia, 1922), pp. 67–68.

[18] And hence the incompatibility of Eurasianist thinking with the old Romanov dynastic slogan, enunciated under Nikolai I, of "orthodoxy, autocracy, nationality," which it superficially resembles. As the Eurasianists repeatedly pointed out, this was actually a statist doctrine that virtually turned the church into a government agency. As the living body of Christ, "the church is really everything—state and culture, religion and church, all in one" (*Vostok, zapad i russkaya ideya*, p. 70).

All-embracing or ecumenical, pan-ecclesiastical activity is not the same as abstract, uniform, automatic action produced by everyone in unison. It is all-embracing in that it is accomplished through everyone, but in each differently according to the individual. But it is nevertheless an activity undertaken by everyone, which is to say it presupposes the coordination and the agreement of all.[19]

Such concord can be achieved neither where the church is separated off from the "worldly" nor where the church is actually split. Hence the hopelessness of post-Reformation Europe, and hence the messianic role of Russia—by means of its vision of *vseyedinstvo* "to reinstitute the unity that Western tendencies have checked."[20]

By the time he emigrated and began contributing to the Eurasianist press, Karsavin had come up with a name for his Russian utopia, and had gone from religious to overtly political theorizing. In an article that appeared in the *Eurasian Record* under the title "The Foundations of Politics," Karsavin unveiled the phrase now most firmly attached to his name. There, for the first time, he called the ideal condition to which Russian Orthodoxy aspired a "symphonic society," incorporating not a polity of individuals in the blasphemous Western sense, but instead a "higher symphonic personality" or "symphonic subject." The concordance between Karsavin's symphonic society and Trubetskoy's Turanian (mental) state is unmistakable, but Karsavin generalizes the notion far beyond the level of ethnicity.

A symphonic subject is not an agglomeration or simply the sum of individual subjects, but rather their *concord* (symphony), the *coordination of the one and many* and—in the ideal and at the limit—the *all-in-one*. Accordingly a nation is not a mere sum of social groups (estates, classes, etc.) but their organized and coordinated hierarchical unity. The culture of a nation is no mere sum but a symphonic unity of more local cultures, and it does not exist otherwise than as a real and concrete unity that is larger than the sum of its parts. Similarly, national cultures can constitute a larger cultural unity (Hellenistic, European, Eurasian), presupposing the existence of a particular communal subject at this level. Insofar as we speak of *human culture*, we presuppose no mere abstract unity, irrespective of multinational or national cultures, nor do we mean any one of them, but rather *the real and concrete unity of all of them, apportioned in time and space*.[21]

Karsavin's theory of symphonic culture and symphonic society is thus a theory of a pleroma, an all-encompassing unitary hierarchy, mirroring the divine order on the human plane. In its rejection of the autonomous individual

[19] Ibid., pp. 70–71.
[20] Ibid., p. 74.
[21] L. P. Karsavin, "Osnovï politiki," *Yevraziyskiy vremennik* 5 (1927): 188.

it is an explicitly antihumanistic theory. "The individual, as usually imagined"—that is, in "liberal" Romano-Germanic societies—"simply does not exist and is nothing more than a notion or a fiction," Karsavin asserted, calling for something akin to Vyscheslav Ivanov's (and Scriabin's) transcendence of the "petty 'I.'"

> A person is "individual" not at all because he is separate or separable from others or from the whole and is closed off in himself, but only insofar as *in himself, particularly and specifically*, he expresses and realizes *the communal or symphonic subject*, which is to say the whole, the higher superindividual consciousness and the higher superindividual will. . . . Therefore the "communal" [*sobornoye*] does not negate or constrain the individual the way the individual is negated and constrained by the "collective" [*kollektivnoye*], which is to say the "massed" [*sobrannoye*] or the "merged" [*sbornoye*].[22]

Thus the higher "symphonic personality" (*simfonicheskaya lichnost'*) realizes its potential (in words practically borrowed from Ivanov) by "renouncing the 'I' of the lower or smaller sphere for the sake of the higher." To drive the point home Karsavin invokes a supplementary musical metaphor, comparing the "individuum" to a single voice ("the carrier of a 'cantus firmus,'" as Karsavin puts it) within the vast polyphonic texture of the total-unity, the pleroma.[23] When successfully harmonized in this way, the individual, being absorbed in an all-embracing "symphonic personality," achieves true freedom. "In its fullness," Karsavin declared,

> symphonic identity transcends all dichotomies of time and space, freedom and necessity, being and nonbeing. Such fullness can be attained in the church, but not in the domain of the empirical. The empirical is limited. In the empirical world incompleteness is inevitable, identity and freedom are imperfect. In the empirical world some will be passive and oppressed, others resistant and violent; there will be conditions and coercion.[24]

The "symphonic society" of Karsavin's utopian vision, then, was a society that existed in a perfect harmony of individuals who were subjectively free but who functioned within it without ever having to make a decision or exercise choice.

It is often assumed that Karsavin derived his symphonic metaphor from the notorious defense of the Russian autocracy in Gogol's *Selected Passages from Correspondence with Friends*, wherein a harmonious society is likened to an orchestra under the baton of a supreme conductor.[25] But that is not the case.

---

[22] Ibid., p. 189.

[23] Ibid., p. 191.

[24] L. P. Karsavin, "Fenomenologiya revolyutsii," *Yevraziyskiy vremennik* 5 (1927): 34.

[25] See N. V. Gogol, *Vïbrannïye mesta iz perepiski s druz'yami*, in *Polnoye sobraniye sochineniy*, vol. 8 (Moscow: Izdatel'stvo Akademii nauk SSSR, 1952), p. 253.

In an anonymous—which is to say communally authored—"attempt at a systematic outline" of Eurasianism to which Karsavin undoubtedly contributed the passage in question, the actual etymology of the term is revealed in the course of a vehement condemnation of the "enlightened" separation of church and state. It is a passage rife with startling Stravinskian resonance.

> We would seek the resolution of this question [of the proper relationship of church and state] in a term used by the hymn-writers [*kanonisti*] of Byzantium: *simfoniya*, that is, concinnity [*soglasovaniye*] and coordinated activity [*soglasovannaya deyatel'nost'*]. When there is a clear understanding of what the Church is and what the state is, and of their true relationship, the theory of "symphony" should present no problems.[26]

Nor will Stravinsky's seemingly recondite appropriation of the word *symphony* in its esoteric Byzantine-Greek etymology (and in the plural), in his Symphonies of [rather than "for"] Wind Instruments (*Symphonies d'instruments à vent*), present problems to those who have a clear understanding of the composer's relationship with the promulgators of proto-Eurasianist thought and his need to take refuge in "Turania," their ideocratic utopia, during the early years of his deracination. The *Symphonies*, composed in 1919–20 as a memorial for Claude Debussy, was first published in 1926 (the year both of the Eurasianist manifesto and of Arthur Lourié's tribute to the composer in *Vyorstï*) in a piano arrangement by Lourié himself that until 1952 was the only score in print. The idea of *soglasovannaya deyatel'nost'* (coordinated activity) is especially relevant to this piece, in which the music constantly shifts among three precisely calibrated proportional tempos. Indeed the form of the work has already been identified, on other evidence, as being modeled on another sort of coordinated activity—the liturgy, replete with interacting celebrants and choir, and with strophes interacting with refrains, of the Russian Orthodox funeral service (*panikhida*), the longest individual component of which is the long strophic hymn known as the *kanon*, to which Karsavin made specific reference in the philological fantasy out of which he constructed his mystique of "symphonic" social order.[27]

Turanian Anhemitony

In laying out his ideocratic utopia, Prince Trubetskoy had placed particular emphasis, as we have seen, on what his research in comparative philology had

---

[26] *Yevraziystvo: Opït sistematicheskogo izlozhenii* (Paris: Yevraziyskoye knigoizdatel'stvo, 1926), p. 43.

[27] See R. Taruskin, review of Igor Stravinsky, *Symphonies d'instruments à vent: Faksimileausgabe des Particells und der Partitur der Erstfassung (1920)*, ed. André Baltensperger and Felix Meyer, *Music Library Association Notes* 49 (1992–93): 1617–21; full details in R. Taruskin, *Stravinsky and the Russian Traditions* (Berkeley and Los Angeles: University of California Press, 1996), pp. 1486–93.

led him to identify as the cardinal trait of Turanian psychology: an inclination to accept restriction gratefully and to make much of little, patterning unquestionable givens with resourcefulness and intensity within inviolable limits. As a sidelight on the restricted phonology of Turanian languages Trubetskoy adduced some observations on Turanian musical idioms, again with an eye toward forging a link with those of Russia, and bolstering the idea of the Russian's natural predisposition to an organic (or "symphonic") society at loggerheads with Romano-Germanic legalistic liberalism.

According to Trubetskoy, real Turkic melodies—that is, melodies unsullied by the Arabian or Persian influences that came by way of Islam (and available for collection, for that reason, only in the Ural and Siberian regions of the Russian empire)—are characterized by the use of what he called "the anhemitonic-pentatonic (alias Indo-Chinese) scale." He further emphasized that such melodies are rhythmically symmetrical and "pair-periodic," breaking down into "parts with an equal number of measures, that number usually being 2, 4, 8, etc." All this, plus a highly repetitive manner of elaboration, is aesthetically most salubrious, resulting in

> a peculiar clarity and lucidity in harmony and rhythm. Every such melody presents one or two similar and very simple musical phrases, but these phrases may be endlessly repeated, forming a long, monotonous song. In other words, the same basic psychological traits that we have already observed in the structure of Turkic languages are again suggested: relative poverty and plainness of material, and a complete submission to simple and schematic rules, which welds the material into a unified whole and imparts to the whole a certain schematic clarity and lucidity.[28]

In a study that purported to reveal the dependence of Russian "high" culture on the indigenous "low" culture, Trubetskoy had made explicit what in his later, more general explorations of Turanian lore he would be content merely to imply: that every Turanian stylistic/psychological trait is also a Russian trait, provided that one penetrate to cultural strata beneath those at which borrowings reflective of recent, deplorable, cultural contacts had taken place; and that these shared stylistic/psychological traits, together with their social and political implications, collectively adumbrate Russia's disengagement from Europe.

> A significant portion of Great-Russian folk songs (including the most ancient, that is, the ritual and wedding songs) are composed in the so-called "pentatonic" or "Indo-Chinese" scale, that is, as if in the major mode without the fourth and seventh steps. This scale exists (and is in fact the only one used) among the Turkic tribes in the Volga and the Kama basins, and also among the Bashkirs, the

---

[28] "O turanskom elemente v russkoy kul'ture," *Yevraziyskiy vremennik* 4 (1925): 358–59; *K probleme russkogo samopoznaniya*, p. 39.

Siberian "Tatars," the Turks in Russian and Chinese Turkestan, and all the Mongol peoples. Apparently this scale once existed even in China: Chinese music theory, at least, presupposes its existence, and the musical notation used in China is based on it. In Siam, Burma, Cambodia, and Indochina it dominates to this day. Thus we have in this case an unbroken line coming from the East, and ending with the Great-Russian. Among the Little-Russians [i.e., Ukrainians] the pentatonic scale is found only in a few very rare old songs, and one notes only isolated instances of it among the remaining Slavs. Among Romanic and Germanic peoples it is unknown, and only in the extreme northwest corner of Europe is it encountered again among the Brittanic Celts (Scots, Irish, Bretons). In rhythm Russian songs are also fundamentally distinct not only from the Romano-Germanic but also from the Slavic, as is evidenced (to pick just one example) by the complete lack of triple meters (the meter of waltzes and mazurkas).[29]

Any ethnomusicologist reading these lines would surely point out, between giggles, that they are pure folklore in their own right, the work of an amateur with a pressing agenda. Drollest of all, in its way, is Trubetskoy's citation, for the benefit of "readers unfamiliar with music theory," of Rachmaninoff's recital favorite "Lilacs" (*Siren'*), Op. 21, no. 5 (composed 1902), an item presumably in every literate Russian's humming repertoire, as an example of pure, anhemitonic "Turanian" style (example 13.1).[30] In his collected essays, Trubetskoy appended a page of musical illustrations, reproduced in figure 13.2, that shows, respectively, a wedding song from the Archangel district in northern Russia, cited to illustrate the "Indo-Chinese (pentatonic) scale"; a pair of Turkic songs—Meshcheryak (Ural/Bashkir) and Kazan-Tatar, respectively—that illustrate the same scale, establishing kinship with the Russian; and a pair of Finno-Ugric songs (Ostyak-Siberian and Estonian, respectively) that demonstrate not an anhemitonic intervallic structure but the narrow ambitus ("diapason no wider than a fifth," as the author puts it) that Trubetskoy had adduced as an additional facet of purebred Turanian style.

Risible all this may be in its musical naivety, especially the conclusive genetic connection Trubetskoy purports to draw between the Russian and the Turkic melodies, so utterly dissimilar in style despite their single, arbitrarily stressed shared characteristic. And yet it is all crucial to any sophisticated understanding of the music of Stravinsky's so-called Swiss period, both as regards the specific nature of its facture and as regards its cultural meaning. Stravinsky made it all true. Just as he realized in his art the "symphonic" *soglasovannaya deyatel'nost'* of which Karsavin could only dream, so, too, in his art he forged the solid Eurasian stylistic bonds about which Prince

---

[29] "Verkhi i nizï, russkoy kul'turï," *Iskhod k vostoku* [= *Yevraziyskiy vremmenik*, vol. 1] (Sofia: Rossiysko-bolgarskoye knigoizdatel'stvo, 1921), pp. 97–98; *K probleme russkogo samopoznaniya*, p. 29.

[30] Ibid., p. 97/29.

EXAMPLE 13.1. Rachmaninoff, *Siren'* (Lilacs), Op. 21, no. 5 (pitches not referable to the anhemitonic set are circled

EXAMPLE 13.1, *continued*

kat'.

*("At morn, at dawn, over the dewy grass, I'll go to breathe the fresh morning air;
and in the fragrant shade, where the lilacs grow thick, I'll go seek my bliss . . .")*

Trubetskoy could only fantasize. He, and he alone, composed genuine "Turanian" music, for among composers he, and he alone, shared Prince Trubetskoy's, and Suvchinsky's, and Karsavin's cultural agenda.

". . . LA BELLE ET SAINE BARBARIE"

The sources of that agenda, where Stravinsky was concerned, were a complex amalgam of the aesthetic, the personal, and the political. Stravinsky's Swiss period was a time of relative isolation and eventual hardship. At its beginning he was a Russian aristocrat and (in the West, at least) the undisputed heir to his country's magnificent half-century of achievement as purveyor of exotic orchestral and theatrical spectacle to the world. At its end he was a stateless person facing uncertain prospects, whose dominating position in the world of modern music no longer went unchallenged, and who, as a result of manifold tilts and turns in the surrounding world, found himself in the throes of a stylistic quandary.

The decision to sit out the First World War on neutral territory had been primarily a career move. Stravinsky's last prewar première was that of *The Nightingale*, the last and most stunning production of the Diaghilev enterprise's opulent first phase. The final performance of the Ballets Russes' 1914 season took place in London on the evening of 25 July. Three days later Austria and Serbia were at war. By the time the company got around to shipping its rented music back to Koussevitzky's Berlin-based Russische Musikverlag, France, England, and Russia had all joined with Serbia against Germany, Austria's main ally. *The Nightingale* nearly became an early casualty of the conflagration. In the theatrical gossip column of the newspaper *Golos Moskvï* (Voice of Moscow), the following item appeared on 26 August (Old Style):

ПРИЛОЖЕНИЕ II.

Великорусская народная песнь в «индокитайской» (пятитонной) гаммѣ:

Свадебновеличальная песнь (Арханг. губ.):

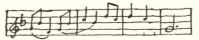

(к ст. «Верхи и Низы Русской культуры»)

Тюркские песни

в «индокитайской» (пятитонной) гамме:

Мещеряцкая:

Казанско-татарская:

Угрофиннские песни

(диапазон-не шире квинты)

Остяцкая:

Эстонская:

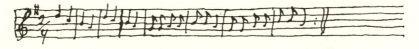

к ст. «Туранский элемент в русской культуре»

FIGURE 13.2. Appendix 2 from Nikolai Sergeyevich Trubetskoy, *K probleme russkogo samopoznaniya* (Paris: Yevraziyskoye knigoizdatel'stvo, 1927). The examples, in the author's hand, are headed as follows:
1) Great-Russian folk song in the "Indo-Chinese" (pentatonic) scale: a wedding praise song (Archang[el] dist[rict])
2) Turkish songs in the "Indo-Chinese" (pentatonic) scale:
   a. Meshcheryak   b. Kazan-Tatar
3) Finno-Ugric songs (no more than a fifth in range):
   a. Ostyak   b. Estonian

Before the war many newspapers carried stories about the impending production in Moscow of Igor Stravinsky's *The Nightingale*, which had gained a noisy celebrity in France and England through Diaghilev's operatic productions. Now, however, unforeseen circumstances have altered all plans. *The Nightingale* is lost. The score, the parts, and the piano arrangements of this opera, following its London performances, were sent to Berlin, where the central office of the company that has undertaken to publish Stravinsky's *Nightingale* is located. At this very time the war broke out, and our countryman's opera did not get to Berlin. The composer has kept neither rough drafts nor copies of the opera. He is beside himself with grief. To restore the whole opera from memory will not be possible.[31]

The embroideries were fanciful. Not only had Stravinsky retained copious sketches and drafts, which may be seen to this day in his archive (Paul Sacher Stiftung, Basel), but the vocal score of *The Nightingale* had been printed at least two months earlier. Indeed, the St. Petersburg musical magazine *Russkaya muzïkal'naya gazeta* thoughtlessly picked up this sensational account from *Golos Moskvï* and ran it in their issue of 7/14 September, which on another page carried an advertisement for the opera.[32] Yet Stravinsky must have suffered a genuine fright, and it must have contributed to his decision to remain in Switzerland as much for the sake of his business affairs as for the sake of his consumptive spouse's health. The Bolshevik coup thus found him abroad, and Russia lost Stravinsky in fact as well as spirit.

It was Stravinsky who felt the loss more keenly. The early years of his exile, fraught in equal measure with homesickness for his country and disgust at the delinquency of its government, led to an access of sharpened nationalism in the name not of the Russia that was but of an imaginary *ur*-Russia that he enthusiastically described to Romain Rolland, whom he chanced to meet in Geneva on 26 September 1914, and who recorded their conversation in his diary. Even Rolland's physical description of his interlocutor bears the impress of Stravinsky's proto-Eurasianist posture:

A long visit with Igor Stravinsky. We spend three hours chatting in the garden of the Hotel Mooser. Stravinsky is about thirty; he is small, has a puny, ugly appearance, a yellow complexion, a weak, exhausted look, a narrow brow, thin, receding hair, eyes wrinkling behind his glasses, a fleshy nose, thick lips, a disporportionately long face. He is very intelligent and direct; he speaks easily, though he sometimes has to search for his words in French, and everything he says is personal and considered (whether true or false). The first part of our conversation had to do with politics. Stravinsky declares that Germany is not a barbarian state but a decrepit and degenerate one. He claims for Russia the role of

[31] "Brut" (pseud.), "Okolo teatra," *Golos Moskvï*, no. 195 (26 August/8 September 1914): 6.
[32] "Raznïye izvestiya," *Russkaya muzïkal'naya gazeta* 21, no. 36–37 (7–14 September 1914), col. 714.

a splendid, healthy barbarism, heavy with germs that will inseminate the thinking of the world. He is counting on a revolution to follow the war, which will topple the dynasty and found a Slavic United States. Moreover, he attributes the cruelties of the Tsarist system in part to German elements that have been incorporated into Russia and run the main wheels of the government or the administration. The attitude of German intellectuals inspires him with boundless contempt. Hauptmann and Strauss, he says, have the souls of lackeys. He touts the old Russian civilization, unknown in the West, the artistic and literary monuments of northern and eastern cities. He also defends the Cossacks against their reputation for brutality . . .[33]

But for the explicitly religious component, which would come soon enough, every one of the tenets in the Eurasian platform is adumbrated, plank by plank: the decadence of the panromanogermanic West, the messianic role of a newly purified Russia of which the communally governed Cossacks were avatars, and all the rest. "Russia must emancipate the world from its slavery to the latest Romano-Germanic fashion," the Eurasianists declared.[34] The form of government they envisioned to replace monarchism as the optimum vehicle for supranational pan-Eurasian self-realization was modeled, just as Stravinsky had foretold to Rolland, on a tortured understanding of the American federal system, implying a "Turanian United States" in which an organic, preternatural unanimity of popular aspiration (*soglasiye*, *simfonichnost'*) would replace merely constitutional or legal authority.[35]

The first Stravinsky composition to be written entirely in Switzerland, and the composer's first attempt at writing in a purified, explicitly "antiromanogermanic" style ("heavy with germs that will inseminate the thinking of the world"), was the Three Pieces for String Quartet, completed exactly one month before the colloquy with Rolland. Only the first of them, completed before the war, was "Russian" in any familiar, folkish sense. The Russianness of the other two went deeper, radically intensifying certain tendencies of structure and facture that were already present or implicit in his earlier music, and giving evidence of an attempt deliberately to exclude or excrete all references to general "European" forms, media, or traditions.

Nineteenth-century Russian composers, however "nationalist," had always implicitly accepted European musical institutions, media, and genres. Once one is writing, say, for the symphony orchestra, one's basic commitment to

[33] Romain Rolland, *Journal des années de guerre 1914–1919* (Paris: Éditions Albin Michel, 1952), p. 59.

[34] Pyotr Savitsky, "Poddanstvo idei," *Yevraziyskiy vremennik* 3 (1923): 15.

[35] *Yevrasiystvo: opït sistematicheskogo izlozheniya*, p. 53: "After all, not only does the federal model take formal or external note of the manifold nature of Eurasian culture, it also vouchsafes its unity. It facilitates the development and flowering of individual national-cultural regions, decisively and conclusively preventing mindless Russification. This in fact advances cultural self-realization."

the musical Europeanization of Russia—her "Westernization," to put it in terms of the classic dualism of nineteenth-century Russian intellectual history—has been made and shown, regardless of the source of one's subject matter. Not so the "Swiss" Stravinsky, for all that by 1914 he was known the world over for his mastery of panromanogermanic genres and media. Between *The Nightingale* and *Pulcinella* (1919) he would write no new orchestral music at all (excepting only his balletic adaptation of the former as *Le Chant du rossignol* in 1917); nor, after the Three Pieces, would he write for any standardized "Western" ensemble.[36] More characteristic of the period were compositions that used "four musicians, one of whom can only be found in Honolulu, another in Budapest, and the other two God knows where!" as Diaghilev cracked to Ansermet in mock-exasperation one day in 1919.[37] He was probably thinking of one of the preliminary versions of *Svadebka*, made that same year, scored for a truly outlandish ensemble of folkish and mechanical instruments—cimbaloms, harmonium, pianola, percussion—that were expressly chosen and deployed so as to emit specifically Turanian noises.

Even where Stravinsky's media were traditional in those years, as in the Three Pieces for String Quartet, genre was radically odd. During the Swiss years his works took shapes that baffled even him. In a letter to Nikolai Struve, his editor at Koussevitsky's publishing house, Stravinsky tried to convey some idea of what *Svadebka* was like: "a cantata or oratorio, or I do not know what, for four soloists and an instrumental ensemble that I am in too great a hurry to describe."[38] Writing to Ansermet a bit later, he called it "a *divertissement* (for it is not a ballet)."[39] Far easier to say what a thing is not than to say what it is, if your vocabulary is panromanogermanic but the thing you are trying to describe is Turanian.

Turanian, too, were the words Stravinsky set during the period of his Swiss

---

[36] Stravinsky's eschewal of the standard orchestra during the Swiss years has often been viewed as an accommodation of wartime conditions, when the large orchestras of the European capitals had been decimated by conscription. Yet Stravinsky did not lack for orchestral outlets during the war. His friendship with Ernest Ansermet, who was exceedingly active all through this period—with the Kursaal orchestra at Montreux (1911–15), the Geneva Symphony Orchestra (1915–18), and finally his own Orchestre de la Suisse Romande—vouchsafed Stravinsky many orchestral performances, and even opportunities to conduct (for the first time) himself. (He led the Kursaal orchestra through a rehearsal of his early Symphony in E♭ in April 1914; his public podium debut was with the Geneva orchestra at a charity matinée for the Red Cross on 20 December 1915; Stravinsky conducted the 1910 *Firebird* Suite, plus Berceuse and Finale [see White, *Stravinsky: The Composer and His Works*, pp. 31, 37].) Nor did the Ballets Russes cease their operations during the war. Diaghilev commissioned the *Chant du rossignol* while the war was raging, and Stravinsky wrote the piece in the early months of 1917, fully expecting a speedy première.

[37] Ernest Ansermet to Stravinsky, 18 July 1919; quoted in *Stravinsky in Pictures and Documents*, p. 155.

[38] Letter of 6 April 1919; ibid., p. 154.

[39] Letter of 23 July 1919; ibid., p. 154.

exile. Between 1913 (*Souvenirs de mon enfance*) and 1919 (*Quatre chants russes*) he wrote no fewer than eight compositions, two of them large-scale concerted works, on Russian folk texts, many of them in nonstandard, local peasant idioms that would have been hard even for native Russian audiences to understand. There was a great quantity of such material in print by the early twentieth century, collected by the Slavophile philosophers and ethnographers of the mid–nineteenth century, much of it (including most of the *Svadebka* texts) published posthumously, but very little of it had been set to original music by the Russian "nationalist" composers of the same period, for to do so would have violated their notion of what "art" was.

Even in their visual aspects, Stravinsky's manuscripts of the Swiss years were "Turanian." He copied their titles and texts in a pseudoarchaic calligraphy modeled on the pre-Petrine Slavic alphabet—that is, the true Old Bulgarian *kirillitsa*, the alphabet of SS. Cyril and Methodius that had been introduced to Russia along with Christianity in the tenth century, but was replaced in the eighteenth by a streamlined, deliberately romanized style of writing (the so-called *grazhdanskiy shrift*, or "civil hand") that has remained current (see figure 13.3).

As for the quartet pieces, they were so obviously and willfully written against the traditions of their medium as to prompt one British critic to comment (of the last of them) that "if this type of passage has any proper place in the art of the string quartet, then the end is near."[40] More sympathetic and perceptive, yet in no way dissimilar, were the recollections of Otto Luening, the American composer, who at the time was working as a young (indeed, teenaged) flutist in the orchestra of the Zürich Tonhalle. He, too, saw that the Russian composer was reacting to what he perceived as the decrepitude of the West, and trying to supersede it. The wartime compositions, Luening thought, "indicated that Stravinsky was thinning out his style considerably. Rumor had it that this mysterious Russian who lived in Morges *had turned his back on all previous music* and had . . . reduced his musical statement to an economical, essential style just sufficient to say what he meant."[41]

Just as Eurasianism was a radical intensification of earlier movements (Slavophilism, "Scythianism"), brought about by the fact and circumstances of forced emigration, so too the newly intensified Stravinskianisms that marked the period of Swiss exile had their origins in the composer's prewar "neonationalist" work. This earlier style was an adaptation, the only musical adaptation ever made, of a tendency in the Russian visual arts with which Stravinsky had made contact through the members of the Diaghilev circle. What modern art historians call "neonationalism" consisted in the profes-

[40] George Dyson, *The New Music* (1924), quoted in White, *Stravinsky*, p. 195.
[41] Untitled memoir in *Perspectives of New Music* 9, no. 2–10, no. 1 (1971): 131 (italics added).

FIGURE 13.3. The fourth song in Stravinsky's set of lullabies (published as *Berceuses du chat*), with a calligraphic dedication in "neo-Cyrillic" style to the neonationalist painter Mikhail Fyodorovich Larionov, 2 November 1915 (André Meyer collection)

sional assimilation of style characteristics, not just subject matter, from folk art. "The folk," the art critic Yakov Tugenhold had written in a review of *The Firebird*, "formerly the object of the artist's pity, is becoming more and more the subject of artistic style."[42] Stravinsky's neonationalist orientation gave rise to the neoprimitivist traits—*drobnost'*, *nepodvizhnost'*, *uproshcheniye*—that were identified and discussed in the earlier part of this chapter. They came to their neo-Turanian peak in the works of the Swiss years.

The second of the Three Pieces for String Quartet, with its radical shifts of tempo, its sectional juxtapositions without transition, and its avoidance of any apparent formal teleology, can serve as a defining epitome of *drobnost'*. Like the *Symphonies d'Instruments à vent* (1920), composed at the other end of the Swiss period, it has resisted conventional analytical methods that assume, and seek to confirm, an ideal of routinized formal unity, and has prompted the backward extension of Stockhausen's concept of "moment form" as an explanatory paradigm.[43] Respect for *drobnost'* as a positive Russian-Eurasian value can serve to mitigate the anachronistic analytical impulse, just as study of Stravinsky's sketches for the piece, and some knowledge of its genesis, can reveal just what it is that holds the piece together in spite of everything. It is worth going into in some analytical detail at this point, as it will provide an important clue for uncovering the macrostructure of *Svadebka*.

Stravinsky was in London in June 1914, to attend the Ballets Russes' performances of *The Nightingale*. (The first London performance took place at the Theater Royal, Drury Lane, on 18 June, the composer's thirty-second birthday.) During that stay, he seems to have gone with Benois to the circus, where they saw the famous juggler and clown Little Tich (1868–1928, alias Little Tichborne, *né* Harry Relph), who was actually a dwarf, and whose chief prop was a pair of elongated shoes on which, by shifting his weight, he could rise up as if on stilts (figure 13.4). As early as 1919, Stravinsky acknowledged this performance as the source of his inspiration for the second quartet piece, completed on 2 July 1914. At first acknowledgment was indirect, through a program note by Ansermet according to which the second piece "represents an unhappy juggler, who must hide his grief while he performs his feats before the crowd."[44] In *Memories and Commentaries*, the second book of "conversa-

---

[42] "Russkiy sezon v Parizhe," *Apollon*, no. 10 (1910): 21; for a detailed discussion of neonationalism and its early impact on Stravinsky, see Taruskin, *Stravinsky and the Russian Traditions*, chapters 8 and 10.

[43] For the concept, see "Momentform" (1960), in Karlheinz Stockhausen, *Texte zur elektronischen und instrumentale Musik*, vol. 1 (Cologne, 1963), pp. 189–210; on behalf of back-extension of the concept, see Jonathan D. Kramer, "Moment Form in Twentieth-Century Music," *Musical Quarterly* 64 (1978): 177–94; on the second Piece for String Quartet, see Marianne Kielian-Gilbert, "Relationships of Symmetrical Pitch-Class Sets and Stravinsky's Metaphor of Polarity," *Perspectives of New Music* 21 (1982–83): 210–221.

[44] It is reprinted in Igor Stravinsky, *Selected Correspondence*, vol. 1, ed. Robert Craft (New York: Knopf, 1982), p. 407n.

FIGURE 13.4. Little Tich (Harry Relph, 1868–1928) (Mary Tich and Richard Findlater, *Little Tich: Giant of the Music Hall* [London, 1979])

tions" with Robert Craft, Stravinsky gave a more straightforward account of the composition's wellspring, albeit now tinged with a characteristic squeamishness:

Q: Has music ever been suggested to you by, or has a musical idea ever occurred to you from, a purely visual experience of movement, line or pattern?

A: Countless times, I suppose, though I remember only one instance in which I was aware of such a thing. This was during the composition of the second of my *Three Pieces* for string quartet. I had been fascinated by the movements of Little Tich whom I had seen in London in 1914, and the jerky, spastic movement, the ups and downs, the rhythm—even the mood or joke of the music—which I later called *Eccentric*, was suggested by the art of this great clown (and suggested seems to me the right word, for it does not try to *approfondir* the relationship, whatever it is).[45]

What Stravinsky was, as usual, careful to withhold was the concreteness of his musical source. The evidence for this is a loose sheet of paper now tucked into a pocket in the back cover of a sketchbook in the Stravinsky archive at the Sacher Foundation otherwise given over to the *Pribaoutki* and the *Pièces faciles* for piano duet, also compositions of 1914 (figure 13.5). The sheet con-

[45] *Memories and Commentaries* (Garden City, N.Y.: Doubleday, 1960), p. 89. On Little Tich see Tristan Rémy, *Les Clowns* (Paris: Bernard Grasset, 1945), pp. 376–80.

FIGURE 13.5. Two homemade sketch leaves with jottings made by Stravinsky in 1914 (Paul Sacher Stiftung, Basel)

First page, recto: under a melody headed "Lullaby" is the "Breton song imparted to me by Shura Benois—and they danced, while a clarinettist sitting on a stone in the rain played this little song with all his might"

First page, verso: the topmost jotting is headed "Dancing girl—horseback rider"

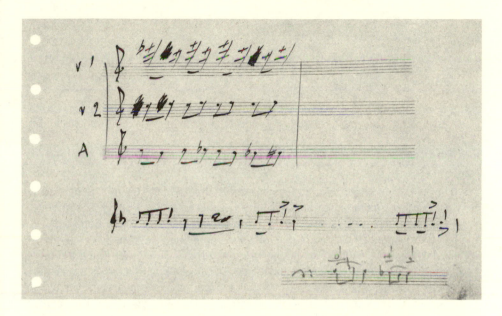

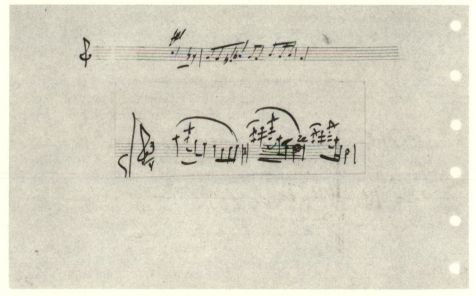

Second page, recto: the single-line jotting across the leaf near the bottom seems equally a derivation from the Breton song or the dancing girl tune, or a conflation of the two

Second page, verso

EXAMPLE 13.2. Stravinsky, "Breton Song," in sketchbook for Three Pieces for String Quartet

tains three notations of relevance to the quartet piece. The first is headed "Breton song imparted to me by Shura [i.e., Alexandre] Benois" (example 13.2) and followed by a description of the circumstances in which Benois had heard it: "And they danced, while on a rock in the rain a clarinet[tist] sat and played this song with all his might." Following this Stravinsky jotted a motivic derivative from the Breton tune (example 13.3). Finally there is a snatch labeled "Dancing Girl: Bareback Rider," evidently taken down at the circus, possibly at the same performance at which Stravinsky saw Little Tich and received the Breton melody from Benois (example 13.4).

A remarkable cloud of disinformation surrounds this innocent bit of paper in the Stravinsky/Craft literature. Robert Craft, forgetting that Stravinsky and Benois were together in London 1914, and ignoring the bareback rider motif, associates the Breton song with Benois's visit to the composer in La Baule, Brittany, in August 1910.[46] (But why, then, is it found among Stravinsky's 1914 sketches?) Even more curiously, Stravinsky himself, in a very late program note for the *Pribaoutki*, cited the plainly labeled Breton tune as an example of an "unused Russian theme" in his sketchbooks.[47]

But it was neither Russian nor unused. Together with the other jottings on the loose leaf, it furnished the thematic basis for Stravinsky's portrait of Little Tich. What all three notations have conspicuously in common is the rising-/falling-fourth motive (bracketed in examples 13.2–4), which, in the context of these tonal melodies, represents a progression from the fifth scale degree to the tonic and back. In the bareback rider phrase the progression is extended to reach the tonic through a repetition of the concluding fifth degree (bracketed from beneath in example 13.4), and in this form the motive found a home amid the motley assortment of phrases from which Stravinsky's famously disjointed composition was assembled.

Its three appearances are at mm. 4–5, 9–10, and 45–46, the last of them especially close to example 13.4. Two pitch levels are employed, as summarized in example 13.5. The four notes thus invoked form a versatile tetrachord

[46] *Selected Correspondence*, vol. 1, p. 408.

[47] Igor Stravinsky and Robert Craft, *Themes and Episodes* (New York: Knopf, 1966) p. 27.

EXAMPLE 13.3. Derivation from the "Breton Song"

EXAMPLE 13.4. Stravinsky, "Bareback
Rider," in sketchbook for
Three Pieces for String Quartet

EXAMPLE 13.5. Stravinsky, "Bareback Rider," derivations and their modal
affinities

that may be embedded in any of three different scale formations that characteristically interacted like chemical agents in Stravinsky's compositions of the
period: the "white key" pentatonic (or, more properly, anhemitonic) scale;
various ordinary diatonic scales (including the tonic scales of all the notations
on the sketch leaf, plus the scale with one sharp); and the octatonic (or "tone-
semitone") scale, in this case the one called "Collection III" in Pieter van den
Toorn's fundamental study. Add to this complex the ubiquitous use of acciaccaturas, without which no Stravinsky composition of the period is complete,
and one arrives at the tonal and thematic recipe, more or less, from which this

enigmatic little "grotesque" was concocted.[48] It is the anhemitonic component, of course, that attracts notice from a Turanian/Trubetskoyan perspective; it will provide the promised link with *Svadebka*.

The quality of *nepodvizhnost'*, or immobility, is the one associated with the
device of ostinato, which reached something of an experimental apex in some
of Stravinsky's short pieces of the "Swiss" decade, notably the little piano
duets, the recently recovered "Valse des fleurs" (*Tsvetochniy val's*) for two
pianos, the 1917 children's waltz published in May 1922 as "Une Valse pour
les petits lecteurs du 'Figaro,'"[49] and other one- or two-chord "vamping"
pieces in which "tonality" seems superficially to have made a comeback in
Stravinsky's music, but in which goal-oriented form and directed voice-
leading are manifestly in abeyance. Some of these pieces are virtually reduced
to the level of windup toy automata by the maintenance of a single ostinato for
the duration. When a more "complex" structure is wanted, it is achieved by
juxtaposing a series of unrelated ostinatos, producing the effect designated by
the use of the word *drobnost'*.

But the category of "automata" or "vamping pieces" is not simply coextensive with that of "easy" or "children's" pieces. The first of the Three Pieces
for String Quartet carries the device to an extreme, presenting a multiplicity of
hypostatized ostinatos, each having its own pitch collection and registral
space, the whole making up as straightforward a bit of imitation folk music as
Stravinsky (or anyone) ever composed, as would be perfectly evident even
without Ansermet's program note, according to which the piece "represents a
group of peasants singing and dancing against the monotonous setting of the
steppes."[50]

The sustained D in the viola (paired at the unaccompanied beginning and
end with a characteristic acciaccatura C♯) is the drone of a *volïnka* (or *duda*),
the Russian bagpipe Stravinsky must have heard every day at his summer
home in Ustilug. The extremely recursive four-note dance tune (*naigrïsh*)
tootled up above on the chanter (first violin) might well have been a variant of
the popular *Perepyolushka* ("Little Quail") (example 13.6), or some other
actual peasant dance of its ilk. Beneath the folkish surface lies an interesting,
and much analyzed, technical study. On the one hand it develops and extends
the *nepodvizhnost'*, the frozen rhythmic immobility, created in *Le Sacre du
printemps* by the use of ostinatos. Here there are two frozen levels: the
twenty-three-beat violin tune and the seven-beat percussive pattern in the
cello, which determines the barring. Since seven does not go evenly into
twenty-three, the violin melody falls behind the cello pattern by the remain-

---

[48] For details see Taruskin, *Stravinsky and the Russian Traditions*, pp. 1467–73. Van den
Toorn's seminal discussion of the octatonic collections is in Pieter C. van den Toorn, *The Music
of Igor Stravinsky* (New Haven: Yale University Press, 1983), pp. 31–60.

[49] Reprinted from the Paris newspaper in White, *Stravinsky*, p. 210.

[50] *Selected Correspondence*, vol. 1, p. 407n.

EXAMPLE 13.6. Russian folk song, *Perepyolushka* (Little Quail)

der, two beats, on each repetition. And since two does not divide seven evenly, the falling-behind effect crosscuts the cello pattern. Stravinsky lets the music play itself out just long enough for this phenomenon to run its course, then lets the air out of the conceptual bagpipe.

The result may be compared with a mobile, a sculpture with moving parts, anticipating the genre pioneered two decades later by Alexander Calder. Two fixed elements here course through time (= space) within independent orbits, passing in and out of phase with one another. The second violin punctuates the texture with an element all its own, just as fixed as the others, but with its recurrences unevenly distributed so as to inject a modicum of (human?) caprice to offset the counterpoint of impersonal automata running above and below.

The pitch material is as strictly hypostatized in this piece as the rhythmic. It is partitioned into two tetrachords separated by the octave-bisecting interval of a tritone, the one (G–A–B–C) assigned to the first violin, the other (C♯–D♯–E–F♯) to the second.[51] Partitions of this kind, originating in the "tone-semitone" practice of the St. Petersburg school under Rimsky-Korsakov, could be applied either to harmonic triads or to melodic tetrachords. The triadic partitioning had reached an early Stravinskian peak in the second tableau of *Petrushka* (composed three years prior to the quartet pieces), with its famous "bitonal" chord associated with the title character. The tetrachordal partition would achieve its Stravinskian zenith in *Svadebka*, complete but for scoring by the middle of 1917, three years later.[52]

As discussed in the first part of this chapter, both the *drobnost'* of the second piece and the *nepodvizhnost'* of the first were aspects of the general stripdown, the radical simplification of means, that was part and parcel of the neoprimitivist ideal, the basic cultural crux that had been so passionately debated in Stravinsky's Russia between those who regarded the shedding of the conventional complexities of linear thinking to vouchsafe a higher unity of thought and feeling (*uproshcheniye*) and those who regarded it as mere

[51] The cello's drum pattern partakes of both tetrachords and could be said to bridge them; the viola's drone D supports the scale segment in the first-violin tune, vouchsafing it an unmistakable tonal priority over the punctuating motif in the second.

[52] When tetrachords rather than triads were the partitioning agents, Stravinsky normally preferred to use "minor" tetrachords, with the intervallic structure tone-semitone-tone (T-S-T). Two such tetrachords placed a tritone apart would together form a complete octatonic scale. Here, however, the first-violin music has been modified, perhaps in keeping with its folk source, to the configuration T-T-S, coinciding with the defining tetrachord of the major scale. Substitutions of this kind were not unprecedented even in the work of Rimsky-Korsakov.

dehumanization (*oproshcheniye*). The absolutely homorhythmic, formally strophic, and harmonically static third Piece for String Quartet is a programmatic exemplification of *uproshcheniye* (or *oproshcheniye*). Its plainly cultic or ritualistic disposition offers scant comfort to defenders of humanistic values, for Stravinsky seemed to be putting into musical practice that notorious call of Pascal's for a dogmatic discipline that should, by lulling, quell the voice of reason.[53]

Adorno's strictures about the "permanent regression" embodied in Stravinskian musical form again come forcibly to mind; and while Adorno did not comment on the Three Pieces, the closely related Concertino (1920), written at the other end of Stravinsky's maximally Turanian phase, enraged him: "The composer insisted that the Concertino for String Quartet should hum along like a sewing machine," Adorno protested. "This he demanded of that combination of instruments once more purely suited than any other to musical humanism, to the absolute enspiritualization of the instrumental medium."[54] Thus spake the voice of Romano-Germany—a highly offended Romano-Germany—assuming, as it will, the voice of (outraged) humanity. It was no universal or "absolute" property of music to represent individualistic subjectivity, but it was a musical potential that Romano-Germany had developed to its pinnacle, for which accomplishment it took an intense and justifiable pride. Romano-Germany had invested heavily in the autonomy of "das Individuum," the individual sentient agent. That autonomy was both (flatteringly) mirrored and protected in panromanogermanic music by structural complexity and profusion of highly differentiated detail. The acutely sentient, autonomous, reflective self represented Romano-Germany's ideal of humanity—a human identity that had reached a peak representation in the Beethoven of the late quartets, with their special quality, as Kerman has so eloquently described it, of "voice."[55] Stravinskian *uproshcheniye* reflected and protected something else—a "symphonic," unreflective identity that Romano-Germany could only regard as subhuman.[56]

---

[53] Blaise Pascal, "Le Pari," in *Pensées et Opuscules* (Paris: Larousse, 1934), p. 62 (quoted in the preface to this book, xxviii).

[54] *Philosophy of Modern Music*, pp. 165–67, 170; translation modified on comparison with the original (Frankfurt: Suhrkamp, 1976).

[55] See Joseph Kerman, *The Beethoven Quartets* (New York: Knopf, 1967; reprint, New York: Norton, 1979), chapter 7.

[56] Perhaps the most caustic of (self-)commentaries on Stravinsky's repudiation of his own past in the wake of his "conversion" to serialism (entailing his conversion to what Prince Trubetskoy would have called "panromanogermanic chauvinism") was his enthusiastic review, written through Robert Craft, of Kerman's book, in which discussion is confined entirely to the late quartets, and in which Stravinsky/Craft unwittingly (or could it have even been wittingly?) assumes the very voice of Adorno, Stravinsky's own chief detractor. (For instance: "The String Quartet was the most lucid conveyor of musical ideas ever fashioned, and the most singing—*i.e.*,

STRAVINSKIAN ANHEMITONY

That subhuman something, of course, was what Prince Trubetskoy lauded as the Turanian psychological type; and Stravinsky embodied it musically in a work that brought the Turanian type and the symphonic personality to a peak of emblematic artistic representation, altogether comparable to the way in which Beethoven's quartets had emblematized the humanistic values Eurasianists now sought to discredit, and did it in a manner uncannily faithful to Prince Trubetskoy's prescription. The most striking feature of *Svadebka* as a musical composition is its unprecedented reliance on anhemitony, the musical idiom that, according to Trubetskoy, ideally reflected Turanian mentality in its "relative poverty and plainness," its "complete submission to simple schematic rules," and its "schematic clarity and lucidity," all amounting, in the modern context, to a cleansing spiritual *uproshcheniye*.

A thematic survey reveals a far higher proportion of anhemitonic melodies in *Svadebka* than is statistically representative of Russian folk melodies, and far higher, too, than the accustomed level of anhemitony in Stravinsky's neonationalist scores. Out of twenty "themes" (a theme being identified, for the purposes of this survey, as a melody or motif that recurs), a total of six, which is to say more than one-quarter, are anhemitonic. Another six (for a cumulative total of twelve, or 60 percent) belong to a class that may be designated "embellished anhemitonic": when represented as scales, the pitch inventories of such melodies contain one semitone, but the pitch that creates it operates under restrictions that subordinate it structurally (or, which amounts to the same thing, perceptually) to one of its neighbors.[57] Thus the two melodies given in example 13.7 (counted as two versions of one theme in the foregoing summary) may be regarded as representing a single anhemitonic scale—/0 3 5 8/ if the lowest pitch of the narrowest possible scalar arrangement of the collection is arbitrarily labeled zero and the remaining pitches counted thence by semitones—with a semitonal adjacency between 5 and 8 that functions either as an upper neighbor to 5 or as a descending (never ascending!) passing tone. In no case is the note in question ever approached by skip. Whether this embellishing note is semitonally adjacent to 5 or to 8 (that is, whether at the given pitch level it is represented by F or F♯) is immaterial to the mode's identity. That this was Stravinsky's own criterion is shown by the fact that he

---

human—of instrumental means; or, rather, if it was not that natively and necessarily, Beethoven made it so.") See "A Realm of Truth," in Igor Stravinsky and Robert Craft, *Retrospectives and Conclusions* (New York: Knopf, 1969), pp. 130–42. (The quoted sentence is on p. 133; the review originally appeared in the *New York Review of Books*, 26 September 1968.)

[57] For the full tabulation on which these figures are based, see table 4, "*Svadebka*: Ethnographic Sources, Action, and Musical Themes," in *Stravinsky and the Russian Traditions*, pp. 1423–40.

EXAMPLE 13.7. "Embellished anhemitony" in Stravinsky's *Svadebka*

modal paradigm

0   3   5   [6/7]   8

used the two melodies in example 13.7 to carry two variants (one from Kireyevsky, the other from Tereshchenko) of a single song text. Thus he regarded the two tunes, despite the superficial discrepancy in their scales, as variants of a single tune, representing a single anhemitonic pitch field, variously embellished.

It should be emphasized once more that all the anhemitonic themes and motifs (*popevki*) in *Svadebka*, however authentic they may sound, were invented by Stravinsky. None was a found object. In *The Rite of Spring*, by contrast, there is only a tiny number of anhemitonic motifs—seven by the most generous count[58]—of which only a single one, the "Incantation" at the beginning of the "Rondes printanières" (rehearsal figure 48) is drawn from a known folk source, and even there the "embellished anhemitony" is the result of an alteration to the original tune.[59]

Thus it transpires that Stravinsky's anhemitony is not so much a "Russian" as an invented Eurasian/Turanian trait; and so it is no longer quite correct to speak of "nationalism" here, or even "neonationalism." Those who have noted the prevalence of anhemitony in *Svadebka* have attributed it to what

[58] Generous because to get this number the criteria of selection have been somewhat eased by comparison with those applied to the *Svadebka* themes. To the /0 2 5 7/ anhemitonic tetrachord played by the English horn at figure 2 a fifth note is added, turning the mode into the diatonic segment /0 2 3 5 7/; the anhemitonic trichord played by the English horn at figure 6 is compromised by a chromatic continuation after three measures; the famous ostinato figure at 14 (first prefigured fifteen measures earlier) is more often thought of as a vamp or an accompaniment than as a tune; the melody first heard at 27 in the alto flute may be classified as "embellished anhemitonic," but the embellishing pitch is far more prominent in the melody than such pitches are anywhere in *Svadebka*, and the semitone is far more conspicuous. The remaining anhemitonic tunes are at figures 48, 83ff., and 121; the last, the main theme of the "Evocation des Ancêtres," consists of a mere dyad, an oscillation of two tones a whole tone apart.

[59] See R. Taruskin, "Russian Folk Melodies in *The Rite of Spring*," *Journal of the American Musicological Society* 33 (1980): 516 (example 3); the source melody was first identified by Lawrence Morton.

they have assumed to be an archaistic tendency. Victor Belaiev, the author of the earliest published analysis of the score, who perhaps hyperbolically considered the /0 3 5/ configuration at the outset "the fundamental motif from which the whole of its melos is developed," identified that melos explicitly with "the old way of Russian life."[60] Boris Asafyev emphasized the "union of archaic musical elements with formal principles derived . . . from the Renaissance."[61] But it is evident (and demonstrable) that the whole category of "embellished anhemitony" was something Stravinsky had never observed but contrived.

It is also demonstrable that Stravinsky's range of ethnographic awareness and even observation extended beyond the frontiers of Russia, into other parts of the "Turanian" domain. As early as March 1914, before a note of *Svadebka* had been committed to paper, Stravinsky clipped from the pages of the newspaper *Rech'* a lengthy article by the famous linguist and academician Nikolai Yakovlevich Marr (1864–1934, the very one over whose theories of Marxian linguistics Stalin would become so comically exercised near the end of his life), entitled "Thoughts on the Religious Singing of the Ancient East: On the Occasion of a Concert of Georgian Sacred Music at the Hall of Nobles on the Sixteenth of March."[62] Marr's thesis, related to his linguistic theories, which traced the origins of human speech to the languages of the Caucasus, was that "the religious singing of the Georgians and related tribes represents a vestige of the religion of the Ancient Orient [i.e., the Near East], neither Semitic nor Aryan, but of the Japhetic tribes that have newly emerged as a focus of scientific research"—that is, what more recent scholars would call the hypothetical primeval "Indo-European" culture. Marr chides the scholars of the humanistic disciplines for failing to recognize this heritage as philologists and archeologists had done, and calls upon artists to "develop these precious artifacts before they perish in obscurity."

It was a typical neonationalist plea on behalf of a cultural heritage that would hold a special appeal for an artist with proto-Eurasianist leanings; in fact it was a point of special emphasis for the Trubetskoys and Karsavins to

[60] *Igor Stravinsky's "Les Noces:" An Outline*, trans. S. W. Pring (London: Oxford University Press, 1928), table of contents and p. 2. This analysis was not published in its original language until 1972 (*Musorgskiy, Skryabin, Stravinskiy: Sbornik statey* [Moscow: Muzïka]).

[61] *A Book about Stravinsky*, trans. Richard F. French (Ann Arbor: UMI Research Press, 1982), p. 129; Asafyev's reference to "Renaissance" principles has to do with his strange conviction that *Svadebka* was modeled on "the old madrigal comedies of the seventeenth [*sic*] century (like the *Amfiparnasso* of Orazio Vecchi)." Alfredo Casella, too, had likened *Svadebka* to *L'Amfiparnasso*, which caused Robert Craft to wonder whether the "farfetched comparison" might not have been "suggested by Stravinsky himself, who was fond of throwing out false scents of this kind" (*Stravinsky in Pictures and Documents*, p. 619n.236).

[62] "Mïsli o religioznom penii Drevnego Vostoka: Po povodu gruzinskogo dukhovnogo kontserta v zale Dvoryanskogo sobraniya 16-go marta," *Rech'*, no. 73 (16/29 March 1914). The clipping is in Stravinsky's 1912–14 scrapbook, now at the Paul Sacher Stiftung in Basel.

insist on the community of Eurasian cultures. Hence it is not surprising to find that Stravinsky showed an interest in Georgian folk and religious music, or that this interest should have left its mark on *Svadebka*.

"Scientific" folklore anthologies that we know Stravinsky to have consulted contained studies of Georgian and other Caucasian musics, the work mainly of Dmitriy Ignat'yevich Arakchiyev (Arakishvili, 1873–1953), a Georgian composer and folklorist who was the first to investigate the local ethnic music with the aid of the phonograph.[63] It was because he knew these publications by Arakchiyev that Stravinsky made a point, in a letter to his mother of 10/23 February 1916, to request "folk songs of the Caucasian peoples that have been phonographically recorded."[64] His mother must have sent him the collection "Georgian Folk Songs and Verses" (*Kartuli khalkuri khimgebi* [Tiflis, 1909]), by Iya (Ilya) Kargareteli (1867–1939), because the entire contents of this volume, consisting of sixteen polyphonic songs calligraphically transcribed by the composer on high-quality card stock, survives today in the Stravinsky archive, the composer having become fascinated, it seems, not just with the music but with the Georgian alphabet.[65] These songs evidently came into Stravinsky's possession too late to have had any direct influence on the composition of most of *Svadebka*; but comparison with Arakchiyev's publications, particularly the group of religious songs published under the title "Georgian Canticles for the Liturgy of St. John of Damascus in Folk Harmonization," will show the source of certain devices of harmony and voice leading— parallel triads, upward-resolving sevenths—that crop up now and again in Stravinsky's score, and will also provide an ethnographic validation for some of his "anhemitonic consonances" (chords in which seconds and fourths are treated as stable) (example 13.8). The passage in *Svadebka* closest to this "Japhetic" style is the one at figures 12–14 in the first tableau, where the women's voices sing an extended diatonic melody in parallel major and minor triads, the pianists' left hands meanwhile thumping out acciaccaturas with a special insistence (example 13.9).

---

[63] These were "Kratkiy ocherk razvitiya gruzinskoy, karatalino-kakhetinskoy, narodnoy pesni," in *Trudï muzïkal'no-ètnograficheskoy komissii*, vol. 1 (Moscow: Moscow University, 1906), pp. 269–344, and "Sravnitel'nïy obzor narodnoy pesni i muzïkal'nïkh instrumentov zapadnoy Gruzii (Imeretii)," in *Trudï muzïkal'no-ètnograficheskoy komissii*, vol. 2 (Moscow: Moscow University, 1911), pp. 119–203.

[64] L. S. D'yachkova and B. M. Yarustovsky, ed., *I. F. Stravinskiy: Stat'i i materialï* (Moscow: Sovetskiy kompozitor, 1973), p. 488.

[65] See Victor Varunts, supplementary note to Stravinsky's letters to his mother in *Muzïkal'naya akademiya*, no. 4 (1992): 118. The first page of this manuscript is illustrated in *Stravinsky in Pictures and Documents*, p. 44, erroneously dated "c. 1904." This date is contradicted not only by the date of Kargareteli's publication but also by the paper Stravinsky used, which bears a Swiss watermark and which was also used for the fair copy of the Peasant Choruses of 1914–17. On the basis of these observations this Georgian transcription would most likely date from late 1916 or early 1917, when Stravinsky was hard at the fourth tableau of *Svadebka*.

EXAMPLE 13.8. Selected passages from D. I. Arakchiyev, *Gruzinskiye pesnopeniya na liturgiyu sv. Ioanna Zlatoustogo v narodnoy garmonizatsii* (Papers of the Musico-Ethnographic Commission of Moscow University), vol. 1, pp. 337–60

EXAMPLE 13.8, *continued*

EXAMPLE 13.9. Stravinsky, *Svadebka*, first tableau, figure 12

THE PLEROMA

The extraordinary preference for anhemitony in *Svadebka* had a technical motivation as well as an ethnographic or metaphorical one. Again, it was a motivation that arose out of no mere archaistic vision but an urgent contemporary one. Actual Russian "calendar" or ritual tunes—a category that includes wedding songs, and the one to which Stravinsky was most attracted when it came to actually mining ethnographic anthologies for neonationalist appropriation—are generally constructed on diatonic segments of small ambitus rather than on the kind of gapped scale tendentiously adduced by Prince Trubetskoy. Though possibly prompted in the first instance by the lexicographer Dahl's description of an unspecified three-tone lament formula (which Stravinsky inevitably fashioned for himself by "gapping" the /0 2 3 5/ minor tetrachord he had exploited so extensively in *The Rite* to produce the /0 3 5/ trichord that dominates the first tableau of *Svadebka*), what accounted for the prevalence of anhemitonic motifs in the later score was their suitability to the all-embracing tonal system Stravinsky devised for it, one of his greatest, if hidden, achievements. Through it, Stravinsky solved once and for all the central problem of his "Swiss" period, namely, that of creating the authentic folklore of an imaginary *ur*-Russia, not the real Russia but one "realer than the real."

What made anhemitonic constructs indispensable to this scheme was precisely their tonally suspensive character. The absence of semitones bars implicit cadential functions (at least in the ordinary "Western," Romano-Germanic sense), thus rendering the melodic surface of the score "nonprogressive" and "non-implicative," as one perceptive writer has termed it.[66] Tonal "implication" in *Svadebka* comes about, on those rare occasions where Stravinsky resorts to it, by specific gesture. The most traditional cadence— the only really traditional cadence in the score, it seems—comes early on, where the bridesmaids finish their combing song in the first tableau with a clear-cut cadential flourish that identifies the pitch E as a soon-to-be-superseded tonic (example 13.10). This gesture seems a vestige of the kind of quasi-tonal or conventionally "modal" thinking Stravinsky would abandon as he worked further into the score, and as he evolved the unique ground plan we are to trace, which would obviate the necessity for such explicit cadential gestures.

The quality of "acentricity," the tonal ambiguity inherent in anhemitonic melodies, was the key to fashioning a convincingly antiromanogermanic idiom, and Stravinsky reinforced it in every way he could. Thus for example the semitonal adjacencies in his "embellished anhemitonic" tunes are never ap-

[66] David Schulenberg, "Modes, Prolongations, and Analysis," *Journal of Musicology* 4 (1985–86): 324.

EXAMPLE 13.10. Stravinsky, *Svadebka*, first tableau, figure 8, voices only

(*"I'll wind a blue [ribbon]!"*)

plied to their neighboring pitches by direct upward step progression, which might lend them the character of leading tones. And so they never compromise the tonally "non-implicative" status of the tunes in which they occur. Stravinsky was interested in another kind of implication, the kind he had developed in *Petrushka* and *The Rite of Spring*, which Pieter van den Toorn has christened "octatonic/diatonic interaction." In *Svadebka*, this interaction acquired an unprecedented scope and integrity, maximalized and systematized far beyond anything Stravinsky had previously essayed, utterly replacing traditional tonal functions and governing every aspect of tonal organization in this greatest of all neoprimitivist scores. By using diatonic or anhemitonic melodies devoid of conventional tonal orientation at the surface of that score, Stravinsky avoided any contradiction with the symmetrically conceived and balanced Turanian ground plan it will now be our business to uncover and describe.

The themes presented and analyzed for their /0 3 5 8/ modal background structure in example 13.7 share that structural configuration with the pitch matrix of the second Piece for String Quartet as given above in example 13.5. Other themes from *Svadebka* built on that anhemitonic tetrachord or on one of its subsets are given in example 13.11. They include some of the ballet's most prominent tunes, including the opening bridal lament (on the trichord /0 3 5/); the song of consolation from the first tableau, on the same trichord; the invocation of the Virgin Mary at the beginning of the second tableau (on the full /0 3 5 8/ tetrachord, embellished); and the *lyuli-lyuli* refrain at the beginning of the fourth tableau (its /0 2 5/ structure corresponding to the /3 5 8/ members of the original tetrachord, minus the "zero" pitch).

What was said of the tonal matrix in the second quartet piece is true of these invented folk melodies as well: their /0 3 5 8/ pitch/intervallic content is equally a subset of the pentatonic (/0 3 5 8 10/), diatonic (/0 2 3 5 7 8 10/)

EXAMPLE 13.11. The [0, 3, 5, 8] tetrachord in Stravinsky's *Svadebka*

and octatonic (/*0 2 3 5 6 8 9 11*/) collections. Another way of saying this is that their pitch content can be variously supplemented to produce pentatonic, diatonic, or octatonic collections; or that such melodies can be inserted ad libitum into pentatonic, diatonic, or octatonic contexts and can therefore bridge them. With these observations we have taken the first step toward understanding the globally worked-out tonal organization of Stravinsky's Turanian masterpiece, as well as the representational or metaphorical purpose that global organization served.[67]

[67] Because the pentatonic collection is a subset of the diatonic collection—that is, because every member of the pentatonic collection as represented above is included in the similar representation of the diatonic (with /2/ and /7/ left over)—it will not be necessary to refer to it separately in the discussion that follows. Anything said in the course of that discussion about the diatonic collection will be true of its subsets as well.

If nothing else, the experience of composing *The Rite of Spring* taught Stravinsky to regard the /0 2 3 5/ T-S-T (tone-semitone-tone) or "minor" tetrachord, of which the *Svadebka* lament (/0 3 5/) was an anhemitonic sub-set, as the most potent agent of linearly conceived diatonic/octatonic inter-penetration. Replicated disjunctly at the major second it produces what Mily Balakirev had called the "Russian minor" (more generally, if loosely, known as the "Dorian" scale). At the minor second it generates the octatonic scale. The T-S-T tetrachord itself being palindromic, the octave species it generates are likewise self-inverting. The modal properties discussed thus far hold true whether one "reads up" or "reads down." Here we already have the concep-tual nub of the matrix that generated the melodic/harmonic texture of *Svadebka* (example 13.12).

EXAMPLE 13.12. Interaction of diatonic and octatonic scales around T-S-T tetrachordal pivots

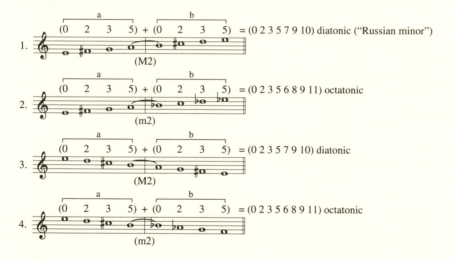

Example 13.12 is notated at the pitch of the opening melody in *Svadebka*, the bride's *plach* (lament), so as to facilitate a number of preliminary observa-tions, including the derivation of the first harmony in the score (if, as seems reasonable, we disregard as harmony the percussive acciaccaturas at the very beginning). At figure 1, the entering pianos harmonize the melody of the *plach*, the tones of which are found within the upper tetrachord of the diatonic scales in example 13.12, with the pitches that enclose its octatonic comple-ment, as shown there in scale 4. The nature of the spacing, with the fourth inverted to a fifth, suggests another sort of enclosure, or infixing: the symmet-rical bounding of the *plach* melody by the defining pitches of the complemen-tary tetrachord, both of which are semitonally adjacent to an outer pitch of the *plach* (example 13.13).

EXAMPLE 13.13. First harmony in Stravinsky's *Svadebka*, figure 1

Thus the *plach* tetrachord is harmonically embellished by its octatonic complement at the same time that its melodic embellishment (the grace note F♯) is drawn from its diatonic complement. In a small way this "polytonal" example already illustrates a basic principle of harmonic/contrapuntal construction in *Svadebka*: the superimposition of two pitch fields that intersect around the notes of the *plach*.

As for scale 2 in example 13.12, the "ascending" octatonic extension of the focal tetrachord, it coincides with the pitch content of the most important octatonic theme in *Svadebka*, the parental lament from the second tableau that returns so poignantly to conclude the third (example 13.14). This theme (plus the piano accompaniment, which supplies in the form of an ostinato the two pitches required to exhaust the scale of reference) was the very passage from which Arthur Berger inferred the octatonic scale as a referential collection for Stravinsky's music in his seminal article of 1963.[68] Having observed the octatonic source of this melody, and its relationship to the complex of scales given in example 13.12, and recalling the way the diatonic grace notes had peacefully coexisted with the octatonic harmony at figure 1 on the basis of the shared upper tetrachord of scale 3 in the example, we may go on to note a similar interaction that takes place between figures 35 and 39 in the second

[68] For the relevant discussion see Benjamin Boretz and Edward T. Cone, eds., *Perspectives on Schoenberg and Stravinsky* (Princeton: Princeton University Press, 1968), pp. 130–31.

EXAMPLE 13.14. Stravinsky, *Svadebka*, second tableau, figure 35

tableau. As shown in example 13.15, a few tones foreign to the octatonic scale of the parental lament occur in the lines set in counterpoint against it. These are the ones, as noted in passing in the previous section of this chapter, that Berger had ignored as "ornamental"; and yet example 13.12 furnishes a means of accounting for them. In example 13.15a, the extraneous pitch (B) is part of a diatonic motif referable to scale 1 and hence related to the octatonic main theme (derived from scale 2) by virtue of their common possession of the all-important T-S-T tetrachord on E. Stravinsky's contrapuntal usage here points up the kinship between the octatonic and diatonic sets as extensions of the same tonality-defining basic tetrachordal cell, precisely as illustrated in example 13.12. In example 13.15b, both elements, octatonic as well as diatonic, have been transposed by minor thirds, albeit in opposite directions. Under such a transposition the pitch content of the octatonic component is invariant. The diatonic counterpoint, while no longer referable to any single scale in example 13.12, remains referable to scale 2 except for the newly introduced "foreign" pitch, D, which is referable to scale 1.

EXAMPLE 13.15. Stravinsky, *Svadebka*, second tableau (notes foreign to scale 2 circled)

a.

b.

A similar octatonic/diatonic interaction, involving one of *Svadebka*'s most prominent anhemitonic tunes, may be observed beginning at figure 68, near the beginning of the third tableau. The melody in question (originally sung as a "consolation song" to the bride at figure 9 in the first tableau) is initiated by the bass soloist at the pitch level originally associated with the bridal *plach*: that is, on an /0 3 5/ configuration referable to the generating tetrachord of scale 3 in example 13.12. The motif is immediately taken through a complete rotation by minor thirds that implicates and exhausts scale 4, the "descending" octatonic collection cognate to scale 3 (see example 13.16a). Meanwhile, the pianos noodle an ostinato, the bass of which sums up the same rotation by minor thirds (reading from the bottom up in scale 4), coinciding with the starting pitches of each transposition of the anhemitonic motif. The newsworthy event is what happens at figure 69: the mezzo-soprano soloist chimes in with a transposition of the motif beginning on F♯, the constituent notes of which—D♯, F♯, G♯—are not to be found in any one scale in example 13.12. They do, however, link up with the concurrent transposition of the same motif in the soprano and tenor parts to form an anhemitonic subset of scale 1 at a transposition precisely analogous to that of the soprano at figure 69 + 2 with respect to the initiating pitch level in the bass (see example 13.16b).

To this observation we may add the striking fact that the groom's concluding address to the bride, which is based on a cyclic (and embellished) reprise of the opening *plach*, is pitched at the level of the first transposition shown in example 13.16a, and the tintinnabulating instrumental coda that derives from it is harmonized exclusively with pitches referable to an anhemitonic subset of the scale given in example 13.16b. The two "ornamental" tones in the voice part (E and D, regularly applied as anacrusis to C♯) derive from scale 4 (see example 13.17). The whole ending tonality of the score, then, is adumbrated by the mezzo's seemingly anomalous entrance at figure 69.

All these wide-ranging if somewhat desultory observations, drawn from all four tableaux, are in fact converging on a single very significant point. They identify the array presented in example 13.12 as something more than a heuristic tool. We seem to be dealing, as forecast, with a global *complexe sonore* (to borrow a term from Stravinsky's *Poétique musicale*) that governs, at both short range and long, the pitch relations of the entire work. The habits

EXAMPLE 13.16. Linkage of *plach* motif transpositions in third tableau (figure 68 onward)

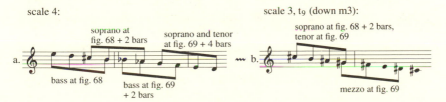

EXAMPLE 13.17. Groom's recapitulation of *plach* motif at end, scalar/harmonic abstract

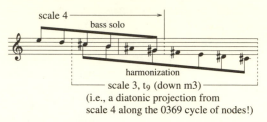

(i.e., a diatonic projection from
scale 4 along the 0369 cycle of nodes!)

of transposition we have been observing suggest that Stravinsky viewed his anhemitonic and diatonic motifs (and their implied scales) against an octatonic background. That is, he considered them to be in a perpetual state of potential symmetrical rotation by minor thirds (hereafter represented by the figures /0 3 6 9/) under which the octatonic background scale is invariant. Thus in order fully to represent the *complexe sonore* governing *Svadebka*, the "Dorian" scales in example 13.12 have to be conceived in terms of a fourfold /0 3 6 9/ multiplication. They are in effect mapped as diatonic projections onto an octatonic background scale, represented by scales 2 and 4 in example 13.12, at each node of invariance-producing transposition. Since scales 2 and 4 differ only in their "filler" pitches, not their nodes, either an ascending or a descending representation of this mapping process will have an identical pitch content so far as the diatonic projections are concerned (see example 13.18).

As newly represented in example 13.18, scale A seems to be identical to what has up to now been designated scale 1. Scale 1, however, was an ascending sequence only, whereas scale A is more properly (and neutrally) a *collection*, encompassing both scale 1 and its descending counterpart, scale 3, from which an identical array might have been generated. One need only imagine, then, an array of descending diatonic scales (replications of scale 3 at each of the /0 3 6 9/ nodes) mapped onto scale 4 in order to have a technically complete, though in practice redundant, representation of the *complexe sonore* that governs the score. The fourfold diatonic array (scales A through D in example 13.18) represents not four different keys (for the melodies fashioned for them, we may recall, are all tonally "non-implicative") but four functionally equivalent diatonic projections of a single /0 3 6 9/ matrix representing the invariance nodes of the octatonic background collection. And so their starting and finishing notes (that is, the nodal points) are not to be regarded as tonics, because the intervallic structure of the various, predominantly anhemitonic, motifs derived from these scales is designed, as we have seen, precisely to preclude such identification. By the same token, the two octatonic scales are best regarded not as representing—in Van den Toorn's nomenclature—"Collection I" (descending) and "Collection III" (ascending),

EXAMPLE 13.18. Diatonic projections of octatonic background

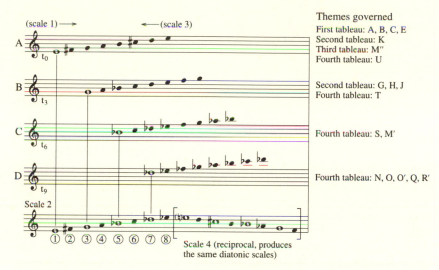

Themes governed

First tableau: A, B, C, E
Second tableau: K
Third tableau: M″
Fourth tableau: U

Second tableau: G, H, J
Fourth tableau: T

Fourth tableau: S, M′

Fourth tableau: N, O, O′, Q, R′

but simply as alternative ways of filling out the same /0 3 6 9/ cycle of nodes. Thus despite the differing local pitch collections, it can be said that *Svadebka* begins and ends in the same tonality, here defined as an octatonic pitch field with multiple local diatonic projections, which comprises and controls a unified tonal system by means of strategic, controlled departures and returns.

A sense of tonal motion can be achieved by means of transitions ("modulations") among the diatonic nodal projections (scales A through D in example 13.18). Indeed, this was Stravinsky's primary means of tonally articulating and differentiating the four tableaux. The main themes of the first (bride's) tableau are all referable to scale A. Those in the first part of the second (groom's) tableau all refer to scale B, representing the next "higher" notch along the /0 3 6 9/ circle. (The second part of the second tableau contains the chant material originally intended for the *Liturgiya* ballet; it constitutes the one extended apparent departure from the governing *complexe sonore*, and we shall pass over it here.)[69]

The third tableau is dominated, like the first, by scale A (we are back at the bride's), except for the mothers' lament at the end, one of the few spots in the score where the octatonic background scale breaks the surface. The fourth tableau places the greatest emphasis on scale D, which occupies a position as far "down" the /0 3 6 9/ circle from A as B is "up." It may be regarded, then, as scale B's reciprocal. Scale C comes briefly into its own at figure 110, where it is entrusted with the first statement of the quoted folk song that will

[69] It is fully described and analyzed in *Stravinsky and the Russian Traditions*, pp. 1378–81.

eventually bring the ballet to its climax (example 13.19). The theme never comes back in this scale, though, and except for a single brief passage after figure 128, scale C is not heard again. The short shrift given this scale in Stravinsky's deployment of this *complexe sonore* enhances the status of scale A, its tritone antipode, as first among equals, shadowed on either side by scales B and D, and, by providing a point of equilibrium between them, signifying harmonic repose.

Its primacy is asserted in another way as well, one that will entail a further refinement in the representation of the *complexe sonore*. Besides the diatonic scales in their normal forms as represented in example 13.18, which we may term "authentic," Stravinsky makes occasional telling use of modal extensions, whereby an extra T-S-T tetrachord is attached at the lower or upper end to form a new scale (example 13.20). On a loose analogy with medieval mode theory, we may christen these extensions "plagal" and "pluperfect," respectively. (On an even looser analogy with the theory of Russian church chant, they could be called "dark" and "thrice bright.") In principle these extensions could be applied to any of the four diatonic scales in the *complexe sonore*, and instances involving each of them do occur. (The bass solo at figure 53, for one example, is built on the plagal extension of scale B—see example 13.21.) Such events are sporadic, however, and of only transient significance. They

EXAMPLE 13.19. Stravinsky, *Svadebka*, fourth tableau, two bars after figure 110

EXAMPLE 13.20. Diatonic projections extended

do not seem to possess any long-range implication for the tonal structure of the ballet. It is another matter with the basic scale, A. Its modal extensions are numerous, recurrent, and thematically crucial. Moreover, they provide Stravinsky with the means to achieve a genuine tonal climax at the conclusion of the fourth tableau.

The plagal extension is heard frequently throughout the "First Part" of the score, comprising the first three tableaux. Its first appearance is the tenor solo (the bride's mother) at figure 21. The fact that Stravinsky doubles the tune at the lower fourth at figure 23 proves its "plagal" status: the bass's part is in A-authentic, and the doubling underscores the modal affinity (example 13.22). The climax of the third tableau (figure 78ff.), which is to say the culmination of the whole "First Part" (where the metaphorical "rivers" come

EXAMPLE 13.21. Stravinsky, *Svadebka*, second tableau, figure 53 (bass solo)

Smo - trel' -shchi - ki, glya -del' -shchi -ki,   ze -va -ki i   pa -losh -nï ko - lyu -ba - ki

EXAMPLE 13.22. Stravinsky, *Svadebka*, first tableau

a. Figure 21 (bride's mother)

Pre - chi - sta - ya Ma - ter', kho - di k nam u

khat'   sva-khe po - mo - gat'.

b. Figure 23

Na - sta - s'yush-ki ko - su Ti -

ma - fe - yev - nï ru - su.

together and where a motif derived from the quoted "Mitusov" folk song is heard for the first time), is also cast strategically in A-plagal.

"Strategically," because of what happens at the corresponding climax of the "Second Part" (fourth tableau). This climax is very elaborately prepared. Scale D having been established as the undisputed local governor at the outset of the tableau (figure 87ff.), its hegemony is challenged in a contrapuntal tour de force at figure 97, where choral parts based on scale A are accompanied by a bass line drawn from scale C, its tritone antipode. Scale D, in other words, has been encircled (example 13.23). By the time the embellished reprise of the bridal *plach* has made it into the choral parts (figure 114), scale A has reasserted its primacy. At figure 119 scale D attempts a comeback via a reprise of the opening theme of the fourth tableau, only to be rebuffed once again by the *plach* in its home scale (figure 121). Unexpectedly, at figure 122, the *plach* theme is taken over by scale C, the tritone antipode. It will never sound again in its home scale. As a matter of fact, at figure 126 (piano parts) it is acquired by scale D, with which it had formerly contended, and in that scale it will remain (though not on the same pitches) for the groom's grand peroration (figure 133).

Why the sudden switch? Because of a third element, one that since figure 110 had been vying for thematic dominance with the others—namely, the quoted ("Mitusov") folk song.[70] Its first, tactically inconspicuous statement is

[70] For some reason Stravinsky (or more likely Craft) referred to this song in a late memoir as "a worker's melody, a proletarian song" (*Memories and Commentaries* [Berkeley and Los Angeles: University of California Press, 1981], p. 97; the phrase is not found in the original edition of the book [Garden City, N.Y.: Doubleday, 1960]), and claimed that it had been so identified by

EXAMPLE 13.23. "Encircling" of scale D at figure 97

made in the tonally peripheral orbit of scale C. Thereafter, it is quickly brought into more central tonal ground. All future statements of the theme (beginning with the bass solo six measures after 111) will be pitched on scales B or A. The first statement on A comes at 120, right before the *plach* melody leaves that scale. In effect, the position of the opening lament as representative of scale A has been preempted by the Mitusov tune. From this point on the place of the quoted folk song—and with it, of scale A—at center stage is vigorously upheld and reinforced. The reinforcement consists in the elaborate mirroring of scale A with its plagal and, for once, pluperfect extensions. The use of the latter, being the unique occurrence of a "thrice bright" region in the entire score, lends the ultimate in exaltation to the climax of the "Second Part" of the ballet, especially by comparison with the climax of the "First Part" at the end of the third tableau, which had adumbrated the same melody in a plagal region.

The mirroring process works as follows. At figure 120, the bass soloist enters with the folk tune in the plagal extension of scale A. After two measures, half of the choral basses intrude with a continuation of the theme in the authentic scale, which runs briefly in canon with the plagal form before the two join at the end in parallel motion (example 13.24a). At figure 124 the

---

his friend Mitusov, from whose singing he had taken it down. That Mitusov did dictate the song to Stravinsky is confirmed by the existence of a bifolium, still extant in the composer's Basel archive, containing the transcription. And yet the song is found in an anthology—*Pesni russkogo naroda* (Songs of the Russian People), texts collected by Fyodor Istomin, tunes collected by Georgiy Ottonovich Dyutsh (St. Petersburg, 1886)—on which Stravinsky had already drawn for a number of earlier works, and where the song is classified as a "love song" (i.e., a wedding song). Stravinsky, who took down its words from Mitusov's singing along with the tune, must have known that it was that. A love song belongs at the procreational climax of *Svadebka*. What would a "workers' melody" have been doing there?

EXAMPLE 13.24. Interaction of plagal and pluperfect with authentic scales as climax of fourth tableau approaches

tenor sounds the theme for the last time on scale B before it is remanded once and for all to scale A. One measure before figure 125, the instruments, in their one-and-only explosive solo measure, strike up the tune in the plagal before shifting abruptly into the pluperfect (example 13.24b); the focal note E furnishes the pivot. The whole climactic passage, from 130 to 133, is devoted to multiple statements of the folk tune, it being buffeted like a soccer ball from one form of the mode to another, sometimes with the help of pivots like the one introduced at figure 125 (example 13.24c). The reiterated use of the note B as cadential pitch implies the ascendency of the pluperfect mode, as befits the score's crowning moment.

Example 13.24c is an especially good illustration of the way Stravinsky exploits contrasting modal scales as dramatic foils. Between 131 and 132 he dips unexpectedly into the plagal region, and even beyond it to scale B, meanwhile bringing in the *plach* motif in an extremely remote pitch area (underscoring in yet another way the dramatic situation: the words here hint at the bride's precoital distress). The harmonic region—C-plagal—could not have been made any more remote: the pitches to which the *plach* motif is sung here are not present in the authentic or pluperfect forms of scale A, from which the passage from 130 to 133 is otherwise exclusively constructed. Thus the reassertion of A-pluperfect at figure 132 comes as a fresh jolt that enhances the sense of its brightness beyond anything that had gone before. Scale A, the scale that had started *Svadebka* on its way, returns in glory at the end, rounding off what is tonally one of the most originally and compellingly integrated scores Stravinsky ever composed.

At the broadest level, the tonal flow of *Svadebka* may be compared with the movement of a pendulum. Beginning stably within scale A (first tableau), the tonal pendulum swings out to a position of greater tension or potential energy along the /0 3 6 9/ circle to scale B (first half of the second tableau); regains equilibrium by returning to scale A (end of the second tableau and into the third), its "downward" motion emphasized by the plagal region; swings out again in the opposite direction to scale D (first part of the fourth tableau); finally regains equilibrium triumphantly at the climax of the fourth tableau, its "upward" kinetic energy dramatized by the breakthrough to the pluperfect form of the concluding tonal region.

The tones of the groom's final address to the bride, though related earlier to scale D, can also be referred to the tonally neutral descending octatonic scale (scale 4 in example 13.12), out of which the opening bridal *plach* had been constructed, thus bringing things emphatically full circle. The ambiguity created by the harmonization, which refers exclusively to scale D, can be construed as a reinforcement of cyclicity through the explicit denial of tonal closure, that is, the sense of an ending—a reading amply supported by the bell sonorities, which, as so often pointed out, symbolize the cycle of church sacraments of which marriage (and its procreative consummation) is but one, thus bracketing the ballet's action within the perpetual round of birth and death that comes from God. The scenario with its collage of abstracted ritual actions, the libretto with its collage of abstracted popular texts, and the music with its collage of abstracted "folk" motifs and tunelets (*popevki*, to use the Russian *mot juste*), together metonymically represent not the mere folk-specific but the human universal.

The tonal plan uncovered and described here must be radically distinguished from the usual concept of a functional harmonic plan or a system of key relationships. It is worth reiterating one last time that the four scales on which *Svadebka* is built have little in common with what is usually meant by a key, for there is no basis for assigning pitch priority either within the scales themselves or, in most cases, within the individual *popevki* that are extracted from them. In most cases, as we have seen, the intervallic structure of Stravinsky's *popevki* inherently precludes the establishment of priority by any but factitious means; in different environments, one and the same *popevka* can support a variety of centric tendencies. Individual *popevki*, moreover, can appear at various pitch levels within a given scale, sometimes with altered intervallic content, sometimes without, but in all cases without any appreciable difference in their tonal implication or lack of it. (Compare, for example, the various pitch levels at which "authentic" tune fragments appear before and after figure 131 in example 13.24c.) Thus the degrees of the four basic diatonic scales in *Svadebka*, unlike the degrees in any tonal, key-defining scale, are not functionally differentiated a priori. Rather than keys, then, the four *Svadebka* scales represent four diatonic projections from a single—that is, universal—octatonic background matrix. They are the four quadrants, so to speak, of a cyclic, periodic, symmetrically apportioned musical space, as depicted in fully elaborated form in example 13.25.

Thus although *Svadebka* contains relatively little in the way of surface octatonics—far less than *The Rite of Spring* or even *Petrushka*—the deeper structure that rules the variegated diatonic surface is more thoroughly and systematically derived from a single /0 3 6 9/ octatonic matrix than that of any other Stravinsky composition of comparable size and scope. Background matrix and diatonic surface are linked through the ubiquitous T-S-T tetrachords. The lower tetrachord in each "authentic" diatonic scale (corresponding to the upper tetrachord in the "plagal" extensions) is referable to the "ascending" octatonic background scale; the upper authentic tetrachords (= lower "pluperfect" tetrachords) refer to the "descending" background scale. Octatonic melodic and harmonic patterns that had played gaudily on the surface of earlier neonationalist scores were submerged to work their influence at the deepest strata of structure and style. The deeper they went—the more they thus, as it were, receded from view—the more pervasive and determinant their influence became.

In fine, example 13.25 is the map of a musical pleroma, a closed-off,

EXAMPLE 13.25. The organization of musical space in Stravinsky's *Svadebka*

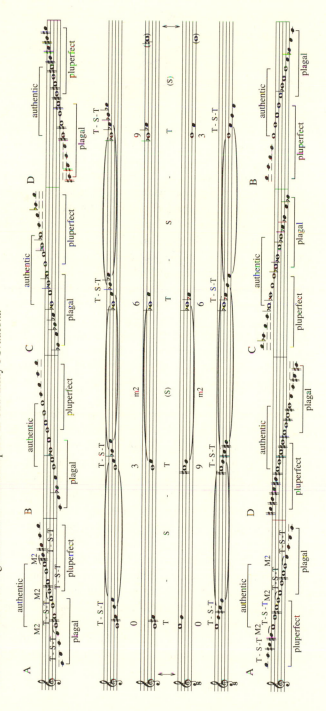

strictly delimited yet all-encompassing hierarchically structured musical universe. All Russian (or Turanian) folk songs have a potential place on its diatonic surface, as all Russians have a potential place in Eurasian symphonic society. That surface, in turn, encompasses all possible diatonic scales, hence not just Russian, but all oral musical cultures, and gives them all an ideal potential ordering that, in its symmetrical apportionment of an octatonic background, is fundamentally opposed to the asymmetrical, fifth-related panromanogermanic norm. Never before had a musical utopia been so expressly modeled on a social utopia. The harmonic space encompassed by example 13.25 analogizes the harmonious concinnity (*soglasovannost'*) of human actions and purposes comprehended by the Eurasianists' symphonically harmonized society. The hidden octatonic background that harmonizes and controls the audible diatonic surface is a perfect metaphor for the constraints of immemorial custom that invisibly rule the day-to-day subjectively free-flowing currents of life in Stravinsky's imagined folk world, harmonizing the thoughts and actions of individuals with the transcendent organic community of the composer's dreams, just as the long-sought and triumphantly successful final scoring for four keyboards and punctuating percussion captures to perfection the nature of symphonic society, as something "perfectly impersonal, perfectly homogeneous, and perfectly mechanical."[71] Together, these symbols of ideally harmonized existence lend *Svadebka* both its incomparably compelling aesthetic integrity and its ominously compelling political allure.

UTOPIA AND ITS DISCONTENTS

Why ominously? Because "perfectly homogeneous" societies exist only in the imaginations of artists and political aesthetes. Conditions in the world fall short of such perfection, and so utopians must either adapt to the world (that is, give up utopia) or correct the shortfall. Utopia cannot tolerate difference or nonconformity, and any nostalgic utopianism must necessarily entail bigotry. The history of the twentieth century has provided sufficient examples of the kind of corrective measures futuristic utopians (e.g., in Russia) and nostalgic utopians (e.g., in Germany) have been prepared to take in order to adapt the world to their aesthetic vision—sufficient, one would think, to make us wary of visions like the one so stunningly represented in *Svadebka*.

Leaving Germany to one side, one can locate the difference between futuristic and nostalgic utopia within Russian thought as that between (pre-Stalinist) Bolsheviks and Eurasianists. And yet Germany still forces its way back into the picture, because the principal scapegoat of nostalgic utopians, at least in Europe, has rarely varied. A polemical essay in the *Eurasian Record*, published in the year of *Svadebka*'s first performances, purported to meet

[71] *Expositions and Developments*, p. 134.

head-on, but only met aslant, the accusation that Eurasianists were anti-Semites.

"We are nationalists," declared the author, a young economist named Yakov Dmitriyevich Sadovsky, "the most outspoken of Russian nationalists." As such, he announced, Eurasianists were bound to hold in contempt the tepid policies of the liberal provisional government that had held the reins of the Russian state between the Tsar's abdication and the Bolshevik coup—policies associated with Pavel Milyukov, the liberal foreign minister, who encouraged the protection of minority rights ("defending every national movement against Russian nationalism"). Still less could Eurasianists support the Bolshevik "nationalities" policy, which would establish "dozens of republics, right down to a Jewish one," Sadovsky sneered, "with Minsk as its capital." Nor was nationalism Eurasian-style a grassroots movement: the people needed to be guided toward national self-realization by an intellectual avant-garde, a "nationalist intelligentsia" (a rank oxymoron for Russia, but invoked here without apparent irony). And so the first task was to cleanse the Russian intelligentsia of its long-standing "internationalist" (read: Jewish) infestation. Like the Stalinists of the late 1940s, the Eurasianists cast their anti-Semitism as anticosmopolitanism, further masked (and with an irony that later events made bitter) as anticommunism. Although no anti-Semites, Sadovsky declared,

> we do part company with the majority of the Jewish community on one question. We part company with them in their evaluation of our political disturbances. For the majority of the Jewish people and for Jewish youth without exception, the Russian revolution is "The Great Russian Revolution," which has given them everything, even the dominant position within the existing Russian revolutionary power, something of which not a single Jew in the world could possibly have dreamed before the revolution. The Jews have greeted the "Great Revolution" and all it stands for and have become its very cement. . . . For us, though, the revolution is above all a Black Death, a plague combined with all the most horrible miseries of nature.[72]

There was no place for such a dissonance in any properly symphonic society. The mask worn by Sadovsky's anti-Semitism, moreover, was only one of many such masks (antimercantilism in the nineteenth century, anti-Zionism in the mid-twentieth) that have given cover to traditional Slavic racial hostility toward Jews.

Given their maximalized, top-down (and therefore topsy-turvy) revival of the Slavophile ideal of *sobornost'*, the organic, pre-cognitive experience of total-unity (manifested socially in what Prince Sergey Trubetskoy, the father of the Eurasianist leader, actually called "corporate consciousness"), their

---

[72] Yakov Sadovsky, "Opponentam yevraziystva (pis'mo v redaktsiyu)," *Yevraziyskiy vremennik* 3 (1923): 159, 161–62.

contempt for democracy, their insistence on audacious leadership as instrument of national self-realization,[73] and their horror of Bolshevism as a godless Western positivism run rampant in their midst, Eurasianists would seem potentially susceptible, when the time came, to the blandishments of fascism. And when the time came, the Eurasianist press amply bore out that grim surmise. Books expounding and explicating fascism were regularly and sympathetically reviewed, especially by Karsavin, whose only reservation was the fact that Italian fascism was a wholly secular movement operating within a Catholic country and therefore could not promote symphonic society in all its fullness.[74] The tragic flaw in fascism, for Eurasianists, was the fact that it had taken shape in a country where religious authority was vested in another, competing, hierarchical institution.

Nevertheless, the only contemporary political figure whom these Russian exiles dependably praised was Mussolini, "who has given Italy much and who may give yet more," in the words of Sadovsky, who went on to declare that "many countries might well envy Italy." The unsubtle hint about Russia is confirmed and extended when Sadovsky upholds Italian fascism as an example of "healthy reaction" and an explicit model for (violent) political action in his own country.

> Bolshevism and fascism have shown that revolution is no creative force; it is a disease, but over its grave a nation's creative power can yet flower. By now it is clear to every right-thinking person that one cannot simply and categorically oppose "revolution" to "counterrevolution" on the prior assumption that the one is a healthy manifestation and the other a morbid one. Nowadays one often hears that revolution means "swimming with the tide," or "riding the wheels of history," while counterrevolution is reaction, movement against the tide, "reversing the wheels of history." How unfounded all this is, and yet how strongly lodged it has become in so many heads! But meanwhile, can one apply this "axiom" to the

[73] Karsavin: "National ideas, ambitions, aspirations . . . gain realization not by crowds, not through mass demonstrations, popular votes, programs and principles, but by guiding spirits. . . . The results of elections to the Constituent Assembly never expressed anything of the national will, but Peter the Great, [the eighteenth-century court poet and scientist Mikhail] Lomonosov, Pushkin were authentic expressers of the national will and the national spirit. Speaking for the nation in the sobbing voice of a provincial tragedian, no Kerensky ever expressed anything national, whereas Lenin, oppressing the Russian people in the name of the International, did manage to express something, as did [the White commander] General Kornilov from the other side" ("Fenomenologiya revolyutsii," p. 38). In fine, even Bolsheviks were preferable to constitutional liberals.

[74] He wrote prophetically, eight years before the invasion of Ethiopia: "The secular cult of the nation leads to imperialism, more dangerous to the nation itself than to its neighbors, and it soon betrays itself as narcissism and worship of relative values" (review of G. Gentile, *Che cosa è il fascismo: Discori e polemiche, Yevraziyskaya khronika* 8 [1927]: 55). Compare Sadovsky: "Fascism might play a role of world significance if it could realize within itself an organic union of the religious and national principles. The fascist *nazia deificata* is not enough" ("Iz dnevnika 'Yevraziysta,'" *Yevraziyskiy vremennik* 4 (1925): 404).

communist revolution in Russia, or to the fascist counterrevolution in Italy? Obviously not. Fascism is certainly a reaction to Bolshevism, but full of energy. There are reactions and reactions. There are pernicious reactions and creative ones. In a creative reaction life throws off the wrongs and the falsehoods of revolution and shows other ways to well-being and prosperity.

The Russian healthy reaction will shed the whole revolutionary husk that is impeding Russia's development. But that's not all. It will have to take over and assimilate the new ruling class and the milieu on which it draws. Of course the purulent communist pustule will have to be lanced: the higher-ups of this internationalist party (alien by blood) will be pruned cleanly away. For this no special laws need be passed; the elimination of this clique will simply happen. But the broad body of the ruling class, the whole executive component, the "actual heros" who find resonance among the people—they will stay.[75]

This warped and woolly revanchiste fantasy is, sadly, an indispensable document for understanding the composer of *Svadebka,* for it shows how the nostalgic utopianism of the Russian émigré right modulated into a barbaric futuristic utopianism (still alarmingly tinged with anti-Semitism) that unwittingly aped its adversary (not for nothing did the Eurasianists acquire the sobriquet "national Bolsheviks" in the 1930s), and that, no longer seeking its validation except delusionally in Russian history or pseudohistory, sought it, rather, in the fascist renewal of Italy. The human pleroma, the symphonic society of the Eurasianist dream, would be enforced—no longer precognitively—with big sticks. The vision was no longer of a pristine society but of a cleansed one.

The Eurasianist trajectory described here was Stravinsky's, too. Enthusiasm for Mussolini peeps indirectly through the lines of *Chroniques de ma vie,* when, speaking of his "traditional" Russian attachment to Italy, he gives it a contemporary political twist by lauding "the marvelous regenerative effort which has manifested itself there for the last ten years, and is still manifesting itself in every direction."[76] This was the tip of an iceberg. Enthusiasm had already erupted in full cry when the composer told a Rome newspaperman, right before an audience with the Duce in 1930,

> I don't believe that anyone venerates Mussolini more than I. To me, he is the *one man who counts* nowadays in the whole world. I have traveled a great deal: I know many exalted personages, and my artist's mind does not shrink from political and social issues. Well, after having seen so many events and so many more or less representative men, I have an overpowering urge to render homage to your Duce. He is the savior of Italy and—let us hope—the world.[77]

[75] "Iz dnevnika 'Yevraziysta,'" pp. 400–401.

[76] Igor Stravinsky, *An Autobiography* (New York: Simon and Schuster, 1936), p. 270.

[77] Alberto Gasco, *Da Cimarosa a Stravinsky* (Rome: De Santis, 1939), p. 452, quoted in Harvey Sachs, *Music in Fascist Italy* (New York: Norton, 1988), p. 168. In 1935, after another audience with Mussolini, Stravinsky told reporters that he had gone so far as actually to confess

A year later, Stravinsky allowed himself to be described in print by Arthur Lourié, who had previously touted him in the Eurasianist press and who was then serving (much as Robert Craft would later do) as his live-in musical factotum and publicist, as being the "dictator of the reaction against the anarchy into which modernism degenerated."[78] Stravinsky had consciously cast himself as the Mussolini of music, who wanted to do for modern music what the Duce promised to do for modern Europe.[79] This was the subtext and the motivation for his "neoclassicism."[80]

Of course enthusiasm for Mussolini or a profession of fascist sympathies in the 1920s should not be confused with what a similar enthusiasm for Hitler, or a similar profession, would have implied a decade later, let alone two. In the decade and a half between his accession to power and the establishment of the Rome-Berlin Axis, Mussolini had many enthusiasts, among them Wallace Stevens, Bernard Shaw, even Winston Churchill. Until 1935, the fascist state did not begin to bear out Karsavin's prognostication that it would turn imperialist. Until 1938, fascism had no necessary racist component, and the institution of racist laws in that year was a concession to the Axis ally, not a matter of fascist doctrine. One still occasionally encounters nostalgia for the "pure" fascism of the 1920s—a "comprehensive rightist doctrine" and an "intellectual reservoir" as yet unpolluted "by World War II, Vichy, Nazism, and the

---

his political loyalty to the Duce in person (quoted from *Il Piccolo*, 27 May 1935, in *Stravinsky in Pictures and Documents*, p. 552). Predictably enough, Sachs attempts to excuse Stravinsky's attraction to Mussolini on the basis of the composer's having been "bamboozled" by the attention paid him (*Music in Fascist Italy*, p. 167). But of course attention was paid him everywhere. The same explanation, political (or "apolitical") naiveté, is dependably adduced to rationalize Prokofiev's return to Soviet Russia, Furtwängler's cooperation with the Nazis, and so on. But these are not explanations; they are in every case tautologies. Backing losers, or those held retrospectively in opprobrium, is merely the working definition here of political "naiveté." If the Axis had won the war, if the world we lived in now looked more like the world Stravinsky dreamed of then, he would look shrewd enough. His biographers would now be praising his political acumen and foresight, just as revisionist biographers of Shostakovich have been doing since the proclamation of "glasnost'" (see the following chapters).

[78] Arthur Lourié, *Sergei Koussevitzky and His Epoch* (New York: Knopf, 1931), p. 196.

[79] For additional information and documentation of Stravinsky's flirtation with fascism, see Robert Craft, "Stravinsky's Politics: Left, Right, Left," in *Stravinsky in Pictures and Documents*, pp. 547–58.

[80] See R. Taruskin, "Back to Whom? Neoclassicism as Ideology," *19th-Century Music* 15 (1992–93): 286–302, esp. pp. 297–99. The prickly *Sonate* for piano, the paradigmatic early neoclassic score in which Stravinsky strove more assiduously than ever as if to exemplify T. E. Hulme's dictum that "they [who] hate the revolution . . . hate romanticism," and to capture what Hulme called "the dry hardness which you get in the classics," was first performed by the composer in 1925 in Venice's Teatro La Fenice at a contemporary music festival organized "sotto il patronato di S. E. Benito Mussolini" (*Stravinsky in Pictures and Documents*, p. 551; for the Hulme quotes see T. E. Hulme, *Speculations: Essays on Humanism and the Philosophy of Art*, ed. Herbert Read [London: Kegan Paul, 1936], pp. 115, 126–27).

Holocaust"—in the writings of conservative communitarians discouraged at the splintered condition of the contemporary intellectual right.[81] This sort of fascism was the "aesthetic" sort—fascism as a fantasy, not a clanking state bureaucracy, and a fascism without consequences. It was the sort of fascism that attracted many modern artists along with intellectuals and dreamy revanchists.[82]

Nor did the Mussolini regime's arts policy in any way discourage such an attraction. Unlike the Stalinist and Hitlerite regimes, the fascist state did not (at first) exercise totalitarian control over the arts; repressions were few.[83] Quite the contrary: cooperative artists enjoyed a bottomless feeding trough, modernists emphatically included. Mussolini was proud to have Italy play host to international festivals of contemporary music such as the one at which Stravinsky performed his *Sonate*, festivals at which every modern master was *persona grata*. Fascist cultural bureaucrats were as philistine as their counterparts anywhere, authoring blustery, well-publicized manifestos against "atonal and polytonal honking" and "so-called objective music."[84] And yet Schoenberg, atonal honker par excellence, toured Italy with *Pierrot lunaire* in 1924, and his music continued to be performed there under prestigious auspices until 1938, five years after the composer had been forced to leave Germany. Alban Berg's concert aria *Der Wein* had its Italian première at the Venice Biennale in 1934 (the composer, in attendance, was loudly fêted). *Wozzeck* was given at the Rome Opera as unbelievably late as 1942.[85]

Also performed during that wartime season was *The Miraculous Mandarin*, a ballet by Bartók, easily the most outspoken antifascist among modernists, who by then had for two years been a voluntary exile from Europe. These examples of artistic tolerance, moreover, were more than matched by the racial tolerance that the fascist government quite demonstratively exhibited,

[81] Norman F. Cantor, "The Reagan Right: No Bark, No Bite," *New York Times*, 22 August 1988 (op-ed page).

[82] For general considerations see Alastair Hamilton, *The Appeal of Fascism* (New York: Macmillan, 1971), and Andrew Hewitt, *Fascist Modernism: Aesthetics, Politics, and the Avant-Garde* (Stanford: Stanford University Press, 1993).

[83] There was only one major repression to report where music was concerned: Gian Francesco Malipiero's opera *La favola del figlio cambiato*, to a libretto by Pirandello, banned after its first Italian performance in March 1934. The episode is reminiscent of the way, two years later, Shostakovich's *The Lady Macbeth of the Mtsensk District* was persecuted by the Soviets, as will be described in detail in the second major division of chapter 14. There is a circumstantial parallel insofar as prudery, so endemic to authoritarian regimes, figured in both incidents (though in the case of *La favola*, it was only the libretto that offended, not the music). But Malipiero's difficulties did not come during a general reign of terror. He was not made out a scapegoat and a general example of degeneracy. The suppression of his work was not a calculated assertion of state control. His other works were not affected. Above all, unlike Shostakovich, Malipiero was not mortally threatened.

[84] See Sachs, *Music in Fascist Italy*, p. 24.

[85] Ibid., pp. 135, 142, 147, 198.

in distinction to Germany, until 1938. Refugees from Hitler like Bruno Walter or Otto Klemperer regularly performed in Mussolini's Italy; and Ernest Bloch's *Sacred Service*, a setting of the Reform Jewish liturgy, had its world première over Radio Turin in 1934.[86] The original fascist movement had numerous Jewish adherents, some even occupying positions of leadership, who saw no conflict in their allegiance to Mussolini, and had no premonition of any anti-Semitic policy turn.

But like his Eurasianist counterparts, Stravinsky was well ahead of Italian public policy in this regard. His anti-Semitism was of long standing and went deep. To be sure, it is something he shared with Glinka, Balakirev, Chaikovsky, Musorgsky, and a whole honor roll of musical Russians.[87] It has been characterized as no more than what every Russian "imbibed with mother's milk."[88] And yet, like everything else about Stravinsky, it had its unique characteristics and foundations, and deserves investigation.

The existence of honorable exceptions is enough to justify the conviction that, however widespread among Russians or any other group, anti-Semitism remains an individual choice. As long as one can point to plausible counterparts—Nabokov (like Stravinsky an aristocrat) or Shostakovich, to give two pertinent examples—who did not so opt, one must admit that anti-Semitism is something for which the individual bears responsibility.

In Stravinsky's case the matter is especially poignant; for the one who did not so opt was little short of a surrogate father to him, and a man who exercised in most other ways the most powerful formative influence on Stravinsky's early development. Nikolai Andreyevich Rimsky-Korsakov happened to come from a purebred Russian line more ancient and distinguished than Stravinsky's by far.[89] And yet despite his arms-cum-gentry background,

---

[86] Ibid., pp. 198, 175, 179.

[87] For evidence of Glinka's anti-Semitism and Balakirev's, see Robert C. Ridenour, *Nationalism, Modernism, and Personal Rivalry in Nineteenth-Century Russian Music* (Ann Arbor: UMI Research Press, 1981), pp. 83–85; for evidence of Chaikovsky's, see P. I. Chaikovsky, *Perepiska s N. F. fon-Mekk*, vol. 1 (Moscow: Academia, 1934), p. 297 (letter to Nadezhda von Meck of 12 April 1878 O.S.; given abridged, but not expurgated, in *"To My Best Friend": Correspondence between Tchaikovsky and Nadezhda von Meck, 1876–1878*, trans. Galina von Meck, ed. Edward Garden and Nigel Gotteri (Oxford: Clarendon Press, 1993), p. 242; for evidence of Musorgsky's see R. Taruskin, *Musorgsky: Eight Essays and an Epilogue* (Princeton: Princeton University Press, 1993), pp. 379–83.

[88] Robert Craft, "Jews and Geniuses," *New York Review of Books*, 16 February 1989, p. 35.

[89] Rimsky-Korsakov could trace his lineage back fourteen generations, to boyars of the fourteenth century. By the eighteenth century, the Rimsky-Korsakov clan had risen to the very summit of the Russian social ladder. Yakov Nikitich Rimsky-Korsakov (1679–1734) was named vice-regent of Ingermanland, and became the first governor of St. Petersburg under Peter the Great. His son Voin Yakovlevich (1702–1757; the name Voin means warrior) was the first commander of the Russian fleet to be designated "Marshal." His son, Pyotr Voinovich (d. 1815), the composer's grandfather, bore the rank of lieutenant-general in the army of Alexander I, and was rewarded with a large estate in the Tikhvin district, where the composer was born. Nikolai

Stravinsky's teacher was a lifelong liberal and freethinker, strongly drawn to the Masons. (Compare Stravinsky, in a 1930 letter to his patron, Werner Reinhart: "I had never realized that you were not indifferent to these antichrists, or to the international Jewry to whom the Freemasons are servants.")[90] Rimsky's liberalism was tested and genuine: for his support of the student strikes of 1905 he was suspended from his post at the St. Petersburg Conservatory and became the focus of a cause célèbre. As for tolerance of Jews, he demonstrated it in a proverbial way: he encouraged, indeed practically forced his daughter Nadezhda to marry one.

The Jew in question, Maximilian Steinberg (1883–1946), is a key to understanding Stravinsky's later enthusiastic anti-Semitism. He hailed from Vilna (now Vilnius, the capital of the independent state of Lithuania), then one of the larger Polish cities in the Jewish pale of settlement, and its main educational center. His father, Osey (Hosea) Steinberg, was a leading Hebraist, the head of the Jewish Teachers' College in Vilna, and the compiler of a biblical dictionary that went through many editions. (His annotated Hebrew/Russian Pentateuch was the last Jewish Bible to be published in Russia until the end of Soviet power.)[91]

Maximilian Steinberg was sent to St. Petersburg University in 1901 to pursue what we would now call a premed course. (He graduated in 1906 with a gold medal in biology.) At the same time he entered the conservatory, where he was put in Lyadov's elementary harmony class. (All his hometown training, typically, had been in playing the violin.) By the fall of 1903 he was ready for Rimsky-Korsakov's counterpoint class, and continued with Rimsky into fugue and practical composition. He quickly became the teacher's pet. Moving on to Glazunov's orchestration class, Steinberg made another con-

---

Andreyevich was brought up in privilege; his elder brother Voin Andreyevich was the director of the Imperial Naval Academy where the composer received training for his intended career in the family tradition; and, at the outset of his musical career, he was able to exploit his court connections when it came, for example, to securing dispensations from the censor. See Andrey Nikolayevich Rimsky-Korsakov, *Nikolai Andreyevich Rimskiy-Korsakov: Zhizn' i tvorchestvo*, vol. 1 (Moscow: Ogiz/Muzgiz, 1933), pp. 5–7; N. A. Rimsky-Korsakov, *My Musical Life*, trans. Judah A. Joffe (London: Eulenburg Books, 1974), pp. 125–27; Tatyana Rimskaya Korsakova, "Rodoslovnaya," *Muzïkal'naya akaemiya*, no. 2, special Rimsky-Korsakov issue (1994): 9–23.

[90] Letter of 27 March 1930, quoted from a typescript transcription (by Robert Craft?) of translated passages suppressed from the published correspondence, kindly furnished by the late Lawrence Morton; a copy is deposited in Morton's archive at the University of California, Los Angeles. (The Jewish-Masonic link Stravinsky assumes here follows the traditional Russian line that harks back to the venerable Tsarist forgery, *Protocols of the Elders of Zion*, and lives on in post-Soviet Russia even today, perpetuated by, among others, the anti-Semitic organization known as *Pamyat'*.) An expurgated translation of the letter to Reinhart is in *Selected Correspondence*, vol. 3, p. 168.

[91] *Pyatiknizhiye Moiseyevo, s doslovnïm russkim perevodom* (Vilna: B. Tsionson, 1914).

quest (which earns Glazunov, too, high marks for tolerance). By 1906 he had become one of the select few who were privileged to associate with their conservatory professors outside of the classroom. In this way Steinberg became acquainted with Igor Stravinsky, the Rimsky-Korsakov family mascot, then undergoing his course of pampered private instruction.

Together with Mikhail Gnesin, another Jewish boy from the pale (Stravinsky's preposterous late recollection of Gnesin—very much an "enlightened" and assimilated Jew—as one who dressed in Hasidic garb will bring a choice scene from Woody Allen's *Annie Hall* to mind),[92] Steinberg and Stravinsky formed a recognized troika of late Rimsky-Korsakov protégés. But Steinberg very quickly became first among equals. Marks of special favor were plentiful, and, to Stravinsky, humiliating. Steinberg heard the kind of unqualified praise from Rimsky that Stravinsky never got to hear; he broke into print earlier; his early works were performed under more prestigious auspices.[93] On top of everything, he married Nadezhda Nikolayevna (Robert Craft has speculated with good reason about a possible earlier romantic link between her and Stravinsky),[94] and inherited Rimsky's conservatory position. (He would hold it until his death in Stalin's Leningrad, thirty-eight years later.)

After Rimsky's death, Steinberg's favored status continued with Glazunov, who held Stravinsky in outright (and later, of course, amply reciprocated) contempt. In the eight months between the loss of his teacher and his discovery by Diaghilev, Stravinsky found himself frozen out of the inner circles of the latter-day "New Russian school" while Steinberg continued to prosper. It was a time of major psychological stress, a crisis he never forgot, or forgave.[95]

On the surface, relations between Steinberg and Stravinsky were cordial, even fraternal at this time, and would continue to be so in *tutoyer* correspondence throughout the years of Stravinsky's early successes in Paris.[96] But no amount of success could ever assuage the envy a musical scion of the Polish

---

[92] Igor Stravinsky and Robert Craft, *Dialogues and a Diary* (Garden City, N.Y.: Doubleday, 1963), p. 47.

[93] For details of Steinberg's early career as Rimsky-Korsakov protégé and his relations with Stravinsky, see Taruskin, *Stravinsky and the Russian Traditions*, pp. 384–96.

[94] Robert Craft, *Present Perspectives* (New York: Knopf, 1984), p. 409.

[95] For one indicative example, Steinberg received an official commission through Glazunov for a memorial composition for Rimsky-Korsakov, while Stravinsky had to write a similar piece on his own initiative and (with difficulty) arrange for its performance himself. Steinberg's memorial, *Prélude symphonique*, Op. 7, was published by the Belyayev firm, of which Rimsky had been the publications director, while Stravinsky's (the *Pogrebal'naya pesn'*, Op. 8), remained unpublished, and in indirect consequence of the composer's emigration, has been lost. Details in Taruskin, *Stravinsky and the Russian Traditions*, pp. 396–408.

[96] For examples, see L. D'yachova, ed., *I. F. Stravinskiy: Stat'i i materialï*, pp. 446–47, 471, 473–74, 478–79.

nobility felt toward this upstart Vilna Jew who had displaced him in Rimsky's esteem and in his ménage. More than half a century after Rimsky's death—and sixteen years after Steinberg's own—that envy was still consuming him when Stravinsky wrote of his old rival as "one of these ephemeral, prize-winning, front-page types, in whose eyes conceit for ever burns, like an electric light in daytime."[97] These feelings lay behind Stravinsky's modernist revolt and his anti-Semitism alike, fanned them both, and linked them.

Derision of Jews—silently expunged (both by Robert Craft and by Soviet editors) for public consumption—was a lifelong feature of Stravinsky's private correspondence, especially with other Russians.[98] A 1919 letter quoted in an auction catalog complains about a New York production of *Petrushka* by a trio of unauthorized "Israelites" (one of them Pierre Monteux, to whose efforts Stravinsky owed a large part of his early fame), heaping special scorn on the "horrible Jew-kraut sets" (*des horribles décors judéo-boches*).[99] Like the Eurasianists, Stravinsky tended to lump his antipathies. He resented the Bolshevik revolution as a Jewish plague, the work of "Braunstein" (Trotsky); to an American correspondent he vented his indignation that such Jew-revolutionists are taken for "authentic" Russians.[100]

Even in America, after the Second World War, by which time his political attitudes had mellowed in the California sun ("As far as I am concerned, they can have their Marshals and Fuehrers," he remarked to Nicolas Nabokov in 1947; "Leave me Mr. Truman and I'm quite satisfied"),[101] and despite his benevolent relations with individual Jews (notably a whole "Boston school" of young composers—Arthur Berger, Irving Fine, Harold Shapero, Lukas Foss—who idolized him), Stravinsky retained his accustomed contempt for Jews as a group. When Serge Lifar, Diaghilev's last *premier danseur*, was picketed in New York for his collaborationist activities in wartime Paris, Stravinsky wrote disdainfully to Craft that "if there were some intelligent

[97] *Expositions and Developments*, p. 49; the appalling outburst immediately follows the recollection that Steinberg was "the only composer I ever heard [Rimsky] refer to as talented."

[98] Robert Craft, unpublished letter to James J. Higginson of the law firm Appleton, Rice, and Perrin, 10 February 1981; photocopy courtesy Lawrence Morton. The letter concludes with a plea that Stravinsky's epistolary archive be closed, at least until the deaths of his grandchildren.

[99] To Misia Sert, 18 April 1919; Sotheby's catalog "Collection Boris Kochno: Monaco, 11–12 Octobre 1991," p. 227.

[100] 1 March 1919; typescript in Lawrence Morton archive, UCLA. Another document from roughly the same time is an apology to the composer from Carl van Vechten, now in the Stravinsky archive (Paul Sacher Stiftung), dated 29 February 1916: "Cher monsieur, I am very sorry that an incorrect impression crept into my book [*Music after the Great War* (New York: Knopf, 1915)] (I do not, however, say that you are a Jew. The line reads 'I do *not know*.') — you may be sure, especially sorry that it annoyed you. However, as you asked me to do, I have written to the papers about the affair, and I am enclosing one of the letters" (the enclosure is not at present in the archive).

[101] Nicolas Nabokov, "Christmas with Stravinsky," in *Stravinsky*, ed. Edwin Corle (New York: Duell, Sloan, and Pearce, 1949), p. 143.

Jews picketing before Lifar not for his 'fascism' (or, later on, 'communism,' about which they are silent of course), but for his quite obvious want of talent, I would gladly change my mind about Jews."[102]

Stravinsky's initial reaction to the advent of Nazism was to write to his Russian publisher, Serge Koussevitzky's Russischer Musikverlag, with offices in Berlin, that he was "surprised to have received no proposals from Germany for next season, since my negative attitude toward communism and Judaism—not to put it in stronger terms—is a matter of common knowledge."[103] When active persecutions began, Stravinsky's attitude continued to combine opportunism with disdain for the victims. He wrote again to his Russian publisher for advice: "Is it politically wise vis-à-vis Germany to identify myself with Jews like Klemperer and Walter, who are being exiled? . . . I do not want to risk seeing my name beside such trash as Milhaud."[104] Immediately on completing his Concerto for Two Solo Pianos, which he wrote as a performance vehicle for himself and his son Sviatoslav (Soulima), Stravinsky tried to arrange a German tour for the work, assuring his German publisher, B. Schotts Söhne, that "I would be so happy to resume my musical relations with Germany."[105]

When the Nazi authorities, acting on a reasonable assumption with regard to a Slav-blooded naturalized Parisian, made Stravinsky and his work an exhibit in the notorious "Entartete Musik" (Degenerate Music) display at Düsseldorf in May 1938, the mortified composer, through Schott, protested his inclusion to the German Bureau of Foreign Affairs, explicitly disavowing "Jewish cultural Bolshevism" and objecting in particular to the caption that had been placed under his well-known portrait by Jacques-Émile Blanche: "Whoever invented the story that Stravinsky is descended from Russian noble stock?" As he had previously taken the precaution (as early as the spring of 1933) of submitting an affidavit to his publisher in lieu of the Reichsmusikkammer's official questionnaire establishing Aryan heredity (and as the publisher had placed an item in the papers quoting Richard Strauss on

---

[102] Letter of 8 October 1948. The letter, with the quoted passage silently deleted, is published in Robert Craft, ed., *Stravinsky: Selected Correspondence*, vol. 1 (New York: Knopf, 1981), p. 346. A facsimile of the uncensored letter was displayed, and the quoted passage read, by Charles M. Joseph in "Ellipses, Exclusions, Expurgations: What Do Stravinsky's Letters Really Say?" a paper presented at the fifty-eighth annual meeting of the American Musicological Society in Pittsburgh, 7 November 1992.

[103] To Fyodor Vladimirovich Weber of the Russische Musikverlag in Berlin, June 1933; typescript of suppressed passages from correspondence in the Lawrence Morton archive.

[104] To Gavriyil Païchadze, Russische Musikverlag, 7 September 1933; quoted from the typescript in the Lawrence Morton archive.

[105] Letter to Willy Strecker, 17 November 1935; the quoted sentence is suppressed in Craft's edition of the letter (*Selected Correspondence*, vol. 3, p. 238); it was reported by the Canadian researcher Joan Evans in a paper, "Stravinsky's Music in Hitler's Germany," read at the fifty-seventh annual meeting of the American Musicological Society, Chicago, 9 November 1991.

Stravinsky's enthusiasm for Hitler's ideas), he was able to receive the satisfaction of a declaration from the German government affirming its "benevolent neutrality" toward him, and his career suffered no further setbacks in the
Third Reich until the war.[106]

Stravinsky came to the German capital the same year and recorded his
ballet *Jeu de cartes* with the *ganz judenrein* Berlin Philharmonic Orchestra.
Shortly afterward, he refused to lend his name to a committee that had been
set up in Paris to help Bruno Walter, who had emigrated to France and, like
Stravinsky, had received French citizenship, to form an orchestra in the
French capital.[107] Keeping himself persona grata in "Germany, this Germany
that was always so attentive to my music" was to him a matter of paramount
personal and professional concern.[108]

Finally, there is sad irony in the fact that the only works by Stravinsky to
incorporate overtly anti-Semitic content were written in America, after the
war. The texts of two late vocal works embody slurs of a familiar kind. The
centerpiece of the 1952 *Cantata*, all the texts for which were chosen (at the
compiler's recommendation) from a little group of "Anonymous Lyrics and
Songs" in W. H. Auden's anthology *Poets of the English Language* (New
York: Viking Portable Library, 1950, with Norman Holmes Pearson), is a
ricercar to a fifteenth-century "sacred history" (as adapted by a nineteenth-
century editor), entitled "Tomorrow Shall Be My Dancing Day." A song of
Christ's crucifixion, it rehearses the old guilt libel, after Hitler more intolerable than ever: "The Jews on me they made great suit, / And with me made
great variance, / Because they lov'd the darkness rather than light." The "Narrative" in *A Sermon, a Narrative, and a Prayer* (1961), for which Robert
Craft selected the texts, is an excerpt from the Book of Acts that relates the
stoning of St. Stephen, including Stephen's address to the High Priest of the
Temple (chapter 6, verses 51–52): "Ye do always resist the Holy Ghost: as
your fathers did, so do ye. Which of the prophets have not your fathers per-

---

[106] See Stravinsky's correspondence with Strecker in *Selected Correspondence*, vol. 3,
pp. 265–70; the affidavit on Aryan (and noble) heredity is included in the letter of 14 April 1933,
(dated by Stravinsky "Vendredi saint"), ibid., pp. 235–36.

[107] Members included Valéry, Bergson, Gide, and Giradoux. Details in the typescript in the
Morton archive.

[108] The quoted phrase is from Stravinsky's letter to Strecker, 27 January 1936; it, too, was
suppressed in Craft's edition. Despite Craft's assertion that Stravinsky's single live appearance in
Nazi Germany (the 1936 performance with Soulima of the Concerto) was made "against his will
and under pressure from his German publisher" ("Jews and Geniuses," *New York Review of
Books*, 16 February 1989, p. 35), the letters Craft has published, even in their expurgated form,
show that Stravinsky was eager to appear there right up to the war, and that his failure to do so
was due to impediments not of his making. See, for example, the letter to Strecker of 3 January
1938, regarding an upcoming performance of *Perséphone*: "I greatly appreciate your having
placed this on the program of the music festival in Baden-Baden this spring. I would certainly be
even more pleased if I could conduct it myself, but after what you told me, I realize that financial
difficulties would surely prevent such a possibility" (*Selected Correspondence*, vol. 3, p. 256).

secuted? and they have slain them which shewed before of the coming of the Just One."

It is not that Stravinsky chose these texts for the sake of the anti-Semitic slurs; it is, rather, that for him, after a lifetime of contemning the Jews, the anti-Semitic content was no object. Indeed, it must have been scarcely noticeable to him, for he inscribed a score of the Jew-libeling *Cantata* in August 1953 to Otto Klemperer, his Los Angeles neighbor in the 1940s, a Hitler refugee with whom Stravinsky had made scant common cause in the thirties.[109] By 1953, the moral implications of setting of such a text, and presenting it to a Jew, had doubtless been occluded by the burgeoning discourse of "music itself." Stravinsky by then was only one of many who placed beauty beyond good and evil; only one of many to endorse the implicit claim—still fashionable, alas—that artists are entitled to moral indifference, and that the greater the artist the greater the entitlement. It is a view that has greatly diminished the art of the twentieth century—not in "quality" (however that may be measured) but in value; and it has diminished the humanity of artists and art lovers. The prestige of high art has accordingly, and justifiably, declined in our time.

UNIVERSALIZING THE RUSSIAN

It would be anachronistic, as well as arbitrarily invidious, to claim that the subject matter of the foregoing cheerless discussion were all part of the immediate subtext to *Svadebka*. It is, rather, the long-lingering echo of that subtext. The critical problem, for those troubled by the subtext and its implications, is the way in which what troubles us (if we allow ourselves, or force ourselves, to pay it heed) has contributed to the artistic achievement we treasure. Without the utopian social vision in all its reactionary severity, and the urge to give it the kind of vicarious fulfillment that art can supply, it is unlikely that Stravinsky would have found it necessary to devise the all-encompassing, all-uniting scheme of Russo-Eurasian tonal relations that so distinguishes *Svadebka* not only from the surfacey work of its many imitators but also from Stravinsky's own earlier neonationalist ventures. Without that scheme, there would not be that quality of rigorous construction that so attracts the sophisticated ear and tantalizes the analytical intelligence. And that quality, despite all their ostensible differences of style, aesthetic, and motivation, is what Stravinsky's pleromic art so notably shares with Scriabin's. It begins to suggest the special blind and blinding Russian predilections—for the maximal, the single, the supernal—that ally them beneath or behind their openly de-

---

[109] See the Alain Nicolas auction catalog "Autographes-Livres-Documents" (Paris: Librairie les neuf Muses, 1993), lot no. 196.

clared antagonisms, and that give them their enduring, unsettling power over our imaginations, resist it as we may.

What makes *Svadebka* not merely the culmination but the crisis of Stravinsky's "Russian" period, and arguably his creative acme, is the fact that, even before the means of its explication were recovered (a process of that for all practical purposes began only with Berger's potent inferences in the 1960s), it so clearly possessed a "background," hence a syntax, a language, a structure. The relationship between background and surface in Stravinsky is far more diverse and dialectical (hence, for some, more interesting) than the one governing Scriabin's more singleminded and limited (hence, for some, more adequate) syntax. In both cases, however, the artistic qualities of the music, however narrowly they may be defined or evaluated, are decisively— indeed, *internally*—connected with its conceptual metaphors. In Scriabin's case these metaphors were overtly and transcendently spiritual; in Stravinsky's, they were tacitly sociopolitical, but with a no less transcendent spiritual component, albeit a more orthodox one. More palpable than in any other Stravinsky composition, perhaps, is the absence in *Svadebka* of any line dividing "the music itself" from "the extramusical."

Unless, of course, we insist upon drawing one. *Svadebka* supremely crys- tallizes in music what has emerged as a dire crux in twentieth-century aes- thetics: the symbiosis of beautiful art and ugly politics. Any easy assumption that we can vote for the art while rejecting (or ignoring) the politics is heedless of the price that the sanitizing process exacts: the art is drastically reduced as the other is syphoned off. Leonard Bernstein, with the best of anticensorial intentions, pled for the reduction: "The 'Horst Wessel Lied' may have been a Nazi hymn," he argued, "but divorced from its words it's just a pretty song."[110] Exactly so. But is that the level to which we would like to see works of art like *Svadebka* reduced?

I would argue, on the contrary, that those of us (those non-Eurasianists, that is) who place *Svadebka* above the level of just a pretty song, who react to it with gooseflesh and to an exceptional performance with tears, are respond- ing to more than a potent aural stimulus or a novel, ingenious patterning of sound. It is precisely the recognition of the danger in the work's allure, the heart of darkness that lurks behind and conditions its gravely joyous affirma- tions, that so intensifies reaction. The ballet, especially as originally staged, speaks to the utopian that lives within each of us, nostalgic for a past that never was, desirous of a future harmony that can never be achieved within the parameters of what we recognize as human justice. The wrenching conflict between *Svadebka*'s enrapturing, consummately realized aesthetics and our

---

[110] Leonard Bernstein, "Wagner's Music Isn't Racist," *New York Times*, 26 December 1991, section A (op-ed), p. 25.

unsexy, unmagical, and often unsatisfying ethical allegiances is what renders us, precisely because of its alienness to the values we have learned to cherish as our heritage, so piercingly alive to the work. And it is what has kept the work so powerfully alive in repertoire despite its cumbersome, nonstandard performance medium and its enormous textual difficulties.

But this is only another way of delineating *Svadebka*'s (and Stravinsky's) alienness to the panromanogermanic world—our world, for better or worse— that they so decisively, if vicariously, conquered and transformed. No one ever came closer to realizing the goals of Eurasianism than did Stravinsky, and nowhere did he ever come closer to the core tenets of the movement than in this ballet, this implied call to Russianize and orthodoxly Christianize the world in response to Russia's capitulation to the modern, atheistic, positivistic, "European" (yes, Jewish) heresy of Marxism.

As Prince Trubetskoy had put it in "Us and Them," the most bilious and provocative of all his essays, Bolshevik "construction" meant "the transfer to Russian soil of yet even more and newer elements of Romano-Germanic civilization, and for Eurasians the least palatable ones of all, since they carry with them the manifest symptoms of Romano-Germanic civilization's decline and fall."[111] *"The communist Bacchanalia,"* wrote Pyotr Savitsky, grimly italicizing every word, *"has arrived in Russia as the culmination of more than two centuries of 'Europeanization.' "*[112] Defeating communism meant defeating "Europe," and defeating Europe would save not only Russia, and not only Europe, but the world.

This—"to emancipate the world from its slavery to the latest Romano-Germanic fashion"[113]—was Russia's true historical mission. Eurasianism was its vanguard. It fell to Stravinsky, with *Svadebka*, hugely influential as it as been on Romano-Germanic musicians, actually to accomplish within the world of art what Eurasianists whose activities were confined to the world at large could only dream about. For the critic Émile Vuillermoz, on the romance side, Stravinsky's Turanian marvel was "that dazzling meteor that crosses our Western sky," spreading a fecundating "dynamic influence."[114] "I love and admire Stravinsky," chimed Satie, in the year of the *Svadebka* première, and in terms virtually borrowed from the Eurasianist vocabulary, "because I perceive also that he is a liberator."[115] For Carl Orff, on the Germanic side, *Svadebka* was nothing less than the wellspring of a lifelong career as bard of Aryan neoprimitivism. It was Stravinsky, of all Russians, who did the

[111] Prince N. S. Trubetskoy, "Mï i drugiye," *Yevraziyskiy vremennik* 4 (1925): 79.

[112] Pyotr Savitsky, "Yevraziystvo," ibid., p. 16.

[113] P. Savitsky, "Poddanstvo ideyi," ibid., vol. 3 (1923): 15.

[114] "Noces.—Igor Strawinsky," *Revue musicale* 4, no. 10 (August 1923): 69.

[115] Erik Satie, "A Composer's Conviction" (*Vanity Fair*, 1923), reprinted in Corle, *Stravinsky*, p. 31.

most to turn the tables on Romano-Germanic hegemony, to stem the tide of what he would later call "defilement of the true foundations of culture."[116]

But these are ends that cannot be met unless *Svadebka*'s own dialectical nature—that is to say, the presence within it of its own Romano-Germanic component—is recognized and respected. That component is the performing medium. Stravinsky's invented peasant lore was meant to be filtered through the familiar, unmarked timbres of "normal," cultivated Western voices, voices with which normal, cultivated Western listeners can identify without any special reflection. The familiarly human vocal presence effectively channels the subversive antihumanistic message of the music. The recent tendency to perform the work with "authentically" ethnic (read: exotic) voices works against the threatened universalization of the Russian. Far from enhancing communication, it mutes or at least moderates the vital, disquieting subtext. What is enhanced, ironically, is "the music itself."

And that seems, after all, to be the intention. Dmitry Pokrovsky, the expert Russian folklorist and performer whose ensemble has recorded a dazzlingly proficient exotic reading of this type,[117] rejects the notion that *Svadebka* embodies a social or political agenda with a plea that has an oddly familiar ring: "After so many years of Soviet rule, I'm uncomfortable with this kind of interpretation," he has told an interviewer. Instead, he has suggested, Stravinsky's neonationalism and neoprimitivism exemplify "a desire to present an unbiased view" of "the customs of societies based on mythological consciousness."[118] It is hard to square this view either with the composer's intentions or with his achievement, given what we know of the boldly tendentious creative hand that shaped *Svadebka*, and the extent of his knowing divergence from his folk sources. Pokrovsky's conception of the work testifies, rather, to the aesthetics and the politics of a later age, described in the earlier part of this chapter—aesthetics and politics that an older Stravinsky, no longer the one who composed *Svadebka*, was happy to endorse.

One of the very last writings to be published over Stravinsky's byline was an account, written for the program book of its "première" performance under Craft, of the most folklike preliminary scoring of *Svadebka*, the one with cimbaloms, pianola, harmonium, and percussion, that is complete through the end of the second tableau.[119] This version, "the most extensive of the abandoned ones" as the author of the late writeup termed it, was also, in his

---

[116] Igor Stravinsky, *Poetics of Music* (1939), trans. Arthur Knodel and Ingolf Dahl (Cambridge, Mass.: Harvard University Press, 1970), p. 131.

[117] Elektra Nonesuch Explorer Series 9 79335-2 (one CD).

[118] Joseph Horowitz, "An Interview with Dmitri Pokrovsky," in J. Horowitz, ed., *The Russian Stravinsky* (Brooklyn: Brooklyn Philharmonic Orchestra, 1994), p. 23.

[119] Craft's performance of this version, with the Gregg Smith singers and members of the Orpheus Chamber Ensemble, was issued on a short-lived Columbia LP: M 33201 (1974).

opinion, "the most authentic, more so in some ways than the final score which, though streamlined, stronger in volume, and instrumentally more homogeneous, is also, partly for the same reasons, something of a simplification."[120] These pronouncements make especially vivid the aesthetic gulf that separated the Stravinsky who wrote them—an Americanized serial composer who fetishized reconditeness and complexity after the academic fashion of those days[121]—from the Stravinsky who wrote *Svadebka*, who understood, better than any other composer then or since, the terrible power of simplification (*uproshcheniye*). What the Stravinsky who wrote in 1968 had forgotten was that in 1923 the simplification was the end, the rest the means.

What the Stravinsky who wrote *Svadebka* actually desired is accurately measured by the work's creative history, a history of progressive abstraction in which the folk specifics were further attenuated at every stage. Bronislava Nijinska, who choreographed *Svadebka* for Diaghilev, understood how this attenuation magnified the work's communicative power, and did everything she could to abet it, astonishing even Diaghilev in the process, as she recalled in a memoir of their first consultation:

> "Bronia, are you ready to begin rehearsing this ballet? How do you see it? You remember the first scene. We are in the house of the bride. She sits in a big Russian armchair to one side of the stage, while her friends comb and plait her hair." "No, Sergei Pavlovich," I interrupted, "there must be no armchair, no comb and no hair!" I took a sheet of paper and sketched the bride with plaits three meters long. Her friends holding the tresses formed a group around her. Diaghilev burst out laughing—which with him was often a sign of pleasure. "What happens next? How can the girls comb such long plaits of hair" he asked. "They won't comb them," I said. "Their dance on point and hers will express the rhythm of plaiting." I went on drawing and explaining my idea of the choreography and staging. Sergei Pavlovich got more and more amused. "A Russian ballet on point!" he exclaimed.[122]

A Russian ballet on point implied exactly the same thing as peasant melodies from the mouths of all-purpose oratorio singers, accompanied by the most all-purpose and generalized of "Western" instrumental timbres. Nijinska had divined exactly what Stravinsky was after with his streamlined scoring, which replaced the ethnic with the "universal." Like her, Stravinsky was now saying, Away with *gusli*, away with *rozhki* (horn bands); the timbres of my

---

[120] "*Svadebka* (*Les Noces*): An Instrumentation" (signed "I. S., Zürich, October 22, 1968"), in Stravinsky and Craft, *Retrospectives and Conclusions*, p. 118.

[121] He went on to celebrate the unfinished version's "generally more elaborate . . . figuration" and its "contrapuntal tendency" (ibid.).

[122] "Création des Noces," in Tatiana Loguine, ed., *Gontcharova et Larionov* (Paris: Kincksieck, 1971), p. 119; quoted in Richard Buckle, *Diaghilev* (New York: Atheneum, 1979), pp. 410–11.

four grands will abstract and distill their essences. At this point he was after more—or rather, less—than timbres. Whereas the earlier scorings had emphasized a variegated interplay of colors and a consequently antic texture (misunderstood by the serialist Stravinsky as "elaborate figuration" and "contrapuntal tendency"), the four pianos are hitched together, like the members of a Turanian polity, in lockstep. Their deployment emphasizes doublings, and in this sense the last scoring of *Svadebka* was paradoxically the most "orchestral" (not to say "symphonic"!) of all. The doublings demand precision of execution, and precision demands rigidity—or, in a (Russian) word, *nepodvizhnost'*.

Here, too, Nijinska was clairvoyantly attuned to Stravinsky's designs. The most uncannily moving aspect of her choreography is its parsimony of movement, which reaches an unforgettable peak in the fourth tableau, where mounting boisterousness in the pit accompanies a scene of staidly ceremonious near-immobility on stage. The stately, unsmiling final lockstep of bride and groom to the marriage bed makes supremely palpable the "profound gravity and cool inevitable intention" of characters "in the grip of remorseless, inelastic tradition." Jeffrey Mark, in the inspired essay quoted earlier (an essay nearly coetaneous with *Svadebka*), had identified these as "the fundamental qualities of folk music." In a folk singer—that is, in one through whom not a personality but a culture speaks—there is "not the faintest suggestion of the flushed cheek and the sparkling eye," and the performance thus conveyed "is ten times the more impressive because of it."[123] That is the secret of *Svadebka*, the secret of *nepodvizhnost'*, *uproshcheniye*, and all the rest. In Stravinsky's postwar masterpiece all the solid Turanian virtues reached their final conjoint apotheosis under the "universalizing" aegis of abstraction, streamlining, and simplicity.

QU'EST-CE QUE LE (NEO)CLASSICISME?

That is what "neoclassicism," at least at first, was all about. It had nothing to do, at first, with stylistic retrospectivism or revivalism, with "returning to Bach," or with vicarious imperial restoration. It had everything to do with a *style dépouillé*, a stripped-down, denuded style, and with the same antihumanism that had already motivated Stravinsky's Eurasianist phase.

So we may read in the very first journalistic essay to attach the *n*-word to Stravinsky—the very first essay, in fact, to apply the word without irony to modern music. It was written in 1923, the year in which *Svadebka* was first performed, and the man who wrote it was the same Boris de Schloezer whose writings on the art of his brother-in-law, Scriabin, have been so crucial to our

---

[123] Mark, "The Fundamental Qualities of Folk Music," pp. 288–90.

interpretation of its transcendence—altogether comparable, it turns out, to Stravinsky's—of the "petty I." Schloezer can serve us again as a uniquely qualified observer on the scene.

The most revealing aspect of Schloezer's early exposition of Stravinsky's neoclassicism is the work that inspired it: not *Pulcinella*, not the Octet, but the *Symphonies d'instruments à vent*, a work we now tend to look upon (and Stravinsky then surely looked upon) as the composer's valedictory to his "Russian period," and one we have already had cause to associate, through Karsavin's "symphonic" metaphors, with Eurasianist ideology. Nothing could be more critical than this unexpected circumstance to our understanding of Stravinsky's neoclassicism.

What made the *Symphonies d'instruments à vent* "neoclassical" for Schloezer, thence for many others, was the assumption that it was "only a system of sounds, which follow one another and group themselves according to purely musical affinities; the thought of the artist places itself only in the musical plan without ever setting foot in the domain of psychology. Emotions, feelings, desires, aspirations—this is the terrain from which he has pushed his work."[124]

For all that these words might seem irrelevant to the poetic conception underlying the *Symphonies d'instruments à vent* (a tombeau for Debussy that, as mentioned earlier, mimics an Orthodox funeral service),[125] Stravinsky lost no time in appropriating Schloezer's view. As early as the next year he was looking back on the *Symphonies* as the first of his "so-called classical works."[126] Schloezer had, as it were, revealed to Stravinsky the underlying, indeed profound relationship between the Eurasianist rejection of personal "emotions, feelings, desires, and aspirations" in the name of a higher symphonic identity that had found expression in *Svadebka*, and the new aesthetic of abstraction that attracted not only Stravinsky but any number of rightward-leaning modernist artists to the postwar "call to order"[127]—a call they heeded in the name of a resurgent, reformulated "classicism."

From this perspective the *Symphonies d'instruments à vent*, in which Eurasianist metaphors found a purely instrumental expression, was indeed a turning point—or could be one if its "extramusical" content were suppressed. And so, in a program note that accompanied performances of the *Symphonies* in the late 1920s and 1930s, Stravinsky went Schloezer one better, describing

---

[124] Boris de Schloezer, "La musique," *La Revue contemporaine*, 1 February 1923; quoted in Scott Messing, *Neoclassicism in Music: From the Genesis of the Concept through the Schoenberg/Stravinsky Polemic* (Ann Arbor: UMI Research Press, 1988), p. 130.

[125] See n. 27.

[126] Letter to Charles-Ferdinand Ramuz, 23 July 1924; *Selected Correspondence*, vol. 3, p. 83.

[127] To call it by the name of Jean Cocteau's testamentary book of essays written between 1918 and 1926: *Le rappel à l'ordre* (Paris, 1926), trans. Rollo Myers as *A Call to Order* (London: Faber and Gwyer, 1926).

the work as entirely formalist and transcendent: no more and no less than an arrangement of "tonal masses . . . sculptured in marble . . . to be regarded objectively by the ear."[128] We have witnessed the birth of "the music itself" out of the spirit of reaction.

[128] Quoted in Deems Taylor, "Sound—and a Little Fury" (review of the American première under Leopold Stokowski), reprinted in *Of Men and Music* (New York: Simon and Schuster, 1937), pp. 89–90. Taylor wrote with great percipience that "the *Symphonies* is, I think, reactionary music," and that Stravinsky "is now experimenting with simplification" (p. 94).

CHAPTER 14

SHOSTAKOVICH AND THE INHUMAN

SHOSTAKOVICH AND US

I

THE THEATER historian Isaak Glikman's recent edition of Dmitriy Shostakovich's letters to him, which appeared during the second year after the fall of the Soviet empire, was the first major post-Soviet contribution to the enormous literature concerning the greatest of all Soviet artists.[1] Its evidentiary value and its human interest are both self-evident, but it has a curious quirk—namely, the editor's frequent interventions to explain that Shostakovich, you see, was making a joke. A choice specimen is his commentary to a letter Shostakovich sent him from Odessa as a new year's greeting on 29 December 1957. This is the first paragraph:

> I arrived in Odessa on the day of the nationwide celebration of the fortieth anniversary of Soviet Ukraine. This morning I went outdoors. You can well understand, of course, that it is simply impossible to stay at home on such a day. Despite overcast skies, all of Odessa turned out. Everywhere there were portraits of Marx, Engels, Lenin, Stalin, and also Comrades A. I. Belyayev, L. I. Brezhnev, N. A. Bulganin, K. E. Voroshilov, N. G. Ignatov, A. I. Kirilenko, F. R. Kozlov, O. V. Kuusinen, A. I. Mikoyan, N. A. Mukhitdinov, M. A. Suslov, E. A. Furtseva, N. S. Khrushchev, N. M. Shvernik, A. A. Aristov, P. A. Pospelov, Y. E. Kalinberzin, A. P. Kirichenko, A. N. Kosïgin, K. T. Mazurov, V. P. Mzhavanadze, M. G. Pervukhin, N. T. Kal'chenko.

And this is Glikman's annotation: "The whole paragraph, seemingly borrowed from a standard newspaper account of those days, is full of pointed irony. Dmitriy Dmitriyevich with deliberate comic pedantry lists the names alphabetically [*sic*], omitting neither initials nor surnames. Indeed the whole letter maintains a satirical tone."

Here, with apologies, is Shostakovich's second paragraph:

> Everywhere there are flags, slogans, posters. All around are joyful, radiant Russian, Ukrainian, and Jewish faces. Here, there, and everywhere one hears saluta-

[1] *Pis'ma k drugu: Pism'a D. D. Shostakovicha k I. D. Glikmanu*, ed. I. D. Glikman (Moscow: DSCH, 1993).

tions honoring the great banner of Marx, Engels, Lenin, and Stalin, and also in honor of Comrades A. I. Belyayev, L. I. Brezhnev, N. A. Bulganin, K. E. Voroshilov, N. G. Ignatov, A. I. Kirichenko, F. R. Kozlov, O. V. Kuusinen, A. I. Mikoyan, N. A. Mukhitdinov, M. A. Suslov, E. A. Furtseva, N. S. Khrushchev, N. M. Shvernik, A. A. Aristov, P. A. Pospelov, Y. E. Kalinberzin, A. P. Kirilenko, A. N. Kosïgin, K. T. Mazurov, V. P. Mzhavanadze, M. G. Pervukhin, N. T. Kal'chenko, D. S. Korotchenko. Everywhere one hears Russian and Ukrainian speech. Now and then one hears the foreign speech of representatives of progressive humanity, who have come to Odessa to congratulate the Odessans on their great holiday. I walked around and, unable to contain my joy, returned to the hotel and decided to describe to you, as best I can, the nationwide celebration in Odessa.

And here is the commentary: "Shostakovich ridicules the false rejoicing of the crowd of city-dwellers filling the streets of Odessa. The repetition, or in musical terms the recapitulation, powerfully reinforces the humorous effect."[2]

Did we really need this help? Did Glikman really think that we did? He seems so eager to point out what could never be missed that he passes over, or maybe hasn't noticed, a joke that really *is* worth calling attention to. It was only because I had put myself to the trouble of transcribing the whole repetitive farrago word for word that I found the names Kirilenko and Kirichenko interchanged the second time around, identifying the pair as the Ukrainian nomenklatura's Dobchinsky and Bobchinsky, the Tweedledee-Tweedledum bureaucrats in Gogol's farce, *The Inspector General*. Since I got to tell about it, I feel my time was rewarded. But what was Glikman's reward? What was the point of instructing us that the letter contained a global irony so ingenuous and unsubtle?

One's first assumption is that old Soviet habits die hard. Anyone who has worked with Soviet editions of primary sources such as composers' letters will recall similar schoolmasterly interventions—intrusive, mistrustful of the reader, seemingly needless, often verging on the comic in their own right. One that has been stuck in my memory now for decades, owing to what I have to call its grotesque typicality, is the editor's prim retort, in a volume of selected articles by César Cui, to a passing remark Cui made in polemic with his perennial antagonist Hermann Laroche. Cui wrote that "unevenness in the work of artists who are devoid of critical discernment, like Rubinstein or Chaikovsky, can be startling." The editor, writing in the wake of the so-called Zhdanovshchina (after Andrey Zhdanov, the Politburo member who directed the postwar reimposition of strict Stalinist conformism in the arts), jumps in on Laroche's side—on the side, that is, of nineteenth-century Russia's most conservative critic—to notify the reader, in a footnote, that "if this assertion

[2] Ibid., pp. 135–36 (commentaries somewhat abridged and conflated).

can to some extent be justified in the case of A. Rubinstein, it is completely mistaken in the case of P. Chaikovsky."[3]

It often happened that the footnotes in Soviet source publications kept up a sort of running feud with the text; a famous tragicomic instance was hard-liner musicologist Yuriy Keldïsh's 1935 edition of some challenging memoirs by the ostensibly "populist" composer Modest Musorgsky's aristocratic companion and probable lover, Count Arseniy Golenishchev-Kutuzov.[4] Altogether painful was the footnote in which the editors—the Jewish editors, I note regretfully—of a 1971 edition of Musorgsky's letters sought to soften the impact of one of the composer's harsher attacks on the Jews: "In spite of what might seem the blatant anti-Semitic character of these lines," they wrote, "in the light of Musorgsky's worldview, as well as his personal friendships and his creative interests, this sally is to be explained not by any chauvinistic outlook on the part of the composer but by a general aversion to the bourgeoisie and to the mercenary element."[5] Leaving aside the part about some of the composer's best friends, could the editors have believed that their exculpatory equation of Jewishness with moneygrubbing was any less blatantly an anti-Semitic slur than whatever Musorgsky had on offer?

Of course not; but one understands the need for all these intrusions. They were the price of publication; the only alternative, under the conditions of Soviet censorship, was expurgation. (Indeed, the anti-Semitic passage from Musorgsky has been expurgated not only in previous but also in subsequent Russian editions of his correspondence.)

But that does not explain Glikman's commentaries, which were written under no such constraint. Nor have we taken their full measure. For the problem of irony can cut the other way, too. People can be schooled and overschooled in irony, as a Greek shepherd boy found out long ago. So just as often Glikman felt called upon to step in and explain that Shostakovich, you see, was *not* making a joke. In one of the earlier letters in the book, Shostakovich writes, "I'm working a lot, but not composing anything." As Glikman explains, this meant that Shostakovich was doing a lot of film scoring, which he did not take seriously as creative work. Then Shostakovich writes, "I hope that these are only temporary setbacks for my modest and insignificant talent." Glikman insists that we take this literally: "These words are not by any means a pose; he did not like posing." And yet a great deal in the letter

---

[3] César Antonovich Cui, *Izbrannïye stat'i*, ed. Izrail Lazarevich Gusin (Leningrad: Muzgiz, 1952) pp. 238, 592.

[4] A. A. Golenishchev-Kutuzov, "Vospominaniya o M. P. Musorgskom," ed. Yu. V. Keldïsh, in M. V. Ivanov-Boretsky, ed., *Muzïkal'noye nasledstvo: Sbornik materialov po istorii muzïkal'noy kul'turï v Rossii*, vol. 1 (Moscow: Ogiz and Muzgiz [copublication], 1935), pp. 5–49. For an analysis of the commentary see R. Taruskin, *Musorgsky: Eight Essays and an Epilogue* (Princeton: Princeton University Press, 1993), pp. 25–34.

[5] M. P. Musorgsky, *Literaturnoye naslediye*, ed. A. Orlova and M. Pekelis, vol. 1 (Moscow: Muzïka, 1971), p. 354. The passage thus glossed is on p. 245.

seems to contradict this reading. For one thing, Shostakovich himself appears to mock the sentence in question, observing immediately afterward that "modesty becomes a person." For another, the sentence parodies an earlier one in the letter, in which Shostakovich sympathizes with Glikman's reported illness by saying, "I hope that these are only temporary setbacks for your mighty organism."[6]

In any case, as revealed in the letters Glikman has made public, Shostakovich's modesty did not extend to self-denigration. One of the most moving letters of all, for me, and the one that if pressed I would single out as the most significant in the book, is the letter that ends with the following paragraph:

> During my illness, or rather my illnesses, I picked up the score of one of my works. I looked through it from beginning to end. I was astonished at its quality. It seemed to me that having created such a thing I can be proud and serene. It was devastating to think that it was I who composed this composition."[7]

Glikman speculates that the composition in question was the Eighth Symphony, one of the works that were under a tacit but official ban (or "idling," as the expression then went) at the time of writing. "And then one fine day," he writes in his commentary, "on the eve of a new year, there arose in [Shostakovich] the need somehow, in a letter to me, to answer his persecutors, tell them what he thought of their judgment, their verdicts and sentences, and what he thought about himself."[8] What made the letter so moving—for Glikman too, I would hazard a guess (though he does not say so), as well as for me—is not so much what is said within it as the date that stands above it. The "one fine day" on which Shostakovich wrote with such intensity about the value of his work was in fact a day of days: 21 December 1949, Stalin's seventieth birthday, the grand apotheosis to which Solzhenitsïn devoted a whole surrealistic chapter in *The First Circle*, a day that was bloated up from end to end of the Soviet Union in an unprecedented discharge of vaunting orchestrated lies and propaganda.

This letter opens out onto a much broader, more important interpretive terrain than the special, relatively circumscribed case of irony. I mean the general terrain of "polysemy," of subtexts and multivalent meaning. This is the interpretive space in which, for at least half a century, the vast majority of Shostakovich readings have taken place. As in the case of the letter just quoted, knowing the dates of things can be terribly important. Knowing, for example, that the first performance of the Fifth Symphony took place in November 1937, at the very height of the so-called Yezhovshchina (after Nikolai

---

[6] *Pis'ma k drugu*, pp. 72–73.

[7] Ibid., p. 85.

[8] Ibid., p. 86.

Yezhov, the "iron commissar" of internal affairs), perhaps the bloodiest political terror the world had ever seen, provides an indispensable subtext for comprehending the palpable funereal imagery in the slow movement, to be examined in detail in the last section of this chapter. Even if it should turn out that Shostakovich never intended any such thing (though I have no idea how such a fact could be established), perceiving the connection is essential to understanding the way in which the symphony was received—as all reports agree, the slow movement provoked a wave of open weeping in the hall—and why Shostakovich's music was valued the way it was.

That social value, which made Shostakovich's music as controversial outside of Russia as it was precious inside, was precisely the result of the play of subtexts—the uncontrollable play of subtexts, it is important to add. It was one of the very few things the totalitarian regime was powerless to contain short of banning the music, which it occasionally did. And that made it precious. "I always sensed intuitively in it a protest against the regime," says Solomon Volkov, the author of that shameless best-seller *Testimony*, a book that falsely purported to be Shostakovich's transcribed oral memoirs.[9] But this time Volkov was speaking in his own voice, rather than through his little puppet Mitya, and we can believe him.[10] And we can agree: of course he sensed protest in Shostakovich's music—he and millions of his countrymen. They needed to sense it; and music, with its blessed polysemy, afforded them a consolation no other art could provide under conditions of Soviet thought control.

Music was special. Music *is* special. Nothing could prevent Volkov and many other intellectuals—as he reports in the preface to *Testimony*, again written in his own voice—from associating the violent music in the second movement of Shostakovich's Eleventh Symphony not with the events of "Bloody Sunday" in 1905, as the symphony's official program stated, but with the more recent bloody events in Budapest, where Soviet troops had lawlessly put down the 1956 Hungarian rebellion.[11] ("Never mind," an ex-Soviet musicologist of Volkov's generation has assured me, "we *knew* what it meant.") For Volkov, for my friend, and for many others, assembling in a concert hall and listening together to Shostakovich's music gave them an otherwise unavailable sense of solidarity in protest.

Did the composer intend it? The question is naive, unanswerable, and irrelevant. A hundred years earlier, as we know, radical students had loved to forgather in the balcony of St. Petersburg's Great Stone Theater to cheer Italian singers who reached their high notes on words like *libertà*. There was

---

[9] Trans. Antonina W. Bouis (New York: Harper and Row, 1979); its ruses were very effectively exposed by Laurel Fay in "Shostakovich vs. Volkov: Whose Testimony?" *Russian Review* 39 (1980): 484–93.

[10] "Zdes' chelovek sgorel," *Muzïkal'naya akademiya*, no. 3 (1992): 6.

[11] Solomon Volkov, *Testimony*, pp. xi–xii.

nothing Tsar Nikolai I could do to prevent it. Does it make sense to ask whether Rossini or Bellini intended it?

Sometimes the composer's intention is manifestly irrelevant to the meaning of his work, and to insist on limiting meaning to original intention can only, and obviously, impoverish it. The veteran Russian scholar Daniel Zhitomir- sky recently called attention to a gripping instance of this sort involving the song cycle "From Jewish Folk Poetry," long regarded as being, quite inten- tionally, one of Shostakovich's riskiest compositions.[12]

Once again, knowing the date crucially affects not just interpretation but our direct apprehension of the work. "From Jewish Folk Poetry" was written during the black year 1948. That was the year of the Zhdanov crackdown, and of the Communist Party's infamous "Resolution on Music," a document that subjected Shostakovich to his second bout of official persecution. It was also the year in which for the first time anti-Semitism, under the guise of a cam- paign against "cosmopolitanism," became official government policy in the Soviet Union. The actor Solomon Mikhoels was murdered in Minsk. The Jewish Anti-Fascist Committee was liquidated and its leadership arrested. Over the next five years, practically every Jewish cultural activist in the coun- try would be executed. Shostakovich's song cycle was the most demonstrative of his several appropriations of Jewish thematic and subject matter, and when you connect the various events of 1948—even when Stalin's cynical recogni- tion of the infant State of Israel that year and the triumphant arrival of Golda Meir (then Goldie Meyerson), the Israeli ambassador, just in time for the High Holidays are weighed in the balance—it seems more convincing than ever to associate that appropriation of Jewish folklore with the composer's wish covertly to affirm solidarity with the persecuted. Indeed, it was a way of identifying himself and his colleagues, creative artists in Stalin's Russia, with another oppressed minority.

By the time the cycle was completed, the honeymoon with Israel was over, and the work could not be performed except clandestinely (which, according to recent reports, it was, repeatedly, to tearful gatherings of Jews and artists). It was consigned "to the drawer" as one said then, along with the First Violin Concerto, whose scherzo contains another Jewish theme in direct conjunction with the first tentative and somewhat ambiguous occurrence in Shostakovich's work of his musical monogram, D–S–C–H (the pitches D, E♭, C, and B, as they are named in German), that would haunt his music from then on with increasing frequency. Yet even for the drawer, Shostakovich took precau- tions. He changed the words of one song, as the ex-Soviet Israeli musicologist Joachim Braun has pointed out, to name the Tsar explicitly as the force behind a Jewish father's exile to Siberia. And he followed the first eight songs, which paint a uniformly bleak picture of Jewish life in Russia, with a final optimistic

---

[12] See D. Zhitomirsky, "Shostakovich," *Muzïkal'naya akademiya*, no. 3 (1993): 29.

trio depicting life in the "Sovietishe Heymland" (to recall the name of that egregious showcase of a Yiddish journal that appeared briefly during the Khrushchev years).

Braun calls these last three songs "tribute money" and tries, somewhat wishfully in my opinion, to portray them as a thinly veiled, deliberate parody of the authentic Jewish style elsewhere embraced in the cycle.[13] Whether or not a parody, the optimistic songs are definitely an emollient. Even so, the last of them, the exultant song of a Jewish mother about her children's prospects in the land of the Soviets, makes for a rousing, if conventional, finale.

That, at least, seems to have been Shostakovich's intention. But between 1948, when the songs were written, and 1955, when they were first publicly performed in the early days of the "thaw," a great many events had taken place. Among them was the so-called Doctor's Plot, the loudly publicized arrest of six prominent Jewish doctors (along with two token Russians and a Ukrainian) on charges of murdering the Politburo members Zhdanov and Shcherbakov at the behest of the American Jewish Joint Distribution Committee (identified by *Pravda*, in the paranoiac jargon of the day, as an "international Jewish bourgeois national organization"), and plotting to wipe out the rest of "the leading cadres of the Soviet Union."[14] This was widely, and one can only think plausibly, read as a *provokatsiya* intended to justify the wholesale deportation or destruction of the Jews of European Russia, from which only Stalin's providential death a few weeks later saved them. (Among those briefly arrested in the immediate aftermath of the Doctor's Plot was one of Shostakovich's close friends, the Jewish composer Moisey Vainberg, who had fled to the USSR from Poland in the wake of the Nazi-Soviet invasion of 1939. Vainberg was arrested not because he was involved in any organized Jewish activities, but because he had the misfortune of being related by marriage both to Mikhoels and to Professor Miron Vovsi, one of the accused medical assassins.)[15]

Thus by the time Shostakovich's song cycle reached its first public hearing, its culminating words—"Our sons have become doctors! A star shines over our heads!"—had taken on a new and chilling meaning the composer never foresaw. They now pointed, with excruciating irony, to the utter betrayal of the hopes an oppressed people had once vested in the Russian revolution. And the star! Instead of the red star atop the Kremlin one now thought of the six-pointed yellow stars sewn on the garments of the German Jews.

It is clear, I should think, that Shostakovich could never have intended this particular irony, which is now perhaps the most potent jolt his song cycle can administer to an appropriately attuned listener. It is equally clear, I hope, that

[13] Joachim Braun, "The Double Meaning of Jewish Elements in Dimitri Shostakovich's Music," *Musical Quarterly* 71 (1985): 74–75.

[14] *Pravda*, 13 January 1953, p. 6.

[15] On Vainberg's arrest see *Pis'ma k drugu*, p. 100.

it is now as much, and as legitimately, a part of the experience of the music as anything he did intend, and that he could only have welcomed it, if one may put it so, and the contribution it made to the effect of his work on the consciousness of its hearers, and to its value as testimony. As contexts change, subtext accumulates. What made Shostakovich's music the secret diary of a nation was not only what he put into it but what it allowed listeners to draw out.

This is anything but a new idea, and only recently controversial in consequence of the general decline in interpretive intelligence that followed the rise of "the music itself" as a critical category. As early as 1794, when the idea of the aesthetic was in its infancy, Schiller observed that "the real and express content that the poet puts in his work remains always finite; the possible content that he allows us to contribute is an infinite quality."[16] There, in a nutshell, and a century and a half in advance, is the best explanation of Shostakovich's hold on our imagination.

Accordingly, Glikman's book, like Zhitomirsky's article, contains many moving, even wrenching junctures, laced with just the right dose of gallows humor, and a wealth of biographical revelation, much of it directly relevant to the apprehension of Shostakovich's works. And yet there is—I won't say a flaw because it arises out of such honorable circumstances—a pervading predicament about its commentaries to which I have already drawn perhaps enough ungrateful attention, but which I nevertheless feel I must pursue because it has such a bearing on our business not only as scholars and as critics but as members of a great composer's audience.

The power of the book, as well as its dilemma, is summarized when, taking leave of the reader on the last page, Glikman confesses that the memory of Shostakovich is sacred to him. It was in order to protect the memory of his most cherished friend, and protect what *he* knew to be the meaning of his friend's words, that the editor felt called upon to interpose himself so often between the reader and the text. Irony, which is to say contradictions between the manifest sense of an utterance and its latent sense, inevitably became the primary object of his ministrations. In all cases, and regardless of which level of meaning he saw fit to endorse in any given case, his object was the same: to adjudicate and resolve the contradiction.

Like the Soviet readings to which I have compared them, Glikman's was thus an attempt to take possession of the meaning of the text, or perhaps, in his own view, to return possession to the rightful owner. It was an attempt to contain meaning and foreclose interpretation. In that sense it *was* an old Soviet habit, as I have suggested—or rather, it was an attempt to fight Soviet methods of appropriation with Soviet methods. What Glikman tried to do was carry out a sort of preemptive strike not only against the old, opportunistic

---

[16] Friedrich Schiller, review of Friedrich Mattheson's landscape poetry, quoted in Charles Rosen, *The Romantic Generation* (Cambridge, Mass.: Harvard University Press, 1995), p. 93.

official view of Shostakovich, to which the reflexes of a lifetime had understandably rendered him permanently sensitive, but also against the equally opportunistic habits of secret nonconformist interpretation in which he knew his readers, being, like him, survivors of the Soviet system, were thoroughly adept.

But the effort to resolve every contradiction and eliminate every ambiguity or multivalence inevitably produces inconsistencies and contradictions of its own. And the price of certainty is always reduction—reduction not only in meaning but in interest and value. Glikman's presentation of Shostakovich's letters thus crystallizes in a microcosm, and with relatively unproblematical texts, the difficulties and the fascination that have always haunted the experience of Shostakovich's musical works—those vastly problematical texts—and our relationship to them: the problem of "Shostakovich and Us."

II

The fact is, no one owns the meaning of this music, which has always supported (nay invited; nay compelled) multiple opportunistic and contradictory readings, and no one can ever own it. Under the old Soviet dispensation, of course, the Party claimed exclusive interpretive rights. Attempts by Volkov or Glikman, among many others, to return exclusive ownership to the composer are futile at best, dishonest at worst. The "Shostakovich" to whom ownership is returned is an ex post facto construction—as he would remain even if the authenticity of *Testimony* were confirmed—through which latter-day interpreters, potentially including the composer, assert their own authority. Imagine Edgar Bergen making himself very small and trying to sit on Charlie McCarthy's lap.

But that hopelessness of final arbitration is precisely what has given the music its enormous social value, its terrific emotional force, and its staying power. No other music—indeed, I would not hesitate to say, no other body of texts—so radically forces engagement with the most fundamental issues of interpretation. No other body of texts so compellingly demonstrates that meaning is never wholly immanent but arises out of a process of interaction between subject and object, so that interpretation is never wholly subjective or wholly objective to the exclusion of the other. And no other body of texts so fully convinces us that the meaning of an artwork, indeed of any communication, is never wholly stable but is the product of its history, a history that only begins with its creation. (Otherwise, one could maintain, our national anthem is not a patriotic song but only a drinking song.)

And now add to all this the incredibly high stakes of the creative and interpretive game as played within the frontiers of a brutal political tyranny. Whether viewed internally or externally, whether in terms of their content or in light of their context, Shostakovich's works are fraught with horrific subtexts that can never be ignored. That is why his music has always been, and will always be, the object of furious and manifold contention. We can never merely receive its messages; we are always implicated in their making, and therefore we can never be indifferent to them. It is never just Shostakovich. It is always Shostakovich and us.

The fact that not even Shostakovich's devoted confidant can entirely succeed in determining for us the extent to which the composer's texts contain irony, or even when they do, is all the evidence we need that irony, along with every other aspect of meaning, is not something that texts merely "contain." Irony, as Stanley Fish so pithily puts it, "is neither the property of works nor the creation of an unfettered imagination, but a way of reading."[17] I quote Fish because he is the soul of quotability, not because his view of irony is a new one, still less because it is the invention of recent literary theory. It may be new to formalized theory, but it is, and has always been, a standard aspect of informal critical practice. I mean the practice of ordinary, nonprofessional readers and, in the particular and especially pertinent case of music, listeners.

The familiarity of the notion is attested by any number of old jokes, like the one about the two Jews who meet in the Warsaw railway station. "Where are you going," asks one. "To Minsk," answers the other. "Ha!" says the first, "You say you are going to Minsk so that I should think you're going to Pinsk, but I happen to know that you *are* going to Minsk, so what's the point of lying?" Or the one about the two psychoanalysts. "Hello," says the first. "Hmm," thinks the second, "what did he mean by that?" Of course it is no accident that these jokes are peopled by Jews and psychoanalysts, representatives of distinguished gnostic traditions—two traditions (or is it only one?) that radically distinguish between manifest and latent content and radically privilege the truth value of the latent. Many such traditions—the mythographic, the symbolist, the occult—lurk in the background to modern art.

Nor let us forget an occult science that used to be practiced until quite recently, that of Kremlinology, along with its sister discipline, "Aesopian" discourse. All Soviet texts—regardless of their provenance, whether public or private, official or underground, whether the latest photo of the Politburo lineup atop the Lenin mausoleum or the latest tape of clandestine "guitar poetry"—have always been doggedly scrutinized for their latent content. The assumptions have always been that such content is there, that it will contradict the manifest content, and that it is the true content. Armed with such assumptions, one could not fail to find it. Thus it is no accident, either, that the theoretical literature on irony, such as it is, overlaps as much as it does with the literature on censorship and its complicated interactions with artistic expression. True hermeneuticists, though often confused with exegetes who

---

[17] Stanley Fish, "Short People Got No Reason to Live: Reading Irony," in *Doing What Comes Naturally* (Durham: Duke University Press, 1989), p. 194.

merely investigate and defend "original intention," have long been subversive readers who have realized the necessarily arbitrary nature of the choice between manifest and latent content. Hans-Georg Gadamer, for one, long in advance of poststructuralist or reader-response theory, recognized (in *Truth and Method*, his classic treatise on interpretation) that hidden meanings are as much the creation of the reader as of the writer.[18]

---

[18] Gadamer made his comments about irony in the course of a critique of a book by Leo Strauss—*Persecution and the Art of Writing* (New York: Free Press, 1952; reprint, Chicago: University of Chicago Press, 1988)—that has great relevance to the interpretive issues that surround the works of Shostakovich. After a pair of introductory chapters Strauss focuses on Jewish writers—Maimonides, Halévy, Spinoza—who published their work in hostile environments. He stresses sensitivity on the part of the interpreter to internal contradictions (in style, tone, or substance) and violations of stylistic or generic norms. Gadamer comments:

> Is not conscious distortion, camouflage and concealment of the proper meaning in fact the rare extreme case of a frequent, even normal situation? —just as persecution . . . is only an extreme case when compared with the intentional or unintentional pressure that society and public opinion exercise on human thought. Only if we are conscious of the uninterrupted transition from one to the other are we able to estimate the hermeneutic difficulty of Strauss' problem. How are we able to establish clearly that a distortion has taken place? Thus, in my opinion, it is by no means clear that, when we find contradictory statements in a writer, it is correct to take the hidden meaning—as Strauss thinks—for the true one. There is an unconscious conformism of the human mind to considering what is universally obvious as really true. And there is, against this, an unconscious tendency to try extreme possibilities, even if they cannot always be combined into a coherent whole. (*Truth and Method* [originally published 1960; reprint, New York: Crossroad, 1982], p. 488)

What is of greatest moment here is the recognition that ironic and straightforward meanings, like freedom and constraint, are not antithetical categories but are located on a continuum, and are therefore relative to one another, and hence that it is never a question of merely selecting alternatives but of weighing variables, a process that in itself undermines the stability of categories. Failure to recognize these complexities rather vitiates the most sustained recent study of the trope of literary irony. In *A Rhetoric of Irony* (Chicago: University of Chicago Press, 1974), Wayne C. Booth posits what seems in light of Gadamer an unrealistically categorical standard for testing for the presence of "bona fide irony," which (Booth argues) is necessarily 1) intended, 2) covert, 3) stable, and 4) finite.

For a rare attempt to formulate a theoretical framework for detecting or evaluating musical ironies in Shostakovich see the final chapter ("Conclusion: The Language of Doublespeak") in David Fanning, *The Breath of the Symphonist: Shostakovich's Tenth* (RMA Monographs, no. 4; London: Royal Musical Association, 1989), pp. 70–76. While certain Boothian assumptions seem to persist—particularly insofar as the writer seeks explicit authorial confirmation (which, when found, eliminates the irony)—Fanning posits some useful musical analogues to the "internal contradictions" literary critics seek. One is incongruous thematic transformation, which he likens to "a tragic speech delivered with merry inflections" (there are celebrated instances of this in the problematic finale of the Tenth); another is "disjunction between gesture and immediate context," compared with "a smile held beyond its natural [or, maybe better, expected] duration—at first vaguely worrying, then more disturbing and finally frightening" (pp. 71–72). For a gen-

ALL THIS is quite apart from the special status, and the special attributes, of music—especially music in the post-Beethovenian symphonic tradition of which Shostakovich was perhaps the last great master. Such music was arguably the most potent medium of artistic expression ever devised. It was equipped with a sophisticated, highly ramified practice of melodic elaboration and directed harmony, which enabled it both to forecast and to delay points of melodic and harmonic arrival (or "closure," as music theorists call it). Because by means of these techniques symphonic music was always portending its own future and recalling its own past, it could be said to possess a powerful internal sign system—an introversive semiotic, the Russian formalists would say—that enabled it to represent enormous tensions and cathartic releases that elicited corresponding affective responses in the hearer: responses that were controlled and directed more precisely, hence more powerfully, than those evoked by any other art medium.

At the same time symphonic music was often laden with "extroversive" symbols and portents as well. By Beethoven's time there were already many conventions for representing the wider world and its contents, all the way from primitive onomatopoeia to sophisticated "intertextual" allusion. The repertoire of such devices grew rapidly over the next hundred years, with Chaikovsky, Shostakovich's countryman and predecessor, making a signal contribution to its development. But—and this may be the key to its uncanny efficacy—such music resolutely eschewed the establishment within itself of any stable code by which its signs could be read.

Thus while its unfolding could simulate the manner and produce the effects of a drama or a narrative, music (even "program music") eluded conclusive paraphrase. Its inescapable assault on the senses and its dynamism, governed by a compelling syntax but unmediated by any established semantic canon, seemed to present and to evoke emotional intensity in a primal, inchoate fashion. "Music," Schopenhauer was prompted thus to write, "gives the innermost kernel preceding all form, or the heart of things."[19] Wagner, under its (and Schopenhauer's) spell, called music that appeared to do this "absolute music," and the name has stuck.[20] But, as we have just observed, the idea of absolute music, as originally envisaged, did not imply abstraction, still less formalism. It named no names, and was therefore unattached to objects, but it

---

eral broaching of the theme of Aesopian discourse in Soviet music see two overlapping articles by Joachim Braun: "Shostakovich's Song Cycle *From Jewish Folk Poetry*: Aspects of Style and Meaning," in Malcolm H. Brown, ed., *Russian and Soviet Music: Essays for Boris Schwarz* (Ann Arbor: UMI Research Press, 1984), pp. 259–86; and "The Double Meaning of Jewish Elements in Dimitri Shostakovich's Music," *Musical Quarterly* 71 (1985): 68–80.

[19] Arthur Schopenhauer, *The World as Will and Representation* (1819), trans. E.F.J. Payne (New York: Dover, 1969), vol. 1, p. 263.

[20] Richard Wagner, "Beethoven's Ninth Symphony" (1846), quoted in Carl Dahlhaus, *The Idea of Absolute Music*, trans. Roger Lustig (Chicago: University of Chicago Press, 1989), p. 18.

was supremely attached to subjects, to the point where it could seem to take over its beholders' sentient lives for the duration, giving knowledge of a reality that (as Scriabin knew best of all) transcended the sensory and the phenomenal, giving access to a realm of gnosis or revelatory "intuition."

What this amounts to in more mundane interpretive terms is an overwhelmingly fraught surface or manifest content, consisting of the dynamically unfolding sound shapes with all their clamor of introversive and extroversive signification, but a symbology whose referents must be sought in the realm of latent content. These circumstances have given rise to a persistent, heated, and fruitless debate that still rages, on and off, both in and out of the academy. On the one hand are those who would prefer to simplify matters by denying the very existence (or the "reality") of a latent content and claiming for music the status of an inherently or ideally nonreferential medium, unattached to the wider world and beatifically exempt from its vicissitudes. Their outstanding nineteenth-century spokesman was Eduard Hanslick, on whom Wagner modeled the figure of Beckmesser, the eternal pedant in *Die Meistersinger*. The outstanding twentieth-century representative of this position was the uprooted Russian nobleman and White émigré Igor Stravinsky (and so identifying him, as we have seen, identifies the motivation for his aesthetic stance). In retrospect, it seems only predictable that the autonomist or formalist position should have achieved its completest ascendancy in the West during the cold war.

On the other hand are those who not only acknowledge the immanence of a latent musical content but seek, or presume, to define it, to fix it, to make it manifest, to have it name names and propound propositions, to subject it to paraphrase, which means subjecting it to limitation and ultimately to control. It is not difficult to see the political subtext that informs this debate, or why the so-called referentialist side of the argument should have reached ascendancy in the twentieth-century totalitarian states at the same time that the autonomist position triumphed in the liberal democracies.

But both these extreme positions are impoverishing. The position that would eliminate a whole level of meaning from music impoverishes it literally and obviously. Yet the other is hardly better. When fixed and paraphrased, the latent becomes blatant. And when the latent becomes wholly manifest, the manifest becomes superfluous.

For an astonishingly abundant demonstration of that blatancy and that superfluity, consider Ian MacDonald's recent book *The New Shostakovich*.[21] Although published more than a decade after its subject's death, this travesty received its most trenchant critique from Shostakovich himself: "When a critic, in *Worker and Theater* or *The Evening Red Gazette*, writes that in such-and-such a symphony Soviet civil servants are represented by the oboe and the

---

[21] Boston: Northeastern University Press, 1990.

clarinet, and Red Army men by the brass section, you want to scream!" That is what the young Shostakovich said at a symposium, "Soviet Music Criticism Is Lagging," held at the Union of Soviet Composers in 1933, and reported in its official organ, three years before he and all his colleagues were muzzled.[22] And here is what Ian MacDonald has written about a passage in Shostakovich's Fifth Symphony: "Over the thrumming rhythm, flute and horn now converse in a major-key transposition of the second subject: two dazed delegates agreeing that the rally had been splendid and the leader marvellous."[23]

There is MacDonald's book in a nutshell. The author musters all the methods of Soviet music criticism at its most lagging, vulgar, and biased in order to prove that Shostakovich was a "scornful dissident" and that his creative achievement amounted to nothing less, and nothing more, than an obsessively sustained invective against the Soviet regime and against Stalin personally.

The methods are familiar. There is trivializing literary or pictorial paraphrase: an ascending scale to a climax in the first movement of the Fourth Symphony depicts the imagined arrival chez Shostakovich of the NKVD, "audibly climbing the stairs . . . and bursting in through the door on a triumphant crescendo [sic]."[24] There is baby "semiotics": every two-note motif says "STA-LIN" (even when iambic), and every descending anapest means "betrayal." There is guilt by association: in defense of his thesis that Shostakovich was dissident from his early twenties, MacDonald names a few antiutopian writers of the 1920s (Zamyatin, Olesha, Bulgakov, Zoshchenko) and points out that "Shostakovich knew these writers personally . . . and socialized with them."[25] There is the shifting burden of proof ("There is nothing to suggest that the composer . . . opposed the non-Party writers"). There is "verificationism" or confirmation-bias: evidence in support of preconceived conclusions is selectively culled and marshaled; contrary evidence is suppressed or damned. And there is pervasive browbeating: "There can be absolutely no doubt" of the author's readings; all others are "palpably ridiculous." At their most triumphant and peremptory, MacDonald's exegeses might have served as confessions to be shoved under Shostakovich's nose by State Procurator Vïshinsky, together with a pen.

III

Where latent musical meaning is neither negated nor successfully administered—where, in other words, it is acknowledged but contested—the value of its

---

[22] "Sovetskaya muzïkal'naya kritika otstayot," *Sovetskaya muzïka*, no. 3 (1933): 121.

[23] *The New Shostakovich*, p. 130.

[24] Ibid., p. 112.

[25] Letter to the editor, *Times Literary Supplement*, 28 September–4 October 1990, p. 15.

vessel is much enhanced. Nietzsche grasped this truth better than anyone
when he wrote, "Music reaches its high-water mark only among men who
have not the ability or the right to argue."[26] The whole history of the arts in
Russia (not just the Soviet Union), and the whole story of Shostakovich's life,
are encapsulated in that sentence. In few countries have the arts ever mattered
so much, and in few countries have they been subjected to a more terrible
stress, a more terrible contest for ownership. As the preeminent modern master of the post-Beethovenian rhetoric (a rhetoric that declined in the West as
the autonomist aesthetic triumphed) Shostakovich was willy-nilly the most
important artist in the country where the arts were most important—and the
most watchdogged, precisely because his was the medium with the most potential slippage between its manifest and its latent content. Because of this,
Shostakovich was the one and only Soviet artist to be claimed equally by the
official culture and the dissident culture.

He managed this feat, of course, by leaving all interpretation to others. Not
explaining his music—or any music—except under public pressure, in the
vaguest terms, became the Shostakovich defense, and a rule that he carried
over even into his private life. That his letters to Glikman contained little
about his music beyond what Glikman calls "statistics"—number of movements, timings, keys—might have been expected; Soviet letters, after all,
were public documents whether or not they were published. But he was just as
tight-lipped in conversation. A much-repeated anecdote (prized because it
brings together two leading figures whose meetings were few) reproduces
some summer shoptalk between Prokofiev and Shostakovich overheard by the
musicologist Grigoriy Shneyerson at Ivanovo, the Composers' Union retreat,
immediately after the war:

> Prokofiev: You know, I'm really going to get down to work on my Sixth Sym-
> phony. I've written the first movement [here follows a detailed description of
> its form], and now I'm writing the second, with three themes; the third move-
> ment will probably be in sonata form. I feel the need to compensate for the
> absence of sonata form in the previous movements.
> Shostakovich: So, is the weather here always like this?[27]

The later portions of Glikman's book, given over to a Boswellian or Robert
Crafty chronicle of Shostakovich's last years, show the composer growing
more and more noncommittal even as circumstances seemed to favor the low-
ering of his guard. On 24 February 1975, less than half a year before his
death, having listened to a symphony by his former pupil Boris Tishchenko

---

[26] Friedrich Nietzsche, "The Wanderer and His Shadow" (1880), in *The Philosophy of Nietz-sche*, ed. Geoffrey Clive (New York: New American Library, 1965), p. 303.

[27] Quoted in Zhitomirsky, "Shostakovich," pp. 26–27.

and said little, Shostakovich offered a sort of apology that might be taken as his Aesopian credo:

> I am generally closemouthed. I have neither the wish nor the ability to analyze or discuss the pieces I hear. I just listen to the music people give me to listen to. Either I like it or I don't. That's all.[28]

Well, that's not quite all. There is more here than the doer's quarrel with the talker, more than the artist's familiar insistence on sensory immediacy and pleasure over secondary, rationalized response—though in this overanalytical age of ours it's a hint we might do well to consider at times. There is simply too much in Shostakovich's instrumental music that is strongly marked—too much that resonates, like Beethoven's or Chaikovsky's music, with characteristic and functional genres, with the conventional iconicity of emotion, with intertextual allusion, with sheer violence—for us to doubt that at bottom he shared his society's faith in the reality of the latent content. Yet unlike the socialist-realist critics who tried to catalog and thus circumscribe his "imagery" and "intonations,"[29] and unlike the more recent biographical paraphrasts (including the one who scandalously appropriates his name), Shostakovich insisted on keeping the latent content latent, and keeping it labile.

And there is more to that insistence than a mere wish to preserve what Admiral Poindexter notoriously called "deniability." As long as music is left to "speak for itself," it can speak only truth. Janet Malcolm's study of Sylvia Plath's contending biographers contains a passage that cuts remarkably near to the Shostakovichian quick. Whereas "the facts of imaginative literature are as hard as the stone that Dr. Johnson kicked," she writes, there is always "epistemological insecurity" in works of nonfiction, precisely because it is aiming at a literal truth that lies inevitably out of reach.[30] The aspiration to literal truth brings always with it the possibility, indeed the virtual certainty, of falsehood.

Just so, paraphrasts of Shostakovich's symphonies and quartets, who strive to reconcile the latent content of the works with the literal truth of lived experience (the composer's, the people's, their own), cannot hope for a perfect fit, and hence, to the extent that they profess certainty, they will always lie. For the composer's perfect silence we substitute a Babel of partial truths. History has decreed that this particular composer's works are fated to be read in part—but never impartially—as nonfiction.

---

[28] *Pis'ma k drugu*, p. 306.

[29] For explication of these actually quite useful terms, which go back to Boris Asaf'yev (*Muzïkal'naya forma kak protsess*, 1930), and whose meanings are actually disguised by their English cognates, see Malcolm H. Brown, "The Soviet Russian Concepts of 'Intonazia' and 'Musical Imagery,'" *Musical Quarterly* 60 (1974): 557–67 (Shostakovich's Seventh Symphony furnishes the practical illustrations).

[30] Janet Malcolm, "The Silent Woman," (New York: Knopf, 1994), pp. 154–55.

IV

The thickest aura and the loudest Babel—a true international Babel, in many tongues—have surrounded the Seventh ("Leningrad") Symphony, ever since the composer's autograph score was microfilmed and flown by allied military transport to New York by way of Teheran, Cairo, and Buenos Aires in a great fever of war-hysterical publicity, for performance under Arturo Toscanini.[31] Toscanini's performance was broadcast on 19 July 1942 to an audience of millions, including Mr. and Mrs. Stravinsky of Hollywood, who, we learn from Mrs. Stravinsky's posthumously published diary, stayed home in order to listen in.[32]

Aura attached in those days far more to the work and its circumstances than to the composer's person. As Toscanini put it in a letter to Stokowski, whom he had to fight for first-performance rights, "I admire Shostakovich music but I don't feel such a frenzied love for it like you."[33] Stravinsky's regard for Shostakovich likewise fell short of frenzied love, as he lost no opportunity to remind his legions of interlocutors. Yet the very fact that a composer of Stravinsky's stature felt compelled to position himself insistently and repeatedly vis-à-vis a composer universally accorded a lesser stature during Stravinsky's lifetime already suggests something of Shostakovich's emblematic status, and that of the Seventh Symphony among his works. Nor was Bartók immune—else why should he have been so enraged by the symphony that he went to the trouble of parodying its notorious "invasion" theme?[34] What has made both composer and symphony into icons, and the symphony from the very first (though there has been little agreement as to what it is an icon of), is the way their careers have forced critical confrontation with so many cherished assumptions about art music, its values, and its relationship to the world.

Shostakovich, by turns abused and adulated by a totalitarian state to a degree that lies, at both extremes, beyond the power of his benignly neglected Western counterparts to imagine, was in the 1940s a vastly ambivalent emblem. Was he toady or victim? Secret voice of conscience or accomplice to deception? Nation's darling or Party-propped demagogue? Keeper of the Beethovenian flame or cynical manipulator of clichés? He aroused pity and an-

---

[31] That very autograph has now been published in photographic facsimile with an introductory note by Manashir Yakubov, the archivist of the Shostakovich family estate (Tokyo: Zenon, 1992).

[32] See *Dearest Bubushkin*, ed. Robert Craft (New York: Thames and Hudson, 1985), p. 125.

[33] See Harvey Sachs, *Toscanini* (Philadelphia: Lippincott, 1978), p. 279.

[34] There really can be no doubt about this, despite Bartók's wan claim, when pressed, that he was quoting "Da geh' ich zu Maxim" from Lehar's *Merry Widow*, the tune that may in fact have served as Shostakovich's model for caricaturing the Nazis; compare the Seventh Symphony, e.g., at six after figure 35, with Bartók's *Concerto for Orchestra*, third movement, m. 95: the key and the exact note sequence are Shostakovich's, not Lehar's, and so are many details of orchestration and accompaniment.

noyance, envy and condescension, admiration and scorn—but never inhabited the limbo of public disregard that has by and large been the fate of the
modernist generations in the West. He lacked the freedoms of his counterparts
in laissez-faire states, including the freedom to be indifferent and the freedom
to be marginal. He accepted the civic obligations that were thrust upon him
and the rewards that followed.

Although now it is easy enough to see that he had little say in the matter, in
the 1940s this was not so clear. Arnold Schoenberg (again: what compelled
his avid notice?) reproached Shostakovich for having "allowed politics to influence his compositorial style," finally exonerating him on terms that today
can only seem callous: "Heroes can be composers and vice versa, but you
cannot require it."[35] Yet having established which of them was the hero,
Schoenberg could allow himself a certain noblesse-oblige generosity toward
the Soviet composer that contrasted with Bartók's and Stravinsky's furious
rejection. Linking Shostakovich with Sibelius after the habit of contemporary
reviewers like Olin Downes (who cried them up) and Virgil Thomson (who
cried them down), Schoenberg made a pronouncement—"I feel they have the
breath [did he mean breadth?] of symphonists"—that has been pounced upon
ever since by writers eager to issue Shostakovich or Sibelius a passport to
academic respectability.[36] And yet Shostakovich's relationship to the public,
both at home and abroad, was at once a seeming vindication of the ostensible
ideals of socialist realism and a paradigmatic violation of one of Schoenberg's
fundamental postulates: "If it is art, it is not for everybody, and if it is for
everybody, it is not art."[37]

The Seventh brought it all to a head. This hulking programmatic symphony, this bombastic anachronism replete with onomatopoetic battle music
and cyclic thematic dramaturgy, had emerged like some kind of woolly mam-
moth out of the Stalinist deep freeze. Its rhetoric was shamelessly inflated: by
a veritable stage band in its outer movements, by a theatrical travesty of Bach
in its protracted Adagio (Passion chorales, massed violins soliloquizing a
chaconne). Its path to grandiose affirmation opportunistically replayed Beethoven's Napoleonic scenario, and the crass methods by which its message
was mongered seemed an assault on fastidious taste just as brutish as the Nazi
assault on Russia, notoriously represented by a mind-numbingly repetitive
march that, in its slow, inexorable crescendo, brazenly appropriated the surefire formula of Ravel's *Boléro* (even down to the snare drum ostinato and
surprise modulation at the end). Glikman's Shostakovich defiantly confirms
the resemblance: "I don't know what will become of this piece," Glikman

---

[35] Arnold Schoenberg, *Letters*, ed. Erwin Stein (Berkeley and Los Angeles: University of
California Press, 1987), p. 219.

[36] Arnold Schoenberg, *Style and Idea*, ed. Leonard Stein (Berkeley and Lost Angeles: University of California Press, 1984), p. 136; cf. the title of David Fanning's book cited in n. 18.

[37] *Style and Idea*, p. 124.

reports his friend saying after playing through the newly composed first movement in August 1941. "Idle critics will surely rebuke me for imitating *Boléro*. Well, let them; that is how I hear the war."[38]

The war. This debasement of musical values was being carried out in the name of the same holy humanitarian cause that dominated the daily headlines. Shostakovich's symphony was riding both cause's and headlines' coattails to worldwide acclaim. In fact it was making headlines of its own. Its performances, both at home and abroad, were as much political events as musical ones. Was music serving politics or was politics serving music? Was music exploiting politics or was politics exploiting music? Or, worst of all, was the very distinction between the two being undermined?

Toscanini's powerful advocacy of the music was at least partly due to its political implications. "I was deeply taken," he wrote to Stokowski, "by its beauty and its anti-Fascist meanings, and I have to confess to you, by the greatest desire to perform it. . . . Don't you think, my dear Stokowski, it would be very interesting for everybody, and yourself, too, to hear the old Italian conductor (one of the first artists who strenuously fought against fascism) to play this work of a young Russian anti-Nazi composer?"[39] Performing the work, then, would be another antifascist credential for a conductor who, in America, was trading heavily on his political commitments. That "extramusical" appeal was accounting for the symphony's success; and that "extramusical" freight was what conditioned not only "the special meaning of this symphony," as Toscanini called it, and its special privileges, but also its very special blatancy.

Critics took revenge. Virgil Thomson launched his review in the *New York Herald-Tribune* with a really memorable salvo: "Whether one is able to listen without mind-wandering to the Seventh Symphony of Dmitri Shostakovich probably depends on the rapidity of one's musical perceptions. It seems to have been written for the slow-witted, the not very musical and the distracted." And he ended by accusing the composer of cynicism: "That he has so deliberately diluted his matter, adapted it, by both excessive simplification and excessive repetition, to the comprehension of a child of eight, indicates that he is willing to write down to a real or fictitious psychology of mass consumption in a way that may eventually disqualify him for consideration as a serious composer."[40]

B. H. Haggin, less verbally astute but farther out on a limb because he was writing for the *Nation*, then a Stalinist publication, hauled out all his doughtiest pejoratives: derivative, eclectic, unresourceful, crude, pretentious, blatant, banal. What was particularly galling was the barbarization of musical

---

[38] *Pis'ma k drugu*, p. 22.

[39] Sachs, *Toscanini*, p. 279.

[40] 18 October 1942; reprinted in Virgil Thomson, *The Musical Scene* (New York: Knopf, 1945), pp. 101, 104.

values in the name of humanitarian ones, paradoxically embodied in "an hour-and-a-quarter-long symphony concerned with the struggle and final victory of humanity over barbarism." The Russians, Haggin warned, not very real-istically, "can escape this difficulty only by recognizing the unimportance of those external conditions [that is, the unimportance of the war against fas-cism] in relation to the greatness we are aware of in some music, the impor-tance instead of the composer's personal and musical resources."[41]

Aesthetics were thus pitted irreconcilably against ethics; transcendence against commitment; quality against currency; art for the sake of art against art for the sake of people. For so crystallizing the terms of the endless and fruitless debate, Shostakovich's Seventh Symphony surely deserves its status as icon, though it is a status the composer could hardly have sought.

The debate has not been helped by its latest phase, carried out since Shos-takovich's death. The objective has been a dual one: to show, first of all, that the blatant manifest content of these works was a protective screen camouflag-ing a hidden truth that only a musical or moral connoisseur could discern (so much for populism); and to show, second, that the hidden meaning was of a sort that would allow precisely the claim Schoenberg denied, namely the claim of heroism—or rather, in the Soviet context, that of dissidence.

In Volkov's *Testimony*, the first-person narrative included the startling as-sertion that "the Seventh Symphony had been planned before the war and consequently it simply cannot be seen as a reaction to Hitler's attack. The 'invasion theme' has nothing to do with the attack. I was thinking of other enemies of humanity when I composed the theme."[42] From this evidence, Ian MacDonald has dependably managed to read the whole symphony ironically, as "a poker-faced send-up of Socialist Realist symphonism" that satirizes pre-cisely what it was formerly perceived as glorifying. By relating the march theme in the first movement not to Lehar (or to *Deutschland über alles*) but (fleetingly) to Chaikovsky's Fifth Symphony, MacDonald identifies it as "Russian rather than German," hence—like every other work of Shostakovich that MacDonald interprets—a mockery of Stalin, not Hitler.[43]

Like most parti pris interpretations this one has to ignore many salient fea-tures of the object interpreted. To uphold the view of the Seventh as exclu-sively anti-Stalinist one has to disregard the imagery of actual battle, as well as that of repulsion (the horripilating climax at figure 52 in the first move-ment, the symphony's one indubitable stroke of genius), and finally of victory

---

[41] B. H. Haggin, *Music in the Nation* (New York: William Sloane Associates, 1949), pp. 109, 113.

[42] *Testimony*, p. 155.

[43] *The New Shostakovich*, p. 160. Compare Shostakovich at seven bars after figure 49 with the finale of Tchaikovsky's Fifth Symphony at four before figure Z. The resemblance is as demon-strable as the others, but the asserted coincidence of keys is the product of MacDonald's inability to read an orchestral score.

(the cyclic return after the climax near the end of the finale, which reinstates in glory a theme that MacDonald wants to read as satirically insipid). These musical events can hardly be read out of the context of the war and its immediate, overriding urgencies, conditions that could not have been foreseen when Volkov's Shostakovich claimed to have had his first thoughts of the Seventh.

But of course there is something much larger at stake. The Volkov/MacDonald reading merely substitutes one limited and limiting paraphrase for another, in the face of the multivalence that has always been the most special, most valuable property of symphonic music. In a very late Soviet contribution to the Shostakovich debates, the distinguished music theorist Leo Mazel likens this multivalence to that of algebra, wherein a formula containing several unknowns can have various arithmetic solutions.[44] It is an analogy that arises naturally out of Russian historical conditions. "The life experiences that serve as impulse toward the creation of an artwork," Mazel valuably reminds us, "are not tantamount to its content"; nor does "the objective result of an artist's work necessarily conform to its original plan." Whatever Shostakovich may have thought he was signifying by means of his invasion theme, this means, wartime listeners were justified in hearing a representation of Nazis, and we are justified now, if we are still interested in anti-Soviet revisionism, in hearing a representation of Bolsheviks. Such a change in signification, Mazel contends, "is nothing special: life itself had rearranged the emphasis within a generalized and compounded image." (The veteran analyst complicates that image further by demonstrating in detail the derivation—one he does not venture to interpret but is content "to state as fact"—of the invasion theme not from Lehar, not from Chaikovsky, but from the E♭-major episode in the finale of Beethoven's Piano Sonata Op. 10, no. 1.)

Yet so ingrained is the practice of hermeneutic ventriloquism that even Mazel, in seeming contradiction of his own enlightened premises, resorts to documentation in order to invest his interpretation of Shostakovich's "generalized and compounded image" with the composer's ex post facto authority. He reports that upon evacuation to Samara (then Kuybïshev), where he completed the Seventh in the late fall of 1941, Shostakovich and his wife made friends with their neighbor Flora Yasinovskaya, a biologist who was the daughter-in-law of Maxim Litvinov, the early Soviet foreign minister (and the mother of Pavel Litvinov, a prominent dissident of the 1960s). In unpublished notes she made at the time, later made available to Mazel, Yasinovskaya recorded some comments Shostakovich made to her alone, late at night, after he had played the symphony through to an audience of fellow evacuees: "Fascism, yes, but music, real music is never tied literally to any theme. Fascism

[44] L. Mazel, "K sporam o Shostakoviche," *Sovetskaya muzïka*, no. 5 (May 1991): 30–35.

is not simply national socialism, and this is music about terror, slavery, spiritual exhaustion." Later, her notes relate, Shostakovich took her even more fully into his confidence: "The Seventh (and also the Fifth) is not only about fascism but about our system as well, about any tyranny or totalitarianism in general." Thus, Mazel suggests, the varying readings of the Seventh may be harmonized. Within this broadened documentary purview all readings may be authenticated. The putative original identification of the invasion theme with Stalin does not preclude its later use as a symbol for the Nazi aggression. The two ideas are not necessarily in conflict; the same algebraic formula can support either arithmetic solution, or both.

In its allowance for a certain multivalence, and in its refusal to reduce the meaning of the symphony to the meaning of a single theme, or of both to a particular verbal paraphrase, Mazel's view of the Seventh is a distinct improvement over old-line Soviet readings and over the simplistic revisionism of the present day. And yet even it remains ultimately unsatisfactory, because like the other interpretations it insists on identifying meaning, whether of the theme or of the symphony, with the composer's explicit designs, and admits multivalence only insofar as the composer's intention may be so represented. The genetic fallacy remains in place.

V

However "monologically" Shostakovich's works were read by the regime (to borrow an appropriate word from the vocabulary of Mikhail Bakhtin), however passively the silent composer appeared to acquiesce in the readings thus imposed, and however great the consequent propaganda yield, the regime could never fully ignore the power of music (and Shostakovich's music above all) to harbor a potentially anarchic folk hermeneutic. The issue was finally brought to a head in 1948, during the Zhdanovshchina. The Party stooges who were now recruited to vilify Shostakovich—mainly Vladimir Zakharov, the leader of the Pyatnitsky Folk Choir, who inveighed against Shostakovich at the open hearings, and the composer Marian Koval', who did so in a series of calumnious articles in the journal Sovetskaya muzïka, the organ of the Union of Soviet Composers—did so by attacking the monumental instrumental genres that Shostakovich now employed.[45] The overt, quasi-"Tolstoyan" charge now made against him was that such genres, being inaccessible to the broad public and thus elitist, were divisive of society, hence uncommunitarian, hence anti-Soviet. The covert motive, transparent enough but

---

[45] For Zakharov's deposition see *Soveshchaniye deyateley sovetskoy muzïki v TsK VKP(b)* (Moscow: Izd. "Pravda," 1948), pp. 20–25; for excerpts in English translation see Alexander Werth, *Musical Uproar in Moscow* (London: Turnstile Press, 1949; reprint, Westport, Conn.: Greenwood Press, 1973), pp. 53–55. For Koval's denunciations see M. Koval', "Tvorcheskiy put' D. Shostakovicha," *Sovetskaya muzïka* (1948), nos. 2–4.

now documented through the recent efforts of the archivist Leonid Mak-simenkov, among others, was to discourage genres that in their wordlessness were less than ideally subject to ideological control. As Maksimenkov writes, "The ideologues from Agitprop demanded texted music, which could be sub-mitted to censorship on a par with movies, literature, and programmatic, socialist-realist painting."[46]

Early drafts of the Central Committee's Resolution on Music contained explicit formulations designed to render all musical genres safe for censorship—formulations that, had they been published, would have ac-quired the force of law. One read, "Resolved: to liquidate the one-sided, abnormal deviation in Soviet music toward textless instrumental works." A revision substituted the somewhat less baleful verb *osudit'* ("censure" or "judge unfavorably") for "liquidate." Had these passed, one wonders what Shostakovich would have been left with. In the end, though, the formulation was vague and somewhat absurd; no specific genres were condemned, only the "formalist tendency in Soviet music," which was "antipeople and condu-cive in fact to the liquidation of music."[47] Maksimenkov comments that "the laconicism of the final version of the directive portion of the resolution bears Stalin's indelible stamp."[48] It should be added that there was good reason, from the administrative point of view, for imprecision. Specific directives can be complied with. Compliance can be a defense. There can be no defense against the laconic, inscrutable charge of formalism.

So Shostakovich went on writing symphonies, and, increasingly, quartets. And they continued to attract ventriloquists from all sides. More and more prevalently, Shostakovich's post-Zhdanovshchina output was read as so many notes in a bottle. That has certainly contributed to the moral stature they, and he, have achieved—uniquely achieved, I think it is fair to say—in the annals of twentieth-century music. But there is tremendous irony in this, because it is a fate and a stature that Shostakovich could never have sought, but that were conferred on him—thrust upon him—by the powers that tormented him, and by the way in which he responded to his tribulations, the chief response con-sisting precisely in the refocusing of his creative energies on textless instru-mental genres.

To a certain extent, Shostakovich's post-1948 compositions obviously in-vited autobiographical reading. Many of them contained signals that their latent content was private rather than public. The very shift, beginning in the 1950s, from symphony to quartet as the center of gravity for Shostakovich's output was such a hint. It was manifestly an anti-Soviet move of a sort, for, as both the Soviet government and its citizens knew long before it became a trendy slogan in the West, the personal is political. To concentrate on cham-

---

[46] L. Maksimenkov, "'Partiya—nash rulevoy,'" *Muzïkal'naya zhizn'*, nos. 15–16 (1993): 9.
[47] Ibid., pp. 9–10.
[48] Ibid., p. 10.

ber music was not just un-Soviet activity, it was un-Russian. There was never much of a tradition in Russia for chamber music. Under the Soviets it was always vaguely suspect as aristocratic or genteel, and in 1948 it was openly denounced. The official list of Soviet genres, drawn up for official promulgation in one of the superseded resolution drafts, included symphonic, operatic, song, choral, and dance genres only; the final text specifically rejected all styles and genres that appealed only to "narrow circles of specialists and musical epicures."[49] There had never been a Russian composer before Shostakovich to concentrate the way he eventually did on quartets, or to write so many of them. (Nikolai Myaskovsky, another prolific composer who was frightened into abstraction, came closest, with thirteen; but since Myaskovsky wrote twenty-seven symphonies, the quartets do not bulk nearly as large in his output as they do in Shostakovich's. Besides, Myaskovsky's career was practically over by 1948, whereas most of Shostakovich's quartet writing lay ahead.)

There are other hints of politically fraught preoccupation with the private and the personal in Shostakovich's quartets, and his late music in general. They include slow, ruminative, fading finales; the simulation of recitative (often in a demonstratively broken or halting mode, reminiscent of the end of the funeral march in Beethoven's *Eroica* Symphony); or contrariwise, the simulation of voicelessness (the tapping bows in the Thirteenth Quartet) or of screaming (the piercing unison crescendo at the end of the same quartet). The transfer of musical ideas, like the screams, or of whole passages of music, from one work to another, suggesting that different works are chapters in an overarching narrative, also puts us in mind of biography, the most overarching personal narrative of all. The obsessional quotations and self-quotations all but force the prefix "auto-" onto the biographical gesture.

And of course there is the increasingly resolute denial of optimism, of "life affirmation," which is to say denial of the sine qua non of Soviet art. (Here is where the late Shostakovich's surprising recourse to a few superficial trappings of twelve-tone technique, officially denounced for its decadence and pessimism, seems to find its rationale.) As Shostakovich, a world-renowned and much-revered figure, reached the stricken and debilitated end of his road, and as the Soviet state stumbled toward its own debilitated end, the composer could afford to lower his guard, if ever so slightly. Whereas in the Yevtushenko-inspired Thirteenth Symphony he was still manifestly wrestling with Soviet authority, in the Fourteenth Symphony, a fully texted and explicit death affirmation, Shostakovich spat in its face. In the Fifteenth Quartet—a

---

[49] Ibid., p. 9; for the text of the Resolution on Music ("'Ob opere "Velikaya Druzhba" V. Muradeli,' Postanovleniye TsK VKP(b) ot 10 fevralya 1948 g."), see *Sovetskaya muzïka*, no. 1 (1948): 3–8. An English translation is included, as appendix B, in Andrey Olkhovsky, *Music under the Soviets: The Agony of an Art* (London: Routledge and Kegan Paul, 1955), pp. 280–85 (the passage on chamber music is on p. 282).

racking medley of Adagios—he fashioned his personal pain and his pessimism into a tour de force.

VI

I speak of hints within the works, but they are hints that we read in hindsight,
and with ever-increasing knowledge of the events of the composer's life. Ultimately it is difficult—no, it is impossible—to know whether he is forcing his
autobiography on us, or we are forcing it on him. We did not need complacent
poststructuralists to tell us that autobiography, too, is not just a writerly genre
but a way of reading.[50]

The first work of Shostakovich's to end *morendo*, with the dying of the
light, was the Fourth Symphony, on which the composer was at work in 1936
at the time of his first denunciation, and which was withdrawn before its
première (we now know) not at Shostakovich's request but at the bidding of
the Composers' Union leadership.[51] This combination of circumstances made
it inevitable that when the symphony was finally performed twenty-five years
later, in 1961, it was received as the composer's first note-in-a-bottle. Reading the symphony as autobiography reached a predictable height of impertinence (that is, of trivial specificity) with MacDonald,[52] but there is something
about the symphony that does seem naggingly to foreground the issue of individual integrity and social stress—namely, the extremes within it of inward-
ness and extroversion, and the manifestly ironic way in which these extremes
are juxtaposed and even thematically interchanged.

What I am calling "the issue" is one that was framed explicitly by the
doomed poet Osip Mandelstam, who in the 1920s argued that lyric poetry, the
novel, and what he called "psychological prose" were inappropriate for Soviet
art because the historical epoch no longer had any "interest in the human fate
of the individual."[53] One could make a case that the young Shostakovich, a
composer of callous "new objective" symphonies, operas, film scores, and
ballets, shared that outlook, and it was an attitude by no means confined in
those days to the Soviet state. (Its epicenter was Weimar Germany, where the
term *neue Sachlichkeit* was fashionable.) But that was before Mandelstam
discovered what, a couple of years later, Shostakovich, too, would learn: that
when the Soviet state turned against you, you were indeed one man alone; and
your individual human fate still mattered to you, if not to the epoch.

---

[50] See Paul de Man, "Autobiography as Defacement," in *The Rhetoric of Romanticism* (New
York: Columbia University Press, 1984), p. 67.

[51] I. Glikman, "'. . . Ya vsyo ravno budu pisat' muzïku,'" *Sovetskaya muzïka*, no. 9 (1989):
47; *Pis'ma k drugu*, pp. 12–13.

[52] See *The New Shostakovich*, pp. 109–17.

[53] Quoted in Jane Gary Harris, editor's introduction to *Autobiographical Statements in
Twentieth-Century Russian Literature* (Princeton: Princeton University Press, 1990), p. 13.

The last movement of Shostakovich's Fourth Symphony has two codas. The first, which seems a parody of the "Gloria" chorus from Stravinsky's *Oedipus Rex*, may be the most raucous and deafening passage of symphonic music ever composed. The muted, drawn-out whimper that trumps it, though, is what stays in the mind, deliberate echo that it is (right down to the harp and celesta) of Mahler, the most self-absorbed bourgeois neurotic subject of them all. This music, which was almost certainly composed postdenunciation, seems palpably to set the inner and the outer, the public and the private, the manic, turbulent collective and the human fate of the bruised individual, in blunt, easily read (indeed, as it turned out, too easily read) opposition.

But this simple message from the bottle seems foreshadowed—ambiguously, enigmatically, uncertainly, not at all easily—in the first movement, which has not such an obvious ex post facto relationship to the events of the composer's life. After a rude raspberry of an introductory leitmotif, the stomping first theme gets under way in a series of aggressively revolting parade-ground colors: an octave pairing of trumpet and tenor trombone is answered by one of bass trombone and tuba, and finally by a pair of tubas, doubled flatulently by the bassoon and contrabassoon. Though not without detours, the first thematic group continually gathers sonority and stridency until it virtually explodes in a crazy squawking. After a general pause, the second group begins in the tiny voice of a solo bassoon, accompanied by isolated grunts from the cellos and basses, the harp finally entering to mark off the cadence. This is public versus private with a caricatural vengeance. No one could miss it. But when the themes are recapitulated at the other end of the movement, the smug stability of the dualism is undermined. The theme that had been given to the solo bassoon comes back in the paired (and now doubled) trumpet and trombone over the stomping chords, and the theme that had represented the blustery parade ground follows, played pianissimo by the solo bassoon, accompanied by the same low strings, but now with the addition of a quietly insistent bass drum.

Of course I cannot say exactly what it is that this disquieting exchange of roles signifies. I have no ready verbal paraphrase with which to replace it, nor have I a ready answer to a friend of mine, a composer, who asked, "Why couldn't he just have been experimenting?" (except maybe Varèse's answer: "My experiments end up in the wastebasket, not the score"). But my uncertainty may be one reason why the symphony haunts me the way it does. Maybe incertitude—irreducible multivalence—is essential to the experience of the symphony as a work of art. There is more to an artwork, one has to think, than there is to a note in a bottle.

I'm pretty sure I do know what the Eighth Quartet is all about. Shostakovich has seen to that. This is the one composition of his that does ask expressly to be read as autobiography, the one time Shostakovich did put an explicit note in a bottle. And, although my saying so may win me few friends,

I believe that this melancholy, much admired work of 1960 reveals something beyond its intended message—something I, for one, would rather not believe. What it shows is that the need to communicate urgently and with specificity in an atmosphere of threat did at times shrink Shostakovich's creative options.

The wry relationship between the stated program—a requiem for the "victims of war and fascism," allegedly prompted by the viewing of atrocity footage during a sojourn in Dresden—and the music, which consists almost wholly of the D–S–C–H motif in thematic conjunction with allusions to Shostakovich's earlier works (the martyred opera *The Lady Macbeth of the Mtsensk District*, banned by express orders from on high, especially prominent among them), was evident from the start. Shostakovich was clearly identifying himself as victim. The point is made over and over again. The motifs associated with the composer's musical monogram include a Jewish theme from the finale of the Second Piano Trio, which overlaps three of the four notes in D–S–C–H, reinforcing the association Shostakovich had already proclaimed between his personal fate and that of the Soviet Jews, and also the first theme of the First Cello Concerto, which overlaps a different three of the four notes in the monogram. The Cello Concerto idea is confronted with a violent motif that had been associated in a film score, *The Young Guard*, with executions. In the final movement, the D–S–C–H motif is played in exquisitely wrought dissonant counterpoint against the main continuity motif from the last scene of *Lady Macbeth*, which depicts a convoy of prisoners en route to Siberia.

All this, as I say, is clear—and became clearer, in another instance of changing contexts and accumulating subtexts, when *Lady Macbeth* was restored to the active repertoire a year after the quartet's première, with an expanded final scene. And yet, by hooking this self-dramatizing quartet onto "his" side's most hallowed and heavily exploited official propaganda motif of the cold war—namely, that it was the Soviet Union's heroic sacrifices that had saved the world from fascism—Shostakovich forced the work's official acceptance and even its official promotion. This was, in its way, an impressive political coup.

The most searing page in Isaak Glikman's book is the one in which he describes the actual biographical subtext to the Eighth Quartet, corroborating previous reports by Galina Vishnevskaya and Vladimir Ashkenazy, among others, but adding many poignant details.[54] Shostakovich was being pressured to join the Communist Party as a trophy, and had not found within himself the fortitude to resist. It was in an agony of humiliation and self-reproach, as much as an agony of revulsion at fascist atrocities, that he conceived this

[54] *Pis'ma k drugu*, pp. 160–61; see also Jasper Parrott with Vladimir Ashkenazy, *Beyond Frontiers* (London: Collins, 1984), pp. 55–56; and Galina Vishnevskaya, *Galina* (New York: Harcourt Brace Jovanovich, 1984), pp. 399–400.

work, and it was offered as an apologia, in the first instance to his own conscience.

The central strategy, it now seems clear, was to contrive the pointed conjunction, which takes place near the end of the fourth movement, between the D–S–C–H motif and the one extensive quotation that does not come from one of Shostakovich's own works, namely the famous song of revolutionary martyrdom that begins with the words *Zamuchen tyazholoy nevoley*, which mean, literally, "Tortured by grievous unfreedom." The citation was insulated from official suspicion by the fact, known to every Soviet child at school, that this was one of Lenin's favorite songs. Yet by appropriating it, Shostakovich was, as it were, giving his quartet not only a subtext but literally a text, proclaiming his unfreedom and disclaiming responsibility for what he judged in himself to be an act of cowardice, or, rather, a craven failure to act.

The Eighth Quartet is thus a wrenching human document: wrenching the way Glikman's commentary to it is wrenching, or the way . . . well, the way a note in a bottle can be wrenching. But its explicitness exacts a price. The quotations are lengthy and literal, amounting in the crucial fourth movement to a fairly inert medley; the thematic transformations are very demonstratively, perhaps overdemonstratively, elaborated; startling juxtapositions are reiterated until they become familiar. The work provides its own running paraphrase, and the paraphrase moves inevitably into the foreground of consciousness as the note patterns become predictable.

The compulsion to write in this virtually telegraphic or stenographic way was unquestionably an inner compulsion. Its sincerity compels a strong empathic response; and yet the work, I feel, is weakened by it nevertheless. I do not find myself returning to it with renewed anticipation of discovery, and when I do find myself listening to it, I seem to be listening to it the way determined paraphrasts like Ian MacDonald evidently listen to every Shostakovich piece. MacDonald himself reveals the danger of such listening when he comes to evaluate the Ninth and Tenth Quartets, works to which the musical imagination—my musical imagination, at any rate—responds with less coercion and more imaginative energy. Finding in them nothing beyond the same anti-Stalinist program he finds in every Shostakovich piece, MacDonald writes dismissively, "One can be forgiven for thinking that we have been over this ground once too often."[55] Having ears only for the paraphrase, he is unable to distinguish one quartet from another, or distinguish his own hectoring, monotonous voice from Shostakovich's.

Ultimately what is wrong with MacDonald's approach, for all that one may sympathize with readings that respect the reality of the latent content, is the same thing that was wrong with many of the radically revisionist readings of

[55] *The New Shostakovich*, p. 234.

Shostakovich that emanated out of the Soviet Union during the *glasnost'* years that now seem so long ago. In both cases Shostakovich has been assimilated to inappropriate ready-made models. In the failing Soviet Union he was cast as a "dissident" of a sort that simply did not exist during the better (or rather, the worse) part of his lifetime. In the West, he has been cast as an alienated modernist. Both moves reduce him to a stereotype.

To read in MacDonald's book, for example, that the "Leningrad" Symphony was yet another exercise in sarcasm or mockery is painful. In contrast to White émigrés like Stravinsky and Rachmaninoff, who were raising funds and sending supplies for Russian war relief, and even in contrast to Anton Denikin, the White general who had led the campaign on Moscow during the Russian Civil War, who had called upon his fellow exiles not to support Germany in a possible conflict with the Soviet Union, Shostakovich comes across as heartlessly self-absorbed, obsessed with unassuageable feelings of political resentment and personal disaffection.

It is here that Glikman's book, and others like it, can offer the most valuable corrective. The mature Shostakovich was not a dissident. Nor was he a modernist. The mature Shostakovich was an *intelligent* (pronounced, Russian-style, with a hard *g*). He was heir to a noble tradition of artistic and social thought—one that abhorred injustice and political repression, but also one that valued social commitment, participation in one's community, and solidarity with people. Shostakovich's mature idea of art, in contrast to the egoistic traditions of Western modernism, was based not on alienation but on service. He found a way of maintaining public service and personal integrity under unimaginably hard conditions. In this way he remained, in the time-honored Russian if not exactly the Soviet sense of the word, a "civic" artist.

That was the ultimate irony, and the ultimate victory. Like the silenced Akhmatova and the martyred Mandelstam, Shostakovich, as the American Slavist Clare Cavanagh movingly suggests, managed to bear witness "against the state on behalf of its citizenry."[56] This was perhaps the most honorable civic use to which music has ever been put, a use in which the composer and his audience acted in collusion against authority. Music was the only art that could serve this purpose publicly. Never was its value more gloriously affirmed.

And that is why Shostakovich's music, while easy for advanced musicians in the West to deride, has always tugged at their collective conscience, making it necessary for them to deride it. The extreme social value placed on this music—by official ideology, to be sure, but also by disorderly, "carnivalistic" folk tradition (to borrow again from Bakhtin's rich vocabulary)—has made

---

[56] "The Death of the Book *à la russe*: Poetry under Stalin," paper read at the conference "Shostakovich: The Man and His Age, 1906–1975," 30 January 1994 (an unpublished typescript), p. 14.

the overweening technical preoccupations of the West look frivolous. The present rash of opportunistic efforts—by Volkov, by MacDonald, even by Glikman—authoritatively to define the meaning of Shostakovich's work can only diminish that value. Definitive reading, especially biographical reading, locks the music in the past. Better let it remain supple, adaptable, ready to serve the future's needs.

The significance of Dmitriy Dmitriyevich Shostakovich in and for the history of twentieth-century music is immense, possibly unparalleled, and, above all, continuing. Anyone interested in that history or alive to the issues his work so dramatically embodies will listen to it (*pace* Virgil Thomson) without mind-wandering, unless musical perceptions are wholly divorced from moral perceptions. The fact that his work still looms in our consciousness, while that of so many once better-regarded figures has receded unregretted into Lethe, suggests that the divorce is not yet final. The fate of the music, of its composer, and of the society from which they both emerged have made it, quite apart from its composer's designs or those of any critic, precisely into a bulwark against that divorce. Smug paraphrasts notwithstanding, it is unlikely that we who live in more favored times and places can ever fully come to grips with such a legacy. Given our scholarly and critical interests, this may seem lamentable. In the context of our lives as we live them, it is something to rejoice in.

ENTR'ACTE: THE LESSONS OF LADY M.

I

FOR A nineteenth-century author, one surefire device for exposing social ills was to plant a sweet innocent amid injustice and corruption and condemn the environment by contrast. By Charlie Chaplin's day a hackneyed formula that could be redeemed only by farce, in its prime it had motivated works of seriousness and consequence. (Where would Dickens have been without it?) And though it was usually accomplished by transparent contrivance, the technique fueled the whole movement known as "realism."

The classic example of the maneuver in Russian literature was Alexander Ostrovsky's drama *The Storm*, first performed in 1859 and published the next year in the pages of the *Muscovite* (*Moskvityanin*), one of those legendary "thick journals" at the crossroads of literature, philosophy, and politics, around which the nineteenth-century Russian intelligentsia led its busy life of the mind. Several operas have been based on it in addition to the one by Kashperov discussed in chapter 10; the most famous of them is Janácek's *Kát'a Kabanová* (1921).

Ostrovsky's heroine Katerina Kabanova, the wife of a merchant in an unnamed Volga town, is a sensitive, poetic nature, stifled by the prisonlike atmosphere of her husband's family and particularly by her formidable mother-in-law. She becomes infatuated with another man, succumbs to her passion during her husband's absence on a business trip, is forced by conscience to confess, and is driven by her shame to suicide. Her plight is epitomized in the scene of her husband's departure, when, humiliated by her mother-in-law's insinuations and torn by her guilty forebodings, she insists upon swearing a hysterical oath of fidelity the audience knows she will be unable to keep. After this harrowing scene one can only sympathize with Ostrovsky's unhappy adulteress, however one feels about her crime.

And if, like every educated Russian since 1860, one has read Nikolai Dobrolyubov's famous critique of Ostrovsky's play, one cannot think of Katerina without recalling the essay's title: "A Ray of Light in the Dark Kingdom." The precocious Dobrolyubov (1836–61), deified in the Soviet Union as a protorevolutionary "radical democrat," interpreted the plays of Ostrovsky as a sustained yet futile indictment of patriarchal merchant-class mores. He hailed *The Storm* for at last embodying, in Katerina's suicide, a gesture of protest against the "dark kingdom's" backward, oppressive structure, and a prophecy of its fall. For him, as for Soviet readers and writers, Katerina Kabanova was an early martyr of the revolution.

Of a wholly different order from "realistic" plays and novels, which embodied (or were seen to embody) themes of social protest, was another favorite nineteenth-century genre, the horror story. At the beginning of the century such tales generally concerned the supernatural. By century's end their subject matter had shifted to the opposite extreme: to "naturalism," to lurid yet minutely dispassionate descriptions of aberrant human behavior, crime and brutality viewed as if under the pathologist's microscope. Though it was part of the naturalist's technique to appear to take no sides, in fact the horror story tended tacitly to condemn those who upset the established order, natural (*Frankenstein, Dr. Jekyll and Mr. Hyde*) or social (the novels of Zola). This genre had nothing—even less than nothing—to do with protest.

An early Russian classic of naturalism was Nikolai Leskov's famous "sketch" of ungovernable passion and mayhem, first published in 1865 in *Epokha*, Dostoyevsky's own thick journal, under the title "The Lady Macbeth of Our District." On the work's republication as a book, the district was specified—Mtsensk, in South-Central Russia (Oryol Province), about as close to the middle of nowhere as one could get in a country that had more "nowhere" than any other. The plot shares a number of striking surface features with Ostrovsky's *Storm*. The title character is another childless merchant wife named Katerina, whose life is made miserable by a despotic in-law, and who is left behind when her husband takes a business trip. In the grip of boredom and frustration she too takes a lover.

But Katerina Izmailova does not confess. Rather, she is found out, and by none other than her carping father-in-law. To avoid punishment she murders him. Her husband returns. To avoid having to give up her lover, she murders again, this time with "an evil joy." She marries her lover, Sergey (a clerk at the Izmailov mill), conceives his child, and inherits the family business. A complication arises when another heir to the Izmailov fortune unexpectedly surfaces in the person of her late husband's nephew, a saintly little child. To avoid losing her inheritance she murders for a third time, "as though demons had broken loose from their chains." She and Sergey are apprehended *in flagrante* by a crowd of villagers returning from church (not the subtlest way of contriving a collision with the moral order, but hair-raising in its execution). They are sentenced to hard labor. By now, "light and darkness, good and evil, joy and boredom did not exist" for Katerina. On the way to Siberia, Sergey takes up with another woman. In a paroxysm of despair at losing him Katerina murders yet again: she grabs her rival, Sonyetka, and jumps together with her off a ferry into the icy Volga, thus finally murdering herself.

The last glimpse we get of Leskov's creation likens her to a rapacious animal: "Katerina Lvovna appeared out of another wave, rose almost to her waist above the water, hurled herself at Sonyetka like a big pike at a soft little perch and both of them went under." And this had been the beginning: "In our part of the world one sometimes comes across people of such character that one cannot recall them without a shudder even when many years have elapsed since the last encounter."[1] One could hardly say that Leskov had portrayed the monstrous protagonist of his tight-lipped little shocker with "sympathy," or sought to inspire anything of the kind in his reader.

II

And yet that is just what Dmitriy Dmitriyevich Shostakovich tried to do when, sixty-five years and an October Revolution later, he turned Leskov's sketch into his second (and, as things turned out, his last) opera. In an essay published in the program book for the first production, which had its première at the Little State Opera Theater of Leningrad (*Malïy Leningradskiy Gosudarstvennïy Opernïy Teatr*, or "Malegot") on 22 January 1934, the twenty-seven-year-old composer made three startling assertions. First, "there is no work of Russian literature that more vividly or expressively characterizes the position of women in the old prerevolutionary time" than Leskov's. But second, "Leskov, as a brilliant representative of prerevolutionary literature, could not correctly interpret the events that unfold in his story." Therefore Shostakovich's own task was clear: "in every way to justify Katerina so that she would impress the audience as a positive character."[2]

All this was in stark contrast to Leskov, who assumed a calculated air of detachment, on one level parodying the manner of what in Russia is known as a "procurator," an impartial court officer whose job it is to prepare summaries of evidence for criminal cases. Shostakovich passionately embraced the role of counsel for the defense. His strategy was to exonerate his heroine by indicting her surroundings, to turn her from sinner to martyr (or, in Shakespearian terms, from a Lady Macbeth into a Juliet or a Desdemona). Here is how he made his case to the public, addressing them exactly as an attorney might sum up before a jury: "Katerina is an intelligent, talented, and interesting woman. Owing to the nightmarish circumstances in which life has placed her, owing to the cruel, greedy, petty merchant environment that surrounds her, her life has become sad, dull, gloomy. She does not love her husband, she has no joys, no consolations. And all at once there appears the foreman, Sergey."[3]

Intelligent, talented, interesting . . . this is no Katerina Leskov would have recognized. But Ostrovsky would have known her; and as we read Shostakovich's essay and observe the events of her life as he portrays them, it gradually dawns that he has switched heroines on us. He has undertaken to turn Leskov's naturalistic horror tale into a high-minded realist tract. "It

---

[1] "Ledi Makbet Mtsenskogo uyezda," in Nikolai Semyonovich Leskov, *Povesti i Rasskazï* (L'vov: "Kamenyar," 1986), pp. 110, 150.

[2] "Moyo ponimaniye 'Ledi Makbet,'" in *Ledi Makbet Mtsenskogo uyezda: Opera D. D. Shostakovicha* (Leningrad: Gosudarstvennïy Akademicheskiy Malïy Opernïy Teatr, 1934), p. 6.

[3] Ibid., p. 6.

would be fairest of all," the composer wrote of his heroine, "to say that her crimes are a protest against the tenor of the life she is forced to live, against the dark and suffocating atmosphere of the merchant class in the last century." This goes beyond Ostrovsky, all the way to Dobrolyubov. And sure enough, Shostakovich does not fail to call his Katerina "a ray of light in the dark kingdom."[4]

In the opera itself, the Ostrovsky/Dobrolyubov subtext is again brought right to the surface, when the whole husband's-departure episode from *The Storm* is transplanted into Leskov's plot at the end of the first scene. As Shostakovich (with his co-librettist Alexander Preys) recast it, the scene is much less subtle than in Ostrovsky. Now it is the evil in-law, not the heroine herself, who insists on the oath. And since it comes before the love intrigue has even begun to unfold, it carries no foreboding. Instead of revealing the heroine's fatal ambivalence, it merely intensifies what is already a heavy-handed portrayal of her oppression. Like everything else in the opera, it whitens Katerina by darkening the background.

But how white, finally, can she get? How dark must a kingdom be to turn a multiple murderess into a ray of light? How far can elementary moral principles be relativized? And how did Shostakovich hope to bring it off?

First, he eliminated whatever could not be rehabilitated in Leskov's portrayal of his heroine's behavior. This meant, above all, getting rid of the third of the original Katerina's murders; for, as Shostakovich rather exquisitely put it in his program essay, "the murder of a child, no matter how it may be explained, always makes a bad impression."[5] What remained was freely altered to reserve the moral high ground for the heroine. Instead of being discovered by a group of religious villagers with an upstanding engineer from St. Petersburg at their head, the operatic Katerina's crimes are detected by a "seedy lout" who stumbles upon the corpse of Katerina's husband when he breaks into the Izmailov storeroom to steal some vodka. He eagerly runs off to the local constabulary with the news, singing what Shostakovich, in conversation with the now-exiled Soviet soprano Galina Vishnevskaya would characterize in later (post-Stalinist) years as "a hymn to all informers."[6]

In the next scene the police are portrayed as a venal, degenerate lot who spend their days persecuting "nihilists" instead of protecting the rights of citizens, and who are overjoyed to have a pretext to avenge themselves on Katerina Izmailova for not inviting them to her wedding. In an especially odious interpolation (perhaps prompted by another Leskov story, "Kotin the He-Cow and Platonida"), Shostakovich precedes the father-in-law's discovery of Katerina's adultery with a lecherous soliloquy in which the detestable old man

---

[4] Ibid., p. 8.

[5] Ibid., p. 6.

[6] Vishnevskaya, *Galina*, trans. Guy Daniels (New York: Harcourt Brace Jovanovich, 1984), p. 355.

declares his intention of seducing her himself. The only other figure of potential moral authority in the opera, the priest who is summoned to minister to the poisoned father-in-law, is portrayed even more cartoonishly than the police.

Merely to recite these unsubtle devices is to expose them. In cold verbal summary they cannot make the case for Katerina as victim. Shostakovich knew this very well: "It would be fruitless to argue at length the ways I justify all these crimes, since the real justification is to be found in the musical material; for I consider that in an opera it is the music that plays the main, the leading, the decisive role."[7] Of course it does, but only when the composer is equal to the task. Few composers have been as well equipped for it as Shostakovich. In his second opera he shows himself authentic genius of the genre, fully able—like Verdi, like Wagner, like Musorgsky—to create a world in tone that carries complete conviction. And he used his awesome powers to perpetrate a colossal moral inversion. It could well be the most pernicious use to which music has ever been put, and it gives the eternal lie to formalists who would deny music the ethical and expressive powers of which the ancients speak. In the hands of a genius, Shostakovich's accomplishment declares, the art of music is still the potent, dangerous thing about which Plato was the first to warn, and Tolstoy, perhaps, the most recent.

III

The composer maintains control over the emotional projection and reception of his opera's gruesome subject matter in two ways. First there are the overt editorials, in the form of five interludes connecting all scenes not bounded by intermissions. This kind of unmediated author's intervention was obviously something Shostakovich had learned from the third act of Alban Berg's *Wozzeck* (performed in Leningrad in 1927, long before its migration westward). Like Berg, Shostakovich intrudes despotically to instruct the audience (in Joseph Kerman's words): "This is as he feels about the action, and this is as you too shall feel."[8]

Thus one of Shostakovich's interludes tells us, after we have witnessed Katerina's little wrestling match with Sergey in scene 2, and before their lovemaking in scene 3, that her sexual drive has been mobilized, that it will liberate her, and that we are to rejoice at this. The interlude between the discovery of the corpse and the scene in the police station, a boorish if virtuosically sustained circus cancan, tells us just how we are to feel about Katerina's nemesis, the "seedy lout." The most forcible directive of this kind, and the one most obviously reminiscent of *Wozzeck*, is the searing passacaglia between the two scenes of act 2—that is, between the two Izmailov murders—which bursts upon the farcical episode with the village priest like a

---

[7] *Ledi Makbet Mtsenskogo uyezda: Opera D. D. Shostakovicha*, p. 7.

[8] J. Kerman, "Terror and Self-Pity: Alban Berg's *Wozzeck*," *Hudson Review* 5 (1952): 417.

howl of pain, and which seems to reenact the catharsis Katerina has inwardly experienced (but that her onstage deportment has concealed) upon dispatching her hated father-in-law to the next world.

Yet what is overt may be easily resisted. More insidious is Shostakovich's other method. Evoking a wealth of familiar musical genres, deploying a bewilderingly eclectic range of styles, the composer makes sure that one character, and one character only, is perceived by his audience as a human being. From the very first page of the score, Katerina's music is rhapsodic, soaring, and (most telling) imbued with the lyric intonations of Russian folk song. As the curtain rises to reveal Katerina alone, lamenting her fate, the clarinet plays a characteristic cadential phrase (a leap from the fourth degree to the tonic) that had been characterized as "the soul of Russian music" by Glinka, the first great Russian composer, a century earlier. Katerina's music is the only music in the opera that has emotional "life," as traditionally portrayed by composers in the heyday of romantic opera. Like the emotions themselves, it waxes and wanes; it has rhythmic and dynamic flexibility; it reaches climaxes.

In utter contrast, every other member of the cast is portrayed as subhuman. The police, the priest, the "seedy lout," the other minor characters are all presented as repulsive caricatures, their music reeking of operetta, of the music hall, of military bands and circus parades. The orchestral ritornello that precedes each stanza of the "police station waltz" in act 3 is the most conspicuous reversion to the brash "wrong-note" vein so familiar from Shostakovich's earlier music, like the notorious polka from the *Age of Gold* ballet, where it had caricatured top-hatted capitalists. The priest, officiating over the last rites for Katerina's first victim, is too dim-witted even for wrong notes: he lapses into a polka of his own, all the more absurd because all its notes are "right." When Katerina's father-in-law—usually painted in the darkest orchestral hues and the ugliest, most distorted harmonies—muses lecherously right before discovering her adultery, he does so to the incongruous strains of a Viennese waltz. The seedy lout's solo scene must be the most brazen piece of bordello trash ever authored by a "serious" composer.

Most effective of all, though, is Shostakovich's way of accompanying the singing, and above all, the movements of all figures except Katerina with trudging or galloping ostinatos—inflexibly rigorous rhythmic pulsations that characterize them one and all as soulless, insensate automatons, comic-book creatures, incapable of experiencing or inspiring an emotional response of any kind. This applies even to the chorus, the "people," who are represented in this opera as a cynical, apathetic and (in the last scene) downright heartless mob. It is sheer dehumanization.

The technique operates at its most insidious in the fifth scene of the opera, which portrays the murder of Zinoviy Borisovich, Katerina's husband. Up to now his role in the opera had been a tiny one, confined to the first scene, and culminating in his departure. Shostakovich's music for Zinoviy's farewell to Katerina, which parodies the style of a sentimental salon romance, had portrayed him (in contrast to his despicable father) as well-enough intentioned if ineffectual. Katerina, to say nothing of the audience, is given scant reason to hate him. How then is his murder "justified"?

Strictly, as Shostakovich would say, by the "musical material." The scene begins with Katerina and Sergey blissfully in bed, surrounded by the lushest, most lyrical orchestral music in the opera. Three times this mood is broken: first by Sergey himself (whose music gets more and more operettalike as the opera approaches its dénouement); next, by an apparition of Boris Timofeyich, the first victim; and then by the offstage approach of Zinoviy, signaled by a typically "trudging" ostinato. Once he arrives onstage, the trudge gives way, literally, to a gallop—that is, to that maddest of all nineteenth-century ballroom dances, the "galop," of which Shostakovich was the preeminent twentieth-century master. The whole scene of confrontation and murder is played against its unremitting oompah.

The American composer Elliott Carter saw *The Lady Macbeth of Mtsensk* in Germany in 1960 and found this scene utterly baffling. "The relation of the music to the action is unaccountable," he thought, unable to comprehend the reason why Shostakovich would have "the heroine and her lover strangle her husband on a large stage-sized four-poster bed to a lively dance tune."[9] But by now the reason should be clear enough: the dance tune is there to dehumanize the husband and mitigate the heroine's crime to one of cruelty to animals at worst. What condemns Zinoviy is nothing more than his being a part of Katerina's hated environment. He is dehumanized and dispatched not for anything he has done but for what he is. He is the beneficiary of the social system that oppressed his wife, and that is enough "objectively" to justify his liquidation. And all this is conveyed to us by the music alone. Carried away with that music, we cannot fail to be (at least momentarily) convinced.

IV

And now we know why Shostakovich's opera was hailed by its earliest critics as such a praiseworthy advance over its literary source. As Adrian Piotrovsky, the Malegot dramaturg, put it in the program book, Leskov's story had been "a defense of resignation, a defense of self-denial and human endurance" by "the ideologist of patriarchal petty-bourgeois humility." Shostakovich and Preys had boldly exposed the "latent social truth" hidden within Leskov's naturalistic treatment of his subject and made it "profoundly realistic."[10] Their Katerina was no mere ray of light but the full radiance of the Marxist sun.

---

[9] E. Carter, "Current Chronicle: Germany, 1960," *Musical Quarterly* 46, no. 3 (July 1960); reprinted in *The Writings of Elliott Carter*, ed. Else Stone and Kurt Stone (Bloomington: Indiana University Press, 1977), p. 213.

[10] "Ot povesti Leskova k opere Shostakovicha i k spektaklyu Malogo opernogo teatra," in *Ledi Makbet Mtsenskogo uyezda: Opera D. D. Shostakovicha*, pp. 14, 16.

Translating this into simpler Soviet language, Shostakovich had turned the tale into one of class warfare. Katerina's victims were class enemies, creatures at a lower stage of historical development than she, and she had every right, according to the objective laws of historical materialism, to eliminate them. "Yes, she kills, and kills again," wrote Piotrovsky, who a short time later would collaborate with Shostakovich on the ill-fated ballet *The Limpid Stream*, and afterward would perish in one of the early Stalin purges. Shostakovich, he maintained, "has created the seemingly paradoxical figure of the innocent murderess, a criminal of romantic purity. This he does not in a spirit of humanitarian forgiveness, but rather by means of a wide-ranging, acute analysis of the social reality that surrounds his Katerina."[11]

It was this kind of "analysis" that was being advanced, even as Shostakovich was writing his opera, in defense of the lawless extermination of the "kulaks," peasants who were resisting forced collectivization in the brutal period of the first Five Year Plan. It was a time of hideous moral inversions in all walks of Soviet life, when the high tide of Stalinism was coming in and the basest atrocities were being justified in the name of the loftiest humanitarian ideals. In the year *Lady Macbeth* was completed, little Pavlik Morozov, a well-indoctrinated "pioneer" from a farm near Sverdlovsk, denounced his parents to the secret police as "enemies of the people." Lynched by an outraged mob of peasants, he became a Soviet saint, not to be decanonized until the days of Gorbachev. Shostakovich's Katerina was a heroine of similar stripe. His opera is a faithful reflection of that abominable time, and a memento of it.

V

In one way only was Shostakovich entirely faithful to Leskov; and that was in his frank naturalistic portrayal of Katerina's sexual passion. It is lust, pure and simple, that he portrays; ignited by rape, it turns Katerina into a love slave, quite belying the frequent claim that she is a liberated, aggressive woman in an age of feminine passivity, whose audacity further justifies her crimes. The theme of carnal violence is exaggerated in the opera beyond anything in Leskov. The salacious trombone glissandos that portray Sergey's detumescence achieved instant world fame when the critic of the *New York Sun*, encountering Shostakovich's opera in a concert performance at the old Metropolitan Opera House under Artur Rodzinski, dubbed them an exercise in "pornophony."[12]

Even before the first overt encounter with Sergey, Shostakovich's Katerina is shown to be obsessed with animal sex. Sitting by the window right before her future lover knocks on the door (his gambit—"Have you got anything to

---

[11] Ibid., pp. 14–15.

[12] The word gained national recognition and eventual immortality when it was picked up by *Time* magazine: "The Murders of Mtsensk" (unsigned review), 11 February 1935, p. 35.

read?"—ranks with Siegfried's "Das ist kein Mann" in the annals of unintended operatic humor), she sings:

> The foal runs after the filly.
> The tomcat seeks the female,
> The dove hastens to his mate.
> But no one hurries to me.
> The wind caresses the birch tree,
> And the sun warms it with its heat.
> For everyone there's a smile from somewhere.
> But no one will come to me.
> No one will put his hand round my waist,
> No one will press his lips to mine.
> No one will stroke my white breast,
> No one will tire me out with his passionate embraces.

These words were never sung on stage in Russia until 1996. Along with a few other crude or salty lines, they were censored from the libretto before the première and were also omitted from the score published in 1935. In their place Shostakovich and Preys inserted a hymn to the joys of maternity and conjugal domestic bliss. (The original text was imparted by Shostakovich years later to Vishnevskaya, who recorded the uncensored opera in London in 1979, with her husband, Mstislav Rostropovich, conducting.)

Yet despite this precautionary self-censorship, there was more than enough left to scandalize a lapsed seminarian of the Georgian orthodox church who took in a performance of the chief ornament of the Soviet musical stage during the third year of its triumphant run. His reaction was the first step in the process through which Shostakovich, until then the brash genius of a brash young society, thriving in the din of its social upheavals and pampered by its artistic elite, was transformed into "pain personified," as the post-Soviet composer Sofiya Gubaidulina now remembers him, "the epitome of the tragedy and terror of our times."[13]

In January 1936, a festival of Soviet music was held in Moscow. The Malegot lent its two most successful productions for the occasion. One was *Quiet Flows the Don*, a corny "song opera" composed (with Shostakovich's help, it was rumored) by a hack named Ivan Ivanovich Dzerzhinsky after Mikhaíl Sholokhov's famous novel of the postrevolutionary Civil War. The other was *Lady Macbeth*.

On the evening of the 17th, Stalin and Molotov attended a performance of Dzerzhinsky's opera and, according to a Tass dispatch, called the composer, the conductor, and the director to the royal box, where they "gave a positive

---

[13] Recorded interview, transcribed and published in Elizabeth Wilson, *Shostakovich: A Life Remembered* (Princeton: Princeton University Press, 1994), p. 307.

assessment of the theater's efforts on behalf of Soviet opera and noted the considerable ideological and political merits of the production."[14] On the 26th, the same leaders—together with Soviet culture czar Andrey Zhdanov, and Politburo member Anastas Mikoyan—went to see *Lady Macbeth* in its eighty-fourth performance at the Bolshoy Theater's affiliated theater, the Moscow equivalent of the Malegot. Shostakovich, alerted by a telegram, was in the audience. He left the theater perturbed (as he wrote to his friend Ivan Ivanovich Sollertinsky) about "what happened to your namesake [Dzerzhinsky], and what didn't happen to me."[15] For Stalin and company had left without comment before the end.

Two days later, what soon became known as the Historic Document appeared in *Pravda*, the infamous unsigned editorial of 28 January 1936, "Muddle instead of Music" (*Sumbur vmesto muzïki*), which remains one of the great paradigmatic documents of the buffeting the arts have suffered in modern totalitarian states. At a time when newspaper campaigns were rife against the "left deviationism" of old Bolsheviks, and soon-to-be-carried-out calls for their annihilation were rampant, the same merciless rhetoric of political denunciation was directed, for the first time anywhere, at an artist.

The first target was the opera's obscenity:

> The music croaks and hoots and snorts and pants in order to represent love scenes as naturally as possible. And "love" in its most vulgar form is daubed all over the opera. The merchant's double bed is the central point on the stage. On it all the "problems" are solved. . . . This glorification of merchant-class lasciviousness has been described by some critics as a satire. But there can be no question of satire here. The author uses all the means at his disposal and his power of musical and dramatic expression to attract the sympathy of the spectators for the coarse and vulgar aims and actions of the merchant's wife, Katerina Izmailova. *Lady Macbeth* is popular among bourgeois audiences abroad. Is it not because the opera is so confused and so entirely free of political bias [!] that it is praised by bourgeois critics? Is it not perhaps because it titillates the depraved tastes of bourgeois audiences with its witching, clamorous, neurasthenic music?

Criticism next turned to the opera's modernistic style, the real "muddle instead of music." This can be a hard point for a listener of today to grasp, especially a listener who knows *Wozzeck* or *Lulu* or *Moses und Aron*, or even Shostakovich's own earlier opera *The Nose*. Compared with these, *Lady Macbeth* can seem downright tame—"more consonant, more 'melodic,' and more openly tonal," as Robert P. Morgan has put it.[16] The curiously squeamish last

---

[14] "Beseda tovarishchey STALINA i MOLOTOVA s avtorami opernogo spektaklya 'Tikhiy Don,'" *Sovetskaya Muzïka* 4, no. 2 (1936): 3.

[15] Lyudmila Mikheyeva, "Istoriya odnoy druzhbï," ibid., vol. 55, no. 9 (1987): 79 (letter posted from Arkhangelsk, 28 January 1936).

[16] Robert P. Morgan, *Twentieth-Century Music* (New York: Norton, 1991), p. 246.

phrase suggests that Western critics may even be inclined to regard tonality as something a self-respecting twentieth-century composer keeps under wraps. And if so, it may not be entirely because of "progressivist" stylistic prejudices but also because of the way in which consonant, melodic, "openly tonal" styles have been enforced by bloody twentieth-century dictatorships.

But in the Soviet Union of the 1930s, the frame of reference was different. Music, like everything else, was monitored for its political implications. "Positive heroes" were defined lyrically. Negative characters were defined by dissonance. In *Lady Macbeth*, as we have seen, the only lyricism in evidence is that given the disrupter of the social order. Otherwise the music is indiscriminately caricatural, purposely deforming not only her victims but also, and particularly, her possible judges—the priest, the police, even "the people."

"The composer," *Pravda* ranted, "seems to have deliberately encoded his music, twisted all its sounds so that it would appeal only to aesthetes and formalists who have lost all healthy tastes." And now the threat: "Left deviationism in opera grows out of the same source as left deviationism in painting, in poetry, in pedagogy, in science." In a phrase that must have scared the poor composer half to death, the official organ of Soviet power denounced him for "trifling with difficult matters" and hinted that "it might end very badly."

VI

Dmitriy Shostakovich, until then perhaps Soviet Russia's most loyal musical son, and certainly her most talented one, had been made a sacrificial lamb. Though his opera had no doubt given the Leader and Teacher a genuine pain, it had surely been marked for denunciation and suppression before Stalin ever visited the theater. It was a target precisely by reason of its unprecedented success, and Shostakovich was a target by reason of his preeminence among Soviet artists of his generation, the first to be educated under Soviet power.

However much Katerina's deeds might be justified on an "objective" vulgar-Marxist basis, moreover, her anarchic behavior posed an unacceptable implicit threat to totalitarian discipline. Shostakovich and Preys had failed to grasp that totalitarian power, by whatever means entrenched, is reactionary, terrified of the sort of ungovernable "revolutionary" turbulence the opera appeared to endorse. Stalinist violence, as Shostakovich would discover, was (like everything else Stalinist), planned, orderly, and thoroughly determined in its calculated randomness.

The real purpose of the *Pravda* editorial, then, was to demonstrate how directly the arts were to be subject to Party controls in the wake of what the unsuspecting Shostakovich himself had hailed in the program book as "the historic April resolution." This was an action the Central Committee of the Soviet Communist Party had taken on 23 April 1932, in accordance with which all existing Soviet arts associations were dissolved and replaced with "unions" (of writers, artists, composers, and cinematographers) that were directly answerable to the Party bureaucracy. At first it was greeted by serious artists as a positive move, for it removed from contention with them the clamorous "proletarian" associations that during the twenties had been aggressively denouncing the elite culture.[17]

In fact, the resolution had removed all barriers that might have protected the arts from the naked exercise of Stalin's arbitrary rule. Shostakovich, through his opera, was one of the first victims of the new dispensation; and if, as things turned out, he was spared the ultimate Stalinist fate, he had to live for the next seventeen years and more with the constant threat of "a bad end."[18] That this unhappy man nevertheless continued to function as an artist and a citizen has lent his career a heroic luster no Western counterpart can hope—or wish—to attain.

It is inevitably in that heroic light, a light made garish by the books of Volkov and MacDonald, by the films of Tony Palmer, and by literature of the cold war and of *glasnost'*, that we now view *The Lady Macbeth of Mtsensk*. We know it as the work through which the Soviet Union's great composer was disgraced; a work whose suppression was an incalculable loss, for it spelled the end of what would surely have been one of the great operatic careers; and, finally, a work that had to endure a twenty-seven-year ban before it was cautiously let back onstage, retitled *Katerina Izmailova*, in a bowdlerized version sans pornophony, and with an expanded final scene of convicts en route to Siberia that is fraught with a new and bitter subtext relating to its author's tribulations.

So ineluctably has the opera come to symbolize pertinacious resistance to inhumanity that it is virtually impossible now to see it as an embodiment of that very inhumanity. The fate of *Lady Macbeth of Mtsensk* opened Shostakovich's eyes to the nature of the regime under which he was condemned to live. It could be argued that its martyrdom humanized its creator. And yet it remains a profoundly inhumane work of art. Its technique of dehumanizing victims is the perennial method of those who would perpetrate and justify genocide, whether of kulaks in the Ukraine, Jews in Greater Germany, or aborigines in Tasmania.

So, one must admit, if ever an opera deserved to be banned it was this one, and matters are not changed by the fact that its actual ban was for wrong and hateful reasons. In the liberal West we are opposed in principle to banning works of art, and do not believe that an opera can deserve such a fate. Yet if

---

[17] On Shostakovich's early support for the decree, see *Galina*, pp. 205–6.

[18] According to the composer Venyamin Basner, a close friend, Shostakovich narrowly escaped arrest in the aftermath of the Red Army purge of 1937, when his patron, Marshal Mikhaíl Tukhachevsky, was condemned (recorded interview, transcribed and published in Wilson, *Shostakovich: A Life Remembered*, pp. 123–25).

that is so because we believe that an opera cannot threaten life and morals, then we are perhaps more vulnerable than we imagine to the dehumanizing message of this opera, one of our ghastly century's greatest and ghastliest. If it is because we believe that ethics can have no bearing on aesthetics, then our own dehumanization is already far advanced. If for the sake of its inspired music and its dramatic power *The Lady Macbeth of Mtsensk* is to hold the stage today, it should be seen and heard with an awareness of history, with open eyes and ears, and with hearts on guard.

PUBLIC LIES AND UNSPEAKABLE TRUTH:
INTERPRETING THE FIFTH SYMPHONY

―――――――

PERESTROYKAS AND PERESTROYKAS

THE WORD *perestroyka*, perhaps needless to say, hardly describes what is going on now in the lands of the former Soviet Union. The communist institutions that were to undergo preservative restructuring have ceased to exist. The Union of Soviet Composers is one of them. Composers in the former USSR now face the same grave problems confronted by everyone else who (while complaining of its drawbacks) had become used to the illusive advantages of a command-driven, production-oriented economy, the economy the Gorbachev *perestroyka* had tried and failed to rescue. It is ironic, then, to continue reflecting on the circumstances that attended the union's creation. The decree establishing it, promulgated by the Central Committee of the Soviet Communist Party on 23 April 1932 (and which, as we have seen, Shostakovich at first greeted with enthusiasm), was titled "On the Restructuring [*perestroyka*] of Literary and Artistic Organizations." Unlike Gorbachev's this was an entirely cynical *perestroyka* that had its origin in a political coverup.

The first Five Year Plan, Stalin's great push toward the building of "socialism in one country," was inaugurated in 1928. An orgy of totalitarian coercion in which the country was forced headlong into urban industrialization and rural collectivization, it was a time of unprecedented political and economic violence, replete with show trials, mass arrests and punitive mass starvation, ceaselessly accompanied by a din of mass indoctrination that included the hardening of the Stalin personality cult. As part of the general effort, a

THIS chapter, though given as a Gauss lecture in December 1993, was originally prepared for a conference organized around the theme "Soviet Music toward the 21st Century," which took place on the campus of Ohio State University from 24 to 27 October 1991. Between the planning and the convening, of course, the history of Soviet music came dramatically to an end. The conference, envisioned as a hopeful toast to *perestroyka*, celebrated not the meliorating continuity that Russian word implies but instead a great historical divide fraught with peril and uncertainty. (Speaker after speaker at that unforgettable meeting mounted the podium to voice fears for the survival of institutions supporting the creation and performance of contemporary concert music in Russia, and some saw emigration as the only way to carry on with their lives.) My original assignment had been to narrate in detail the early history of the Union of Soviet Composers, now sketched briefly in the first section of this essay; the decision to focus instead on questions of interpretation was a reaction to the march of events. It was my own *perestroyka* (the Russian for "changing course midstream" being *perestroyit' sya na khodu*). For furnishing the immediate pretext to do a job that had been long simmering within me, and for generously allowing me to follow my impulse, I thank Margarita Mazo, the organizer of the conference.

cultural revolution was set in motion. In December 1928 the Central Committee passed a resolution establishing ideological controls over the dissemination of art and literature, and placing members of proletarian organizations in charge of the organs of dissemination and training. In music, executive power was concentrated by decree in the hands of the so-called RAPM, the Russian Association of Proletarian Musicians.

This was the period during which the Moscow Conservatory was renamed the Felix Kon School of Higher Musical Education (*Vïsshaya muzïkal'naya shkola im. F. Kona*), after the editor of the newspaper *Rabochaya gazeta*, the Workers' Gazette.[1] A nonmusician, Boleslaw Przybyszewski, the doctrinaire Marxist son of the Polish decadent writer Stanislaw Przybyszewski, was installed as rector. The composers Myaskovsky, Glière, and Gnesin, stalwarts of the old, prerevolutionary musical elite, were denounced and fired from the faculty. Grades and examinations were abolished, and admission restricted to students of acceptable class background. Ideologists of the RAPM like the young Yuriy Keldïsh consigned the composers of the past wholesale to the dustbin of history, excepting only Beethoven, the voice of the French revolution, and Musorgsky, the proto-Bolshevist "radical democrat." Chaikovsky, virtual court composer to Tsar Alexander III, was a special target of abuse. Composers were exhorted to spurn all styles and genres that had flourished under the Tsars and cultivate instead the only authentically proletarian genre, the marchlike *massovaya pesnya*, the "mass song," through which proletarian ideology could be aggressively disseminated. The only politically correct concept of authorship was collective, epitomized in the so-called Prokoll (*Proizvodstvennïy kollektiv*), a group of Moscow Conservatory students who banded together to produce revolutionary operas and oratorios that were in essence medleys of mass songs.

The joyous declaration of a prematurely successful completion to the first Five Year Plan was the leadership's way of retreating from a ruinous situation without admitting error. The country was in misery—a misery that could be conveniently blamed on local administrators and "wreckers" in the case of the real tragedies such as forced collectivization (hence the show trials), and on survivals of "left" deviationism on the intellectual and artistic fronts. The reining-in of the proletarian cultural organizations became necessary in order to regain the good will of an alienated intelligentsia, but especially in order to woo back émigré luminaries like Gorky and Prokofiev, who were fearful of proletarianist opposition. (Prokofiev, whose eventual decision to return to Soviet Russia had been sparked by the triumphant success of his first post-emigration visit in 1927, had been frightened off by the RAPM, which all but wrecked his second tour in 1929.) So the same party that had installed the

---

[1] Juri Jelagin, *The Taming of the Arts* (New York: Dutton, 1951), pp. 188–90; Yuriy Keldïsh, *100 let Moskovskoy Konservatorii 1866–1966* (Moscow: Muzïka, 1966), pp. 127–29.

proletarianists at the beginning of the Cultural Revolution now suppressed them in the name of benign *perestroyka*. The RAPM and its sister organizations in the other arts were dissolved, and replaced by all-encompassing unions of art workers. The Union of Soviet Composers was established at first in Moscow and Leningrad, and over the next sixteen years grew geographically and organizationally to encompass the entire country, becoming fully centralized just in time for the Zhdanovshchina, the musical show trials of 1948.

At first the 1932 *perestroyka* was seen and touted (like Gorbachev's, at first) as a liberalizing move, for it meant the removal from the scene of the fractious radicals who since Lenin's time had hectored Soviet artists of the academic tradition (as well as their heirs, the elite modernists), and who had lately been allowed to tyrannize them. Now the radicals were stripped of power and their leaders forced to make satisfying public recantations.[2] Nominal power reverted to the old guard, from whose standpoint the 1932 *perestroyka* meant salvation from chaos and obscurantism—an obscurantism that was now officially labeled *levatskoye* ("left," for which read "Trotskyite") and thus politically tainted.[3] The grateful old professors were given back their classrooms and installed as willing figureheads in the organizational structure of the union—along, eventually (and very significantly), with the pupils of their pupils. To all appearances, the Composers' Union was a service organization, even a fraternal club.

The real power, of course, lay elsewhere, and the real purpose of the organization, though this was not immediately apparent, was to be a conduit of centralized authority and largesse. As the guarantor of its members' right to work, as the channeler of state patronage through commissions (*kontraktatsiya*, as it was called), and as dispenser of material assistance through the so-called Muzfond, the union was ostensibly engaged in protecting the interests of composers, but by the same token it was implicitly endowed with the power to enforce conformity.[4] The union's chief social functions were the so-

[2] See the article by two leading RAPMists, Lev Lebedinsky and Viktor Belïy (the latter the editor of the RAPM organ, *Za proletarskuyu muzïku*), entitled "Posle aprelya: Sovetskoye muzïkal'naya pod'yom" ("After April: The Soviet Musical Upsurge"), *Sovetskoye iskusstvo*, no. 22 (1933). Lebedinsky (1904–93) lived long enough to take part in the recent Shostakovich debates: see "O nekotorïkh muzïkal'nïkh tsitatakh v proizvedeniyakh D. Shostakovicha," *Novïy mir*, no. 3 (March 1990): 262–67 (on Shostakovich's use of musical quotations and in particular about the meaning of the "invasion theme" in the Seventh Symphony); the article was later attacked in *Pravda* by the composer Yuriy Levitin ("Fal'shivaya nota, ili Grustnïye razmïshleniya o delakh muzïkal'nïkh" [11 November 1990]; Lebedinsky's rebuttal ["O chesti mastera: vozvrashchayas' k teme"] was published in the issue of 19 March 1991).

[3] See "Vïvodï po chistke yacheyki VKP(b) Moskovskoy Gosudarstvennoy Konservatorii v 1933 g.," *Sovetskaya muzïka* 1, no. 5 (1933): 161–64.

[4] For organizational details see the report by Levon Atovm'yan, "God rabotï Soyuza sovetskikh kompozitorov," ibid., pp. 131–41. A similar report for Leningrad, by A. Ashkenazi, appeared in ibid., vol. 2, no. 6 (1934): 61–64.

called internal *pokazï*—meetings at which composers submitted their work in progress to peer review in the spirit of idealistic "Bolshevik self-criticism"[5]— and open forums at which composers and musical intellectuals shared the floor discussing topics like Soviet opera or "symphonism" for eventual publication in *Sovetskaya muzïka*, the union's official organ, which began appearing early in 1933.

Acting through an Organizational Bureau set up to implement the April decree, the Central Committee installed one Nikolai Ivanovich Chelyapov (1889–1941) as chairman of the Moscow union and editor of *Sovetskaya muzïka*. He was not a musician. A jurist by training, Chelyapov was an all-purpose bureaucrat (what in Soviet jargon was called an *obshchestvennïy deyatel'*, a "public figure") by profession. He functioned as a sort of middle manager, presiding at meetings, articulating official policy in his editorials, and organizing the union's formal activities. From the beginning of 1936 he reported directly to the future Ministry of Culture, then called the All-Union Committee on Artistic Affairs (*Vsesoyuznïy komitet po delam iskusstv*), a subdivision of the Sovnarkom, the Council of People's Commissars (later the Council of Ministers). Centralized totalitarian control of the arts was now complete. The command structure was in place. The next year Chelyapov, a superfluous Old Bolshevik, shared the general fate of his cohort. He disappeared into Lethe, not to be mentioned again in print until the 1960s.

For the new control system was one of the many harbingers of the coming storm, and the Composers' Union assumed the role for which it had been created. It all happened very dramatically. The February 1936 issue of *Sovetskaya muzïka* opened with what editor Chelyapov called "three historic documents," consisting of the TASS communiqué, quoted in the previous chapter, reporting a friendly conversation between comrades Stalin and Molotov and the creators of the opera *The Quiet Don* (composer Ivan Dzerzhinsky, conductor Samuil Samosud, and the director M. A. Tereshkovich), and two unsigned editorials reprinted from *Pravda*, both of them vilifying one composer, not yet thirty years old: "Muddle instead of Music" (*Sumbur vmesto muzïki*) attacked Shostakovich's wildly successful opera *The Lady Macbeth of the Mtsensk District*, and "Balletic Falsehood" (*Baletnaya fal'sh*) denounced his ballet *The Limpid Stream*, then in the repertory of the Bolshoy Theater. These articles were indeed historic documents. They were unprecedented, not because of the militant philistinism for which they are chiefly remembered but because they are couched in terms of political denunciation and threats of violence, indistinguishable in diction from the scattershot attacks on the so-called "Zinovievite faction" that had by then become

---

[5] See Victor Gorodinsky and Vladimir Iokhelson, "Za bol'shevistskuyu samokritiku na muzïkal'nom fronte," ibid., vol. 2, no. 5 (1934): 6–12, where the internal review of Shostakovich's *Lady Macbeth* is described in detail. (The authors express dissatisfaction at the lack of aggression on the part of the critics and at the lack of receptivity on the part of the composer.)

ubiquitous in the Soviet press in advance of the great show trials of 1937 and 1938. Shostakovich was simultaneously accused of *levatskoye uródstvo*—"left deformation"—and "petit-bourgeois" sympathies.

Needless to say, his union offered Shostakovich the very opposite of protection. For what the *Pravda* editorials signaled above all was an end to even the semblance of public debate or discussion. The March and May issues of *Sovetskaya muzïka* were devoted practically in toto to zealous ratification of the attack, in a manner exactly paralleling the unanimous endorsement of war whoops against the "Zinovievites" that had been appearing in *Sovetskaya muzïka*, as in every other Soviet publication, since the middle of 1935.

The format of the old union "discussions" was retained, but only as a vehicle for a campaign of organized slander. Under the heading "Against Formalism and Falsehood" (*Protiv formalizma i fal'shi*), the members of the Moscow and Leningrad unions were marched to the rostrum one by one in the February days following the second of the *Pravda* editorials to deliver denunciations of their fallen colleague and fulsome praise of the historic documents. The mobilization of such demonstrations of "solidarity" would henceforth be among the unions' paramount functions. The dire period thus ushered in was hailed as a new *perestroyka*.[6]

Among the individual contributions to the "discussions," two stand out as especially poignant and revealing. Maximilian Steinberg, Rimsky-Korsakov's son-in-law and successor as professor of composition at the Leningrad Conservatory, took the floor to declare that "insofar as he was my best pupil . . . the drama of Shostakovich is my personal drama, and I cannot look with indifference upon what my pupil is going through in his creative work." The tone is quickly modulated, however, into one not of defense but of personal exculpation and distance, illustrating the quintessential Stalinist theme: the fraying of the social fabric in the face of fear. "The utmost expression of Shostakovich's 'new' direction was his 'Aphorisms' [for piano, Op. 13 (1927)]," Steinberg testified. "When Shostakovich came to me with the 'Aphorisms,' I told him that I understood nothing in them, that they are alien to me. After this he stopped coming to see me."[7] In Moscow, the twenty-two-year-old Tikhon Khrennikov spoke for "the rising generation of Soviet composing youth": "How did the youth react to *Lady Macbeth*? In the opera there are some big melodic numbers that opened up for us some creative vistas. The entr'actes and a lot of other things called forth total antipathy. In general, our youth is healthy. A certain faction has succumbed to formalist influences, but this is being overcome; it does not represent any principal objective on our part."[8] The oldest generation and the youngest were being deployed as pincers

---

[6] "Na vïsokom pod'yome," ibid., vol. 4, no. 7 (1936): 4–12.

[7] "Protiv formalizma i fal'shi: Vïstupleniye tov. SHTEYNBERGA," ibid., vol. 4, no. 5 (1936): 38.

[8] "Protiv formalizma i fal'shi: Vïstupleniye tov. KHRENNIKOVA," ibid., vol. 4, no. 3, (1936): 45.

against the most vital one, as represented by its outstanding member, who had been chosen as sacrificial victim not only as a demonstration of the might of Soviet power but because his precocious fame and his phenomenal talent had made him the object of the greatest envy.

CODE WITHOUT KEY

That is enough about the phoney *perestroyka*. It is an ugly story and a much-rehearsed (if still underdocumented) one, and I have recalled it only as preface to the *perestroyka* that is my subject, Shostakovich's own. That story is very much worth telling, because we do not fully understand it yet, and because its many repercussions still affect our lives.

We do not fully understand it, and perhaps we never will, because no one alive today can imagine the sort of extreme mortal duress to which artists in the Soviet Union were then subjected, and Shostakovich more than any other. The only possible analogy is to the experience of condemned prisoners or hostages or kidnap victims. The nearest thing to it in the prerevolutionary history of the arts in Russia was the case of Dostoyevsky, who, condemned to death for political subversion and granted a last-minute reprieve, became a fervent believer in the Russian autocracy and a religious mystic. The nearest parallel in today's world is the case of Salman Rushdie, whose response to dire death threats has included reconfirmation in the faith of his oppressors.

It is with thoughts like these in mind that I want to examine Shostakovich's Fifth Symphony, notoriously designated "a Soviet artist's creative response to just criticism" and first performed in Leningrad on 21 November 1937, in the midst of mass arrests, disappearances, and executions. Its tumultuous, ecstatic reception has become legend. It led to the composer's rehabilitation—or would have, were it not that his forgiveness was surely just as foreordained as his fall. Thanks to the system of *pokazï* and the need for securing performance clearance from the Committee on Artistic Affairs, Shostakovich's work was known on high before its public unveiling. Its status as apology and as promise of a personal *perestroyka* was a conferred status, bestowed from above as if to show that the same power that condemned and repressed could also restore and reward.

Shostakovich's rehabilitation became an opportunity for fulsome official self-congratulation. "One feels that Shostakovich has been through and thought through a great deal," wrote Mikhail Mikhailovich Gromov, the polar aviator and Hero of the Soviet Union, who in a fashion so typical of the day was serving as all-purpose Party mouthpiece. "He has grown as an artist. His growth, one cannot doubt, was abetted by stern, just criticism."[9] "Shos-

---

[9] M. Gromov, "Zametki slushatelya (O 5-y simfonii D. Shostakovicha)," ibid., vol. 6, no. 3 (1938): 29. (The quoted comment echoes the one attributed to the composer; see the text that follows.) One can still find similar heartless claims in the literature on Shostakovich, though now

takovich is a great, truly Soviet artist," wrote the very *partïynïy* critic Georgiy Khubov on behalf of the union in its official organ. He was at pains to note that Shostakovich's *perestroyka* went beyond mere style to the profoundest levels of consciousness.[10] The theme of ongoing personal *perestroyka*, beginning precisely with the Fifth Symphony, was sounded again a year later by Yuliy Kremlyov, writing in the official organ about Shostakovich's First String Quartet.[11] The word continued to resound in Soviet critiques of the Fifth Symphony to the end of the Stalin period.[12]

The same critics who wrote about Shostakovich's *perestroyka* also wrote about his "realism," which gives a clue to their meaning. By realism, of course, they meant socialist realism. The theory of socialist realism has always been an occult subject, especially when applied to music. The critic Victor Gorodinsky had tried, soon after its coining, to explicate it theoretically in the very first issue of *Sovetskaya muzïka*,[13] only to have his waffling efforts derided by none other than Shostakovich in the days when the union still functioned as something resembling a forum.[14] Over the next few years the idea had been roughly defined in practice. The recipe, to put it bluntly and oxymoronically, was heroic classicism.

That Soviet reality required a monumental scale and a high rhetorical tone for its proper celebration was an old proviso. It had been the topic of Chelyapov's first sermon as editor of *Sovetskaya muzïka*. Distinguishing the union's aims from the program of the old discredited RAPM—no mean task, actually—Chelyapov fastened on scale. "At a time," he sneered, "when proletarian literature was giving us great canvases of socialist construction, beginning with Gladkov's *Cement* and [Serafimovich's] *The Iron Flood* [*Zheleznïy potok*], continuing with *The Quiet Don*, [Panfyorov's] *Ingots* [*Bruskí*], and so forth, . . . in the realm of music we were told: large forms are something for the future; now let us work on the small forms of mass song; first vocal works, afterward we will get to writing instrumental music."[15] One might say that the future of Soviet music, fated to preserve in a totalitarian

---

only in the uncomprehending West—cf. Malcolm Barry, "Ideology and Form: Shostakovich East and West," in Christopher Norris, ed., *Music and the Politics of Culture* (New York: St. Martins Press, 1989), p. 181: "If, for example, a substantial body of expert opinion declared that the revision [of *Lady Macbeth* as *Katerina Izmailova*] was a finer work (based on whatever criteria), might there not have to be a revision of the critical commonplace about the reprehensibility of 'Chaos instead of Music'? Could it be that the intervention, brutal and traumatic as it was, might have been *helpful* to the *composer*, even within the context of a 'value-free' approach to the music *as such*?"

[10] "5-aya simfoniya D. Shostakovicha," *Sovetskaya muzïka* 6, no. 3 (1938): 14–28.

[11] "Strunnïy kvartet D. Shostakovicha," ibid., vol. 7, no. 11 (1939): 46–54.

[12] See, for example, Ivan Martïnov, *Dmitriy Shostakovich* (Moscow: Muzgiz, 1946), p. 43.

[13] "K voprosu o sotsialisticheskom realizme v muzïke," *Sovetskaya muzïka* 1, no. 1 (1933): 6–18.

[14] "Sovetskaya muzïkal'naya kritika otstayot," ibid., vol. 1, no. 3 (1933): 120–21.

[15] "O zadachakh zhurnala 'Sovetskaya muzïka,'" ibid., vol. 1, no. 1 (1933): 5.

aspic all the mammoths and mastodons of the Western classical tradition—the program symphony, the oratorio, the grand historical opera—was decided right here.

Except for his withdrawn Fourth Symphony, Shostakovich's Fifth was his first really heroic symphonic work. And while the unconventionally structured, maximalistic Fourth had been grandiose (or so the composer would later put it) to the point of mania, it was anything but "classical"—which is exactly why it could not be performed in the aftermath of his denunciation. For it was precisely at this point, the very apex of political pressure, that Soviet composers were first directed to emulate *russkaya klassika* as a timeless model, signifying a return to healthy, "normal" musical values after the excesses of early-Soviet modernism.[16] With its ample yet conventional four-movement form, even down to an improbably minuetish scherzo, its unextravagant yet sonorous scoring, and its notable harmonic restraint, the Fifth Symphony amounted to a paradigm of Stalinist neoclassicism, testifying, so far as the powers were concerned, to the composer's obedient submission to discipline. It was time to reward him.

The immediate reward was an orgy of public praise (later there would be Stalin prizes and titles and honorary posts). It went on for months, to the point where Isaak Dunayevsky, the songwriter who was then president of the Leningrad Composers Union, tried to apply the brakes. On 29 January 1938, the day of the Moscow première, he circulated a memorandum comparing the Fifth's reception to a stock speculation, a ballyhoo, even a psychosis that threatened to lead Soviet music into a climate of "creative laissez-faire" in which the union might not be able to exercise its police function.[17] (It was inevitable that Shostakovich's Sixth Symphony would meet a hostile reception—and so his career would go on, yo-yo fashion, practically to the end.) Typical of the composer's official welcome back into the fold (and typical as well of the tone of groveling civic panegyric that inevitably accompanied Soviet public rhetoric) was a pronouncement by the composers Anatoliy Alexandrov and Vasiliy Nechayev: "A work of such philosophical depth and emotional force," they wrote, "could only be created here in the USSR."[18]

---

[16] See Anna Shteynberg, "Pushkin v tvorchestve sovetskikh kompozitorov," ibid., vol. 5, no. 1 (1937): 53–59. The Pushkin centenary, first marked at the Union of Soviet Composers with a conference on 11 and 12 December 1936, was the occasion for the earliest explicit exhortations to revive "classical" models.

[17] Sofiya Khentova, *Molodïye godï Shostakovicha*, vol. 2 (Leningrad: Sovetskiy kompozitor, 1980), p. 192. The political threat was overt: referring to Leonid Entlelis's remarks (see n. 27), Dunayevsky warned against any suggestion that "the Party may have wrongly judged Shostakovich's work, that there had been no formalist high-jinks, no muddle, but just the innocent mistakes of youth." (My thanks to Laurel Fay for Dunayevsky's text.)

[18] "Vpechatleniya slushateley," *Muzïka*, 26 November 1937; quoted in Genrikh Orlov, *Simfonii Shostakovicha* (Leningrad: Muzgiz, 1961), p. 64.

There were many, both at home and abroad, who willingly granted the last point, though not necessarily in a spirit of praise. The symphony's manifest philosophical and emotional freight, far more than its traditional form, made not only it but Soviet music generally seem backward and provincial to many Western musicians in an age of burgeoning formalism. Many will recall how bitterly Igor Stravinsky mocked it in his Harvard lectures of 1939, later published as *Poetics of Music*. And he mocked it through the prism of the famous review by Count Alexey Tolstoy—"a consummate masterpiece of bad taste, mental infirmity, and complete disorientation in the recognition of the fundamental values of life," as Stravinsky described it—in which the celebrated Soviet novelist attempted an inventory of that philosophical and emotional cargo:

> Here we have the "Symphony of Socialism." It begins with the *Largo* of the masses working underground, an *accelerando* corresponds to the subway system; the *Allegro*, in its turn symbolizes gigantic factory machinery and its victory over nature. The *Adagio* represents the synthesis of Soviet culture, science, and art. The *Scherzo* reflects the athletic life of the happy inhabitants of the union. As for the *Finale*, it is the image of the gratitude and the enthusiasm of the masses.[19]

"What I have just read to you is not a joke which I myself thought up," Stravinsky assured his audience. But this was true only to the extent that the joke had been thought up not by Stravinsky himself but by his ghostwriter, Pierre Souvtchinsky. Yet for over half a century now Stravinsky's jape has been believed, even though as fabrications go it is very crude, with the movements misnamed and in the wrong order.[20] Stravinsky has been believed not only because he was Stravinsky (hardly an assurance), and not only because one is ready to attribute any sort of statement about music to a literary man (especially one named Tolstoy), but because we accept the notion that Shostakovich's symphony not only invites but requires an interpretation, if not this particular one. More than that, it is obvious that there is no way of rejecting the kind of interpretation Stravinsky derides (whatever we may make of the given reading), without rejecting the music outright.

So before addressing the vital matter of interpreting Shostakovich's Fifth, before examining past interpretations (beginning with Tolstoy's actual one) or proposing new ones, it is worth reopening briefly, and from a somewhat narrowed perspective, the question that pervaded the first section ("Shostakovich

---

[19] Igor Stravinsky, *Poetics of Music in the Form of Six Lessons*, trans. Arthur Knodel and Ingolf Dahl (Cambridge, Mass.: Harvard University Press, 1970), pp. 153–55.

[20] James Billington actually reproduced Stravinsky's parody, accepting it at face value as "Alexis Tolstoy's paean to Shostakovich's Fifth Symphony as the 'Symphony of Socialism,'" as a paradigm to illustrate "the role of music in the Stalin era." See *The Icon and the Axe: An Interpretive History of Russian Culture* (New York: Vintage, 1970), p. 478.

and Us") of this chapter, and inquire into just what it is that makes interpretation of Shostakovich's Fifth Symphony so necessary.

Like the symphonies of Mahler, with whom Shostakovich is constantly compared, and the late ones of Chaikovsky (only recently rehabilitated in the Russia of the purge years, and shortly to be deified on his centenary), Shostakovich's Fifth Symphony self-evidently belongs to the tradition established in the wake of Beethoven's Ninth, whereby the music unfolds a series of components, gestures, or events that are immediately recognizable as signs or symbols, but signs and symbols whose referents are not specified by any universally recognized and stable code (though they may, and obviously do, participate to some finally undeterminable extent in such codes).[21] Such signs are often said to exist on two broad levels, defined as "syntactic" vs. "semantic," or, following Russian formalism, as "introversive" vs. "extroversive," related in "Shostakovich and Us" to the familiar interpretive levels of "manifest content" and "latent content."[22] Syntactic or introversive signs are those with referents that are perceived to lie within the boundaries of the work itself. In the case of music they include reprises, transformations, and recombinations of previously heard events or gestures such as motives and themes, culminating in broad sectional repeats and "recapitulations." Semantic or extroversive signs are those with referents that lie outside of the work in which they occur. They cover a range all the way from primitive onomatopoeia to imitation of speech to metaphors, at times quite subtle, of physical motion or distance or modes of temporality (time consciousness). Very often they invoke other music, whether by allusion to specific pieces or by more general reference to "topics," genres, and styles.

But this distinction—syntactic vs. semantic, introversive vs. extroversive—can be maintained only in theory. It is not usually possible, or even desirable, to distinguish them in practice, in the actual act of listening. While thematic or motivic recurrences are in themselves defined as syntactic, their interpretation often depends on semantic codes. The climactic unisons at figure 36 in the first movement of Shostakovich's Fifth, for example, derive their significance equally from both perceptual spheres. Their loudness speaks—or shouts—for itself. At the same time, they remind us of the famous passages *all'unisono* in Beethoven's Ninth, with which Shostakovich's symphony shares its key. These are obviously extroversive references (or, to be precise, intertextual ones). But hardly less significant is the fact that the climactic unisons are a reprise of some of the quiet music from the first thematic group (cf. the music from figure 3 to figure 5). That may be a syntactic feature, but

---

[21] For a fuller discussion of Beethoven's role in establishing this stylistic and critical heritage, see R. Taruskin, "Resisting the Ninth," *19th-Century Music* 12, no. 3 (Spring 1989): 241–56.

[22] For extensive discussion of the musical significance of this distinction, see V. Kofi Agawu, *Playing with Signs: A Semiotic Interpretation of Classic Music* (Princeton: Princeton University Press, 1991), chapters 2 and 3.

the huge contrast in dynamics and texture asks to be read semantically, in relation to some mimetic or iconic convention. Another apparently syntactic observation concerns the tonal significance of the passage at figure 36: it marks the arrival at the tonic key after a long series of modulations and an elaborate preparation. Yet when we recognize the effect as that of a sonata-form recapitulation, which we think is an introversive observation, we are instantly reminded of other recapitulations and of their expressive effect—semantics again.

To pick another example: surely the most conspicuous structural or syntactic peculiarity of the symphony as a whole is its use of a pervasive rhythmic cell, presented interchangeably as dactyl or anapest, unifying all four movements. Yet the same feature is simultaneously a heavily laden intertextual reference to Beethoven's Fifth Symphony and its motivic "dramaturgy," to use the Soviet jargon. Add to that an exceptionally wide-ranging panoply of suggestive generic or topical references (pastoral, rustic, military, religious)—again curiously paralleling those in Beethoven's Ninth—plus a network of specific allusions that includes conspicuous self-reference as well as more oblique yet still specific reference to passages in works by other composers, and it is clear that this symphony is a richly coded utterance, but one whose meaning can never be wholly encompassed or definitively paraphrased.

Given the conditions in Russia in 1937, this last was a saving, not to say a lifesaving, grace. It opened up the work to varying readings, which is precisely what made for the seeming unanimity of response at its première. Each listener could inscribe a different, personalized construction on the work's network of references and participate, as a result, in the same general enthusiasm. The process of continual, heavily fraught inscription and reinscription has gone on to this day, surely one of the circumstances that has kept the Fifth, of all of Shostakovich's symphonies, the most alive. The obvious questions: What constrains interpretation? What validates or invalidates a reading? What, finally, does the symphony mean? Answers cannot be asserted from general principles—at least, none I've ever seen—only deduced from practice and from the specific case.

"ALL THAT I HAVE THOUGHT AND FELT"

The most obvious early constraint was the symphony's inescapable relationship to its composer's recent life experience (viz., the 1936 denunciations), a connection almost immediately bolstered by the composer's public testimony, amounting to a plea—not to say a demand—that the symphony be read as autobiography. This "conferred status," as I would call it, surely furnished Alexey Tolstoy—the real Count Tolstoy, not the one invented by Stravinsky—with the point of departure for his very influential critique. Solomon Volkov, speaking through the first-person voice in *Testimony*, has speculated that the article was ghostwritten by "musicologists . . . summoned to Tolstoy's dacha [who] helped him through the morass of violins and oboes and other confusing things that a count couldn't possibly fathom."[23] In fact, the review, which avoids all technicalities, is just what might have been expected from a writer. Combining the autobiographical assumption with what he must have taken to be the "Beethovenian" mood sequence of the symphony's four movements (Beethoven, that is, construed in his "revolutionary" guise), Tolstoy assimilated the music to a literary prototype: the Soviet *Bildungsroman*, a very popular genre of the period, exemplified by such prestigious books as Valentin Katayev's *I Am the Son of Laboring Folk* (*Ya—sïn trudovogo naroda*), on which Prokofiev would later base his opera *Semyon Kotko*, or Nikolai Virtá's *Loneliness* (*Odinochestvo*), on which Khrennikov would base his opera *Into the Storm*, or—most famous of all—Nikolai Ostrovsky's *How the Steel Was Tempered* (*Kak zakalyalas' stal'*). These novels concerned the formation of new consciousness—personal *perestroyka*—on the part of "searching heroes," honest blunderers whose life experiences teach them to embrace revolutionary ideals.

Tolstoy viewed the composer of the Fifth Symphony as such a one, and proceeded to paraphrase the work in terms of the catchphrase *stanovleniye lichnosti*, "the formation of a personality (within a social environment)." In the first movement the author-hero's "psychological torments reach their crisis and give way to ardor," the use of the percussion instruments suggesting mounting energy. The second movement, a sort of breather, is followed by the most profound moment, the Largo. "Here the *stanovleniye lichnosti* begins. It is like a flapping of the wings before takeoff. Here the personality submerges itself in the great epoch that surrounds it, and begins to resonate with the epoch." The finale is the culmination, in which "the profundity of the composer's conception and the orchestral sonority coincide," producing "an enormous optimistic lift," which, Tolstoy reports (and his report is corroborated), literally lifted the spectators out of their seats at the first performance, many of them before the piece was over.[24] That response, Tolstoy averred, was at once proof that his reading of the symphony was correct, and proof that the composer's *perestroyka* was sincere: "Our audience is organically incapable of accepting decadent, gloomy, pessimistic art. Our audience responds enthusiastically to all that is bright, optimistic, life-affirming."

[23] Solomon Volkov, *Testimony: The Memoirs of Dmitri Shostakovich*, trans. Antonina W. Bouis (New York: Harper and Row, 1979), p. 224.

[24] "Pyataya simfoniya Shostakovicha," *Izvestiya*, 28 December 1937, p. 5. For descriptions of the reactions of the audience at the première, see Jelagin, *The Taming of the Arts* pp. 167–68 (thirty-minute ovation); A. N. Glumov, *Nestertïye stroki* (Moscow, 1977), p. 316, quoted in Khentova, *Molodïye godï Shostakovicha*, vol. 2, p. 186 (rising from seats during finale); Isaak Glikman, ". . . Ya vsyo ravno budu pisat' muzïku," *Sovetskaya muzïka* 57, no. 9 (1989): 48; *Pis'ma k drugu*, p. 14 (open weeping during the third movement).

The whole review, in fact, is one enormous tautology, not only for the way the audience reaction is construed, but because it amounts throughout to a rehash of ready-made socialist-realist clichés. Compare, for example, a passage from a speech the former RAPMist critic (and union boss) Vladimir Iokhelson delivered at one of the Leningrad meetings at which *Lady Macbeth of Mtsensk* had been denounced the year before. Socialist realism, Iokhelson proclaimed,

> is above all a style of profound optimism. The whole historical experience of the proletariat is optimistic in essence. And we can and must affirm that optimism is intended as an obligatory feature of this style, its very essence. It is a style that includes heroics, but a heroics that is not merely tied to narrow personal interests. Here we mean a heroics of an individual connected with the mass, and of a mass that is capable of bringing forth such a hero. It is necessary that the connection between the hero and the mass be made intelligible.[25]

"A mass that is capable of bringing forth such a hero . . ." Tolstoy ended his review with a toast, not to Shostakovich but to "our people, who bring forth such artists."

No wonder Tolstoy's review was influential. Its tenets were, to quote Iokhelson, obligatory. And no wonder, then, that the composer was among those whom it "influenced," for Shostakovich was quick to seek (or to be granted) its protection. In an article that appeared over the composer's name in a Moscow newspaper shortly before the first performance in the capital— its headline, "My Creative Response," became the symphony's informal subtitle—we read: "Very true were the words of Alexey Tolstoy, that the theme of my symphony is the formation of a personality. At the center of the work's conception I envisioned just that: *a man* in all his suffering. . . . The symphony's finale resolves the tense and tragic moments of the preceding movements in a joyous, optimistic fashion." That man, the symphony's hero, is explicitly identified with the composer and his recent past: "If I have really succeeded in embodying in musical images all that I have thought and felt since the critical articles in *Pravda*, if the demanding listener will detect in my music a turn toward greater clarity and simplicity, I will be satisfied." A special effort was made to dissociate the symphony's "tense and tragic moments" from any hint of "pessimism":

> I think that Soviet tragedy, as a genre, has every right to exist; but its content must be suffused with a *positive idea*, comparable, for example, to the life-affirming ardor of Shakespeare's tragedies. In the literature of music we are likewise familiar with many inspired pages in which [for example] the severe

---

[25] "Tvorcheskaya diskussiya v Leningrade," *Sovetskaya muzïka* 4, no. 4 (1936): 5–15.

images of suffering in Verdi's or Mozart's Requiems manage to arouse not weakness or despair in the human spirit but courage and the will to fight."[26]

In keeping with this last idea, Shostakovich's Fifth was assimilated to yet another factitious literary model. At a special performance for Leningrad Party activists, the musicologist Leonid Entelis first attached to it a phrase that would become another unofficial emblem, one that perfectly summed up the whole oxymoronic essence of socialist realism: recalling Vsevolod Vishnevsky's bombastic play about Bolshevik maritime heroism during the Civil War, Entelis declared Shostakovich's symphony an "optimistic tragedy."[27]

HERMENEUTIC FOLKLORE

Thus the official reading. The author of *Testimony* was of course at special pains to repudiate it, especially as concerned the "joyous, optimistic" finale:

> I think that it is clear to everyone what happens in the Fifth. The rejoicing is forced, created under threat, as in *Boris Godunov*. It's as if someone were beating you with a stick and saying, "Your business is rejoicing, your business is rejoicing," and you rise, shaky, and go marching off, muttering, "Our business is rejoicing, our business is rejoicing." What kind of apotheosis is that? You have to be a complete oaf not to hear that.[28]

As a matter of fact, this was not news. People did hear that, and even wrote about it—but in private or obliquely. It, too, was a standard, if at first hidden, interpretation, which eventually reached public print in the Soviet Union around the time of the so-called post-Stalin "thaw." Volkov mentions Alexander Fadeyev, the head of the Writers Union, whose diary, published posthumously in 1957, contains his reaction to the 1938 Moscow première: "A work of astonishing strength. The third movement is beautiful. But the ending does not sound like a resolution (still less like a triumph or victory), but rather

---

[26] "Moy tvorcheskiy otvet," *Vechernyaya Moskva*, 25 January 1938, p. 30. It is often stated that the "subtitle" was Shostakovich's own, but near the beginning of this article there is a specific statement to the contrary: "Among the often very substantial responses [*otzïvï*] that have analyzed this work [after its Leningrad performances], one that particularly gratified me said that 'the Fifth Symphony is a Soviet artist's practical creative answer to just criticism' [*pyataya simfoniya—eto delovoy tvorcheskiy otvet sovetskogo khudozhnika na spravedlivuyu kritiku*]." I have not seen this comment or review, nor (rather strangely, in view of its significance) has it been traced to its source in the huge subsequent literature. One might therefore suspect that Shostakovich coined his symphony's sobriquet after all, then cautiously attributed it to an unnamed reviewer or discussant. But to assume this would be to assume that Shostakovich was in fact the author of the article that appeared over his name, and that of course is a great deal to assume.

[27] Quoted in Khentova, *Molodïye godï Shostakovicha*, vol. 2, p. 187.

[28] *Testimony*, p. 183.

like a punishment or vengeance on someone. A terrible emotional force, but a tragic force. It arouses painful feelings."[29]

Four years after this avowal appeared in print, the musicologist Genrikh Orlov, who has since emigrated from the USSR, came forth with the startling suggestion—of a type unheard of in Soviet criticism—that the composer's own commentary be set aside. "It is well known," he argued, "how often the objective results of a creative effort fail to coincide with the artist's subjective intentions. And if pretentious conceptions often lead to insignificant results, so, more rarely, a modest autobiographical theme may assume the dimensions of a broad generalization about life." Avoiding any awkwardly direct challenge to the veracity of Shostakovich's commentary, still less to its authenticity, Orlov nonetheless succeeded in challenging its relevance. The symphony's great strength, he asserted, lay in its ability "to engrave in broad artistic generalizations the typical ideas, sensations, conflicts, and hopes of its epoch."[30]

That was letting in a great deal between the lines. Over the five years that had elapsed since Khrushchev's "secret speech" at the twentieth Party congress, the "epoch" of Shostakovich's Fifth Symphony had received a far harsher public evaluation in the Soviet Union than was possible before. The subtext to Orlov's remarks was unmistakable. And there was more:

> In the years preceding the creation of the Fifth Symphony, Shostakovich had grown not only as a master but as a thinking artist-citizen. He grew up together with his country, his people, sharing their fate, their aspirations and their hopes, intently scrutinizing the life around him, sensing with all his being its inner pulse."[31]

This places an altogether new and different construction on "My Creative Response," with its famous allusion to "all that I have thought and felt since the critical articles in *Pravda*." Shostakovich's last Soviet biographer, writing under less liberal conditions than Orlov had enjoyed, went farther yet, managing through a fleeting aside at once to enlarge the ambit of Orlov's interpretation of the symphony and to project it onto the early audiences. "Shostakovich had created a universal portrait," wrote Sofiya Khentova. "The people of the thirties recognized themselves, grasping not only the music's explicit content but also its general feeling."[32]

---

[29] *Za tridtsat' let* (Moscow: Sovetskiy pisatel', 1957), p. 891; quoted in G. Ordzhonikidze et al., eds., *Dmitriy Shostakovich* (Moscow: Sovetskiy kompozitor, 1967), p. 43. The Ordzhonikidze collection also contains the 1966 memoir by Yevgeniy Mravinsky ("Tridtsat' let s muzïkoy Shostakovicha," pp. 103–16) that occasioned the Brahms-like animadversion in *Testimony*; it will be quoted in what follows.

[30] Orlov, *Simfonii Shostakovicha*, pp. 68–69.

[31] Ibid., pp. 69–70.

[32] Khentova, *Molodïye godï Shostakovicha*, vol. 2, p. 189.

This was classic "Aesopian" language, describing what was undescribable: a symphony that spoke the unspeakable. We can understand it only if we make the requisite adjustments, translating "people of the thirties" as "people in the grip of the Terror"; "explicit content" as "official interpretation"; "general feeling" as "unstated message." And that is why they wept, then stood up and cheered, grateful for the pain.

There are contemporary witnesses to this reaction, the most explicit, if somewhat tentative, from a defector, the violinist Juri Jelagin, who had attended the première:

> Later when I tried to analyze the reason for the devastating impression the Fifth Symphony made on me and on the entire audience I came to the conclusion that its musical qualities, no matter how great, were by themselves not enough to create that effect. The complex background of events and moods had to combine with the beautiful music of the Fifth Symphony to arouse the audience to the pitch of emotion which broke in the Leningrad auditorium. . . . The Soviet Government had set the stage for the incredible triumph of the gifted composer with long months of persecution and with the senseless attacks on his work. The educated Russians who had gathered in the auditorium that night had staged a demonstration expressing their love for his music, as well as their indignation at the pressure that had been exerted in the field of art and their sympathy and understanding for the victim.[33]

"The complex background of events and moods . . ." Jelagin, from his musician's perspective, construed it narrowly. For a fuller contemporary reading of the symphony's "broad artistic generalizations," we must turn to what on its face seems the unlikeliest of sources.

Georgiy Khubov's review, first delivered orally at an official Composers Union "discussion" on 8 February 1938 (eleven days after the Moscow première), was published in the March issue of the union's official organ. Adopting the repellent tone and language of officious bureaucracy, the union reviewer began by chiding those who had overpraised the symphony in their eagerness prematurely to exonerate the composer from all the old ideological charges. His overall strategy was to compare Shostakovich's actual musical performance with the Tolstoy-derived platitudes affirmed over his signature in the Moscow press, and to note the ways in which the music fell short of the stated goals. Pointedly, and very significantly, Khubov fastened on the "static and drawn out" Largo (which the author of "My Creative Response" had called the movement that best satisfied him), protesting the way other critics had overemphasized and overrated it. "The problem of the *stanovleniye lichnosti*," Khubov pompously concluded, "viewed from the point of view of

---

[33] *The Taming of the Arts*, pp. 167–68. Jelagin's memoir was finally published in the Soviet Union in the weekly *Ogonyok* in October 1990.

genuine tragedy—that is, tragedy informed by a *life-affirming idea*—is in point of fact resolved in Shostakovich's symphony (the Largo and the finale) only *formally*, in any case inorganically, with great strain."

The symphony, the critic declared, was an attempt to find a way out of existential "loneliness" (again compare Nikolai Virtá's *Bildungsroman*), a loneliness stated as a dialectical thesis in the first movement's first thematic group (dubbed the "epigraph theme"). The masterly development depicts the composer's "strenuous contest" with his alienation until a powerful proclamation of the epigraph theme—the massive unisons described above—temporarily stills the struggle. So far the critic entirely approves, as he approves of the scherzo, where in place of the composer's former manner ("specious urbanity, flaunting of cheap effects") there are "new traits of fresh, hearty humor, naivety, and even tenderness."

Now the problems begin. Khubov calls the Largo a "poem of torpidity," (*poèma otsepeneniya*), in which "a pallor of deathly despondency reigns." According to the terms of Shostakovich's stated program, this cannot be called tragic, "since the truly tragic in art can only be expressed by great, inwardly motivated struggle, in which the high life-affirming idea plays the decisive role, determining the bright outcome through catharsis." Complaint is piled upon complaint with unbelievable repetitiveness, the tone meanwhile turning sinisterly prosecutorial:

> Precisely this is what the Largo lacks. And therefore, for all the expressivity of its thematic material, for all its crushing emotional impact on the listener, the third movement lowers precipitously the high level of symphonic development [attained in the first movement]. . . . The listener had a right to expect a further, even more determined dramatic development of the symphony's underlying idea. But instead the composer has revealed to the listener with naked candor a motionless little world of subjectively lyrical sufferings and . . . tearful apothegms. Instead of a great symphonic canvas . . . he has set out an expressionistic etching depicting "numb horror."
>
> Let us put it to the author straight out: what does it say, where does it lead, . . . this numb, torpid Largo? Could it be an organic link in the process of the life-affirming *stanovleniye lichnosti*? Even the composer could hardly give an affirmative answer to this question. For what he shows with such expressionistic exaggeration in his Largo is torpidity, numbness, a condition of spiritual prostration, in which the will is annihilated along with the strength to resist or overcome. This numbness, this torpidity is the *negation* of the life-affirming principle. This is clear to all and does not require any special proof. . . . What is the way out? What is the ultimate solution going to be?

The finale. The "answer," as "My Creative Response" had put it, "to all the questions posed in the earlier movements." The critic is obdurate:

It breaks in upon the symphony *from without*, like some terrible, shattering force. . . . Having analyzed the third movement, we understand that Shostakovich had no other choice; for there was no way to develop that mood of torpidity and bring it to life affirmation. It could only be *broken*. . . . And this function the main theme of the finale fulfills. It definitely makes an impression, and no small one. But at the same time, precisely because of its unexpectedness, its lack of logical preparation, it *lacks conviction*. . . . And similarly lacking in conviction, therefore, is the loud coda with its hammering over a span of thirty-five measures at the opening motive of the main theme in D major! . . . A perceptive, attentive listener feels all the while that this theme is not the result of an organic development of the symphony's idea, that for the composer this theme is the embodiment of a superb but *external*, elemental, subjugating force . . .

And that is why the general impression of this symphony's finale is not so much bright and optimistic as it is severe and threatening.[34]

Solomon Volkov could not have put it better. Khubov, writing from the depths of the Stalinist freeze, leads his "perceptive, attentive listener" to all the unmentionable truths adumbrated by Orlov and Khentova after the thaw, and stated outright (but to himself alone) by Fadeyev, all the while proclaiming their falsehood. By insisting on the probity of "Shostakovich's" commentary, he exposes its untruth. He and Orlov have a common strategy; they both dwell upon the music's incongruity with the stated program. Where Orlov could risk upholding the music, Khubov must uphold the muddle. But both rely on "the complex background of events and moods" to right the score. I do not think it merely wishful to see in Khubov's bullying review—the work of a critic who remained a Party stalwart to the end, who was widely suspected of having helped draft the *Pravda* editorials of 1936, and whom therefore Isaak Glikman, half a century later, still remembered as a "reptilian musician"[35]—a rich vein of rhetorical ambiguity inviting readerly irony—in short, of doublespeak as classically defined.[36]

SOUND EVIDENCE

Confronted with two diametrically opposing perspectives on the symphony, the one public and canonical, the other a sort of folk tradition that could be

---

[34] Georgiy Khubov, "5-ya simfoniya D. Shostakovicha," *Sovetskaya muzïka* 6, no. 3 (1938): 14–28.

[35] *Pis'ma k drugu*, p. 323.

[36] Khubov was careful to conclude on an explicitly positive note so as to mitigate the risk of his review being read as a political denunciation (doubly an embarrassment if official approval, as suggested above, had been mandated): the symphony, despite its flaws, "tells us that the composer has decisively thrown over all tawdry formalistic affectation and stunt, has made a brave turn onto the high road of realistic art. Sincerely, truthfully, with great force of unfeigned feeling he has told his own story in the Fifth Symphony, the story of his recent doleful meditations and perturbations, of his inward, strenuous and complicated creative struggle" ("5-ya simfoniya D. Shostakovicha," p. 28).

only alluded to or hinted at, it is fair to assume that nowadays few will hesitate to choose the second. But is it only Kremlinological habit or bourgeois prejudice that so inclines us? Is there evidence to support the choice?

There is, of course, and Khubov even cites it for us. "Numb horror" . . . "torpidity" . . . "spiritual prostration, in which the will is annihilated along with the strength to resist or overcome" . . . these were the dominant moods of the Yezhovshchina, the peak purge years, as a whole library of émigré, samizdat, and *glasnost'*-inspired memoirs by now openly attests. Anna Akhmatova, in the prose preface she added in 1957 to the poem "Requiem," which she began composing mentally in 1935, chose the very same word that Khubov so conspicuously overused—*otsepenenie*, "torpidity"—to characterize the mood that reigned in the endless queues of women that gathered daily at the prisons of Leningrad to learn the fates of their arrested loved ones.[37] The "life-asserting principle" demanded by the theorists of socialist realism, and embodied in such exemplary musical compositions of the period as Dunayevsky's *Marsh èntuziastov* (with which Shostakovich's symphony was often invidiously compared, incredible as that may seem), or with Vasiliy Lebedev-Kumach's "Song of the Motherland" (*Pesnya o rodine*, 1935), the egregious mass song that Akhmatova parodied in the verse dedication of her "Requiem"[38]—that was the public lie. Count Tolstoy and the author of "My Creative Response," writing virtually without reference to musical particulars, enthusiastically identified the symphony with the public lie. Khubov, whose ostensively chilly review is full of musical examples and precise descriptions, managed, wittingly or unwittingly, to identify the work with the unmentionable truth.[39]

One could go much farther with description—farther than any Soviet writer before the officially proclaimed age of *glasnost'* dared go—toward identify-

[37] The preface (actually titled "Vmesto predisloviya," or "In place of a preface") in full: "In the terrible years of the Yezhovshchina I spent seventeen months in the Leningrad prison lines. One day someone 'fingered' me. Then the blue-lipped woman standing behind me, who of course had never heard my name, roused herself out of the torpor [*ot otsepeneniya*] we all shared and whispered in my ear (everyone there spoke in whispers): 'But can you describe this?' And I said, 'I can.' Then something like a smile slid across what had once been her face." Anna Akhmatova, *Sochineniya*, 2d ed. (Munich: International Literary Associates), vol. 1, p. 361.

[38] See Susan Amert, "Akhmatova's 'Song of the Motherland': Rereading the Opening Texts of *Rekviem*," *Slavic Review* 49 (1990): 374–89.

[39] Glikman seems to allege that the composer (reacting, perhaps, to its rhetorical camouflage or to the author's reputation) was put out by Khubov's interpretation of the Largo, though many ambiguities in the wording of the relevant passage defeat evaluation of the claim: "One day Dmitriy Dmitriyevich thrust toward me a magazine that had fallen into his hands and pointed to a page on which I read that the trouble with the Largo was its coloration of 'deathly despondency.' Dmitriy Dmitriyevich said nothing about this 'revelation' by the famous critic, but his face very graphically reflected a bewildered question" (". . . Ya vsyo ravno budu pisat' muzïku," p. 48; *Pis'ma k drugu*, p. 15). On the same page Glikman records that at the first performance "I was shaken to see that during the Largo . . . many, very many were weeping: both women and men" (cf. n. 24).

ing the Largo with publicly inexpressible sentiments. The movement is saturated with what, adopting the familiar Soviet jargon, we might call the "intonations" and the "imagery" of leave-taking and of funerals, ironically disguised by the suppression of the brass instruments (anyone who has attended a Soviet secular funeral with its obligatory lugubrious brass quintet will know what I mean). But that very suppression works together with multiple extroversive references to invoke the all-vocal Orthodox obsequy, the *panikhida*. At figure 86 the imitation is so literal that you can almost hear the string instruments intone the *vechnaya pamyat'* (Eternal Remembrance), the concluding requiem hymn (example 14.1). This near-citation comes in the second half of the movement, in the midst of a process that could be described thus: "The solo instruments of the orchestra file past . . . in succession, each laying down its . . . melody . . . against a . . . background of tremolo murmurings." That is Stravinsky's description, from his *Chroniques de ma Vie*, of his *Pogrebal'naya pesn'*, the funerary chant he composed in memory of Rimsky-Korsakov.[40] Performed once only, in 1909, it is now lost and obviously can have had no influence on Shostakovich. But it was a representative of a distinct genre of Russian orchestral pieces that Shostakovich surely did know: in memory of Rimsky-Korsakov there were also compositions of this type by Glazunov and Steinberg, Shostakovich's teachers, and there were also well-known "symphonic preludes," as the genre was called, in memory of the publisher Mitrofan Belyayev, the arts publicist Vladimir Stasov, and others. They all quoted from the *panikhida*; it was a defining attribute of the genre.

In the Largo of Shostakovich's Fifth, the evocation of the *panikhida* comes amid a sequence of woodwind solos—first the oboe, then the clarinet (accompanied by flutes), then the flute, all accompanied by a steady violin tremolo. The melody these instruments play resonates neither with the orthodox liturgy nor with Russian folk song (as some Soviet writers have maintained), but with Mahler—specifically, with two movements from *Das Lied von der Erde*: "Der Einsame im Herbst" (The Lonely One in Autumn), and, of course, "Der Abschied" (The Farewell) (example 14.2). That Shostakovich's movement was a mourning piece cannot be doubted—and surely was not doubted, though it could not be affirmed openly. It has been suggested that the movement was a memorial to Mikhail Nikolayevich Tukhachevsky, Marshal of the Soviet Union and Shostakovich's protector, whose infamous execution—now the very emblem of the Yezhovshchina and perhaps its single most terrifying event—had taken place during the symphony's gestation. But why limit its significance? Every member of the symphony's early audiences had lost friends and family members during the black year 1937, loved ones whose deaths they had had to endure in numb horror.

The agony of suppressed grief comes to the fore in a searing fortissimo at

---

[40] Igor Stravinsky, *An Autobiography* (New York: Norton, 1962), p. 24.

EXAMPLE 14.1

a. Shostakovich, Symphony no. 5, third movement, figure 86

b. *Obikhod notnogo tserkovnogo peniya,* ed. N. I. Bakhmetev (St. Petersburg: Pridvornaya pevcheskaya Kapèlla, 1869), vol. 2, p. 330, transposed up a semitone to facilitate comparison

EXAMPLE 14.2. Mahler, *Das Lied von der Erde,* second movement ("Der Einsame im Herbst"), one bar after figure 3; and sixth movement ("Der Abschied"), two measures after figure 41

figure 90, when the farewell melody is transferred to the cellos, the clarinets reinforcing the liturgical tremolo, and the double basses emitting violent barks of pain (to which only Leonard Bernstein's, among recorded performances, have done justice).[41] One would think no one could miss the significance of this passage, but someone did. Prokofiev, a composer of prodigious invention and facility but a man of small feeling, sent Shostakovich a grudging note of congratulations on the Fifth, reproaching him however for one detail: "Why so much tremolo in the strings? Just like *Aida*."[42]

As for the finale, the quality of intrusion from without, which Khubov found "severe and threatening" and therefore unconvincing as optimistic life affirmation, applies not only to the beginning, in which the brass section, silent throughout the Largo, bursts in upon and destroys its elegiac mood. It is explicitly confirmed within the movement. The long, quiet stretch in the middle, from 112 to 121 (and could it be a coincidence that it is cast in the key of B♭ major, the alternative tonality of Beethoven's Ninth and the key of its visionary slow movement?), culminates, at figure 120, in self-quotation, the violins, and later the harp, alluding to the accompaniment to the final quatrain in Shostakovich's setting of Pushkin's poem "Rebirth" (*Vozrozhdeniye*, Op. 46, no. 1), composed immediately before the Fifth Symphony, Op. 47 (example 14.3).

In this poem a painting that had been defaced but is restored by time is compared to a spiritual regeneration: "So," the final quatrain runs, "do delusions vanish from my wearied soul, and visions arise within it of pure primeval days" (*Tak ischezayut zabluzhden'ya / s izmuchennoy dushi moyey, / i voznikayut v ney viden'ya / pervonachal'nïkh, chistïkh dney*). The image suggests not the promise of a bright future but an escape into the past.[43] When the local tonic chord is resolved as a submediant to the dominant of the main key in the restless six-four position; when that dominant, A, is hammered out by the timpani as a tattoo, reinforced by the military side drum, over a span of fifteen measures; and when the woodwinds bring back the main theme to the

---

[41] Particularly worthy of recommendation is Columbia MS 6115 (1959), with the New York Philharmonic, recorded immediately after returning from a Soviet tour in which the orchestra had performed the symphony in the composer's presence.

[42] M. G. Kozlova, ed., *Vstrechi s proshlïm*, vol. 3 (Moscow: Sovetskaya Rossiya, 1978), p. 255.

[43] The point is worth insisting on, since the English-language literature on Shostakovich, however it has construed the passage, has consistently relied on the inaccurate rendering of Pushkin's quatrain in George Hanna's translation of David Rabinovich's *Shostakovich* (Moscow: Foreign Languages Publishing House, 1959), p. 49: "And the waverings pass away / From my tormented soul / As a new and brighter day / Brings visions of pure gold." See, inter alia, Ian MacDonald, *The New Shostakovich* (Boston: Northeastern University Press, 1990), p. 132. In a radio talk delivered in January 1993, the composer and Shostakovich scholar Gerard McBurney made the intriguing observation that the first four notes of the "menacing" main theme of the finale coincide in pitch (and almost in rhythm) with the first four notes of the song, which carry the words *khudozhnik-varvar*, "artist-barbarian." See Elizabeth Wilson, *Shostakovich: A Life Remembered*, p. 127, n. 32.

EXAMPLE 14.3

a. Shostakovich, Symphony no. 5, fourth movement, figure 120

accompaniment of a pedal on all four horns (the whole maneuver replaying the approach to the coda in the finale of Chaikovsky's Fourth Symphony), the effect is that of puncture, of sudden encroachment (of the present, of unsettling objective reality, of the "artist-barbarian") on that subjective escape into the past. The resulting affect of grim passivity mounts into ostensible resolution as the coda is approached.

That coda, emulating a whole genre of triumphant "Fifth Symphony" finales from Beethoven's to Chaikovsky's to Mahler's, has been a special bone

EXAMPLE 14.3, *continued*

b. Shostakovich, *Vozrozhdeniye* ("Rebirth"), Op. 46, no. 1, mm. 18–29 (end)

of interpretive contention from the beginning. Many musicians have found it—like Chaikovsky's and Mahler's!—simply inadequate or perfunctory: Myaskovsky, writing to Prokofiev (describing rehearsals he had attended) shortly before the Moscow première, pronounced it "altogether flat."[44] Yevgeniy Mravinsky, the conductor of the première, offended the author of *Testimony* when, comparing the finale of the Fifth with that of the masterly Tenth (where "there is a full synthesis of the objective and the subjective"), he wrote that in the earlier work

> Shostakovich makes a great effort to make the finale the authentic confirmation of an objectively affirmative conclusion. But in my view this confirmation is achieved to a large extent by external devices: somewhere in the middle of the movement the quick tempo spends itself and the music seemingly leans against some sort of obstacle, following which the composer leads it out of the cul-de-sac, subjecting it to a big dynamic buildup, applying an "induction coil."[45]

Untouched by the Forces of Evil?

The question, of course, is whether the coda fails on purpose, as, in the wake of *Testimony*, many writers now contend. Is the ultimate meaning of the symphony, or its method, one of mockery? Behind that question lurks a much larger one; for if we claim to find defiant ridicule in the Fifth Symphony, we necessarily adjudge its composer, at this point in his career, to have been a "dissident." That characterization, popular as it has become, and attractive as it will always be to many, has got to be rejected as a self-gratifying anachronism.

There were no dissidents in Stalin's Russia. There were old opponents, to be sure, but by late 1937 they were all dead or behind bars. There were the forlorn and the malcontented, but they were silent. Public dissent or even principled criticism were simply unknown. "People's minds were benumbed by official propaganda or fear," Adam B. Ulam has written, continuing: "How could there be any public protest against the inhuman regime when even a casual critical remark to an old acquaintance would often lead to dire consequences, not only for the incautious critic but for his family and friends?"[46]

Precisely with the collapse of Soviet power and the opening up of the past has come (or should come) the painful realization that the repressive Stalinist

---

[44] S. S. Prokofiev and N. Ya. Myaskovsky, *Perepiska* (Moscow: Sovetskiy kompozitor, 1977), p. 455.

[45] "Tridtsat' let s muzïkoy Shostakovicha," p. 109. Of course the Tenth has an equally famous "finale problem" (see David Fanning, *The Breath of the Symphonist: Shostakovich's Tenth* [RMA Monographs, no. 4; London: Royal Musical Association, 1989], chapters 5 and 6).

[46] Review of Yuri Orlov, *Dangerous Thoughts: Memoirs of a Russian Life*, *New York Times Book Review*, 7 July 1991, p. 6.

apparatus left few of its hostages uncoopted. It is all too convenient to forget that pervasiveness now. "Anyone who did not wish to take part" in the evil of those days, as honest late- and post-Soviet writers admit, "either left this world or went to the Gulag."[47] The warning is most often addressed to those who would accuse their fathers, but it applies with equal pertinence to would-be romanticizers.

Dissidence resulted from the loosening of controls, not the other way around. It began very mildly, under Khrushchev, with circumspect critiques of the bureaucracy like Vladimir Dúdintsev's novel *Not by Bread Alone* (1956); it gained momentum with *samizdat* (clandestine self-publication in typescript) and *tamizdat* (unauthorized publication abroad), and only flared into open conflict when the Brezhnevite regime tried to reinstitute Stalinist controls (most visibly in the 1966 trial of Andrey Sinyavsky and Yuliy Daniel for *tamizdat*) but lacked the will or the wherewithal to reinstitute full Stalinist repressions. Even so, outspoken anti-Communism—as against specific policy critique, vindication of victims, or defense of the historical record—did not make its real debut until the Gorbachev years. Even Solzhenitsïn preached explicit anti-Communism only from abroad. And yet Shostakovich is now portrayed, both in Russia and in the West, as if he had done so at the height of the Terror.

It is natural that latter-day dissidents would like him for an ancestor. It is also understandable, should it ever turn out that Shostakovich was in fact the author of *Testimony*, that he, who though mercilessly threatened never suffered a dissident's trials but ended his career a multiple Hero of Socialist Labor, should have wished, late in life, to portray himself in another light. The self-loathing of the formerly silent and the formerly deluded has long been a salient feature of Soviet intellectual life. But genuine dissidents like Sakharov and Solzhenitsïn, having paid for their dissent with reprisals, have not been ashamed to admit that they had once been silent or deluded. Lev Kopelev, the exiled scholar, confessed to having as an idealistic young Communist participated enthusiastically in forced collectivization, starvation tactics, and denunciations during the winter of 1932–33. In a chilling passage from his memoirs, he even admitted to having collaborated—precisely out of misguided idealism—with the secret police.[48]

<hr>

[47] Andrey Ustinov, "Pravda i lozh' odnoy istorii" ("The Truth and Falsehood of a Certain Story"—concerning the authorship of "Muddle instead of Music"), *Muzïkal'noye obozreniye* (July–August 1991): 3, trans. David Fanning.

[48] Lev Kopelev, *To Be Preserved Forever*, trans. Anthony Austin (Philadelphia: Lippincott, 1977), p. 111: "The GPU representative at the factory, a stern but good-natured veteran of the Cheká, would often visit us in he evenings, asking us to take note of the workers' attitudes, keep an eye out for kulak propaganda, and expose any remnants of Trotskyist and Bukharinist thoughts. I wrote several reports on conditions at the plant, although there was little I told him that I had not already said at meetings or written in our paper. My editorial colleagues did the same. The GPU man would chide us for our frankness in public. 'Don't you see, now they'll hide

Yet now that the dissidents have won, it seems nobody ever really believed in the Soviet way of life. Commonplace now are media interviews in which comfortably situated post-Soviet intellectuals and celebrities like Tatyana Tolstaya or Vasiliy Korotich, to say nothing of the egregious Yevtushenko, blandly assure their interlocutors that everyone had always seen through everything.

It is to that pharisaical pretense, so forgetful of the way things were in the Soviet Union until so very recently, that Shostakovich is now being eagerly assimilated. How pleasant and comforting it is to portray him as we would like to imagine ourselves acting in his shoes. For a vivid illustration of the process, we need only survey chronologically a few readings of one of the most striking pages in the Fifth Symphony—the march episode in the first movement's development section (figures 27–29)—beginning with Alexey Tolstoy, who like General Grant evidently knew only two tunes (one the "International," the other not). For him, a march was a march. "It is like a short discharge of the whole orchestra's breath," he wrote, "foreshadowing the symphony's finale, a finale of grandiose optimistic exaltation."[49]

For those who could actually hear music, and could appreciate the march's discordance and its harsh timbre, there could be no question of optimism. The interpretations grow progressively more negative. Alexander Ostretsov, writing in 1938, saw frustration: "In this passage all human willpower and fortitude are concentrated, but they can find no outlet."[50] For Georgiy Khubov, committed to an autobiographical reading, the march epitomized "the sharply dynamic, troubled, anxious character of the development (and of the whole first movement), some kind of strained craving to find *within oneself* the positive, life-affirming strength of creative victory."[51] Ivan Martïnov, in the mid-1940s, comparing Shostakovich's methods to Chaikovsky's (in the *Symphonie pathétique*) or Scriabin's (in the Ninth Sonata), calls the march a "tragic grotesque. . . . In this transformation of the main theme there is something incongruous. It is like a monstrous mask, a deformed grimace frozen on one's face."[52]

By the Khrushchev period, as we have seen, the symphony's meaning had been divorced from autobiography. Genrikh Orlov interprets the march as "the source of tormenting premonitions," a generalized, disembodied "image of aggression and annihilation," suggesting that, in contradistinction to the

---

things from you—they'll give you a wide berth. No, fellows, you've got to learn Chekist tactics.' These words didn't jar us. To be a Chekist in those days seemed worthy of the highest respect, and to cooperate secretly with the Cheká was only doing what had to be done in the struggle against a crafty foe."

[49] "Pyataya simfoniya Shostakovicha," *Izvestiya*, 28 December 1937, p. 6.

[50] "Pyataya simfoniya Shostakovicha," *Sovetskoye iskusstvo*, 2 February 1938.

[51] *Sovetskaya muzïka* 6, no. 3 (1938): 21–22.

[52] *Dmitriy Shostakovich*, p. 46.

Seventh Symphony, which treats of actual military conflict, the Fifth concerns the struggles "of daily life, and within the human soul, the struggle that defines the essence of life." He, too, sees Shostakovich's march in terms of a tradition—the tradition of Berlioz's "Marche au supplice" from the *Symphonie fantastique*, or the menacing fanfares in Chaikovsky's Fourth Symphony. In all of these symphonies, "the moment of the decisive onslaught of the forces of evil is given a martial, bellicose character."[53] By the time of Khentova's biography, of which the relevant volume was published in 1980, the march has been effectively pigeonholed. She calls it, simply, "the march of the forces of evil," and, contradicting Orlov, equates its purpose and effect with those of the invasion episode in the Seventh Symphony.[54]

It remained for the post-*Testimony* literature to define those forces. The definition is altogether predictable, but the assertive self-assurance with which it is advanced is nevertheless extraordinary. Ian MacDonald, whose colorfully written recent book puts him at the forefront of this latest revisionism, has brought the Emperor's-new-clothes rhetoric of *Testimony* to a supreme pitch. His commentary on the Fifth Symphony is riddled with intimidating echoes of Volkov's Shostakovich ("You have to be a complete oaf . . . ," etc.). Here is how he paraphrases the lengthy passage that proceeds from the march episode on into the recapitulation:

> A startling cinematic cut sends us tumbling out of the world of abstraction and into representation of the most coarsely literal kind. We are at a political rally, the leader making his entrance through the audience like a boxer flanked by a phalanx of thugs. This passage (the menace theme dissonantly harmonised on grotesquely smirking low brass to the two-note goosestep of timpani and basses) is a shocking intrusion of cartoon satire. Given the time and place in which it was written, the target can only be Stalin—an amazingly bold stroke.
>
> The appearance of the Vozhd [Leader] evokes an extraordinary musical image of obeisance, the orchestra thrumming the one-note motto in excited unison before bowing down to the symphony's keynote D. . . . At the peak of a wildly struggling crescendo, [the main theme's] basic two-note component abruptly, and with vertiginous ambiguity, turns into a flourish of colossal might on drums and brass, punctuating a frenzied unison declamation of the motto rhythm. . . . There can be absolutely no doubt that introspection plays no part in this, that it is objective description—Shostakovichian, as opposed to Socialist, realism.
>
> As this declamatory passage ends, the brass and drums de-crescendo in triumph on the three-note pattern from bar 4, as if grimly satisfied with their brutalisation of the rest of the orchestra and of the symphony's earnestly questing opening bars, all elements of which have been deformed during this convulsion. Over the thrumming rhythm, flute and horn now converse in a major-key trans-

---

[53] *Simfonii Shostakovicha*, pp. 80–82.
[54] *Molodïye godï Shostakovicha*, vol. 2, p. 181.

position of the second subject: two dazed delegates agreeing that the rally had been splendid and the leader marvellous. (A typical stroke of black comedy here has the horn doggedly copying everything the flute says, to the point of reaching for a B clearly too high for it.)[55]

Perhaps needless to say, this apodictic paraphrase cannot be refuted on its own terms. Every one of MacDonald's points has its referent in the score; with one exception, the musical events he describes are undeniably "there." It does no good to point out that his characterization of the melody first heard quietly at figure 1 as the "menace theme" is arbitrary, and that the reading of the march passage is therefore tautological. That will not dislodge the interpretation from its internal consistency, and internal consistency is what always "proves" a verificationist thesis or a conspiracy theory. One cannot empirically determine that a snatch of music does not represent Stalin. But all of this is as true of Tolstoy's reading of the symphony (or even of Stravinsky's version of Tolstoy's) as it is of MacDonald's. They are all internally consistent, and all therefore tautologically true, impervious to empirical refutation.

The exception, the one point in the cited passage that can be empirically "falsified," is the last point, about the horn's high B. It is based on a footnote in the score: "If the hornist cannot play the top 'B' piano, then [the] lower octave should be played, as indicated."[56] But what the footnote shows is that Shostakovich wished to avoid the very effect to which MacDonald calls attention. The only performance he sanctions is one in which the horn's high B does *not* sound "clearly too high for it."

So there is no black comedy at that point. What about the rest? One could easily and, I think, rightly object on grounds of anachronism, as outlined earlier with respect to "dissidence" in general: if it is indeed true that "there can be absolutely no doubt that . . . it is objective" mockery of Stalin Shostakovich meant to perpetrate, then it would have been more than "an amazingly bold stroke" to have had the Fifth Symphony performed. Like Osip Mandelstam's reckless recitations of his little poem about Stalin, it would have been suicide. The considerations that caused Shostakovich to withdraw his Fourth Symphony under duress on the eve of its première were no less relevant a year later, when the political atmosphere had grown incomparably more stringent. If any oaf could hear the "shocking intrusion of cartoon satire," so could any informer.

But even this is not the really decisive argument against MacDonald's interpretation. The question was raised earlier as to what in principle can validate or refute an interpretation of music. It seems to me that the standards one applies to musical interpretations of this kind should be no different from those one applies to any theory. That theory is better which better organizes

---

[55] *The New Shostakovich*, pp. 129–30.

[56] Edition Eulenburg, no. 579, p. 58. The concert pitch in question, of course, is E.

the available information, or organizes more information. MacDonald's reading pays attention only to the most local extroversive referents. Every one of the events that make up the caricature of Stalin entering the hall (and, by the way, were grand entrances his style?) and delivering a thunderous Hitlerian oration (and, by the way, wasn't his a tremulous high-pitched Georgian-accented voice, and weren't his public speeches few?) is a transformation of previously presented material, as is the purported exchange between the two delegates that follows. Any convincing exegesis, therefore, should account for the introversive semiotic along with the extroversive; it should relate the various thematic or motivic appearances to one another, not merely take note of the immediate musical environment—the local dynamic level, the local instrumentation, or the locally characteristic harmonies—surrounding a single one.

Leaving aside the motives that carry loaded labels in MacDonald's analysis, there is the theme that constitutes the actual content of Stalin's purported "declamation." It had been heard only once before, between figure 3 and figure 5, a quiet passage in the violins that links up with others (such as the one that comes four measures before figure 12) that have the characteristics of recitative, musical "speech." When recitative appears in an instrumental context (e.g., in Beethoven's late quartets, or Shostakovich's) it is well understood to be an iconic convention, one that creates a sense, as Kerman puts it, of "direct communication" from the author, a special "immediacy of address."[57] There is an inescapably subjective, self-referential component to the expression; the melody MacDonald associates with Stalin's farcical harangue had already been marked for us as the composer's own voice. Failure to note the thematic relationship here—the introversive semiotic—has led, I believe, to a fatal misconstrual of the extroversive. I am convinced that those critics—Khubov, for one—are right who have seen the climactic unison passages as representing the efforts of the buffeted, brutalized subject—the hostage, if you will—to regain a sense of control at any cost.

The same point, writ much larger, applies to the much-debated coda. Leo Mazel has recently contributed a convincing, and very moving, *intonatsionnïy análiz* of the very last gesture in the symphony, in which the stereotyped manifestations of rejoicing give way to a sudden modal mixture that introduces not only dissonances but also a melodic progression Shostakovich frequently employed in other works, including texted ones, to evoke "a sorrowful, gloomy, or angrily plaintive character."[58] This may be viewed as irony, perhaps; but it is not mockery. Like the funereal third movement, it is an act of witness that gives voice to the silent wounded. And it does so not by "objective description" but by the purposeful intrusion of subjective feeling,

[57] Joseph Kerman, *The Beethoven Quartets* (New York: Norton, 1979), pp. 199–200.
[58] "K sporam o Shostakoviche," *Sovetskaya muzïka* 5 (1991): 35.

the composer having learned that this subjectivity alone is what gives art—his art—its enduring value.

This is what sensitive Soviet listeners perceived from the beginning. It is what Georgiy Khubov sensed and signaled to his readers even in 1938, though he had to do so under cover of ostensible censure. It is what Alexander Ostretsov sensed and signaled when, also under cover of complaint, he informed his readers that "the pathos of suffering in a whole series of places is driven to the point of naturalistic wails and howls; in some episodes the music seems almost capable of evoking physical pain."[59] It is what Leo Mazel recorded in 1960, though he had to do so under cover of ostensible reference to the Patriotic War, trusting that his readers would remember the Fifth Symphony's actual date:

> A sense of responsibility, consciousness that "the struggle of progressive humanity with reaction is not over," that one must remember fallen heroes and think of future generations, that into our thoughts of victory our former grievous anxiety and the tormenting pain of former misfortunes must flow like a living current— all this permeates the work of this composer. And it is important for understanding him—for understanding, for example, why there is a mournful episode in the finale of the Seventh Symphony, and why even the dazzlingly bright major-mode conclusions to the finales of the Fifth and Seventh symphonies are interspersed with intimations of the minor and sharp dissonances.[60]

And it is what has kept Shostakovich's Fifth Symphony, alone among the products of Soviet music from the time of the Terror, alive not only in repertory but in critical discourse and debate.

AN UNHAPPY CONVERGENCE

So Ian MacDonald's reading is no honorable error. It is a vile trivialization, graphically exemplifying the *poshlost'*—the smug vulgarity, the insipid pretension—that always informs a high moral dudgeon that comes so cheap. What level of criticism is it that seeks to anthropomorphize every fugitive instrumental color and every dynamic shade, and from these analogies assemble a literalistic narrative paraphrase of the unfolding music? Shostakovich himself, as we recall, wanted to scream when he found critics writing "that in such-and-such a symphony Soviet civil servants are represented by the oboe and the clarinet, and Red Army men by the brass section." The same holds, one may assume, for the flute and horn. And what kind of investigator builds

---

[59] "Pyataya simfoniya Shostakovicha," *Sovetskoye iskusstvo*, 2 February 1938; quoted in Khentova, *Molodïye godï Shostakovicha*, vol. 2, p. 190.

[60] Lev Abramovich Mazel, *Simfonii D. D. Shostakovicha* (Moscow: Sovetskiy kompozitor, 1960), pp. 8–9.

sweeping forensic cases on such selectively marshaled evidence? To that question the answer is obvious, and sinister. MacDonald's method is precisely what is known in this country as McCarthyism. It is our own, our homegrown Stalinist manner. Ian MacDonald, it thus transpires, is the very model of a Stalinist critic.

All of which would be merely comical to relate, were it not that the same reversed stereotype is now being applied to Shostakovich in his homeland, too, in the spirit (or in memory) of *glasnost'*. The politically correct late- or post-Soviet position on Shostakovich has become a facile inversion of the old official view (but still no gray). The new inverted or negative portrait came strikingly into view in the September 1989 issue of *Sovetskaya muzïka*, which contained a quintet of revisionist pieces on the composer that portrayed him as a martyr to his beliefs, a romantically heroic resister from the start. "He was not afraid of Stalin," proclaims the title of one of these articles, by Rudolf Barshai, the now-emigrated conductor who gave the first performance of the Fourteenth Symphony. Isaak Glikman's piece takes its title from a remark the composer is said to have made in response to the martyrdom of *Lady Macbeth* in 1936: "Even if they cut off both my hands, I'll go on writing music just the same, holding the pen between my teeth." A third, entitled "His Greatness and His Mission," places the world-renowned and decorated Shostakovich in the same category as Roslavets and Mosolov, silenced composers, and compares them all with repressed literary figures such as Bulgakov, Zamyatin, Pasternak, and Pilnyak.

An essay by a self-styled "kulturólog" named Georgiy Gachev practices a familiar form of ventriloquism on the music. For him, as for Ian MacDonald, the Fifth Symphony is an objective narrative, wholly reducible to paraphrase: "And now, 1937—to the howl of mass demonstrations, marching, demanding the execution of the 'enemies of the people,' the guillotine machinery of the State goes resoundingly into action—and there it is in the finale of the Fifth: the USSR is building—only it is unclear what it is building, a bright future or a Gulag."[61] The height of impertinence is reached when Gachev begins playing compulsively, irresponsibly, and untranslatably with words: *Ne prosto muzïkoVED—Shostakovich, no muzïkoVOD, vozhd' muzïki* ("No simple musicologist was Shostakovich but a music-leader, the Führer of music").[62] *Vozhd'*—Führer—was Stalin's sobriquet. Gachev makes Shostakovich the anti-Stalin—Stalin's equal, Stalin's match, the musical Stalin—but, needless to say, a good Stalin.

One understands the motives—or rather, the compulsion. The author's father, Dmitriy Gachev, a Bulgarian-born Communist and an old RAPMist who crusaded for *partiynost'* in musical criticism in the early days of the Com-

---

[61] "V zhanre filosofskikh variatsiy," *Sovetskaya muzïka* 57, no. 9 (1989): 36.
[62] Ibid., p. 39.

posers Union,[63] had fallen victim to that roaring guillotine the Fifth Symphony is supposed to illustrate. Romanticizing Shostakovich as an avenging angel is for members of Georgiy Gachev's generation a cathartic. But now that anything can be said in Russia, the inevitable inflation of rhetoric has produced correspondingly diminished returns. The hedged, risky, guarded statements of the past were so much more powerful, so much richer. Viewing Shostakovich through them brought a measure of understanding and exhilaration. The discourse of *glasnost'* produces a sense of futility. It is not, after all, by egoistically trivializing the agonies of the Stalin years that whatever replaces Soviet music will find its way to the twenty-first century.

To me, the most heartening bit of writing on Shostakovich in quite some time was a piece by Liana Genina, the deputy editor of *Sovetskaya muzïka*, writing this time in a rival journal, *Muzïkal'naya zhizn'*. It is called "Hoping for Justice," and it calls a halt to cheap inversionism: to the insistence on reading formulaic ideological programs or primitive story lines into every Shostakovich composition—only the reverse of what was read before—and especially to the easy presumption that Shostakovich, "in the grip of horror, said, signed and did one thing, but *always* thought another."[64] So far, most commentators, both in and out of Russia, have followed the line of least resistance to a specious, falsely comforting sense of purification. But as Caryl Emerson has written, "the genuine de-Stalinization of Shostakovich, like the de-Stalinization of the [former] Soviet Union in every other area, will require a much more critical look at the ethical dimension, and a much more painful catharsis."[65]

We can learn a great deal from the cultural artifacts of the Stalin period, but only if we are prepared to receive them in their full spectrum of grays. The lessons may be discomforting, unpalatable, even repellent, but all the more necessary and valuable for their being so. The chief ones may well be the moral ambiguity of idealism, the inescapable ethical responsibilities of artists, and the need to resist the blandishments of utopia. Stalinism was a double thing, as Irving Howe, an impeccable anti-Stalinist, had the courage to remind us shortly before he died. I want to end this chapter, and this book, by quoting, in tribute, some eloquent words of his:

> If humanity cannot live without a measure of idealism, idealism can turn upon
> humanity. Prompted by impatience with the laggard pace of history, idealism

[63] See D. Gachev, "Za partiynost' khudozhestvenno-muzïkal'noy kritiki," *Sovetskaya muzïka* 11, no. 5 (1933): 152–58.

[64] "S nadezhdoy na spravedlivost'," *Muzïkal'naya zhizn'*, no. 5 (1991): 3.

[65] Caryl Emerson, "Grotesque Modernism in Opera: Shostakovich's *Nose* and *Lady Macbeth*," paper read at a panel ("Russian Modernism: Art and Literature") at the annual convention of the American Association of Teachers of Slavic and East European Languages, Washington D.C., 1989. My thanks to Prof. Emerson for allowing me to quote from the typescript (p. 13).

generated a counterforce within itself, an involuntary poisonous secretion. Dostoyevsky understood this brilliantly when he wrote in *A Raw Youth* about man's "faculty of cherishing in his soul the loftiest ideal side by side with the greatest baseness, and all quite sincerely." The last four words are the words that count.[66]

[66] Irving Howe, "The Great Seduction," *New Republic*, 15 October 1991, p. 47.

INDEX

ABOUT THE AUTHOR

Richard Taruskin, Professor of Music at the University of California, Berkeley,
is a regular contributor to *New Republic*, *The New York Times*,
The New York Review of Books, *Opera News*, and many scholarly publications.
His books include *Opera and Drama in Russia*, *Stravinsky and the
Russian Traditions*, and *Musorgsky: Eight Essays and an Epilogue*,
published by Princeton University Press.